Native Peoples

The Canadian Experience

Third Edition

Edited by

R. BRUCE MORRISON

AND

C. RODERICK WILSON

OXFORD
UNIVERSITY PRESS

1904 ✦ 2004

100 YEARS OF
CANADIAN PUBLISHING

OXFORD

UNIVERSITY PRESS

8 Sampson Mews, Suite 204, Don Mills, Ontario M3C 0H5
www.oupcanada.com

Oxford University Press is a department of the University of Oxford.
It furthers the University's objective of excellence in research, scholarship,
and education by publishing worldwide in

Oxford New York

Auckland   Cape Town   Dar es Salaam   Hong Kong   Karachi
Kuala Lumpur   Madrid   Melbourne   Mexico City   Nairobi
New Delhi   Shanghai   Taipei   Toronto

With offices in

Argentina   Austria   Brazil   Chile   Czech Republic   France   Greece
Guatemala   Hungary   Italy   Japan   Poland   Portugal   Singapore
South Korea   Switzerland   Thailand   Turkey   Ukraine   Vietnam

Oxford is a trade mark of Oxford University Press
in the UK and in certain other countries

Published in Canada
by Oxford University Press

National Library of Canada Cataloguing in Publication

Native peoples : the Canadian experience / edited by R. Bruce Morrison and C. Roderick Wilson.—3rd ed.
Includes bibliographical references and index

ISBN-10: 0-19-541819-0
ISBN-13: 978-0-19-541819-4

1. Native peoples—Canada—History.   I. Morrison, R. Bruce   II. Wilson, C. Roderick
E78.C2N335 2004   971'.00497   C2003–907333–5

7 8 9 – 14 13 12 11
This book is printed on permanent (acid-free) paper ∞.
Printed in Canada

MIX
Paper from
responsible sources

FSC
www.fsc.org   FSC® C004071

TABLE OF CONTENTS

Part IX Conclusion

ACKNOWLEDGEMENTS

A scholarly effort reaches completion only with the dedication and co-operation of more people than could possibly be mentioned. So while we mention only a few, our appreciation extends to all who contributed in myriad ways.

The contributors to this volume have endured a great deal of editorial constraint and comment from us. Yet they still managed to produce manuscripts of exceptional quality. We thank them. We particularly appreciated the excellent editorial advice and encouragement offered by Megan Mueller. It sometimes takes longer to get a manuscript together than one anticipates at the beginning. We appreciate her patience as well. We would like to thank Richard Tallman for his thoughtful and thorough copy-editing. The care he took with the manuscript significantly enhanced the book. Our agent, Joanne Kellock passed away before this volume was published; we are grateful for the support and encouragement she gave to us.

Our wives, Joyce Morrison and Keithal Wilson, were always there when we really needed them, and that's not always easy.

Finally, and of most central importance, the many Aboriginal persons and groups whose co-operation made these chapters possible are gratefully acknowledged.

CONTRIBUTORS

Margaret Seguin Anderson (Ph.D., Michigan) is Professor of First Nations Studies at the University of Northern British Columbia. She lives and works in UNBC's Northwest Region, in the centre of Tsimshian territory. She continues to work with Tsimshian, Gitksan, and Nisga'a communities to develop resources for language revitalization, including 'talking dictionaries', and has also served as an expert witness in several court cases on Tsimshian land and resource rights. She has written and edited three books, the most recent being *Potlatch at Gitsegukla: William Beynon's 1945 Field Notebooks*, co-edited with Marjorie Halpin.

Michael Asch (Ph.D., Columbia) is Professor Emeritus in Anthropology at the University of Alberta. He is currently teaching in the Indigenous Governance Program of the Anthropology Department at the University of Victoria. He is author of *Home and Native Land: Aboriginal Rights and the Canadian Constitution* (1984) and *Kinship and the Drum Dance in a Northern Dene Community* (1988), and editor of *Aboriginal and Treaty Rights in Canada: Essays on Law, Equality and Respect for Difference* (1997). Dr Asch gave testimony on the Dene economy at the Berger Inquiry, directed the Dene/Metis Mapping Project, and served as Senior Research Associate for Anthropology with the Royal Commission on Aboriginal Peoples.

Mary Druke Becker (Ph.D., Chicago) is Research Associate at the Iroquois Indian Museum in Howes Cave, New York. Her research activities have focused on Native history and culture. She is organizer of the Conference on Iroquois Research; is author of a number of scholarly articles; and is associate editor of *The History and Culture of Iroquois Diplomacy: An Interdisciplinary Guide to the Treaties of the Six Nations and Their League* (1985).

Jennifer S.H. Brown (Ph.D., Chicago) is Professor of History at the University of Winnipeg. As an anthropologist specializing in ethnohistory her work has focused on the Canadian fur trade. *Strangers in Blood* (1980) dealt with the significance of Native families in the fur trade. More recently she co-edited, with Jacqueline Peterson, *The New Peoples: Being and Becoming Metis in North America* (1985).

Ernest S. Burch Jr (Ph.D., Chicago) is Research Associate, Arctic Studies Center, Smithsonian Institution. For the past 40 years he has pursued his interest in the structure of hunter-gatherer societies through ethnographic and ethnohistorical research on early contact northern populations. He is author of *The Eskimos* (1988), in addition to other more technical studies.

Sarah A. Carter (Ph.D., Manitoba) is Professor of History at the University of Calgary. Her publications include: *Lost Harvests: Reserve Farmers and Government Policy* (1990), *Capturing Women: The Manipulation of Cultural Imagery in Canada's Prairie West* (1997), and *Aboriginal People and Colonizers of Western Canada to 1900* (1999).

Hugh A. Dempsey (LL.D., Calgary) retired in 1991 as Associate Director of the Glenbow Museum in Calgary after 30 years with the organization. He is the author and editor of several books relating to Indians and western Canadian history, including *Crowfoot, Chief of the Blackfoot* (1972), *Red Crow, Warrior Chief* (1980), and *Big Bear: The End of Freedom* (1984). He was awarded the Order of Canada, and received an honorary doctorate from the University of Calgary in recognition of his work with Native people. He is an honorary chief of the Blood tribe.

Harvey A. Feit (Ph.D., McGill) is Professor of Anthropology at McMaster University. He has written regularly on the historical and contemporary culture and ecology of the James Bay Cree and on Cree efforts to reshape their relations to the Canadian and Quebec states and to the other peoples of Canada and Quebec. Through the 1970s he served as senior social science adviser to the James Bay Cree during their court case and the negotiation and implementation of the James Bay and Northern Quebec Agreement. Since, he has consulted with other indigenous organizations across Canada, Alaska, and

Australia. Recent articles include 'Hunting, Nature and Metaphor: Political and Discursive Strategies in James Bay Cree Resistance and Autonomy' (2001), and, with Robert Beaulieu, 'Voices from a Disappearing Forest: Government, Corporate and Cree Participatory Forest Management Practices' (2001).

Christopher Fletcher (Ph.D., Université de Montréal) is an Assistant Professor in the Department of Anthropology at the University of Alberta. He has diverse research interests in medical and ecological anthropology. He has worked in Nunavik, Nunavut, and Nitassinan (Labrador) with Inuit and Innu people. His research interests focus on Aboriginal health and healing, cultural concepts and practices in social and mental health, cultural landscape, kinship, and cross-cultural dissemination of research results. His publications include: 'Spirit Work: Nunavimmiut Experiences of Affliction and Healing' (1997) and 'Community Based Participatory Research Relationships with Aboriginal Communities in Canada: An Overview of Context and Process' (2003).

John E. Foster (Ph.D., Alberta) was Professor of History at the University of Alberta before his death in 1996. His research interests focus on the pre-1870 Canadian West with an emphasis on the history of Metis peoples. He was the author of numerous scholarly articles that helped change the direction of Canadian historical studies.

Elizabeth Furniss (Ph.D., British Columbia) is Assistant Professor of Anthropology at the University of Calgary. She has carried out ethnographic and ethnohistorical research with the Secwepemc and southern Carrier of central British Columbia, and her scholarly interests include the anthropology of colonialism and Aboriginal/settler relations in Canada, Australia, and New Zealand. She is the author of *The Burden of History: Colonialism and the Frontier Myth in a Rural Canadian Community* (1999) and *Victims of Benevolence: The Dark Legacy of the Williams Lake Residential School* (1995).

Jean-Guy A. Goulet (Ph.D., Yale) is Professor of Anthropology and Dean of the Faculty of Human Sciences at Saint Paul University (Ottawa). He has learned from Aboriginal peoples in Latin America and the Canadian Subarctic. His publications include *Ways of Knowing: Experience, Knowledge and Power Among the Dene Tha* (1998). He is co-editor (with David Young) of *Being Changed by Cross-Cultural Encounters*, 2nd edn (1998).

Douglas Hudson (Ph.D., Alberta) teaches anthropology at the University College of the Fraser Valley, with a special interest in Pacific Northwest indigenous cultures, resource use and environment issues, social organization, and culture change. He has carried out fieldwork with a number of indigenous groups in BC, including Dakelh (Carrier), Nisga'a, Taku River Tlingit, Okanagan, Stl'at'imx (Lillooet), Dunne-za, Sekani, and Coast Salish. His publications include a co-authored article on the Nisga'a in the *Handbook of North American Indians*, as well as articles on Aboriginal rights in British Columbia.

Marianne Ignace (Ph.D., Simon Fraser) is Associate Professor of Anthropology and First Nations at Simon Fraser University as well as Academic Co-ordinator of the Simon Fraser/Secwepemc Cultural Education Society Partnership. She lives in the Secwepemc Nation with her husband and children, and has carried out research on Secwepemc traditional resource use, language, discourse, and social organization. Some of her work with the Haida was published in the monograph *The Curtain Within*. She is currently collaborating with Haida Elders on a volume of Haida oratory and stories.

Ron Ignace (Ph.D. candidate, British Columbia) was chief of the Skeetchestn band from 1982 to 2002. He was also chairman of the Shuswap Tribal Council and until recently was chair of the Assembly of First Nations Chief's Committee on Aboriginal Languages. Since 1987 he has served as president of the Secwepemc Cultural Education Society and co-chairs the Aboriginal-University partnership between SCES and Simon Fraser University in Kamloops, BC. He has authored articles on Secwepemc history, traditional ecological knowledge, and language.

Peter Macnair (BA, British Columbia) was Curator of Ethnology at the Royal British Columbia Museum for more than 30 years. The acclaimed exhibits on First Nations peoples were designed and installed under his guidance. Recently he curated 'Down From the Shimmering Sky: Masks of the Northwest Coast' and 'To the Totem Forests: Emily Carr and Contemporaries Interpret Coastal Villages'. Currently he is consulting curator on a major research and exhibit development project for the National Museum of the American Indian at the Smithsonian Institution. His scholarly publications have focused on Northwest Coast material culture, art, and artists.

Virginia P. Miller (Ph.D., California) is retired from the Department of Sociology and Anthropology at Dalhousie University. She now lives on the South Shore of Nova Scotia where she divides her time between writing on the Mi'kmaq of Nova Scotia and the Yuki people of northern California, and sailing.

R. Bruce Morrison (Ph.D., Alberta) is Adjunct Professor of Anthropology at Athabasca University. His applied and scholarly interests have taken him to the Caribbean, Southeast Asia, and South Asia. Most recently he has conducted ethnographic and ethnohistorical research in Nepal. He is co-editor with C. Roderick Wilson of *Ethnographic Essays in Cultural Anthropology.*

Sylvie Poirier (Ph.D., Laval) is Professor of Anthropology at Université Laval. She has done fieldwork with Australian Aboriginals (Western Desert groups) and with the Atikamekw, focusing on their relations to the land and social and cultural change. Her present research interests include comparative analysis between indigenous claims and rights in Canada and Australia. Among her publications are *Les jardins du nomade: Cosmologie, Territoire et Personne dans le desert occidental australien* (1996, soon to be published in English). She is co-editor, with John Clammer and Eric Schwimmer, of *Figured*

Worlds: Ontological Obstacles in Intercultural Relations (forthcoming).

Carl Urion (Ph.D., Alberta) is Professor Emeritus of Anthropology at the University of Alberta. His research interests are widespread, but have focused on the study of Algonquian languages. Until his retirement he was co-editor of the *Canadian Journal of Native Education.* His major focus as an academic has been working with students.

C. Roderick Wilson (Ph.D., Colorado) is Adjunct Professor at the University of Alberta. He has done anthropological research among Papago and Navaho in the American Southwest, Cree and Metis in Alberta, Waorani in Ecuador, and pastoral nomads in Kenya. He is co-editor with R. Bruce Morrison of *Ethnographic Essays in Cultural Anthropology.* He has a long term involvement with an international NGO that actively complements his research interests.

Robert Wishart (Ph.D. candidate, Alberta) has recently been researching the relationship between narrative and landscape among Tetlit Gwich'in hunters in the Northwest Territories and how these relationships are used by them as a critique of colonial efforts. Using methods and theory from ethnohistory and oral history, he has written about hunting practices among Ojibway and Potawatomi in southwestern Ontario.

PART I

Introduction

CHAPTER 1

On the Study of Native Peoples

R. BRUCE MORRISON and C. RODERICK WILSON

National attention in recent years has frequently been given to such issues as Aboriginal land claims, unfulfilled treaty promises, and the constitutional status of Native peoples.[1] As a result one often hears questions such as: 'Just what do Native people want?' and 'Why don't we simply get rid of the reserves?'

Such questions reveal that most Canadians have some interest in Indians, but they share stereotypes that are not well founded, show little appreciation for the role of Native peoples in our history, and do not understand the basis for Native land or other claims. Canadians are not necessarily ill-disposed towards Natives, but there is currently little basis for real understanding.

Many Canadians revel in a national self-image as a mosaic—each ethnic group maintaining its distinctive character while still being essential to the whole. The image has some validity, but it seriously underplays pressures towards cultural conformity, especially at the regional level. How many immigrant children have been ridiculed because they spoke French or English with an accent? How many of us learned more British history in school than Canadian?

Being Ukrainian is marvellous, if it is limited to matters primarily aesthetic: grandmothers dyeing Easter eggs, teenagers folk dancing, and so on. At this level, being Native is fully acceptable, if rather quaint: totem poles and Inuit prints are widely recognized as striking art forms and a few chiefs in Plains-style regalia dress up a parade. Unlike other groups, Natives are not content simply to be Canadians or even to be hyphenated Canadians. They generally recognize that they are in Canada and are necessarily Canadians, but they also insist that they are first of all Indian—or Inuit, or Metis. In so doing they place themselves beyond the experience and understanding of most Canadians.

The Book's Approach

This book is based on three assertions. First, an understanding of Native peoples must start from an appreciation of Aboriginal society as it existed and as it continues, in its own terms and not as an appendage to that larger conglomeration of peoples and provinces that we call Canada. It is a fundamental anthropological premise that cultures are best understood within their own frameworks. One cannot comprehend, far less evaluate or judge, behaviour grounded in one cultural system by the standards of another. Much that follows is therefore an attempt to understand Canadian Native societies as, first of all, *Native* societies.

Second, any explication of either the objective conditions of contemporary Canadian Native peoples or the perceptions they have of themselves and of their place in the larger Canadian society must also take into account the history of relationships between Indians and Canadian

FIGURE 1.1. Dr C.M. Barbeau, Quebec's first university-trained anthropologist, transcribing Native folksongs. (© Canadian Museum of Civilization J4840)

society—particularly in its governmental aspects. Native societies have not existed within the last century simply as Native societies, but to greater or lesser extents have functioned (or been forced to function) as parts of Canadian society: Natives have become tribal peoples encapsulated within a colonial state. That the life of Canadian Indians is defined by the Indian Act—legislation enacted by the federal government without consultation, which is amendable and enforceable without Indian consent—unambiguously indicates that the subjects of the legislation have literally been created by government. From this point of view, status Indians, those people recognized as Indians by the Indian Act, are Canadian in a way that none of the rest of us are. Ironically, the life of non-Inuit Native people declared by the Indian Act not to be Indians (the Metis and non-status Indians) has largely come to be defined by the absence of that legislation. This equally speaks of their embeddedness within Canadian society, of inextricable links and connections.

Third, the scholars who here present their views of Native society and history are not simply recording devices mechanically reproducing data to which they have been exposed. They are people—who happen to be social scientists, who find themselves in interactive situations with other people who happen to be Indians. The resulting analysis is in this sense not an objective reality but a product shaped by shared experiences. This interaction is influenced by the nature of the Native community and also by the anthropologist's background. Most immediately, that background includes a particular kind of professional training and an interest in specific kinds of theoretical problems. It also includes a personal, social, and cultural background. All of these factors affect research in numerous and subtle ways. Ultimately, anthropological analysis is a creative act. By emphasizing the human elements in the research process we are not suggesting whimsy or speculation. The point, rather, is that critical rigour is obtained not by mechanizing the field-work process but by openly recognizing its interactive nature: greater knowledge of the 'subjective' factors tends to increase a study's validity and reliability.

This work is not encyclopedic, but it does discuss representative groups[2] from each region of Canada. Not all that is known about each society is presented; each chapter most completely presents that aspect of the culture of particular interest to the author. Cumulatively, this allows the reader some sense of the richness and complexity of Native life. Finally, each author examines Native life from one particular theoretical perspective. Thus, the reader gains a broad knowledge of the current state of Canadian anthropology.

It goes almost without saying that the authors believe that efforts to further the public understanding and awareness of the ways of life of the Native peoples, of the history of relationships between the original inhabitants and later immigrant peoples in Canada, and something of how various anthropological pictures of Aboriginal people are constructed are all worthwhile goals in themselves. At a very practical level, the future of Canada for both Indians and non-Indians alike may hinge on how well we have learned the lessons of our past.

Anthropological Concepts

This book is written for the general reader; it does not assume extensive knowledge either of Natives or of anthropology. Most concepts are explained as they arise, but some general comments may help. This book uses the notion of culture area as a general organizing principle—and the reader will note that each of the culture areas represented by Parts II to VIII begins with a brief overview chapter. Canada is a very large country, possessing diverse environments, and the Native population exhibits great variety. Nevertheless, within this spectrum of variability are regional similarities, and neighbouring groups tend to have features in common. This regional patterning of Aboriginal societies results from two major factors. First, primary food resources are regionally distributed: salmon is the prime resource in some areas, caribou or moose in others, and so on. Since each is taken by techniques that have different social as well as technological requirements—some require communal activity, while others reward individual effort—regional patterns of subsistence developed. The second factor is that neighbouring groups, especially ones that inhabit essentially the same kind of environment, tend to influence each other. As ideas and techniques spread from one group to another the regional patterns tend to become intensified: while each group remained unique, areal patterns of life emerged that persisted for millennia.

Regional patterns were not, however, simply the automatic response of people adjusting to a specific environment. New World prehistory was dynamic: populations moved from one region to another; major environmental changes occurred, as did technological and social innovation. Throughout, regional patterns developed, persisted, and changed.

Although European colonization disrupted Aboriginal patterns, the disruptions themselves were patterned areally. Various regions and cultures experienced first contact with European explorers and settlers at different times, in differing ways, and by varying groups. The first sustained contacts for most Inuit were with whalers, while on the west coast they were with traders seeking sea otter pelts and on the east coast they were with fishermen. Each group had different economic interests that strongly affected relationships with local Natives. Furthermore, the interests of all three contrasted strongly with those of Europeans who penetrated the interior of the continent in a fur trade that required major inputs of labour and material goods by the indigenous population. Although colonialism in whatever guise tends to produce parallel patterns of events, and although Canada's recent past has featured numerous national events that affected all Native people, much Native-European interaction has had a decidedly regional quality.

Having argued that it is sensible to think of Indians in regional terms, it is necessary to warn against taking the concept of culture area too literally. 'Culture area' is only a generalization, an indication of central tendency: each group also possesses unique practices. Arguments about boundaries (are the Mi'kmaq really Eastern Woodland or Eastern Subarctic Indians?) are essentially spurious, giving to a line on the map a specificity that is not present in reality. This particular boundary, for example, could with equal logic be drawn north or south of the Mi'kmaq; we have chosen to run the line through them! A further danger of the culture-area concept is that it tends to shape our thinking, leading us to ignore other possibilities.

Culture areas are a set of mental boxes. Some boxes are necessary to do anthropology, to attempt to explain human behaviour, or to talk about anything. We cannot forget, however, that we ourselves have created the mental boxes: another set of such organizing categories would likely put things in a different perspective.

It is fairly clear that culture areas are mental constructs, not visible in the natural world. It is less obvious for seemingly more concrete realities, such as 'tribe'. At a nineteenth-century Blackfoot Sun Dance, for instance, one could have encountered virtually the entire tribe. Other groups that never gathered together or acted as political units, however, are also customarily spoken of as tribes. Cree and Ojibway, for instance, both stretch for thousands of kilometres across the landscape. They clearly are not and never have been political units. What unites them, and what separates them, is primarily degree of linguistic similarity. The concept of tribe is thus quite loose: it can refer to people who think of themselves as a clearly identified political unit and to people who do not. It can refer merely to people designated a tribe by ethnographers essentially on the basis of common language and generally similar behaviour.

Even with this flexible understanding, it is tempting to think of tribes too narrowly. Partly this stems from what is, generally, the European heritage—a Europe of nation-states and fixed boundaries—of those writing about Natives. Tribal boundaries often were permeable, with joint-use areas between more central zones, and fluid, as tribal fortunes changed. Maps of Indian societies usually are not dated, implying a timeless fixity to the boundaries; chapters on the Iroquois, Cree, and Blackfoot indicate otherwise.

In conclusion, the argument here is not that anthropological concepts are deficient. Rather, the world is a complex place where human behaviour does not come pre-packaged. In attempting to explain behaviour, anthropologists have devised various concepts, some of which have proven to be useful, all of which are limited, and none of which provides final answers.

On Doing Anthropology: Agreements and Disagreements

This is a book about Native people; it is necessarily also a book about Canada. Further, it is a book about anthropology, or at least about how some anthropologists work and think, and the analytic frameworks are anthropological. As such, they differ from ones used by sociologists, political scientists, or economists. One should not think of one of these disciplines as right and the others wrong. Rather, they present complementary perspectives, different windows into the complex reality of human life. Similarly, anthropologists have diverse perspectives. Some anthropologists focus on the words that people use, others on how they make a living, still others on the rise or fall of their numbers. All are potentially useful topics of investigation that add to our knowledge of how societies and cultures survive.

A more troublesome matter arises. At times Native people are in profound disagreement with what has been written about them. Sometimes this is not a matter of differing perspectives but of the researcher's being wrong. This can occur in a number of ways: a linguist analyzing an unwritten language once spent hundreds of hours working with an informant who had a speech impediment. The resultant analysis was correct—but only for that informant. This is a case of sampling error, in principle a simple matter to avoid. But since anthropologists may well have good reasons for working intensively with very few people in a community, it is a recurrent problem. (In a village of 100 people, how many can speak personally of events that took place 60 years ago?) Or what if the anthropologist is the victim of a practical joke but never discovers it? What if (s)he simply misunderstands what happens? The anthropologist should validate or cross check all information—but errors can occur.

Error may be difficult to determine. The earliest substantial sources of information on the Chipewyan, for instance, are the journals of the fur trader Samuel Hearne. In numerous ways he pictures their women as drudges, the victims of abusive and domineering men. Since this seems not to fit what is known of more recent Chipewyan society or of other boreal forest people at the time of first contact, what should be made of his account? Was he misinterpreting what he saw because of his European background and his unfamiliarity with the semi-nomadic hunting and trapping life? Or was his account essentially correct, but he happened to be with a small band that, in taking up a fur-trading life, had dropped much of traditional Chipewyan values and was now composed of social deviants? Or was Hearne describing behaviour typical for the Chipewyan of that time? Contemporary Chipewyan, women in particular, may well take umbrage at anthropologists and historians who accept Hearne's account, but the question is not capable of definitive resolution.

In other instances where Natives object to anthropological interpretations, it seems parallel to the disagreement between two scholars. A classic case would be those who object to archaeological accounts, particularly to the notion that Amerindians ultimately derive from Siberian populations or that there have been relatively recent shifts of Aboriginal peoples from one region to another. These accounts are seen to be in opposition to the traditions of the Elders, to the view that they have occupied this land from the time of creation. At a time when Indians are increasingly turning to the Elders for leadership, an apparent challenge from archaeologists cannot be tolerated. The position taken here is that the two kinds of accounts regarding the past do not confront each other because they cannot. They are different kinds of truth and both can have relevance to contemporary Native people.

A related feature of anthropological writing that Native peoples (and others) frequently find unsettling is that truth seems to change through time. It seems self-evident that truth, particularly scientific truth, should be immutable. However, new data continuously arise, making necessary the re-evaluation of previous conclusions. Second, conclusions are always tentative because

BOX 1.1

Pithouses or Bunkers?

How do anthropologists study representations of Aboriginal peoples? Extensive ethnographic interviews and archival data allowed one anthropologist to analyze the media coverage of the 1995 standoff at Gustafsen Lake, British Columbia, revealing factors promoting media stereotyping. What set the Gustafsen Lake standoff apart from other conflicts involving Natives was that it was the largest Royal Canadian Mounted Police (RCMP) operation in history, with cultural misperceptions and misinformation spread across the country.

The case study of the media coverage of the 1995 Gustafsen Lake standoff demonstrates the depths of understanding attainable with anthropological methods. Many journalistic errors were the result of inadequate cultural knowledge and sensitivity towards Native people. A widely circulated untruth was that the standoff was caused by a spiritual vision. Across Canada, newspaper stories repeated stock phrases providing an oversimplified interpretation about a conflict between Aboriginal spirituality and Euro-Canadian concepts of property ownership. The media used cultural differences to cast the protestors as 'the enemy', but could not restrict this characterization to people inside the camp. Several newspapers incorporated perspectives of Sun Dance practitioners and academic sources to explain the Sun Dance, but emphasized its secretive and violent aspects. Others noted the recent introduction of this ritualistic dance at Gustafsen Lake and used this to question the authenticity of protestors' demands. Assumptions about the 'barbaric' practices of the Sun Dance and the ulterior motives of those who introduced this Plains ritual into BC exacerbated existing suspicions about those in the camp and Natives in general. One news story written with sensitivity and respect nevertheless served to denigrate a traditional sweat lodge ceremony at Alkali Lake—with the added headline 'Natives Steamed'. The media publicly voiced doubts about a local chief who broadcast a surrender message to the protestors in Shuswap over the radio—simply because they could not understand it!

For the RCMP, Hollywood stereotypes often replaced what they did not know. Some assumed that Natives in the camp had an inherent ability to stalk through heavily wooded areas undetected. Members of the RCMP tactical unit stated that they feared sleeping at night in the bush, lest they be 'scalped'. After the conflict, the RCMP conducted a media tour of the camp, misidentifying traditional pithouses as 'bunkers'.

Although the RCMP operation concerned itself with weapons and shooting offences and not with religious practices or the dispute over landownership, nevertheless the media and RCMP co-constructed stereotypes of Native people and their cultures that were mutually reinforcing.

Cultural misperceptions grow out of fear and ignorance, and these prevailed during the standoff. The RCMP frame of reference was that Native resistance had become so radicalized that the lives of law enforcement officers were at risk. Journalists who lacked an understanding of Native cultural traditions were more likely to sensationalize unfamiliar religious practices, make simplistic inferences, and represent Native traditions insensitively. And once these misunderstandings about Native spirituality, Sun Dances, pithouses, and Hollywood myths were transmitted as news, they took on lives of their own. There is little doubt that these misunderstandings could encourage intolerance towards Native people.

SOURCE: Sandra Lambertus, *Wartime Images, Peacetime Wounds: The Media and the Gustafsen Lake Standoff* (Toronto: University of Toronto Press, 2003).

they are interpretive. Folk explanations, of course, also change, but not so visibly, nor are the contradictions sudden.

Indians have criticized some anthropology as irrelevant to their needs. Mandelbaum's *The Plains Cree*, the standard work on that group, presents their life during the buffalo-hunting days of the late nineteenth century, as remembered by elderly people in the 1930s. Nowhere does it mention the trauma of everyday life on the reserves of that period. For some, a political and economic analysis of reserve life would seem more to the point. In Mandelbaum's defence it must be noted that his fieldwork could not have been duplicated at a later date and that one's sense of relevance can change. Many contemporary Cree have found the book to be a treasure house. Several of our authors have been hired to collect precisely this kind of material. One cannot be sure which book would have been more relevant, the one Mandelbaum wrote or the one his critics wanted.

A final criticism is that some ideas propounded by anthropologists have actively harmed Native people, a charge made both by Indians and by anthropologists. The most obvious examples involve acculturation theory. The general argument is that in focusing so exclusively on how Indian culture changes to accommodate to Euro-Canadian culture, anthropologists have unwittingly supported the ideas that such change is inevitable and that ultimately Indians will be totally assimilated. The issues are complex, but some preliminary comments may be helpful. First, whatever the merits or faults of acculturation theory, its practitioners as a group were actively involved in working with and for Native peoples. Second, neither scholars nor Natives can afford tests of orthodoxy. The issue should not be whether a conclusion is 'politically correct' but whether the analysis is sound.[3] Interestingly, good analysis seems to lead to anti-assimilationist conclusions. Third, anthropologists, like nuclear physicists, cannot guarantee that their work will not be misused.

One means of minimizing the misuse of anthropology is to increase the involvement of the Native community in the process of doing anthropology. Several authors touch on this, including Anderson, Hudson, the Ignaces, Macnair, Poirier, and Wilson, and still others could have. Macnair is quite explicit in speaking of training Native people in the doing of anthropology. He makes it clear that not all community members saw this as relevant to their interests. Increasingly, though, it has been seen as important to the community in terms of its own internal dynamics; it is particularly important to the process of reviving pride in being Indian.

Attention has been given recently to the relevance of anthropology in the external relations of Native communities. Anderson, Asch, Feit, Furniss, Hudson, the Ignaces, and Poirier all mention this explicitly as something they have done. Again, others could have mentioned it, but did not. We mention Feit's case illustratively. When threatened by proposed development, the James Bay Cree turned to him to provide expert witness in court. They were able to do so because they had an understanding of this research. It was not that the Cree acquired his academic, ecological understanding of their life, but that his acquisition of their understanding of hunting necessarily involved communicating to them in their terms something of what he was doing.

This discussion has focused on the anthropologist-Indian relationship. The anthropological audience also includes other anthropologists, students, the general public, and, at times, client agencies. The concerns expressed here have also had an impact, in somewhat different forms, on these audiences: the issues are not merely specific to Native peoples; they are general. As an example, we mention the treaties that various First Nations have signed. They are centrally of concern to the signatories, and have so been mentioned in a number of chapters. They also impact all other Canadians, but usually this is not noticed. On occasion, however, treaties become front-page news, often in ways that leave many

BOX 1.2

On Being an Aboriginal Graduate Student

[Editor's Note: Becoming an archaeologist is difficult for anyone, but for an Aboriginal student it has its own special difficulties. Tara Million, a Cree of the Saddle Lake First Nation and a Ph.D. student in anthropology at the University of Alberta, has grappled with some of these difficulties, rethinking for herself aspects of the archaeological paradigm. Here, however, she has chosen to write on something even more basic.]

Rod Wilson asked me to say something about my 'Aboriginal graduate student experience'. I am having a difficult time doing this. I could tell you about my experiences as an Aboriginal student in archaeology, but they may be different from others' experiences. I could try to come up with a generic Aboriginal graduate experience, but it might not be truthful or complete. So what can I do? I think that the only thing I can do is to tell you what I believe.

I believe that when you decide to become an Aboriginal graduate student you decide to go on a vision quest. I believe that you need a supervisor with a generous and confident spirit so that he or she can provide proper guidance on your quest. I believe that you need to be a member of an academic community that accepts you and hears your words, and that you need to be willing to hear their words, too. I believe that you need to belong to an Aboriginal community that respects your choices, values the contributions you are making to First Nations, and supports you in your vision quest both culturally and financially. I believe that you need a family to give you assistance in your quest through their love and encouragement. I believe that you need determination and endurance and flexibility in order to see your vision. I believe that this will be the most painful experience of your life and it will mark you forever.

I tell you here and now, that I know my vision is worth everything I have gone through.

—Tara Million

people mystified because they really have little basis for understanding them. We have included a typical treaty in Appendix I. To help readers understand that the written treaty is inherently a one-sided document and must be read in a historical and cultural context, we include as Appendix II a commentary on a recent court decision interpreting one aspect of Treaty No. 8.

In summary, anthropologists have always been concerned with accuracy, or more technically, reliability and validity. This has been one of the factors in the search for new methods and new ideas and in the introspective analysis of past problems. Our current understandings are hope-

fully neither a defence nor a rejection of the past, but a building upon successful parts of the past. Anthropology started in the belief that it was possible to comprehend other cultures if one sought an insider's understanding and that this was possible through objectively recording material gained by the technique of participant observation. This involved participating in many activities of the daily life of a community. Like a child, the fieldworker learned the lessons required to be a member of the community, to see the world as they saw it. The insider's viewpoint remains a valid ideal, but we are now more aware of its unattainability. Participant observation is still a basic technique, but we no longer assume that our presence does not alter what happens. The community being studied is not simply there as an object, but actively and purposively interacts with the researcher. Writing of one's field experiences, including emotional responses to the very demanding task of fieldwork, demands both courage and personal insight, but it creates a more human ethnography and allows the reader to judge more fully its merit.

This volume, then, is both a discussion of some current perspectives on Canadian Native peoples and a comment on the scholarly enterprise in itself.

Notes

1. We have attempted to be consistent and straightforward in our use of terminology. 'Native', 'Aboriginal', and 'indigenous' are terms that emphasize that the people to whom they are applied, all people tracing their ancestry to the pre-Columbian inhabitants of Canada (and all of North and South America), were here before the arrival of the rest of us. 'Amerindian' and an early meaning of 'Indian' are almost as broad in scope, excluding only the northernmost layer of people stretching from the tip of Siberia to Greenland. In Canada these northernmost indigenous people are known as 'Inuit'. In Alaska and Siberia they are more likely to be 'Aleuts' or 'Eskimos'. Collectively, they can be referred to as 'Eskaleuts'. The usual meaning of 'Indian' in Canada refers to those Native people who are recognized by the federal government as having 'Indian status' by virtue of the Indian Act. In recent decades such people are more likely to refer to themselves formally as being 'First Nations'. In addition to 'Indians' and 'Inuit', the Canadian Constitution recognizes 'Metis' as a third category of Aboriginal person. A broad definition of 'Metis' includes communities of people with mixed Indian and European descent.

2. The book covers all culture areas of Canada and two or three societies within each area. Within each area we are also representative. The basic distinction in the Arctic, for instance, is between maritime and inland societies. On the Northwest Coast it is between northern and southern societies. In both cases we selected one of each. Finally, we chose authors who are recognized for the quality of their work and for their ability to communicate their findings forcefully.

3. Good analysis is predicated upon information being rigorously collected and validated. Further, for the analysis to work it must reach conclusions whose logic is supported by the data.

CHAPTER 2

First Nations Prehistory and Canadian History

C. RODERICK WILSON and CARL URION

Beginnings[1]

If we were to peer through the mists of time to the Age of the Ancestors, the First Americans, what would we see? Probably we would see a small group of people, about 15 or 20. At times they might be joined by people from other bands, but usually that was about the right number of people to live together. Mostly they lived near the sea. They might follow streams to places where it was easy to spear salmon or go inland to hunt deer or bear, or to gather berries on hillsides, but they were seldom far from water. They had spears and baskets, warm clothing, and sleeping robes, and, especially in the winter, shelter from the Subarctic storms. But they moved frequently and did not have much else by way of physical possessions.

What they mostly had was not things, but knowledge, the knowledge to find what was needed, that which was provided. Anthropologists for the most part would say that they had environmental knowledge (what do the land and sea provide and how can they be used?) and social knowledge (how do members of the group relate to each other in order to get things done?). Anthropologists might also state that the Ancestors themselves (to judge from their descendants) would have given primacy not to environmental knowledge or to social knowledge but to religious knowledge as being more fundamental.

In our view, however, the Ancestors (again inferring from their descendants' views) would have put it still differently. They would not have thought of hunting or gathering or even of knowledge as things unto themselves. They would not have thought of hunting as a specialized skill to be learned so much as an expression of the hunter's spirituality.

In sum, we are suggesting that: (1) just as contemporary Native people are the biological descendants of the Ancestors, and hence we can infer that the Ancestors had straight black hair, skin that tanned easily, and so on, so can we look to the traditional ways of thinking of Native people across the New World to get some sense of what their world view was; (2) the Ancestors were real people in time and space about whom we will never know many things but about whom some matters of importance and interest may be said; and (3) Native peoples and anthropologists frequently see things differently and speak about things with different vocabularies, but dialogue on these matters is both possible and important.

Native peoples have their own ways of speaking of beginnings. Tsimshian groups, for instance, consider that they are descended from an ancestress who was carried away and married by one or another supernatural (for example, grizzly or killer whale) in the form of a man, but who eventually returned to her homeland with her children. Such stories, among other things, define the nature of reality and (spiritual) power, the basis for relationships within the group, and the nature of relationships with external groups.

Just as we noted in the first chapter that one should not think of one academic discipline as right and the others wrong, so one should not think of one origin story as right and another wrong. For one thing, each story is told in its own vocabulary; the resulting conflicts in view are more apparent than real. For instance, Native Elders commonly assert that the First Nations have been here forever, since the creation of the world. This view is seen as being in conflict with those of archaeologists, some of whom place the original peopling of the New World as recently as 12,000[2] years ago. How does one relate the archaeological discourse of hypothetical carbon-dated years to the discourse of Aboriginal origin myths? One approach is to ask what even 12,000 years means, not in the scientific language of radiometric dating (where it seems almost as yesterday), but in the language of culture. What does 12,000 years mean in terms of the history of Western culture, the cultural frame for most of us? Two meaningful comparisons, of the many possible, would be to point out that the Judeo-Christian-Islamic tradition is usually seen to begin with Abraham, only some 4,000 years ago, or to point out that the proto-Indo-Europeans, the small horticultural group ancestral to speakers of modern languages ranging from Hindi and Russian in the East to Icelandic and Portuguese in Western Europe, began their migrations, as best as we can now reconstruct, some 8,000 years ago. In other words, the most recent suggested date for the inhabiting of North America is far more distant than most ancestral events in Western culture for which there is any glimmering of cultural memory. Thus, the Native Elder and the archaeologist, in their different ways, seem to be saying much the same thing: 12,000 years ago is, in almost any sense, at the beginning of the world.

In the following sections we will discuss, without making exclusive truth-claims, first, what various kinds of anthropologists have to say about

the original settling of the continent and about how Native societies developed in the millennia prior to European discovery, and, second, some general issues from the history of Native–Euro-Canadian relationships that will help the reader form a context for the following chapters.

The Settling of the Continent

Viewpoints from Physical Anthropology

All humans are related, forming one species. But some of us are more alike and some are less alike. It is in this perspective that we use the term 'Amerindian'. It suggests that in general the Aboriginal inhabitants of North and South America are more like each other than they are like people deriving from elsewhere on the globe. This in turn implies that Amerindians have been here for a long time, long enough to become somewhat distinct from other peoples.

The perspective of relatedness also suggests, however, that Amerindians are more like people from eastern Asia than anywhere else. This does not prove that the long-distant ancestors of Native peoples came here from Asia, but it does suggest it as the strongest possibility.

Even to a casual observer, Amerindians and people from eastern Asia share features that link them together and separate them from the rest of the world. People from both areas tend to have straight black hair, a lack of male-pattern baldness, and little facial or body hair; they have skin that tans easily, rarely have blue eyes, and may have epicanthic eye folds ('slanted' eyes). Less visible traits linking these peoples include the Inca bone (the occipital bone at the back of the skull is divided in two, the smaller, upper portion being referred to as the Inca bone, in commemoration of its first being noticed by archaeologists working in Peru) and the Mongolian spot, a purplish spot about the size of a dollar coin on the skin at the base of the spine. Such a list could be expanded at some length. It is not that everyone in these populations has all these characteristics, but these heritable traits are found more or less frequently among these people and are not found among other peoples.

While the relative biological affinity of New World and East Asian peoples is visible to the layperson, we are not limited to the approach of simply listing points of physical connectedness. For instance, large numbers of heritable traits, including non-visible characteristics such as blood proteins, can be treated mathematically to create an index of genetic similarity. While the specific numbers generated in such an approach depend on exactly which characteristics are included, such studies generally attempt to be broadly inclusive and typically conclude both that there are interesting variations within New World peoples and that they are linked more closely to eastern Asia than elsewhere. In fact, the people of the far northwestern part of North America are genetically closer to the people of Siberia than they are to the people of South America.

Ultimately, the question of New World origins must be placed in the context of human evolution generally. The present evidence is that North and South America, like Oceania and Australia, have been inhabited only by fully modern human beings. That is, the evolution of human beings took place primarily in Africa, secondarily in Asia and Europe, and not at all in the rest of the world. While this line of thought categorically concludes that the ancestors of Amerindians must have come here from somewhere, with respect to time it is vague.

The most exciting recent research bearing on this issue is undoubtedly the study of human DNA, with the promise of much more detailed studies soon to come. Looking at the big picture, the most definitive line of research involves Y chromosomes (the study of male lines of descent). The startling conclusion is that all non-African humans are descended from an individual who lived in east Africa about 60,000 years ago. If people reached the Americas before then, as they certainly reached Asia and Europe, they apparently left no male descendants.

The study of mitochondrial DNA (mtDNA, inherited through the female line) is revealing a more complex picture. Several genetic lineages have been isolated connecting modern Native Americans to other populations. The main hypotheses at this time seem to be that: (1) the initial peopling of the Americas probably occurred some 20,000 to 40,000 years ago; (2) modern Native Americans may have multiple points of origin, or the founding population included several mtDNA lineages; and (3) most but not all of these genetic groupings trace back to East Asia and Siberia, but specific lineages within each major group originated within the Americas.

Teeth have played a special role in the study of evolution (human and non-human alike) for two reasons. First, they tend more often than other parts of animal anatomy to be preserved. Second, they are evolutionarily conservative; that is, they tend to vary less within populations and to change more slowly over long periods of time than many other anatomical features. This becomes relevant for us in a comparative study of tooth morphology by Christy Turner. He studied the shape of fossil teeth in museum collections around the world and also contemporary teeth. He found a small number of major types, including what he called the sinodont pattern, encompassing the prehistoric and contemporary peoples of China, northeastern Asia generally, and the New World. Within the sinodont pattern, he distinguished a number of subtypes. New World peoples divide into three subtypes: the Eskimoan peoples, the Athapaskans and some other Northwest Coast groups, and all other Aboriginal New World peoples. Each of these subtypes in turn is most closely associated with fossil populations coming from distinct areas of northeast Asia. The implication (not accepted by all) is that there were three separate migratory streams into the New World from that area, with the Eskimoans being the most recent, preceded by the Athapaskans, in turn preceded by the original stream.

In summing up the evidence from the sub-discipline of physical anthropology that relates to the question of the settling of the New World, one can firmly state that the ancestral populations came here from eastern Asia in what seems to any living person a very long time ago but in evolutionarily modern times. It can further be stated, though with less certainty, that they probably came over long periods of time in at least three separate streams of migration.

Viewpoints from Linguistic Anthropology

Language Classification Systems
It has always been clear to people that some languages are closely related. A shared or similar vocabulary leads easily to the conclusion that there must be a shared past. Reversing this equation, the widespread existence of dialects suggests that contemporary languages might over time evolve into separate languages; the widespread existence of families of related languages suggests that processes of linguistic fission have been going on for a long time.

As early as 1786 Sir William Jones, a British colonial official in India, reported structural similarities between some European languages (by then common knowledge) and the Asian languages Sanskrit and Persian (at the time quite surprising). The idea that peoples who looked quite different and who had very different cultures might nevertheless share, at least in part, a common linguistic ancestry was electrifying.

In North America the first comprehensive attempt at classifying Aboriginal languages was made in 1891 by John Wesley Powell of the Bureau of American Ethnology. He classified the Aboriginal languages of North America into 58 (later revised to 51) different stocks. We can now see that his classification was very much a product of the times: there was virtually no information on some of the languages; he assumed that all Amerindian languages represented a single stage of evolutionary development and therefore ignored grammar as a factor in determining relationships; and, because the primary purpose of making the classification was to provide a basis

for the placement of tribes on specific reservations, there was no particular interest in the degree of relationship but only in the fact of a relationship. In spite of these rather severe defects it is still regarded as a foundational, if conservative, statement. In the context of this particular discussion, it is a minimalist statement about the past.

In 1921 Edward Sapir constructed a classification that dramatically reduced the number of stocks to six. Although much linguistic work had been done in the intervening 30 years, and Sapir himself had by then worked on 17 Native languages, the difference between the two classifications lies less in the quality of analysis than in the fact that Powell was a 'splitter' and Sapir was by inclination a 'lumper' who was willing to go beyond the hard evidence and who had an eye on the grand sweep of historical processes. For instance, he classified Beothuk, the extinct language of Newfoundland, as Algonquian, largely because its Indian neighbours are. It may well have been, but we will never know. He attempted to link the Na-Dene phylum to Sino-Tibetan. He even suggested that Hokan-Siouan was the basic North American Indian language and implied that an ancestral proto-language might at some point be reconstructed.

This is not to suggest that Sapir was indifferent to the question of to what extent the suggested connections between various languages had been demonstrated. The 1929 version of his classification contains two separate lists (see Table 2.1, compiled by Darnell). The first is the six-unit radical classification; the second is a more conservative grouping into 23 units. The premise for the second list was that by this date linguistic analysis had proceeded to the point where even the most conservative would now accept some linking of units listed separately by Powell; 12 of the 23 represent this kind of well-substantiated clumping.

Until recently the lists of Sapir and Powell more or less defined the parameters of the classificatory discussion. In 1986, Darnell noted that to an unfortunate extent linguists usually chose one

Table 2.1. North American Linguistic Classifications (after Darnell 1986)

Sapir 1929-A	Sapir-B	Powell 1891
Eskimo-Aleut	Eskimo	Eskimo
Algonquian-Ritwan	Algonquian-Ritwan*	Algonquian, Beothukan, Wiyot, Yurok
	Mosan*	Wakashan, Chemakuan, Salish
	Kutenai	Kutenai
Na-Dene	Tlingit-Athapaskan*	Haida, Tlingit, Athapaskan Haida
Penutian	California Penutian*	Miwok, Costanoan, Yokuts, Maidu, Wintun
	Oregon Penutian*	Takelma, Coos (-Siuslaw), Yakonan, Kalapuya
	Plateau Penutian*	Waiilatpuan, Lutuamian, Sahaptin
	Chinook	Chinook
	Tsimshian	Tsimshian
	(Mexican Penutian)	—
Hokan-Siouan	Hokan*	Karok, Chimariko, Salinan, Yana, Pomo, Washo, Esselen, Yuman, Chumash
	Coahuiltecan*	Tonkawa, Karankawa, Coahuiltecan
	Tunican*	Tunica, Atakapa, Chitimacha
	Iroquois-Caddoan*	Iroquois, Caddoan
	Yuki	Yuki
	Keres	Keres
	Timucua	Timucua
	Muskhogean	Muskhogean
	Siouan	Siouan, Yuchi
Aztec-Tanoan	Uto-Aztecan*	Nahuatl, Pima, Shoshonean
	Tanoan-Kiowan*	Tanoan, Kiowa
	Zuni	Zuni

*Twelve units that Sapir considered to be accepted by his colleagues. The reduction of Powell's 55 units to 23 reflected the work of a generation of linguists, largely trained by Franz Boas. The further reduction to six units Sapir saw as being his own work.

list or another but that the field was now generally conservative in that there was growing insistence on thoroughly demonstrating relationships. Table 2.2 is a modified version of her chart showing established linguistic groupings for Canadian languages.

This picture was challenged in 1987 with Joseph H. Greenberg's radical proposal that there are three basic groupings in the New World: Eskimo-Aleut stretching across the Arctic rim from eastern Siberia to Greenland; Na-Dene running from central Alaska to Hudson Bay with outliers as far south as Arizona; and Amerind covering all the rest of North and South America. The first two groupings are not new and are fairly conventional; the proposal of an Amerind macrophylum is startling (as is including Eskimo-Aleut in another macrophylum, Eurasiatic, which also includes stocks as diverse as Chukchi-Kamchatkan, Altaic, Uralic, and Indo-European).

Greenberg's groups are startling for at least two reasons. One is that they link geographically distant peoples whose separation would have taken place well over 20,000 years ago. The other reason is methodological: instead of a painstaking point-by-point analysis of the sound, word, and

Table 2.2. Languages and Language Families in Canada

Family	Language	Number of Speakers In Canada	Number of Speakers Outside Canada
Algonquian			
Eastern Branch	Abenaki	10	few
	Maliseet	655	850
	Mi'kmaq	7,300	1,200
	Munsee (Delaware)	8	few
	Potawatomi	few	50
Central Branch	Cree	91,500	1,100
	Innu (Montagnais-Naskapi)	9,100	
	Ojibway	35,000	5,000
	Algonkin	2,275	
	Odawa	5,000	330
	Saulteaux (W. Ojibway)		
Plains Branch	Blackfoot	4,800	1,100
Athapaskan			
	Babine	1,600	
	Dunne Za (Beaver)	300	
	Carrier	1,500	
	Southern Carrier	700	
	Ts'ilqot'in (Chilcotin)	705	
	Chipewyan	4,000	
	Dogrib	2,100	
	Gwich'in (Kutchin)	430	300
	Han	few	20
	Kaska	400	
	Tsuu T'ina (Sarsi)	50	
	Sekani	1-500	
	Northern Slavey	290	
	Southern Slavey	2,620	
	Tagish	2	
	Tahltan	40	
	Tutchone	400	
	Upper Tanana	10	105
Eskimo-Aleut	Inuktitut	32,000	48,000
	N. Alaskan Inupiat	840	2,700
Haida	Haida	40	15
Iroquoian	Cayuga	360	10
	Mohawk	350	3,000
	Oneida	200	50
	Onondaga	80	15

Table 2.2 (continued):

Family	Language	Number of Speakers	
		In Canada	Outside Canada
	Seneca	25	175
	Tuscarora	8	10
Ktunaxa	Ktunaxa (Kutenai)	120	100
Salishan			
Interior	Okanagan	500	110
	Ntlakapmuk (Thompson)	150	
	Sepwepemc (Shuswap)	200	
	St'at'imcets (Lillooet)	200	
Coastal	Comox	400	
	Halkomelem	500	
	Nuxalk (Bella Coola)	180	
	Pentlatch	none	
	Sechelt	40	
	Squamish	20	
	Straits	25	few
Siouan	Dakota	5,000	15,300
	Stoney (Assiniboine)	1,500	few
Tlingit	Tlingit	145	700
Tsimshian	Gitxsan	400	
	Nisga'a (Nishga)	2,000	
	Tsimshian	432	70
Wakashan			
Northern Branch	Haisla	200	
	Heiltsuk	300	
	Kwak'wala (Kwakiutl)	250	45
Southern Branch	Nuuchahnulth (Nootka)	590	
	Nitinaht	30	

grammatical subsystems, comparing two languages at a time, repeating the process for possibly numerous diads, and eventually reconstructing an hypothesized proto-language, Greenberg looks at words only and does so for large numbers of languages at the same time. His work is controversial and points to a far horizon. While the overall picture may turn out to be generally valid, the work itself has serious flaws (some of it is simply sloppy) and the apparent congruence with Turner's model of dental groups is superficial.

Implications of Typological and Distributional Data

In considering the implications for us of the various classification systems and the distribution of language families across the New World map, let us start with some of the points that linguists agree on.

One such point is that the map of Canada is virtually covered by only three language families. The languages of most Canadian Natives, and the vast majority in southern Canada east of the Rockies, are members of the Algonquian family. Cree and Ojibwa are very closely related, implying very recent separation; Blackfoot is more distantly related, implying an earlier independent history. Much of interior northwestern Canada and Alaska is occupied by Athapaskan speakers. The many similarities among Athapaskan languages imply relatively recent division into separate languages. Their greatest linguistic diversity is found on the southeast coast of Alaska; an implication is that they spread from there into the Alaskan interior and thence eastward across northern Canada and that subsequently some groups moved southward, with some (ancestral to the Navajos and Apaches) reaching the American Southwest. The third family is Eskimo-Aleut, represented in Canada by Inupik (Inuktitut). It is an extreme case, a single language continuum spread from northern Alaska across to eastern Greenland. Apart from any archaeological evidence, this is a strong indication of relatively recent occupation of the region.

The British Columbia coast stands out as the one region of Canada characterized by linguistic diversity. On principle, then, one would expect that the BC and Alaskan coasts were inhabited earlier than the other parts of Canada. This is entirely likely when one considers that parts of the coast were virtually the only regions in the country to escape glaciation, *if the continent generally was inhabited prior to the last ice age* (the Pleistocene). At this point we have moved to the controversial.

It should be noted that the controversy here is not really linguistic. It arises because what has been the dominant archaeological model has the New World settled very quickly and very late (post-Pleistocene). Since for the most part linguists are more concerned with establishing rela-

tionships than with establishing how old the relationships are, the issue of time is often not considered.

We have already noted that on grounds relating to where the most linguistic diversity is to be found within their language family, the Eskimo-Aleut generally are thought to have reached their present distribution from points of origin on the Alaska coast. This is both orthodox linguistics and consistent with the standard archaeological view; it should also be noted that both groups are thought to be relatively late arrivals on the continent and that the point of origin of both would have been on the Beringian side of the ice age glaciers.

The point here is that the pattern of inferred historic dispersal presented by both the Eskimo-Aleut and the Athapaskans is not exceptional but is very much the general pattern. In plotting the distribution of the likely centres of major Amerindian language families and language isolates, Gruhn (1988) notes that 42 of 47 such centres are to be found in coastal regions, virtually all of them on the Pacific or Gulf of Mexico coasts. In other words, the distributional evidence is that the original settlement of the Americas was along the coastal areas, with interior areas being settled later. The linguistic evidence does not support the notion of people funnelling into an empty North American continent from a northern corridor between mountains of ice, but of people moving eastward from the Pacific and northward from the Caribbean.

Gruhn also argues that the shallow time depth of the standard archaeological model is not sufficient to generate the linguistic diversification found within many language families. It should also be noted that if Greenberg's picture is at all correct, the point is even more nearly valid. If 12,000 years is thought to be inadequate to generate the linguistic diversity found within the Hokan or Penutian groups, for instance, is it sufficient time for the entire Amerind macrophylum—all of the diverse languages and language families south of the Athapaskans—to have developed?

Viewpoints from Archaeological Anthropology

Archaeologists all agree that people have lived in the New World for at least 12,000 years. That general time frame was established in 1927 when a magnificently crafted stone spear point, to be named Folsom, was found still embedded within the ribs of an extinct form of bison, itself lying in a datable geological formation. That direct association of a human artifact with a datable object in an undisturbed context forever silenced the then dominant conservative view that people had been here for only some 3,000 years. Since then other Folsom sites have been found across the High Plains, dated from about 10,600 to 10,000 years BP (before the present), along with numerous other 'Early Man' sites of undisputed authenticity across virtually the entire continent, so that an entry date of 12,000 BP has now become the conservative position. The Early Man debate is now centred on the question of whether there is really good evidence for an earlier date. Part of this question, naturally, is also the question of what constitutes good evidence.

The late-entry view is that there is no shortage of sites for which claims have been made for earlier dates, but that a careful examination of these sites raises questions that have not been fully answered. Old Crow in the northern Yukon is an example. The most famous Old Crow artifact is a hide flesher made from a caribou leg bone. Originally dated at 27,000 BP, improved technical knowledge has led to it being reassessed at only 1350 BP. Numerous other bones, many of extinct animals, from the area showing unmistakable evidence of having been worked on or made into tools are dated from 45,000 to 25,000 BP. The problem for some is that these artifacts have been washed out of their original context by the Old Crow River (to which one could ask, 'Is not a tool out of context still a tool?'). Lastly, modified bones have been found in contexts reliably dated at 80,000 BP and earlier, but there is not universal agreement that the cuts were made by humans.

The view of those advocating very early entry to the Americas is that although it is true that in the past some unsubstantiated claims for extreme antiquity were made in a few cases, and although some sites like Old Crow are less than perfect in some regards, there is an ever-growing list of sites from much of North and South America that have been reliably dated as being older than 12,000 BP. Bluefish Cave, for instance, 'next door' to Old Crow, has *in situ* mammoth bone cores and flakes dated to 24,000 BP. Another of these sites is Monte Verde, in southern Chile. The main site is exceptionally well preserved because of its water-logged condition and includes a series of wooden hide-covered houses with numerous wooden artifacts and even some food remains in wooden mortars. It is dated at 12,800 BP. Given its far southern location, not just in terms of distance, but in terms of a sequence of major environmental adjustments that people must have made as they made their way south, one can only speculate at what a reasonable starting time would have been. But below this site is an earlier occupation floor with simple stone artifacts that have been dated at 33,000 BP. The implications of such an early date this far south are staggering.

The situation just described, with two opposing 'camps' of archaeologists (with many, of course, not fully subscribing to either view), has existed for decades. In the past few years, however, the situation has become newly complicated and lively. The precipitating event was the 1996 discovery of a virtually complete human skeleton washing out of the bank of the Columbia River near Kennewick, Washington. Kennewick Man was a middle-aged male about 174 centimetres tall who died about 8,400 BP, and whose long, narrow face and brain case and a projecting mid-facial region appear to some archaeologists not to be 'typically Amerindian'. Relatively little is still known about him because he has been immobilized in a series of legal actions. His existence has nevertheless stirred considerable re-examination of the whole field (but not, as reported in the media, a revolution). It turns out that the handful of relatively complete New World skulls of roughly this age share the specific features mentioned but differ in other ways; more importantly, they differ substantially from living Amerindians as a group. The biological history of people in the New World thus seems more complex than previously thought. The most likely explanations involve recognizing that the peopling of America may have involved multiple groups over a long period of time and/or started early enough for genetic changes to take place in local populations. There is at this point no need to conclude that Kennewick Man and his contemporaries were not ancestral to living Amerindians even though they looked quite different.

The controversy generated by the Kennewick discovery need not have led to questions about what route(s) were used in settling the Americas, but it has. As a consequence, the dominance of the conservative position involving a late and mid-continental entry quickly leading to Clovis culture has been substantially weakened. A glacier-free corridor east of the Rockies apparently did not exist prior to about 11,000 BP, so that a Pacific coast entry, possibly but not necessarily involving boats, seems most likely. There are also serious advocates of other possibilities, such as the Solutrean culture of about 20,000 BP on the north coast of Spain leading to the Clovis culture of America.

One other factor in this controversy must be mentioned, even in such a brief summary. The lifestyle of the oldest 'Early Americans' about which archaeologists generally agree, in western North America from about 11,500 to 7500 BP, is often referred to as big-game hunting. The sites giving rise to this designation are characterized by the remains of large animals and the tools to kill and process them. These killing tools are fluted, lanceolate spear points, the earliest being termed Clovis (in use from 11,500 to 11,000 BP). The early-entry advocates think that the late-entry advocates simply project this lifestyle into the older past and assume that the very first Amerinds must also have been big-game hunters and must also have been using the same type of stone hunting tools. There are alternatives,

including bone tools, fire-hardened wood tools, and other types of stone tools. In fact, in South America most of the early people contemporary with Clovis in North America were foragers, and not specialized hunters. The argument is that the 'Clovis first' people are not finding pre-Clovis sites in North America because they are not looking for the right kinds of things.

It is entirely appropriate to end this discussion of the settling of the New World on this note because we need to remind ourselves that the past is not there simply to be dug up; rather, anthropologists are actively reconstructing the past. The patterns upon which reconstructions are based are not only in the data but in the minds of those doing the reconstruction. If the radicals and conservatives can resolve their differences, perhaps we can start paying more attention to the mental patterns of those who originally provided the data.

The Time before History or Canada

The view taken here is that the first people came to this continent from what is now Siberia earlier than conventionally thought, via a land bridge known as Beringia that existed intermittently from 70,000 to 12,000 BP, and first spread down the Pacific coast and then into the continent's interior. Most of what is now Canada was either abandoned when the glaciers came or was not settled at all until they melted. At that point ancestors of the people now known as Ktunaxa and Salish could move into the BC interior from the west coast, the Algonquians and then the Siouans and Iroquoians into central and eastern Canada from the south, and the Athapaskans into the interior northwest from the coast. Still later, the Eskimoans moved across the Arctic in a series of west-to-east migrations.

The Paleo-Indian Stage (11,500–7500 BP)

The Paleo-Indians are the earliest people about whom there is relative agreement, both because

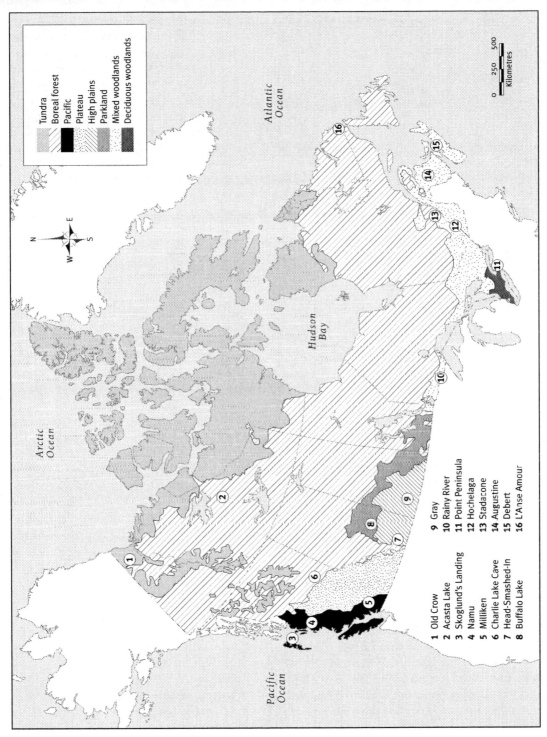

Legend:
- Tundra
- Boreal forest
- Pacific
- Plateau
- High plains
- Parkland
- Mixed woodlands
- Deciduous woodlands

Arctic Ocean

Atlantic Ocean

Hudson Bay

Pacific Ocean

1 Old Crow
2 Acasta Lake
3 Skoglund's Landing
4 Namu
5 Milliken
6 Charlie Lake Cave
7 Head-Smashed-In
8 Buffalo Lake
9 Gray
10 Rainy River
11 Point Peninsula
12 Hochelaga
13 Stadacone
14 Augustine
15 Debert
16 L'Anse Amour

0 250 500
Kilometres

MAP 2.1. Vegetation Zones and Archaeological Sites of Canada

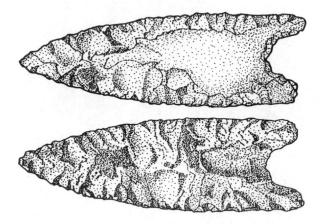

FIGURE 2.1. Fluted projectile point from the Debert site in Nova Scotia. Given what we know of the ecological context, these particular points were most likely used to hunt caribou. (© Canadian Museum of Civilization, image from James A. Tuck, *Maritime Provinces Prehistory*, illustrator Dave Laverie, 1984, p. 5)

there is more evidence and because they produced 'diagnostic' forms of projectile points. We have already mentioned two of these, Folsom and Clovis. They are both bifacially flaked (worked on both sides), fluted projectile points, a style found widely across the continent. Fluted points have been dated in Canada from the Debert site in central Nova Scotia (10,600 BP), Sibbald Creek near Calgary, Alberta (9570 BP), and Charlie Lake Cave north of Fort St John, BC (10,500 BP). The Debert site included 140 artifacts, including spear points, drills, knives, wedges, and scrapers, providing a fuller view of the range of activities and skills of these people than most sites. The distribution of fluted points extends to the Yukon and Alaska, but is most extensive in the US.

Microblades, very small, unifacial, parallel-sided flakes that presumably were often inset into bone or wood tools, are found in Alaska and the Yukon before 11,000 BP. Part of their interest is that they appear in Siberia from 17,000 to 11,000 BP, and hence they quite directly link peoples on the two continents. They are also of interest because their use persists so long, on the BC coast

and interior until after 4000 BP and in the Arctic (where they are associated with people called Paleo-Eskimos, or the Arctic Small Tool tradition) until about 2800 BP.

About 10,000 BP fluted points were replaced on the Plains by stemmed points that are quite thick in cross-section. Collectively called Plano points, they were developed in the US Great Basin around 12,000 BP. They were then used on the Plains, on the northern barren grounds by 8000 BP, and as far east as the Gaspé Peninsula. While they generally seem not to have been used after about 7500 BP, their use persisted in northern Ontario until as recently as 5000 BP. One needs to be cautious in assuming that their persistence in the Subarctic has to do with cultural isolation; Plano style points at Acasta Lake in the Keewatin District dated at 6900 BP have side notches, presumably showing an awareness of a new hafting style developed on the Plains.

Canadian Paleo-Indians east of the Rockies concentrated on hunting big game. In the Far West a more diversified economy developed, although from quite early times salmon constituted the primary resource. The productivity of specific locations has led to spectacular archaeological sequences. The Milliken site near Hell's Gate, the narrowest part of the Fraser River and a natural location for fishing, provides an almost continuous record of occupation dating from 9000 BP. Farther north, the Namu site provides the longest essentially continuous record of occupation, dating from 9700 BP. The deepest level provides the earliest microblades on the coast. Recent work at On Your Knees Cave on Alaska's Prince of Wales Island has revealed human remains and artifacts dating to 10,000 BP made from material that could only have been transported by boat, as well as other tools (not microblades) dating to 10,300 BP. Sites on Haida Gwaii (the Queen Charlotte Islands off the northern British Columbia coast) go back to 10,000 BP and also indicate a strongly developed maritime

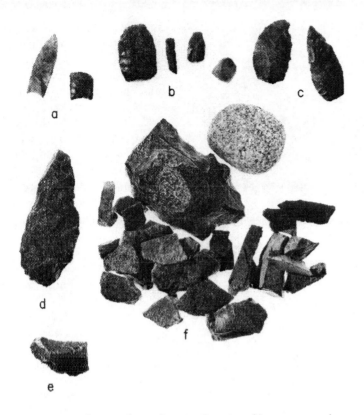

FIGURE 2.2. Plano artifacts: a) projectile points; b) scrapers used to work various materials such as hide, wood, and bone; c) knives; d) roughly shaped 'preform', an early step in making projectile points, knives, and other tools; e) a tool used for slotting bone and wood; f) hammerstone, core, and flakes (typical of quarry sites where tools were 'mass-produced'). (© Canadian Museum of Civilization, from J.V. Wright, *Ontario Prehistory*, 1984, p. 14)

begins about 5000 BP and leads directly to the Tsimshian. Because the site was waterlogged, there is remarkable preservation of perishables after 2000 BP, including whole houses and canoes (the large rectangular planked houses typical of the historic period appear on the coast at about this time). Farther south on the coast, Wakashan history can be inferred to extend to at least 4500 BP and Salish to 3500 BP. That is not to say, of course, that these people did not exist earlier as distinct groups.

The Interior Plateau of BC is less well known, partly because people tended to live in the same places as earlier people did, and making a new semi-subterranean pit house often meant digging up an old one. In any case, small villages appear by about 6000 BP, located near good fishing sites (and as salmon re-established themselves on these streams in the post-glacial environment). Houses of much the same style were still used in the last century.

The Plains appear to be relatively depopulated from about 7500 to 5000 BP, possibly due to the effects of the hypothesized hotter and drier period known as the Altithermal. If so, this was merely an extreme example of the standard Plains adaptational pattern: both the buffalo and those who lived off them moved from the Plains to the adjacent mountains and parkland during times of stress, including the average winter. Head-Smashed-In, a buffalo jump in southern Alberta, was in use from at least 5700 BP. Such sites, where massive quantities of meat were processed repeatedly, leave an interesting chronology, but of only one aspect of life.

Pottery appeared on the Canadian Plains somewhat before arrowheads. It is found as far northwest as central Alberta and, like burial

culture. There are also tantalizing finds of artifacts from underwater beaches that may be even older.

After the Paleo-Indians: Western Canada

Not only are the sequences on the west coast very old, they link at early stages to the area's contemporary residents. That the Haida are a linguistic isolate living on partially unglaciated islands and that sites such as Skoglund's Landing show a growing cultural complexity without significant intrusions suggest that the Haida have occupied the islands for at least the last 10,000 years. The sequence in Prince Rupert harbour

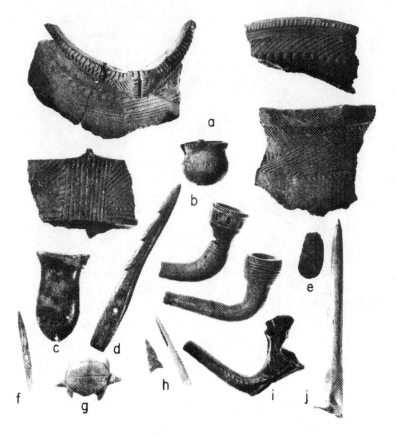

FIGURE 2.3. Iroquoian (Huron-Petun) artifacts: a) rim fragments from pots; b) pot, probably made by a small girl; c) stone pipe bowl; d) antler harpoon; e) scraper; f) netting needle; g) turtle amulet made of stone; h) stone and bone arrowheads; i) clay pipes; j) dagger made from human bone. (© Canadian Museum of Civilization, from J.V. Wright, *Ontario Prehistory*, 1984, p. 80)

L'Anse Amour is the earliest known burial mound in North America (7500 BP). Located in southern Labrador, it is associated with the Maritime Archaic culture. It contains the body of a young teenager and numerous grave goods, including points, knives, needles, a flute, and a toggle carved from an antler. Key interpretations are that the grave goods indicate not only a belief system including an afterlife, but: (1) a productive maritime hunting economy (a toggle harpoon head pivots inside the hide of a speared animal after the attached line is pulled, allowing the offshore hunting of sea mammals), and (2) the subsequent development of some degree of social differentiation. By 5000 BP Maritime Archaic people had expanded to Newfoundland, indicating they had seaworthy craft.

The Laurentian Archaic developed in southern Ontario and Quebec, later expanding to New Brunswick and Maine. Few campsites have been found (they moved a lot), but about 6000 BP they started placing grave goods in burial sites. These goods indicate an extensive trade network, including conch shells from the Gulf of Mexico, copper work from west of Lake Superior, and ground slate points from Maritime Archaic people.

mounds (found as far northwest as southeastern Saskatchewan) and farming (as far northwest as North Dakota), was derived from the Woodland culture of southern Ontario and the Mississippi Valley and ultimately from the cultures of Mexico, or even Colombia.

Eastern Canada: Archaic Period (9500–3000 BP)

'Archaic' is an unfortunate term, but it is thoroughly embedded in the literature. It generally refers to people who have a broadly based foraging lifestyle of hunting, fishing, and gathering.

Eastern Canada: Woodland Period (3300 BP–Historic Era)

Woodland culture is primarily a culture of the eastern US, extending into the southern part of

FIGURE 2.4. These are examples of the kinds of stone tools made by people in Alaska early in the post-glacial period. At lower left is a microblade core from which sharp, parallel-sided blades (lower right) were removed. Microblades could be used as knife blades or further modified to form small points on weapons. Above these artifacts are a larger stone core and a spear point. Few other artifacts have been preserved from this time period. (© Canadian Museum of Civilization, from Robert McGhee, *Canadian Arctic Prehistory*, 1978, photographer Don E. Edmond, p. 11)

eastern Canada. It is a northern extension of a settled, agricultural way of life largely originating in Mexico (although local plants were domesticated before they adopted more southerly cultigens) but achieving a regional cultural focus in the central Mississippi Valley. The archaeological convention (arising out of the incorrect assumption that only agriculturalists made pottery) is to refer to people as Woodland if they made pottery even if they were not actually agriculturalists.

About 3300 BP Laurentian Archaic people started making ceramic beakers with pointed bottoms and cord-marked walls. This marks the beginning of Woodland culture in Canada, although the people continued to be nomadic hunters.

The Point Peninsula phase began about 2750 BP. The pottery marking this phase clearly was strongly influenced by the Adena culture of the Ohio Valley; it also demonstrates local affinities (like cord marking) and influences from northern Ontario ('toothed' markings). As time goes on, the extensive trade in regionally identifiable goods indicates complex and continuing connections spanning half the continent.

Canadian Woodland culture clearly developed in part out of local antecedents generally thought to be associated with the Algonquian language family. Just as clearly, southern Ontario has also been inhabited for some time by Iroquoian speakers. Although there are reasons to think that Iroquoians may have reached the area as early as 3500 BP, only by 1100 BP are there palisaded villages with corn fields and large ossuaries clearly identifiable as Iroquoian. About 700 years ago these people experienced a significant geographic expansion from a southern Ontario base leading to their historically known territories.

From earliest times this has been a region of hunters living in small bands that moved frequently. It is also a region of acidic soils that quickly destroy most of the things that humans leave behind. It is not surprising, then, that we know relatively little about the area.

Boreal Forest and Subarctic Tundra

As noted earlier, Paleo-Indians moved into the Subarctic tundra and boreal forest as the glaciers melted. The lanceolate points characteristic of the Paleo-Indians continued to characterize this region after the side-notched points that archaeologists use to define the Shield Archaic (6000 BP to historic times) were introduced. About 2200 BP Shield Archaic people living in eastern Manitoba and the adjacent Rainy River region of northern

Ontario started making Laurel pottery. The Rainy River region is also known for burial mounds with especially rich grave goods. This is most unusual for boreal forest hunters, but perhaps the point is more that the area is relatively close both to the Great Lakes and to the Plains and, therefore, to people living different lifestyles. About AD 700 other types of pottery originating in southern Ontario came into use.

The Arctic

The Arctic is the most recently inhabited part of Canada. Only 4,000 years ago did people spread eastward from what is now Alaska, moving quite rapidly across the High Arctic islands to northern Greenland. These first inhabitants of Canada's Arctic are known as Independence I people, from the Greenlandic fjord where they were first identified. They were part of a cultural tradition known both as Paleo-Eskimo and as the Arctic Small Tool tradition, from their use of microblades as tool components. The use of microblades and a complex of other features link the Paleo-Eskimo both to earlier Alaskan cultures and ultimately to the Djuktai culture of northeastern Siberia. Djuktai, formerly dated to 35,000 BP, is now understood to be only 17,000 years old, making it less interesting but still ancestral to these people. The rapid movement of the first Paleo-Eskimos across previously uninhabited areas seems to require some explanation. One possible factor may be that, although people had been living in the North for some time, their annual cycle had them moving seasonally back and forth between forest and shore; only now had they learned to live throughout the year near the Arctic shoreline.

Another factor may be that the shore region was now habitable for the first time since the glacial age due to a stabilized sea level and increasing (although still low) stocks of maritime resources. This may be reflected in the apparently greater reliance of the Independence I people on land resources like caribou and muskox than on seals and walrus. Since the number of land animals living on islands is limited and since these land animals reproduce slowly, an explanation for why the people kept moving from island to island and why they disappeared shortly after reaching the eastern end of the High Arctic island chain may be that they simply ran out of food and in the end literally had nowhere to go.

Only 300 years after the Independence I people, however, a second wave of Paleo-Eskimos, known as Pre-Dorset people, moved eastward out of Alaska. Perhaps because they had a more balanced reliance on land and sea resources, their colonization of the Arctic was successful. In any case, for about 1,000 years small, mobile groups of these people occupied the Far North. This is not to say they occupied all the territory all the time. Richer areas seem to have been used continuously; other areas were occupied or abandoned as local conditions warranted. The cultural variability one would expect under these conditions did in fact arise. In general, we can say that these people lived in skin tents for much of the year. They also used snow houses (they may have invented them) and heated them with oil lamps. They may have used skin-covered boats. They had dogs, but not dog sleds. They used sinew-backed bows much like more modern ones.

Life in the Arctic is never easy, but life for the Pre-Dorset became harder as the decades went by because their entry into the Arctic coincided with a long-term cooling trend. With game becoming scarcer, even good hunters may go hungry. By 3000 BP the Pre-Dorset range seems to have become restricted to Foxe Basin and Hudson Strait.

Given these circumstances, we are not surprised to find that people turned increasingly to hunting sea mammals, particularly those, such as seals and walrus, that are 'ice-loving' and hence fairly accessible. With this orientation there is a concomitant decline in the number of dogs, bows and arrows are abandoned, the snow knife is invented, oil lamps are used more, stone cooking pots are used, ice creepers (to strap on the feet while walking on ice) are found, and the kayak is definitely used.

BOX 2.1

Kwädäy Dän Ts'ìnchi—
'This is a man, not an experiment'

In August 1999, human remains were discovered melting out of a glacier in Tatshenshini-Alsek Park, located in the extreme northwest corner of British Columbia. Concurrently, a number of artifacts (clothing, tools, food items) made of perishable materials were found in direct association with the remains. Immediately after the discovery was reported to authorities, the site was visited and evaluated by archaeologists and representatives of the Champagne and Aishihik First Nations (CAFN). The discovery was named Kwädäy Dän Ts'ìnchi, 'Long Ago Person Found'. As a recovery and research plan started to evolve, a unique, co-operative, and collaborative relationship, culminating in a formal agreement, was struck between the CAFN and the government of BC (Archaeology Branch). The committee thus formed was responsible for overseeing the recovery and proper handling of the remains and the subsequent proposed research. Priority issues involved quickly planning and co-ordinating a safe, contamination-free recovery and determining where the remains and artifacts would be housed. They decided that the best location would be specially altered facilities at the Royal BC Museum in Victoria. The preservation protocol was a customized version of the methods used at the University of Innsbruck to protect and preserve the 5,300-year-old Neolithic man found in an Italian glacier in 1991.

During late 1999 and early 2000, the committee evaluated many research proposals submitted by scientists from a number of countries, and selected some to conduct studies. Projects included dating the human remains and artifacts (about 450 years old), the forensic evaluation of the body, determination of the individual's diet, and examination of DNA evidence. The needs of these research projects were met by the committee agreeing to the collection and retention of the required samples from the individual and artifacts, and providing access to the discoveries. CAFN members enthusiastically volunteered for DNA testing in hope of establishing a connection to Kwädäy Dän Ts'ìnchi. Some results are starting to be published (Beattie et al., 2000; Monsalve et al., 2002), but much work is still in progress.

Many difficult issues and important decisions were made regarding the modern cultural and scientific needs and sensitivities inherent in such a discovery. No perfect solutions exist, but the real possibility that this man could be documented in oral histories highlighted the need to approach the discovery with the same respect and sensitivity that a coroner or medical examiner would show to a recently deceased body. This can be seen to contrast with the need of science to be allowed the unrestricted freedom to pursue the collection of scientific data. Some controversy will always be associated with the natural tension that exits between conflicting needs. But to paraphrase a colleague commenting on these needs, 'This is a man, not an experiment.' That sentiment has been the guiding philosophy in the research on Kwädäy Dän Ts'ìnchi. His remains were returned to the site of discovery in August 2001 and interred.

—Owen Beattie, Department of Anthropology,
University of Alberta

FIGURE 2.5. These Pre-Dorset artifacts are quite similar to those of the Independence I culture, except for some stylistic features and the two harpoon heads (upper left). Proceeding clockwise, the other items are: what is probably a broken fish spear head, two harpoon or spear points, side blades for insetting into the sides of weapon heads, two burins for working bone or antler, microblades, two scrapers, a bone needle, and a bone pin. (© Canadian Museum of Civilization, photographer Harry Foster, 1978, 77–30)

animal skins. By acting as a drag and a marker, the device greatly improved the efficiency of walrus and whale hunting. After this the population expanded greatly and society became more complex. The resultant cultural tradition is referred to by archaeologists as Thule culture. For a variety of reasons, but certainly in part because it was effective both economically and socially, Thule culture spread into southwestern Alaska, into the interior of Alaska, and eastward across Canada to Greenland.

The bearers of Thule culture into Canada were Inupik speakers, ancestral to the modern Inuit. While it is clear that their sweep across the Arctic was rapid, we know very little about the nature of their relationship with the Dorset populations already there. It is easy to envision hostile encounters between bands of armed hunters, but there is no direct evidence of such conflict. Perhaps the Dorset simply retreated. Or, as Hickey (1986)

By 2500 BP the cumulative effect of these changes had become transformative; the new society is referred to as Dorset. Dorset culture flourished and recolonized the sea margins of the North from Labrador to Greenland and westward toward Alaska.

While our narrative is focused on the Canadian Arctic, we must now turn to Alaska. The archaeology of Alaska is complex, in part because it was a meeting ground between North Pacific and Arctic peoples. A critical event was the adaptation in the ninth century by northwestern Alaskan peoples of a Japanese innovation—making large floats out of

thinks more likely, the Thule incorporated at least some Dorset people (although recent DNA studies suggest not).

In Hickey's scenario, it would be advantageous to the immigrant Thule to take advantage of the detailed local environmental knowledge of Dorset men. Dorset women would be valued as domestic and procreative assets, but more importantly as a medium for social alliances. Such a process would leave little archaeological evidence. An intriguing line of evidence in favour of Dorset people being incorporated into Thule society is the continued tradition of women in

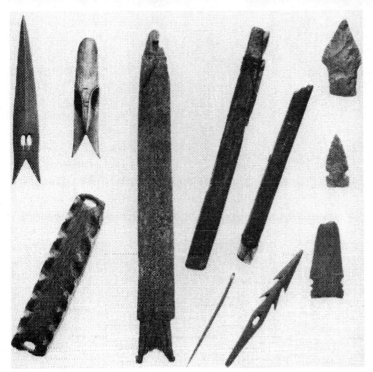

FIGURE 2.6. These are examples of the more 'sophisticated' technology of the Dorset people. Clockwise from the upper left: two harpoon heads, a large lance head, a knife utilizing a microblade, a ground burin-like implement with its handle, two flaked stone and one ground stone points, a fish arrow or spear head, a bone needle, and an ivory ice-creeper. (© Canadian Museum of Civilization, photographer Harry Foster, 1978, 77–28)

course, did not think of their experiences in those terms, for their frames of reference were different. Nevertheless, they created a series of diverse and successful adaptations to the entire range of environments to be found. And here, in turn, they were 'found' by another kind of migrant.

A Millennium of European Immigration

European immigration began with at least one aborted attempt at settlement by the Norse about 1,000 years ago. There is scant but tantalizing evidence for contact between Europeans and indigenous Americans over the next 500 years. European and African immigration to the territory that is now Canada began building in the sixteenth century, accelerated dramatically in the seventeenth century, increased even more dramati-

the eastern Arctic making special 'dress-up' clothing that is much more complex in construction than are utilitarian garments. This seems more consistent with the ornate Dorset artistic aesthetic than with the generally austere Thule taste. In this view, Dorset women in Thule households would generally have raised their children as Thule, but might well also pass on special skills and aesthetic judgements that they valued highly. In any case, Thule people prospered and for roughly 1,000 years evolved into the several historic Inuit societies.

In sum, North and South America were inhabited an unimaginably long time ago by people who migrated over the land mass that now constitutes Asia and the Americas. They, of

cally in the eighteenth century, and became overwhelming in the nineteenth century. The human migration from Europe between the early 1600s and 1930 was probably the largest ever, and it changed the face of the Americas. The history of the First Nations of Canada in the face of that massive immigration of Europeans is one of survival. It is first of all a history of physical survival, given the effects that European diseases had on indigenous populations. An aspect of history that is resonant with our own era has to do with another kind of survival: the history of the relations between indigenous Canadians and the Europeans, Africans, and Asians who migrated here after 1600 is one of the struggle for survival of

FIGURE 2.7. Illustrating the great difference between Thule and the earlier Paleo-Eskimo technology, we see clockwise from the right: an adze handle, an adze head with a ground stone blade, a man's knife with a ground stone blade, a woman's knife (ulu) with an iron blade, a whalebone snow knife, a bone scraper for skin working, an engraving tool with an iron point, and a drill bit with a ground stone point. (© Canadian Museum of Civilization, photographer Harry Foster, 1978, 77–27)

Treaty of Utrecht in 1713 they completely ignored consideration of Mi'kmaq or Maliseet interest or opinion in the French relinquishment of Acadia to the English.

In the European conception of things, America was a wilderness and Natives were part of that wilderness. That idea could be maintained despite all the evidence: the obvious concentration of indigenous populations, the obvious control and management of unfenced pasture areas in which many Native people harvested mammals for food, the practice of agriculture, the military power and skills of indigenous groups, and the extensive trade networks. The country was no wilderness, and given the evidence it is a wonder that Europeans could see it as one. It was a European legal and moral convention to assume that land that had not been extensively used and modified by 'civilized' peoples was in fact empty, and so could be claimed by Christian, civilized Europeans. That idea may have been a powerful constraint on European understanding of how American indigenous groups occupied and used land.

The period of sustained contact began in Canada in Newfoundland and the Maritimes, followed shortly thereafter by the Gaspé and the immediate St Lawrence watershed. During the sixteenth century European settlement in North America was focused on the subtropical regions, but Europeans had become familiar with the North Atlantic coast through the activity of the Atlantic fishery. Portuguese, Basque, and English exploitation of the Newfoundland fishery accelerated during the 1500s, until every summer saw

sovereignty within a European Christian conception of land rights.

The paradox was that during the first century of sustained contact, it was obvious that Europeans stayed on at the sufferance of their hosts and trading partners. While explorers could claim a territory for a European crown, the reality of control over the territory was not always coincident with the claim. Recognition of the reality of Amerindian control made it necessary to purchase land from Indians or for Europeans to ally themselves with Indians for trade and warfare. Europeans professed dual postures to their Indian allies, trading with them, even adopting indigenous forms of negotiation and trade protocols, but claiming European sovereignty in law. Thus, more than 150 years after the beginning of sustained contact, the French could claim to the English that French presence in Acadia was by right of Indian invitation to be there, yet in negotiating the around 17,000 European males along the north-east coast. Though occasionally some crew members wintered over, there was no really permanent settlement. Trade in furs, at first an adjunct to exploration, began in earnest during this time, with French and English voyages of trade and exploration along the coast and up the St Lawrence River.

The first and lasting effect of sustained contact was disease. No one knows the extent of the first great smallpox epidemic in 1520–4. It began in the West Indies and Mexico and spread northward to affect most of North America. It was followed by a devastating epidemic of measles just seven years later. An epidemic caused by an unknown pathogen affected people of the St Lawrence Valley in 1535, and smallpox struck again in the eastern Great Lakes region in the early 1590s. European diseases took a crushing toll: smallpox, for example, seemed to hit every other generation, as each generation that had gained some immunity was replaced by a new, susceptible one.

The number of people who died or who were permanently disabled by disease is a matter of speculation. Estimates of the population of North America north of the cities of Mexico in the early sixteenth century vary from 4.5 million to as high as 18 million, and one of the difficulties in making the estimate is the incalculably devastating effects of the early epidemics. The cost in human life has been very great: susceptibility to European disease was a major factor in the decline of the indigenous population until the 1920s, to the extent that by the last part of the nineteenth century the indigenous population of the US and Canada dropped to around 300,000. Epidemics of smallpox, measles, influenza, and bubonic plague were the greatest killers, and diphtheria, cholera, typhus, scarlet fever, and typhoid also caused high mortality. The early epidemics preceded initial European settlement in the Northeast, so when that settlement began in earnest in the early 1600s it was among an indigenous population already seriously affected by European diseases.

Alliances in Trade and Warfare

Acceleration of the trade in furs was coincident with the first sustained European settlement in the early seventeenth century in the areas that now comprise Canada and the United States. European immigration began building in the 1630s, with French, English, Dutch, and Swedish establishment of fur-trading posts and with experiments in agricultural settlement by the French and English. Trade relationships begun during the sixteenth century formed the basis for the initial pattern of European settlement, with the various European nations establishing colonies in territory controlled by the indigenous nations with which each European nation had regularly allied itself in trade.

We tend to look at those alliances nowadays in terms of their lasting significance rather than in terms of what motivated them at the time. Perhaps we lend too much relevance to those alliances that seem to have endured and to have changed history because of the eventual balance of power between European nations. The seventeenth century was a time of huge increase in trade between Europeans and Amerindians as well as of European encroachment on Indian land. Our discussions cloud a very complex period of competition among the European groups themselves for control of land for expansion and of competition among indigenous nations, both in economic terms and for favourable terms of survival given the European onslaught.

The alliances built on, exploited, and irrevocably disrupted ancient trade patterns between indigenous nations. Indigenous trade patterns had been predominantly north and south, but the French inroad had been east to west, from Acadia to Gaspé, the St Lawrence Valley, and then the Great Lakes and south through the Ohio and Mississippi River systems. The French were allied initially in the Maritimes with the Mi'kmaq and Maliseet, then with factions of those groups' occasional enemies, the Eastern Abenaki. Their allies north of the St Lawrence were the Montagnais and, in the interior, the Algonquians and a major group of Huron nations. The Dutch were initially allied with the Algonquian groups around the Hudson River, but sought alliance with the group that became known as the Five Nations Iroquois. England's beachhead was first in New England and then in its settlements south of Chesapeake Bay.

The Iroquois of the Five Nations gained tremendous political power by challenging the French and their allies to control trade on the St Lawrence and then by allying themselves with the British. As the English took over Indian land in New England and along the Hudson River, groups displaced by British encroachment moved westward and some former enemies of the Five Nations put themselves under the protection of their erstwhile foes. Five Nations ascendancy was clearly realized when they destroyed the strongest interior trading partners to the north, the Huron allies of the French, during the mid-1600s.

Disease was a continuing major factor in the European expansion of the seventeenth century, with epidemics of bubonic plague in New England during the years 1612–19, measles in 1633–4 throughout the whole Northeast and again in 1658–9, scarlet fever in 1637 among the Hurons, diphtheria in 1659 in New England and eastern Canada, and smallpox, which racked the entire Northeast at least once during each decade from the 1630s to the 1690s. Military action against Indians was usually along lines consistent with the pattern of European alliance, but in New England there was military action against Indians for control of land. The military action, from the European colonizers' standpoint, was probably not as effective as disease. The effects of disease on Native populations were so obvious that English colonists could interpret the devastation brought by epidemics as divine sanction for European possession and repopulation of the land.

Control over territory and trade was clearly the cause of war. France and England were at war during much of the seventeenth century. The Five Nations Iroquois fought the French for nearly the entire century, the Abenaki fought the English for

control of northern New England, and New England Algonquians went to war to attempt to remove the English from their territory.

European Expansion into the Interior during the Eighteenth Century

The eighteenth century was a time of continued conflict between European powers and conflict between England and her American colonies. A significant part of that conflict was played out in America. The Five Nations Iroquois established peace with French colonists in 1701, but their allies the Fox, in the area that is now Wisconsin, continued hostile action against the French and their Dakota allies. The French sought to maintain a continental sphere of influence through the Great Lakes to the Mississippi, and fought with the English over control of trade in Hudson Bay. During the early part of the eighteenth century French interests were well served by Mi'kmaq military conflict with the English in the Maritimes.

If the focus is on European conflict, the history of relationships between European colonists and the different Indian nations during the seventeenth and eighteenth centuries is one of shifting alliances and unclear national boundaries: for example, during the last era of formal conflict between the French and the Five Nations Iroquois, many Christianized Iroquois settled in villages near Montreal. That illustrates two aspects of Amerindian-European relationship: (1) missionization had become important as a policy of control and pacification; (2) Amerindian political organization was markedly different from that of Europeans. Indian military strategy, patterns of alliance, social movement, and migration are more clearly explicable if the focus is not on European spheres of influence and power balances but on Amerindian groups' own attempts to control trade and land on their own terms, to adapt to the presence of Europeans, and above all to retain a land base for themselves that they might control. In other words, Indian political alliance was not a matter of less powerful nations aligning with more powerful European partners, but was instead a series of strategic partnerships, negotiations, diplomatic ventures, and armed hostility, all oriented towards maximizing each Amerindian group's interests.

Relationships among Indian nations were oriented to the same end—maximizing the specific national interest of the individual nation. The nations of New England and the American Atlantic seaboard, displaced and decimated by European disease and finding refuge with other groups, were among the first to couch the struggles of the seventeenth and eighteenth centuries in terms of a conflict of a duality, Indians against Europeans. Groups such as the Delaware, formed as a collectivity from Algonquian survivors of groups north of Chesapeake Bay, first moved west to put themselves under the protection of their former antagonists, the Five Nations Iroquois, and then further west to the continental interior and to Upper Canada. Some of their leaders were influential in attempts to bring Indian nations together to fight in common cause against European colonists.

The English Royal Proclamation of 1763, requiring that any alienation of Indian land be negotiated and that the Crown be the sole European agency in negotiation, was a central component of an Imperial strategy to ally Indian nations with Britain. When English domination was established in Quebec and the Maritimes during the last half of the eighteenth century, the possibility for Indian nations to play off one power against the other was removed, but during the war between England and the 13 American colonies Indian nations were fighting on both sides, and they continued to face other Indian nations in battle in alliances with Europeans until the cessation of hostilities between Canada and the US in 1814.

Patterns of European migration changed as well. Until the establishment of the United States, around two-thirds of the immigrants other than slaves had been indentured labourers. After the American Revolution, European immigration to North America was predominantly by free

persons, and there was a large one-time immigration of British Loyalists from the US to Canada.

The last part of the eighteenth century saw increased direct trade between Europeans and Indians in the interior, building on primarily east-west trade routes that had been established in the fur trade among Indian groups. That trade was extended through the watersheds that led to Hudson Bay.

Trade with the Pacific Northwest began during the last part of the eighteenth century. It was joined by the Russians, who established permanent trading and missionary ventures with their claim to Alaska. English and American trading in the Northwest was initially by ship, and the commodities bought from Indians were primarily maritime products, such as sea otter pelts. By 1821, when the Montreal-based North West Company and the London-based Hudson's Bay Company amalgamated, the fur trade relied primarily on land mammals and was conducted in trading posts, and the HBC had extended its domain to the coast with the amalgamation. The decade of the 1830s saw the beginning of European settlement in the area that is now British Columbia. Though conflict between west coast Indians and individual traders could be bloody, the pattern of alliances and warfare of the east coast was not repeated in the West, except for the battles fought between Tlingits and Russians.

Before any appreciable contact, around 1770, the first of the great smallpox epidemics hit the Northwest Coast. It may have reduced the total population by 30 per cent. Before the introduction of European disease, the area had been the most highly populated of any non-agricultural area in the world, with as many as 180,000 inhabitants. Losses from a single epidemic would claim as much as two-thirds of the population of a single community, and as each succeeding epidemic claimed lives the Native population was reduced to just over 30,000 by the late 1800s.

The eighteenth century was also a time of displacement and migration. In the West, some nations whose way of life and habitation had been primarily in woodlands and parklands saw some of their people move onto the Plains. In the south, adoption of the horse as a central part of the culture facilitated that movement. Some groups whose livelihood had been in agriculture and the harvest of land mammals abandoned agriculture to hunt with horses and to trade for agriculture products and European goods with indigenous agriculturalists in the river valleys. In the northern Plains, the move was facilitated by a growing market to provision the fur trade with food and other supplies.

A Tide of Immigration and the Beginning of the Reserve Era

The nineteenth century, by contrast to the preceding 200 years, was a period of relative peace between European powers and a period of wholesale change in the Americas. The United States and Canada had used Aboriginal groups as buffers along their common border. When the possibility of war between the two countries diminished after the signing of a formal treaty in 1817, the importance of Indians as military allies decreased and a period of oppressive attempts to control them began. The US began relocating Indians westward, including groups who had lived near the eastern international border with Canada, and by the 1820s the strategic importance of Indian nations in that area, as military allies of Canada, was diminished.

The intensification of industrialization in Europe displaced many of its own people and created a world demand for agricultural land and agricultural products. Between 1814 and World War I around 50 million people migrated from Europe to the 'new Europes' of the Americas and Australasia. Two-thirds of them came to the United States and 4 million to Canada, where the largest tide of immigration was to the West after the 1890s.

The policies of both the US and Canada were westward expansion and the alienation of ever more Indian land to provide a place for Europeans to farm. Populations of Amerindians continued to decline in the face of repeated epidemics, but the birth rate of new immigrants was one of the highest ever recorded, especially among Caucasians. The African-American population increased as well, through natural increase and the importation of slaves, so that their population in North America went from 1 million in 1800 to around 12 million by 1930.

Policies that became pre-eminent in the early 1800s seem to have driven Canadian government interaction with indigenous nations for the next two centuries. It appeared to most non-Native observers that indigenous groups were dying out. The continuing dramatic toll of disease in Native populations appeared to make their eventual demise inevitable. Social philosophy as it developed during the nineteenth century saw all human groups as developing through inevitably sequenced stages, and Native cultures were thought to be in a stage of 'savagery'. In that conception of things, Euro-Canadian culture was an aspect of Western Europe's pre-eminent development to 'civilization'. During the last half of the nineteenth century the concept of social Darwinism expanded on the assumption that Indian cultures represented less progress and less cultural development than European cultures, and it was assumed that 'civilized' cultures were 'fittest' to survive in any context of cultural conflict over resources.

Peace between the United States and British North America after 1817 brought an end to the long period of military and political alliance among First Nations and European, colonial, and American governments. No longer needed as political allies, Native people became objects of altruism: European social philosophers saw them as being in need of 'advancement' to participate in 'civilization'. Churches and missionary societies defined Natives as needy in economic, social, moral, and spiritual terms. Indians, in areas where Europeans wanted land, needed to be protected and, eventually, assimilated. Churches and philanthropic organizations, primarily in Britain but also in the US, focused on Canadian indigenous nations as subjects of concerted missionary activity. From the 1820s until mid-century, British missionary organizations were a powerful lobby in the British Parliament for reorienting colonial policy towards the philanthropic end of Christianizing and civilizing Indians and Eskimos.

Since the Royal Proclamation of 1763, the management of the relationship between Indians and the government had been the responsibility of the British government rather than any colonial government. An imperial policy of 'civilization' of Indians as communities began in 1830. It marked the beginning of the reserve period in Canada. Indians were to congregate on land reserved for them, apart from the rest of Canadian society, and, as communities, to adapt to Canada's changing social order by learning to farm. The government encouraged missionary activity and the nineteenth-century debate over which came first, civilization or Christianization, seems to have had its popular origins in this period. The policy had its greatest impact east of Lake Superior. Rupert's Land was still the domain of the Hudson's Bay Company and the indigenous nations there were autonomous and relatively self-sufficient through participation in the fur trade and through traditional harvest of food and other resources. They effectively controlled the Plains, the western and northern woodlands and parklands, and the Arctic. European settlement began to increase in BC in the 1840s, and the first reserves in that colony were established during this early period of increased government control of Indians.

In the last few years of 1870s the policy changed from one of assimilation by community to one of outright assimilation as individuals: the policy of establishing isolated reserves changed, and it was thought that reserves should be close enough to non-Native communities for individuals to have an incentive to become 'enfranchised', that is, to have the same legal status (and way of life) as individuals as non-Native Canadians. Though provision was made for individual enfranchisement, the number of people who opted for it was minuscule.

When Canada took over control of Indian affairs at the time of Confederation, indigenous nations became internal colonies. Until then, Indian groups had maintained control over their land, financial arrangements, membership, business dealings with outsiders, and internal governance. The first legislation about Indians in post-Confederation Canada, the Indian Act of 1876, effectively removed their control in all those areas and imposed systems of band governance that allowed the federal government exclusive control over Indian national leadership, land, membership, and money. Another challenge to internal band authority and First Nations community integrity was the policy's manifest orientation towards individual enfranchisement. Canada had no effective control over those matters in the North and West, so at first the policies applied only to those bands east of the Lakehead.

The issue for all indigenous nations in Canada where they were in contact with Europeans became one of maintaining the integrity of their individual communities. During the last few years of 1860s, Native community integrity was at the heart of the conflict surrounding the admission of Manitoba as a province, and it was most surely the issue in the 1885 Rebellion. In the case of Manitoba, an attempt was made to resolve the issue by negotiating terms for the admission of the province that appeared favourable to the retention of Metis community structures. The almost immediate failure of those provisions was one of the origins of the tension that resulted in the 1885 uprising.

During the 1870s pressure to alienate Indian lands in western Ontario and in Manitoba motivated the federal government to enter into formal treaties, as had been done earlier in Ontario with the Robinson Huron and Robinson Superior treaties of 1850. An added federal government impetus as the treaty process moved west was to attempt to extinguish Metis claims. The self-sufficiency of the nations of the prairies and western parklands was threatened during the decade after Confederation because of the dramatic decrease, then absence, of the great buffalo herds upon which they depended. During the 1870s the Plains nations joined treaty negotiations as an alternative to starvation, though some groups of Cree, Assiniboine, and Saulteaux attempted to maintain autonomy through coalition by congregating in the Cypress Hills in Assiniboia, near the present boundaries of Alberta, Saskatchewan, and Montana.

In 1871 British Columbia entered Confederation with the federal government assuming responsibility for the administration of Indian affairs, but with a proviso for provincial involvement in any Indian land settlements. (Except for a few early treaties on Vancouver Island and the extension of Treaty No. 8 into the northeastern part of the province, the alienation of Indian land in BC has not involved treaties.)

Thus the establishment of reserves and the policy of wardship of Indians during an anticipated period of assimilation were cornerstones of the policies governing indigenous nations within Confederation. The policies that characterize the reserve period were begun in the 1830s, were modified in the 1850s and again in the late 1860s, and then were implemented as each area of the country was alienated from effective Native control. A most interesting aspect of the policies was the uniformity with which they were applied. The policies directed governmental relations with groups such as the Mi'kmaq and Iroquois, who had been trading with and fighting alongside Europeans for almost 300 years; with groups such as the Cree and Blackfoot, who had had completely different trading relationships with Europeans; and with groups in the Mackenzie watershed and northern BC, some of whom were entering their first sustained relationships with Europeans.

If we focus on the government's rationale for the institution of such policies, it is possible to accept Tobias's (1991) interpretation that the policies were directed by a concern for the 'protection, civilization, and assimilation' of indigenous people. If, instead, we look at the legislation itself,

the way policies were carried out, and the effect of the policies 'on the ground', the idea of protection is not an acceptable interpretation. The reserve era was one of control and containment of Indians, primarily under authority provided by the Indian Act. Characteristics of the era are:

- duplicity in the alienation of even more land, including land previously reserved for Indians;
- heavy-handedness and arbitrary judgement in the definition of who was an Indian, both through the Indian Act itself and most particularly in the way recognition as being Indian was effected in individual cases;
- control over internal governance of bands, the election and recognition of leadership, and the definition of band responsibilities;
- corruption in the provision of goods and services to bands;
- legal sanctions against the practice of indigenous religion and spirituality;
- the establishment of industrial schools, then residential schools operated by churches, in which Indian custom was denigrated and in which an attempt was made to wipe out the use of indigenous languages;
- the institutionalization and structuring of schooling, generally, that made academic success and achievement extremely difficult;
- control over persons and individual movement and mobility, with the institution of 'passes' for leaving reserves;
- control over the finances of individuals and bands;
- the institution of policies that made early Indian successes at farming impossible to maintain; and
- legal sanctions against meeting and organizing.

Though the reserve era is characterized by the Indian Act, federal administration of reserves, and oppressive policies, it is in fact simply a name that characterizes oppression over a period of time, whether or not the people affected were resident on reserves. Reserves were not established in the North for either Inuit or northern Dene, and some bands whose treaties provide for reserves have still to see them established, but the Indian Act has applied to all people recognized as Indian under the Act, and the constraint and regulation of the reserve era have been as oppressive to off-reserve Indians as to those who live on reserves. Exclusion from identification as Indian, under the Act, had the effect of socially defining a significant number of 'non-status Indians' as 'Metis'. During the early part of the twentieth century, Inuit were specifically excluded from definition as Indian but nonetheless had their affairs administered by the same department as Indians. The Metis, the large community of mixed-ancestry people who had begun forming indigenous communities west of the Great Lakes as early as the late 1600s, did not have reserves, as their rights to land were supposed to have been recognized by the issuance to individuals of 'scrip', which was to be exchanged for land.

Resistance

The record of First Nations resistance to the measures of the reserve era is a long and detailed one. From the very beginning of the reserve era, individual leaders approached the government with complaints, protests, and constructive suggestions. The kind of control exerted by government agencies over the lives of Indians and whatever Inuit were in the orbit of government influence militated against either economic development or individual achievement. The era between the two world wars was one of particular economic hardship for many Canadians, and particularly so for the many First Nations people whose traditional subsistence base of agriculture and resource harvest had been destroyed.

Pan-Canadian organization of Indians began in 1919 with the efforts of F.O. Loft, a Mohawk army officer who was an organizer of the League of Indians of Canada (Cuthand, 1991). Regional coalitions of First Nations groups began organiz-ing in the 1920s and 1930s, one of which in Alberta was responsible for eventual government establishment of Metis settlements in the only province to set such land aside.

After World War II it became increasingly clear to government that the inequities perpetuated in the name of wardship had to change, but change was slow and often apparently in the wrong direction. As after World War I, returning Indian veterans were in the vanguard of organization and protest. For the first time since sustained contact, the rate of increase in the indigenous population was accelerating but post-war economic development largely excluded Indians, so the economic distinctions between Euro-Canadians and Indians became more marked. The middle part of the century brought the last relatively isolated groups of indigenous people into sustained contact with government agencies, and yet another revision of the Indian Act in 1951 reinformed policies of control. The concept of wardship was still firmly entrenched in its provisions. A major change came in 1960 when registered and treaty Indians—quite abruptly and with negligible consultation—were recognized as citizens of Canada. The federal government took over administration of Indian and territorial schools from the missionary groups who had operated them since at least the 1850s, and many of the residential schools were phased out. The courts took on more importance as contentious issues were increasingly being settled there.

In 1969 a major change in governance was proposed in a government White Paper: the Indian Act and reserves were to be phased out and provinces would take over administration of Indian affairs. Echoing the policy changes of the 1850s, indigenous people were to be dealt with individually by government, not as groups. The government professed the changes to be a movement towards equality and justice.

A very strong indigenous protest, particularly from the National Indian Brotherhood (later to become the Assembly of First Nations), came in response: the message was that injustice had indeed been perpetuated but that government had not got the main point about the nature of the injustice. Rather than an equality in law as assimilated individuals, indigenous people—as groups and not as individuals—had rights that derived from their status as indigenous people. There were rights to land that had never been ceded, rights that derived from treaties, rights that inhered in the nature of indigenous peoples' relationship with land, and rights to govern themselves. Those rights had not been granted by the government and could not be removed by government: treaty rights had been negotiated and could not be unilaterally changed; other rights were inherent in Aboriginal status in Canada.

In the 1970s, two important court decisions in Canada about land, one brought by the Nisga'a in BC and the other by Cree and Inuit in northern Quebec, made First Nations' claims about land and rights credible to the federal government. For the first time since Confederation there was a government willingness to discuss a remedy for the negative consequences of the policies of the reserve era. The federal government instituted processes whereby claims for compensation and land could be heard, and those claims were to be distinguished as either comprehensive or specific. Comprehensive claims were primarily those where rights to Euro-Canadian use of land had not been negotiated and specific claims were for cases in which specific obligations had not been met by the government. The claims process continues, but the system set up to deal with claims has been overwhelmed by the several hundred claims brought to it, and should it continue to work at its present pace, claims will not be resolved for centuries.

The policy foundation for a return to First Nations self-government was established in the 1970s, though it was laid piecemeal. The substantive foundation was the persistent will of First Nations leaders and Aboriginal people generally to demonstrate that the right and responsibility for self-governance had never been relinquished. One of the first government policy objectives was

to mandate control of First Nations schools by First Nations peoples. A corollary was the provision of funding for legal treaty research in connection with claims processes, as well as the federal provision of funding for national and regional First Nations organizations to represent indigenous interests to government.

As a result of those measures, the nature of schooling has changed dramatically since the 1960s. Most schools on reserves, for example, are now run under the authority of band councils; access to post-secondary schooling, while still a problem, has improved dramatically; and there has been a movement to make curriculum consistent with First Nations interests and cultures. Another result of those measures is that Aboriginal organizations have become key players in constitutional issues.

First Nations issues were front and centre in negotiations to patriate the Canadian Constitution in the early 1980s, not because of a priority placed on those issues by government but because of strong and effective First Nations representation to the Canadian public and to the Parliament of the UK, which was required to pass the measure as a last vestigial act of Canadian colonialism. The constitutional conferences of the mid-1980s between federal, provincial, and territorial governments and First Nations leadership came to no formal definition of the 'existing rights' of indigenous people—rights that had been codified in the new Constitution—but media attention to those conferences brought the concept of First Nations self-government to public awareness. One of the lasting consequences of those debates is that Aboriginal self-government is now a putative objective of the Department of Indian Affairs.

It is a rocky road. A good example of the complexities of establishing First Nations self-government within Canadian Confederation is the debate over reinstatement of Indians who had been forced to enfranchise at marriage. Bill C-31 was passed in 1985 as a measure that recognized gender equality: Indian women who had married non-Indians had been forced to enfranchise, while

Indian men who married non-Indians brought legal recognition as Indian to the spouse. The complex question was whether or not the principle of gender equality was paramount over the principle that First Nations, as all nations, have the right to determine membership and affiliation. Parliament imposed a resolution by passing legislation reinstating large groups of people as Indian and requiring bands to establish clear membership criteria.

When the Meech Lake Accord of 1987 sought to bring Quebec to agreement on constitutional issues, it was couched in terms of recognition of Canada's having been created by 'two founding nations', British and French. The response of the Assembly of First Nations and of other Aboriginal groups was to recall a long history of alliance, trade, negotiation, and participation in the establishment of the current Canadian polity. It was more than symbolic that a treaty Indian member of the Manitoba legislature, Elijah Harper, was able in 1990 to delay—and thus obviate—passage of the Accord and its acceptance by the rest of Canada. The subsequent attempt through the Charlottetown Accord of 1992 to reconcile differences between Quebec and the rest of Canada, an effort that included a national referendum, saw First Nations people vote with the majority for rejection, even though national First Nations leadership had been instrumental in fashioning the Accord, and even though it included measures that were supposed to lead to self-government.

The federal government professes a commitment to First Nations self-government but there is no clear agreement among the various levels of government and Canadian First Nations about how to accomplish it. During the first few years of the twenty-first century the federal government attempted to specify legislation that would define the terms of self-government, but all but a few First Nations leaders voiced strong objection to what they said was an inappropriate and unilateral imposition of terms. The discussion is much more complex now than it was 15 years ago. In the first place, indigenous peoples from all over the world are working in concert with each other to effect international political change and to effect social changes that reflect indigenous values. The United Nations has played an important role in an international and intergovernmental discourse about indigenous peoples' right to self-government and self-determination. Post-secondary specialization in Native studies has been possible in Canada since the 1970s: now there is an academic and legal specialization focusing specifically on indigenous governance. Courts are currently playing a large part in redefining the relationship between Canadian indigenous peoples and others. It is almost impossible to predict how that relationship will evolve, but one generalization that can be made is that the field is very complex. Self-government within the territory of Nunavut, for example, will be realized differently than in urban communities or on reserves.

Self-government is not a right that can be granted by any other government. Thus it is not something for which any formula or policy can apply across the board. It is instead a principle. The long history of First Nations on this part of the continent and the important place that self-directed First Nations have had in the creation of Canada are evidence of the principle that the rights and responsibilities of self-government are inherent and have never been compromised. Except for the most oppressive period of the reserve era, between the 1870s and 1970s, First Nations have in fact been self-governing. In the twenty-first century, individual First Nations will reaffirm self-government in a modern Canadian social context.

In the past 100 years the effects of Europe's diseases have been diminished. Physical survival is no longer in question. Survival in terms of community integrity is a continuing struggle, even in the face of federal government commitment to a move to First Nations self-government. Survival as nations honours the Ancestors who established those nations thousands of years ago, as well as those who have struggled to maintain the integrity and autonomy of First Nations communities.

BOX 2.2

Rossdale Flats

Rossdale Flats, just down from the provincial legislature on the north bank of the North Saskatchewan River in downtown Edmonton, was from 1801 to 1830 the site of a series of fur trade posts. It first saw Edmonton House and later Fort Augustus II and IV. The associated cemetery was in use until the 1880s. As the years went by floods ripped away grave markers and civic development changed the area. A common understanding has been that the bodies in the cemetery were removed and re-interred in the new Edmonton Cemetery.

However, upwards of 40 burials have been uncovered in utility construction along Rossdale Road since 1940. No one knows how many more remain. Although some have seen this as a problem for decades, what primarily brought it to the public eye was the proposal to expand and redevelop the old Rossdale Power Plant, which had been slated for decommissioning and preservation as a historic building. Various civic groups think that no city needs a power plant at its centre. Aboriginal groups think that respect must be shown for the dead. Both groups note that nothing permanent commemorates the site and its history.

While the controversy is multi-faceted, the issue of human remains is central. Archaeologists indicate that up to 200 people, including First Nations, Metis, and Europeans, may have been interred. As recently as 2001 human remains were found under a parking lot. Some remains have been re-interred at the Edmonton Cemetery, some may be with a provincial agency, and some are with the Department of Anthropology at the University of Alberta, which is committed to their repatriation.

The City of Edmonton is now committed to working with various organizations, including the Edmonton Aboriginal Urban Affairs Committee (EAUAC) and the Rossdale Stakeholders' Group. The latter is comprised of the Cree and Blackfoot Nations, Metis Nation of Alberta, St Joachim's Parish, Association Canadienne-francaise de l'Alberta, the Rossdale Descendants Group, and others. A historical land-use study is underway, in part to determine the cemetery's boundaries and to make recommendations about the site's future. The initial guidelines made no reference to the need to conduct oral history research, as had previously been agreed. To remedy this, EAUAC approached the city administration and secured funding for an oral history project to complement the historical land-use study. A side project is a review of the process conducted by city administration, local Aboriginal groups, and other interested parties. It is hoped that a model of co-operative research will emerge.

—Pamela M. Cunningham

(Miss Cunningham is from one of St Albert's founding Metis families, a member of EAUAC, and a graduate student in the Department of Anthropology, University of Alberta.)

References and Recommended Readings

Beattie, Owen, et al. 2000. 'The Kwaday Dan Ts'inchi Discovery from a Glacier in British Columbia', *Canadian Journal of Archaeology* 24: 129–48.

Bryan, Alan Lyle. 1986. 'The Prehistory of Canadian Indians', in R. Bruce Morrison and C. Roderick Wilson, eds, *Native Peoples: The Canadian Experience*. Toronto: McClelland & Stewart. One of the very few brief synopses on the topic. Written from an early entry, hemispheric perspective.

Campbell, Lyle. 1997. *American Indian Languages: The Historical Linguistics of Native America*. New York: Oxford University Press. The standard reference on this topic.

Cuthand, Stan. 1991. 'The Native Peoples of the Prairie Provinces in the 1920s and 1930s', in J.R. Miller, ed., *Sweet Promises: A Reader on Indian-White Relations in Canada*. Toronto: University of Toronto Press.

Darnell, Regna. 1986. 'A Linguistic Classification of Canadian Native Peoples: Issues, Problems, and Theoretical Implications', in R. Bruce Morrison and C. Roderick Wilson, eds, *Native Peoples: The Canadian Experience*. Toronto: McClelland & Stewart. A theoretically and historically focused survey.

Dickason, Olive Patricia. 2002. *Canada's First Nations: A History of Founding Peoples*, 3rd edn. Toronto: Oxford University Press. Now the standard reference for Canadian First Nations history.

Dobyns, Henry F., and William R. Swagerty. 1983. *Their Number Become Thinned: Native American Population Dynamics in Eastern North America*. Native American Historic Demographic Series. Knoxville: University of Tennessee Press in co-operation with the Newberry Library Center for the History of the American Indian. Dobyns is known for his relatively high estimates of pre-contact Aboriginal population levels. This work details the effects of European disease in eastern North America.

Francis, Daniel. 1992. *The Imaginary Indian: The Image of the Indian in Canadian Culture*. Vancouver: Arsenal Pulp Press. This history of popular and scholarly Euro-Canadian perceptions of First Nations peoples provides a valuable background for contemporary studies.

Greenburg, Joseph H. 1986. *Language in the Americas*. Stanford, Calif.: Stanford University Press.

Grant, Shelagh D. 2002. *Arctic Justice: On Trial for Murder, Pond Inlet, 1923*. Montreal and Kingston: McGill-Queen's University Press. This story of the eastern Arctic's first criminal trial, or, the price paid by a small indigenous community for Canadian imperial ambitions, reminds the reader of the many narrowly focused histories available.

Hickey, Clifford G. 1986. 'The Archaeology of Arctic Canada', in R. Bruce Morrison and C. Roderick Wilson, eds, Native Peoples: *The Canadian Experience*. Toronto: McClelland & Stewart. Presents both a cultural history of the region and a regionally focused perspective on the work of archaeology.

Kehoe, Alice Beck. 2002. *America Before the European Invasions*. London: Longman. Kehoe places Canadian material into a Mexican-centred continentalist context, but this is nevertheless a very useful survey.

Kinkade, M. Dale. 1991. 'The Decline of Native Languages in Canada', in, R.H. Robins and E.M. Uhlenbeck, eds, *Endangered Languages*. Oxford: Berg.

McGhee, Robert. 1996. *Ancient People of the Arctic*. Vancouver: University of British Columbia Press. The most recent overview by the dean of Canadian Arctic archaeologists.

Miller, J.R., ed. 1991. *Sweet Promises: A Reader on Indian-White Relations in Canada*. Toronto: University of Toronto Press. Essays explaining government policies in changing social and political contexts through time.

Monsalve, M.V., et al. 2002. 'Molecular Analysis of the Kwaday Dan Ts'inchi Ancient Remains Found in a Glacier in Canada', *American Journal of Physical Anthropology* 119: 288–91.

Powell, John Wesley. 1891. *Linguistic Families of America North of Mexico*. Washington: Bureau of Ethnology Annual Report for 1885–6: 7–139.

Sapir, Edward. 1929. 'Central and North American Languages', *Encyclopaedia Britannica*, 14th edition, 5: 138–41.

Thomas, David Hurst. 2000. *Skull Wars*. New York: Basic Books. A balanced account of the Kennewick controversy and its underlying issues.

Tobias, John L. 1991. 'Protection, Civilization, Assimilation: An Outline History of Canada's Indian Policy', in J.R. Miller, ed, *Sweet Promises: A Reader on Indian-White Relations in Canada*. Toronto: University of Toronto Press.

Trigger, Bruce C. 1983. *Natives and Newcomers: Canada's 'Heroic Age' Reconsidered*. Montreal and Kingston: McGill-Queen's University Press. A ground-breaking account of Canadian history giving attention to its Native aspects.

Washburn, Wilcomb E., ed. 1986. *History of Indian-White Relations*, vol. 4, *Handbook of North American Indians*. Washington: Smithsonian Institution. Almost half the articles in this large collection are about Canadian First Nations. Of direct interest also in this series are vol. 5, *Arctic*, vol. 6, *Subarctic*, vol. 7, *Northwest Coast*, and vol. 15, *Northeast*.

Suggested Web Sites

Canadian Museum of Civilization:
www.civilization.ca/cmc/cmce.asp
Home page for one of the very best broad sources of information on Aboriginal and other topics.

Ethnologue: www.ethnologue.com
A current summary of the world's languages compiled by the Summer Institute of Linguistics.

Indian Affairs Annual Reports:
www.nic-bnc.ca/2/23/index-e.html
The complete annual reports for the Indian Affairs portfolio from 1864 to 1990.
Kennewick Man: www.washington.edu/burkemuseum/ kman_homc.htm
The Burke Museum in Seattle maintains excellent coverage of the Kennewick controversy.

Notes

1. The first edition of *Native Peoples* had three chapters at this point, one on Canadian Native languages by Regna Darnell, one on the prehistory of Canadian Indians by Alan Bryan, and one on the archaeology of Arctic Canada by Cliff Hickey. The reader wishing a survey of these topics is directed to them; they are thorough and still relevant. We chose to drop them because we realized that the average reader did not require this detailed background. At the same time, we also felt that we had to provide readers with an overview of key issues in Canadian history as they related to Native peoples generally before taking up the stories of specific peoples.

Many Natives, it should be noted, object to the term 'prehistory' on the assumption that it implies that First Nations have no past worth talking about. We have used the term deliberately to emphasize that the term's referent is not really what kind of past a people has had but rather that it describes how things are done in a particular kind of academic discussion. Within the anthropological tradition, Native peoples have a very substantial past, but one not knowable by the same methods as the more recent past.

2. This appears to be a straightforward statement but is not. Like all the other archaelogical dates in this chapter, what it really refers to is radiocarbon years. It is now clear that carbon-dated years in the time range discussed here are younger than calendar years by from about 900 to 2,000 years. Since there is not yet consensus on precisely how to convert radiocarbon years into calendar years, we have left all dates in radiocarbon years.

PART II

The Arctic

CHAPTER 3

The Eskaleuts:
A Regional Overview

ERNEST S. BURCH JR and CHRISTOPHER FLETCHER

An Aboriginal population, known to science as the 'Eskaleuts', extended from the western tip of the Aleutian Islands and the Asiatic coast of the Bering Sea around the western portion of Alaska, across northern Canada to the Atlantic Ocean, and further still to the shores of Greenland. This immense region, some 20,000 kilometres (12,000 miles) in breadth, was inhabited in the eighteenth century by about 81,000 people speaking at least seven related, but different, languages.

The diversity of Eskaleut peoples in the eighteenth century was much greater than most people realize, but it is not really surprising given their extensive geographic distribution. 'Eskaleut', of course, is an artificial word derived from the names of the two major linguistic divisions of the general population, Eskimos and Aleuts.

Aleuts

The Aleuts occupied the Aleutian Islands and a portion of the adjacent Alaska Peninsula. Their natural environment is characterized by a maritime climate noted for its perpetual strong winds, overcast skies, frequent fog, and violent storms. Although the area receives a fair amount of snow in winter, the ocean remains ice-free year-round. Aleutian waters are home to a rich and diverse marine fauna. Whales, sea lions, seals, sea otters, walrus, several varieties of fish and shellfish, sea birds, and seaweed provided a reliable resource base for a relatively dense human population. Aleut hunting technology was admirably developed to harvest these resources.

The estimated 14,000 Aleuts of the mid-eighteenth century were divided into three major groups: Eastern Aleuts, numbering some 9,000 people; Central Aleuts, numbering perhaps 4,000; and Western Aleuts, numbering about 1,000.

Rather little is known about the traditional life of the Central and Western Aleuts. The Eastern Aleuts, who have been more thoroughly described, were organized in terms of relatively large-scale (for hunters) societies of up to some 2,000 people, and these societies generally were more complex in structure than any Eskimo society. They were divided into a series of hereditary, ranked classes consisting of chiefs, nobles, commoners, and slaves. Aleut societies were apparently divided into matrilineal lineages whose major orientation was towards child-rearing and marriage practices. Girls were raised in their mother's household, but boys were brought up by their mother's brother. Residence was matri-patrilocal; newly married spouses lived with the wife's parents until a child was born, at which point they joined the household of the husband's parents. Aleut societies were also divided into patrilineal lineages, whose major function was to own land. Ritual, folklore, and art (particularly work with grass) were highly developed among the Aleuts. Inter-societal relations, too, were

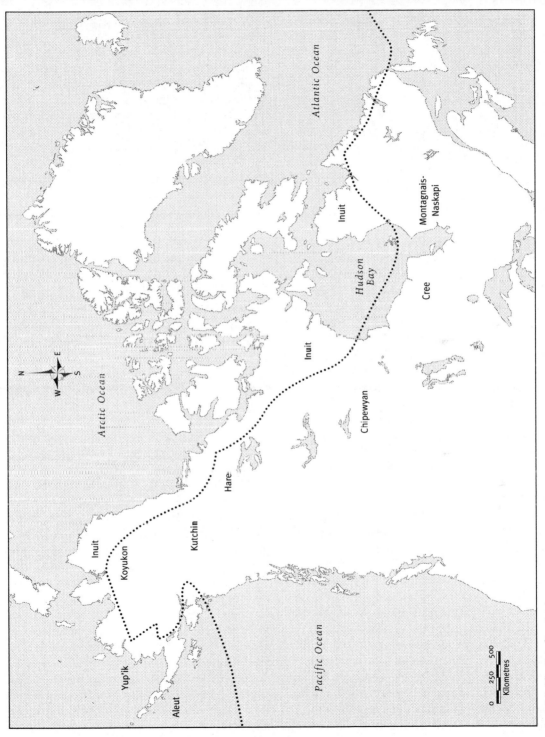

MAP 3.1. The Canadian Arctic

relatively complex, and included an extensive network of trade, a framework of relatively formal political alliances, and a complementary pattern of active warfare.

Eskimos

The second major branch of the Eskaleut language family is Eskimo. Eskimo-speaking peoples inhabit by far the largest portion of the Eskaleut area and are divided into several language groups. The most fundamental division within the Eskimo language family is between Yup'ik and Inuit. Yup'ik speakers live in south-central and southwestern Alaska, and on portions of the Asiatic shore of the Bering Sea and Bering Strait. Inuit speakers are distributed the whole way across North America, from Bering Strait to Greenland and Labrador.

Linguistic variation is much greater among the Yup'ik Eskimos than among their Inuit cousins. The Inuit language forms a continuum that is divided into a number of dialects among native speakers of the language, all of which share enough similarity that basic comprehension is possible after a brief period of familiarization. Yup'ik, on the other hand, is divided into at least five distinct languages: Pacific, Central Alaskan, Naukanski, Chaplinski, and Sirenikski.

Pacific Yup'ik was spoken in south-central Alaska by perhaps as many as 10,000 people in the mid-eighteenth century. There were two groups of dialects: Chugach and Koniag. Like the Aleuts, Pacific Yup'ik societies had economies oriented to the harvest of marine mammals, although fish were also important. Their societies also were characterized by a system of ranked classes, by relatively elaborate art and ritual, and by complex inter-societal relations. Unlike the Aleuts, they apparently lacked any sort of lineage system.

A second Yup'ik language, Central Alaskan Yup'ik, was spoken in southwest Alaska, along the Bering Sea coast, and for a considerable distance inland along the major river systems. The region includes scattered ranges of hills and mountains, but most of it consists of an immense delta.

The Central Alaskan Yup'ik population of some 14,000 people in the mid-eighteenth century was concentrated along the rivers and along portions of the Bering Sea coast. There were three major dialect areas—Bristol Bay, Kuskokwim, and Yukon—and a number of small, local dialect areas. The relatively dense human population was sustained by salmon and several other types of fish, by caribou, by sea mammals along the coast, and by a variety of plant and other animal foods. Unlike the Aleuts and Pacific Yup'ik peoples, the Central Alaskan Yup'ik Eskimos did not have a system of hereditary, ranked classes, and, in most respects, their social system was less complex than that of their southern relatives.

The other three Yup'ik languages are often lumped together under the heading of 'Asiatic Yup'ik', although that is strictly a geographic designation, not a linguistic one: the three languages were quite distinct from one another, and Sirenikski was the most divergent of all Eskimo languages.

The northernmost of the three Asiatic Yup'ik languages was Naukanski Yup'ik. In the mid-eighteenth century it was spoken by perhaps 1,000 people living on or near East Cape (on the west side of the strait), and possibly at scattered points along the coast for another 50 kilometres or so on either side of the cape area. Chaplinski Yup'ik was spoken by perhaps 6,000 people who lived on St Lawrence Island and on the adjacent Asiatic mainland. Sirenikski was spoken by only 150 to 200 people who lived along the southern shore of the Chukchi Peninsula, just west of the Chaplinski language area. This language is now extinct.

All three Asiatic Yup'ik-speaking groups occupied rugged, barren coastal regions, and their economies were nearly as marine-oriented as those of Aleut societies. They had little access to fish resources, and they acquired virtually all of their reindeer (Eurasian caribou) skins and meat through trade with neighbouring Chukchi. Asiatic Yup'ik societies are distinguished from all other Eskimo societies in that most of them were organized in terms of exogamous, patrilineal clans.

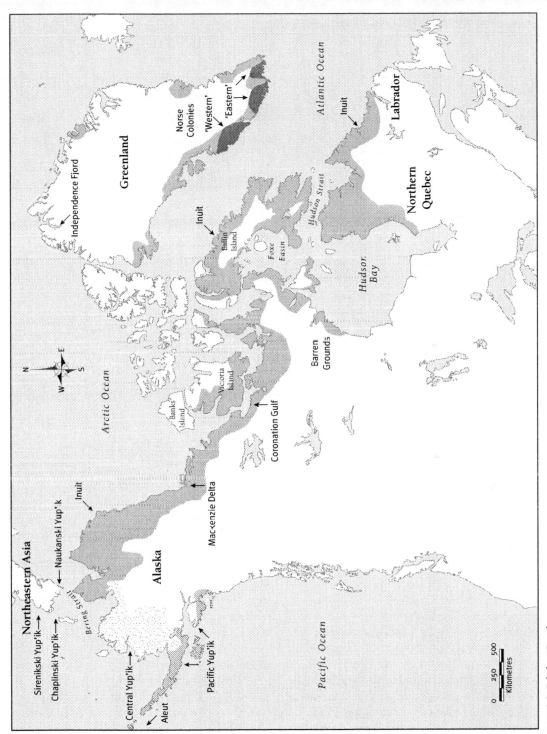

The Eskaleuts: A Regional Overview

Greenland

Norse
Colonies

'Western'
'Eastern'

Atlantic Ocean

Inuit

Labrador

Independence Fjord

Inuit

Baffin
Island

Foxe
Basin

Hudson Strait

Northern
Quebec

Hudson
Bay

Arctic Ocean

Barren
Grounds

Victoria
Island

Banks
Island

Coronation Gulf

Inuit

Mackenzie Delta

Alaska

Northeastern Asia

Sirenikski Yup'ik

Chaplinski Yup'ik

Naukanski Yup'k

Inuit

Bering Strait

Central Yup'ik

Aleut

Pacific Yup'ik

Pacific Ocean

0   250   500
Kilometres

MAP 3.2. Eskaleut Peoples

Table 3.1. Major Divisions of Inuit Eskimos, *circa* 1750

Group	General Location	Approximate Numbers
Northwest Alaska	Bering Strait to the mouth of the Colville River, Alaska	10,000
Mackenzie Delta	Herschel Island to the Baillie Islands	2,000
Copper	Cape Parry to Queen Maude Gulf, including much of Victoria Island	1,300
Netsilik	Adelaide Peninsula, King William Island, Boothia Peninsula, and Pelly Bay	650
Caribou	West central coast of Hudson Bay	400
Satlirmiut	Southern portion of Southampton Island	200
Iglulik	Wager Bay, Repulse Bay, west side of Foxe Basin, and northern Baffin Island	700
Baffin Island	East, south, and west coasts of Baffin Island	2,750
Labrador Peninsula	Coastal area from Great Whale River, on west, to Sandwich Bay, on east, including Ungava Peninsula	4,200
Polar	Extreme northwestern Greenland	200
Southwest Greenland	West coast of Greenland south of Baffin Bay	12,000
East Greenland	Southeast coast of Greenland	1,000
	Total	35,500

All other Eskimos, some 35,000 people, spoke the Inuit language, which also has been referred to as Inupik and as Eastern Eskimo. Inuit speakers were spread the whole way across the top of the continental land mass, many portions of the Arctic Archipelago, and along most of coastal Greenland. They were organized into several dozen societies, which anthropologists have lumped together for descriptive convenience into geographic groups, which are listed in Table 3.1.

The Inuit generally have been thought of as maritime peoples. In fact, few Inuit were as dependent on marine resources as the Aleuts, the Pacific Yup'ik, or the Asiatic Yup'ik Eskimos. Almost all Inuit relied to a significant extent on caribou as a source of raw materials, and anadro-

mous fish were very important in some regions. A few Inuit groups—in northwest Alaska, in the region just west of Hudson Bay, and in northern Quebec—had economies oriented more towards terrestrial than towards maritime resources. The precise combination of animal and plant species available to Inuit populations varied considerably from one section of their vast territory to another, as did the climate and the topography. With few exceptions, Inuit economies, yearly cycles of movement, and lifestyles were precisely adjusted to deal with both the assets and the liabilities each local environment had to offer.

Inuit Eskimo culture, in general, was less complex than that of either the Aleuts or the Yup'ik Eskimos. Inuit societies were not divided

FIGURE 3.1. Ahiarmiut caribou hunters in their kayaks on the upper Kazan River, 1894. They are taking a break from spearing caribou crossing the river. The man in the foreground is smoking a pipe, a habit the Inuit acquired very early in the historic period. (By permission of the J.B. Tyrrell Papers, Thomas Fisher Rare Book Library, University of Toronto)

into ranked classes of any kind, and neither clan nor lineage organizations have been reported for any Inuit group. Art and ritual also were not as well developed among the Inuit as among their Aleut and Yup'ik relatives. On the other hand, Inuit culture was more complex in some areas than most Westerners generally realize, particularly in northwest Alaska and in the Mackenzie Delta region of Canada.

Contact with Europeans

The first definite encounters between Europeans and Eskaleuts took place about 800 years ago, when Norse settlers encountered Inuit in Greenland—although encounters may have taken place somewhat earlier, when Norse explorers first visited Greenland, Baffin Island, Labrador, and Newfoundland.

The second period of Eskaleut-European contact also occurred in the East. In the late 1400s, Portuguese and Basque fishermen and whalers began to frequent the waters of the western North Atlantic. They were followed by explorers, and in 1501 Gaspar Corte-Real's expedition encountered Inuit in Labrador and captured several dozen of them to take back to Europe. Other explorers and increasing numbers of whalers and fishermen from several European countries followed. They encountered Inuit in Greenland, Baffin Island, and Labrador with increasing frequency over the course of the fifteenth and sixteenth centuries.

The eighteenth century saw a new phase of Eskaleut-European contacts when permanent European outposts began to be built in Native territory. In the eastern Arctic these outposts were established by missionaries and traders, for the most part, and their relations with the Inuit were usually peaceful, if not always friendly. In the West, outposts were first established in the 1740s, when Russians began to move into Alaska. The Russians were bent on conquest and plunder, and Aleuts, Pacific Yup'ik Eskimos, and Tlingit Indians mounted a formidable armed resistance to them. Ultimately the Russians prevailed, and missionaries and traders were able to begin working in the area well before the end of the eighteenth century.

Over the course of the eighteenth and nineteenth centuries, explorers, missionaries, traders, and some few other people of European descent gradually pushed forward into Eskimo territory, proceeding from both the East and West towards the centre. Despite their generally good intentions towards the Natives, they spread disaster in their wake in the form of diseases for which the Natives had neither immunity nor cure. Smallpox, measles, influenza, mumps, and many other diseases wrought terrible havoc, particularly in the more densely populated areas of Alaska and the Atlantic coast. By the beginning of the twentieth century, the overall Eskaleut population may have been reduced to only half its size of 1750.

By about 1920, outposts of non-Natives had been established at key points over the entire length and breadth of Eskaleut country. With few exceptions, each of these tiny settlements included one or two missionaries and traders, and, in the Canadian North, a detachment of the Royal Canadian Mounted Police. In some areas there were schools as well, typically run by missionaries. In most cases there was also a small resident population of Natives, but the great majority still spent most of the year living in small, widely dispersed camps; they made periodic visits to the mission/trading post settlements during the winter, but came in for a month or two in the summer. This general pattern prevailed, particularly in Canadian Inuit territory, until the end of World War II.

World War II and the Cold War that followed it heightened American and Canadian interest in northern regions, leading to the construction of military bases and radar sites all across northern North America. The labour requirements of this work led to the hiring of hundreds of Natives for varying periods of time and to contacts with outsiders of a type and on a scale never before seen in the North. The resulting changes, combined with increasing concern for Native health and welfare and a growing sense of obligation on the part of governments to provide better schooling

for Native children, led to still greater government involvement in Native affairs in the 1950s. However, it was impossible to deliver the necessary services to people living in widely dispersed camps, so a systematic effort was made to encourage the Natives to abandon their camps for the administrative centres. This campaign had been largely successful by the late 1960s.

At the end of the twentieth century, there were approximately 2,200 Aleuts in Alaska, another 700 in Russia, 900 Yup'ik Eskimos in Russia, and about 25,100 in Alaska. Of the Inuit, there were some 13,500 in Alaska, 45,000 in Canada, and 48,000 in Greenland. The great majority of these people lived in small, widely dispersed communities in or near their traditional homelands. Although geographically isolated, most villages are connected to the rest of the world by satellite communications (television, telephone, Internet) and are readily reached by scheduled and charter air service. The situation in Russian communities is less clear, as the northeast of Russia has suffered significant changes as a result of the effects of the post-Communist era restructuring of government. With the advent of full-time community living the growing interdependence of the subsistence and cash economies became a permanent feature of northern community life. Despite the importance of cash and wage labour in Eskaleut life today, hunting, fishing, and trapping by individuals and family groups remain fundamental to cultural identity and provide a considerable portion of the food people consume.

The transition to a mixed economy has brought the legitimacy and sustainability of Eskaleut land-use and subsistence practices into question and has politicized them in the process. For example, animal rights organizations had a profound impact on the viability of indigenous subsistence hunting in the 1970s and 1980s. Using sophisticated media portrayals of trapping, which was depicted as cruel to animals, these organizations caused the market for furs to collapse. While well intentioned, these campaigns failed to consider the devastating financial effects that a loss of the economic viability of trapping would have on indigenous peoples, the cultural practices designed to reduce animal suffering, and the place of people in the ecosystem generally. If taken to its logical conclusion, the philosophy of some animal rights groups would stop indigenous wildlife harvesting altogether.

Similarly, the growing knowledge about the presence of high levels of chemicals in the Arctic food chain has caused widespread concern about the health effects of maintaining a traditional diet. Inuit organizations have supported and sponsored research into these issues as they are critical to traditional practices in the present day.

The impact that people far from the Arctic can have on Eskaleut lives demonstrates how closely tied all peoples are today. For Inuit, Yup'ik, and Aleut peoples these effects are part of a continuum of change imposed from outside of their own political and social structures. In response to these and other events, the Arctic peoples have organized politically at regional, national, and international levels to defend their rights as indigenous peoples and to protect their traditions from erosion by global events. In Canada, Inuit Tapiriit Katatami represents the interests of the various Inuit regions within the country. The Inuit Circumpolar Conference encompasses Canadian, Greenlandic, Alaskan, and Russian Eskaleut peoples and represents them internationally.

The continued growth in importance of these organizations stems in part from the successes that Inuit have had in establishing land claim agreements with national governments. Many of the Arctic peoples have undergone a process of redefining their indigenous land rights in the countries in which they live. The land claims process has afforded people renewed control over their territories and new tools to promote and maintain their traditional lifestyles. The first land claim agreement in the North was the Alaska Native Claims Settlement Act of 1971, under which Eskimos and Aleuts, along with other Alaska Natives, could select nearly 18 million hectares of land and receive a significant cash compensation for surrendering their Aboriginal claims to the land. In 1975 the Inuit of Quebec signed the James Bay and Northern Quebec Agreement establishing the region of Nunavik and beginning a process of increasing Inuit control over municipal and regional matters. In 1978 the Home Rule Act granted a high degree of local autonomy to Greenlanders, and in 1984 the Inuvialuit of the western Canadian Arctic also signed a land claim agreement. Finally, in 1999 the territory of Nunavut in the eastern Arctic of Canada was created out of the existing Northwest Territories and includes an Inuit-dominated system of public government, based on consensus, with full territorial legislative powers. These developments are discussed in greater detail in Chapter 4 of this volume. In Russia, the Eskimos and Aleuts have not yet signed land rights agreements. Their situation is quite difficult as their traditions and land base suffered during the Soviet era and now face new challenges in the post-Soviet period as government has largely abandoned the services it once provided and on which people depended.

Recommended Readings

Burch, Ernest S., Jr. 1988. *The Eskimos*, with photographs by Werner Forman. Norman: University of Oklahoma Press. A lavishly illustrated, comprehensive description of Eskaleut ways of life during the early 1800s. Intended for a general audience.

Damas, David, ed. 1904. *Handbook of North American Indians*, vol. 5, *Arctic*. Washington: Smithsonian Institution. An encyclopedic source of information on Eskaleut peoples.

Duffy, R. Quinn. 1988. *The Road to Nunavut*. Montreal and Kingston: McGill-Queen's University Press. A comprehensive and accessible account of the process leading to the creation of Nunavut.

Wenzel, George. 1991. *Animal Rights, Human Rights: Ecology, Economy and Ideology in the Canadian Arctic*. Toronto: University of Toronto Press. An excellent analysis of the impact of the animal rights movement on the Inuit of the eastern Canadian Arctic.

CHAPTER 4

Continuity and Change in Inuit Society

CHRISTOPHER FLETCHER

Introduction

The Arctic holds a particular fascination for Canadians. Few Canadians ever see it, yet everyone is at least dimly aware that it exists as a massive and cold space, 'up there' somewhere. The people who live in the Arctic have been the subject of a lot of scrutiny by scientists, writers, artists, explorers, and eccentrics of various kinds. They are objects of fascination to those of us who can barely imagine living in such a place. I am astonished by how widespread the stereotypes of Inuit life are. I get into a taxi at the Montreal airport after returning from fieldwork and the driver asks me where I am coming from. When I say, 'The Arctic', he asks, 'Is it true that they share wives? or eat raw meat? or have a thousand words for snow?' It seems everyone knows some ethnographic details about the Inuit. Why is this kind of knowledge about them so widespread?

A good part of the answer comes from the contrast that the Arctic presents in the popular imagination as a hostile place and the Inuit ability to survive in such a climate. How do they do it? The ability of Inuit to live off the land is a source of amazement to us who cannot. This background knowledge points to two things: first is the tendency to romanticize the lifestyle of the Inuit in a mythologized 'traditional' period and second is the question of the continuity of tradition in the contemporary context.

An alternative image of Inuit has also become widespread, and is not flattering. A monotonous number of news and research reports picture a people who are losing their grasp on the value of life. A recent headline in the *Edmonton Journal* (26 Apr. 2002, B11) was 'Another Monday night, another big drunk. Rage for alcohol grips many Quebec Inuit, sets off health disaster'. Social problems including alcohol abuse, sexual abuse, youth suicide, and accidental deaths are presented as overwhelming. Inuit society is pictured as chaotic, with past values seemingly lost. Alcohol does have serious consequences in Inuit communities, but it also does in southern society. Yet this characterization of their society tends to dominate. There are important implications to these kinds of general knowledge. They suggest that values of the past have no place in a present where people live in communities, have jobs, or not, and have many of the same preoccupations as southern Canadians. They also suggest that Inuit are not responsible enough to run their own affairs, a discourse that historically has been used to justify Aboriginal disempowerment.

But, of course, they are and do. As I write this, all Canadian Inuit with the exception of those in Labrador have signed land rights agreements with the federal and provincial governments. In the Labrador case, a settlement is in place and working its way through the ratification process. Once implemented the Labrador Inuit Land Claims

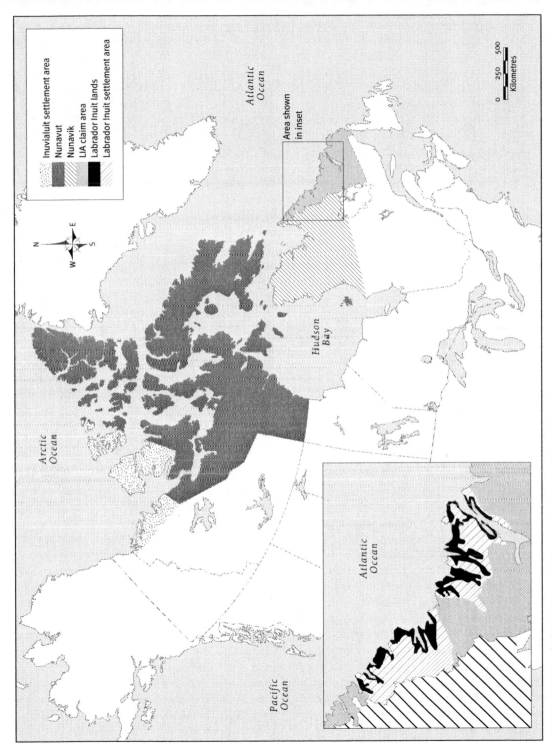

MAP 4.1. Inuit Land Claims Areas

Agreement (LILCA) will provide the legal basis on which Inuit rights and governance will be structured. The LILCA follows on the heels of the Nunavut Agreement (NA), the James Bay and Northern Quebec Agreement (JBNQA), and the Inuvialuit Final Agreement (IFA). Each defines relationships between Inuit and their ancestral territories and provides for Inuit control over sectors of regional economic, justice, environment, education, employment, and cultural policy. As a result of their settled territorial claims (see Map 4.1) and the breadth of experience they have with regional control, Inuit have a unique position as indigenous people within Canada.

When in the North I am struck by the density and quality of Inuit kinship and friendship links and how these serve to create cohesive and inclusive society. My experience in Inuit communities, particularly Kangiqsujuaq, Quebec, is not reflected in the newspapers. People are supportive towards each other and protective of me because of my lack of experience. The community works well and the municipal government is involved in the betterment of the community. People volunteer to help on local education, youth, and cultural committees. Children are cherished. People are active on the land. Life in the camps is a source of great pleasure; young and old hunt, eat, sleep, and play together, communicating in their own language. Hunting is a full-time occupation for some; everyone enjoys eating food from the bountiful land. Social problems are everyone's concern and suffering people are cared for by friends and family. People participate in a lifestyle that, while clearly different from that of three or four generations ago, is grounded in viable and strong cultural and social principals. It is not surprising, then, that people in the North often ask me why anthropologists and other researchers seem to concentrate only on negative aspects of their lives. This chapter is, in part, a response to this question. What we know about Inuit life and how we know it are influenced by what we consider to be true about ourselves, first, and then about them. In my perspective, under-

standing the Inuit requires that we look at our conceptions of their place in the world and its significance for what they say about our own lives.

This chapter examines Inuit cultural and social persistence. By looking at the ways people lived in the past and live today, I will address the questions I have raised. How does the northern landscape figure in southern understandings of the Inuit? What is the relationship between this understanding and an Inuit comprehension of themselves and the North? How did and do Inuit survive in the Arctic? What is their place in the world today?

Neither the stereotype of the traditional lifestyle nor the rhetoric of modern social decay is an accurate reflection of Inuit life. To understand Inuit in the Canadian context we must consider the interaction of their culture and society with others over time and space. We will find a people who are generous to each other and outsiders, confident in their abilities, grounded in tradition, and forward-looking. Inuit have faced challenges in the past and continue to do so. The way they approach these is rooted in their relations with each other and with place.

Becoming an Anthropologist

For those Canadians who grew up in the relatively thin band of densely populated territory hugging the US, the North represents a wild and 'natural' counterbalance to the industrial and political giant to the south. In this sense Canada is suspended perpetually between two states of being: the industrial and natural. Growing up in southern Canada in the 1960s and 1970s involved navigating these ideas about wilderness and civilization in everyday life. In school we drew pictures of fast cars and igloos, but never in the same frame. Inuit—they were 'Eskimos' back then—were stereotyped as people of perpetual winter who lived without need of what we had: houses, record players, skateboards, and TV dinners. We were fascinated by them for their difference and their distance from our lives.

FIGURE 4.1. Kangiqsujuaq, Quebec, 1994. (Courtesy C. Fletcher)

The foundations of my anthropology were laid when I read Farley Mowat's *Never Cry Wolf* three times between the ages of about 8 and 12 and got something completely different from it each time. That I remember each reading demonstrates how much the book resonated with particular interests I developed in my professional life: the relations between humans and the environment, modernity in Aboriginal culture, and relations between governmental institutions and the everyday lives of people. Mowat is one of Canada's most widely read authors. He brought the North to the south and had an impact on the role that government played in creating northern communities. Rarely does a writer engage both the imagination and the action of a nation. In this respect, my experience with *Never Cry Wolf* was not uncommon and reflects a broader characterization of the role of the North in Canadian imagination.

After I had finished my undergraduate degree in geography/environmental studies I found a job in Montreal driving a bus for Native Patients Services. Every day I would collect people at the airport who were coming for tertiary care in the south and take them to boarding houses or hospitals. Over the six years I did this

I met hundreds of Inuit and Cree from northern Quebec. Some people came regularly to the hospital and, over time, I made a few friends. I became interested in the relationship between Aboriginal culture and health through my contacts with people in the bus and eventually returned to university to pursue graduate studies. My first fieldwork trip was in 1990 when I went to Kangiqsujuaq for four months to collect data for my Master's degree. I had mentioned to a friend that I would like to stay with a family when I was in the North. She set things up with her parents and off I went.

When I arrived I found I was miserably unprepared, with little idea of what to do. I had read lots of ethnography that now seemed to be about somewhere else. Unlike the classical ethnographies or the more contemporary structuralist approaches that placed Inuit myth and traditional social organization into beautifully rendered analytical frameworks, I landed in a North that was resolutely and comfortably modern. Finding the connections between what I was seeing and what I had read would take ages. This is the point of long-term fieldwork in anthropology. It takes a lot of direct experience to get past first appearances and into the realities of how people live, think, talk, and act.

I spent a couple of months trying to interview people about kinship. The interviews were awkward and the questions much too structured. I had worked too hard on the formal aspects of my study and not enough on the observational. I was being much too *Qallunnaq* (European) to understand Inuit. Finally, in early June, the family I was staying with said, 'Come with us to the camp.' I went, leaving the tape recorder behind, and finally began to learn something. I slept in the family tent, ate food that people captured, watched the ice slowly decay, and was fixated on the beauty of the landscape. I learned that Inuit are thoroughly modern in outlook and firmly planted in their culture at the same time. The literature on social problems alluded to earlier tends to portray Inuit between two worlds, making them 'stuck' and somehow pathogenic. Noted linguist Louis-Jacques Dorais notes that the interaction of tradition and modernity is not automatically problematic. It is what people make of the two that counts.

I eventually got through the Master's degree after changing topics, and then earned a Ph.D.— and 10 years later, have sat down to do some work on kinship. Anthropology is not for the impatient.

The People and Their Landscape

Defining 'North' in Canada is difficult. We could use an arbitrary latitude, the Arctic Circle, for example, or the line of continuous permafrost, or the treeline. Each case would miss people who are northerners or places that seem northern. If we take North to mean all areas occupied by Inuit, that includes everything north of the treeline from Yukon to Labrador and the north shore of the St Lawrence River. In effect Inuit occupied all the land that was largely treeless and connected to ocean that would freeze over.

The emphasis on land is a bit misleading in depicting Inuit territory. They also lived on the ice in winter and continue to take much of the

food they eat from under it. The Inuit are the indigenous inhabitants of this particular ecological condition and remain the majority population of it today. But Inuit are not restricted to living in these areas. There are important Inuit communities in Montreal, Ottawa, Winnipeg, and other places throughout the country. The lives of southern Inuit are informed equally by the values of their ancestors as they are shaped by contemporary reality. Likewise, Inuit people are not restricted to Canada; they are also indigenous inhabitants of eastern Russia, northern Alaska, and all of Greenland. To my knowledge the Inuit are the only indigenous culture to occupy portions of two continents and four countries. Because of the breadth of their territorial and aquatic occupation, describing a generic form of Inuit lifestyle glosses over a lot of important regional variation.

In popular and academic works we find repeated references to Inuit-occupied territories as representing the edge of human existence and the available resources as meagre. A good question to ask is how much of this view derives from the emptiness of the landscape to the foreign observer?

The Arctic landscape is difficult to seize with the senses without a lot of experience within it. During the first months I spent in the North, people seemed constantly to be pointing out animals I could not see. Someone would say, 'Look, 10 caribou on the hillside', and I would strain to catch a glimpse. Were they close or far? I could not tell. Eventually I realized that I had no frame of reference to judge distances. There are no trees or buildings to allow me to judge how big the animals would be in my field of vision. To make matters worse, caribou blend in with the lichen-speckled rock and juniper brush. The landscape appears meagre if you cannot see what it holds.

The Inuit, their ancestors, and their predecessors have survived well in the North. There have been three different waves of technological and cultural change in the Arctic. The first, known as the Arctic Small Tool Tradition, arose in the west and moved quickly east. Sites in eastern Alaska attest that Arctic inhabitants, who were culturally and more than likely biologically distinct from contemporary Amerindians, lived there some 9,000 years ago. As the Arctic glaciers retreated about 4,000 years ago, these people applied their distinct hunting, travelling, and dwelling technologies in the new landmass and ocean areas to move across and occupy all the land from present-day Alaska to eastern Greenland. This seems to have happened very rapidly, perhaps in only a few hundred years. In Canada this original technological-cultural tradition is thought to have developed into the second phase, known as the Dorset culture.

Contemporary Inuit are descendants of people who developed what archaeologists call the Thule tradition. Thule people seem to have displaced the Dorset, perhaps through a superior technology including the use of harpoons with floats attached and the invention of large skin-covered boats (*umiaq*) and the use of dogs for labour. These would have allowed them more easily to access and kill large marine mammals including walrus, seals, and beluga, narwhal, and bowhead whales. The size of these animals allowed for the storage of large quantities of meat and fat to cover lean periods. This technology first appears in the archaeological record some 2,000 years ago on islands in Bering Strait. By 1,000 years ago, Thule culture bearers had displaced the Dorset people already occupying the Arctic.

Inuit oral tradition on the distant past acknowledges the existence of *Tuniit*, described as people who inhabited the Arctic but who were not Inuit. Throughout the North the material remains of past human occupation are quite evident. Very little soil accumulates so that while simply walking around one often finds harpoon points, bits of broken cutters, soapstone bowls, and flakes from tool production. The remains of tent rings, meat caches, and semi-subterranean houses are plainly evident. The Inuktitut word for 'artifacts' is *Tunirtait*, 'things of the Tuniit'. Some archaeologists take the Inuit mythology and oral history of the Tuniit to be evidence that groups of Dorset people persisted until relatively recently. While this may be the case, Inuit descriptions of Tuniit emphasize superhuman capacities that suggest they are not a literal retelling of contact with other peoples.

Tuniit are renowned for remarkable strength. They could move enormous boulders and run over deep, soft snow with ease. Some lived inside mountains that were bright and crystalline inside. Tuniit were capable of changing their size, of being very small or huge, and of becoming invisible. What's more, many Inuit have had encounters with Tuniit. In some cases they see them at a distance but are unable to catch up with them. In others the Tuniit come to play jokes on Inuit in their camps or while hunting alone on the land. People have told me of getting up in the morning to find a large rock in front of the entrance to their tent. Others find things strewn about camp when there was no wind the night before. Tuniit will frustrate or tease a lone hunter by calling his name from a hiding place. While invisible they may throw rocks near a hunter, surprising him, or push him off balance. Tuniit are alternately mischievous and timid. Few people alive today have spoken with them, although I have heard stories of people who did. It seems that Tuniit are quite sensitive to Inuit. They will not directly approach someone they know to be afraid or tense but will come to those who are without trepidation about them. The qualities that Tuniit look for in meeting Inuit are those highly valued by Inuit themselves.

There is an Inuit way of distinguishing among the people of the Arctic, as I have heard from a number of Elders. They talk of three phases or styles of Arctic occupation: Tuniit, Eskimo, and Inuit. The Tuniit, as described above, were there before Inuit arrived. Today the word 'Eskimo' is often taken to be derogatory and no longer used to identify Inuit. However, when used by Elders it is not pejorative, but an important marker of identity for those who were born and lived on the land before there were communities. It defines a kind of life experience that cannot now be reproduced. Their knowledge and experience was generated by a lifestyle of continuous hunting and movement on the land. In contrast to 'Eskimo', 'Inuit' has come to mean 'people born once communities existed' and signifies a distinct break in lifestyle among people who nonetheless share a language and culture. Inuit, then, are politically modern, comfortable with community living, and can move from city to city anywhere in the world. For Elders the framing of time in this way distinguishes historical periods relevant to them and asserts a cultural continuity of territorial occupation in the North despite changes in lifestyle.

The Arctic is an enormous territory that, contrary to popular conception, must have been quite rich in order to support the population growth and expansion that occurred. Indeed, Inuit today point to the wealth of the land that surrounds them as the most important element in their persistence as a people. Elders will say that, whatever happens to the rest of us, Inuit will survive because they have the knowledge to do so. From an Inuit perspective the Arctic is far from barren; rather, it is lush, comforting, and supportive. The landscape is inhabited by birds in huge numbers and large numbers of mammals—muskoxen, caribou, several species of fat-rich seals—in the sea, lakes, and rivers are fish, and in the sea are whales big and small (one of which can support a large family for months). The land is not poor unless the people lose their knowledge of it.

The Pursuit of Animals

For Inuit, like hunting peoples everywhere, relations with animals are fundamental to the way they understand the world. Hunting provides food, which permits the continuation of society. It also forms the basis for organizing the social, spiritual, and cultural worlds. Animals figure prominently in Inuit mythology and the relations between people and animals are often represented like those of kin. Indeed, the distinctions between animals and people are ambiguous in

mythology, as many stories concern animals who transform into people and vice versa.

Traditional Perspectives

In earliest time, once humans had been created, people and animals could exist by eating earth. They spoke with one another and experienced no violence. The boundaries between animals and people were flexible as transformations and marriages between them were common. With time the world became overpopulated and animals and people began to kill and consume each other.

The origins of the animals and the distinctions between them are found in transgressions of social orders. The classic myth of Nuliajuk (also known as Sedna and Napaaluk) accounts for the creation of sea mammals. There are many variations of this myth and the following version is condensed.

> A woman disobeyed her father by refusing to marry the man he arranged for her. She chooses one of his dogs instead and leaves with him to live on an island. Her father kills the dog, which is providing well for her, while she is pregnant. She bears the children; they are both human and dog. The father pities his daughter's life on the island and goes to bring her back in his *qajaq* (*kayak*). The husband has been transformed into a bird and swoops down on the qajaq to kill the father. In his terror, or seeing duplicity in his daughter, he throws her overboard. She clings to the edge of the *qajaq*. He cuts off her fingers one by one and each turns into an animal: seals, whales, and walruses. She sinks to the bottom of the sea where she becomes a human-fish creature controlling the animals of the sea that were created from her body.

The annual cycle of hunting is also an annual social cycle. Animal spirits associate with individuals who may travel to lands where animals and humans converse. Protector spirits (*turngait*) help people who treat them appropriately and thus help people to help others through successful hunting and sharing of game. *Turngait* can also be evil and intentionally cause misfortune. They can mislead people into thinking they are helpful. In many accounts the role of the shaman in Inuit society was to mediate between the invisible realms of the *turngait* and other spirits and that of the mundane world. Like *turngait*, shamans are seen as possibly being a positive force for people or possibly negative. In general, the intensity and complexity of human–animal relations is mirrored by the complexity of knowledge that successful hunting requires.

For people on Baffin Island the year is divided into 13 moon months[1] and six to eight seasons. With the input of Elders, John MacDonald of the Nunavut Research Institute has published a comprehensive survey of Inuit astronomy that includes a description of the months and seasons along with their corresponding ecological and social activities. Eight of the 13 'months' are named after ecological characteristics of food animals: three for seals (*Avunniit*: March or April, *Nattian*: April or May, *Tirigluit*: May or June), four for caribou (*Nurrait*: June, *Saggaruut*: July or August, *Akullirut*: August or September, and *Amiraijaut*: September or October), and one for eggs (*Manniit*: June or July). Four moon months refer to light characteristics. *Tauvikjuaq* (December or January) means great darkness. Two names mark the re-emergence of the sun, *Siqinnaarut* (January or February) and *Qangattaasan* (February or March), while *Ukiulirut* (October or November) simply means the beginning of winter. Only one makes reference to social life: *Tusartuut* ('Hearing' about other people), in November or December, marks the end of a transitional season when sea ice is forming but not thick enough to travel on. The significance of the names lies in their descriptive qualities and in the implication that social interaction is taken for granted throughout the year except during *Tusartuut*.

As parts of the year are either continuously dark or light above the Arctic Circle, clock-based time is relevant mainly to the requirements of the communities. On the land, time markers are established by the pragmatics of travel and animal behaviours. It is easier to travel from the ice to the land when the tide is high because the transition is smoother. In Hudson Strait, tides rival those of the Bay of Fundy and getting over or between huge hummocks of broken ice at low tide is very difficult. At low tide during full moons in winter, the heaving of the ice leaves sizable air pockets underneath. Mussels and clams can be collected by making a hole between two slabs large enough to squeeze through and climbing under the ice. In hunting it is not the amount of time that matters but the level of success. Hunters will hunt 24 or more hours continuously and sleep after they get the catch back to camp. In the warmth of late spring the snow loses its friction, making travel difficult. People covering long distances by dog team or by skidoo will wait until 10 or 11 p.m. to leave, as it is colder then and the snow a bit more solid.

The seasonal round of hunting and gathering provides a wide variety of foods, almost all of it meat-based. Inuit distinguish between store-bought foods and *niqituinnaq*, 'genuine food' that is hunted. An important component of the hunting lifestyle is expressed in cultural conceptions of health. Country food is good—wild food that has lived without human constraints. Its meat and fat provide the kind of energy people need to feel comfortable on the land. The blood of animals restores the energy in human blood that is depleted when *niqituinnaq* is unavailable. Store food appears to have no blood in it and provides less energy. For Inuit, domestication of food animals was never undertaken and people are generally disdainful of food raised on farms. In the hunter's perspective, animals in these conditions are like pets. Dogs are the only domesticated animal in the North and were a food of absolute last resort. Elderly people today remark that modern youth are much bigger than people of their generation, something they correctly attribute to the eating of carbohydrates during growth, but the young people have no endurance and little strength for their size. *Niqituinnaq* gives you strength just as it requires strength to capture it.

FIGURE 4.2. Surveying for animals at the edge of the ice—Ukiivik polynia, Hudson Strait, 1998. (Courtesy C. Fletcher)

Above the Arctic Circle the return of the sun marks the beginning of spring. Below the Circle the short periods of daylight begin to lengthen and it is noticeably warmer. It is a productive time for hunters, who use the breathing holes maintained by seals along the cracks and thinned areas of the sea ice to wait with harpoons. The later in spring, the more likely that seals will be found on the ice as well as in the fissures and areas of open water. When ring seal pups are born, their mothers scrape out little ice domes next to breathing holes. Pups rest under a thin layer of ice while mother searches for food. Experienced hunters can spot these small rises on the surface of the ice and wait for the mother to return or simply take the pup if it is there. Later, when days are warmer, the pups and mother bask in the sun. Several breathing holes are established and a mother seal will call her pup from a 'learning hole' to condition it to swim. At this time of the year they are approached using canvas or skin blinds to hide the human presence or by slowly creeping up to the seal while lying on one's side and waving one hand as if it were a flipper. This technique works particularly well for bearded seals. Another technique uses the labour of the entire family hunting group by placing one person at each hole. As the seal rises it will be scared away until it is forced to rise at the hole of a waiting hunter. Seal-hunting at breathing holes can be undertaken in winter but is very demanding because of the temperatures. In spring it is easier to wait quietly behind a windbreak made of snow. Early spring is also a good time for hunting ptarmigan, when they gather together in willows or brush.

In late spring migratory birds begin to arrive as areas of open water appear along the shore of the ocean and on the lakes and rivers. The birds are looking for nesting grounds and hunters wait by good spots. Before rifles were available, people would use small bird spears and thongs weighted with stones to immobilize or kill them. As the sea ice rots, jigging along the edge for the formidable-looking *Kanajuk* (sculpin) or 'ugly fish' is common. The occasional northern cod is caught as well. When the ice has broken but is still floating in large pans, sleeping walrus can be caught.

Before the arrival of rifles, it was difficult to kill them in the water at this time of year.

Once the birds have settled in and laid their eggs, usually after ice has broken on the ocean, parties of men, women, and children will make collecting trips to the near-shore islands favoured by eider ducks in particular. On a good day a group of five or six people can find 50 or more eggs. A goose egg is two to three times the size of a chicken egg. Beluga whales move east to west following the ice breakup through Hudson Straits into Hudson Bay. They are harpooned from *kayaks* or the shore. Belugas return to the same estuaries yearly to moult their skins by rubbing on the gravel bottom and to bear their young. Hunters today wait at the same well-used spots as their ancestors did. The harpoon head detaches from the shaft as it is driven under the animal's skin. The shape of the head is such that it flips up as it enters and secures behind the skin as a button does on a coat. A cord, normally made of a single strip of bearded seal skin, is attached to the harpoon head and has a float (*avataq*) made of an inflated ringed seal skin attached to the far end. The harpooned whale is easy to spot when it surfaces with the float and tires quickly because of the drag. Today harpoons are used in conjunction with rifles and the float is often an empty five-gallon gasoline container.

With the ice largely gone, bowhead whales were sought by large parties of hunters in *qajaqs*. Numerous solid harpoon hits and *avataq* were needed to kill these animals. In some places, bays with narrow entrances were used as traps. Hunters would prevent the animal from leaving the bay as the tide went out. It would become trapped in a small area and killed by several hunters.

As summer gives way to the cooling temperatures of fall, preparations for winter are made. Before the widespread use of snowmobiles, a major concern was acquiring enough food for the dogs. While in the summer they are generally left to their own devices on small islands, they work hard in winter. Walrus is a good source of dog food. Walrus tend to congregate on the ocean side

of islands and on specific points of land, but hunting them is dangerous because they are enormous and agile in the water. Several men were required to provide enough strength to hold the harpoon line once it had struck a walrus. Late summer and early fall are also good for hunting caribou. They are fat from the summer's grazing and the skins have healed from fly infestations. An adequate supply of caribou was important for meat and fat as well as for the clothing and other materials produced from the skins. In late fall, once the ice had set on lakes, fishing for Arctic char was undertaken. The most significant vegetable source in the Inuit diet comes from berries. In the fall women and children collect blueberries, juniper, and cloudberries. They are so abundant in some areas that the pickers' footwear will turn purple while picking.

While the annual cycle emphasized hunting of specific species when they were most likely to be found, many food sources were available much of the year. Fish, particularly Arctic char, can be caught year-round in lakes and the ocean, although they were taken in largest numbers at stone weirs while they were making their runs to and from the sea. Likewise, caribou and seals are often hunted throughout the year.

Without dogs winter travel was very difficult. Distances covered to locate and kill game are substantial and walking often requires more energy than it can produce in game. Seals are hunted through their breathing holes and caribou may be found close to the coast in some areas and inland from the west coast of Hudson Bay. In northern Quebec the Leaf River and George River herds have recovered from a population crash in the early 1900s that was disastrous to the Inuit of the region, and now number in the hundreds of thousands. Population cycles of all the animals are familiar to the Inuit and they have strategies to concentrate on more abundant species. The timing of the last caribou crash, however, had significant impacts as it coincided with the early arrival of southern administrators and the increasing reliance of

Inuit on trade goods. With the availability of some limited relief, and an increasing interest by non-Inuit in the North, the people adopted the beginnings of a community lifestyle.

Multiple preservation techniques allow for surpluses to be stored and periods of lean harvesting to be covered. Air-dried fish, thinly sliced meats, and seal entrails last for long periods of time. Beluga and seal fat are collected in containers and fermented to produce *misirak*, eaten as a dip for fish, and caribou meat and fat are buried under rocks and sod for preservation. Of course, in winter food is frozen as well. Taken together these techniques provide for the levelling out of periods of abundance and scarcity.

Modern Hunting

All of the above animals, with the exception of bowhead whales, still are hunted regularly. Knowledge of wildlife behaviour is still as important. Only the technology has changed. The same is true of preservation and storage practices. Caches are filled and emptied. This I take to be evidence of the abundance of animals in the Arctic and testimony to the importance of self-sufficiency and *niqituinnaq* in the maintenance of Inuit culture.

Hunting today is undertaken in a broader context that includes people from other cultures with other preoccupations. For example, Inuit have experienced considerable economic hardship as a result of animal rights organizations, prompting the European Union in 1982 to ban the importation of sealskins. This has essentially eliminated the trade in sealskins and made trapping unviable for most Inuit. The number of seals taken has not likely fallen very much, however, as they remain a staple food source. A small trade in fox, wolf, and polar bear skins still exists but does not cover the cost of hunting. Inuit are exempt from an international ban on whale-harvesting because they conduct a subsistence hunt. Regardless, they are obliged to monitor their hunts and respect quotas drawn up by wildlife management agencies. It is surprising, given their expert and

multi-generational knowledge of animal populations, but the role of Inuit hunters in these organizations has until recently been marginal. Only with the conclusion of land claims agreements across the Canadian Arctic has Inuit participation with wildlife management boards become commonplace. One of the most significant effects of the creation of Nunavut is that Inuit now have effective control over, and responsibility for, the management of wildlife on their territory. There are still disagreements between hunters and scientists as to the status of a number of species, but in general co-operation in managing wildlife wins out over antagonism.

The settlement of land claims agreements has played an important role in maintaining the viability of hunting and gathering as a lifestyle, or what is now termed the 'subsistence economy'. Despite the enormity of the North, there are increasing pressures on the land from industrial developers, tourism and hunting outfitters, and a growing indigenous population. It has become necessary to define who can do what, where, when, and how in order to regulate land activities and avoid unintended ecological damage. Inuit have consistently defended their right to continue hunting without restrictions from outside their own cultural system. They have also developed hunter support programs that allow people to continue these activities. In northern Quebec each municipality has a hunter support budget to benefit hunters and the community at large. Communal freezers store meat brought in through hunter support and all can help themselves, although the elderly and incapacitated have priority. In this we see the reinvention of the Inuit ethos of sharing in a community setting.

In each of the four Inuit regions the land base has been classified into several categories in which Inuit have varying rights and exemptions from the hunting, fishing, and trapping legislation that applies to others. In Nunavik, for example, the JBNQA established three basic categories of lands. Category I lands immediately surround communities and their resources are reserved

BOX 4.1

Whale Hunting

Bowhead whales had been hunted almost to extinction by the early twentieth century. They were prime targets for commercial whaling expeditions because of their size and the relative ease of killing them. For decades they were rarely seen and even more rarely hunted. Tight government restrictions on the remaining animals formally ended the hunt. For the Inuit, it was the loss of an important part of their culture, not to mention a significant food source.

In 1996 it was back on. A large bowhead was killed close to Repulse Bay in an intensely scrutinized and somewhat disappointing hunt. The animal sank in deep water only to resurface two days later, the meat largely spoiled. Some of the *muktuk*, the thick skin and a favoured food of most Inuit, was distributed to Inuit communities as planned. The hunt was repeated in Pangnirtung two years later with new equipment and more success. The whale was landed at the old whaling station at Kekkerten and distributed widely throughout Nunavut.

The right to harvest at least one bowhead was negotiated into the Nunavut Land Claim Agreement subject to federal ministerial approval. The symbolic importance of a renewed hunt in a new, Inuit-run territory is clear. It asserts Inuit political authority over sea mammals they have always used, demonstrates traditional values of sharing, and attributes prestige to those associated with hunting success.

There are long-standing tensions between Inuit hunters and fisheries and wildlife officials regarding the status of a variety of animal populations and the Inuit obligation to respect quotas and other hunting restrictions. Inuit have always felt they were the experts and the responsible hunters. It was largely non-Inuit who brought species to dangerously low levels and yet it is Inuit who must restrict their traditional activities to save them. The Nunavut Wildlife Management Board conducted a large-scale study of the eastern Arctic bowhead using the traditional methods of science and Inuit knowledge. They think an ongoing but limited hunt is sustainable. The tide seems to have turned towards an era of cooperation and mutual respect when it comes to managing these animals.

The return of bowhead whaling in Nunavut has international political ramifications. Pro- and anti-whaling nations and organizations have deeply entrenched positions about the legitimacy and ecological viability of whaling. The subsistence hunts of the Inuit and other indigenous peoples are contested by some and are used by others to argue for the resumption of commercial hunts. Inuit are represented on many international whaling organizations to monitor these debates and to make sure that their voice is heard. Inuit hunting is now a global occupation.

exclusively for Inuit. They comprise 8,152 square kilometres. All land-use activities on Category I lands are under the jurisdiction of the landholding corporations of the communities. On Category II lands Inuit retain exclusive hunting, fishing, and trapping rights, including commercial exploitation. Category II lands constitute 82,597 square kilometres and include the most productive hunting and fishing areas. Category III lands are Crown

lands on which the public at large has access as they do elsewhere. Certain species are reserved for Native use on Category III lands.

In Nunavut a similar system of land categories and Inuit rights to animals exists. An additional feature of the Nunavut Agreement is that Inuit have subsurface rights on some lands. The land claim negotiators were clearly looking for broadly based economic sustainability. Having subsurface rights allows for Inuit control over mines and other developments that could have significant implications for their economy. Should development prove viable, it will lessen their dependence on transfers from the federal government. This is the only Inuit territory where the Crown has ceded mineral potential to the people.

The land claims have not settled all the territorial questions or concerns of the Inuit. Jurisdiction over oceans and navigable waters still remains in the hands of the federal government, as it does for the rest of the country, even though Inuit have a legitimate ancestral claim to seasonal (winter) occupation of the ice. There is no legal mechanism to deal with these issues and they largely remain uninvestigated. The issue of offshore islands, however, is subject to some negotiation. When the borders of Quebec were extended north to their present locations in 1912, relatively little was known about the geography of the province. Consequently, the question of islands close to the coast was not considered. Inuit from Quebec now find themselves in the curious position of travelling from a province to a territory with completely different legal and jurisdictional requirements when they paddle five minutes to an island from which they have always hunted. Likewise, Inuit from the Belcher Islands in Hudson Bay are part of Nunavut—the capital, Iqaluit, is 1,000 kilometres away—even though they are related through family ties, culture, history, geography, and language to Quebec Inuit only165 kilometres east. These are accidents of history that have become political issues between the Inuit and federal and provincial governments, and increasingly between Inuit regional governments.

Global assessments of wildlife status are also an issue. The global transport of pollutants has important repercussions in the North. Global weather patterns concentrate many dangerous pollutants in the North, where they are consumed by animals. PCBs and mercury, for example, are found in high concentrations in the fat and skin of some marine mammals. Inuit generally eat at the top of the food chain: animals that eat other animals. There have to date been no demonstrated effects on people in the North from these chemicals and the biophysical mechanisms that create health problems are still poorly understood. However, the potential for health risks is undeniable and quite disconcerting to Inuit. In some instances pregnant and breast-feeding women have been advised to avoid certain parts of animals. In the case of mercury, not eating seal would have a complicating effect because seal meat also contains selenium, which negates the effect of mercury. The risks of *niqituinnaq* have to be evaluated in comparison to the alternatives. Overall, people who eat country food are better nourished, have a healthier body weight, and are more active than those who do not. If people were told to stop eating *niqituinnaq*, they would eat more junk food and do less physical activity. These are the major factors in the lifestyle diseases afflicting people in industrial countries. In fact, there is already evidence that rates of diabetes and heart disease are rising among Inuit for exactly these reasons. A final effect would be on social cohesion and intergenerational communication. Social problems are already pronounced in the North. If people stopped doing what they have always done there would be further erosion of the qualities of life that make people feel good.

At a political level, Inuit are very active in national and global environmental policy. Organizations like Inuit Tapiriit Kanatami and the Inuit Circumpolar Conference have been effective at representing Inuit interests and in influencing environmental policy. They regularly promote the reduction of pollutants and greenhouse gas emissions that undermine their traditions and the quality of the environment for everyone. The Inuit are not a passive people. Rather, they connect local traditions to global discourses and actions in a unique and productive way.

Leadership, Individuality, and Social Solidarity

Accounts of Inuit social organization point to two distinct and quite different systems, based on the seasons. Winter life in some regions was focused around the multi-chambered snow house, *illu* (igloo), or semi-subterranean dwelling, *qarmaq*. Several extended families would winter together, particularly when a surplus of meat had been collected. At this time of the year ritual activity was frequent and intense. Spousal exchanges, shamanic divinations, competitions of strength, and so on occurred within the concentrated space of the igloo. Authority in social matters, including marriage, hunting, division of game, naming children, and the adoption of children, was concentrated in a single socially acknowledged, powerful, and knowledgeable person know as *isumataaq*. Social interaction was at its height and the people's attentions were focused indoors. Several anthropologists have described the igloo as a female realm dominated by the symbolic symmetry between domestic space and female bodies.

In contrast to winter's social organization, summer was typified by dispersal into small, autonomous family groups consisting of father and sons, or brothers and wives, and children. Older people and others who were unable to move around easily, and those who were not wanted as travel companions, tended to stay close to the winter sites, fishing and hunting seals throughout the summer. The authority in decision-making shifted from the *isumataaq* to family heads and there was much more room for individual independence. In the warm months people were mobile and life was focused outward, onto the land and sea. Relations between people and animals displaced relations among people and the female symbolic realm gave over to the male. The social distinctions between summer and winter patterns are reproduced in categorizations of summer-born and winter-born people, between the continual pursuit of the sun and the moon in mythology, and in the tensions between individual autonomy and social obligation.

This last point is quite important, as it seems from a variety of accounts that Inuit people experienced significant tensions embedded in the structures of authority and individuality. Throughout Inuit rituals we see an emphasis on sharing and giving. The first time a young hunter caught an animal of each species, he was obliged to give it to others in particular sequence. In most cases he could consume none of it himself. These gestures acknowledged the importance of elders, midwives, and namesakes and continuously demonstrated individual subservience to the group. Deference to familial authority, the *isumataaq*, and the shaman led to tensions when disagreement was suppressed or ignored. There are numerous stories of people who rebelled and adopted a self-oriented, perhaps selfish, position. Sometimes they went on to become leaders through the fear they invoked, but in other cases they were ostracized or even murdered.

Denial of the self and deference to socially recognized authority continue to be important Inuit traits. While these traits had an important role in maintaining group cohesion in the past, when the first non-Inuit came into the North bearing governmental authority their decisions, even dangerously poor ones, were often met with quiet acquiescence. People today talk about how they could not speak their minds to *Qallunaaq* in the past, even when asked to do so, because they had no authority to do so within their own social system. In contemporary society we see an easing of these absolute hierarchies. There is much greater latitude for Inuit to voice their opinions and, consequently, to control their own destinies.

What has happened to this way of organizing life? At one level all would seem different: people live in permanent communities, have jobs, and participate in the opportunities available today in Canada. However, it is also possible to see the reproduction of older patterns. The community has replaced the large igloo and ritual activity now includes shopping, schooling, and church-going. In summer, particularly in smaller communities, seasonal dispersal of family groups to hunting camps still occurs much as it always did. Hunting and consuming marine mammals, caribou, birds, and fish remain vitally important to physical and social health, as Inuit readily affirm. In this instance traditions are easily transplanted to a new context.

There are limits to the community-igloo analogy. The most obvious difference is in the pluralization of Arctic society and the roles that people can occupy. For example, the characteristic leader of the past, the *isumataaq*, is now paralleled by formally elected leadership. 'Paralleled' is the key word here, as formal government has neither replaced family-based authority nor does it threaten to. Instead, it would appear that a basic challenge to the Inuit regional and territorial governments is to acknowledge the importance of that system, incorporate its cultural power into effective policy-making, and draw society into that process by linking tradition with governance.

There have been attempts to acknowledge the role of social leadership by incorporating an Elders' area into the Nunavut legislature. The area chosen was felt by some to be disrespectful of elders because it was located behind the Premier's and Speaker's areas. Elders do not generally get pushed to the side. More important than seating arrangements is the role that Elders' knowledge and experience brings to the process of government. Nunavut government has adopted as policy *Inuit Qaujimajatuqangit*, 'Inuit ways and knowledge'. Many feel that decisions and policies should be examined from the perspective of Inuit traditions and philosophy before being acted upon. The logic is that Inuit government should contribute to and respect traditions rather than ignore or undermine them.

Socially vested authority and formalized authority sometimes correspond, sometimes coexist, and sometimes conflict. Leadership is now specialized and rarely carries the same all-encompassing social importance it did. Solutions to problems are increasingly sought in processes located in institutions and not in a society consisting of small groups, where all problems were once managed. A complex division of labour has developed with the cash economy. Where once one would have gone to see a leader whatever the problem, now an Inuk can seek out specialists in social matters, hunting, mechanical repairs, or medicine.

Contemporary lifestyle brings with it inescapable effects on social and familial organization. Having permanent dwellings imputes a specific kind of social structure onto its inhabitants, restricting and shaping social organization. In effect, the predominant housing style emulates that of the nuclear family and reifies that kinship system. This has impacts on the way Inuit social organization is conceptualized in administrative systems and these in turn affect families. Of course, there are social problems in some families in the North, and it is through the management of tragic and complex events that we most readily see where change in Inuit society is taking place. Also, the structure of governance now in the hands of Inuit is inherited from English common law. It brings with it assumptions about the nature of society, productivity, property, and kin that in some instances counter those of Inuit customary practice. It is common to hear leaders talking about the antithesis of the idea of landownership to Inuit cultural values, for example, yet ownership is exactly what has been determined in the land claims agreements.

An aspect of the incompatibility of Inuit and Canadian systems of social organization that I have studied closely is child adoption. The largely unacknowledged assumptions of the child welfare system, which is grounded in national legal standards rather than Inuit social or moral ones, are a continuing source of friction. In Nunavut and Nunavik roughly one child in four is adopted by customary arrangements. I define 'adopted' in

Inuit society as 'not primarily socialized by the biological parents'. Adoption is a cornerstone of Inuit social organization and essentially everyone takes part as a giver, receiver, brother, sister, and so on of adopted children. Older people in particular adopt children. Often elderly adopters talk about having young children in their lives as a requirement to staying healthy. Without them they feel unproductive, lazy, and even ill. Inuit customary adoption challenges basic assumptions about motherhood, childhood, and elderhood held in southern Canada and beyond.

These social arrangements of child-rearing run counter to fundamental truths held in the legal system and reflect back on non-Inuit ideas of property and ownership. Children *belong* to their biological parents and to give away a child imputes negligence on the part of the parents. Old people are supposed to be quiet, unproductive, and relieved that they no longer have to bear the burden of child rearing. Rarely would we see elderly people seeking children to adopt. Inuit clearly do not experience adoption this way. They see giving children as a sign of respect to people they have known all their lives and care for deeply. It is, as one woman told me, 'the nicest thing I could do for them'. Inuit adopt into pre-existing and often multi-generational relationships. The quality of parenting an adopted child would receive is rarely in question and people who are seen as irresponsible are less likely to be given the opportunity to adopt. Checks and balances relying on social knowledge and historical association are built into the system. Regardless, the role of government institutions has grown and there are clear conflicts grounded in the differences between Inuit social and bureaucratic systems. Attempts to resolve social problems involving children occur in both realms. Customary adoption practices stand out in these instances and are probed for their contribution to social problems. Rarely, however, have they been examined by the bureaucratic system for their contributions to social harmony. While there is more to say about this, it is sufficient to say that even in the context of renewed Inuit political authority, there are restrictions on the space that cultural practices can take.

The Historical Context: Communities and Coercion

Historians of English Canada have said that we stopped thinking like a colony and began acting like a nation in the wake of the collective loss and horrors of two world wars. As a nation we grew up. In World War I, Canadians began to emerge from the mentality of imperial colonials and into the mindset of independent nationals. World War II cemented a growing vision of nationhood and initiated the consolidation of national territory, including the Arctic. Our attention turned inward to our own geography and its meaning.

The changes in Canadian self-image are seen in the corresponding shifts in how the North has been represented and acted upon. In the age of exploration the Arctic grail that drove the exploration of the North was the fabled Northwest Passage. Finding a sea route from the Atlantic to the Pacific had enormous symbolic importance and potential economic significance. Heroes of this period expanded the horizons of empire and some lived to tell the tale. Others, such as Sir John Franklin and his crew of 128, disappeared (in 1848) in the High Arctic. More than 40 expeditions tried to find them, none successfully. The only evidence of their fate came from Dr John Rae, who travelled with Inuit in the mid-1800s as a surveyor for the Hudson's Bay Company. He heard from them of a group of white men, who could only have been Franklin's crew, hauling a large boat over the ice. He collected stories of their fate and relayed them to England, where they were largely disbelieved (Woodman, 1991).

The relevance of this episode is in the extent to which the Inuit testimony was correct and the degree to which it was ignored. This pattern of interaction between peoples has endured for some time, although its substance has changed. This episode demonstrates that what we think we know is often determined by what we assume to be possible. Only recently has Inuit testimony regarding Franklin's fate been tested against objective criteria, primarily the discovery of artifacts and graves from the Franklin crew. In the end the Inuit testimony was found to have been highly accurate. That it was doubted for so long says something about the durability of preconceptions.

The Franklin expedition marks the beginning of the end of the imperial North and the dawn of the Canadianization of the Arctic. Early in the twentieth century a new way of talking about the North emerged, one that began to acknowledge Inuit cultural and technological mastery of the Arctic. In popular culture, notably the hugely successful film *Nanook of the North*, the technological ingenuity of the Inuit was marvelled at, although it seemed to emerge from childlike explorations with simple objects: stones, bone, and small pieces of wood. Others in this period, notably Vilhjalmur Stefansson, argued that the North is amenable to occupation and exploitation and, more importantly, that this should be a national objective. In the period between the wars, Inuit were not considered active participants in northern development. In fact, they existed on the margins of the story, almost invisible to those who were imagining it. The leap from a passive observation of the Inuit to an active intervention in their lives would come later.

The end of World War II marked a new era. The nation had barely worked out where it stood in the world when the world crowded in on it. Americans had strategic claims to portions of the Arctic Archipelago, Danes were looking across Baffin Strait to Ellesmere Island, and Russians suddenly were capable of attacking the West by coming over Arctic Canada. Perhaps the most significant event in the ongoing relationship between the state and the Inuit occurred when the US built radar bases across the North. In the process, Canada's Arctic peoples came to be seen by the world. In many instances what was seen were resolutely traditional-looking people, almost entirely self-reliant, living from the land. The post-war boom brought unimagined technology and comparative wealth to almost all of North America, yet the Inuit were stubbornly unchanging. Well into the 1950s many clothed themselves in skins and lived off the land, with no need of government or nation. The new sense of national confidence was threatened by the transformation of geopolitics, by the absence in Canada of knowledge about its own territory, and by the apparent indifference of Inuit to material prosperity. The earlier imaginings about the Arctic and its peoples were outdated and in need of revision. Where formerly Canada had no means of demonstrating sovereignty over its territory and little interaction with its indigenous inhabitants, the post-war period was marked by the arrival of the state in the lives of the Inuit. They became, in the eyes of government, people needing administration.

Not only did Canada begin to think like a nation in the post-war period, it acted like one. The development and implementation of national social policies had a profound effect. The presence of government in the daily lives of people, seen through the development of education, health, economic, and social policies, increased dramatically. The post-war period saw Canada transformed into a wealthy, modern country. For Aboriginal peoples generally, the same period is marked by an intensification of the systematic undermining of their indigenous social structures and cultural principles. The Arctic and the Inuit posed a particular difficulty in this modernization. Transportation was erratic and distances enormous. The few non-Inuit living in the North were largely traders, priests, and the occasional RCMP officer. There was little government in the North and most people lived outside the cash economy.

Anthropology and Arctic Modernity

Anthropology has played an important role in building the national sense of the North and in criticizing it. For a period from the 1950s to the late 1970s when Inuit were being drawn into permanent settlements, applied anthropologists addressed the question of how they were adapting to life in communities and looked at social and cultural change. Throughout the past 40–50 years the discourse of cultural contact and subsequent change in indigenous lifeways has been invoked as an encompassing explanatory model in applied anthropology, and in psychological and psychiatric investigations of individual distress and social dysfunction. Change, as it has been expressed as a result of the encounters between Inuit and Euro-Canadians, is generally taken to be pathogenic. But change is not an accident of nature. People make decisions about what will change and how. Enforced change means that some people have authority over others.

Anthropologists took a role in analyzing the effects of change on Inuit and in making certain changes happen. Diamond Jenness, an anthropologist who travelled with Knud Rasmussen, the Danish explorer and ethnologist, in the ground-breaking Fifth Thule Expedition, later undertook a large study called *Eskimo Administration* (1964) that supported the development of a government policy of settling Inuit into new and permanent communities. It was generally taken for granted that they would ultimately be acculturated into pan-Canadian values, abandoning the subsistence economy to participate in industrial society. Throughout this period anthropologists examined the social changes resulting from community living with an eye towards easing and understanding the adjustment of Inuit to this new arrangement.

In retrospect it seems that the disappearance of traditional cultures was taken to be inevitable by government and researchers alike. Inuit today speak of this time with great sadness. They were told repeatedly that they would have to change and were better off not pursuing traditional activities. Children were encouraged to learn English and came to devalue their parents through an educational system that portrayed their lives as primitive. This period produced a disjuncture between generations that has come to be seen as a source of social distance and disintegration that people are only now coming to terms with.

The presumed inevitability and direction of change in Inuit society were a force shaping their relations with government. Early studies of Inuit social change were naive to the politics at play in describing the apparent dissolution of traditional ways in the face of new modes of social organization imposed from outside. The basic assumptions about the future of Inuit life were in effect self-fulfilling prophecies. As evidence of social dysfunction mounted, new programs and policies were created to shape and mitigate the changes. In each case Inuit were pulled further from the sources of social order and authority that had informed their lives, in many instances making things worse. Few people with authority were suggesting alternatives to the policies that disempowered Inuit.

The settlement of Inuit into communities did not happen overnight. Rudimentary towns had grown up around Hudson's Bay Company posts and missions since the turn of the twentieth century. In some cases people would gather there, usually in winter, and then return to other hunting areas in spring. In this respect social organization emulated that of the past. However, with World War II, trade goods became scarce and fur prices fell for lack of demand. Inuit who had become accustomed to semi-annual trading sessions, and the goods these provided, were often left destitute. No ammunition meant no hunting, so they were increasingly reliant on relief through the missions, the HBC, or the RCMP. From the point of view of people providing relief, the situation was chaotic. They could not plan for the future and had no idea what would happen next. Inuit were still highly mobile but when game became scarce they would arrive, needing relief, far from where they had been last encountered. It became increasingly important to control the movements of people so they could be provided for when necessary.

In the early 1950s the RCMP systematically shot all dogs in several communities in northern

Quebec and the Northwest Territories. This was explained as necessary due to rabies among the dogs and the danger this posed to people. Inuit, who are knowledgeable about rabies in wildlife populations, disagree. They view these incidents as intentional efforts to stop them from going on the land. They have also come to symbolize their powerlessness in relations with the state. Dog teams were the principal means of winter locomotion. Without them people were forced to remain in the communities. They could not hunt and became more dependent on imported goods.

The demonstration of Canadian sovereignty over the Arctic was also wrapped up in these efforts. Creating recognizable and permanent communities involved, in some instances, relocating people from one part of the North to very distant places. People in Inukjuak, Quebec, a relatively southern Inuit community, were moved to Grise Fjord in the High Arctic under the guise of providing them access to more productive hunting grounds. The people had no experience with this landscape and the hunting was unfamiliar and certainly no more productive than where they came from. In the end, the real reason seems to have been to show the flag in a contested part of the North.

Throughout this period of transition to community living, locally pertinent alternatives to a seemingly irrevocable process of settlement and modernization were never explored by those in charge. They were being put forth by Inuit, however. The rise of co-operative movements and new forms of culturally defined political representation were undertaken even before the communities of today had been formalized.

Recently, a critique of the relations of power inherent in the internal colonialism of Aboriginal peoples in Canada has pointed to the devastating effects of enforced social change. One example comes from the institutionalization of Inuit health service delivery. Epidemic tuberculosis was responsible for many deaths throughout the North in the twentieth century. Treatment involved sending people south on an annual medical survey ship for treatment in sanatoriums. The separation of families, sometimes for years and sometimes permanently as many died and a few were even lost in the 'system', had an important impact on the ability of Inuit to be independent. By necessity many Inuit remained close to the trading posts, mission houses, and RCMP stations to receive relief. This pattern became regularized as their dependence on non-Inuit grew and they could not re-establish their traditional economy.

The policy of evacuating people with chronic illness for hospital treatment was eventually extended to include women in the third trimester of pregnancy. As in the case of TB, sending women to hospitals separated them from the familial and social support already in place, and isolated fathers from caring for the family and from the birth itself. It also severed cultural practices around birth that were important in establishing the child's social context. Inuit midwives had an important place in the life of children they helped deliver. Similarly, cutting the umbilical cord created a lifelong special relationship between the child and *Sanajiik*, the one who cut the cord. Hospital births for healthy women ruptured these social ties. Sending women out of their communities was done under the guise of helping people, a justification that made it easier to intervene in cultural practice and demonstrate authority. The anthropological literature discussing these events generally supports returning control over policy to the Inuit. Regaining the power to make decisions that affect people's lives will allow for more culturally appropriate policy to be established and for the wounds of the past to be healed.

Conclusion

The past 25 years have witnessed the resolution of that process with land claims agreements across the Arctic. The most significant for the country at large was the creation of Nunavut. This is the first change in Canadian political bound-

BOX 4.2

Inuit Language and Writing

Inuktitut is one of the most vigorous indigenous languages in North America. It is widely spoken within Inuit communities and is the language of everyday life in most. Inuktitut, Inuinaqtung, Inuttut, and Inuttitut are, respectively, the regional dialects of the majority of native speakers in Nunavut, the Inuvialuit Settlement Area, Labrador, and Nunavik. There are sub-dialects within each region as well, but all are largely mutually intelligible. Language and culture are closely linked and Inuit are keenly aware of the challenges that Inuktitut faces in a sea of Anglo North American culture. The Nunavut government has implemented a policy of three official languages in the territory: Inuktitut, French, and English. A major challenge in Nunavut is encouraging the use of Inuktitut in the workplace. As the government workforce is heavily populated by non-Inuit, many of whom grew up elsewhere, and Inuit tend to be bilingual, the tendency is to favour English. In some instances Nunavut government employees are encouraged to take Inuktitut language courses.

In Nunavik the situation is more complex as provincial authority has grown since the signing of the JBNQA and there is a mix of Inuktitut, French, and English speakers in the workplace. In some instances Inuit have chosen to educate their children alternately in English and French in order to have a full spectrum of language skills within the family. Many young people are growing up functionally trilingual. In Kuujjuaraapik in southern Hudson Bay the community is roughly half Inuit and half Cree. Here there are some people who are comfortable in four languages.

Writing in Inuktitut is a relatively new invention brought by Anglican missionaries in the nineteenth century. The majority of Inuit in Nunavut and Nunavik use a syllabic script based on modified shorthand. In Labrador the roman script is used with some modifications for sounds not found in English. For example, a capital 'K' anywhere in a word indicates a combined q and h sound produced deep in the throat. In western Nunavut and the Inuvialuit settlement area a standard roman script is used for writing. When Inuit from around the world gather they also add the Cyrillic script (Russia) and Greenlandic versions of roman Kallalisut (the Greenlandic name for their language) writing to the menu. Not surprisingly, there have been efforts to produce a unified Inuit writing form that would allow for simple written communication across the Circumpolar North. To date this has not happened, and it appears unlikely to occur in the near future. Instead, people look increasingly to digital technology to make transliteration between the various scripts instantaneous and automatic.

The cultural and political dimensions of language use in the North are complex. Variations in written and spoken language signal regional and national differences that correspond both to particular historical trajectories and senses of identity and tradition.

aries since 1949, when Newfoundland joined Confederation. Nunavut has a public government, meaning any resident may participate in it, dominated by Inuit because of their overwhelming numbers. This achievement is the culmination of more than 30 years of work by a class of politically astute Inuit that emerged in the 1960s shortly after people had been settled into communities and by Elders and others who supported them. Nunavut represents a return to Inuit regional autonomy, but its creation obviously is not a return to the past. Instead, it reflects a hybrid of Inuit and southern ways of doing things. Consequently, social and political tensions inherent to the new structure of governance place demands on Inuit that are unique in the country and serve as a model for others.

The changes that Inuit have experienced in a lifetime are profound and irrevocable. It was clear even at the turn of the nineteenth century that many of them were going to happen. This has led to almost 100 years of anthropological research that was explicitly or implicitly underpinned by the idea that, eventually, the Inuit would lose or abandon their culture to adopt that of the majority population. This is to say that they would cease to exist as a distinct cultural group. To be fair, it was not just anthropologists who assumed this process was inevitable. It was the dominant way of conceiving the future of all non-Western cultures since at least the Victorian era. Certainly, the assumption of cultural loss and assimilation was central to how government operated until relatively recently. Not only were the Inuit 'disappearing', but the role of government was to facilitate their transformation. Rarely were Inuit themselves consulted or considered.

Well, we all seem to have been wrong. Since regional political autonomy has been regained and as Inuit take charge of their governments, Inuit culture is undergoing a renaissance. Inuit culture has taken its place on a world stage and it is not uncommon to see throat singing and drum dance performances in Paris or Osaka, or to hear Inuit popular music being played alongside American and British tunes. Not only are there more Inuit alive today than at any time in the past, but the use of the various dialects of the Inuit language is strong in most areas, particularly the eastern Arctic. Where the use of Inuktitut has declined and been replaced by English, there are now government-funded programs and voluntary associations of people working to expand its use. Permanent housing, wage-paying jobs, television, the Internet, school buses, and airplanes have not made the Inuit any less Inuit. These are simply material things that people incorporate into their everyday lives. What is relevant to a discussion of Inuit cultural continuity and change is how their everyday lives are constrained and broadened by the flow of information and continual contact with ideas, values, rules, and laws that people are surrounded with.

Note

1. Although the terms 'month' and 'moon month' are commonly used, technically they are neither, but rather are named mini-seasons that follow each other in regular order. In any particular year they may come sooner or later than usual.

References and Recommended Readings

Briggs, Jean. 1970. *Never in Anger: Portrait of an Eskimo Family*. Cambridge, Mass.: Harvard University Press. A groundbreaking and sensitive ethnography of Inuit family life, this study broke the formalist and descriptive tradition to focus on the emotional lives of a small group and includes excellent detail on children and women.

Dorais, Louis-Jacques. 1997. *Quaqtaq: Modernity and Identity in an Inuit Community*. Toronto: University of Toronto Press. Examines the process of community development and the influence of family alliances on contemporary political and social organization. A very accessible ethnography/ethnohistory of a small Nunavik community.

Grace, Sherrill E. 2001. *Canada and the Idea of North*. Montreal and Kingston: McGill-Queen's University Press. A comprehensive overview of Canada's fascination with the North. Includes consideration of poetry, performing arts, painting, and literature in attempting to grasp what the North means to us.

Jenness, Diamond. 1964. *Eskimo Administration, vol. II*. Canada: Arctic Institute of North America.

Mowat, Farley. 1963. *Never Cry Wolf*. Toronto: McClelland & Stewart.

Pitseolak, Peter, and Dorothy Eber. 1993. *People From Our Side*. Montreal and Kingston: McGill-Queen's University Press. An autobiography with accompanying photographs by Peter Pitseolak. The original manuscript was complemented with interview citations and synthesized into a genuinely Inuit view of history in the twentieth century.

Honigman, John, and Irma Honigman. 1970. *Arctic Townsmen: Ethnic Background and Modernization*.

Ottawa: St Paul's University, Canadian Research Centre for Anthropology. A culture change study by two of the leading anthropologists of the period.

Nunavut Arctic College. 1999–2001. *Interviewing Inuit Elders*, 5 vols. Iqaluit: Nunavut Arctic College. A remarkable series (vol. 1, *Introduction*; vol. 2, *Perspectives on Tradtional Law*; vol. 3, *Childrearing Perspectives*; vol. 4, *Cosmology and Shamanism*; vol. 5, *Health Practices*) exploring the experiences of Elders with Inuit traditions and change in their lifetimes. Presented as extended interview transcripts, these are accessible first-person accounts. Selected texts available as downloads from <http://www.nunavut.com/traditionalknowledge>.

MacDonald, John. 1998. *The Arctic Sky*. Toronto: Royal Ontario Museum and Nunavut Research Institute. A thematic approach to Inuit cosmogony that emphasizes the role of human-animal relations in Inuit representations of the heavens.

Rasmussen, Knud. 1976 [1932]. *Intellectual Culture of the Copper Eskimos*, trans. W.E. Calvert. New York: AMS Press.

———. 1976 [1930]. *Intellectual Culture of the Iglulik Eskimos*, trans. W.E. Calvert. New York: AMS Press. These two volumes of the Fifth Thule Expedition Reports (1921–4) are some of the most comprehensive descriptions of Inuit life, custom, and myth in the early twentieth century. Rasmussen was part Greenlandic Inuit and spoke Inuktitut, providing an unparalleled window into the Inuit world of the time.

Tester, Frank James, and Peter Kulchyski. 1994. *Tammarniit (Mistakes): Inuit Relocation in the Eastern Arctic*. Vancouver: University of British Columbia Press. A finely researched and scathing reconstruction of the role of government ineptitude in the events leading up to starvation and murder in two Inuit regions.

Turner, Lucien. 1979 [1894]. *Indians and Eskimos in the Quebec-Labrador Peninsula*. The first comprehensive ethnography of Inuit in Labrador and Ungava Bay (Quebec). It has methodological problems but is an important benchmark.

Wenzel, George. 1991. *Animal Rights, Human Rights: Ecology, Economy and Ideology in the Canadian Arctic*. Toronto: University of Toronto Press.

Woodman, David C. 1991. *Unravelling the Franklin Mystery: Inuit Testimony*. Montreal and Kingston: McGill-Queen's University Press.

Suggested Web Sites

Nunatsiaq News: www.nunatsiaq.com
   Northern news from Nunavut, Nunavik, and elsewhere weekly. Has a searchable archive that is useful for gaining a sense of what is happening.

Inuit Tapiriit Kanatami: www.itk.ca
   ITK is the national organization representing Canadian Inuit interests. Since the early 1970s, ITK has guided the social, economic, and political development of Inuit regions and communities.

The National Library of Canada—North: Landscape of the Imagination: www.nlc-bnc.ca/nord/index-e.html
   A comprehensive and intelligent Web site devoted to exploring Canada's North in historical perspective.

Arctic Circle: www.arcticcircle.uconn.edu
   A Web site devoted to exploring issues around natural resources, history and culture, and social equity and environmental justice in the Circumpolar North. Solid content by a dedicated team lead by Norman Chance.

CHAPTER 5

The Caribou Inuit

ERNEST S. BURCH JR

Introduction

The people called 'Caribou Eskimos' lived on and near the west coast of Hudson Bay in what is now the southern portion of the Kivalliq Region, Nunavut Territory. The label was coined in the early 1920s by the Danish ethnographers Knud Rasmussen and Kaj Birket-Smith, who were fascinated by the obsession the Inuit-speaking residents of the region had with caribou as a source of food and other raw materials, to the near exclusion of everything else. In this respect they contrasted markedly with other Eskimo groups in the ethnographic record, most of which depended primarily on sea mammals.[1]

From the perspective of the early twenty-first century, the interesting question is less that these people were obsessed with caribou than with how they came to be that way. Also of interest is the fact that, as we now know, the members of these relatively simple hunter-gatherer societies increased in numbers and expanded their territory for nearly two centuries after European contact. This placed them in direct contrast to the experience of small-scale societies in almost every other part of the world.

Field and archival research conducted during the second half of the twentieth century significantly enhanced our understanding of Caribou Inuit history, ecology, and social organization. Birket-Smith's and Rasmussen's accounts will always be essential elements in our record of

Caribou Inuit life, but we now realize that those authors overlooked several important aspects of it, and they failed completely to understand the unusual historical circumstances in which they made their observations.

My own introduction to the Caribou Inuit came in 1968. I was interested in learning how people living in extreme environments were organized prior to the time of Western contact. I was looking for an Inuit group that was different enough from the Iñupiaq Eskimos of northwestern Alaska, with whom I was already familiar, to provide me with an instructive contrast.[2] On more practical grounds, I had just joined the Anthropology Department at the University of Manitoba and, as a condition of getting the job, had agreed to do research among Canadian Inuit. A literature review suggested that the Caribou Inuit might solve both problems. That view was confirmed by a colleague at Manitoba, Thomas C. Correll, who had spent several years among the Caribou Inuit as a missionary-linguist before entering anthropology. Between 1968 and 1971, Correll and I spent about 14 months interviewing Elders in both northwestern Alaska and on the west coast of Hudson Bay, trying to learn what they knew about their ancestors' ways of life. Then I turned to historical documents, both published and unpublished.

The primary unpublished documents relevant to the Caribou Inuit region were the Hudson's Bay Company (HBC) records, which spanned the entire era between the late seventeenth and early twentieth centuries. These were not made available to the general public until the mid-1970s. As I examined these amazingly informative documents, what began as a relatively straightforward exercise in sociology developed into a rather complicated project in ethnohistory. My original interest in the general structure of early twentieth-century Caribou Inuit societies expanded to include an equal, if not greater, fascination with the changes occurring in that structure over the previous 250 years. Both of those interests are reflected in the present account.

The Country

The Caribou Inuit region is located about halfway down the west side of Hudson Bay, between approximately 60° and 65° N. It extends roughly 600 kilometres from north to south and 500 kilometres inland from the coast. The landscape is an undulating plain of generally low relief that rises gradually from the shallow waters of Hudson Bay towards the west and south, where it reaches a maximum elevation of some 500 metres above sea level. A heavily glaciated portion of the Canadian Shield, the region is characterized by a variety of post-glacial landforms, such as eskers and rocky outcrops, and countless marshlands, rivers, lakes, streams, and ponds. The land is still rebounding from the release of the great continental glacier's weight, with the result that the shoreline has changed considerably over the past 300 years.

The treeline angles irregularly across the region from southeast to northwest (see Map 5.1). North of this line, the country is blanketed by barren or lichen- and moss-covered outcrops and boulders interspersed with grass and sedge meadows, and copses of dwarf trees and shrubs, which seldom exceed one metre in height. Here and there in the southern and western portions, in a sheltered valley or hollow, are islands of spruce that remained behind when the forest retreated southward during the bitter weather of the Little Ice Age, some 400 years ago. (Currently the treeline is moving north again.) Below the treeline, spruce fill the valleys and hollows, and grow progressively farther up the hillsides as one proceeds from northeast to southwest.

Plant growth even in southern Kivalliq is severely restricted by the harsh climate. Frost occurs on an average of more than 260 days per year, and the average temperature, reckoned for a 12-month period, ranges from about −5°C in the southwest to −6°C in the north.[3] Precipitation, which fluctuates considerably from year to year, is at near-desert levels most of the time, averaging between about 20 and 30 centimetres a year; 60 per cent of this usually falls as rain between early June and early October. The dominant feature of the weather, however, is the wind, which blows incessantly across the land, day and night, all year long.

The harsh climate and lack of vegetation mean that relatively few species of animals are found in the region. Historically, barren ground caribou and muskoxen were the dominant terrestrial species. Both have experienced dramatic fluctuations in numbers over the past 300 years, ranging between great abundance and near-extinction. Several varieties of fish—most notably Arctic char, lake trout, and whitefish—are found in the lakes and rivers.

The shallow coastal waters of western Hudson Bay are home to several kinds of sea mammal. The most common is the small ringed seal, but the much larger bearded seal is also present in some numbers. Walrus formerly were numerous in the central and northern sections of the coast, and belugas were abundant in some areas in early summer. Bowhead whales frequented the waters off the mouth of Chesterfield Inlet before they were nearly exterminated by American whalers in the nineteenth century. Arctic foxes, wolverines, wolves, polar bears, and several varieties of birds—particularly ptarmigan, ducks, and geese—constitute the remaining faunal resources of the area.

Origins and Early History

Precisely when and how the Caribou Inuit originated as a distinct population have long been the subject of debate. Birket-Smith maintained that they were living representatives of the earliest Eskimos, and that they still occupied the original homeland of all Eskimo-speaking peoples when he visited them in the early 1920s. Birket-Smith's conclusion followed in part from his belief that social and technological change can proceed only from less to more complex over time. He showed, through an exhaustive comparative analysis of the material culture of various historic Eskimo (including non-Inuit) groups, that the Caribou Inuit had a less complex social structure and technology than almost all of the others. Hence, they must represent the 'original' Inuit. All others, therefore, had to be descendant populations. Unfortunately, while his argument was logically valid, its conclusion was wrong because its basic premise was flawed. In fact, as we now know, change can go from more to less complex; indeed, it actually *did* do so in the specific case of the Caribou Inuit.

A contrary view was developed by Birket-Smith's colleague on the Fifth Thule Expedition, Therkel Mathiassen. He contended that his archaeological research demonstrated that all historic Inuit were descended from rather sophisticated prehistoric immigrants who brought the Thule culture eastward from Alaska. Subsequent research has shown that Mathiassen was correct.

The Caribou Inuit are definitely the biological and cultural descendants of Thule people, but just how and when they reached the west coast of Hudson Bay is still being debated. My own view is that they migrated overland from the north Canadian coast sometime in the seventeenth century. However, regardless of when they arrived or how they got there, they were firmly ensconced in the central portion of the west Hudson Bay coast by the summer of 1719, where they were encountered by HBC traders Henry Kelsey and John Hancock.

The Founder Society

The eighteenth-century Inuit population of southern Kivalliq seems to have ranged between about 250 and 450 people, as good times alternated with bad to keep their numbers in a state of flux.[4] Their territory extended along the coast from Eskimo Point to Rankin Inlet, and probably continued inland for several tens of kilometres. A few families also wintered periodically on or near Baker Lake. The greatest concentration of people was in the vicinity of Whale Cove, in the richest sector of the southern Kivalliq coast. Observations of the location and movements of specific individuals and families, made over several decades by HBC traders, suggest that all of the eighteenth-century Inuit inhabitants of the region were members of a single social system. Lacking an Inuit name for this society, I call it the 'Founder Society' of Caribou Inuit.

The Founder Society way of life was an adaptation to local conditions of the Thule culture they brought with them from the west and north. Their winter houses, made of stone chinked with moss and dirt and covered with snow, were situated on the mainland coast. In spring they moved out to islands and points of land, where they lived in conical, skin-covered tents. There they hunted seals, walrus, belugas, and an occasional bowhead whale, and fished for char. They dried the meat and fish in the sun, and stored it, along with blubber, in sealskin bags. The supplies they accumulated between May and early August probably formed the bulk of their food during the following winter. In mid- to late August they walked inland to hunt caribou, acquiring skins for clothing, and meat and fat for food. In fall, they returned to their winter dwellings near the coast with the dried meat and hides. After the ocean froze, they retrieved from the islands the supplies of sea mammal oil and meat stored there since early summer. During winter they hunted caribou or seals, as need required and conditions permitted. Overland transportation must have been by foot, since there are no references to dogs or sleds in any of the observations made of their camps by eighteenth-century explorers and traders. On water, they traveled by *kayak*, frequently lashing several together to form a raft when carrying bulk goods or large numbers of people.

The members of the Founder Society apparently were rather isolated from other Inuit. However, they were in intermittent contact with Chipewyan Indians, hundreds of whom ventured onto the tundra each summer to hunt caribou. Relations between the Chipewyan and Inuit during this period usually are depicted as invariably hostile, often violently so. HBC traders later took credit for establishing peace between the two groups. A careful examination of the archival sources, however, indicates that, while Chipewyan–Inuit relations did indeed sometimes result in bloodshed, contacts were peaceful more often than not. If anything, the HBC made things worse because members of the two groups began to compete for the traders' attention. After a smallpox epidemic decimated the Chipewyan population in the early 1780s, contacts became less frequent and overt hostility between Chipewyan and Inuit largely disappeared.

The early trade between the Caribou Inuit and the HBC was conducted from sloops sent north from Churchill during the summer. The trade was so meagre that one has to wonder why the HBC pursued it. The only furs southern Kivalliq has in quantity are those of the Arctic fox, with some wolf and wolverine, and the market for all of them was very weak during the eighteenth and nineteenth centuries. The bulk of the trade was in caribou skins and sea-mammal products, primarily blubber, with some baleen and walrus ivory. In exchange, the Inuit received knives, hatchets, fish hooks, pots, files, beads, and tobacco. After about 1770, guns, powder, and shot were also traded. The balance of the coastal trade was much to the advantage of the Inuit, a fact realized early on by the HBC traders at Churchill, but overlooked or ignored by their superiors in London. It was finally halted in 1790, after which the Inuit had to make the long trek to Churchill if they desired goods of European manufacture.

Expansion

The end of the coastal trade, which apparently occurred during a period of increasing population—the reasons for the increase are not known—led the Caribou Inuit to expand their geographic horizons. For much of the eighteenth century, and especially after 1750, they had moved to the coast each spring to hunt seals. The HBC had kindly delivered a boatload of trade goods to their very door, receiving in return a variety of miscellaneous items having little value to the Inuit. The Inuit did not become dependent on this trade, for they headed inland as soon as caribou-hunting season arrived whether or not the trading vessel had been there.

The people whose winter houses were situated in the northern sector of Caribou Inuit territory were understandably loath to make the 700–800-kilometre round trip to Churchill to acquire trade goods after 1790. Such goods were nice to have, but they were not crucial to survival. When the coastal trade was broken off, the inhabitants of this sector began to spend more time hunting, fishing, and exploring in the Chesterfield Inlet and Baker Lake area than formerly. They probably also travelled more extensively north along the Hudson Bay coast.

About the same time that the Caribou Inuit were expanding the scope and frequency of their journeys north, the Aivilik branch of the Iglulik Inuit was expanding southward from Foxe Basin. Members of the two populations apparently came into contact for the first time around 1800. This was a major event for the Caribou Inuit because, evidently from the Aivilik, they learned the art of making a snow house, a vastly more suitable winter habitation for life on the barrens than a rock house. They may also have acquired their first dogs from the Aivilik. Conversely, the Aivilik gained their first access to iron tools and containers, which they purchased from the Caribou Inuit.

While people in the northern segment of the Founder Society were gradually reorienting their activities towards Chesterfield Inlet and Baker Lake, those in the southern segment were beginning to focus their attention on Churchill, 250–300 kilometres to the south. On 9 June 1791, 20 Caribou Inuit arrived in Churchill, bringing 50 caribou skins, six fox skins, and a wolf skin to trade. They were hired by the HBC to hunt seals until the ice left the coast, and subsequently to hunt beluga whales for the HBC for a week or so before returning to their own country. When they departed, the chief factor told them that, henceforth, all trade would be done at Churchill, and he asked them to tell that to their friends. They did so, and another group of Inuit arrived at Churchill on 22 August of that same summer. These two visits initiated a trend that was to persist, with occasional modifications, for more than 130 years.

By 1810, the members of the northern and southern segments of the Founder Society were not getting along, and by the mid-1820s they had split. HBC people at Churchill learned of this development and began to refer to them as the 'Distant' and 'Homeguard' Esquimaux, respectively. The former spent the winter in the interior, near Baker Lake, and the summer along the shores of Chesterfield Inlet and Marble Island. A few made the long trip to Churchill each year, but they headed back north in time for caribou-hunting season. The 'Homeguards' probably spent the winter along the Lower Maguse River and the spring on the islands near Eskimo Point. Several of them visited Churchill each spring, then hunted beluga for the HBC during the summer. The area around Whale Cove, the geographic centre of Founder Society and the area with the greatest supply of sea mammals, became a sparsely inhabited borderland. It was apparently during this period that the trend towards the later obsession with caribou began.

The Caribou Inuit population grew rapidly, albeit with occasional setbacks, over the next century or so. At this point reasons for this increase are purely speculative. The population reached a total of perhaps 1,100 in 1881 and some 1,500 in 1915. As the population grew in size, it also expanded in space, particularly towards the interior.

Several developments, in addition to population growth, contributed to the inland expansion. The first involved the Chipewyan, who had dominated the interior, at least in summer, until the smallpox epidemic of 1781. The lure of the fur trade led many of the survivors to move southwest, further into the forest and closer to the trading posts, and away from the Inuit. Their departure left the country open to the Inuit, although groups of Chipewyan continued to make annual summer trips into the Barren Lands in the western part of the region until at least the 1870s.

A second important development was the adoption of the snow house as a winter dwelling. As noted above, this apparently occurred between 1790 and 1810. Much warmer in the winter wind than a tent, but equally suited to a nomadic way of life, snow houses were a vast improvement over stone houses. In 1750, people had had to stay fairly close to their (stone) houses whether there was any food there or not, or else live in tents all winter long. By 1820, if food ran short, they could go anywhere they wished and be relatively comfortably housed.

A third development was a crisis, in the form of a caribou decline, along the coast. Lasting for most of the 1840s, this event led to considerable hardship, particularly among the Homeguard Esquimaux. In an effort to locate caribou, several families apparently moved west to the middle Kazan River, where they discovered an abundance of muskoxen, enough to sustain them through the crisis. Finding the country to their liking, they simply stayed there after the caribou population recovered.

As the Caribou Inuit population grew numerically and expanded geographically, it also became further divided socially. The two societies of 1850 had become five only 30 years later. I have been

BOX 5.1

Caribou

'. . . the importance of caribou hunting as far as the Caribou Eskimos are concerned cannot be rated high enough. To them the caribou occupies at least the same position as the seal and the walrus to their kinsmen, or as the bison of the past to the Plains Indians. The caribou is the pivot round which life turns. When it fails, the mechanism of culture comes to a stop and hunger and cold are the consequences for those tribes which, relying upon it, have created an almost incredibly one-sided culture' (Birket-Smith, 1929: 9).

unable to learn what one of them was called by HBC personnel, but the others were known as the 'Homeguard', 'Distant', 'Inland', and 'Middle' Esquimaux. These societies were in operation during what I call the 'Classic Period' of Caribou Inuit history.

The Classic Period

Caribou Inuit culture, as a distinctive way of life, was marked by a general emphasis on terrestrial, as opposed to marine, resources, and by an overwhelming reliance on caribou as the specific resource with which material needs were satisfied. European recognition of these characteristics in the descriptive label 'Caribou Inuit' was closely paralleled in the Inuit term *nunamiut*, 'inland People', which other Inuit used to designate even those groups who spent some of the year on the coast.

The economic orientation of the late nineteenth-century Caribou Inuit was markedly different from the one prevailing 150 years earlier. In the 1750s, HBC traders literally had to beg them to give up even a small portion of their precious supply of seal oil. A century later they still killed hundreds of seals and belugas each summer, but they sold virtually their entire production to the HBC and relied almost entirely on caribou, muskoxen, and fish for their sustenance. Just why this change occurred and particularly why it took such an extreme form remain mysteries.

The change from a diversified economy to a highly specialized one occurred gradually during the demographic and geographic expansion of the mid-nineteenth century and definitely was completed by 1880. That year, therefore, may be designated as the beginning of the 'Classic Period'. The end of the period may be designated, less arbitrarily, as 1915, the first year of the 'Great Famine'.

The period 1880–1915 has a number of features that commend it for special treatment. During those years the Caribou Inuit population in general was high and still growing; the extent of their territory was greater than at any other time, before or since, and, despite more than a century and a half of contact, the people remained extraordinarily uninfluenced by Western culture. Finally, this is the earliest period for which the documentary records of traders and explorers can be enriched by information obtained directly from Caribou Inuit themselves.[5]

Societies

During most of the Classic Period the Caribou Inuit were organized in five societies, the Ahiarmiut, Harvaqturmiut, Hauniqturmiut, Paatlirmiut, and Qairnirmiut (see Table 5.1). A sixth group, the Tahiuyarmiut, may have become a society before 1915, but too little is known about it to establish that as fact; it was all but wiped out by famine almost as soon as it emerged.

Table 5.1. Caribou Inuit Societies, *circa* 1890

Inuit Name	Est. Founded	HBC Name	Population	General Location
Paatlirmiut	by 1825	Homeguard Esquimaux	450	Maguse River and nearby coast
Qairnirmiut	by 1825	Distant Esquimaux	200*	Thelon River, Baker Lake, and Chesterfield Inlet
Ahiarmiut	by 1858	Inland Esquimaux	350	Middle Kazan River
Hauniqturmiut	by 1871	Middle Esquimaux	175	Wilson River and nearby coast
Harvaqturmiut	by 1890	None	200	Lower Kazan River
Estimated total population, 1890			1,375	

*The Qairnirmiut population was already being affected by European diseases in 1890.

All five societies had developed out of the Founder Society, but they had become separate social systems—the hunter-gatherer equivalent of different countries—by 1880. Each society was a relatively (although not absolutely) discrete network of families connected to one another by marriage, descent, and partnership ties. In addition to holding dominion over a separate territory (see Map 5.1), the members of each spoke a distinctive variant of the Caribou Inuit dialect, wore clothes that were distinctive in one or more respects, and held to a general ideology of uniqueness and a sense of superiority over other peoples.

Families

The organizational core of a Caribou Inuit society was the extended family. This type of organization took a variety of forms. Some examples are: a group of adult male and/or female siblings, their spouses, and children; two adult brothers, their widowed mother, spouses, and children; or an aged couple, an adult offspring (of either sex), an adult nephew or niece, and their spouses and children. There were many other variations along these same general lines.

Children were betrothed early in life, often while still infants. The arrangements were made by the parents of the prospective spouses, and the principals had no say in the matter. According to Caribou Inuit belief, the best marriages were those of first cousins, and the very best arrangement of all was a brother–sister exchange (*akigiik*) between two sets of cousins; thus, a brother and sister of one family would marry a sister and brother of another, the two sibling pairs being cousins to begin with. When a cousin marriage occurred, people who started life as siblings, cousins, nieces, and nephews suddenly became spouses and in-laws of various kinds as well, thus building one layer of kin relationships upon another. The condition in which a small number of individuals became related to one another in several different ways simultaneously was known as *tamalrutit*, and was regarded as a highly desirable state of affairs.

If Caribou Inuit ideology was carried to its logical conclusion, all the members of an entire society would have lived together in one place, intermarrying, having children, and generally operating as one huge family. However, tight limitations on the food supply and inevitable personality conflicts prevented them from even remotely achieving this ideal. Actual families ranged in size from simple conjugal units comprised of just a

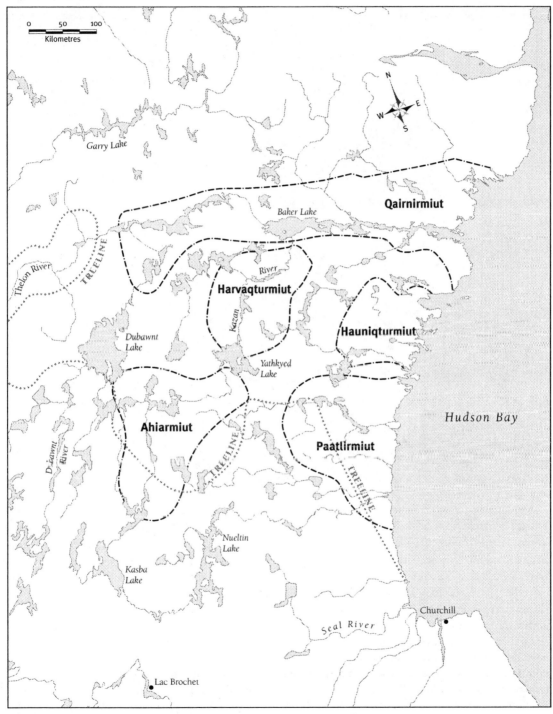

MAP 5.1. Caribou Inuit Societal Territories

FIGURE 5.1. A Paatlirmiut woman carrying her baby on her back, inside her parka, not as commonly supposed, in her hood. (By permission of the National Museum of Denmark, Department of Ethnography)

tent. The average family seems to have involved nearly 20 people living in three tents in summer and fall, or in two snow houses in winter and spring.

Most settlements were occupied by the members of only one extended family. In times of hunger even these might split up, the constituent households spreading out over the country in the hope of finding game. In late spring or summer, though, when food supplies were greater, two or more related families often joined forces. Aggregations of more than 75 people sometimes occurred, but they were unusual and temporary, generally associated with the arrival of an HBC trading vessel, a whaling ship, or an unusually large caribou kill.

A Caribou Inuit society was entirely lacking in political, economic, or other specialized institutions, such as governments, businesses, churches, or schools. Almost all functions required to sustain life were performed within the extended family. To a degree that most Canadians could scarcely comprehend, the life of a Caribou Inuk (singular of 'Inuit') revolved around family—from birth until death.

married couple (or sometimes a man and two wives) and their non-adult children to relatively complex extended families of up to 35 people. Caribou Inuit had no ideological preference for either the male or female line, and so developed neither lineages nor clans.

The members of a small family could live comfortably in a single dwelling. The larger the family, the greater its need to have two or more dwellings, since there are fairly narrow limits on the size of a snow house and more so on that of a

Other Social Bonds

Extended family ties were supplemented in the Caribou Inuit social system by only two other types of social bond. One consisted of a series of special kin relationships created through a co-marriage; the other was a dancing partnership.

A co-marriage was established when two married couples agreed to exchange sexual partners for a night or two. This was not the casual, lustful affair implied by the common phrase 'wife trading', because it really was a form of marriage. The arrangement created a number of relationships in addition to the original husband-wife ties. *All* of these relationships were imbued with rights and obligations of mutual support and assistance, and these rights and obligations were binding for the rest of one's life.

A dancing partnership was established in a more elaborate way. After agreeing to become partners, two people, usually men, struck each other on the face and shoulders as hard as they could, often raising large welts. Eventually one gave up, at which point they exchanged gifts. The third and final stage was to dance together, beating drums, while the onlookers sang. By the time exhaustion finally overcame them, they had become *mumiqatigiik*, dancing partners.

Dancing partners were members of different families who normally lived in different settlements but visited each other from time to time. When they met after a prolonged absence, they repeated the initiation ceremony with only slight modification. At first sight they hit each other and tried to knock each other down. Later they danced and exchanged gifts. In addition to the ceremonial features, a dancing partnership was imbued with a great deal of joking and horseplay, each member trying to outdo the other in, say, an exchange of jibes or in a shoving match. *Mumiqatigiik* were very fond of each other and eagerly looked forward to their meetings.

The Political Process

Politically, each family was a hierarchical system based primarily on generation and relative age, and, to some extent, on gender differences. In general, people of a senior generation had authority over those in junior generations, older individuals had authority over younger ones, and, within a given generation or age category, males had authority over females. At the pinnacle of each of these tiny hierarchies was an *ihumataq*, or 'chieftain'.

An *ihumataq* was a mature adult, usually a middle-aged or older man who had lived long enough to have experienced life, acquired wisdom, and demonstrated in practice that he was qualified for the responsibilities of leadership. An *ihumataq* was also a very close relative of most of the people over whom he wielded authority. He was related to them as husband, father, older brother, older cousin, uncle, grandfather, and/or senior in-law. In short, the *ihumataq* typically was a person who wielded authority automatically by virtue of the fact that he filled a superior position in a whole series of hierarchical kin relationships. But the role always carried greater authority than would be conveyed by age, generation, and gender considerations alone, and it could be filled by any man whose extraordinary ability overrode those considerations. In a family large enough for there to be more than one candidate for the position, the actual *ihumataq* was likely to be a physically powerful individual, an excellent hunter, an understanding counsellor, an expert at human relations, and often a shaman as well. He would have more wives, more living children, better clothing, and generally more and better of everything than anyone else in the group.

An *ihumataq* led by a combination of demonstrated wisdom and ability. Where he was lacking those qualities, he might try to wield authority by brute strength, but a family headed by such a person would not stay intact for long. Individuals or conjugal family subunits could leave at any time. But where could they go? They either had to set out on their own or join another group of relatives belonging to the same type of organization as the one they left, but with different personnel. These alternatives combined to act as a check on the abuse of power by an *ihumataq*, while at the same time helping concentrate people around the most effective leaders.

An *ihumataq* had no institutionalized authority over anyone outside his own family. At the interfamily level, therefore, power and responsibility were allocated in a very haphazard manner. Families whose members could not get along very well together either had to fight or stay apart. Most of the time, they chose the latter course.

Subsistence

Caribou are remarkably useful. Their skins provide raw material for excellent cold-weather clothing, footgear, rope, tents, boat covers, sleeping bags, mattresses, insulating materials, house covers, knapsacks, blankets, and storage bags. Thread can be made from their sinew, and components of tools, weapons, and utensils can be manufactured from their antlers and bones. People who consume all of the meat, viscera, stomach contents (rich in vitamin C), and fat of caribou are able to satisfy all of their nutritional requirements from that species alone. If caribou are available in sufficient numbers at appropriate times of year, and if they are fully utilized, they can provide for the *total* subsistence requirements of a human population.

Given the real benefits that an adequate harvest of caribou can bestow, it is not surprising that hunting peoples living on or near the boreal forest-tundra border all the way around the world had economies based heavily on this species (which includes Eurasian reindeer). But barren ground caribou are highly migratory animals, travelling hundreds or even thousands of kilometres each year. The only predictable feature of these movements for herds whose ranges straddle the treeline is that the majority of animals in a herd move onto the tundra for the calving season in early summer and return to the boreal forest for the winter. Hunters have three alternatives: (1) try to follow the animals over immense distances; (2) harvest caribou in great quantities when they are present and store enough meat and skins to last the rest of the year; or (3) harvest other species when caribou are not available. Within the region and time period of interest here, the Chipewyan emphasized the first strategy, while the Caribou Inuit employed a combination of the other two.

The main caribou hunt was from mid-August to late September, when the hides are in prime condition and the animals are normally fat. Hunters waited at places where caribou were likely to cross rivers or lakes, then speared the swimming animals from *kayaks*. While women processed the meat and hides, men continued to hunt, killing as many animals as they could. Meat, bones, and viscera not required for immediate use were wrapped in skins and cached under rocks. If the meat putrefied a bit before frost halted the process that only enhanced its taste—from the Inuit perspective. The success or failure of this late-summer hunt generally determined how comfortable life would be during the following winter.

Caribou hunting for most of the rest of the year was erratic. Whenever caribou were present they were pursued—with bow and arrow or with pitfalls dug in deep banks of snow. Occasionally they were hunted with muzzle-loading guns. But the Inuit were frequently out of ammunition, and their weapons apparently were not well maintained, so firearms provided little benefit. Sometimes thousands of caribou remained on the tundra all winter, but sometimes there were none at all. When there were not enough caribou, the people turned to muskoxen.

Muskoxen generally live in small groups of perhaps 12 to 24 animals. These groups, which travel only short distances, were widely distributed across southern Kivalliq at the beginning of the nineteenth century. They apparently were not heavily hunted by the Chipewyan. But when the Inuit moved inland in mid-century, they killed muskoxen whenever they ran out of caribou. This happened in mid- to late winter almost every year. During the Classic Period they are known (from HBC records) to have killed at least 3,000 muskoxen, and the real number must have been much higher. In the process, they all but exterminated their most important source of emergency food.

Fish also played a part in their diet, particularly in spring, when char run out to sea, and again in August and September, when they return to the rivers and lakes. Char were caught with stone weirs, leisters, and hook and line. But fish were needed most in late winter, when the supply of caribou meat was often exhausted. Although the lakes of southern Kivalliq contained large populations of whitefish and other species, none of the Caribou Inuit techniques was very effective for winter fishing. Schools of fish are difficult to locate in large, deep, ice-covered lakes. Gill nets, set under the ice, are relatively productive on lakes, and particularly so on rivers. Yet almost every March found people chopping holes through the thick ice and jigging with hook and line. Sometimes they found fish, but often they did not.

The Caribou Inuit had been exposed (by the HBC) to the use of gill nets since at least 1720. They had been shown how to use them, and nets were available to them in trade. But it was not until the 1930s that they were widely adopted. Why? Birket-Smith provided the answer, which has three parts. First, they had a powerful taboo against eating fish taken dead from the water—and fish often drown in gill nets unless removed quickly. Prompt removal is very difficult in cold winter weather. Second, it was just about impossible to dry and mend nets in a snow house, where the temperature was below or near freezing most of the time. Finally, nets are heavy, bulky items to carry around, and Caribou Inuit moved quite often over the course of their yearly cycle. For all of these reasons, but particularly the first, extensive use of nets was out of the question.

The Ahiarmiut and Harvaqturmiut, who remained inland year-round, lived almost exclusively on caribou, muskoxen, and fish, supplemented by ptarmigan in early spring, other birds in summer, fur-bearing animals such as foxes and wolves, and such other small game as they might encounter—right down to and including mice in extreme situations. Most members of the other three societies moved to the coast each spring. There they fished for char and hunted seals and beluga—unless caribou or other game was available.

It is worth repeating that, throughout the Classic Period, Qairnirmiut, Hauniqturmiut, and Paatlirmiut men remained active and competent sea-mammal hunters. But most of their harvest was sold to the HBC in Churchill or to whalers farther north. They regarded sea-mammal meat as suitable for dogs, but as little more than emergency food for humans. Even the blubber was hardly used. This is surprising because the meat of northern mammals is much leaner than beef, and people must have some fat in their diet. Blubber is also an efficient fuel for lamps and an excellent medium in which to store dried meat and fish for prolonged periods. However, for fatty food the Caribou Inuit relied on fish and caribou—or went without; for fuel they depended on dwarf willows and moss—or went without; and for a food preservative they relied primarily on cold temperatures. And whenever caribou, fish, or, say, geese appeared on the scene, sea mammals were all but forgotten. This utter disdain for sea-mammal blubber and oil, not the obsession with caribou as such, made the Caribou Inuit unique in the Eskaleut world.

Yearly Cycle

Caribou Inuit societies followed one of two forms of yearly cycle. One, followed by most Ahiarmiut and Harvaqturmiut, involved year-round residence in the interior of the country. The other, followed by most Qairnirmiut, Hauniqturmiut, and Paatlirmiut, involved residence in the interior from late summer to early spring, and settlement on the coast in spring and early summer. This second pattern obviously required extensive travel between the two areas. Beyond that, the similarities among the five societies were much more numerous than the differences; the similarities receive treatment here.

In summer the Caribou Inuit lived in conical tents consisting of a frame of poles over which a cover made from several caribou skins was stretched. Cooking was done outside on a fire made of dwarf trees and shrubs. The smoke also helped to drive away some of the billions of

FIGURE 5.2. Moving camp near Yathkyed Lake, early July 1922. The women and children move out first to be followed by the men and dogs. (By permission of the National Museum of Denmark, Department of Ethnography)

mosquitoes that infest the country each summer. Light was provided by the sun. Although southern Kivalliq is well south of the Arctic Circle, it is still far enough north to have relatively little darkness during the late spring and early summer months.

Children amused themselves or helped their parents, women tended to their babysitting, sewing, or butchering chores, and men roamed the country searching for game. Individuals ate whenever they were hungry (if food was available), although a cooked meal was usually prepared for the entire family each evening. When food was abundant and there were no pressing matters to attend to, the members of the tiny community often came together in the largest tent, or perhaps in two tents linked together, and danced, sang, told stories, and generally enjoyed themselves.

People usually stayed in one place as long as the hunting or fishing was good, although

hunters often covered a tremendous area in their excursions around the camp. If a large kill was made at some distance from the tents, or if the hunting appeared to be better somewhere else, camp was moved.

Movement in summer was primarily on foot. People and dogs had to carry literally everything; what they could not carry, they cached under rocks. Each man carried his *kayak* upside down on his shoulders, his head inserted into the cockpit, while the women, children, and dogs carried almost everything else. When people reached a river or small lake, they ferried themselves and their equipment across by making repeated trips in the *kayak*. If two or more *kayaks* were available, they were rafted together. By alternately walking and camping, moving slowly but steadily across the country, an entire family, including infants and old people, could cover hundreds of kilometres in just a few weeks. Caribou Inuit were marvellous walkers.

People lived in their unheated tents until, in the fall, snowdrifts of the right depth and quality formed on the downwind side of the countless eskers and ridges. Usually the right snow conditions did not develop until November or even December. The snow houses that they could then build were of the general central Canadian Inuit type—dome-shaped structures perhaps four to five metres across at the base, made by stacking progressively smaller rows of snow blocks on top of one another in a circle until they converged at the top. To the basic house was added a long entrance tunnel, off which was built an alcove for cooking and perhaps one or two others for storage. Often the two or more houses occupied by a single extended family were linked by tunnels made of snow blocks.

Unlike all other snow-house dwellers, and, indeed, unlike most other Eskaleuts, Caribou Inuit did not normally heat or light their winter houses. A few people used seal-oil lamps, but they usually ran out of fuel by early winter. Light generally was provided by sunlight, which came directly through the translucent snow walls and through a window of clear ice placed in the roof on the south side of the building. But during the short days of early winter the Caribou Inuit spent most of their inside hours in total darkness. They did without heat altogether, except for that provided by the bodies of the house's occupants. Any cooking was done over a fire of dwarf willows built in the alcove. At most there was one cooked meal (of boiled meat or fish) a day, but during the winter months most food was consumed raw and frozen. During daylight hours people occupied themselves much as they did in the summer, but during the long hours of darkness they lay in their warm sleeping bags and chatted, told stories, sang songs, or just slept. Boredom must have been a major problem, which may account at least in part for their willingness to make long winter excursions to trade at Churchill, on the coast, or at Brochet, in the interior.

When people travelled they hauled their baggage on long (c. 750 cm), low (10 cm), narrow (42 cm) sleds, which looked more like ladders than sleds capable of hauling 500 kilograms. In the morning, people loaded the sleds and, pushing and pulling along with the dogs, moved out slowly. When travelling downwind they erected sails and let the wind do the work. When darkness began to fall, they built new snow houses and created a new settlement within an hour or two.

Religion

The Caribou Inuit believed that a spirit called Hila constituted the supreme force underlying all phenomena. This general force also had a special female form, Pinga, which dwelt somewhere in space. It was Pinga who made it possible for people to live in the world, who kept a close watch on human activities, and who intervened from time to time in people's affairs. Hila determined which acts were good and which were bad, but Pinga was the spirit who monitored people's behaviour. The soul of a person who had lived according to the rules laid down by Hila was believed to ascend at death to Pinga. That spirit received it in space and subsequently returned it to earth in the body of an animal, human, or otherwise. The souls of persons who had not lived properly, on the other hand, were condemned to eternal misery, somewhere outside the earthly domain.

Caribou Inuit did not pretend to know much about the spirit world. What knowledge they did have was acquired by their shamans, or *angakut* (plural). The primary duty of a shaman was to act as intermediary between the human and spiritual worlds. By communicating with Hila, a shaman could determine the cause of a problem and ascertain its solution. The latter invariably involved adherence to one or more taboos stipulated by the spirit. In addition, a shaman could perform magic of various kinds and make certain kinds of predictions about the future.

Caribou Inuit religion, while ostensibly quite otherworldly, had a considerable immediacy about it. One did not spend time worshipping an intangible and dimly perceived God or contemplating a satisfactory reincarnation in the next life. Rather, one tried to sustain oneself in this difficult life by conforming to an extensive set of rules governing quite specific acts. Indeed, practically every act was governed by some taboo: the technique, timing, and location of the hunt; the technique and timing of butchering; birth and death; menstruation; eating—these and more were governed by taboos so numerous that no one could remember them all.

Taboos were laid down by Hila, and obedience to them helped maintain a balance of amicable relations with that power. If people disobeyed them, on the other hand, Hila subjected them to hunger, sickness, bad weather, or other calamity. Observance of the rules was basically an individual matter, but a transgression by one person often resulted in punishment being visited upon an entire settlement. It was therefore in everyone's best interest not only to watch one's own behaviour but also to monitor that of one's neighbours.

Misfortune was usually interpreted as a sign that a taboo had been broken. In order to determine what was involved, a shaman went into a trance to contact Hila, who specified who had committed what particular offence and stipulated the procedures necessary to rectify the situation (and perhaps also to prevent its recurrence). It was through this oft-repeated sequence that the extensive body of taboos governing Caribou Inuit life gradually developed, probably over hundreds of years. Since Hila apparently would not entertain general questions, the shamans were denied the kind of comprehensive revelation that has led to the development of more complex religions in other parts of the world.

Concluding Remarks

This brief summary of the structure of Caribou Inuit societies during the Classic Period depicts a system that, even after nearly two centuries of contact with Westerners, was thoroughly non-European, not only in its basic structure but in almost every detail. The Caribou Inuit were still very much in control of their own affairs. Despite the fact that their land was one of the least

hospitable areas in the world, they remained in their own country, dealt with life's problems in their own ways, and generally remained aloof from the wider world of whose existence they had long been at least vaguely aware.

Denouement

From the time of first known contact in 1631, when Luke Foxe sailed down the west coast of Hudson Bay, until 1903, when the government of Canada decided to assert its control over the region, Europeans had little interest in Caribou Inuit territory or in the people who occupied it. A few outsiders had visited the region to explore, while others had come to hunt whales or trade for furs, but all remained for just a little while, then left.

This geographic isolation began to be broken when the North-West (later, Royal Canadian) Mounted Police established a post at Cape Fullerton, on the northeastern fringe of Caribou Inuit territory, in the summer of 1903. The police established the post partly to keep an eye on American whalers, and partly to establish an official Canadian presence in a land whose ownership was not yet established in international law.

In the summer of 1912, both the Roman Catholic Church and the HBC established permanent posts on the south side of Chesterfield Inlet, right in Caribou Inuit country. Over the next two decades tiny Euro-Canadian settlements sprang up at a few widely scattered points across the region. The largest contained an RCMP post, an HBC trading post, sometimes a competing trader or two, and two missions, one Anglican, the other Roman Catholic. The missionaries often ran schools, in addition to trying to convert the Inuit to Christianity. Traders, police, and missionaries all tried to influence the Inuit in one way or another, and they competed in attempting to achieve a dominant position. During the early years, however, the Inuit remained almost as aloof as ever.

The event that did more than anything else to terminate Caribou Inuit societies was the 'Great

BOX 5.2

On Doing Anthropology

It is one of the great ironies of Arctic ethnography that Kaj Birket-Smith and Knud Rasmussen made their observations near the end of the Great Famine of 1915–25, probably the lowest point for the Caribou Inuit in 200 years. Their 'definitive ethnography', which has been widely cited in the anthropological literature, was actually a description of a people on the verge of extinction.

Famine' that began in 1915. For reasons that remain unclear, caribou fled the country. Unfortunately for the Inuit, the muskoxen, which had played a crucial role in their original inland expansion, had been all but exterminated.

People turned to fish, but they had only hook and line with which to catch them. Weakened by hunger, they chopped holes through the thick ice in the lakes and jigged their lures, but with little success. Eventually they slaughtered their dogs and ate them, and even ate pieces of boiled skin clothing. The famine continued for years. It was not until the fall of 1924 that caribou returned in some numbers to the Qairnirmiut sector, and not until the following summer that they reached Ahiarmiut country again. The precise figures remain debatable, but in 1915 there were probably some 1,500 Caribou Inuit. In 1925 only about 500 remained.

In desperation, the Inuit turned to outsiders for help. Police, missionaries, and traders tried to assist them, but there was little they could do. The Inuit starved and died in their isolated camps as they had lived, on their own.

Eventually, the Great Famine led the Caribou Inuit to become trappers. Previously, they believed that, despite periodic fluctuations, caribou would never forsake them for long. And if they ran out of caribou meat for awhile, they could always turn to muskoxen, which did not travel far, were easily killed, and whose general whereabouts were well-known. By 1915, however, the muskoxen were gone, and by 1920

people realized that total reliance on caribou was fatal. But, as luck would have it, the price of a white fox pelt, which was the only fur the Barren Lands had in abundance, increased significantly after World War I. Thus, for the first time in their history, the Caribou Inuit could turn to fur-trapping as a realistic way to make a living.

Somehow a few people managed to survive, but the societies to which they belonged did not. Their populations were so reduced in size that they could not maintain their independence. By 1922, what in 1915 had been five and possibly six societies had merged into a single unit consisting of five regional bands. Each of the latter was the remnant of a former society. The Tahiuyarmiut, who were in the process of splitting off from the Paatlirmiut and becoming a sixth society when the famine began, were reduced to only a few individuals.

During the period from 1915 to 1945, several additional developments contributed to the erosion of Caribou Inuit autonomy. One, noted previously, was the gradual expansion of police, missionary, and trading operations all across what was then the southern part of the Keewatin District of the Northwest Territories. Another was the migration of members of other Inuit groups to the northern fringe of the region. Some of them came from the northern Hudson Bay and Foxe Basin coasts. These were members of the Aivilik branch of the Iglulingmiut and descendants of Netsilingmiut, who previously had migrated eastward to the Hudson Bay coast, attracted there by the prospect of trade with American whalers. Both groups were drawn by the trading post at Cape Fullerton, and later by the one at Chesterfield Inlet. Somewhat later still, other Netsilingmiut from the Back River area also moved south, attracted by the timber along the Thelon River and by the opportunities for trade at Baker Lake.

While these incursions were taking place in the northeastern and northwestern sectors of the region, the people continued to suffer periodic famine farther south. None of these misfortunes was as geographically extensive or as prolonged as the disaster of 1915–25, but each regional band was struck by more than one period of extreme hunger during which many people died. The Qairnirmiut, and particularly the Hauniq-turmiut, began to fragment under the pressure, and the surviving families began to disperse in an effort to find game. Epidemics took an even greater toll.

The nadir was reached in 1948, when a combination of tuberculosis, influenza, and infantile paralysis reached such an extreme state that the entire district was placed under quarantine for almost two years by the Canadian government. Seriously ill people cannot hunt, so epidemics were invariably accompanied by famine.

Concern on the part of missionaries, police, and government officials, and a storm of public outrage stimulated by the writings of Farley Mowat and Richard Harrington, led the government to take a more active interest in the early 1950s. Administrative centres were set up in the old communities of Baker Lake, Chesterfield Inlet, and Eskimo Point, and new settlements were established at Whale Cove and Rankin Inlet, the latter in conjunction with a mining operation.

In the late 1950s, the government confronted a dilemma. On the one hand, the combination of genuine concern and political pressure dictated that something be done to help the starving Inuit. On the other hand, Canadian taxpayers did not want to foot much of a bill for whatever action was taken. Regular monitoring of conditions in and

the provision of adequate medical and other assistance to the tiny, widely scattered camps would have been prohibitively expensive. Consequently, officials decided to concentrate both the Caribou Inuit and the Netsilik and Aivilik immigrants in the five administrative centres.

By 1968 the centralization process was complete. Of the five settlements, only Arviat (formerly Eskimo Point) was inhabited primarily by people of Caribou Inuit extraction. Baker Lake and Whale Cove each contained, in addition to Caribou Inuit, significant numbers of Netsilik, Aivilik, and other Inuit immigrants. Rankin Inlet was largely Aivilik, and Chesterfield Inlet was primarily Netsilik.

Vastly improved medical care and other government services helped the Inuit population of the region rise dramatically during the final decades of the twentieth century. In 1996, nearly 4,900 Inuit lived in the five administrative centres, along with some 760 non-Inuit. Thirty years of living together in the same settlements and of intermarriage had blurred the ancient boundaries between Inuit groups. Elders had not forgotten their roots, but people came to be identified more by the settlement in which they lived than by the society or regional band to which their ancestors once belonged. As this transition occurred, 'Caribou Inuit', which was not an Inuit concept but a useful anthropological referent until the late 1960s, rapidly lost its currency. The label remains useful with reference to the past, but not to the present.

Recent Period

On 1 April 1999, the area of interest here became the southern portion of the Kivalliq Region, Nunavut Territory, instead of the southern portion of the District of Keewatin, NWT. The population is now distributed among the five previously existing administrative centres, which are now designated as 'hamlets' (see Map 5.2). Locally elected councils, chaired by mayors, give the residents of each community a relatively high

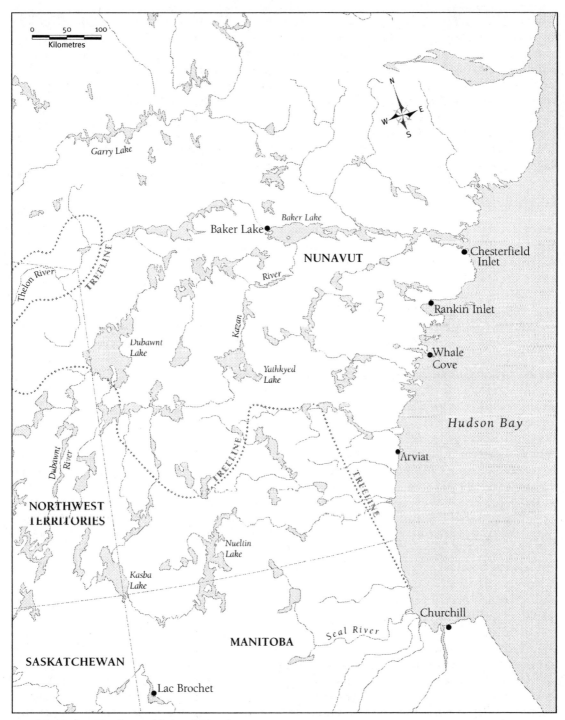

MAP 5.2. Modern Hamlets and Political Boundaries

level of self-government. Offences against local regulations are dealt with by Inuit bylaw officers and justices, although the RCMP remains responsible for dealing with more serious issues. Formal education and health care are provided by the territorial government. Roman Catholic and Anglican missions have been supplemented by those of a number of other religious groups. Inuktitut is still the first language, but is being replaced rapidly by English.

The biggest problem facing the people of southern Kivalliq today is how to make a living without leaving their traditional homeland. Inuit can still meet many of their food needs by hunting and fishing, and they travel long distances across their territory, especially by snowmobile, to find game. However, they need a cash income to acquire equipment and fuel, not to mention clothing, and houses to keep themselves in a semi-urban setting.

Fur-hunting can provide some cash, but not enough to live on. The country is rich in minerals, but at current price levels no one can afford to extract them and take them to market. Located far from population centres, industries of even modest size are unlikely to locate here at any time in the foreseeable future. The rivers and lakes can provide excitement for a few adventuresome canoeists and fishermen as well as income for outfitters who look after them, but the landscape is too bleak and homogeneous to attract large numbers of tourists. The production of carvings and other forms of art is one possibility—and, indeed, some of the finest artists in Canada live in the region—but this can never support more than a small percentage of the population. Considerable effort is devoted to preparing Inuit to fill locally available jobs, but there are not enough positions to go around.

The Inuit residents of southern Kivalliq enter the twenty-first century in complex and generally difficult circumstances. On the one hand, they have regained a measure of local and regional control over their affairs, which they had nearly lost after they were concentrated in hamlets. Most live on or near lands inhabited by their ancestors, and the extended family remains a central focus of people's social networks. On the other hand, they have been forced by hard times and a rapidly changing cultural environment to abandon their traditional way of life. Because of their geographic isolation, they cannot participate as constructively as they might like in the modern Canadian way of life. As a result, apathy is widespread, and rates of sexual abuse, substance abuse, domestic violence, parental neglect, and suicide are at comparatively high levels.

The obvious alternative—leaving the North for cities in the south—does not offer much promise. Only slightly prepared by training and experience for urban life, confronted by widespread discrimination, and isolated from family and friends, the urban Inuk often has an even harder time than his rural counterpart. Most people living in northern settlements have heard about these difficulties and are reluctant to try city life themselves.

Conclusion

Having information on even the general outlines of the lifeways of a particular population of hunter-gatherers over nearly 300 years is very rare in anthropology. That it is possible in the Caribou Inuit case is due to fortuitous circumstances. Among them are the following: (1) the frequent but peculiarly casual contacts between Inuit and HBC traders during the eighteenth and nineteenth centuries; (2) splendid HBC record-keeping during that era; (3) the fact that the Caribou Inuit homeland did not offer enough attractions to Westerners to draw them there on a permanent basis until well into the twentieth century; and (4) the fact that the Inuit were content enough with life in their homeland to resist the temptation to move elsewhere.

One general lesson we can take away from the history of southern Kivalliq is that change is continuous in all human societies. This is true even of those that, like the Caribou Inuit, are organized along very simple lines. Therefore, it is incumbent on the author of every ethnographic account to state the specific period to which that account pertains. It is incorrect to treat the past as an undifferentiated whole, no matter what society is involved. Separate descriptions of Caribou Inuit societies in 1750, 1825, 1890, and 1925 would produce significantly different pictures. This is so even though the people were members of relatively simple hunter-gatherer societies throughout, and even though the people living in later periods were direct cultural and biological descendants of those in the earlier ones.

Notes

1. In the 1970s, the Native term 'Inuit' began to be used instead of the foreign term 'Eskimo' for the Inuit-speaking residents of the central and eastern Canadian Arctic, with the result that 'Caribou Inuit' replaced 'Caribou Eskimo'.
2. From 1968 to 1974 the research on which this chapter is based was supported by the Canada Council (now the Social Sciences and Humanities Research Council of Canada). Since 1974, I have continued it on my own as time and resources permitted.
3. At the beginning of the twenty-first century, the climate is probably warmer than these late twentieth-century temperature figures indicate. In the eighteenth and nineteenth centuries, the climate was noticeably colder.
4. The sources on which this historical summary is based include a number of published documents, and the following unpublished records: (a) HBC Archives: Churchill post journals, sloop and ship logs, correspondence, accounts of trade, and miscellaneous other records, from 1717 to the early twentieth century; (b) National Archives of Canada: Record Group 18, Records of the RCMP; Record Group 85, and Records of the Northern Administration Branch; (c) original field journals and other records compiled by J. Burr Tyrrell in 1893 and 1894, housed at the National Archives of Canada, Record Group 45, Reports of the Geological Survey of Canada, and in Manuscript Collection No. 26, in the Thomas Fisher Rare Book Library, John P. Robarts Research Library Complex, University of Toronto.

5. This reconstruction of the 'classic period' is based primarily on information acquired from Inuit Elders interviewed by T.C. Correll or me from 1968 to 1970, on HBC records of the period, and on Birket-Smith (1929, I), Boas (1901, 1907), Rasmussen (1930), Turquetil (1907, 1926), J.B. Tyrrell (1897), and J.W. Tyrrell (1898).

References and Recommended Readings

Birket-Smith, Kaj. 1929. *The Caribou Eskimos: Material and Social Life and Their Cultural Position*. Copenhagen: Report of the Fifth Thule Expedition 1921–4, vol. 5, pts I and II. Part I of this substantial work, together with Rasmussen's 1930 volume, constitutes the basic ethnography of the Caribou Inuit. It focuses primarily on economic and technological matters. Part II, a reconstruction of Inuit history and prehistory, is an extraordinary example of reasoning that was outmoded even at the time it was published, using atemporal distributional data to draw temporal conclusions.

Boas, Franz. 1901. *The Eskimo of Baffin Land and Hudson Bay*. Bulletin of the American Museum of Natural History, vol. 15, Part I.

———. 1907. *Second report on the Eskimo of Baffin Land and Hudson Bay*. Bulletin of the American Museum of Natural History, vol. 15, Part II.

Burch, Ernest S., Jr. 1976. 'Caribou Eskimo Origins: An Old Problem Reconsidered', *Arctic Anthropology* 15, 1: 1–35. A comprehensive review of the literature dealing with Caribou Inuit origins. The historical sequence outlined in the present chapter begins where this article ends.

———. 1977. 'Muskox and Man in the Central Canadian Subarctic, 1689–1974', *Arctic* 30, 3: 135–54. This article describes how and why the Caribou Inuit nearly exterminated muskoxen from their country. It was published at a time when most scholars believed that only Westerners were capable of destroying one of their major resources.

Csonka, Yvon. 1995. *Les Ahiarmiut. A l'écart des Inuit Caribous*. Neuchâtel, Switzerland: Editions Victor Attinger. This elegantly written study of the Ahiarmiut concerns a Caribou Inuit group that the Fifth Thule Expedition entirely missed. It contains a thorough literature review, information on social change and Chipewyan–Inuit relations, and many useful maps and photographs.

Fossett, Renée. 2001. *In Order to Live Untroubled: Inuit of the Central Arctic, 1550 to 1940*. Winnipeg: University of Manitoba Press. A general historical summary of most of the Inuit populations of the central and eastern Canadian Arctic. The sections dealing with the Caribou Inuit region are particularly well-informed.

Rasmussen, Knud. 1930. *Observations on the Intellectual Culture of the Caribou Eskimos*. Copenhagen: Report of the Fifth Thule Expedition 1921–4, vol. 7, no. 2. This monograph is a companion to Birket-Smith's. The two stand together as the major ethnographic account of Caribou Inuit culture. Rasmussen, like Birket-Smith, was a poor historian, but he had as much insight into Inuit thought processes as anyone who ever wrote on the subject.

Smith, James G.E., and Ernest S. Burch Jr. 1979. 'Chipewyan and Inuit in the Central Canadian Subarctic, 1613–1977', *Arctic Anthropology* 16, 2: 76–101. The Chipewyan and Caribou Inuit were invariably described in the pre-1979 literature as having been in a state of perpetual armed conflict. This article shows that Chipewyan–Caribou Inuit relations were more complex than previously thought, and were often peaceful.

Turquetil, Arsène. 1907. 'Première tentative d'apostolat chez les Esquimaux', *Missions de la Congregation des Missionnaires Oblats de Marie Immaculée* 45: 330, 353, 484–503.

———. 1926. 'Notes sur les Esquimaux de Baie Hudson', *Anthropos Ephemeris Internationalis. Ethnologica et Linguistica* 21: 419–34.

Tyrrell, J. Burr. 1897. *Report on the Doobaunt, Kazan and Ferguson Rivers, and the north-west coast of Hudson Bay, and on two overland routes from Hudson Bay to Lake Winnipeg*. Ottawa: Geological Survey of Canada. (Ninth Annual Report, part F.)

Tyrrell, James Williams. 1898. *Across the sub-Arctics of Canada, a journey of 3,200 miles by canoe and snowshoe through the barren lands*. London: T. F. Unwin.

Vallee, Frank G. 1967. *Kabloona and Eskimo in the Central Keewatin*. Ottawa: Canadian Research Centre for Anthropology, St Paul University. The most comprehensive account of the Caribou Inuit in the late 1950s, it is arguably one of the best monographs on any Inuit group from that era. Its focus is on the northern part of Caribou Inuit territory.

VanStone, James W., and Wendell H. Oswalt. 1959. *The Caribou Eskimos of Eskimo Point*. Ottawa: Department of Northern Affairs and National Resources, Northern Co-ordination and Research Centre (NRCRC–59–2). This short monograph describes Caribou Inuit life in or near Eskimo Point (now Arviat) in the middle and late 1950s. It is a useful summary of the southern sector of the Caribou Inuit region at the time.

Suggested Web Sites

Bibliography: www.nunanet.com/~jhicks/nunabib.html/
    Not updated very often, but still a useful source.
Government of Nunavut: www.gov.nu.ca
    The official government site, with many links.
Nunatsiaq News: www.nunatsiaq.com
    The weekly newspaper of Iqaluit.
Qikiqtani Inuit Association: www.qikitani.nu.ca
    QTA is a non-governmental organization that promotes Inuit language and tradition, environmental protection, and Native self-sufficiency.

PART III

The Eastern Subarctic

CHAPTER 6

The Northern Algonquins: A Regional Overview

JENNIFER S.H. BROWN and C. RODERICK WILSON

The Eastern Subarctic is sometimes referred to as the Northern Algonquian culture area because the entire region is occupied by a branch of the widespread Algonquian-speaking peoples. The surviving languages form two series of closely related dialects that can be grouped into two languages, Cree and Ojibway, which are, confusingly, simultaneously also spoken of in English as being two 'tribes' (see Chapter 1). Our usual terminology does not reflect this understanding very well: old-fashioned terms, such as 'Naskapi', implied the status of being a separate language, rather than being a dialect of Cree. Its modern replacement, Innu, has the same implication. Another older term, 'Tête-de-Boule Cree', had the advantage of clearly indicating linguistic affinity, as its contemporary replacement, 'Atikamekw', does not. The latter term, however, has the still greater advantage, like Innu, of being what the people call themselves!

In any case, Cree and Ojibway seem to have developed independently from Proto-Algonquian, possibly separating about 3,000 years ago. The relationship between the dialects of these languages is quite complex, in part because in historic times (and earlier?) whole groups of people have shifted from one dialect to another.

The inhabitants of any region must come to terms with their environment. The Eastern Subarctic is characterized by long winters, short summers, and a continental climate. The generally cold climate is also related to the jet streams, which, passing from west to east, tend to draw arctic high-pressure air masses to the southeast. In spring and summer, intensified sunlight decreases the dominance of arctic air, so seasonal contrasts are strong. Minimum/maximum daily mean temperatures in the Severn River drainage in northern Ontario, for example, range from between −29° and −19°C in January to between 11° and 21°C in July. But even hot summer days may soon be followed by frost, and variations from the average can be considerable in either direction.

Precipitation in much of the area is relatively light. Total annual precipitation in northern Ontario averages only about 60 centimetres, most of it coming in summer thunderstorms. However, the climate east of James Bay is much affected by Hudson Bay. Air currents in fall and early winter pick up moisture from Hudson Bay to dump it along the eastern shores and inland. From midwinter to early summer, the Bay remains ice-covered, depressing temperatures and delaying the coming of spring in lands to the east. As a consequence, this area experiences very heavy snowfall and cold temperatures.

The presence of such extreme climatic conditions in these latitudes was difficult for Europeans to accept. When in 1749 the Hudson's Bay Company faced a parliamentary inquiry into its conduct, critics complained that it had not established agriculture and colonies around Hudson

Bay and asserted that company representatives must be lying about the climate; after all, Fort York was on the same latitude as Stockholm, Sweden, and Bergen, Norway; and the Severn River was on a level with Edinburgh, Copenhagen, and Moscow. The critics' ignorance was pardonable, however. Fuller understandings of the effects of large-scale and even global weather patterns on the region have only recently been developed. Current research, in fact, is drawing on Hudson's Bay Company journals from the eighteenth and nineteenth centuries to trace the regional weather patterns.

Northern Algonquians have therefore long been adapting, with a success that startled their early, ill-equipped European visitors, not only to cold, but to unpredictable and extreme climatic conditions. A late spring, for instance, would mean late breakup of lakes and rivers for travel and late arrival of migrating geese and other birds important as food. Less moisture than usual meant, among other things, less snow cover, meaning in turn less shelter and lower survival rates for some basic food sources such as ptarmigan, hare, and other ground-dwelling animals. Drying of streams is a serious impediment when the movements of people to different seasonally used food resources (between winter hunting camps and summer fishing spots, for example) depend on canoe transport. Excess precipitation would bring floods, mud-filled portages, and swollen rapids dangerous to small vessels.

The landforms, rocks, and soils of the Algonquian Subarctic support many forms of life, but they, too, pose challenges and constraints. The Canadian Shield is the single topographic feature that has most influenced the shape of Northern Algonquian life. Even a casual traveller sees how this rough rock base, polished clean in places by glaciers and overlain in other places by glacial clays, sand, and gravel, provides the contours for countless lakes, streams, and swamps—ideal habitat for beaver, muskrat, and other animal species long important for food and furs. The French who reached present-day Ontario in the

seventeenth century found that the Hurons valued the trade furs and leather they received from the Algonkin, Nipissing, Odawa, Ojibway, and others who made their home in the Shield region. And these Algonquian groups in turn valued their trade with the Hurons, prizing in particular Huron cornmeal.

The Shield country in central Ontario and Quebec is transitional between temperate and Subarctic. The observant traveller notices, going north, that the mixed deciduous trees of the south yield increasingly to evergreens—white and red pines mingled with spruce—then to a predominance of black spruce. Continuing northward the landscape changes again. The rocks of the Canadian Shield mostly disappear. The Hudson Bay Lowland—a spruce-dominated forest on poorly drained, clayey soil—covers an area west and south of the James Bay. The growing season is short and intense throughout the Algonquian Subarctic. People intensify their activities, taking advantage of the open waters, the fisheries and waterfowl, and such plants as blueberries, which can only be harvested for a few short weeks.

The landscape presents limits of various kinds to its occupants, and anthropologists and other Western scientists are only now beginning to appreciate the extent to which Aboriginal peoples interacted with the environment. Europeans, for example, have always described the forests they found in America as 'virgin', 'primeval', 'wilderness', and so on. In contrast, the forests were not only occupied, but their productivity was actively managed and maintained. We have long been aware that one could manage game directly by varying the intensity of hunting; it is now clear that Native peoples also managed game levels indirectly by manipulating the environment, primarily through the selective use of fire.

Small, carefully located and timed fires were extensively used to hasten new growth in the spring, which would attract desired animals and birds, foster desired plants such as blueberries and raspberries, create a more varied habitat that would support larger numbers of animals, and

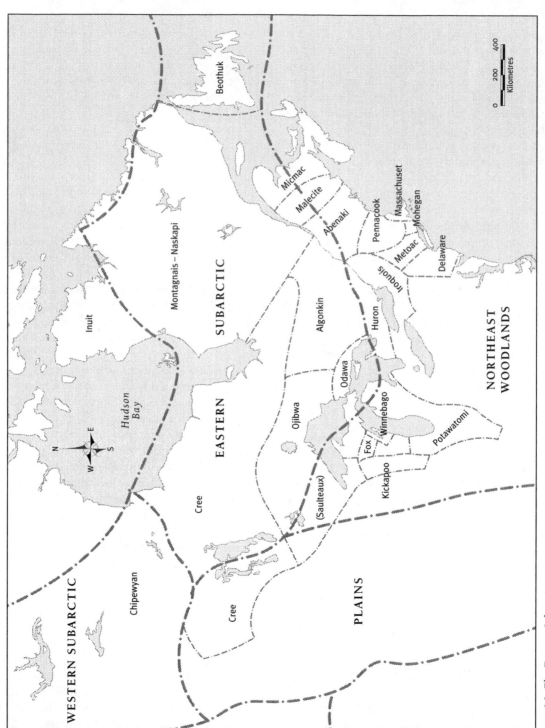

MAP 6.1. The Eastern Subarctic

FIGURE 6.1. Hudson's Bay Company post at Moose Factory on James Bay, 1934. (Courtesy of the Hudson's Bay Company Archives, Archives of Manitoba)

open up areas for travel and hunting. Some species that benefited from controlled burning were moose, deer, beaver, muskrat, bear, and ducks. Other species, notably caribou, require the mosses and lichens of mature, 'climax' forests. Where caribou was the preferred basic resource, as it was in the northerly parts of the region, the use of fire was lessened. The choice was not simply a matter of food preferences but ultimately one of social organization, since the strategies for hunting solitary and herd animals vary substantially. In either case, the forest was not something simply provided by nature.

Changing patterns of human activity have also been major determinants of Northern Algonquian life. Because the following chapters are strongly historical in orientation, the historic context for the region will be limited to two generalizations. First, despite the fact that large numbers of its contemporary inhabitants pursue lifeways that are seen as strongly 'traditional', this region had an extremely long period of contact with Europeans. Almost certainly its southeastern reaches along the St Lawrence River were visited by Bretons before 1500, and by 1670 the Hudson's Bay Company had initiated trade in the more northerly Hudson drainage. First European contact for the Cree in the northwestern corner of the Eastern Subarctic was only a few years prior to the first direct contacts for their closest neighbours in the Western Subarctic, the Chipewyan. As a whole, contact in the east of the region was substantially earlier—in some cases more than 350 years earlier.

Partly because of the length of the cultural contact, people's lives over the years have changed substantially. Again, this is most true of the south and of the coastal regions, but it also places the Eastern Subarctic as a region in contrast to the Western Subarctic. This region saw very early missionizing of its people, early exposure to new diseases, and generally a greater involvement in the fur trade than similar zones further west. As an extreme example, by the end of the era of competitive fur exploitation (1763–1821) between the Hudson's Bay Company and its Montreal rival, the North West Company, in some areas the dominant resource bases, caribou and moose, had been virtually exterminated. A consequence of this longer and more intense period of cultural contact in the Eastern Subarctic than in the West is that we are less sure of what the eastern Aboriginal life patterns and beliefs were. On the other hand, in the East there is substantial historic (European) documentation of events dating from the early seventeenth century, for which there is no parallel in the Western Subarctic.

There follow three final points of general relevance. First, there is always the problem of sources—which voices have spoken to us and why. Native voices are rarely heard from the documentary record, and, when they are, they are often reported at second or third hand.

A second matter is that of homogeneity versus local variability. A superficial observer sees a great sameness: Algonquian hunters inhabiting a vast, cold, mainly spruce-covered region. In fact, local variations—the shape of a lake, the slope of the land, pockets of soil—produce a considerable range of micro-environments. Where local food resources, particularly game, are not evenly distributed, people have reacted in even more complex fashion. Furthermore, their lives have never been solely subsistence-oriented. They evolved distinctive social traditions, world views, and cultural and religious patterns that had their own dynamics of variability and conformity.

Superficial generalization is accordingly to be avoided. The challenge is to get beyond the simple traditional stereotype of hunters in wigwams, or the more modern one of isolated northern villages, to begin to know the Northern Algonquians as complex, diverse human beings whose lives have their own historic richness and vitality. We close with a series of contemporary facts that have implications worth pondering. Cree children who first learn to read in Cree, reading stories produced in their home community, later learn to read English or French better than their older siblings did. Some families strategize by ensuring that some children learn the old bush skills and sending others to university. The Grand Council of the Crees and similar regional Aboriginal governing bodies are rooted in traditional ways of doing things; they also are contemporary political innovations of the first order.

CHAPTER 7

Hunting and the Quest for Power: The James Bay Cree and Whiteman Development

HARVEY A. FEIT

Introduction

Hunting and 'quests for power' mean different things to different people. The 'quest for power' is a metaphor the James Bay Cree might use for the life of a hunter; it is also a metaphor other Canadians might use for the goals of both northern developers and government bureaucracies. 'Whiteman' is a general term James Bay Cree use for non-indigenous people. In this chapter I consider these different ideas of hunting, power, and development, and I show how the way each group uses them is related to their relationships to the environment and to other peoples.

The way I approach these questions is to look at how people typically talk and think about themselves and about others in their world, and at what kind of relationships they create. Relationships are usually unequal because what one group does profoundly limits or aids what others can do. In the second half of this chapter I therefore focus on how the governments of Canada and Quebec have tried to control the James Bay Cree, and how the Cree have sought to exercise their autonomy. This part traces the court challenges, the environmental campaigns, and the negotiations that the Cree have used to maintain control over their lives. In doing this I continue the themes of the first half, showing how environment and politics are inter-

twined in the conflicts over who governs the James Bay region and how it is to be developed.

The James Bay Cree region lies to the east and southeast of James Bay and southeast of Hudson Bay. Cree have lived there since the glaciers left about 9,000 years ago. They now number some 13,000 people and live in nine settlements from which they hunt approximately 375,000 square kilometres of land. (In this chapter the word 'Cree' refers specifically to the James Bay Cree).

I first visited the region in 1968 when I began my doctoral research on hunters of the Cree community of Waswanipi. My interest in hunting arose from a concern for the relationships between Western societies and their environments. I had read often in the human ecology literature that Indians had a different relationship with nature, but I found the accounts in that literature vague and often romantic. I thought an 'on-the-ground' study of Cree/environment relationships could help revise the popular images of Indians as ecological saints or wanton over-exploiters and could develop a practical understanding of the real accomplishments and limitations of one group's approach to the environment. I think I was partially able to accomplish this goal, but with Cree tutelage and encouragement I also learned things I had not foreseen. These are probably best described as lessons in the sacredness of the everyday, the practicality of wisdom, and the importance of reciprocity.

When the Cree began their opposition to the James Bay hydroelectric scheme in 1972, they asked if I would present some of my research to the courts and then use it in the negotiations. It was an unexpected happenstance that my research proved to be of some use to the Cree, and one for which I was thankful. I served as an adviser to Cree organizations during the negotiation and implementation of the James Bay and Northern Quebec Agreement, regularly from 1973 through 1978 and occasionally thereafter.

Contemporary Cree Hunting Culture

Hunting in a Personal and Moral Environment

We can develop an understanding of how the Cree think about hunting and themselves and their world by considering the different meanings conveyed by their word for hunting. Their concept of hunting is very different from the everyday understandings of most North Americans. However odd the Cree conception may appear at first, it not only has logic when understood in the context of Cree life and environment, but also has important affinities with the discoveries of ecological scientists. These analogies may help us to better understand Cree thought, although they will not make the Cree out to be secular scientists or transform scientists into effective hunters.

Animal Gifts

Nitao, the root of the Cree term that is roughly translated as 'hunting, fishing, and trapping in the bush', is found in a series of words related to hunting activities. At least five basic meanings are associated with this root term for hunting: to see or to look at something; to go to get or to fetch something; to need something; to want something; and to grow or continue to grow.

That hunting should be thought of as a process of looking is apparent. Hunting is typically a process of seeing signs of the presence of animals—tracks, spoor, feeding or living areas—

and of then seeking to encounter the animals to kill them. But the proposition that hunting is 'looking' also emphasizes uncertainty. The Cree view is that most animals are shy, retiring, and not easily visible, and hunting therefore involves an expectation as well as an activity.[1] The hunter goes through a process of finding indications of possible encounters with animals; if the hunt is successful they fulfill their anticipation. We will see below how this anticipation plays a role in Cree understandings.

That a successful hunt should also be conceptualized as getting or fetching animals is also apparent, but part of what the Cree mean by this is different from what non-Cree might assume. To get an animal in the Cree view does not mean to encounter it by chance, but to receive it. The animal is given to the hunter. A successful hunt is not simply the result of the intention and work of the hunter; it is also the outcome of the intention and actions of animals. In the process of hunting, a hunter enters into a reciprocal relationship: animals are given to hunters to meet their needs and wants, and in return hunters incur obligations to animals. This conception of hunting involves a complex social and moral relationship of reciprocity in which the outcome of the hunt is a result of the mutual efforts of the hunter and the environment. This is a subtle and accurate perspective, somewhat like the ecological insights that have become prominent recently both in science and popular culture.

It may seem odd that animal kills should be conceptualized as gifts, and it is important therefore to note that Cree do not radically separate the concepts of 'human' and 'animal'. In their everyday experience in the bush they continually observe examples of the intelligence, personalities, and willpower of animals. They say that animals are 'like persons'; animals act, they are capable of independent choices, and they are causally responsible for things they do.

For the Cree hunter this is an everyday observation. Evidence of intelligence is cited from several sources. One type is that each animal has its own way of living and thinking. Each responds to environmental circumstances in ways that humans can recognize as appropriate. Each has its own preparations for winter: beavers build complex lodges; bears, dens; ducks and geese migrate. Each also relates to, and communicates with, members of its species. For example, beavers establish three-generational colonies built around a monogamous couple. Geese mate for life and have complex patterns of flock leadership. And inter-species communication is indicated by the intelligent response of animals to the efforts of hunters. Some beaver will place mud on top of a trap and then eat the poplar branches left as lure and a gift by the hunter. Each animal has special mental characteristics: beavers are stubborn and persistent, bears are intelligent, wolves are fearless, grouse are stupid. Further, animals have emotions and may be 'scared' or 'mad' when they avoid hunters.

That animals give themselves is indicated in part by their typical reactions to hunters. When a bear den is found in winter, a hunter will address the bear and tell it to come out. And bears do awake, come out of their dens sluggishly, and get killed. That such a powerful, intelligent, and potentially dangerous animal can be so docile is significant for the Cree. The behaviour of moose is also telling. Moose bed down facing into the wind, so that air does not penetrate under their hair. When a hunter approaches from down wind, he comes upon it from behind. A moose typically takes flight only after scenting or seeing a source of danger. It therefore rises up when it hears a hunter approach and turns in the direction of the noise to locate and scent the source. In this gesture, taking 10 to 15 seconds, the moose gives itself to the hunter by turning and looking at the hunter.

The extensive knowledge Cree hunters have of animals becomes, therefore, a basis for their understanding that animals are given. The concept of an animal gift indicates that killing an animal is not solely the result of the knowledge, will, and action of humans, however necessary these are, but that the most important reasons for the gift lie in the relationships of the givers and receivers. Because animals are capable of intelligent thought and social action, it is not only possible for them to understand humans, but for humans to understand animals. The actions of animals are events of communication that convey information about intentions. Saying that the animals are gifts therefore emphasizes that the hunter must adapt his hunt to what he learns from and knows about the animals he hunts. To see how this works we must examine the Cree world.

The Hunters' World

Because animals are gifts, it is appropriate to ask Cree hunters, 'Who gives the animal?' Their answers lead us to important features of Cree logic and cosmology. Recurrent answers are that animals do not only give themselves, but they are given by the 'wind persons' and by God or Jesus.

Just as animals are like persons, so are phenomena that we do not consider to be living. Active phenomena such as winds and water, as well as God and various spirit beings, are all considered to be like persons or to be associated with personal beings. Because all sources of action are like persons, the explanations of the causes of events and happenings are not in terms of impersonal forces, but in terms of the actions of persons. Explanations refer to a 'who' that is active, rather than to a 'what' (Hallowell, 1955). The world is volitional, and the perceived regularities of the world are not those of natural law but, rather, are like the habitual behaviour of persons. It is therefore possible to know what will happen before it occurs, because it is habitual. But there is also a fundamental unpredictability in the world: habits make action likely, not certain. This capriciousness is also a result of the diversity of persons, because many phenomena must act in concert for events to occur. The world of personal action is therefore a world neither of mechanistic determination nor of random chance: it is a world of intelligent order, but a very complex order, one not always knowable by humans.

This way of thinking and talking captures the complex interrelationships among phenomena that are experienced in the environment and the world. The environment cannot be perceived or experienced fully by a human being at any one time or at one place—it is too complex and too large and dynamic. In different cultures people understand it using analogies from their own experiences. Scientists, for example, use mechanical metaphors when they talk of the environment as having energy flows, or having nutrient or material cycles, and they employ market metaphors when they talk of investing in the environment or the decline in biological capital. The Cree, for their part, know the environment as a society of persons, and this view emphasizes the relationships humans have to non-human phenomena and the detailed interactions they have within it everyday.

For the Cree, the relationship of the wind persons to animal gifts is constantly confirmed by everyday experience. The wind persons bring cold or warmth and snow or rain, and with the coming and going of predominant winds the seasons change. They are responsible for the variable weather conditions to which animals and hunters respond. The bear hibernates and is docile only in winter when the cold north wind is predominant. The geese and ducks arrive with the increasing frequency of the warm south wind and leave with its departure. In a myriad of ways, the animals and hunters, and the success of the hunt, depend in part on the conditions brought by the winds.

When a hunter is asked by young people who have been away to school why they say that animals are given by the winds, the answer often is that they must live in the bush to see for themselves. These relationships can be discovered by anyone who spends enough time in the bush. The wind persons also link God to the world. They are part of the world 'up there', but they affect the earth down here. They thus link the spirits and God who are up there to the humans and animals who live on earth.

'God' and Jesus are the ultimate explanation for all that happens on earth, but He also gives all the personal beings of the world intelligence and will in order to follow His Way, or abandon it.[2] Persons are responsible for their actions. God therefore plays a key part in the gift of animals to hunters, but only a part. He is the leader of all things, and He is assisted by the wind persons and a hierarchy of leaders extending to most spirits, animals, and humans. The idea of leadership is persuasive in the Waswanipi world, alongside egalitarianism and reciprocity, and the hierarchy of leaders is spoken of as one of power. Hunting therefore depends not only on the hunter and the animals, but on an integrated chain of leaders and helpers acting together to give and to receive animals.

In this chain, human beings fit somewhere in the middle, closely linked to those above and below. Humans are mutually dependent on animals, who are generally less powerful than humans, and on spirit beings, who are generally more powerful. But the linkages are close and the positions flexible. As Cree myths indicate, some less powerful spirit beings were formerly humans who have been transformed into spirits. Animals used to be 'like us', and in the 'long ago' time they could talk with one another and with humans.

The Power of Hunting

The power of God and humans is manifest in the relationship between thought and happenings in the world. What God thinks or knows happens; His thought is one with happenings and thus He is all-powerful. Spirit beings participate in this power to a lesser degree; they know only some of what will happen in the future or at a distance. Their thought and happenings frequently coincide. God and spirit beings may give their powerful knowledge to humans in dreams, in waking thoughts, and by signs in the world, but they never tell all that humans would like to know. People can often be said to 'discover' their understandings rather than create them; and thought or insight may 'come to us' as a gift from God and spirits, in everyday thoughts, or in dreams.

Thinking and prayer may be one. The knowledge that spirits give anticipates the future with some effective, but always unknown, degree of certainty.

Humans not only differ from animals by the degree of power they receive, but also from each other. Powerful and effective knowledge increases with age and with the care and attention individuals give to interpreting and cultivating their communications with God and spirit beings. These differences in power and wisdom are reflected in the patterns of leadership within human communities.

The meaning of power in the Cree perspective, therefore, differs in important ways from that common in North American societies. People in the latter typically think of power as the ability to control others and/or the world. For the Cree it is more complex. Human knowledge is always incomplete, and there is often a gap between what humans think and what actually happens. In hunting, for example, a hunter will frequently dream of an animal that will be given before he or she begins to look for it. When they then go out hunting they may find signs of that animal that confirm this expectation. When the things they think about actually come to be—when they are given the animal—that is an indicator of power. The power is an emerging coincidence between the anticipation (social thought) and the configuration of the world (event), a congruence that this anticipation helps to actualize through action. Thoughts, actions, and events are all social processes. The social person who thinks and the personal environment in which he or she acts are not radically separable. Power is not an individual possession, it is a gift, and a person cannot in this view bring thought to actuality by individually manipulating the world to conform to personal desires. At each phase of happenings, humans, spirit beings, and other beings must sensitively interpret and respond to the communications and actions of other beings around them. 'Power' is a social process, a relationship in thoughts and actions among many beings, whereby potentiality becomes actuality.

Hunting is an occasion of power in this sense, and the expression of this is that animals are gifts, with many givers. Power in this Cree sense may have analogies to a concept of truth, i.e., thoughts that come to be. We might say that in this view the power that is worth seeking is truth unfolding in social relationships, rather than power as a control of one person over another.

This complex understanding of hunting links intimately with basic Cree attitudes towards human life itself. The symbols conveying Cree concepts of hunting also order the Cree understanding of the life and death of animals and of the hunters themselves. The life and ultimate death of both the hunted and the hunters are as enigmatic for the Cree as they are for others. That humans must kill animals to feed themselves and their families in order to live, and that humans themselves all die, are fundamentally mysterious features of life. Cree symbols of hunting elaborate this and bring the wonder of life and death into the world of everyday meanings.

The hunt is conceptualized as an ever-changing cycle at many levels. Successful hunters will bring game back to their families and others in camp. Having received gifts, hunters are obligated to respect them by reciprocating with gifts of their own. These gifts go partly to other Cree, as most large kills are shared with kinsmen, neighbours, or with the wider Cree community. By giving meat to others they are said to find more animal gifts in return. Many hunters also reciprocate to the spirits who have participated in the hunt, often by placing a small portion of meat into the stove at the first meal of each day. The smoke of the gift goes up the stovepipe as a sign of appreciation and respect to the spirits 'up there'. This return offering is part of an ongoing relationship of reciprocity: it not only expresses respect and repays an obligation, it continues the exchange as a statement of anticipation that the hunter will again receive what is wanted when in need. Many Cree rituals follow a similar structure.

In hunting, when bad luck occurs with a particular animal, hunters turn their attention to other species or they hunt in another area until the animals are ready to be caught again. But if animals want to be caught and are not hunted, that is also bad luck, because they have fewer young and more easily succumb to diseases or predation. Thus, proper hunting can lead to increases in the numbers and health of the animals. However, if a hunter kills animals that are not given, if they over-hunt, then the spirits of that species will be 'mad' and the hunter will have no luck. Thus, in hunting, the life and death of animals form a delicate reciprocal process.

The alteration in hunting luck brings us to the last of those meanings of the word 'hunting'. Hunters say that when they decrease their hunting they do so that the animals may cease being mad and may grow again. Hunting involves a reciprocal obligation for hunters to provide the conditions in which animals can grow and survive on the earth. The fulfillment of this responsibility provides the main criterion by which hunters evaluate one another. In everyday conversation people speak extensively about the reputations and actions of hunters. What is emphasized is hunting competence (Preston, 2002). A hunter who masters a difficult skill and through his ties with spirits receives hard-to-get gifts exhibits his competence and participates in power. Men and women who are respected for exceptional competence are contrasted with those who take chances, who fool around with animals by not killing them cleanly, and who seek self-aggrandizement by large kills or wasting animals. Hunters who consistently have good luck but not excessive harvests also demonstrate competence because they maintain that delicate balance with the world in which animals die and are reborn in health and in continuing growth.

This image of the competent hunter serves also as a goal of the good life. The aims of both hunting and of life are, in part, to maintain a continuing sensitivity to and a balanced participation with the world, in which humans and animals reciprocally contribute to the survival of the other. The aim of life is the perpetuation of a healthy, meaningful, and bountiful world. This aim includes those now alive and those yet to be born. The social universe thus extends beyond the human world, beyond the temporal frame of an individual human life.

Hunting is not just a central activity of the Cree, nor is it simply a body of knowledge or a spiritual activity. Hunting is an ongoing experience of truth as power in the course of human lives and in the social world in which they are lived.

Hunting Practices: Subsistence Economy, Kin and Society, and Environmental Conservation

Contemporary studies by anthropologists of hunting and gathering peoples can be dated to the mid-1960s when it was 'discovered' that the hunting and gathering peoples of Africa and Australia efficiently, abundantly, and reliably produced their subsistence. This came as a revelation to both popular and professional images of hunting life. The hunting way of life was often thought to be precisely the opposite—inefficient, impoverished, and unpredictable. Studies of the Cree tended to confirm the application of the new view to Subarctic hunters as well, although with some qualifications.

Efficiency, Abundance, and Reliability

It was found that hunters do not encounter game haphazardly, but by careful planning and organization. Hunting is organized so that each species of game is used at times likely to produce an efficient, abundant, and reliable supply of food. Thus Cree know how to kill moose in almost any season, but they tend to concentrate their hunting at specific periods. One period is during the fall mating season or rut, when moose call to attract partners. Hunters often look along shores for signs indicating the places that moose have visited to drink; they then wait or return at appropriate times to call males to the location. After the rut, moose are not hunted extensively until deep snows have accumulated. As the snow depth increases, the widely dispersed populations progressively concentrate and are often found on hills where wind blows some snow accumulations thin. When the snow in the concentration areas exceeds one metre in depth, moose tend to restrict their movements to a series of trails. Under these conditions Cree know where to look for moose, and moose move outside the trails reluctantly. If moose do take flight, hunters on snowshoes can exhaust them by pursuit until they stand their ground, face the hunter, and give themselves to the hunters.

A third period of intensive moose hunting occurs in late winter when snow may form a crust. Moose can walk, breaking through the crust with each step, but if they run they tear their legs against the jagged edges of the crust. Again, they will often stand their ground and face the hunter.

Cree moose-hunting practices therefore depend on extensive knowledge of the habits of animals in relation to weather, habitat, and the actions of hunters. Hunting is concentrated in periods when moose most clearly give themselves to hunters and when hunters can best fulfill the obligation to kill them with a minimum of suffering.

The proficiency and knowledge of Cree hunters make their hunting quite reliable. They succeed on about 22 per cent of the days they search for moose, 88 per cent of days spent fishing, and about 50 per cent of days hunting beaver. Bush food is also abundant, providing hunters' families with 150 per cent of the calories they require and eight times the daily protein requirement. It also provides more than twice the required intakes of the nine other vitamins and minerals for which calculations could be run. Hunters also take purchased food with them into the bush camps, but the caloric value of bush foods is greater than the calories available from store food. About half the food they harvest is circulated in gift exchanges to kinsmen and friends back in the settlement, and some is kept for later village consumption, so everyone in the community receives some 'bush food'.

Social Relations, Hunting Reciprocity, and Conserving Animals

The Cree have a distinct system of rights and responsibilities concerning land, resources, community, and social relations—a legal system of land and resource tenure, and of self-governance. This system enables hunters to fulfill their responsibilities to animals and spirits and contribute to the conditions necessary for their mutual survival.

Cree society is organized around principles of community, responsible autonomy, and reciprocity. The central resources of land and wildlife are not owned. The land and the animals are God's creations, and, to the extent that humans use or control them, they do so as part of a broad social community united by reciprocal obligations. These gifts and obligations are not solely individual; they involve the wider human community as well, so that all people have a right of access to land and resources to sustain themselves. This right extends to all Cree, and to others, but along with the rights go responsibilities to contribute to the continued well-being of the land and animals. The exercise and fulfillment of such responsibility implies a willingness to exercise self-control and participate in a community of responsibility.

The Cree are efficient enough at hunting that they could deplete the game. Restraint is both an individual and a community responsibility and is assisted through a stewardship system. All hunting land is divided into territories under the stewardship of Elders. The approximately 300 territories vary in size from about 300 to several thousand square kilometres, each supervised by a steward (see Map 7.1). They are part of larger blocks, each associated with a community. While rights to land and resources are distributed to the whole community, as a continuing society extending over generations, the stewards exercise authority over the territories in the name of the community and the common interest. Their authority is, in principle, spiritually sanctioned, thus obligating them to protect and share the resources.

MAP 7.1. Approximate Territory Areas of James Bay Cree Hunters

FIGURE 7.1. The late Joseph Ottereyes from Waswanipi hunting geese while travelling to get wood for his fall bush camp. (Courtesy H. Feit)

In general, all community members have the right to hunt on any land on a short-term basis, while travelling through, while camping for brief periods, or while using small game or fish resources. However, extended and intensive use of the larger game resources is under the supervision of the stewards.

Stewards usually have grown up in a territory on which they hunt repeatedly over many years before they inherit their role. They have built up extensive ties with the spirits of the land and acquired a vast knowledge of its resources. Most are constantly aware of the changing conditions and trends in the game populations. They discuss these trends with other stewards and elder hunters, comparing patterns in different territories and relating them to changes in weather, vegetation, and hunting activity. Some of the trends observed by the stewards are the same ones used by wildlife biologists to monitor game popula-

tions, although few biologists have such long-term and detailed knowledge of a particular area. The trends are also important because they are communications from animals and spirits. Thus, if too many animals were killed in the past, the animals would be 'mad' and have fewer young or make signs of their presence harder to find. This would indicate that the animals wish to give fewer of themselves, and, out of reciprocal respect, the hunters would take less.

Stewards use their knowledge to direct the intensive hunting of the animals on their territories. Each steward has the right to decide if the territory will be used intensively in any season, how many and which people can use it, how much they can hunt of each key species, and where and when they can hunt. However, stewards do not exercise these powers in an authoritarian manner. Stewards usually act by suggestion and by non-personal public commentaries on the situation, and their knowledge, their spiritual ties to the land, and the sacred sanctions for their statements give them considerable influence.

The system is part of the network of social reciprocities. At the individual level, the system of allowing hunters to join groups generally assures each a place to hunt every year. For the community as a whole, the system permits the distribution of hunters to respond to changes in the conditions of the game populations. The right to steward land and animals is inherited as a gift from previous generations, and the present stewards view their own actions as implying the same respect and responsibility to future generations.

In practice, the system of hunting-territory stewardships works to maintain an ongoing balance between harvests and game of those species that can be conserved. Several studies supply quantitative evidence that the Cree system works for the moose, beaver, fish, and geese populations, by keeping harvests below sustainable yields of the game populations. The best indicator of success is the relative stability of game populations over the two decades during which estimates have been made. These data indicate that the long-term ecological balance sought by the Cree is, in general, maintained. Furthermore, the Cree have been highly responsive to changing environmental and historical circumstances in pursuing a balanced hunt.

The Cree have also responded to important demographic, technological, and economic changes. They have generally maintained viable game populations through a period in which their own numbers may have risen fivefold since the early twentieth century. Reasons for this demographic increase are not fully understood. To increase their food production they have intensified and diversified their use of some game populations but have also limited their bush food production to sustainable levels. They therefore now have to purchase a significant proportion of their food.

The more intensive harvesting has occurred with the aid of important additions to their technological repertoire, including improved rifles and shotguns, new traps, and some new means of transportation. But the use of this technology still depends on Cree knowledge, cultural values, and social practices. The technology, therefore, has not led to over-hunting, but rather to a more secure balance between humans and animals. The Cree have also maintained the balance despite periods of a shortage of cash. In such times they have done without some trade goods rather than exhaust animal resources. And they have continued to treat cash and trade goods as socially modified forms of property, using them for co-operative ends by integrating their distribution and consumption into the widespread reciprocal exchange practices.

The Cree have thus maintained their hunting and the animals in their region despite important changes in their environment and in historical circumstances. However, rare periods of breakdown in the balance of hunters and animals have also occurred. The most serious of these happened in the 1920s and 1930s, when beaver were severely depleted. Non-Native trappers, encouraged by temporarily high fur prices, entered the region from the railway 100 miles to the south, trapped out a place, and moved on. Some Cree say that they themselves trapped out the beaver in some areas because they did not see the possibility of maintaining animal populations if non-Native trappers continued to deplete their lands. But they continued to conserve moose and other game that were not hunted by the intruders. This example emphasizes the limits of the means at the disposal of the Cree for maintaining viable long-term balanced relations with animals. The culture and social organization of the Cree are effective aids for their self-governance, but they could not regulate or control the impact of what outsiders do on their lands. Further, where outsiders did not act responsibly and with respect, their activities threatened the animals and the Cree themselves.

The Cree recovered from the impact of these intrusions when non-Native trappers were banned from the area, but a crisis developed again in the

1970s when the government of Quebec started to build a massive hydroelectric project on their hunting lands. To understand the events of this second crisis, we have to turn from an examination of Cree culture and hunting to an account of the relationships of Cree to governments and developers.

The Cree Struggle to Maintain Autonomy in the Face of Government Intervention

Crises in the Fur Trade and the Incorporation of the Cree into Canada and Quebec

Fur traders have been present in the James Bay region since the mid-seventeenth century, and missionaries have visited most trading posts since the mid-nineteenth century; but the arrival of the government and corporate resource developers characterizes the twentieth and twenty-first centuries. In the late 1920s the Quebec government's first intervention in the region occurred when it responded to requests to help solve the beaver crisis created by non-Native trappers. Quebec first made the killing of beaver by non-Indians illegal and then in the mid-1930s outlawed all killing of beaver. The Cree supported this closure, and some communities reached their own agreements to cease taking beaver before the government decision.

When hunting resumed, after 10 to 20 years depending on the region, the response had worked: beaver were numerous, they were no longer 'mad', and they wanted to give themselves again. The Cree and the government thus agreed independently on the means for re-establishing beaver populations and then on the timing for beaver hunting to be reinstituted.

For the Cree, the government was recognizing their system and giving the stewards an additional source of authority that they could use to limit the hunting activities of people from outside their communities, including non-Natives, who often were less responsive to their social and spiritual authority. In this respect, therefore, an important but not yet fully apparent conflict developed between the Cree and the governments. The governments thought that Cree hunting was regulated and supervised by government regulations and authority, and that they determined the Cree rights to hunt. The Cree thought the government had recognized their system of tenure and self-governance.

An element of the government response to the crisis of the 1930s was to establish a band government structure for each community and to start issuing rations and, later, social assistance. In the late 1930s and early 1940s the federal Department of Indian Affairs sent an Indian agent to each community to establish an official list of band membership—one band for each fur trade post—and to supervise the election of band chiefs and band councils. In fact, however, it appears that a chief and council system had been adopted in most communities before this time. Nevertheless, these responses also represented a turning point in Cree society. They bound the Cree within the fabric of Canadian political society, law, and economy for the first time, and in circumstances that did not make the potential threats to their autonomy clear. The Cree were still exercising extensive control and autonomy in their hunting society and on their lands, but they were now doing so as part of the Canadian polity.

Government Assistance Turns To an Assertion of Dominance

Government presence in the region accelerated rapidly throughout the 1950s and 1960s as governments sought to 'open the North'. This involved making the region more accessible to southern Canadians and international corporations. It also involved extending government administration and authority. These changes were not intended to aid the Cree but to promote the interests of corporations and southern Canadians. Programs specifically affecting the Cree were not developed in consultation with them, and were aimed at their assimilation rather than at supporting their culture and economy.

The expansion of the rail and road networks into the southern portions of Cree territory occurred in the 1950s and 1960s, and several mines, mining towns, and commercial logging operations were established. Their impacts on the Cree were neither foreseen nor considered. Hunters said animals became much less calm and less willing to be caught over large areas affected by noise generated by railways, road traffic, and airplanes. Cree reported frequent finds of dead fish and aquatic animals and changes in the taste of animals over large areas. The extensive Cree use of the environment and their knowledge of it made clear to them the extent of the impacts these developments were having, but no mechanism was established by governments or companies to give them a voice in the projects. That the government did not consider the Cree system of land use and management as a system of land tenure and of rights, and that it did not consider that government and developers as well as the Cree had mutual obligations, was becoming clear.

The opening of the region to development projects not only affected the land, it affected the choices open to the Cree. When fur prices declined in the 1950s and 1960s, hunters began to meet the cash shortage by taking summer employment. They chose jobs primarily in projects that were compatible with continued hunting, used their bush skills, allowed them to work in Cree groups, and were not organized by industrial time or authority structures. Although they continued to hunt, the number who did not pursue hunting as their main occupation rose significantly. Other changes also influenced this process: the formation of reserves, the construction of permanent settlements, and the establishment of schools.

Taking these jobs provoked a new crisis. Agents of government saw this as the first step in an irreversible process of abandoning hunting for wage labour. This fit the common image of hunting as an unreliable, unproductive, and insecure means of living, one that any rational person would willingly give up for a steady job. The Cree not only knew differently about hunting, but also about jobs. During their summer jobs in the 1960s they were aware of often being given the hardest work, of being paid lower wages than non-Natives, and of being the first fired. The non-Native sawmills, exploration companies, fisheries, and hunting outfitters for whom they worked were constantly failing or moving.

Although some schooling had been provided earlier, during the 1960s a significant portion of Cree youths began to attend schools. The government tried to force parents to send their children, sometimes threatening to cut off social assistance if they did not. Most parents wanted their children to have some schooling, and an increase in the number of children also affected their willingness to send some to school. The trauma of residential schooling away from the reserves, in programs not significantly adapted to Cree culture, separated parents from their children in more than a physical sense. The longer children stayed in school the harder it was for parents and children to understand each other. As people saw what was happening, up to one-third of a community's children were kept out of school each year to learn bush skills and the hunting way of life. Thus, the Cree kept some control over the education of their children.

The result was not to limit the continuation of the hunting economy but to diversify the range of skills and interests of the young adults. The effect of schooling paralleled that of the crisis in hunting, creating a need for a more diversified economy in which both hunting and employment would be viable activities. However, schooling also created new resources for continuing efforts to define their own future. One effect was to bring a generation of Cree with high school, and some with higher education, back to the communities and into active roles in social and political life.

Cree Opposition to Quebec's Quest for Power

When the government of Quebec announced its plans for hydroelectric development in the James Bay region in 1971, it followed its practice of

FIGURE 7.2 The late Emily Saganash from Waswanipi preparing a beaver as her granddaughter watches. She will remove the pelt for commercial sale and cook the animal for sustenance. (Courtesy H. Feit)

complete opposition to the project, to see if they could establish respectful and reciprocal relationships with governments, and to get modifications to reduce the project's impact. However, the government refused to do anything but inform the Cree as the plans developed. The Cree were left with no choice but to oppose the project (Feit, 1985).

Joined by the Inuit of northern Quebec, some of whom lived on one of the rivers to be diverted by the project, in 1972 they initiated a legal injunction. Basically, they had to prove that they had a *prima facie* claim to rights in the territory, that the project would damage their exercise of these rights, and that these damages would be irreversible and irremediable. They asked the court to stop construction until hearings on their rights could be completed.

The court hearings provided a detailed description of the project planned for the La Grande region. The La Grande complex involved diverting three major rivers into the La Grande River to increase its flow by 80 per cent. The construction of roads and power transmission lines would require cutting three or four corridors 960 kilometres long through the forest. And all this was only the first of three phases.

In the Cree view, many of the damages were like those they had previously identified from earlier developments, although now over a much larger area. In addition, the particular effects of flooding were of special concern because about 50 per cent of the wetlands of the region would be underwater, destroying important beaver, waterfowl, and game habitat. The number of animals would be significantly reduced, and the variability of water levels in the reservoirs would

neither involving the Cree in the decision nor examining its impact on them.

Several young Cree leaders called a meeting of leaders from each village to discuss the project. At the time, the Cree were comprised of eight separate communities and bands having no regional integration or political structure. At the meeting, all were opposed to the project because of the severe damage it would cause to the land, the animals, and the Cree. In their view, the project was to serve non-Natives and they would not benefit substantially. They discussed ways to oppose the project and attempted to get discussions going with the Quebec government and its Crown corporations. They wanted to avoid restrict the ability of many animals, particularly beaver, to re-inhabit the areas. In short, they argued that hunters would suffer a serious and permanent loss of subsistence resources and a major threat to the continuity of their culture and society. Dozens of Cree hunters came to Montreal to testify, explaining to Judge Albert Malouf, government representatives, and the public how they lived on the land and why they had to have a say in what was done there. Their tone was not confrontational, but truthful and firm.

The Cree lawyers then argued that their clients had been exercising rights to the land since time immemorial, including the rights to hunt, fish, and trap, which constituted an Indian title over the land. To that time, the case was one of the most important on the concept of Aboriginal rights and Indian title. It was also one of the strongest such cases.

The government lawyers argued that the project would affect only a small percentage of the land directly, that it would improve its productivity in many respects, and that in any case the damages were temporary or remediable. They claimed that the Cree no longer lived primarily off the land: they lived in settlements, had houses, used manufactured clothes and equipment, and now ate purchased foods predominantly. They argued that Cree culture had been substantially transformed and replaced by Canadian culture. They said the Cree were dependent on government financial assistance and support for their settlements. They argued that the use of wildlife, especially beaver, was completely institutionalized by the government as a result of establishing beaver reserves. They claimed that most Cree now had jobs. Finally, they argued that the Cree had no Aboriginal title to the land, or at most had a right to some monetary compensation and small reserves such as were provided in other treaties made elsewhere in Canada.

In November 1973, Judge Malouf ruled that the Cree and Inuit people did appear to have Aboriginal title to the land; that they had been occupying and using the land to a full extent; that

hunting was still of great importance, constituted a way of life, and provided a portion of their diet and incomes; that they had a unique concept of the land; that they wished to continue their way of life; that any interference with their use compromised their very existence as a people; and that the project was already causing much interference. He ruled that the province was trespassing. The ruling was a stronger affirmation of Cree rights than many people had thought possible at that time and forced the government to negotiate with the Cree.

To people in the villages the ruling was a great victory, but it was also a straightforward recognition of the truth about their way of life and the dangers inherent in development conducted without their involvement and consent. It was also interpreted as a statement of good sense, reaffirming that relations between Cree and non-Natives could be guided by the principle of reciprocity that should inform interrelations among all beings in the Cree world (Scott, 1989). Reciprocity implied mutual respect for the needs and autonomy of others, ongoing obligations and relationships to others, and the possibility of sharing the land responsibly.

Cree Autonomy and the Aboriginal Rights Agreement

Negotiating Recognition of Aboriginal Rights

The Cree approached negotiations cautiously, despite the effort they had put into trying to get discussions started. They were in a difficult position as they were already experiencing the impacts of massive construction work on the project, which had been permitted to continue while Justice Malouf's ruling was appealed.

Early in the negotiations the Cree formed their own political association, the Grand Council of the Crees (GCC) with the chief and another leader from each community on its Board of Directors. The full Cree name for the Grand Council means roughly 'the people from inland and the people from the coast helping each other'.

Negotiations continued for nearly two years through 1974 and 1975 until there was a sense that neither the government nor the Cree would go further.[3] The negotiations included several changes to project plans. The location of a main dam was changed. Funds were provided for remedial work to be undertaken as future impacts were experienced, and the negotiators agreed that any future changes would require new approvals.[4] These limited compromises meant very substantial impacts on the land and wildlife of the region. Despite major efforts by the Cree, no other major modifications could be agreed upon.

The government agreed to recognize the right of all Cree to hunt, fish, and trap all kinds of animals at all times, over all the lands traditionally harvested by them, on the understanding that their harvesting rights would be subject to conservation of wildlife. Conservation was an objective Cree were pursuing in any case, and they were careful to get agreement on a definition that recognized their needs. In addition, it was agreed that Cree harvesting would take precedence over sport hunting and fishing by non-indigenous hunters, but not that they had priority over other uses of natural resources (see below). Approximately 16 per cent of the land area, called Category II lands, was set aside for exclusive Cree use. From the government point of view the Cree recognition of the principle of conservation and of some non-indigenous access to game made the wildlife provisions acceptable. From the Cree point of view the government recognition of their rights and of their priority of access to wildlife over sport hunters made the provisions acceptable.

Differences then arose over whether the governments or the Cree would have jurisdiction to implement these provisions. The terms agreed to would have to be interpreted and applied each year, as game populations shifted and hunting activities varied. The Cree argued that the fact that game existed in the region today demonstrated the effectiveness of their management, and they claimed a right to manage the wildlife. The representatives of Quebec and Canada argued that parliamentary legislation gave the responsibility to manage wildlife to the governments.

This conflict was resolved through two procedures. It was agreed that all parties would recognize the Cree system of hunting territories and that there would be a minimum of government regulation. Second, the provincial and federal governments would exercise legal authority and enforcement powers over most of the region, but only after receiving the advice of a co-ordinating committee composed equally of Cree, Inuit, and government appointees. On areas reserved exclusively for Cree, the Cree governments would act with the advice of the committee.

Both the Cree and the governments agreed that development had to be controlled. The Cree did not oppose all development, envisioning sharing the land with non-Natives, but they wanted the right to decide on whether specific projects should be permitted, and if so, under what terms and conditions. The governments argued that they had the right to final decisions authorizing future developments, and they wanted to avoid situations in which the Cree could tie up projects in court. The conflict over this issue was not fully resolvable.

The insistence of the governments that the region be open for development limited the land base over which the Cree could negotiate control. The province took the position that land under Cree control should be limited to areas immediately around the settlements and to the adjacent hunting locations. The greatest amount of land the province would transfer to Cree control, Category I lands, was only 5,500 square kilometres of the approximately 375,000-square-kilometre region.

The Cree sought to reduce their dependence on governmental authority and administration during the negotiations and to take more control of their own affairs through increased self-government. They therefore sought regional autonomy and self-determination through the formation of distinctive, ethnically defined governments and boards for education, health, and other social services. At the community level, the

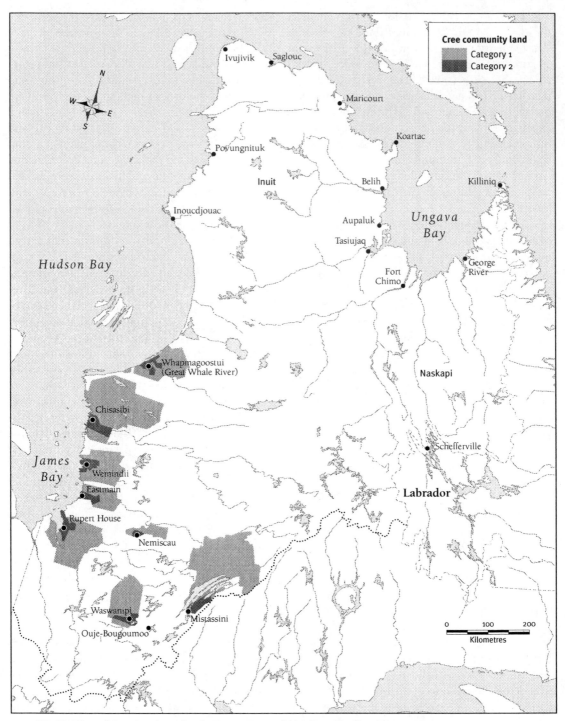

MAP. 7.2. Division of Cree Lands under the James Bay and Northern Quebec Agreement

Cree got agreement to special legislation for a Cree-Naskapi Act, extending the powers of their band councils as new community governments and replacing the provisions of the Indian Act.

The Agreement in Principle, reached after eight months of negotiation, was discussed periodically in each Cree community, where the provisions were outlined in detail. People did not consider the draft agreement to be fair or just but thought it would increase their chances of maintaining their culture, society, and economy, given the alternatives. The final agreement followed a year later. The outcome was summarized by Chief Billy Diamond of the GCC, announcing to the press that all Cree communities had accepted the Agreement in Principle:

> The Cree People were very reluctant to sign an Agreement in Principle. . . . We feel, as Cree People, that by coming to an Agreement in Principle, that it is the best way to see that our rights and that our land are protected as much as possible from white man's intrusion and white man's use. We . . . believe this agreement supports and strengthens the hunting, fishing and trapping rights in/over all of the territory, and restricts non-Native activity in that area. . . . I hope you can all understand our feelings, that it has been a tough fight, and our people are still very much opposed to the project, but they realize that they must share the resources. That is why we have come to a decision to sign an Agreement in Principle with the Quebec Government. (Diamond, 1977)

Implemention: Enhancing Cree Autonomy Despite Government Dishonesty

A definitive account of the results of the James Bay and Northern Quebec Agreement (JNBQA) has not been made. Nevertheless, I emphasize five general aspects: (1) the agreement has considerably aided Cree hunting; (2) it has strengthened the Cree socially and politically; (3) the economic provisions of the agreement have failed; (4) government respect and support for the agreement have been very mixed and often absent; (5) the Cree are more autonomous than before the agreement, but real threats to Cree autonomy remain.

The protection and recognition of Cree hunting rights and the provision of income security payments for hunters have enhanced the perceived viability of hunting as a way of life, and participation in hunting has intensified. In 1975, about 700 families or single adults were hunting as a way of life. The number of intensive hunters increased following the agreement to approximately 900 and has since risen to about 1,200. The time spent in hunting camps has also increased, and the average number of days intensive hunters stayed in the bush hunting during a year increased by about 25 per cent after the income security program was begun. Most of these families now live seven months or more in bush camps.

The increased number of intensive hunters and the increased time they spend in bush camps present complex challenges to the stewards of hunting territories, who want to assure these changes do not result in over-hunting of game. In the initial year after the JBNQA, harvests of the most intensively used wildlife—goose, beaver, and moose—increased significantly. Stewards responded quickly, speaking widely of the problems in the villages, and reorganized their hunting groups accordingly. By the second and third years, harvests had returned to earlier levels. This adjustment to a significant and rapid increase in the numbers of hunters and the length of time people spent in bush camps was a dramatic test and confirmation of Cree conservation practices.

In terms of changes in social relations, several commentators anticipated that the increased cash available to both hunters and to the growing number of employed Cree might result in widespread increases in the independence of individual nuclear families and in reduction in extended social relations and reciprocity. These changes have been modest or non-existent. All sectors of

Cree society maintain a high value and a strong preference for locally produced 'bush foods'. The desire for bush foods reflects pride in the specialized knowledge, skill, and work that go into harvesting animals and the recognition of nutritional and health benefits of a fresh bush food diet. The majority of families who hunt intensively continue to do the work necessary to make additional harvests of foods that they give to kin, friends, and those who do not hunt so intensively. Customary stewardship therefore continues to express social responsibility and mutual aid despite considerably more intensive use of lands (Feit, 1991).

In a society in which animals are sacred and labour is highly valued and a source of respect, social exchanges of bush foods and access to hunting lands are highly valued. The gifts of bush foods are a sign both of the continuing value of those foods and of the value of the social bonds that motivate the distribution and are confirmed by it. The fact that such exchange is less of a material necessity today highlights its social value.

The rapid increase in Cree population has meant that while the number of intensive hunters has stabilized in recent years, the total population continues to grow, so that now between one-quarter and one-fifth of the adult resident population are intensive hunters. Almost all other Cree hunt, but on a variety of arrangements. Extensive linkages exist between families living most of the year in the settlements—who hunt part-time in the evenings, on weekends, school breaks, and holidays, and between jobs—and those kin and friends who live most of the year in bush camps and for whom hunting is their primary activity. Those in the settlements often provide equipment and cash for those in the bush, while the latter provide access to hunting camps and lands, advice and knowledge of hunting conditions, and regular gifts of food to the former. Hunting is critical to the identities and relations of nearly all Cree, and it binds together the diverse sectors of the communities. Rather than cash and market conditions leading to an attenuation of social relations, hunting reciprocity continues to recreate wider social relationships and reciprocity, which are dominated by a desire to enhance collective local autonomy in the face of market forces that might otherwise radically transform Cree society.

Social linkages are also expressed in the growth of more formal community-based decision-making institutions. Under the agreement and the supplementary federal legislation—the Cree-Naskapi Act of Quebec, 1984—the Cree no longer were under the formal jurisdiction of the Indian Act and took over formal control of the many organizations that provided services in their communities. Initially, organizations were taken over more or less as they had existed, but as Cree received on-the-job training, Cree control has grown and policies and programs have become increasingly innovative (Salisbury, 1986).

In the villages, more and more school and health committees composed of local Cree users have started to play decisive decision-making roles. This has empowered local people and provided them with enhanced skills and experience. These processes have not been easy, and numerous mistakes have been made. Nevertheless, the overall process has showed how effective self-government can be established.

This process has had important consequences for community economies. The Cree takeover and expansion of administrative services and programs have increased employment opportunities in the communities. The 30 or so Cree who were fully employed as administrators before the agreement have grown to some 800 administrators and supporting employees. It is clear, however, that the number of administrative positions is insufficient to employ fully all those Cree in the rapidly growing population who do not hunt as their primary activity. The Cree have therefore recently begun to emphasize the creation of Cree economic enterprises in the communities. The structures being developed frequently combine elements of modern business practices with structures adapted from Cree hunting society. However, these enterprises are not sufficient to employ the growing numbers of Cree youth, and there are still many obstacles to full Cree participation in the regional resource-based economy. Most limiting is the small land base of the Cree and their inability to access natural resources for their development, as almost all resources continue to be allocated to large corporations.

The economic development provisions of the agreement have not greatly benefited the Cree. Nor has the hydroelectric project contributed systematically to community-level economic development within the villages. The economic benefits of the project have been directed to southern urban centres. Indeed, nearly all monetary provisions of the agreement have suffered negligence on the part of governments, and in some cases explicit subversion.

When the first major parliamentary review of the implementation of the agreement was conducted in 1981, five years after the signing, it was clear that the federal government had not budgeted any special funds to meet its new obligations under the agreement, nor had it established any agency with responsibility for overseeing its role in the implementation processes. As a result of this review several initiatives were undertaken, including the passage of the Cree-Naskapi Act. Nevertheless, the Cree-Naskapi Commission, the independent organization set up to report every two years to Parliament on the implementation of the Act putting the JBNQA into law, reported:

> It is difficult to believe that a federal department responsible for negotiating and implementing self-government arrangements with Indian nations, and charged with improving their conditions, could persistently misinterpret a negotiated arrangement of this nature. The Department's attempt to circumvent clear obligations . . . is unjust, and must not be allowed to continue. Such actions cannot be dismissed as merely an honest difference of opinion. (Cree-Naskapi Commission, 1986: 27–8)

Similar attitudes and actions prevail with respect to the exploitation of natural resources.

The governments of Quebec and Canada have repeatedly tried to avoid their obligations to the Cree, and to the wider public, in the interests of facilitating large-scale projects that primarily meet the interests of corporations.

Billy Diamond (1990: 28) wrote, 'If I had known in 1975 what I know now about the way solemn commitments become twisted and interpreted, I would have refused to sign the Agreement.' These failures led to new conflicts between the Cree and the governments of Quebec and Canada in the early 1990s and also to new negotiations in 2001.

A New Kind of Campaign, and a New Agreement

Creating a Transnational Campaign Against Development

In 1989 Hydro-Québec announced that it would build the second phase of its hydroelectric projects for James Bay, the Great Whale River (GWR) project north of the La Grande (McCutcheon, 1991). Its view was that with the JBNQA some rights of the Cree had been recognized, but the agreement also recognized the right of the government to develop the hydroelectric resources of the region, with or without Cree participation or agreement.

The Cree decided to oppose the project and embarked on a campaign that lasted five years and created innovative ways of seeking recognition for indigenous rights. At the heart of their campaign was a sophisticated linking of indigenous rights to the environmental movement. Opposition to the project was led by Whapmagoostui, the community at the mouth of Great Whale River, but was supported broadly. Nevertheless, it was not an easy decision to stand against further development in the region. The failure of the social and economic development provisions of the JBNQA meant that there was a widely felt need for jobs and contracts that the development could bring, and there were now some Cree with businesses and jobs who voiced support for the development.

BOX 7.1

Testimony of Alan Saganash Sr

I am the *Ndoho Ouchimau* ['hunting boss' or steward] . . . I am 80 years old this year. All my life has been spent on the land. . . .

Our land is uncut now but a Hydro Road passes close to it. . . .

Poachers use that road now. . . . Many people come there now. There is garbage left everywhere. . . . The lake is over-fished. . . . Our camps in that area have been vandalized and things are stolen.

Our land is very rich elsewhere. There are all kinds of animals and fish . . . but I know [a forestry company] plans to build a road into it. They want to put a camp . . .

The road will change all that [it] will damage the habitat and open it up. . . .

I am afraid once the road comes there will be many mines opened. . . .

I want all of this considered in a full environmental assessment but they won't do it. I know the government well. I have seen how they work throughout my life. They refuse to consider all the development together. I have no chance to get all these issues looked at. I worry all the time about what will happen when the road comes.

The road is not to come to the heart of my land. I don't want it. The government is not trustworthy . . . We are pushed out of our land again and again. We are told to move our hunting grounds. I have seen this happen many times in Waswanipi.

The companies and the government don't listen to us. They take what is ours and push us aside. This must stop.

—From an affidavit of 22 July 1999 by Allan Saganash Sr of Waswanipi submitted in the court case the Cree initiated against forestry companies and the governments[5]

The discussion was wide-ranging, and in the end there was strong support not just to oppose the project but to stop it.

The Cree people and leadership were in a better position to try to do this than they had been in the early 1970s, but there are few examples of small communities stopping multi-billion dollar development projects. The Cree had a strong organization, experienced leadership, and a broad base of community support for the campaign. They also had some funds as a result of the JBNQA. The provisions of both the JBNQA and general environmental legislation that had been passed since 1970 required that environmental and social impacts of large-scale developments be assessed before construction could begin. The governments tried to bypass key requirements, but the Cree challenged them in court to assure the full application of the law because this would assure construction would not begin while the Cree campaign was being initiated.

The Cree strategy was not, however, to fight mainly in the courts, but to carry their campaign to the public, the politicians, and the public utility decision-makers in the US where the energy would be sold, and to the international investors whose capital Hydro-Québec needed. The Cree reasoned that if US contracts for the bulk purchase of this electricity could be blocked, it would make the investment of billions of dollars in Hydro-Québec bonds look less attractive to the managers of capital from world markets in New York and Europe, thereby making it harder for Hydro-Québec to finance the project.

The Cree set out a multi-scale campaign, developing it as they went along. Leaders spoke to environment groups in the US and built campaign plans with national and international groups who opposed the project on environmental and social grounds. They commissioned slide shows, videos, Web presentations, and newspaper and magazine articles, and gave talks at massive environmental rallies such as Earth Day in New York City. All were aimed at convincing environmentalists and the public at large that hydroelectricity from northern Quebec was not 'clean' power just because it did not burn fossil fuels or was generated outside the US. They pointed out the project involved damming and diverting rivers that in the US would be protected by environmental legislation. They also noted it would disrupt habitats and wildlife, including migratory waterfowl protected by US and international treaties. They also said it would endanger the 'way of life' of Cree hunters.

Not only leaders were involved. Hunters and their families, especially from communities threatened by the project or who had experienced the effects of development on the La Grande River, travelled to the US to speak directly with people in towns and cities in the northeast states where the electricity would be consumed. They travelled down the river systems of Vermont, Massachusetts, and New York, stopping each night to meet environmentalists, church groups, and social activists. They built understanding, support, and long-term friendships, and some of the people they met made return journeys to James Bay. Some of those they met say that working with the Cree and seeing the connections between communities so far apart, yet struggling with similar issues of how to keep control of their lands and their lives, has changed how they live and work in their own communities (McRae, forthcoming).

The diverse strands of the Cree campaign argued so successfully that Americans must care about what was being done to provide them with power that a significant number of new members joined the US environmental group that led the campaign. The Cree commissioned pollsters to survey public opinion and show that there was growing public opposition in the US to buying power from Hydro-Québec. They made sure that US politicians up for re-election saw these results and they urged candidates privately and publicly to stand against the contracts.

But public and political support was not enough. The Cree also sought to show that the contracts did not make good economic sense, and that there were alternatives. They were convinced that, without these economic arguments, the political pressure would be undermined by power utilities and US companies needing electricity. The Cree commissioned US experts to evaluate critically the Hydro-Québec and US utility company figures on how quickly energy demand would grow and what prices could be charged for it. They studied how demand could be met if more electricity were not available from Hydro-Québec. These technical studies showed that it would be cheaper to apply conservation measures in the US than to buy Great Whale River power, and that energy conservation could fully meet the expected demand. They also showed energy conservation would create jobs in the US. These studies helped to convince some senior officials in US electric utility companies that new contracts with Hydro-Québec were not economically viable.

The multi-year campaign had many twists and turns, but the Cree renewed their commitment to it each year and pursued an extraordinarily diverse set of means to their goal of preventing the new dams (Craik, forthcoming). They lost fights opposing contracts and won others. The New York state power authority cancelled a large contract with Hydro-Québec, and several months later, early in 1995, the Premier of Quebec, Jacques Parizeau, announced that the Great Whale Project would be delayed indefinitely.

It was an extraordinary victory, and it had ramifications for everyone involved. It was now clear that groups like the Cree could not be simply ignored. Over the next few years both the Quebec provincial government and Hydro-Québec acknowledged that it would be better to involve the Cree in development planning than to try to ignore them, although their ways of involving the Cree were not always measures the Cree thought appropriate.

Hydro-Québec opened offices in New York and in Europe, realizing it needed an ongoing presence in the political and economic centres where its power was sold or where it sought to raise capital. This was partly in response to realizing that the victory of the Cree and their international environmental allies had damaged the corporation's image. The innovativeness and success of the Cree campaign has also led to its being a case study problem for law students at the Harvard Business School (Dumont, 1998), presumably in the hope that companies could better oppose similar campaigns in future. The Cree campaign changed things transnationally, for social, environmental, and indigenous rights activists, and in corporate boardrooms and law firms.

Shortly after the decision cancelling the Great Whale River Project, the referendum campaign on whether Quebec should separate from Canada went into high gear, and the Cree were drawn into it. They argued that they were not objects that could be incorporated into an independent Quebec against their will, that they were a nation with indigenous rights. They also argued that their lands would not necessarily become part of an independent Quebec, should Quebecers separate from Canada (GCC, 1998). The Cree used some of the techniques they had learned in the Great Whale River campaign during the referendum debates. They commissioned a public opinion poll that showed the percentage of Quebecers supporting separation was significantly lower if a separate Quebec would not include the northern Cree and Inuit lands. Some Cree leaders were told that this survey was one of the factors that influenced the federal government to argue more publicly against separation. When the referendum to separate was defeated by the narrowest of margins, the Cree leadership thought that its campaign had played a role in that outcome.

Trying to Build a New Relationship, Again

Following this intense five years of political action, Cree and Quebec slowly sought to rebuild relations. For the Cree it became increasingly urgent during the later 1990s that the overexploitation of forests and wildlife by industry and sport hunters be dealt with. Commercial cutting of forests and sport hunting were both increasing, despite Cree attempts over many years to raise concerns and despite provisions of the JBNQA.

Under the JBNQA, forestry development was to be reviewed through Cree input to Quebec government forestry management plans. In practice, Cree input has not been sought at critical stages of the planning, and discussions that have been held have not resulted in any significant modification to forestry practices or plans. Consistent with Quebec's denials that forestry clear-cutting has a significant impact on the Cree, it permitted forestry companies to cut without regard to the Cree hunting territory system. The scale of this exploitation now threatens some Cree hunting territories as effective hunting and conservation units. Over 40 per cent of several hunting territories have already been cut, and the cut on one is already 80 per cent of the commercially forested land (Feit and Beaulieu, 2001). The rapid development of logging and significant increases in non-Cree hunting directly threaten the Cree use of lands and the fabric of Cree society and economy. Nevertheless, Cree hunters are convinced that if they have a say in how the forests are cut and at what pace, timber harvesting could be compatible with forest and wildlife regeneration and conservation.

Cree also wanted greater economic participation in forestry activities. Few Cree worked for the major companies, and those who did were in unskilled jobs. The Cree set up logging and sawmill operations to meet some of their economic development needs, but they were allocated limited forest resources and were kept to a very small scale by Quebec.

In the late 1990s Hydro-Québec began talking to Cree communities about building a smaller hydroelectric diversion to the south of the La Grande River complex, which would divert the water from more rivers through dams on the La Grande. These discussions, and some preparatory work, extended over several years. However, in 2001 Waskaganish, the Cree community at the mouth of the Rupert River, told Hydro-Québec that it would not agree to a diversion of the river. Within a few weeks the government of Quebec proposed new negotiations about Cree and Quebec relations. Only weeks later an agreement in principle was completed, and Cree negotiators and regional leaders took it back to the communities to explain it, to consult the people, and to raise support for it.

When the agreement was made public, it surprised many Cree and their supporters in the environmental community, because the Cree negotiators proposed to allow new dams that would divert additional rivers into the existing La Grande hydroelectric dams. But Quebec had made important concessions, too, agreeing not to build the much larger Nottaway-Broadback-Rupert project, which could have flooded up to 20 times the area that the approved diversion would flood.

The proposed agreement involved important concessions by both sides. Forestry practices in the region would be modified, under the supervision of a joint government-Cree committee, so that logging would be planned in relation to Cree hunting territories, and limits were established for how much land could be logged on a territory before there was adequate regeneration.

In addition, the Cree would be guaranteed funds needed for economic and social development. This was of vital concern, as JBNQA provisions for programs had been largely ignored by governments. This time the Cree undertook to do it themselves and Quebec guaranteed annual block funding. Funding would come throughout the 50-year term of the agreement through payments from royalties and incomes collected by government from development of natural resources in the region, with a minimum amount

guaranteed and increased payments if resource exploitation exceeded certain levels. The Cree also agreed to withdraw the numerous lawsuits that were pending over forestry, other development activities, and unfulfilled JBNQA undertakings. The Quebec government agreed that its relationship with the Cree would henceforth be on a nation-to-nation basis, a principle that had previously been refused.

The Cree negotiators believed the agreement met needs that previously they had been unable to address. In their view, the main challenge they faced was to balance protecting the land with creating the social and economic conditions for healthy, viable communities for those who were not full-time hunters. This would require jobs and new Cree businesses. The agreement would help to achieve these goals.

In the Cree communities people faced one of the most difficult decisions they ever had to make. On one hand, Cree have participated in commercial trade and market relations for 350 years. They have repeatedly been able to create a balance between their ties and obligations to the land and their production of commodities and wage labour for commercial trade. For centuries this trade has allowed them to secure from external markets the goods and services they need to build more viable communities and lives. Yet, the failure of social and economic development programs in recent decades was clearly taking a high toll on community health, sanitation, housing, and the ability of village-based Cree to have productive and meaningful lives. The whole history of marginalizing indigenous people in Canada on reserve lands, with limited ownership of natural resources on their traditional lands, has condemned them to communities ridden with severe economic, health, and social limitations. This agreement promised new resources and means for trying to meet these challenges.

Nevertheless, many Cree did not support permitting more dams, nor were they sure the right balance had been struck between economic development resources and protecting the land.

BOX 7.2

Grand Chief Ted Moses

On the 7th of February [2002], Premier Landry and I signed a nation-to-nation agreement establishing a New Relationship between the Crees and Québec. . . .

It is the recognition of our nationhood that has made this agreement possible; and it is this principle of nationhood that in a very pragmatic way creates the common ground for our partnership with Québec. . . .

Ultimately . . . the fundamental concerns of Aboriginal peoples in Québec are reflected by the concerns of Québec society. . . .

I told Premier Landry that we were not opposed to development. We want to be included in a way which will be respectful of our nationhood and our right to maintain our own way of life. . . .

Why has this pragmatic approach not been taken before? I can only say that for some people we are still viewed as strangers, and the idea persists that the benefits from any revenue that we earn will somehow mysteriously disappear from the economy and from Québec. But this is nonsense.

Our agreement with Québec establishes a partnership based on the mutual recognition of rights. Everyone in Québec has heightened sensitivity on the issue of rights. . . .

We want to determine the pace of our own development. We want to choose for ourselves what is best for our communities and our people. . . .

We know, however, that we cannot make our choices without appreciating the interests and concerns of Québec society. We have far too many common interests to be able to do that, and we live, after all, on the same land. . . .

We Crees still attach great reverence to the land. We continue to hunt, fish, and trap, and none of this will really change. . . .

[The agreement] is a Québec-Cree production. Québec society and the Cree Nation are the winners.

—'La société québécoise et les Autochtones', Notes for a statement by Grand Chief Dr Ted Moses, Grand Council of the Crees (Eeyou Istchee), on 26 March 2002[6]

There were also concerns that by accepting money tied to new developments, they could weaken their resolve, and their public support, in future negotiations with governments over projects they might oppose. There was some feeling that the Cree should seek to have good working relationships with governments, but that they should also be careful not to endanger their autonomy. In addition, the speed with which the draft agreement had been reached, without prior consultation, was a concern.

There were, and are, many questions about the agreement, and many Cree viewpoints on it. In early 2002, 55 per cent of the voters turned out for the referendum, and 70 per cent voted in favour of the agreement. Their votes expressed diverse thinking: outright support, a desire to build a new relationship with 'whitemen' based more on mutual respect and reciprocity, and a desire for the Cree to stay united. When elections were held for leadership of the GCC later in 2002, those who most strongly supported the agreement were re-elected by the slimmest of margins. One gets the sense that most Cree want to try to make the relationship with non-Natives work better, using this new agreement, but they remain uncomfortable about what will happen. They have taken a risk in the hope that something better for themselves, the government, and the land can be created.

Having signed the agreement, the Cree still face formidable challenges, and many Cree are well aware of them. The new financial resources and access to development opportunities are vitally needed, but turning cash and opportunities into local or regional development that benefits Cree has not proved any easier for Cree than for other First Nations. It is clear that standard development planning does not work. Very few Cree presently work for regional companies and innovative measures will be needed. One challenge is how to make regional corporate employers responsive to the scale of Cree employment needs, while adapting job requirements to the social and cultural responsibilities and values of Cree workers who live in reciprocity-based small communities. Employees in Cree administrative positions typically have flexible working hours to meet family and community obligations, community-wide holiday breaks for hunting seasons, and non-authoritarian working relationships. Many Cree seek similar opportunities wherever they work. Another problem is how to create viable enterprises in the communities that are controlled locally. It is also a challenge to develop new Cree enterprises that use natural resources in ways that maximize their compatibility with the protection of the land, and that maintain the relatively egalitarian fabric of Cree community social life, while remaining economically viable.

Another challenge is that the new agreement does not resolve the limitations of the colonial dispossession of indigenous peoples. A consequence of whiteman development is that Cree control and have access to so few of the natural resources of the region. As a result many will benefit only as employees of resource development corporations, and corporate development in northern Canada has a history of boom and bust. Furthermore, the federal government has not done anything to meet its obligations. Clearly, the agreement does not provide solutions for these problems, but it provides the Cree with new means to try to find more effective answers.

Part of the long-term success or failure of this agreement will depend on the government of Quebec. Premier Bernard Landry hinted that he was aware that the failure of Quebec to deal justly with the indigenous nations within its borders was a blemish on Quebec separatists' claims to national sovereignty. The Quebec government has also recognized that the Cree might again stop the new development plans, as they had done 10 years earlier, and it clearly wanted to avoid this with the new hydroelectric diversions. But it must also have wanted to create the conditions in which it would avoid such crises arising again. This could be done by pursuing the 'new relationship' with the Cree in a way that gives them an effective voice in future decisions about development. Alternatively, the government could try to tie the communities so closely to the income from new developments that they could not say 'no' to development again. The agreement is not clear on what say Cree will have in future developments, nor is it clear at this point if the recent election of a provincial Liberal government led by Jean Charest will alter Quebec-Native relations in any way.

The outcomes will also depend in part on government-corporate relationships. It is likely that the government wanted to demonstrate to the investment community that it could 'manage' the conflict with the Cree, making some concessions but assuring investors that resource developments could go ahead smoothly in the future. If these compromises continue, it would mean that some development might go ahead on a smaller scale, or more slowly, and that Cree would have some say in how they went ahead, as in the case of forestry under the new agreement. If the government is willing to implement the forestry provisions and show companies that compromises to avoid conflicts can create a better investment climate, then the forestry experience may serve as an example for companies to agree to development projects in which Cree have a say. But if corporations and the government still seek simply to maximize all resource developments, then they will surely come into irreconcilable conflicts with Cree hunters and communities. If this is the government strategy, now or in the future, then the Cree willingness to initiate new campaigns against development, at considerable social and economic cost, will again be required.

Conclusions: Continuing Autonomy, Seeking Reciprocity

Over the last three decades, the autonomy of Cree communities has clearly been enhanced by strengthening the hunting economy and society, by their greater control of regional government, services, and resources, and by their ability to take political, legal, and economic initiatives. The ability to sustain their autonomy, and to enhance that autonomy in the face of repeated government attempts to erode and manage Cree power and rights, is also clear. The new agreement will challenge both the government and the Cree.

The Cree continue to face major threats. For one, large-scale resource exploitation projects are continuing on Cree lands. The regulation of resource development has been addressed with new commitments in the forestry provisions of the recent agreement, but they need to be fully implemented, and other resource developments remain major threats to the revitalized hunting sector. Hunting remains central to the viable identities and reciprocal social relationships that bind the people together in relatively egalitarian diversity and give them their unique character. Alternatively, the Cree ability to maintain broad consensus on how to achieve both protection of the land and community-based development will need to continue to be created as the agreement is implemented and as more Cree become involved in the regional economy.

The Cree have repeatedly sought and hoped for a new relationship with other Canadians and Quebecers, based on mutual respect, on reciprocal and responsible sharing of land, resources, and wealth, and on a process of enhancing the mutual power to make aspirations come true. They have sought to achieve this while retaining considerable personal and collective autonomy. In the most recent agreement they have again committed themselves to renewing the quest for relationships with whiteman governments and developers based on reciprocity.

Acknowledgements

This chapter draws on the work of many Cree people and scholars from whom I have drawn insights, including: Philip Awashish, Mario Blaser, Matthew Coon Come, Brian Craik, Paul Dixon, Sam Gull Sr, Peter Hutchins, Ted Moses, Alan Penn, and Colin Scott. I also want to acknowledge financial support from: the Social Sciences and Humanities Research Council, and the Arts Research Board of McMaster University.

Notes

1. The term 'hunter' includes both men and women hunters and their spouses. Women are typically active in fishing and small-game hunting, but some engage in all types of hunting. Some also say that they anticipate where game may be caught and assist their husbands with this knowledge. How animals are butchered, prepared, distributed, and consumed can also affect the hunt. So post-harvest tasks that are typically, but not exclusively, done by women are an integral part of the hunting process.

2. In Cree the word for God does not specify gender. But Cree, who are mostly Christians, generally use the masculine pronoun when speaking English. I follow their usage when paraphrasing their statements.

3. The negotiations were conducted jointly with the Inuit of Quebec, but this discussion only addresses aspects relevant to the Cree.

4. As it turned out, later changes were agreed to on several occasions, including an agreement to relocate the dam that had been moved and to build it on its original site. The move was requested by Hydro-Québec because construction at the new site proved to be technically impossible. The developers also

claimed that it was nearly impossible to protect the village on Fort George Island from erosion by the greater flow in the river, and they funded the construction of a new site on the shore of the river at Chisasibi, which the Cree agreed to.

5. *Mario Lord et al. v. The Attorney General of Quebec et al. and Domtar Inc. et al.*, Superior Court, District of Montreal, No. 500–05–043203–981.

6. www.gcc.ca/news/moses_speech5_151812002.htm

References and Recommended Readings

Blaser, Mario, Harvey Feit, and Glenn McCrae, eds. Forthcoming. *In the Way of Development: Indigenous Peoples, Life Projects and Globalization*. London and Ottawa: Zed Books.

Craik, Brian. Forthcoming. 'The Importance of Working Together: Exclusions, Conflicts and Participation in James Bay Quebec', in Blaser et al. (forthcoming).

Cree-Naskapi Commission. 1986. *1986 Report of the Cree-Naskapi Commission*. Ottawa: Cree-Naskapi Commission.

Diamond, Billy. 1977. *Highlights Leading to the James Bay and Northern Quebec Agreement*. Val d'Or, Que.: Grand Council of the Crees.

———. 1990. 'Villages of the Damned: The James Bay Agreement Leaves a Trail of Broken Promises', *Arctic Circle* (Nov.–Dec.): 24–34. An invaluable account of the JBNQA by the foremost Cree leader of the period, and a critique of its implementation.

Dumont, James A. 1998. 'Environmental Law and Environmental Lawyers—Problems or Solutions for Native Peoples?', paper presented at the 'In the Way of Development' Conference, McMaster University.

Feit, Harvey A. 1985. 'Hydroelectric Development', in Noel Dyck, ed., *Indigenous Peoples and the Nation-State: Fourth World Politics in Canada, Australia and Norway*. Social and Economic Papers No. 14. St John's: Memorial University of Newfoundland, ISER Books.

———. 1989. 'James Bay Cree Self-Governance and Land Management', in Edwin N. Wilmsen, ed., *We Are Here: Politics of Aboriginal Land Tenure*. Berkeley: University of California Press. A review and assessment of relations between the Cree and Quebec governments in the decade following the JBNQA.

———. 1991. 'Gifts of the Land: Hunting Territories, Guaranteed Incomes and the Construction of Social Relations in James Bay Cree Society', *Senri Ethnological Studies* 30: 223–68.

Francis, Daniel, and Toby Morantz. 1983. *Partners in Fur: A History of the Fur Trade in Eastern James Bay, 1600–1870*. Montreal and Kingston: McGill-Queen's University Press. The first comprehensive history of the James Bay Cree in the period up to the twentieth century. An informative and readable account that challenges widely held assumptions.

Grand Council of the Crees. 1998. *Never Without Consent: James Bay Crees' Stand Against Forcible Inclusion into an Independent Quebec*. Toronto: ECW Press.

Hallowell, A. Irving. 1955. *Culture and Experience*. Philadelphia: University of Pennsylvania Press.

McCrae, Glenn. Forthcoming. 'Grassroots Transnationalism and Life Projects of Vermonters in the Great Whale Campaign', in Blaser et al. (forthcoming).

McCutcheon, Sean. 1991. *Electric Rivers: The Story of the James Bay Project*. Montreal: Black Rose Books. An account of the James Bay hydroelectric project and its initial environmental and social impacts by an independent science writer.

Morantz, Toby. 2002. *The White Man's Gonna Getcha: The Colonial Challenge to the Crees in Quebec*. Montreal and Kingston: McGill-Queen's University Press. A history of the James Bay Cree in the twentieth century and how they responded to Canadian and Quebec colonialism.

Niezen, Ronald. 1998. *Defending the Land: Sovereignty and Forest Life in James Bay*. Boston: Allyn and Bacon. A very readable account of the changes and continuities in Cree society and culture from the 1970s to the 1990s.

Preston, Richard J. 2002. *Cree Narrative: Expressing the Personal Meanings of Events*, 2nd edn. Montreal and Kingston: McGill-Queen's University Press. An extensive exploration of core Cree symbolic meanings and knowledge as revealed through the analysis of myths, songs, stories, and conjuring performances.

Richardson, Boyce. 1979. *Strangers Devour the Land*. Vancouver: Douglas & McIntyre. A richly personalized account, by a skilled journalist, of Cree hunting and the court case against the hydroelectric project.

Salisbury, Richard F. 1986. *A Homeland for the Cree: Regional Development in James Bay, 1971–1981*. Montreal and Kingston: McGill-Queen's University Press. A major review and synthesis of the organizational and economic changes in Cree society in the initial years following the signing of the JBNQA.

Scott, Colin H. 1989. 'Ideology of Reciprocity between the James Bay Cree and the Whiteman State', in Peter Skalnik, ed., *Outwitting the State*. New Brunswick, NJ: Transaction Books.

————, ed. 2001. *Aboriginal Autonomy and Development in Northern Quebec and Labrador*. Vancouver: University of British Columbia Press. The most up-to-date collection of papers reviewing the relations of Cree and neighbouring indigenous societies with the nation-state and world markets in changing times.

Tanner, Adrian. 1979. *Bringing Home Animals: Religious Ideology and Mode of Production of the Mistassini Cree Hunters*. Social and Economic Studies No. 23. St John's: Memorial University of Newfoundland, ISER Books. A detailed ethnography of Cree hunting, emphasizing the ritualization of productive activities and the symbolic organization of the social life of hunters.

Recommended Web Sites

Grand Council of the Crees (Eeyou Istchee): www.gcc.ca
    The James Bay Cree political organization, a source of much current information.

Arctic Circle, on the James Bay Cree: www.arcticcircle.uconn.edu/history/culture/cree/
    A student-oriented site at the University of Connecticut with background articles and connections.

James Bay Cree Culture: www.creeculture.ca
    A site on Cree language, culture, and arts.

Cree School Board: www.cscree.qc.ca.csb
    Education-related information.

CHAPTER 8

The Atikamekw:
Reflections on Their Changing World

SYLVIE POIRIER

Introduction

The Atikamekw live in the boreal forest and rich watershed of the upper St-Maurice River of north-central Quebec (see Map 8.1). In traditional times, these waterways facilitated numerous contacts and exchanges with neighbouring groups. These include the Innu of Lac St-Jean to the east, the James Bay Cree to the north (mostly Waswanipi and Mistassini), and the Algonkins to the west. All these groups are Northern Algonquians, and they share strong linguistic, social, cultural, and territorial affiliations. Their alliance and exchange networks may, however, have extended far beyond these groups, including some Ojibwa bands. In contrast to their neighbours, who are well known in the literature through the writings and records left by missionaries and traders as well as through anthropological studies, there are very few such records of or studies on the Atikamekw. Today, they number about 5,000 people, living in the three communities of Wemotaci, Manawan, and Opitciwan, manifestations of their colonial history.

In this chapter, I present some facets of my understanding, as an anthropologist, of the Atikamekw world. In the face of many challenges that confront them, the Atikamekw are involved in a dynamic redefinition of their culture and its institutions. Their intimate and complex relationship with the land forms a focal point for much of their struggle. They have experienced decades of colonial denigration and dispossession in an unequal struggle. Nevertheless, they persist and practise what some would call the art of resistance, a process I am profoundly moved by. I am particularly interested in the methods they creatively employ to preserve and pass on their ways and their knowledge, methods that involve reinterpreting their culture and devising new initiatives and strategies in the hope of taking their rightful place in today's world.

A discussion of the Atikamekw people necessarily involves a consideration of the forest and their intimate relationships with it, a forest that for the last hundred years has been coveted and transformed by loggers and the builders of dams, with little consideration for the 'original people', *Nehirowisiw*. As a result, the contemporary reality of the Atikamekw cannot be grasped without an understanding of their prolonged contact with the *Ka Wapisitcik*, literally, 'the whites'. That reality provides the context for the persistence and transformation of their language,[1] their knowledge, and their practices as semi-nomadic hunters and gatherers, and of their specific way of engaging with the land (*aski*) and with the forest (*notcimik*), as a social space containing networks of living places. What I wish to describe here are some of the ways in which the Atikamekw are rethinking their new realities in relation with the dominant society and some of the strategies they are developing to accommodate to these new realities.

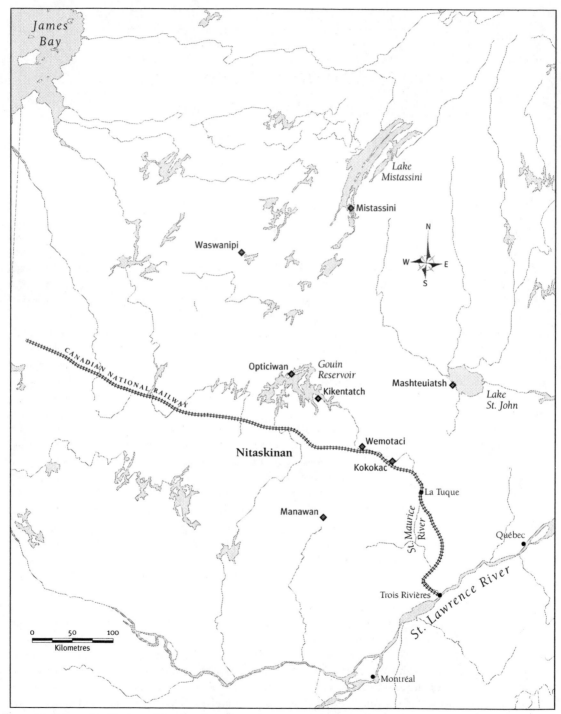

MAP 8.1. Atikamekw Territory (*Nitaskinan*) and Contemporary Communities

Doing Fieldwork

Before I began doing research with the Atikamekw in the early nineties, I underwent an enriching initiatory journey in the Australian Western Desert with the Kukatja and neighbouring groups. My research and long-standing relationship with these Australian Aborigines (since 1980) had introduced me to many of the realities of contemporary hunters and gatherers and of Fourth World peoples (colonized indigenous peoples within contemporary states). The experience and knowledge I gained as an individual and as an ethnographer with my Kukatja friends, and the comparative basis it has given me, were invaluable when I decided to pursue my anthropological research itinerary with the Atikamekw. Although the path from the Australian Western Desert to the Canadian boreal forest is a long one, the social worlds of the Kukatja and the Atikamekw nonetheless share much in common. For example, they both come from a hunting and gathering tradition that entails a nomadic or semi-nomadic (in the case of the Atikamekw) way of life. Flexible and dynamic social and territorial networks inform their respective social orders and identities, each in their own ways. Both value an intimate and reciprocal relationship with the land and with non-human agencies, including animals, plants, spirits, or places. Both come from an oral tradition, where their knowledge and their history are best expressed and passed down through the idiom of stories.

As for their respective colonial encounters, colonial histories, and current experiences as indigenous peoples in modern liberal nation-states, there are both similarities and differences. For both, the gradual yet irreversible process of settling in confined communities started in the 1950s, with all the accompanying bewilderment and sense of loss felt at the time and during the following decades. For both, that process also gave rise to economic dependence on the state. However, then as now, both groups have continued to have access, at least to some degree, to their ancestral territories, giving them a sense of continuity as well as a medium through which they can express and hand down their knowledge, values, and memories. For both, in spite of two decades of a residential school regime, the local languages are still very much alive.

By the turn of the twentieth century the Atikamekw had converted to Christianity and Catholic beliefs and practices became an intrinsic dimension of their culture. Their contact with travelling missionaries—people who would only stay a few days during the summer at Atikamekw gathering places—had been sporadic until the end of the nineteenth century. Nevertheless, the Atikamekw were sensitive and to some extent receptive to their messages, liking in particular the practice of prayer. They were comfortable integrating elements of Christian doctrine, practices, and prayer within their own indigenous religious beliefs. From the end of the nineteenth century Oblate missionaries stayed permanently with them in the newly established reserves, even though the Atikamekw themselves would only gather there during the summer. The influence and 'power' of the missionaries increased over the following decades. There, as elsewhere, they strongly forbade and denigrated all traditional ritual because it was identified with the devil. They also forbade polygamy. According to Atikamekw oral tradition, in the 1890s, the last man living in a polygamous relationship engaged in open confrontations with the priest.

By the 1950s the Atikamekw not only had converted to Catholicism, but it became an intrinsic part of their identity and culture. Some of them, however, continued to practise hunting rituals while on their territories, when they were a long way from the missionary. The Atikamekw, like the Innu, have a particular affection for Sainte-Anne. In today's context, Elders who have grown up in a solely Atikamekw Catholic tradition sometimes look with suspicion on the renewal rituals (sweat lodge, drumming, first-step ceremonies, etc.) favoured by many of the younger people who have abandoned Catholicism.

The Kukatja, in contrast, strongly resisted missionary attempts to convert them. Very few identify themselves as Christians and their cosmology and ritual life still follow their Ancestral Law (commonly known as the 'Dreaming'). To some extent, the same is true of their attitude towards political structures imposed from the outside. While the Atikamekw seem to have readily adopted the band council system, as stipulated under the Indian Act, the Kukatja still refuse to adopt a political structure (the Aboriginal community councils implemented by the Australian government in the 1970s) that runs counter to their own decision-making processes. Since the late 1970s, following a major change in Canadian policies towards indigenous people, the Atikamekw Nation has been negotiating with the federal and provincial governments towards a comprehensive land claim. A similar possibility was presented to the Kukatja and neighbouring groups only in 1993 with the implementation of the Native Title Act by the Australian government.

I first encountered the Atikamekw in the early 1990s. In 1992, while a post-doctoral fellow at the University of Montreal, I took a small contract with the Atikamekw and Montagnais Council.[2] At the time, there was a dispute between some Atikamekw families who had built permanent camps on their ancestral lands and a local town council over municipal taxes for resort leases. The town council wanted these Atikamekw families to pay annual taxes just like the few Euro-Canadians families who had resort leases and cottages along the river. From the perspective of the Quebec government and the town council, these Atikamekw were outside the law unless they agreed to pay taxes. According to the government, the only area where the Atikamekw are allowed to build permanent camps on public Crown lands is within the beaver reserve, an area reserved exclusively for Atikamekw trapping and hunting (see below). As for the Atikamekw, they argued that on the basis of the families' historical and customary affiliation with that particular territory, they should be treated differently from the vacationers.

In addition to these permanent camps, a number of temporary campsites in the same area were being used by members of related families. The mere presence of 'Indians' was a great irritation, not only to the authorities but also to the cottage owners and sport hunters.

My task was to demonstrate the historical presence of these Atikamekw families in the area, at least since the middle of the nineteenth century. Alongside a number of written (and official) records, the oral testimony and memory of Elders, men and women, were central to the research. I met with Elders at their house in La Tuque (the neighbouring Euro-Canadian town), in Wemotaci, or at their camps. With the help of an Atikamekw research assistant who introduced me to them and acted as interpreter, I drew up genealogical charts and recorded the oral life histories of these families. The genealogies covered at least six generations (from the great-grandparents of today's Elders to their own grandchildren) and were most helpful in showing the matrimonial alliances between the families.

It turned out that all of the families still frequenting the disputed area were related to the band formerly connected to Kokokac. The Hudson's Bay Company had operated a trading post at Kokokac from 1863 to 1911. In 1894, following an official request by the Atikamekw chiefs, an area of 388 acres was surveyed and Kokokac officially became reserved land. However, in 1931, Kokokac was flooded following construction of the Rapide Blanc dam, at a time when indigenous land rights were not recognized and there was no possibility of land claims; no compensation was received. The families affected by the flooding, who had used Kokokac as a summer gathering site and whose ancestral affiliations and hunting territories lay in the vicinity, nonetheless continued to occupy the area, as do their descendants to this day. According to official records, the band of Kokokac no longer exists; its members had been transferred to the Wemotaci band. After our report was completed (Poirier, 1992), the town council (following a recommendation by the

FIGURE 8.1. Once a year the Atikamekw Elders of the three communities gather for a few days to discuss and exchange views on social and political issues. (Courtesy of the Conseil de la Nation Atikamekw)

Quebec Ministry of Municipal Affairs) agreed to the Atikamekw demands. No taxes on their permanent camps have since been requested. However, the Atikamekw refusal to pay taxes was motivated more by politics than economics (the tax bill was rather low). For the Atikamekw Nation, it was a small yet significant victory within their broader political agenda of achieving recognition of their land rights.

During the research I was introduced not only to the struggle of the Atikamekw for their land rights, but also to their recent history and their life as contemporary hunters and gatherers. Since then, I have returned many times to the Atikamekw lands, visiting their communities and conducting research on customary practices, local knowledge, and oral traditions in their changing contemporary expressions. Over the years, my work and relationship with them have

evolved into an exchange: whatever I produce in terms of anthropological knowledge may be used by their leaders as anthropological proof of their enduring and ever-changing relationship with the land and the forest. I view my role and my responsibility as an anthropologist as a mediator and translator between worlds (a cultural broker). I hope that my role may eventually contribute to the empowerment of indigenous peoples. Escobar (1997: 510) has aptly identified such a position as 'a new ethics of anthropological knowledge as political practice'. As an anthropologist, I believe that we have to embrace this role if we are to continue to have a dialogue with indigenous peoples. As ethnographers, we have to continue to explore and take seriously the manifold forms and expressions of cultural differences if we are to meet our responsibilities as 'translators between worlds'.

Atikamekw Colonial History

Due to a lack of written reports, very little is known of Atikamekw early contact history. A first and brief mention of the 'Attikamègues', a name given to them by the Algonkins, is found in the *Jesuit Relations* of 1636, written by Father Le Jeune (Gélinas, 2000: 32). It was reported that a few of these hunters who lived in the north basin of the Saint-Maurice River had travelled to the trading post of Trois-Rivières, founded in 1634, to trade their furs. There is no doubt that like their Cree, Innu, and Algonkin neighbours, the Atikamekw had been engaged in the fur trade for some time. In the absence of trading posts in their own territory, however, they travelled to those of the Lac St-Jean and James Bay areas and, after 1634, to the one established at Trois-Rivières. During the last quarter of the seventeenth century, Atikamekw families suffered significant losses due to smallpox epidemics and to raids by the Iroquois, who ventured into their territory in search of furs. According to oral tradition, some families decided to travel further north into Cree territory for a few decades before coming back to their own lands. Between 1775 and 1821, a few short-lived trading posts were established in Atikamekw territory, mostly by the North West Company. In 1821, the HBC established a trading post at Wemotaci (not far from the present-day community), and two others, at Kikentatch and Kokokac, were established in the following decades. Atikamekw families already used these places as summer gathering camps. Well into the 1960s, the Atikamekw continued to be involved in trapping; to a great extent it guaranteed their autonomy and pride as hunters. Today, while hunting, fishing, trapping, and gathering remain intrinsic dimensions of their experience and of their relationship with the forest, no one earns a living as a trapper.

With traders generally came missionaries. In 1651, Father Buteux, a Jesuit, was the first to venture into Atikamekw territory. During his three months of perilous travels, he met with three Atikamekw 'assemblées'. On a subsequent visit, a few years later, he was killed in an Iroquois raid. During the eighteenth century there seem not to have been any missionaries in Atikamekw territory, which does not, however, mean that they were not influenced by Christian ritual and belief. From 1837 onward, priests from Trois-Rivières visited Kikentatch and Wemotaci annually in July, when Atikamekw families were gathered there. By the turn of the twentieth century the Oblates maintained a permanent presence in the newly established Atikamekw 'reserves'. Catholicism became an intrinsic dimension of Atikamekw culture; they appropriated Catholic cosmology, ceremonies, and praying practices. Some people continued, however, to perform traditional hunting ritual and ceremonies such as the first-steps ceremony (*orowitowasowin*), the sweat lodge (*marotsowin*), and drum beating, all of which they practised on a sporadic basis while out on their territories and unbeknownst to the missionaries.

In the 1850s, when the first timber concessions were granted to a logging company, the Atikamekw were confronted with what was to become a major activity on their land. Logging has grown significantly since then, and with the introduction of heavy equipment in the 1970s the forest industry has transformed the Atikamekw forest-scape on a larger and different scale than any of the area's forest fires had ever done. Significantly, one of the Atikamekw words for Euro-Canadian people (particularly the Québécois) is *emitcikocic*, 'the ones who use wood'; some Atikamekw like to translate the word as 'the wood eaters'.

Their involvement with the forestry industry has evolved over the decades. Until the 1970s, a fair number of Atikamekw men worked seasonally as lumberjacks. Today, faced with the increasing presence of forestry activities, the Atikamekw have developed a bold strategy. They not only want to participate in the decision-making processes concerning the forest, but they also want to share the economic benefits. To achieve these ends, two communities have started joint ventures with forestry companies operating in the area. Opitciwan has been operating a small sawmill for several years now, and Wemotaci is in the process of building one. In spite of these initiatives, it is still too early to speak of an indigenous forestry industry since the Quebec government and forestry companies still control the industry. One can sense mixed feelings and growing concerns among the Atikamekw regarding forestry activities.

In 1881, concerned by the growing presence of Euro-Canadian people and interests on their land, the council of chiefs, *Kice Okimaw*, of the then four Atikamekw bands of Wemotaci, Manawan, Kokokac, and Kikentatch, petitioned the federal government to set aside lands for them. Four communities ('reserves') were surveyed shortly thereafter. The sites of Kikentatch and Kokokac have since been flooded by the construction of the La Loutre hydroelectric dam in 1918 (which created the vast Gouin reservoir) and the Rapide Blanc dam in 1930. The families who frequented Kikentatch asked to be relocated at Opitciwan; those from Kokokac, as we have seen, officially merged with the Wemotaci band while maintaining their activities and presence in the Kokokac area.

It must be stressed, however, that the Atikamekw did not settle in communities right away. Until the 1950s, and for some families well into the 1960s, the communities were simply places where they established their summer camps for a few weeks. There, the children would attend summer school while their parents fulfilled their commitments as Catholics. By the end of the summer they would start travelling back to their territories, their places of belonging, their 'homes'. As a general rule, it was only in the 1970s that Atikamekw really began living on a permanent basis on the 'reserves', and even then many of the adult men went back to their territories during the winter months, often accompanied by their wives. However, that practice declined significantly in the following decades.

The first decades of the twentieth century brought about other changes, including construc-

tion of a railroad through Atikamekw territory. While the railroad meant an increase of Euro-Canadian workers and visitors, it also made it easier for Atikamekw to travel to trading and supply posts. In spite of an increased infringement of *Ka Wapisitcik* activities on their land, the Atikamekw adapted fairly well to the changes while maintaining their autonomy and self-determination as semi-nomadic hunters. Up until the 1970s, many of the men worked seasonally as lumberjacks or guides for the (mostly) American sport hunters and fishermen who came to the private clubs. These activities gave them some income but did not significantly infringe on their lives as hunters. They maintained their camp lives and trapping activities, as well as their responsibilities towards their ancestral territories. The flexibility that characterizes the world of hunters—an openness to change that allows them to reassess constantly the resources and potentialities of the land and of their social environment and to act accordingly—served them well.

Government Policies of Assimilation

The Canadian policies of assimilation of indigenous people that were implemented more systematically from the 1950s to the 1970s marked a turning point in the world of the Atikamekw. The impacts of those policies, wherein Natives were pressured to move into permanent settlements (reserves) to 'take advantage' of educational and health services, for instance, are still felt. One of these policies, the off-reserve residential schools, created a breach in the local processes of handing down knowledge, skills, and practices to younger generations. Several men and women, now in their forties and fifties, shared with me their memories of childhood, when they were taken away from the security and warmth of camp life to faraway and foreign places. One of them recalled the sadness and loneliness he felt around Christmastime when his parents would send him a two-dollar bill that smelled of the reassuring scents of the forest and of camp life, of the wood stove and the fir ground cover. He kept it secretly and affectionately under his pillow. Another recalled the awkwardness he felt when he returned to live with his parents during the summer holidays. He would try to assist his father in making wooden snowshoe frames, unable to understand the technical Atikamekw terms of his father. Paradoxically, the residential school generation is now the one involved in the reaffirmation and the revitalization of the Atikamekw ways, language, and traditional ritual practices. They are also the ones pushing for political change and land claims. It is the students of the residential schools who established a bilingual program in elementary schools. Only at this point in their lives—after many hardships and many painful experiences in the Euro-Canadian world—have they been able to establish a dialogue with their Elders, and now they are learning from these Elders.

In the early 1950s, at a time when the beaver population was declining dramatically to the point of jeopardizing the fur market, the Quebec government implemented beaver reserves over large areas of central and northern Quebec. The reserves were intended as a resource management strategy; the government believed the beaver population could recover by delimiting and securing areas of land where only Aboriginal people could hunt and trap. The Abitibi beaver reserve covered just over half the territories used by Atikamekw families, thus reducing significantly the territories where the Atikamekw were legally allowed to hunt and trap. At the time, the government also imposed a five-year ban on beaver trapping and even brought some beavers from elsewhere to allow the resource to regenerate. According to the Elders, these measures were not necessary.

According to the Atikamekw, the decline was the result of over-trapping by Euro-Canadians who did not have the necessary knowledge to ensure the reproduction of the species. As early as the 1930s, the Atikamekw, accompanied by Father Guinard, a missionary, had brought their

concerns about the abuses of Euro-Canadian trappers to the attention of Quebec Premier Louis-Alexandre Taschereau. Most Atikamekw, however, also explained this disappearance as a result of the beaver's decision. The following comment made in 1997 by an Elder of Manawan, who was a young man at the time, is revealing:

The Elders had told us. One day, the beaver will come back. He has dived into the water, but one day he will surface again. He stays underground, but we don't know where. And when they know that their number has increased, they will surface again. When they know that they are sufficiently numerous to give themselves as food. All the animals do that, even the moose. They disappear for a while, unwilling to give themselves as food, and then they come back.

In the late 1940s and 1950s, in the absence of the beaver and until he decided to 'surface' again, the Atikamekw trapped other species, such as marten, muskrat, mink, fox, lynx, otter, and a few others. While the focus of trapping has varied, throughout the same time period the moose has remained central to hunting activities.

Within the beaver reserve, trapping lots were granted to the heads of family groups, more or less respecting traditional territorial affiliations. The beaver reserve represented the first tangible gesture by the Quebec government to set limits on Atikamekw hunting (and living) territories. As a result, the Atikamekw were directly confronted, perhaps for the first time, with Western ways of mapping and drawing boundaries. Again, they adjusted to this new reality, evolving a synthesis between these new regulations and their own customary practices of sharing and handing down territories, including resource management practices and ethics. Those families whose ancestral territories lay outside the beaver reserve continued, whenever possible, to use them as before.

This brief overview of Atikamekw colonial history is meant to outline the main events and

---

BOX 8.1

Reserved Lands

The reserved lands of the Atikamekw communities of Wemotaci, Manawan, and Opitciwan occupy 7,410 acres, 1,970 acres, and 2,287 acres. These reduced spaces contrast sharply with the amount of territory that not so long ago they occupied as semi-nomadic hunters. Such spatial reduction has meant a rethinking of interpersonal and inter-group relationships and a transformation in gender and generational relationships. At the political level, as stipulated under the Indian Act, every three years each community elects a band council, that is, a chief and councillors. Until recently, the council was solely a male domain. This contrasts with traditionally egalitarian gender relationships and contradicts somehow the fact that *kokum*, the grandmother, to this day stands as a most respected, knowledgeable, and even authoritative figure. In the last five years, however, women have been increasingly present in local and 'national' political bodies and agendas, putting forward their concerns on community matters and on social healing, re-establishing a more egalitarian balance in the decision-making processes. Following the implementation of federal policies of self-determination towards First Nations, Atikamekw communities have gained increased autonomy in dealing with their own affairs, particularly on issues of health and social services, justice, and education. This leaves political and legal recognition of their rights and title on ancestral territories as their most important struggle.

---

policies that have shaped recent Atikamekw experiences and the forms that their resistance has taken. These events and policies have played a significant role in the transformation of their world. Their social order, their cultural consciousness and identity, and the ways in which they relate with the forest have all been affected.

Contemporary Social and Political Structures

The Atikamekw Nation, as a modern social and political entity, took shape gradually throughout the twentieth century as the semi-nomadic bands and families of this vast territory consolidated their alliances and united their forces in the face of the intruders. Over the last three decades and in their struggle for self-determination, the Atikamekw have created institutional structures and representative bodies that allow them to relate to and negotiate with the state and the dominant society in ways that they feel they can be heard. These

structures and bodies give them an opportunity to reaffirm their difference and the vitality of their dynamic tradition. From the 1970s onward, following on the Canadian government's policies of self-determination for indigenous people, the Atikamekw founded institutions that have enabled them to assert themselves as a distinct social, cultural, historical, and political entity. Among these are: Atikamekw Sipi, the Council of the Atikamekw Nation; Nehirowisiw Wasikahikan, the Atikamekw language institute; and Mamo Atoskewin, the Atikamekw trapper's association. Through these institutions, the Atikamekw are able to represent their interests vis-à-vis the dominant society.

Among themselves, however, at both the individual and collective levels, Atikamekw affiliation is community-based, as in Wemotaci Iriniwok (the people of Wemotaci), Manawan Iriniwok (the people of Manawan), and Opitciwan Iriniwok (the people of Opitciwan). Within each one of these community-based identities are a number of family groups, which some people today refer to as 'clans'. Each family group strongly identifies with its ancestral territory. The guardianships and responsibilities towards these territories are still being passed down according to Atikamekw customary practices, even for the territories that cannot be used anymore because of clear-cutting or other *Ka Wapisitcik* activities or regulations. An Elder expressed this in the following manner:

> We have to maintain our territories, always and irrespective of what happens. We have to do all what is in our power to maintain (our relationships to) those territories. . . . My territory that was my grandfather's and father's before me, even if today it is clear-cut, it will always be my territory. . . . One day the animals will come back. They always come back.

Gradually, over recent decades, the place where people camped in the summer has become their central living place year-round. For the Atikamekw, as for other First Nations, there is a direct correlation between the loss of territories, the loss of self-determination, and their confinement in 'reserves' and a significant increase in a variety of social problems. These include, in the last few years, a high rate of suicide among young people.

Even in the confines of the new communities, however, the Atikamekw have evolved a different sense of belonging, interacting, and moving about that still reflects some aspects of their semi-nomadic traditional ways and values. They have redefined their hunting and nomadic traditions to meet the requirements of today's world. Ancestral territories are now visited only on a sporadic basis. This does not, however, mean that their ties and sense of responsibility towards the land have diminished; territorial affiliations sometimes may be neglected, but they are never denied. The Atikamekw social order still values and recognizes each person's identification with the family territory inherited from their fathers and grandfathers. People still visit their territories, even if it is only on weekends, on holidays, or during cultural

weeks.[3] These visits are facilitated by motorized transport (outboard motor, four-wheel drive vehicle, and snowmobile). Over the years, some Atikamekw hunters have been fined or arrested and their hunting equipment has been confiscated for hunting outside the beaver reserve, such as within the limits of an outfitting camp that has been given exclusive rights to the area by the government. Far from being discouraged, more and more Atikamekw are now 'occupying' their family territories. They are making their presence known by establishing both temporary and permanent camps, in spite of the tensions it may create with the sport hunters and fishermen they encounter. These signs of their presence and activities in the forest represent for them the most tangible evidence of their rights and responsibilities towards their ancestral territories. The traditional identification of land with family groups still lies at the core of Atikamekw identity, social networks, and interpersonal relationships, and is an intrinsic part of their sense of responsibility towards the land. Even the territories that cannot be used anymore, for example, because of clear-cutting, are still identified with their traditional owners.

Atikamekw Land: Identity and Knowledge

In societies like that of the Atikamekw that value oral traditions, storytelling plays a paramount role in the process of individual socialization. It is also a means of sharing knowledge and skills. Through the telling of stories, including myths, life histories, personal experiences, and anecdotes, children learn the values and moral codes of the group. For the ethnographer, stories represent a privileged medium through which one can access a culture and the way a group of people understand their own history. This section is inspired mostly by stories told by elderly women and men of the three communities, as they recalled their lives in the first half of the twentieth century and well into the 1960s.[4]

These narratives refer to a time when the Atikamekw were still living independently on the land and the signs of *Ka Wapisitcik* presence were few. Through stories, these Elders share their experiences, knowledge, practices, and interactions, not so much on the land and in the forest, but with the land and within the forest, and with the trees, animals, and plants. As hunters, the Elders acquired the art of deciphering the various sounds, signs, and traces left by all living beings that share the land with them; it is a fundamental dimension of their intimate and knowledgeable relationship with their dwelt-in world. From their point of view, the decrease in recent decades in the various signs and traces left by the Atikamekw (the campsites, for example) and the increase in the signs and traces now left by the Euro-Canadians represent the most tangible indication of their dispossession. Interestingly, in their narratives, they never referred to themselves as Atikamekw. They used instead the word *Nehirowisiw*, that is, the first human inhabitants, which also means those who have an intimate and knowledgeable relationship with the land and the forest. It is precisely such a relationship that has made it possible for them to live autonomously on their territories. *Notcimik*, the Atikamekw word for 'forest', can be translated by 'where I come from'.

Ancestral Territories

The Atikamekw language distinguishes between an inclusive 'us' that encompasses the one who speaks (and other related persons) and the listener, and an exclusive 'us' that includes only the one who speaks (and other related persons) but excludes the listener. This distinction is evident in the different ways they designate their ancestral territory. In the context of land claims and negotiations with Euro-Canadian people, Atikamekw refer to their ancestral territory by using the word *nitaskinan*: the listeners are here excluded from territorial affiliation. When, on the other hand, they speak between themselves of their ancestral territory, they use the word *kitaskino*: the speakers and the listeners share then the territorial affiliation.

The territory of a multi-family group can be defined as a more or less bounded area delimited by permanent landmarks (rivers, lakes, or mountains). Overlapping between different territories was (and is) frequent. These rather large multi-family territories may in turn be divided into extended family hunting territories, which are sometimes called *nehirowisiw aski*, 'the land within which one can be autonomous'. From the Atikamekw point of view, territorial boundaries are permeable and flexible, something that can be reassessed according to needs, events, or the accessibility of resources. These areas of land, as areas of responsibility, are inherited, usually along the father's line, but again some flexibility is needed. For example, some people have inherited rights over their mother's father's territory, while others have inherited areas of land from their adoptive father. The Atikamekw rules of sharing, delimiting, and passing down territories—rules that are grounded and recognized solely through oral tradition—are flexible and dynamic, constantly adapting to circumstances, perhaps more so in today's context. But now as before, what is most important for the Atikamekw is that no territories be left alone without a traditional 'guardian' to look after them. The main guardian, the head of a family territory, who must be an accomplished hunter, is called *kanikaniwitc*, 'the one who walks in front' or 'the one who leads the way', referring to portaging. His main responsibilities are to ensure that the territory is well looked after, that local resource management practices are respected, and that every hunter within the extended family has his hunting and trapping area. If someone from outside the extended family wishes to use an area within the territory for a season, permission must be requested orally of the *kanikaniwitc*.

What is handed down is not so much a bounded area of land as a series of named places along travelling routes, as well as campsites and traplines. All of these are imbued with memories, stories, and traces from the ancestors (*kimocomnok*), those who lived there before, taking care of the land and leaving their mark on it. An Elder from Manawan expressed it in the following manner, 'When you give your territory to your son and your grandson . . . you give your *onehirowisiwin* (a way or a place for being autonomous). You don't give the territory itself but everything that lives and grows on the territory . . . so people can in turn live from it. My grandfather did not "give" his territory to anyone, he simply said, "This is where you will find whatever you need to feed yourselves and to live."' The importance of the territory in providing food is crucial. A way of life and a path to self-sufficiency, and thus to autonomy and pride, are also passed down with the territory. From the point of view of the Elders, the responsibility and commitment to one's territory make an individual a *nehirowisiw*.

Delimiting and Sharing Traplines

Extended family territories, within the larger multi-family domains, must in turn be distinguished from the traplines. Within each extended family territory are a number of traplines (*atoske meskano*) that are shared among the hunters of an extended family and reassessed every year according to Atikamekw resource management strategies and ethics. It is the responsibility of the main guardian to ensure that the hunting and trapping areas are shared among hunters. Each year, in August or early September, before the trapping season, hunters visit their territories—and the hunting and trapping areas they know best—to evaluate the state of the land and its resources, paying particular attention to the beaver population. Circling around their territory (*waskackan*), they identify the lakes and streams where there are families of beavers. At each place, they evaluate the number of beavers and know how many can be taken and how many should be left to ensure reproduction. Along the way—and Atikamekw insist that traplines are always circular—in order to mark the identified places but also to delimit trapping areas for the coming season, hunters make notches on the trees (*wasikahikan*). They may even make as many notches as the corresponding number of beavers they plan to trap

there. These notches—signs—represent a highly efficient system of communicating to other hunters that this place, and this colony of beavers, is already set aside for the coming season. In no way, according to Atikamekw customary rules, should these trapping spots be infringed upon. Once the trapping season is over, these seasonal boundaries are lifted and will be reassessed the following year. An Elder from Wemotaci described the marking of territory:

I have seen my father. He made a notch on a tree, and planted a branch in it, meaning that this is as far as he would go. The other hunter does the same thing; he comes to the limits of his trapping area and does a notch next to my father's. Like that, they both know their respective limits where their trapping territories meet, so they would not encroach on each other's territory. *It is not the territory itself that they were measuring, it is the streams and the lakes where they trapped that they were indicating* (my emphasis).

It is worth noting that it was (and is) common for a group of hunters to share the same trapping and hunting area for a season. The group of hunters (*mamo atoskewin*) may be composed of a father and his adult sons (or grandsons, or nephews), a man and his brothers-in-law, or a hunter and some friends he has invited for the season. This brings us to a widespread practice embedded in the Atikamekw social order and in resource management strategies: the practice (or institution) of inviting other hunters to share one's territory for a season. This principle (*wicakemowin*) serves mainly as a resource management strategy. It means that whenever one's territory, or trapping area, has to be left for a season to replenish itself, the hunter can seek an invitation to share another territory. Or, whenever a hunter considers that he has surplus resources on his territory, he can invite family members or friends to share the trapping season (and resources, and income from the sale of furs) with him.

Learning the Languages of the Forest

In handing over the responsibility for an extended family territory or a hunting area within it, a number of factors are taken into account, among them the degree of knowledge one has of the territory. One knows a country when one has walked over it; when one can name and recognize the myriad places and the trails connecting them; when one knows the paths and travelling routes according to the seasons, over the land (*icawin* or *motewin*), along the water ways (*itohiin*), and across the snow in winter; when one has the skills to evaluate the state of the land and its various resources. This knowledge must be balanced with an equivalent degree of respect towards the land and its non-human inhabitants. In the past, a boy of 10 would start following his grandfather during the trapping and hunting season. After five years of learning from his grandfather, he would go hunting with his father for a few seasons. Not only did he have to acquire hunting skills, but he had to be able to make the necessary materials out of local resources (bark canoe, snowshoes, sledge, axe handles, etc.). This meant, for example, that to make a frame for snowshoes, he had to be able to recognize the right birch tree, one that would bend easily and not split during the process. In his early twenties, once he had acquired the skills and values to be self-sufficient, he would be given responsibility for an area within the family territory. Throughout the learning process, each time he killed a type of game for the first time, the event was underlined by a *makocan*, a ceremonial meal. An Elder from Opitciwan told the story of his own experience:

> I was a boy, and I was helping my mother to lift the fishing net. My father and my brother had gone to trap muskrat. I saw the loon. I took the gun, it was a short one, and shot it. This was the first time that I killed a loon. With my mother, we took it and brought it to the camp. My grandfather was there; he was blind. He told us to prepare it right away. My mother plucked it, cleaned it, and cooked it.

> Then, when everybody had come back, we made the *makocan*. We all sat in a circle. I sat next to my grandfather, and we ate and shared the loon. During the meal, I was asked to sit in the middle of the circle; they gave me the fat and they told me to rub my hair with it. This is what they did.

In the meantime, young girls were initiated by their grandmothers, mothers, or aunts into the skills and knowledge needed by women. While the men were out on their traplines or travelling to and from the trading posts, often for weeks at a time, the women stayed at the winter camp and had to ensure the well-being of the household. Among others things, women's skills included setting snares for hares and other small game; fishing; preparing the game men brought back from hunting; cooking, smoking, or drying the meat or fish; gathering medicinal plants; tanning the hides (mostly moose hides); making snowshoes; and making and decorating leather clothing, etc. These skills and practices are not simply things of the past. Although they are no longer part of everyday life, many women from all generations still have these skills.

It would be wrong to believe that this knowledge, these practices, and these values are things of the past, or that they have been eroded or become obsolete as a result of the major changes in the Atikamekw way of life and the growing constraints on using their territories. While some of the knowledge and skills that used to sustain a nomadic and self-sufficient way of life have indeed disappeared, most of them are still very much alive. They remain part of contemporary Atikamekw reality, in spite of the fact that the knowledge is acquired and practised differently by the younger generations and may have different meanings for them.

The Seasonal Cycle

The Atikamekw recognize six seasons, rather than four, and whenever the opportunity arises, they are proud to point out this difference to

FIGURE 8.2. An Elder stretching a beaver skin to dry it. The skin will be used for making various items of clothing. These skills, though less widespread than in earlier generations, are still part of Atikamekw reality. (Photo, 1965, by Camil Guy. Courtesy of the Conseil de la Nation Atikamekw)

non-indigenous people. Each season corresponds to a state of the land, to the availability of particular resources, and thus to specific hunting, trapping, fishing, and gathering skills and practices. *Miroskamin*—'new earth, new shoot'—corresponds to May and June and marks the beginning of a new year. In addition to fishing and trapping and hunting animals, it is also a time for hunting geese and other migratory birds. *Nipin* (July and August), a word derived from 'water', is the summer season. Fishing is the main activity, with no trapping and very little hunting being done, aside from duck hunting and some snaring. It is the time to gather bark (mostly from birch, to make baskets and canoes in traditional times), medicinal plants, and blueberries. The latter are abundant in the area. They are cooked, made into a paste, mixed with bear fat, and stored for the winter. Traditionally, it was the time when families, who were spread over a wide

territory the rest of the year, would gather together to socialize and meet with friends and family members. *Takwakin* (September and October) is the season of 'chilly times'. The family groups would start their journey back 'home' to their respective hunting grounds. They had gathered the necessary material (food, hunting equipment, clothing, etc.) and would take a few weeks to get to their winter camps. They would establish temporary camps along the way, travelling on rivers and lakes, portaging, etc. *Takwakin* is also the best time for moose hunting; the bulk of the meat would be smoked and kept for later and harder times. *Pitci pipon* (November and December) is the 'false winter'. By this time, families usually had arrived at their winter camps; hunting, fishing, and trapping are the main activities during this season. *Pipon*, 'winter' or 'coldest times' (January and February), is the best time for trapping. Some fishing is done by cutting holes in the ice. *Sikon* (March and April) is the period before the new year, when the lakes start to break up; travelling on the land during this season is problematic. It is the time for collecting and making maple syrup, a traditional activity. During *sikon* the Atikamekw start the journey to their summer gathering place. *Takwakin*, *pitci pipon*, and *pipon* are the best seasons for trapping, when an animal's fur is thickest. The best seasons for fishing are *miroskamin*, *nipin*, and *takwakin*. Today, Atikamekw still strongly identify with the six-season cycle and its associated activities.

Named Places and Campsites

The Atikamekw have an intimate relationship with the forest as a social space and a series of living places. Their deep knowledge of it is eloquently expressed in a rich profusion of place names for locales that, not so long ago, were home to those who are Elders today. Nomads are not content to name only the most obvious features of the landscape; instead, they name the smallest meaningful unit. Place names are inspired by a permanent or peculiar feature of the landscape, by whatever can be gathered or hunted there, or by a particular event or action that occurred there. The comments of two Elders of Opitciwan in regard to a small portion of their ancestral territory help us to understand this reality:

> There is a place, it is a shortcut; it is all covered with a lot of moss. There is only moss at that place, so we call it Mickekonikimici. At another place, the water level is higher, so we call it Eskowipew or Eskowpekw. There is a trail that we call Miro Mitiso Meskano, which means 'the trail where one eats well'. Another place, it is a long portage and over the years as people walked over and over, the roots have been coming out, so we call it Ka Otapihocomokw, 'the trail of roots'. Another place where they come up to with the canoe for a portage; there are a lot of cypress at that place, so we call it Ka Oskikecimokw.

> There is a place where a female Elder once prepared some strips out of moose hides for snowshoes, so we call it Ackimin. There is another place where the passage to go from one lake to another is very narrow; we call it Ka Arokopetciwokw. A place where the edge of the forest is scattered, we call it Ka Meskwaskokamak. Another one, it is the highest point in the area where one can see all around; it is as if there were waves, as if one could hear the humming of the waves, we call it Ka Mokwaskak. Another place is called Ka Atikamekwskak—this is where there is cisco [a fish]. There is a mountain we name Ka Nicokotewci Matana because it is as if the mountain had two peaks.

From the Atikamekw point of view, these place names represent signs of their intimate and enduring relationship with the land and the forest. Other signs of Atikamekw presence and dwelling within *notcimik* are also highly valued. Such traces include sites of old and more recent temporary camps, places where imprints left on the ground by tents are visible. Another sign is the *tecpitukun*, a wooden structure used to store hunting and trapping materials (traps, snowshoes, canoes, sledges, etc.) in the bush at the end of the hunting season. Atikamekw stopped building and using these caches about 20 years ago because of Euro-Canadian break-ins and vandalism. The decrease in these signs of Atikamekw activity, as expression and proof of their connection to the land, makes the Elders, both women and men, quite nostalgic. Part of their nostalgia is also due to their observation that Euro-Canadians perceive and act upon the forest in ways that lack the basic values of respect and reciprocity that formerly orchestrated the relationship between the human and non-human inhabitants of the land.

A Sentient Forest

At the beginning of the chapter, I mentioned that an anthropologist acts as a translator between worlds. This role becomes especially challenging when we come to radical cultural differences, particularly when they relate to questions of ontology and epistemology. An example of this radical difference is seen in how the Atikamekw view, experience, and relate to the forest and its non-human constituents. An answer to this question can be found by exploring and taking seriously local ontological (ways of being) and epistemological (ways of knowing) principles and comparing them with those dominant in the West. Western thought, and by extension its scientific models, establishes a clear distinction, if not an absolute dichotomy, between the world of 'natural' objects and the world of 'cultural' (human) subjects. This mode of thought is based on an anthropocentric view of the world, giving humans priority over the rest of nature. As members of a community that embraces that view, we see it as normal, as the 'logical' way to look at the world. However, such a dualistic mode of thought is far from universal. One has only to look at the world of hunters, as well as the world view of many other non-Western societies around the world, to realize that the Western scientific outlook is but one way of defining reality.

What anthropological studies seem to emphasize, insofar as the world view of hunters is concerned, is the centrality of relatedness (Bird-David, 1999; Ingold, 1996; Viveoiros de Castro, 1998), that is, the relational nature of being, knowing, and becoming. Relationships dynamically unfold in time and space through the interactions between interconnected constituents, whether these are human or non-human. Hunters engage in intimate and reciprocal relationships with the animals they hunt insofar as they share the same land, trees, and waters, breathe the same air, and walk over the same ground. Furthermore, the non-human constituents of the world are considered sentient entities that act consciously upon their world. Animals, for example, are endowed with intentionality. They have purposes, identities, and points of view so that they experience the world from their own perspectives and act

accordingly. Let us see now how these considerations find echoes in the world of the Atikamekw.

In a hunting tradition, like that of the Atikamekw, knowledge and practices, ethics and aesthetics, and values and emotions are all closely intertwined. The Elders also make it clear that sharing and reciprocity are at the core of their understanding of their relations with the animals. As hunters, the Atikamekw value and engage in an intimate and reciprocal relationship with the non-human constituents of their world—animals, trees, plants, mountains. Atikamekw ethics, their resource management strategies and practices, and even their aesthetic sense can only be understood by taking into account this particular dialogue with the forest and its inhabitants. The land, as a sentient landscape, 'speaks' to the hunter. Asked about the beauty of the mountain, as part of a landscape, an Elder answered that 'the mountain is delicious', referring to all the different food that the mountain offers to humans. The animals *are* food, but the Atikamekw hunter is always reminded that the animals 'give themselves' and by that conscious gesture they earn the hunter's respect. It is in that sense that their relationship is said to be reciprocal. If humans do not act properly, the animals may decide to go away and not give themselves anymore. The trees and plants, as food for animals and humans, are just as valued and respected. An Elder spoke of the trees as the sole 'guardians' and 'chiefs' of the *nehirowisiw*.

These examples suggest that, for the Atikamekw, the animals, plants, trees, and waters are resources. But they are also sentient entities who share the forest with humans. This view contrasts with the Western one in which only humans are said to be conscious agents who have a mandate to act as sole masters over an objectified world of 'nature'. The Atikamekw concept thus entails a different code of ethics and a different mode of resource management based on a holistic system of knowledge. The Atikamekw system of knowledge is holistic in the sense that it is not specialized and compartmentalized. Trees, bears, and people are not put into separate 'boxes'. When

walking in the forest or visiting a hunting territory, a knowledgeable person should be able to
read, both qualitatively and quantitatively, the
state of the land as a whole. The availability of so-
called resources as well as the state of their interrelations and interactions, and thus of their
becoming, should be apparent. Such a qualitative
and quantitative process of assessment implies
listening to, reading, and interpreting the different languages within the forest, and responding
to them appropriately.

In the Atikamekw language, this holistic
process of assessment and reconnaissance over the
extent of one's territory is referred to as *tipahiskan*.
Tipahiskan implies a whole range of knowledge
and practices, from visiting a territory and evaluating its resources to passing on knowledge and
telling stories. It can be translated as 'land and
resource management', though the term has a different meaning from what Westerners, or scientific
models, usually understand by it. The main difference between the Western concept of resource
management and that of the Atikamekw is that the
former aims to modify the land and exploit
resources through technical manipulation of the
natural world in order to suit the needs and purposes of humans. From an Atikamekw perspective, considering the principles of relatedness and
reciprocity, management and ethics mean adapting one's behaviour or future purposes and actions
on the basis of the information received from the
forest, including the needs and well-being of non-
human others. If the needs and purposes of the
latter are not taken into account, the well-being of
humans will be affected. From the perspective of
Euro-Canadian 'users', whether logging companies or sport hunters, the forest is viewed as a
commodity and as 'raw nature'; it is neither a
'home' nor a 'sharing partner'. Furthermore,
tipahiskan implies the whole person, as a centre of
relationships, and his or her engagement within
notcimik, not merely a disembodied, technical
knowledge over an objectified world of 'nature'.
Even the concept of 'sustainable development' is
inadequate to express all that is implied in the

concept of *tipahiskan* because it usually is construed in a dualistic manner and so limits what is
taken into account in assessing resource needs. In
the rhetoric of sustainable development, resources
remain merely resources; they are not non-human
agents who interact with humans and share the
forest. *Tipahiskan*—the Atikamekw mode of
resource and land management—currently must
take into account the Euro-Canadian presence,
activities, and boundaries, demonstrating once
more their tremendous ability and willingness to
transform their ways in order to adapt to the new
conditions of their changing world.

Conclusion

In this chapter, I have portrayed some aspects of
the changing world of the Atikamekw. We have
reviewed their colonial history, their participation in the fur trade, and their gradual passage
from a nomadic way of life to settled communities subsequent to the narrowing of their hunting and living territories. Elders' stories have
offered some understanding of the lives, values,
and seasonal practices of the Atikamekw prior to
the 1960s, at a time when they still felt they
could live autonomously, following in the foot-
steps of their ancestors. We have also tried to
understand how Atikamekw hunters view and
experience their relationship with the forest, as a
world of interacting and interconnected sentient
entities. With the same determination and flexibility as their ancestors, but also with much dis-
illusion, frustration, and suffering, today's
Atikamekw have accommodated to their new
realities and adjusted their practices. In their
ongoing attempts to accommodate *Ka Wapisitcik*
activities and interests on their land, they have
made many compromises, while others they
have resisted.

After decades of colonial negation and humiliation, Atikamekw women and men are involved
in a number of initiatives in an effort to build a
meaningful future and to regain their dignity and
pride. I have already referred to the creation of

BOX 8.2

Ancestral Territories

In the 1970s, public access to Crown lands was democratized by the Quebec government and private hunting and fishing clubs were suppressed. Since then, Atikamekw ancestral territories, apart from the reserves, have been subject to an administrative system that places them in one of four categories: controlled harvesting zones, outfitting camps (with either exclusive or non-exclusive rights), resort leases, or logging leases. This means that, on the ground, the Atikamekw must deal with two systems for 'mapping' the land and for setting boundaries: theirs and that of the *Ka Wapisitcik*. While the Euro-Canadians' boundaries and regulations contrast with Atikamekw ways of sharing, delimiting, and passing down family and hunting territories, a synthesis—or compromise—between the two has evolved. However, all the decisions about policies, leases, and boundaries have taken place with almost no consultation with the Atikamekw, let alone their active participation. This seems to deny not only their history, but their very existence. On the other hand, the Atikamekw Nation has been negotiating with the federal and the provincial governments since the mid-1970s towards a comprehensive land claims agreement over the extent of their ancestral territories, but with no tangible results to this day. The Atikamekw refuse to comply with the federal policy of extinguishing indigenous rights and title. Like other First Nations, they seek a form of modern treaty based on a mutual recognition and affirmation of rights and interconnections between them, the state, and the dominant society; they seek to shape a relationship based on sharing (Asch, 1997).

The following statement by César Néwashish, a most respected Elder who died in 1994 at the age of 91, is emblematic of Atikamekw territorial claims:

Witamowikok aka wiskat e ki otci pakitinamokw kitaskino, nama wiskat ki otci atawanano, nama wiskat ki otci meckotonenano, name kaie wiskat ki otci pitoc irakonenano kitaskino. (Tell them we have never given up our territory, tell them we have never sold or traded it, tell them that we have never reached any other sort of agreement concerning our territory.)

political, cultural, and linguistic bodies and institutions at the level of the Atikamekw Nation. In order to promote the Atikamekw language and ways, a primary school bilingual program has been implemented. Smaller-scale programs aim to initiate young people to life in the forest and to hunting skills. Alongside these initiatives, a growing number of Atikamekw are involved in the revitalization of traditional ritual practices such as the first-steps ceremony, the sweat lodge, and drum beating, all practices that were strongly denigrated and forbidden by the Roman Catholic Church. To these practices we could add also the reactivation of networks of ritual exchange with neighbouring First Nations such as the Ojibwa. While some Atikamekw express opposition to these practices, they are gaining momentum and contributing to the process of social healing. The revitalization and reinterpretation of these ritual practices are not only culturally interesting, but are also politically empowering as significant gestures in the struggle towards self-determination. All these initiatives, along with their territorial claims, are political statements insofar as they are contemporary expressions of their identity and of their unique relationship with the land.

As a rule, the Atikamekw are conscious that their relationship with the land is the only guarantee of the vitality of their language, and thus of the Atikamekw ways. Indeed, it is a leit-motif in the various claims, strategies, and struggles to regain their self-determination. The initiatives and strategies being developed today by the Atikamekw aim to maintain and reconfigure their relationship to their territories while accommodating the dictates of modernity and development. They are waiting, patiently but not passively, for the political recognition of their land rights. In so doing they hope to gain their rightful place as equal 'partners' within the decision-making processes that govern their territories and preside over the destinies of *notcimik*.

Acknowledgement

The research on which this chapter is based was supported by the Social Sciences and Humanities Research Council of Canada.

Notes

1. The Atikamekw language is an *r*-dialect of Cree, using 'r' where other dialects might use a 'th' or an 'l'. Sometimes they are simply included among the Cree. From the end of the eighteenth century until the 1950s, they were known as the Tete-de-Boule Cree. The phoneme *kw* is pronounced *ak*.

2. The Atikamekw and Montagnais Council was founded in 1975 as a political and representative body. It was dissolved in 1994, each of the nations preferring to negotiate separately (see Charest, 1992).

3. Fifteen years ago, the Atikamekw instituted cultural weeks—two weeks in spring and autumn when schools and offices are closed so people can set up camps on their territories during the hunting seasons for migrating birds.

4. These narratives were collected between 1995 and 2000 by myself, two Atikamekw research assistants, Jean-Marc Niquay and Gilles Ottawa, and two MA anthropology students, Kathia Lavoie and Marie-Josée Roussy.

References and Recommended Readings

Asch, Michael. 1997. 'Affirming Aboriginal Title: A New Basis for Comprehensive Claims Negotiations', in Asch, ed., *Aboriginal and Treaty Rights in Canada: Essays on Law, Equality, and Respect for Difference*. Vancouver: University of British Columbia Press.

Béland, Jean-Pierre. 1978. 'Atikamekw Morphology and Lexicon', Ph.D. thesis, University of California, Berkeley. This is the only thorough description and analysis of the Atikamekw language, with some analysis of contemporary dialects and comparisons with neighbouring Cree and Innu.

Bird-David, Nurit. 1999. 'Animism Revisited', *Current Anthropology* 40, Supplement: S67–S91.

Charest, Paul. 1992. 'La prise en charge donne-t-elle du pouvoir? L'exemple des Atikamekw et des Montagnais', *Anthropologie et sociétés* 16, 3: 55–76.

Clermont, Norman. 1977. *Ma femme, ma hache et mon couteau croche: Deux siècles d'histoire à Weymontachie*. Québec: Ministère des Affaires Culturelles. A comprehensive analysis of Wemotaci from the end of the eighteenth century to the 1950s, this study offers historical data and information on social organization, material culture, and hunting practices.

———. 1977. 'Les Kokotchés à Weymontachie', *Recherches amérindiennes au Québec* 8, 2: 139–46. Information about Atikamekw oral tradition, myths, and cosmology are rare. The Kokotchés are strong and malevolent beings who look like humans but are cannibals and masters of the wind.

Cooper, John M. 1926. 'The Obidjiwan Band of the Têtes de Boule', *Anthropos* 21, 3/4: 616–17. A historical, social, and territorial overview of Opitciwan hunting groups. Cooper conducted extensive fieldwork and underlines the linguistic, social, and cultural affiliations among northern Algonquians.

———. 1928. 'Field Notes on Northern Algonkian Magic', *XXIII International Congress of Americanists*: 513–18. Based mostly on ethnographic data from Opitciwan, a short and unique early description of Atikamekw hunting rituals, including notes about the shaking tent.

———. 1945. 'Tête-de-Boule Cree', *International Journal of American Linguistics* 11, 1: 36–44. The evidence of the Atikamekw language being a Cree dialect is presented here. Mention is made of sub-dialectic differences between Atikamekw bands.

Davidson, D.S. 1928. 'Notes on Tête de Boule Ethnology', *American Anthropologist* 30, 1: 18–46. One of the first anthropologists, with Cooper, to conduct fieldwork among the Atikamekw, Davidson provides invaluable data on their social and territorial organization in the early twentieth century.

———. 1928. 'Decorative Art of the Têtes de Boule of Quebec', Museum of the American Indian, *Indian Notes and Monograph* 10, 9: 115–43. A thorough analysis of Atikamekw material culture and art designs, with a focus on birchbark containers, cradleboards, and moccasins. Makes some comparisons with Cree and Innu.

———. 1928. 'Some Tête de Boule Tales', *Journal of American Folklore* 41: 262–74. An early account of Atikamekw oral tradition, with a number of stories about the Iroquois raids. One tale about an old woman who finally succeeded in cheating and killing them is widespread among Algonquians.

Escobar, Arturo. 'Anthropology and Development', *International Journal of Social Sciences* 154: 497–515.

Gélinas, Claude. 2000. *La gestion de l'étranger: Les Atikamekw et la présence eurocanadienne en Haute-Mauricie, 1760–1870*. Québec: Septentrion. The first comprehensive ethnohistorical study of the Atikamekw. Gélinas analyzes the organization of hunting groups, material culture (including the trade of imported goods), relations with Euro-Canadians, and their changing character over 100 years.

Guinard, J.E. 1945. 'Mémoires: Journal des missions', manuscript in Seminaire de Trois-Rivières, Québec. Father Guinard was an Oblate missionary in the upper St-Maurice from 1899 to 1940. His narration contains information on daily social realities in the communities. It is most instructive regarding Catholic and French-Canadian attitudes towards 'Indians' in the early twentieth century.

Ingold, Tim. 1996. 'Hunting and Gathering as Ways of Perceiving the Environment', in R. Ellen and K. Fukui, eds, *Redefining Nature: Ecology, Culture and Domestication*. Oxford: Berg.

Labrecque, Marie-France. 1984. 'Des femmes de Weymontachie', *Recherches amérindiennes au Québec* 14, 3: 3–16. This work is based on the life stories of Atikamekw women from four generations. The author shows some of the changes in their lives and their main concerns.

———. 1984. 'Développement du capitalisme dans la région de Weymontachie (Haute-Mauricie): Incidences sur la condition des femmes Attikamèques', *Recherches amérindiennes au Québec* 14, 3: 75–87. A Marxist analysis of the fur trade, colonial history, and the development of capitalism in Atikamekw territory and how such external influences have affected the sexual division of labour and the social roles of women.

McNulty, Gérard E., and Louis Gilbert. 1981. 'Attikamek (Tête de Boule)', in June Helm, ed., *Handbook of North American Indians*, vol. 6, *The Subarctic*. Washington: Smithsonian Institution. A useful summary of Atikamekw history, population movement during the fur trade period, and material culture, with bibliographic sources.

Poirier, Sylvie. 1992. 'L'occupation et l'utilisation du territoire dans la région du Lac Flamand, McTavis et Windigo', report filed with Conseil Atikamekw et Montagnais, Québec. An analysis of the occupation of the Kokokac area and the merging of the Kokokac and Wemotaci bands, including maps showing family hunting territories and detailed genealogical charts.

———. 2000. 'Contemporanéités autochtones, territoires et (post)colonialisme: Réflexions sur des exemples Canadiens et Australiens', *Anthropologie et Sociétés* 24, 1: 137–53. A critical approach to colonial doctrines, such as *terra nullius*, and their current effects through a comparative analysis of the Atikamekw and Kukatja (Australian Western Desert): their dealings with 'modernity', their land claims processes, and their cultural consciousness and resistance.

———. 2001. 'Territories, Identity, and Modernity among the Atikamekw (Haut St-Maurice, Quebec)', in C.H. Scott, ed., *Aboriginal Autonomy and Development in Northern Quebec and Labrador*. Vancouver: University of British Columbia Press. The Atikamekw as contemporary hunters and gatherers: the consolidation of their nation, their perceptions of the land, and their resistance to Euro-Canadian activities and interest on their land.

Viveoiros de Castro, Eduardo. 1998. 'Cosmological Deixis and Amerindian Perspectivism', *Journal of the Royal Anthropological Institute* 4, 3: 469–88.

Suggested Web Sites

Conseil de la Nation Atikamekw: www.cnalatuque.com
> The official site of the Council of the Atikamekw Nation (Atikamekw Sipi). It offers historical, social, and cultural information on the three Atikamekw communities.

La piste amérindienne—The Native Trail: www.autochtones.com
> Prepared by the 11 First Nations of Quebec in collaboration with the Quebec government. Aside from a large range of topics, it gives access to Quebec First Nation sites.

Le Musée de la civilisation (Québec): www.mcq.org/mcq/
> This site includes a permanent exhibition on the 11 First Nations of Quebec.

Innu Nation/Mamit Innuat: www.innu.ca
> A bilingual, up-to-date, and informative site on the 13 communities of the Innu Nation. It covers a wide range of topics, including political and environmental issues, and gives access to international sites on indigenous issues.

PART IV

The Western Subarctic

CHAPTER 9

The Northern Athapaskans: A Regional Overview

C. RODERICK WILSON

Although the region strikes most southerners as definitely inhospitable, people have lived in the Western Subarctic longer than in any other part of Canada. As discussed in Chapter 2, bone tools discovered in the Old Crow region of Yukon have been widely accepted as indicating human presence some 25,000 years ago. Some archaeologists think that other artifacts found in the region are much older. Whatever dates are ultimately demonstrated, Amerindian people have clearly lived in the region from 'time immemorial'.

The physical environment of the region can be characterized as the zone of discontinuous permafrost in western Canada. The southern half is boreal forest (spruce, fir, and pine, with some poplar and white birch) and the rest is primarily a transitional zone of boreal vegetation intermixed with patches of lichen-dominated tundra. (As a cultural region the Western Subarctic in places extends north of the treeline into the tundra because some Subarctic societies made extensive use of tundra resources.) In absolute terms the region receives little precipitation (annual average about 40 cm), yet it has two of the largest river systems on the continent and innumerable lakes. The ground is snow-covered six months of the year, and few places have more than 50 frost-free days. Temperature extremes typically range from lows of -50° C to summer highs of over 20° C.

Large game animals, particularly caribou, constituted the primary resource base for Aboriginal peoples. Moose, goats, sheep, and even bison were locally important. Small animals (especially the snowshoe hare), fish, migratory waterfowl, and grouse were of secondary importance.

The entire Western Subarctic culture area is inhabited by people speaking a series of closely related Athapaskan languages. Linguists believe that these languages were undifferentiated as recently as 2,500 years ago and that from their 'ancestral' homeland they expanded further west in Alaska and eastward into the Northwest Territories and then southward. Some, notably the Apacheans, became physically separated from the others and ended up thousands of miles to the south, but for Northern Athapaskans, because of limited linguistic variation, communication is still possible across considerable distances. This implies frequent communication between people from different localities throughout the prehistoric past. Correlatively, the ethnographic evidence is that few Northern Athapaskan groups had significant relationships with non-Athapaskans. The exceptions are the Chipewyan (with Cree), the Gwich'in (now Kutchin) and Hare (with Inuit), and the Kaska (with Northwest Coast groups).

In this context it seems significant that Northern Athapaskan kinship systems could be extended in such a way that usually one could find a 'relative' even in bands quite far distant, and hence a legitimate basis for establishing a relationship. In general these people developed

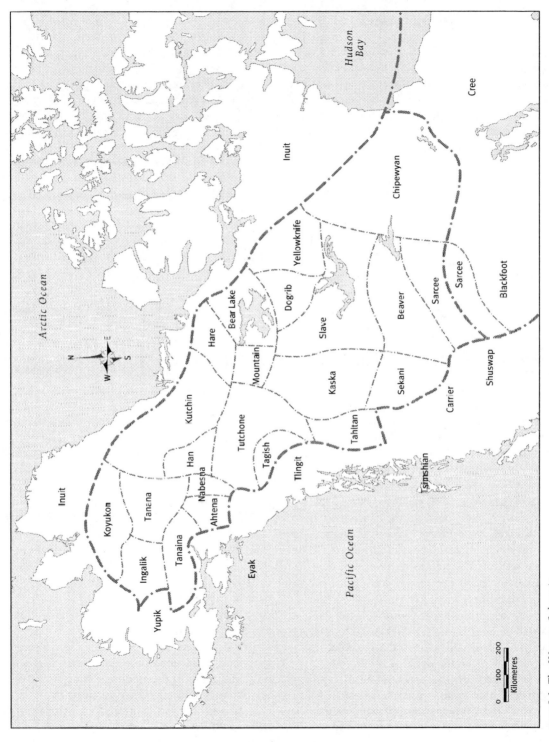

MAP 9.1. The Western Subarctic

social strategies characterized by great flexibility and informal institutional arrangements. For example, leadership among the eastern Northern Athapaskans was largely situational: people were listened to or followed not because they had the power to make people obey but because they had demonstrated an ability to lead in that particular activity. An outstanding hunter might attract a considerable following; nevertheless, he had no permanent power. The overall picture thus was of individuals, family groups, and even larger groupings making short-term decisions about where and how they would live. These decisions were based on a large number of factors: the local supply of game, reports from elsewhere, degree of satisfaction with fellow band members, which relatives lived where, and so on. In the western part of the region, the existence of clans correlated with a more complex and formal social life; nevertheless, that life also was characterized by remarkable social flexibility.

Another key to Aboriginal Athapaskan society is its egalitarianism (autonomy and self-reliance are closely associated). This was true even among the most westerly Athapaskans who, like their maritime neighbours, had 'chiefs'. As McClellan and Denniston (1981: 384–5) point out, these positions were conditional, and stratified rank was not possible for them until the fur trade period. The staples necessary for life were, in general, equally accessible, and the skills necessary to transform them into finished products were shared widely in the community. Although some people were more competent than others, and more respected, there was no basis from which an exclusive control over goods, and hence people, could develop. Even in the realm of spiritual power, the ultimate basis for any success and an aspect of life in which people varied conspicuously, the possibility of becoming a shaman was in principle open to all.

The initial contact of Canadian Athapaskans with Europeans was consistent with the general trend of the frontier moving from east to west. Direct trading contacts were made by the eastern-most group, the Chipewyan, in 1714, while none of the westernmost tier of Canadian Athapaskans had direct contacts prior to 1850. There was not, however, a single frontier: Athapaskans in southern Alaska had trading contacts from 1741.

Helm (1975) makes the following points concerning the early contact process: European goods and diseases usually preceded direct contact with traders; the first-contacted tribes obtained guns and expanded their fur-collecting operations at the expense of their western neighbours; trading posts were welcomed by those living in the 'new' territories; traders tended to act as peacemakers in this newly competitive context. The latter three points particularly contrast with Russian-Native relationships in Alaska.

The fur trade had numerous consequences, and it constituted a social revolution. The introduction of new goods, especially guns and traps, is salient. New social roles, such as trading chiefs, and changing social relationships are also striking. Perhaps most startling are features that are now identified as traditional, such as dogsleds, which were introduced during this period. Somewhat simplified, the guns, traps, and sleds enabled people to engage in old and new bush activities more efficiently, and the trading chiefs allowed traders to deal with the people more efficiently. However, the new elements made their own demands: a dog team in a year would eat thousands of pounds of fish, thereby increasing the 'need' to obtain new goods such as fish nets and to harvest bush resources at a higher level. Further, an innovation frequently had a cumulative impact. The effect of the gun, an early trade item, in contributing to higher harvest levels becomes most evident after 1900. Nevertheless, these early changes were limited in scope, and continuity with the past was evident. The ensuing way of life was remarkably stable for many groups for almost a century and a half. Even the general acceptance of Christianity resulting from the activities of Oblate and Anglican missionaries was as notable for people's continued adherence to old beliefs as to new.

FIGURE 9.1. Chipewayan hunter with caribou he has shot, northern Manitoba. (Courtesy Hudson's Bay Company Archives, Archives of Manitoba)

demographic change until recently. With the advent of modern medicine some 50 years ago, the Yukon and Northwest Territories have experienced the highest rates of population increase in Canada.

For most of the area, the fact that Native societies had become incorporated into Canada did not become a social reality until the early 1950s. There were two major exceptions. Much of Dunne-za (Beaver) traditional territory, the Peace River country of northern British Columbia and Alberta, is arable. Farmers began displacing Natives in this area *circa* 1890. Even more dramatic was the Klondike gold rush. Dawson alone had grown to 25,000 by 1898, while the Han 'tribe', occupying adjacent portions of Alaska and the Yukon, numbered only about 1,000. The gold rush, and the government and commercial presence it created, resulted in an early marginalization of Native people in the Yukon to a degree that the people of the Northwest Territories generally have still not experienced.

A few generalizations about contemporary life are in order. First, for much of the region, most adults over about age 50 have personal memory of what life was like before significant government-industrial presence. For some the 'traditional life' is a still present reality. Second, even for severely impacted groups, truly significant features of traditional life remain important.

Third, the treaties continue to be living documents. As Asch notes, there is active debate over how Treaties No. 8 and No. 11 should currently be interpreted, but both sides agree that they help define the constitutional debate on what it means

The impact of introduced diseases is not clear. Aboriginal population levels are not well known, nor are the consequences of the various outbreaks. Are they isolated events, as a narrow reading of the sources would indicate, or do they represent merely the documented cases of widespread epidemics? What is evident is that a number of new diseases (smallpox, scarlet fever, influenza, measles, venereal diseases, and tuberculosis—in rough chronological order) became common and that there were at times very high mortality rates, both because the new diseases were in themselves devastating and because in their wake small groups might well starve to death. Nevertheless, the recuperative powers of the population were such that the region as a whole appears not to have experienced significant to be Native in those regions. A unique element of this debate is Judge Morrow's 1973 investigation of the circumstances under which Treaty No. 11 had been signed in 1921, unique because at the time there were signatories to the treaty still alive and able to testify in court that the treaty had been everywhere presented as a gesture of friendship and goodwill and not, as a literal reading of the English-language written text would indicate, as a means of extinguishing Aboriginal title.

A fourth point is that Athapaskans have attempted both to maintain themselves as distinctive peoples and to accommodate the powerful forces for change thrust upon them. In the late twentieth century the primary mechanism in the Northwest Territories for doing this, the Dene National Assembly, was profoundly rooted in traditional values. Events, however, have overtaken it, so that currently regional organizations and the Territorial Assembly are the primary arenas in which Aboriginal people attempt to regain effective control over their lives. As Asch documents for the NWT (and as Goulet shows for Alberta and Furniss for BC), political and economic control are intimately connected, and currently are being negotiated in various venues, including both formal treaty processes and commercial deal-making.

The end result will not be something closely resembling Nunavut. The Inuit case is unique for Canadian Natives; they are numerically dominant in their region and therefore a politically open system is very workable. The Dene, like most Natives in Canada, must find mechanisms other than a territorially based legislature for political accommodation. Presumably that means some form of limited, shared, or joint arrangement with Euro-Canadians. Their recent history demonstrates a willingness to seek workable solutions. A wide range of options has been actively explored by the various Native groups in recent years. The question that remains, however, is whether or not Euro-Canadians will be as open to accommodation.

References

Helm, June, et al. 1975. 'The contact history of the subarctic Athapaskans: an overview', in A. McFayden Clarke, ed., *Proceedings: Northern Athapaskan Conference*, vol. 1. Ottawa: Canadian Ethnology Service Paper No. 27.

McClellan, C., and G. Denniston. 1981. 'Environment and Culture in the Cordillera', in June Helm, ed., *Handbook of North American Indians*, vol. 6, *Subarctic*. Washington: Smithsonian Institution.

CHAPTER 10

The Dene Tha of Chateh:
Continuities and Transformations

JEAN-GUY A. GOULET

Introduction

Young Dene in high school or university are taught about Canada, a Canada with a life expectancy of over 80 years for women and over 75 years for men. The Canada they know, however, is strikingly different. Their average life expectancy is 20 to 30 years less, largely due to a high rate of tragic juvenile and adult deaths related to alcohol abuse. Many Dene Tha end their days in conditions that were unknown only one generation ago. They strive to live meaningful lives in the midst of grieving their lost ones. They do so in the light of their Aboriginal knowledge and convictions. They also do so in the midst of Euro-Canadian institutions established over the last century: the church, the store, the residential school, and later the government-operated day school, the RCMP detachment, and the nursing station.

I first visited Chateh in northwest Alberta in the summer of 1979 to ask the Dene Tha if they would teach me their language and way of life. I explained that I intended to spend six months of each year with them as part of an extended research project. My goal was to find out if the Dene Tha had repudiated their own institutions and values as they were exposed to Euro-Canadian institutions in the fields of politics, economy, religion, education, and health. During six years of close association with them, I found that a century of interaction with Euro-Canadians has not eradicated or rendered obsolete Dene ways of knowing and living. The Dene Tha saw Western institutions as a complement to, rather than a substitute for, their Aboriginal ways.

The presentation of contemporary Dene Tha lives proceeds in four steps. First, I offer a brief historical sketch of events to explain how the Dene Tha of Chateh came to live in their present location. Second, I explore their understanding of the world, including their relationship to individuals who are reincarnated and their recourse to healing powers received from animals. Third, I examine Dene Tha domestic life. I focus on their views of education and learning as well as on the challenge posed over the past 40 years by violent behaviour associated with the consumption of alcohol. Last, I discuss contemporary social, economic, and political issues that are shaping the future. Dene Tha are preparing to invest millions of dollars to exploit vast oil and gas fields in their traditional homeland.

The Slaveys of Alberta Become the Dene Tha of Chateh

In the anthropological literature the people of Chateh are referred to as Slavey, Hay River Indians, Albertan Beaver Indians, the Dene Tha branch of the Beaver Indians, and the Hay Lakes Alberta Dene. Chateh, also known as Assumption,

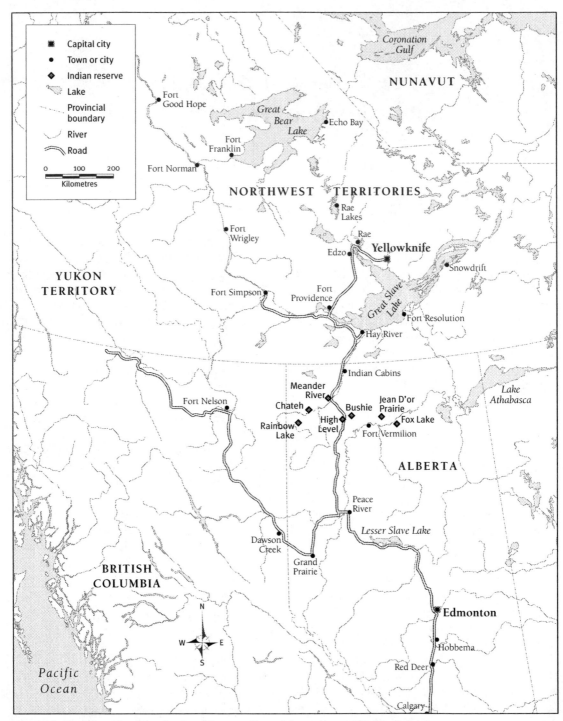

MAP 10.1. The Dene Tha: Homeland and Surroundings. (Map courtesy of Robin Poitras)

is listed by the Department of Indian and Northern Affairs as the Hay Lakes Reserve (the name given to the band in 1953 by the federal government), with a population 838 in 1996.

Three Names, Three Historical Phases of Dene Tha Life

Hay Lakes, Assumption, and Chateh are names that reflect distinct phases in the history of the Dene Tha. Following battles lost to the Cree in the nineteenth century, the Dene Tha moved northward from the Lesser Slave region. Contemporary Dene Tha know the place along the Hay River where they last battled with the Cree. They remember that a Dene Tha woman survived by hiding on the riverbank. Elder Louison Ahkimnatchie comments, 'Today, if you want to camp there, you have to make an offering of tobacco. If you don't, you will hear crying and screaming of people who were killed in the battle. Dene Tha have tried to stay there without making an offering and they had to leave before morning—they couldn't stand the terrible noises' (Dene Tha' First Nation, 1997: 40).

In 1900 the Dene Tha signed Treaty No. 8. Unknowingly, they became subject to the Indian Act. A band membership list was drawn, specifying who could live on the land set aside for them. They received patronyms. Adult male members were called upon to elect a chief and a council to act as counterparts to federal officials whose primary mandate was to open Aboriginal territories to peaceful settlement and exploitation.

The Dene Tha understanding of the treaty was as a means of establishing a kinship-like alliance between themselves and the government. The treaty-signing ceremony had been concluded with a gift of money from the federal government to each band member. This money, Elder Jean-Marie Tally told me, was 'not to sell anything but to make us brothers and sisters [and therefore inclined to assist each other]. That is what my father, who saw them give money to the people, used to say. It [the treaty] will not be a lie for God as long as night follows night, and as long as the sun lasts, and as long

as the water flows.' Every year since, in midsummer, Dene Tha line up to receive from an officer of the RCMP the five-dollar bill promised annually to each band member. In Dene Dhah, the language of the Dene, treaty day is appropriately called 'the day they give money to people'.

Following the signing of Treaty 8, Dene Tha had little exposure to Euro-Canadians since they spent most of the year making a living on the land. Contact was limited to occasional visits to the Hudson's Bay Company trading post in Fort Vermillion. There they sold furs and purchased supplies of flour, lard, tea, sugar, ammunition, and the like for the next round of trapping. Until about 1950, government policy throughout the Subarctic, in the absence of economic development, was to preserve unchanged the 'traditional' fur-trading way of life as much as possible. In this way indigenous populations contributed to the market economy while providing for all their needs at a minimal cost to the Canadian government.

The Dene Tha then lived and hunted over a wide expanse extending into northeast British Columbia and the Northwest Territories. Until the mid-1940s, Hay Lakes, some 13 kilometres north of the present-day site of Chateh, was an important gathering place. In spring and fall Dene Tha found in Hay Lakes plentiful wildlife (fish, moose, deer, beaver, muskrat, ducks, and geese) and abundant pasture for their horses. When winter set in, extended families dispersed to their traplines.

During that period, anthropologists living with the Dene could not see them as victims or as dispossessed of their land or their means of living. Richard Slobodin (1975: 285), who worked among the Gwich'in, asked how anthropologists could 'depict as mere victims the men, women, and children who had hauled us through the broken ice, disentangled dogs, given us dry clothing, and poured hot caribou soup down our throats.' In those days Dene could well feel superior to the occasional white man who ventured into their midst and who depended on them for food, shelter, and orientation.

Anthropologists were then motivated by the desire to record distinctive ways of life threatened by Euro-Canadian colonization. In the course of these investigations, the Dene Tha of Chateh, along with many other Aboriginal populations north of them, became known as the Slavey. This name, a translation of the Cree term *awahka'n*, 'captive, slave', was already widely used by traders, explorers, and missionaries to refer to Indians in northern Alberta and the NWT. People so designated eventually adopted the term to refer to themselves when communicating in English. A new system of social identity began to coexist with the Aboriginal one, according to which people identified themselves in reference to geographic sites, as 'people of the swift current' or 'the brush-wood people'. When anthropologists adopted Slavey as the English term to refer to all these populations, they collapsed into one general category various groups dispersed over a wide area.

After the Fur Traders, the Missionaries

After the fur traders, the missionaries were the most significant outsiders to enter Dene Tha lives. Roman Catholic missionaries first sought to convert them and later operated a residential school. In 1917 Father Joseph Habay, an Oblate missionary, built a log chapel on the shore of Hay Lakes, where he carried out his missionary work (the site was named after him in 1953). He was followed by Father Arbet, OMI, who built another chapel there in 1927–8. Elders recall how he travelled by dog team to visit families on their traplines. They remember how he ate with them and slept in their house, lying, like them, on the floor. Hospitality was mixed with puzzlement. 'Before we go to mission', that is, the residential school, said a devout Catholic woman, 'Father Arbet used to come to visit us in the bush. We get pictures of Mary and Jesus, but we do not know what they are. We laugh and say, "This woman looks like this woman." We learn to do the sign of the cross when we pray, and we laugh a lot then. It's funny to us. But when we got in mission, then we learned a lot.'

In 1938 and again in 1948, Dene Tha requested a residential school and a hospital. In a letter dated 17 July 1948, the band chief wrote to the Minister of Mines in Ottawa as follows:

We Hay Lakes Indians take the liberty of submitting to you some communications and asking you a few questions. We are Indians, poor, ignorant, and we start to realize our situation among white people. We are trappers, part in Alberta and part in British Columbia. But trapping is getting so poor that some of us might have to find work amongst white people but only 6 of us have been at school at Fort Vermillion and can speak English.

The chief underlined the need for a local hospital, given the band's hardships and the 17 deaths the previous year, '3 of old age, 1 childbirth, 1 pneumonia, the other 12 were TB'. The chief then added that the band wanted a boarding school, 'because it is impossible for us to send our children to a day school' and it was 'very difficult, not to say impossible to carry with dogs enough supplies 80 miles away, for big families like we have'.

Following this petition, construction of a boarding school soon began, not at Hay Lakes but at a site 13 kilometres inland. The missionaries deemed this site, named Assumption, less liable to flooding and more appropriate for a residential school and a farm to support its staff and pupils. In February 1951 the new school received 74 children (28 boys and 46 girls). The following month 16 other children joined them. From 1951 to 1969 the number of students ranged from 72 to 125 (the peak year being 1960). Over these years more families built their log cabins closer to the mission site and residential school. A cemetery was created nearby, and so the people of Hay Lakes became the people of Assumption. The relationship between church, local people, and cemetery continues to this day. Only for a funeral does the church fill with people, before they follow the coffin to their burial ground.

Closing the Residential School, Opening up to Global Developments

In 1965 major discoveries of oil and natural gas west of Assumption led to construction of a road between High Level and what was to become the town of Rainbow Lake. The disparity in living standards between the Dene Tha, who had lived in the area for centuries, and the Euro-Canadians moving into High Level and Rainbow Lake by the hundreds soon became obvious to all. Differences in employment opportunities, housing, types of vehicles, and the like clearly indicated that the Dene Tha were disadvantaged. Band members marched on the steps of the Alberta legislature, asking for jobs and better living conditions. In response, the federal government built simple two- and three-bedroom frame houses in Assumption. These were most often built next to log cabins erected a generation earlier. As they moved into their new homes, families also kept log cabins in the bush. Here men in their fifties and older, along with sons or other relatives, spent extended periods trapping and hunting in winter and spring, a pattern that still continues.

In 1966, 120 Dene Tha were living in Habay and 575 in Assumption. As more people were living permanently around the local store and boarding school, the federal government established a day school there in 1969. That same year, the missionaries closed the boarding school and the band named the settlement Chateh, in honour of the chief who had signed Treaty No. 8. This change of names came at a time of worldwide Aboriginal political mobilization. Other Northern Athapaskans (Slaveys, Chipewyans, Hare, Dogribs, Mountain Indians, Bearlake Indians, and Kutchin) living in the NWT adopted the name 'Dene' to designate themselves in English. In the same breath they referred to the Western Subarctic as Denendeh, 'the land of the Dene', to stand beside Nunavut, 'our land', the land of their Inuit neighbours. This was the context in which the Slaveys of Assumption became the Dene Tha of Chateh.

One could argue that Chateh could have been included in Denendeh. The Dene Tha share many features of social organization, culture, and language with the Slavey of the NWT. The hunting and trapping activities of Dene Tha extended into the Territories. Slaveys from Assumption have many family ties with NWT Dene. Moreover, in the mid-1960s Dene Tha prophets had played an important role in a revitalization movement among Dogribs and other groups in the NWT. In the following years members of these groups travelled regularly to Chateh to consult with local Elders. Why, then, were the Dene Tha not included in the wider project of Dene self-determination? The reason is political. In Canada Aboriginal peoples must claim their Aboriginal rights without challenging provincial and territorial boundaries. This was the condition under which the federal government would negotiate. The claim to nationhood and self-determination can be made only on a political stage defined by Euro-Canadians. If the Dene Tha were to claim Aboriginal rights, they would have to do so in Alberta.

The assertion of Aboriginal nationhood and the adoption of Aboriginal names to identify oneself in the world publicly emphasized the existence in Canada of two categories of people, with a broad semantic contrast between them. One category is comprised of people with Aboriginal rights to land and to self-government, the original inhabitants of Chateh, Denendeh, and Nunavut. The other category is made up of non-Aboriginals, whose privileged economic opportunities in the land of the Dene are due to Canada's control of those territories. As shall be discussed in the last section, these political developments constitute the background to the current agreements between the Dene Tha, government, and business to generate employment and exploit resources in the Dene Tha homeland.

Being at Home in the World

What has been stated so far about the Dene Tha is based on an examination of the historical record and observable reality in northern Alberta. Much of social reality, however, consists not of events and material objects but of people's interpretation or understanding of them. A crucial part of the anthropological endeavour consists precisely in grasping these understandings. For this, anthropologists depend on their hosts to help them learn about what is really going on.

In my experience, an important way to learn from the Dene Tha about how things really were in their lives consisted of asking them to translate into Dene Dhah a statement initially made in English, and then to have them translate this statement back into English. For instance, in English, Dene Tha would sometimes refer to someone's 'superstition'. When translating this into Dene Dhah, people always said *dene wonlin edadihi*, which they translated back to English as 'a person who knows an animal'. Similarly, when speaking in English about individuals dying and being born again, a few Dene Tha spoke of 'reincarnation'. Most, however, would use phrases such as 'he or she was done to us again' or 'he or she was done again'. When translated to Dene Dhah, it became apparent that these phrases were close to the Dene expression denoting such a person: *Dene andat'sindla*, 'a person made again by others'. In these cases, as in countless others, Dene meanings are attached to English vocabulary. These Dene meanings are to a large extent shared by old and young alike and taken for granted by contemporary Dene Tha. To grasp these meanings is to truly enter the Dene Tha world.

Living in Our Land and in the Other Land

Dene Tha differentiate between *ndahdigeh*, 'our land', and *ech'uhdigeh*, 'the other land'. Dene Tha do not draw this distinction in the way Euro-Canadians conceive of binary opposites such as the natural and the supernatural or the field of science and the field of mysticism, magic, and religion. The other land, also referred to as *yake*, 'heaven', is experienced first-hand in dreams when the soul journeys away from the body. It is in the other land that one meets relatives who have passed away, as well as Christian figures such as Mary and Jesus. In conversation, Dene

Tha Elders easily followed an account of a trip to a nearby town with a story of a journey to the other land. To the nearby town in our land they had travelled by car. To the other land they had travelled with their souls. Elders often bring songs back from their journey to 'heaven' and sing them in 'our land' during healing ceremonies. Similarly, young people would describe bouts of acute illness and near-death experiences as a period of time when their soul or spirit had begun to travel on the trail leading to heaven. In such circumstances, individuals called on Elders and their animal helpers to help recover their souls and, hence, their health.

In the Dene Tha world, events in the other land and in our land are intimately associated. For instance, atmospheric events in this land are an expression of someone's condition in the other land or in this land. When a violent storm swept over Chateh the day after a young man was shot to death, people said the storm was his feelings. When low clouds drizzled over Chateh for three days, a Dene Tha healer explained that it was his power (animal helper) feeling let down because his patients had not brought appropriate gifts as promised. When exceptionally bright red northern lights were seen in the sky, Dene Tha said it was because their leading prophet had lost much blood in the course of an operation. Thus, a continuous flow of interpretations accompanies changes in weather patterns, weaving threads of meaning between social and atmospheric events.

In this land the Dene Tha share a deep sense of dependence on animals, to whom signs of respect are faithfully given lest animals stop giving themselves to hunters who seek them as game. A child learns this respect from his parents as they dispose properly of the bones of animals or the feathers of fowl. People also avoid talking negatively about animals since they know how one talks about them and will not present themselves in the bush to those who speak negatively about them. Children learn that the little feathers at the end of a duck's wings are not to be burned. 'If you burn that little feather, real pointed ones, if you

FIGURE 10.1. Drumming and singing from the other land. (Courtesy J.-G. Goulet)

burn them, you don't shoot ducks as you would like to; you miss them. You don't throw them to the dogs. You throw them in the bush or in the water.' And so the child is sent to drop the feathers in the creek behind the house. The guts are removed from a dead moose and its eyes pierced before its head and brain are put high in a tree. 'This is so he will not see where we go. If he knew, he would be mad at us and we would not shoot moose next time around', says a hunter. Eagles are never killed, for they tell hunters where the moose are and in some cases fly very low to look at people and communicate with them. A woman commented, 'We are afraid of the eagle; we do not kill it. If we kill it in the fall, then it comes and kills one of the family the same year. It all goes back to the time when animals were like human beings, and they could talk and everything.' This woman refers to a distant time when animals and human beings spoke the same language, married, and cohabited. Although this is no longer the

case, animals and human beings continue to entertain intimate relationships, particularly in the realm of healing.

Seeking a Power to Heal, Going for a Song

Until very recently, virtually all Dene Tha children, before the onset of adolescence, went on a vision quest and experienced an encounter with an animal who gave them a song and a power to heal. Dene talk little, if at all, of these things, lest they lose their power or have it turn against them. When asked what it means to know an animal and have an animal helper, a woman answered:

I don't really know. Like my older brother, he never talks to us about it, but my mom told us once that one day [he] went in the bush with little provisions, and was supposed to come back the same day, but stayed two days and two nights. On his way he met wolves who had come to meet him, and he had been with them all that time. I guess they became his helpers. But that is all I know. We do not talk about these things.'

This, as we shall see, is also the reason invoked by Dene Tha not to include on maps of their homeland the sites where they collect *yu*, 'powerful medicine'.

In the early and mid-1980s, most Dene Tha were known to have an animal helper even if they had spent years in residential school. As one former student commented, 'You need an animal helper to survive in this community.' Although some children still go for a song, many parents despair that their children will ever get a vision. Pointing to her young son and nephew, who were listening to our conversation, a young woman told me, 'They are always on the road. You get that kind of thing [a vision] in the bush, not on the road.' Voicing her opinion in this manner, the woman was reminding the children that they should get on with it and go for a song. In another Dene Tha family, teenagers admitted that although their grandfather had often told them 'to go and look for medicine, to learn what they had to do and receive a song to sing on people', they had been too scared to go. These adolescents were growing up without a power but in the company of grandparents, parents, and siblings who had animal helpers.

Dene Tha say that, 'Long ago there were no doctors, and people who had visions were like doctors [who] would cure others.' To cure others, Dene Tha would draw on *ech'int'e*, the power to heal received from an animal helper. To this day, every Dene Tha knows someone who has had a vision and has received a power; everyone knows a relative or a friend whose health has recovered through the assistance of someone with a power to heal. When in need, every Dene Tha calls on someone who knows an animal. Dene Tha also use *yu*, substances that have medicinal properties, such as animal parts, herbs, roots, bark, and leaves. For instance, beaver testes are often seen hanging up to dry in homes. The gum-like material inside relieves toothaches, or the whole can be boiled and the potion drunk for a chest cold. It is also used as an efficient bait for lynx. Rat root is used for stomach ache and head colds. Poplar bark is used for headaches. And so on, with a wide variety of parts of animals and plants.

In a sense *yu* is in the public domain. It is part of the knowledge of every family and is in principle accessible to anyone who cares to go into the bush with the proper attitude and knowledge. This knowledge is nevertheless special. To benefit from the medicinal power of these entities, one does not simply take it. One places tobacco where an uprooted plant stood or by a tree from which a part is taken. 'If you pluck a "rat eye" or stinkweed, you don't just take it. You have to put a gift there to replace what you took.' Without this acknowledgement, the plant's power is withheld. So profound is this attitude to *yu* and the places where it may be gathered that these places were not included on any of the Dene Tha maps drawn for their traditional land-use study. As Dene Tha stated, 'Not everyone should know about them [medicine, or powers]' and 'Any person cannot just pick ground medicine. It is dangerous if one does not know how to use it.'

Some Dene Tha men and women are reputed to gather and keep *yu* properly. They dispense it as medicine in exchange for appropriate payment in tobacco, other goods, and sometimes cash. Dene Tha also apply the term *yu* to Western medication—the pills, syrups, and ointments bought in drugstores or administered by doctors and nurses. A medical professional is referred to as *yu dené*, 'medicine person'. In Dene Dhah, *yu koan*, 'medicine house', refers to the local health clinic or to hospitals in urban centres where they are often taken for medical treatment. They never refer to a fellow Dene as *yu dené* or to a dwelling of theirs as *yu koan*.

Reincarnation, or 'Being Made Again'

I have mentioned cases of reincarnation and journeys of the soul that led to near-death experiences. The following account contains all the Dene Tha themes associated with death: grief over the death of a loved one; the apparition of the dead relative in the narrator's dreams; fear that the visitation would cause harm; and reassurance by the deceased relative that it would not.

> You remember my little niece [Lucy, deceased in her early twenties], she died; she had an accident. About two months after she died I was just crying and then I dreamed about her. Just like a person in person. I could hear that foot, foot, you know [with her hands on the kitchen table she makes the movement and noise of footsteps]. She was carrying a paper like this [she rolls the TV guide in her hands to show me]. When I was dreaming, looking at her, first thing I see her, I say, 'She is gone; how come she is back?' First time she says, 'Where's Peter [the narrator's son]?' He was sleeping in the next room. 'I want to see Peter and Rose [his wife]', she said. I was surprised, scared. She could ask for something if she couldn't go to heaven. She said, 'No, I will not do nothing; I just want to see again.'

The narrator went on to explain that when Rose woke up the next morning, she was screaming and shaking, terrified by a dream in which she had seen Lucy coming back. Was Lucy coming back to take someone's soul away and cause another death in the family? A month later Rose found out that she was pregnant. Rose then knew that Lucy had come back to her to be made again and raised once more as a child in our land.

Identification of someone as a reincarnated person may be a gradual process. Prior to Beverly becoming pregnant with her third child, her father had dreams of his late hunting partner. Her father, who suspected that his partner might be made again to his pregnant daughter, nevertheless kept his dreams to himself. The child reached the stage when she was grasping things and taking them to her mouth, when one day she began to cry inconsolably. Many objects were offered to the child, who turned them down and kept on crying. Beverly's father then said, 'Try giving her an onion.' Beverly did so. To everyone's surprise, the child eagerly took the onion, bit into it, ate, and smiled. Beverly's father then explained that following his dreams he had expected other signs that would confirm his suspicion that his close friend was reincarnated. His suggestion that the child be given an onion reflected the fact that his late hunting partner loved onions. The child eagerly eating the onion confirmed that the baby was his hunting partner growing among them as a young girl.

Among Dene Tha, the individual going into a woman to be born again is a known relative. When the child is born in a sex opposite to its previous sex, the latter determines what kinship terms of address are used. A boy may be addressed as my daughter, my sister, or my aunt. Conversely, a girl may be called my son, my brother, or my uncle. In turn, these kinship terms of address trigger a wide range of accounts of the child's previous life that progressively enter the child's sense of its own identity. The grandmother who constantly greets her grandson with the exclamation, 'Ha ha, the child who is made again', sets the stage for others to engage in recollections of events lived by the child in an earlier life. Through such interaction adults teach a child knowledge that is defined as recollection of a past life. Within this process of socialization, one's sense of identity is mediated by others who know who one is because they saw the spirit come back to be made again.

Household and Daily Life

Dene Tha homes in Chateh are distributed over the land in a clear pattern. Bilingual and bicultural Dene Tha, that is, those most closely associated with Euro-Canadian institutions, dwell in the central townsite. This area also includes the day school, the band-owned general store, the police station, the nursing station, and the residences of the non-Dene professionals (school principal, teachers, nurses, police officers, store manager, band office personnel, and missionaries) living on the reserve. Many Dene Tha women who reside in the central townsite find employment with these professionals as receptionists, clerks, teaching aids, secretaries, or cleaning ladies. Families who associate less closely with Euro-Canadians and their institutions tend to live further away from the townsite in houses built along the road to Habay or along the Gun River, running through what is called the First, Second, and Third Prairie. Over the past 20 years, population increase has led to the creation of a trailer park near the airstrip for younger couples and their children.

Households on 'the prairies' most often consist of a three-generation family living under one roof and addressing one another by kinship terms. English is seldom heard in Dene Tha homes, except for the omnipresent voice of the television. Most adults under 40 are fluent in English but raise their children in their native tongue, although some parents now speak English at home. All children eventually attend the local public school where they are instructed in English, but to this day they play in the school-yard speaking Dene Dhah. In Dene Dhah, people refer to individuals according to their relationship to the first-born child. When this child receives a name, for instance Dih, the parents and siblings become known as Dihta, 'the father of Dih'; Dihmo, 'the mother of Dih'; Dihdéédzé, 'the sister of Dih'; Dihchidle, 'the younger brother of Dih'; and so on. The status achieved in parenthood is immediately reflected in the change of kinship terms of reference.

Learning by Observation or by Instruction
In all societies children learn from their elders the knowledge, attitudes, and skills that allow one to live with confidence as a competent individual. The manner in which learning occurs varies, however, according to kinds of social organization. Among the Dene, as among hunters and gatherers generally, learning proceeds through observation and imitation with what appears to outsiders to be a minimum of intervention and instruction. From the Dene point of view, to

explain is to take away someone's opportunity to learn for herself or himself. To the Dene, knowledge derived from others is suspect. True knowledge comes through direct experience.

When I began fieldwork among the Dene Tha, I took up a Dene Tha woman's offer to teach me how to cook bannock. She came to my house, and while we talked in the kitchen about community matters she proceeded to mix flour, water, and lard and to bake the resulting dough without offering a single word by way of instruction. One hour later, while we shared the freshly baked bannock, I asked if she was going to give me the recipe or the instructions necessary to replicate her baking. She immediately told me, 'I just taught you; you've seen me do it!' Obviously, I had not watched as a Dene Tha would have watched. A 40-year-old Dene Tha father asked me once how many sports I could engage in. I mentioned swimming, whitewater canoeing, scuba diving, skiing, and skating. With tears in his eyes he said that we non-Dene Tha could learn so much because we had instructors to teach us all manners of activities, whereas the Dene Tha must take the much longer and more arduous route of personal observation and imitation.

Given this attitude to learning and dispensation of knowledge, it should come as no surprise that schooling organized according to Euro-Canadian principles of education is problematic for Dene Tha. Thirty years ago, anthropologist Catharine McClellan wrote that in regard to schooling Indian children, 'The increasing emphasis on verbal instruction in advanced grades, regardless of subject matter, helps to cause the withdrawal of older native children about which White teachers so often comment' (McClellan, 1972: xvi). The same observation was made recently after the psycho-educational assessment of Dene Tha children. That report stated:

> Assessments revealed, first and foremost, that the students at DTCS [Dene Tha' Community School] are capable and show personal strengths in many areas. The *DTCS students are*

FIGURE 10.2. Self-directed learning on the prairie. (Courtesy J.-G. Goulet)

not 'stupid,' 'dumb,' or lacking in ability. Virtually all students showed strengths in their ability to work with their hands and to learn by doing and seeing. However, *they displayed weaknesses in their ability to learn through language. This pattern of strong visual and poor verbal learning skills was pervasive. This pattern of abilities will have a significantly negative effect on students' abilities to function effectively within the classroom,* particularly when students with these types of abilities are taught via conventional teaching methods (i.e., verbally based teaching methods). (DTCSTI, 1996; my emphasis)

The report clearly states that in the current schooling system Dene Tha children are deficient and disadvantaged. There is no suggestion that one could design an educational system that would build more on Dene values and ways of learning.

Being Autonomous and Responsible

The Dene Tha emphasis on experiential learning through observation and imitation is closely associated with their value of autonomy. People's ability to realize their goals on their own, including the acquisition of personal knowledge, is highly respected. This respect for autonomy is experienced throughout life. It is experienced by the year-old child who moves towards a broken window, pulls himself up onto a chair, moves his hand through the gaping hole, feels the cold outdoor air, and safely withdraws his hand without touching the windowpane's jagged edges. All along, the child's parents and grandparents quietly observe as they carry on with their own activities, while I, not believing my eyes, silently cringe at the thought of an impending injury. At the other end of life, the consideration for one's right to accomplish one's goals on one's own is experienced by elderly people who, in their seventies, climb aboard pickup trucks unaided. It may take them several minutes to pull themselves partially up, slip down, and pull themselves up again, sweating and breathing heavily in the process. As they do so, able-bodied adults casually carry on with their conversation in the vehicle, while I wonder if it would not be more respectful, and easier for everyone, to give the old person a helping hand.

The differences between my view and that of the Dene Tha reflect our very different upbringings. According to the Dene Tha, to interfere with the child's exploration of his environment would violate his right and ability to pursue and achieve his goals. According to my point of view, to stop the child from approaching the broken window is to protect him from possible injury. I must, however, acknowledge that over the years the accidents and the injuries that I expected in the course of the Dene Tha children's free-ranging explorations did not occur. This fact, I believe, accounts for the relaxed attitude of Dene Tha adults, who supervise their children with a minimum of interference in their activities. Children proceed with confidence in their exploration, secure in the knowledge that no one will interfere. Similarly, to help an elderly individual get into a vehicle would be insulting, for it would suggest that he or she cannot climb on board the vehicle on his or her own. What outsiders see as non-interference in other people's lives, Dene see as preserving the other's ability to truly live life to the fullest extent.

To affirm that 'the behavioural mode by which the autonomy rights of others is observed can best be summed up as non-interference' (Helm, 1961: 176) is to view them as not acting as we would act. To engage in this kind of description is to miss the point that in behaving as they do, the Dene promote *their* values and view of life. They consistently maximize the number of occasions in which one can learn by oneself and for oneself what it is to live an autonomous life competently. This is why they do not step in to stop a small child from approaching a broken windowpane, to take a chainsaw and a new pair of gloves from a boy who imitates his father, or to snatch liquor away from young children who are drinking it. The following statements reflect the Dene attitude towards their children and fellow Dene: 'At home I pretty much let them do what they want to do.' 'It's up to this certain person to make up their mind; no one is going to make their mind.' Since it is the Dene world that we anthropologists strive to grasp, the onus is on us to write, as much as possible, in a manner that conveys their view. We should, therefore, write about the Dene ethical principle of personal responsibility for one's own life, where in the past we spoke of non-interference.

Dene Tha children make decisions that non-Dene parents or professionals would never consider letting them make. For example, when a six-year-old girl was bitten by a dog, I expressed my concern about rabies to the parents and suggested the need for a medical examination and, possibly, vaccination. I offered to take them to the nursing station in my vehicle. The parents listened and sat in silence. They then told me that their daughter did not want to go see the doctor. The girl looked at me with a smile. She knew that it was up to her to make up her mind and that everyone would respect her decision. A week later the wound had properly healed, and the girl could be seen merrily playing with her siblings and cousins.

Dene Tha similarly respected another girl's decision when a doctor and a nurse came into a home, explaining that they had flown to Chateh specifically to vaccinate a few children also at risk of contracting tuberculosis. They asked where they might find an eight-year-old girl whose name they had but whom they did not know. It happened that the girl they were looking for was in the house. The five adults present remained silent as six children quietly moved around. The nurse asked if the girl they were looking for was in the house, but no one answered. Growing impatient, the doctor explained that he was on a tight schedule and must soon leave. He reiterated that without the proper vaccination the girl could become very sick. He obviously expected the adults to cooperate and to answer his questions. From the Dene Tha point of view, however, it was the girl's responsibility to identify herself to the doctor. The girl knew that no one would point her out to the doctor. In the end the doctor and nurse left without finding the girl. The parents of the girl looked at me with a smile, happy that I had not stepped in to undermine the child's ability to make up her own mind.

Note that in all of this the Dene responsibility for one's own life is accompanied by a well-developed sense of one's position relative to others. Everywhere the older and more capable individual has a responsibility to exhibit competent and respectful behaviour for younger individuals to observe and learn well. Kinsmen and friends keep an eye on one another to offer protection, important information, or food, when needed, without being asked. Parents are also careful to store firearms and ammunition away from the reach of children. Stories are repeated again and again to illustrate the kind of behaviour that leads to well-being and the kind that leads to undesired consequences or disaster. And so one learns that true knowledge is personal knowledge, that generosity brings general esteem, and that consideration for the well-being of others and for the community is the foundation of a life well lived.

Dene Tha social life is therefore informed by a pattern of subtle verbal and non-verbal interaction oriented towards the well-being of others while respecting each person's own autonomy. This pattern was observed again and again by Peruvian-born anthropologist Kim Harvey-Trigoso in her recent investigation of Dene Tha childhood socialization and the transmission of traditional knowledge. She notes that, 'The more children engaged in traditional subsistence activities with their caretakers, the more they exhibited a positive attitude towards the community based on co-operation and reciprocity' (Harvey-Trigoso, 1999: 18). In her study, the greatest exposure to activities related to hunting, gathering, and trapping are designated as High Traditional Subsistence Activities (High TSA), as opposed to Low TSA, whereby children have little exposure to these activities.

In their drawings, High TSA children drew more scenes of life in the bush, of local and distant hunting grounds, and of service institutions within the community. Important differences between High and Low TSA children were also noted in terms of group process and behaviour when drawing. High TSA groups consulted each other more, engaged in mutual planning, and stimulated each other with humour to co-operate with each other while avoiding conflict. The High and Low TSA groups both spoke about the dark side of life in Chateh. This included fatal car accidents due to drunk driving, people being shot at, people drowning in the river, and so on. Harvey-Trigoso's observation was that the High TSA groups ended their fantasies with positive outcomes. The boy who had fallen in a river would be saved. The one who had been shot at would survive. The one who ventured into the bush would be visited by an animal. This positive outlook on life was absent in the fantasies of Low TSA children, whose 'mutual criticism of what was drawn inhibited interaction, co-operation, and enthusiasm' (ibid., 17).

Yesterday and Tomorrow: The Power of 'Fire Water'

The dark side of life alluded to above is a recent development in the lives of the Dene and of Aboriginal peoples worldwide. Everywhere, the intrusion of Western institutions and officialdom, often supported by military might, into Aboriginal economy, politics, and religion brings about massive social disruption. Aboriginal peoples cease to enjoy unimpeded access to their ancestral land and the resources that supported their way of life. The social fabric of old is torn along generational and gender lines as young and old, men and women, are drawn differently into a new social order. Adults participate as they may as cheap labour in the new frontier economy. Tensions and frustrations increase. Men, especially, take to drinking, vent their anger towards family members, destroy property, and sometimes take their own lives or those of other community members.

It is against this global background of colonization and its aftermath that we can best understand the alternation among the Dene Tha between two contrasting states of affairs: the attentive and joyful climate of sober life, on one hand, and the uninhibited outbursts and violence associated with drinking, on the other. These opposing states I came to see as phases in a continuous, complex process of social interaction. The ideal and practice of respecting each other's autonomy, which is so characteristic of Dene social life, give way, with alcohol, to violent intrusions into the lives of others. Following violent incidents, the most often heard comment is that the person acted when his or her mind was gone. Hence the person is not accountable for these violent actions.

To read generalizations about Dene Tha patterns of behaviour is not the same as coming face to face with individuals whose behaviour fully fits the pattern. This was the case when two strongly built Dene Tha men in their early thirties came to visit me and have tea early one February afternoon. It was our first meeting, as I was in the initial weeks of my first fieldwork. Full of laughter, they introduced themselves as very best friends and sat next to each other, shoulder to shoulder, on the living-room sofa. I could not help but notice one man's bluish, bruised face, the nose covered with a wide bandage. He spontaneously explained his injuries, first telling me that his friend sitting next to him had hurt him. Both men then laughed and elbowed each other. They insisted that they could not get angry over this incident because the broken nose had been unintended.

The circumstances were as follows. While at a drinking party, the drunken victim's friend, who had a large piece of lumber in hand, had waited behind a door to smash it in the face of a drunken foe, who was soon expected. It was not the foe but the friend, however, who entered the room. As they told me about this turn of events, both men broke into laughter. The broken nose and bruised face were really nothing at all, they said. The victim reiterated that his friend did not know who he was when he delivered the blow. Laughing again, both men repeated how much they enjoyed each other's company. Later, when

they walked away, I doubted that it was possible not to feel anger towards someone who had inflicted such injury, friend or not.

Through numerous accounts of this kind I learned that the Dene Tha operate within a complex system of management of self and of social relationships. When a Dene Tha woman reported that the neighbours' drunken son had slashed the four tires of her pickup, I spontaneously asked, 'What have you done?' She immediately replied, 'I'm keeping my niece away from him. We might have to move for a while to Edmonton' (approximately 800 kilometres south of Chateh). In typical Dene fashion, under the cover of drunkenness, a teenager has retaliated against a woman who thwarted his ambitions. Her response is also typically Dene, to withdraw temporarily from the scene with her niece, rather than confront the teenager or to lay charges with the police. Conflict thus is avoided and people's autonomy is respected to the fullest extent.

Contemporary Issues in a Competitive World

As noted earlier, the year 1965 represents a major turning point in the lives of the Dene Tha. The discovery of a vast gas field in Rainbow Lake, a few kilometres southwest of Habay, led to the construction of a major highway linking it to High Level and other economic centres. In the years to follow, government and industry promoted the construction of a major pipeline to connect gas fields in the Beaufort Sea to Zama Lake, in the Dene Tha homeland. It was already the hub of a distribution system extending from northwest Alberta to Canadian and American markets far to the south.

Dene Tha were then eager to see this project go ahead. They hoped to play a significant part in its implementation. In the mid-1970s they trained with heavy equipment in the dense forest around Chateh in anticipation of the contracts they would get to open roads and to dig trenches in which to lay the proposed pipeline between Zama Lake and the NWT. When I arrived in Chateh in 1979, huge mounds of trees and earth piled at one end of the reserve were testimony to the determination with which the Dene Tha had prepared for the economic development to come. That dream failed to materialize, but it is revitalized today.

A Squandered Opportunity?

To speak of revitalization is to posit a relationship between the past and the present interest in building a pipeline from the Beaufort Sea to Zama Lake. Twenty-five years ago, provincial, territorial, and federal governments, allied with powerful business interests, were deciding to open the entire length of the Mackenzie Valley corridor. This would have involved construction of gas and oil pipelines, building a highway and possibly a railway to the Arctic coast, and the massive influx of non-local labour. New towns, more housing, hydroelectric transmission lines, and telecommunication facilities would follow.

In 1973 this socio-economic revolution was in the making without the participation of the Aboriginal communities it would affect most. The response of Aboriginal peoples to the federal government's intentions was to present a caveat to the Supreme Court of the Northwest Territories, asking it to prevent economic developments that did not consider their Aboriginal rights and interests in the land. In June of the same year, following extensive hearings in Dene communities, Judge Morrow ruled in favour of the Dene and upheld their claim to over one million square kilometres of land. In March 1974, the federal government appointed Justice Thomas Berger to conduct an inquiry into the social, ecological, and economic impact of the proposed pipeline project. In his report, released in May 1977, Justice Berger recommended a 10-year moratorium on the development of the project to allow for a satisfactory conclusion to necessary comprehensive negotiations between the federal government and the Aboriginal inhabitants of the land.

Extensive and intensive negotiations followed, and in April 1990 an agreement in principle between the Metis, the Dene, and the federal government was in place. Three months later, however, the agreement was rejected when put to a vote of the Dene Assembly. With the collapse of this comprehensive claim, regional groups soon indicated that they were prepared to sign regional agreements. This was the case first for the Dinjii Zhuh (Gwich'in), who signed a regional agreement with the federal government in September 1991, soon to be followed by the Sahtu (Bearlakers) and the Dogribs. In August 1993 these three groups declared that they no longer recognized themselves as members of the Dene Nation.

Today, provincial, territorial, and federal governments are once more allied with powerful business interests, promoting the construction of a Mackenzie Valley pipeline. They do so, more and more, in partnership with regional and local Dene First Nations. There is, however, one outstanding Dene regional group, the Deh Cho First Nation, that has not settled its claims with the federal government. Their lands comprise 40 per cent of the area along the southern part of the Mackenzie Valley that the pipeline must go through before reaching Alberta. Without participation of the Deh Cho, construction of the pipeline cannot proceed. Their participation hinges on the successful completion of what is known as the Deh Cho Process, negotiations with the federal government entered into by the Deh Cho First Nation to protect their lands and resources and implement their oral understanding of Treaties No. 8 and No. 11. The Dene Tha see the successful outcome of the Deh Cho Process as vital to their interests. It is not surprising, therefore, that at the National Treaty Conference held in Yellowknife in October 1998, Chief James Ahnassay of the Dene Tha First Nation seconded a motion tabled by Chief Rita Cli, Liidli Kue First Nation. This motion asked for the support of the First Nations at the National Treaty Conference and of the First Nation members of the Assembly of First Nations for the Deh Cho First Nation's stated agenda.

Treaty Rights and Aboriginal Rights

The Dene Tha have supported the Deh Cho Process for two main reasons. First, without its successful completion a major economic project they may benefit from cannot proceed. Second, one day they may also, like the Deh Cho First Nation, formally claim their Aboriginal and treaty rights. A recent statement by Chief James Ahnassay reminds people that the Dene Tha 'are still striving to assert ownership of the traditional lands as it was supposed to have been included in the Treaty negotiations back in June 23, 1900.' He adds, 'The true spirit and intent of the Treaty as understood and told by the Elders has yet to be implemented by Canada to this day. The Elders maintain that none of our traditional lands have ever been given up and will never be given up' (DTFN, 1997: 4).

In these matters of treaty rights, the views of the Dene Tha and of the federal government and the provincial government of Alberta are diametrically opposed. These governments maintain that a simple reading of the English-language text of Treaty 8 makes it clear that any rights the Dene Tha may have had to lands outside their reserves were extinguished absolutely. The political implications of this understanding are stark. Building on its view of property rights, the provincial government grants leases of this 'Crown' land (i.e., traditional Dene Tha territory) to corporations for resource extraction. Forestry and oil and gas companies exercising these rights pay royalties to the provincial and federal governments, but none to the Dene Tha. What are the Dene Tha to do when Euro-Canadians claim property rights and exercise these rights over their homeland? How are they to maintain any control over their homeland? To do so they must speak in a language that can be heard by the powerful. That language is the language of property rights.

For Aboriginal people to claim rights in the language of property, however, is to attempt to speak a language that is alien to them. We have seen that the vocabulary of superstition, reincarnation, power, and medicine stands for very different realities in the words and worlds of the Dene Tha and of Euro-Canadians. The differences in meaning are just as significant in regard to such words as 'land', 'animals', 'ownership', and 'right'. Consider this. An Aboriginal leader surveys his community's land to map out what belongs to them and what belongs to others. When he tells his mother what he is up to, she tells him it is 'a crazy thing to do, for no one can own the land—neither white men nor Indians.' She tells him that Aboriginal land claims ought to mean that government and Aboriginal people get 'together to try to figure out how to keep the land and animals safe for their children and grandchildren' (Nasaday, 2002: 247). Is this not the standard against which to measure the value of any Aboriginal people's attempt to co-operate with government and industry, both to create employment and also to preserve its traditional ways for future generations?

Presently, however, the Dene Tha appear to pursue immediate economic benefits. Corporations and governments remind them that hoped-for benefits will be jeopardized if they enter a land claim with the federal government, asking for recognition of Aboriginal rights to the land, or if they initiate a legal case that could take years to come to a conclusion. The time to invest in gas and oil extraction and distribution is now. This view is in sharp contrast with the attitude expressed recently by a Deh Cho Elder: 'We haven't had a pipeline for thousands of years. I don't see why we should be worried about waiting a little longer' (Anderson, 2002).

Dene political leaders are caught between immediate worries and a concern for the long-term well-being of their people. They fear missing out on an imminent economic boom. That is why, in April 1998, the Dene Tha signed with the federal government an Enhanced Co-Management Agreement to build capacity at the band level to prepare for full control of local oil and gas resources. Following this agenda, in September 2002 the Dene Tha accepted $1.96 million in assistance from the federal government to enable

BOX 10.1

Standards of Consultation

The standards of consultation imposed on the Crown acting in its fiduciary capacity [when it acts in its role as *trustee* for Aboriginal peoples] are more onerous than those that arise out of statutory obligations and procedural fairness requirements. Some of the key findings of Monique Ross (1997), a research associate at the Canadian Institute of Resource Law, include:

- The constitutional obligation, and the ability to discharge that obligation, rest squarely with the Crown. As a result, government must be involved in the consultation process and cannot simply delegate that duty to a third party without supervising it. The courts scrutinize how government, not industry, has consulted.
- Aboriginal and treaty rights are collective rights. Therefore, consultation must involve not only individuals directly affected in their exercise of those rights, but also community representatives.
- Government must initiate the consultation process and obtain sufficient information (including information on the practices and

views of the affected First Nation) upon which to base a conclusion regarding the impact of proposed developments and land-use decisions on Aboriginal and treaty rights.
- Government must provide to potentially affected Aboriginal people full information on the proposed action or decision and its expected impacts, so that they have an opportunity to express their concerns and interests.
- Consultation is expected at a minimum to be 'meaningful' and the Crown must be prepared to 'substantially address the concerns of the Aboriginal peoples whose lands [or rights] are at issue'. Depending on the nature of the proposed infringement of the right, this may translate into a duty to obtain full consent, notably in the context of title lands.
- Case law suggests that any decision affecting the balance between Aboriginal and treaty rights and non-Aboriginal interests in natural resources (such as setting harvesting limits and allocating resources between various users) requires prior consultation with Aboriginal people.

the band to acquire a 50 per cent interest in two oil and gas drilling rigs to be used for a minimum of 760 drilling days over the next four years in northern Alberta and northeast BC. As they implement this project that will create 32 new jobs, Chief Stephen Didzena highlights the dilemma facing the Dene Tha. 'We are determined to work with industry and government to maximize economic benefits from resource development, while ensuring the protection of our Treaty rights and the enhancement of our traditional ways.' Significantly, in all existing agreements with governments leading to economic development in the

Dene Tha homeland the federal government has yet to meet fully its obligations towards the people. This may well constitute the basis for an eventual Dene Tha claim against the Crown.

Whether or not such a claim is ever filed, the question remains: will the intensification of oil and gas exploration enhance Dene Tha traditional ways? The new jobs will be held by men who are part-time hunters and trappers. The land continues to provide Dene Tha families with substantial amounts of food (fish, rabbit, duck, moose, etc.) and medicine or *yu*. These life forms are more than material resources; they are vital links to their history and identity. This heritage and land base, however, are rapidly changing. Trappers describe their traplines as being close to or towards 'Mobile Road', 'Esso Road', or 'Husky Road', using the different oil companies as reference points. The impact of this development is further reflected in the fact that when people 'stay for a week or longer in the bush they take drinking water' (since natural water is polluted due to industrial development).

In 1995, in an attempt to bridge the gap between themselves and governments regarding their interests in their homeland, the Dene Tha commissioned a Traditional Land Use and Occupancy Study. It had positive outcomes, particularly growth in community pride, in awareness of the importance of traditional sites and traditional knowledge, and in understanding government and industry perspectives on economic development. Nevertheless, the results have fallen short of expectations. Outsiders' recognition of their traditional lands as Dene Tha territory has not increased. Neither has communication between the community and forestry companies improved.

The Dream of Full Employment

The economic opportunities pursued in recent years may exacerbate rather than improve social problems. It is well-known that drinking is tied to the flow of cash in the community. Dene Tha men, for instance, observe that 'firefighting money is for firewater.' They do not, however, spend all their firefighting money on drink. Typically, they buy gifts for their parents and spouse (a piece of furniture, a major appliance, or a television, for instance), give some money to siblings and cousins, and keep some for drinking in High Level. The same pattern is likely to repeat itself in the years to come in the context of higher male employment.

As we have seen, the Dene Tha continue to privilege observation over instruction and individual autonomy over subordination. In this respect, there is great continuity from generation to generation. The consequences of living by

these values, however, are quite different today than they were in the past because the physical and social environments have changed so drastically. To live by these Dene values in the context of a hunting and gathering economy, in which extended families or small bands were dispersed over a large territory for most of the year, is one thing. To live by these same values on a reserve, where almost 800 people, the majority under 16 years old, dwell in constant proximity, is another. Earlier generations of Dene Tha dealt with their children in the context of a dwelling they had built in the bush, in which their children would fall asleep at night as the fire went out, and everything was dark, indoors and out. Nowadays children may keep their parents awake night after night in a single-family dwelling serviced with electricity, permitting light and television after dark. Children play and watch television in the presence of parents who will not turn off the lights or pick up the children and put them to bed, because that simply is not done. To do so would infringe on their autonomy.

In the past, men and women had clear and complementary productive domestic roles. Through observation, girls would learn from their mothers and sons from their fathers. Dene then experienced themselves as largely autonomous and self-governing. They sought gifts and songs from animal helpers and developed strong minds with which to know how to conduct themselves competently. This is no longer the case, with most men and women unemployed and, to a significant degree, dependent on unemployment and welfare cheques. The tragedy is that for contemporary adults on the reserve, there is a lack of constructive challenges to meet and overcome.

The dream of full employment was vividly expressed by a young girl. Her father had been drinking with his brothers and friends for four consecutive days. One man in the group was paying for all the liquor, since he had received three cheques of $340 each. Once the men were drunk, the girl and her mother hid one of the cheques. When the man asked for his last cheque, the girl told him he would not get it back until he was sober. She added, 'I am tired of you drinking. I will buy the band store, you will be the meat cutter, and your brother will be the meat grinder for hamburger, and your mom, she is old, her, she will work on the food side, and Mom will work on clothes, and my sister will be at the Post Office, and Dad will be the manager. I will buy the nursing station, and I will buy the school too, and Dad's brother will be the principal. And I will buy the coffee shop and I will run it.' In reality, except for the positions of school principal and store manager, held by non-Dene hired by the band, all the positions mentioned by the girl were already held by Dene Tha. In this light, current Dene Tha initiatives to foster a type of economic development that will provide employment opportunities to a greater number of individuals may well represent the lesser of two evils. But such a choice must only be embraced with a view to mitigating as best as possible the potential negative consequences.

Conclusion

For centuries, the Dene Tha have lived in their homeland according to a rich indigenous tradition. This accomplishment is reflected in the comment of an Elder who proudly told his son, 'If our stories and ways were wrong, we would not be here today.' The son, however, faces circumstances that his ancestors did not. Treaty 8 was signed by people thinking they would be able to pursue their traditional way of life with a minimum of external control. Their descendants are now accepting millions of dollars in loans from the federal government to invest in the exploitation of gas and oil fields in their homeland to fuel the economy of the Canadian and American heartland.

Such a development would have been unimaginable 20 years ago. Its occurrence demonstrates the degree to which the Dene Tha have come to shape their lives in the context of Western institutions designed to promote Euro-North American values and standards of life. Up to this point, the various non-Dene institutions have not eradicated or rendered obsolete Dene ways of living in this land and in the other land. The cumulative impact of sustained interaction with non-Dene is nonetheless undermining the relatively homogeneous view of the world and the practices characteristic of Dene life. This is true of the school, the police station, the nursing station, and the church. It is even true of the band office, which now functions more and more as the local gateway to industrial economic development on the Dene Tha homeland.

There is little evidence that Euro-Canadians can truly be receptive to an agenda other than their own. For some time to come outside professionals who are incognizant of much of Dene Tha reality will continue to staff the school, court, hospital, nursing station, and church. These professionals will continue to dispense Eurocentric forms of education, justice, medication, religious service, and employment.

Given current political and economic developments, it is also likely that the differences between families who pursue different economic strategies will increase. In and out of school one will be able to distinguish between children who still know the land and children who do not. The former will continue to have a positive outlook on life; the latter will see only disaster looming before them. The source of this contrasting outlook on life will continue to stem from the children's participation, or lack of participation, in traditional subsistence activities.

In the meantime, the environmental crisis will continue to impact the Dene Tha. People already see damage done to the land undermining their ability to move around their homeland. Water in some streams and lakes is polluted by industrial activity. Vast tracts of forest are harvested by international corporations. The harm being done to their homeland will persist for decades, if not centuries, to come. Throughout the Subarctic, cleaning up the environment in the wake of ecologically insensitive mining, drilling, and harvesting of trees is a huge task that government and industry have yet to undertake seriously. Slow progress on this front means that it will take more than a generation before Dene Tha can hunt and trap in the bush for extended periods and drink again with confidence the water that is now polluted and undrinkable.

Finally, the Dene Tha will continue watching the Deh Cho Process and learn from their northerly neighbours how best to launch their own claims to Aboriginal self-government and Aboriginal stewardship over the land. If they take that route, governments and their legal advisers are likely to argue that the willing participation of the Dene Tha in current agreements governing exploitation of resources indicates their recognition that what exists within the global economy are not Aboriginal rights but economic opportunities open to all regardless of race or creed. Once again, Dene Tha leaders will have to face the deep disjunction between Euro-Canadian and their own understandings of their history and their relationship to the land and its inhabitants. Sadly enough, in the present circumstances I see little likelihood that Euro-Canadians and Dene Tha will be able collectively and jointly to create a just and balanced political and economic environment. Such an environment would truly enhance the quality of life for all the inhabitants of Chateh and beyond. Such an environment would then respect the invisible web of interpretations drawn by the Dene Tha to constitute a distinctively meaningful Aboriginal world that, to this day, is much richer and more complex than ever imagined by outsiders. Such an environment would foster a world in which parents could still proudly say to their children, 'If our stories were not true, we would not be here today.'

Acknowledgements

I want to express my gratitude to Monique Ross of the Canadian Institute for Resource Law and to Kim Harvey-Trigoso for making available to me, on short notice, valuable material they had recently published or written concerning the Dene Tha. Thanks also to Christine Hanssens, who, based on her first-hand experience with the Dene Tha, has provided valuable insights and comments on the organization and content of this chapter. Except for references to events and developments that have taken place since 1987, the ethnographic material (including the map of the Dene Tha homeland) pertaining to the Dene Tha contained in this chapter is adapted from Jean-Guy A. Goulet, *Ways of Knowing: Experience, Knowledge, and Power among the Dene Tha* (Lincoln: University of Nebraska Press, 1997).

References and Recommended Readings

Anderson, M. 2002. 'Not All Aboriginal Groups Support New Developments', *Edmonton Journal*, National Post Supplement, 17 Sept., EJ14. A journalistic account, supported by a wealth of colour photographs, of current economic developments and contemporary actors in the NWT.

Brant, C. 1990. 'Native Ethics and Rules of Behaviour', *Canadian Journal of Psychiatry* 35, 6: 534–9. A Mohawk psychiatrist discusses the ethics of non-interference and individual responsibility among Natives.

Dene Tha' First Nation. 1997. *Dene Tha' Traditional Land-use and Occupancy Study*. Calgary: Arctic Institute of North America. Verbatim statements on issues affecting individuals following their transition from the bush economy to contemporary development and welfare. Many photographs.

Dene Tha' Community School Testing Information. 1996. Unpublished manuscript, 3 Apr.

Goulet, Jean-Guy. 1997. *Ways of Knowing: Experience, Knowledge, and Power among the Dene Tha*. Lincoln: University of Nebraska Press. A study that illustrates with anecdotal accounts how it is possible to understand another culture.

Harvey-Trigoso, Kim. 1997. 'Ecological Knowledge of the Dene Tha': Traditional Subsistence Activities and Childhood Socialization', MA thesis, University of Calgary. A study of childhood socialization among contemporary Dene Tha that reveals the unique perspective of children on their world.

Helm, June. 1994 [1961]. *Prophecy and Power among the Dogrib Indians*. Lincoln: University of Nebraska Press. Traces origins of a revitalization movement among NWT Dene to activity of Dene Tha prophets.

Horvath, S., L. McKinnon, M. Dickerson, and M. Ross. 1997. *The Impact of the Traditional Land-use and Occupancy Study on the Dene Tha' First Nation*. Sustainable Forest Management Network, Project Report 2001–18. Edmonton: University of Alberta. Documents the impact of traditional land-use study on the Dene Tha and on industry and government.

McClellan, C. 1972. *The Girl Who Married the Bear*. Publications in Ethnology No. 2. Ottawa: National Museum of Man.

Mills, Antonia, and Richard Slobodin, eds. 1994. *Amerindian Rebirth: Reincarnation Belief among North American Indians and Inuit*. Toronto: University of Toronto Press. Excellent collection of reincarnation studies among contemporary Native peoples.

Moore, Patrick, and Angela Wheelock, eds. 1990. *Wolverine Myths and Visions: Dene Traditions from Northern Alberta*. Edmonton: University of Alberta Press. Dene Tha stories from when animals and humans talked and intermarried.

Nasaday, P. 1997 '"Property" and Aboriginal Land Claims in the Canadian Subarctic: Some Theoretical Considerations', *American Anthropologist* 104: 247–61.

Ross, Monique M. 1997. 'The Dene Tha' Consultation Pilot Project: An "Appropriate Consultation Process" with First Nations?', *Newsletter of the Canadian Institute for Resource Law* 76 (Fall): 1–7. A legal analysis of current agreements between the provincial government and the Dene Tha from the perspective of the federal government's legal obligations towards Aboriginal peoples.

Slobodin, Richard. 1975. 'Canadian Subarctic Athapaskans in the Literature to 1965', *Canadian Review of Sociology and Anthropology* 12: 276–89.

Smith, D.M. 1993. 'Albert's Power: A Fiction Narrative', *Anthropology and Humanism* 18, 2: 67–73. An insightful narrative based on the Dene understanding of animals as a source of power that humans can draw upon.

Suggested Web Sites

Assumption RCMP:
   www.geocities.com/CapitolHill/Senate/6979/
   assumption.html
   Briefly describes Assumption, occupations of the Dene Tha, and the proposed program to train Dene Tha police officers.

Indian and Northern Affairs Canada:
   www.inac.gc.ca/FNProfiles/FNProfiles_DETAILS.
   asp?BAND_NUMBER=448
   Basic geographic, demographic, social, and political information on the location and size of Dene Tha reserves.

First Nation Forestry Program:
   www.fnfp.gc.ca/sectione/3section/alta/200001/
   denetha.html
   FNFP will provide funding to train equipment operators to scarify and reforest blocks of Dene Tha land. Related sites describe FNFP objectives, governance, successes, and challenges.

CHAPTER 11

The Slavey Indians:
The Relevance of Ethnohistory to Development

MICHAEL ASCH with ROBERT WISHART

Introduction

One important strain in anthropological thought is the notion that disciplinary expertise can be lent to the solution of problems in the 'real world'. As an undergraduate at the University of Chicago, I became acquainted with this perspective through a course I took with Dr Sol Tax, widely known as a proponent of 'action anthropology'. This greatly influenced my decision to become an anthropologist. Yet, it was not until the mid-1970s that I was able to make a contribution to this aspect of the discipline.

The circumstances of my involvement were as follows. In the early 1970s, a consortium of multi-national petroleum corporations decided to construct a pipeline to transport Alaskan and Canadian Arctic gas to markets in southern Canada and the United States. Named Canadian Arctic Gas Pipeline Ltd (CAGPL), the consortium proposed to construct an $8 billion line along the northern coast of North America and up the Mackenzie River Valley to northern Alberta. The region through which the pipeline was to pass included the homeland of two Aboriginal nations: the Dene (Athapaskan-speaking Indians of the Mackenzie corridor) and the Inuvialuit (the most westerly Inuit of Canada). The government of Canada set up a commission of inquiry to ascertain the potential social and economic impact of this pipeline. Under Mr Justice Thomas R. Berger

this commission, called the Mackenzie Valley Pipeline Inquiry, spent more than two years listening to testimony from experts and community people. It concluded that the proposal should be shelved for 10 years, and, in some respects at least, this recommendation was followed.

I became involved in the Berger Inquiry because I had done research among the Slavey regional grouping of the Dene in 1969–70. I had collected much information on the contemporary economy and economic history of the Slavey at Wrigley (Pehdzeh Ki) and Fort Simpson during my fieldwork. Yet the focus of my initial fieldwork had not been economic matters but social organization and music.

My orientation to music and social structure was based on a complex set of factors, a part of which was my belief that understanding how other societies frame their world cognitively is crucial to the anthropological enterprise. I therefore chose in my doctoral research to focus on understanding how the Slavey conceptualized music sound and how they created structured musical compositions. This work resulted in the development of a model that described their music sound system and predicted, with some degree of accuracy, how compositions were structured (Asch, 1972, 1975). Yet I remained uncertain whether the model really mirrored Slavey perceptions or whether it was merely a creation that helped me to understand them. I felt I then had two choices: to try to solve this dilemma or to turn to a different sphere of Slavey life. I took the latter course. In focusing on economic activities I chose an aspect of Slavey life I believed I could understand in a manner similar to the Dene themselves. This was because the things of the economy as they see them are quite similar to the things I can see and, perhaps more importantly, because Dene talk much more about economic matters than they ever do about music.

For all that, I have not abandoned an interest in Dene cognition. In retrospect I see that my concerns ran deeper than just which focus to choose in analysis. The kind of cognitive mindset I find myself interested in is not easily expressed by any group and requires a high degree of 'native intuition'. For this reason (I believe), I shifted my focus away from ferreting out the underlying cognitive framework (in the economic or any other sphere) of the Dene to working it out for our own society. Ultimately I have found that, for me, it is easier to use my intuition to grapple with how we think than it is to figure out the 'deep structure' of people from other cultures. This is not due to a belief that different ways of thinking do not exist or, as Rushforth (1986) attests, cannot be understood or discussed by non-Natives. Rather, it is that I do not seem to have a strong talent in that direction.

The Dene and the Pipeline: Economic Development in the Canadian North

The Berger Inquiry dealt with the social and economic consequences of a major construction project on contemporary Native people. Crucial to this kind of evaluation is the status of the Aboriginal society: is it 'dead' or 'dying', or does it remain 'viable'? At the heart of this matter lies our perception of hunting-gathering society. Dominant in academic thought today is an evolutionary view that sees such societies as of intellectual interest primarily because of the data they provide on the 'past' of human history. Hunter-gatherers are in this view our 'contemporary

ancestors'. Part of the intellectual baggage pertaining to this idea is the belief that such societies today are mere vestiges of their former statuses and, like vestigial organs, are about to self-destruct. Evidence for this conclusion appears to abound in transparently obvious symbols of precipitous assimilation. After all, the Dene now wear Western clothing, speak English, go to school, ride on snowmobiles and in cars, listen to country music, and complain about lack of disposable income. One could easily presume that fundamentally these are just poor people who happen to be Dene and not members of an autonomous culture.

The proponents of the pipeline firmly supported this view. On the basis of studies into the contemporary economy of the Dene and Inuit and by reference to some of the ethnographic literature, expert witnesses (including economists and sociologists) who appeared on behalf of the applicants argued that the traditional way of life was 'dead' or 'dying'. As a consequence, they argued that in the near future the Dene would slip from high unemployment to endemic poverty. Seen in this context the pipeline was a good thing, for it would provide jobs enabling the Dene to make a 'smooth' transition from a traditional existence to a middle-class way of life.

Because of my work at Wrigley, I was asked by the Indian Brotherhood of the Northwest Territories (now renamed the Dene Nation) to provide evidence for the Berger Inquiry. However, it was not supposed to be about evaluating this way of thinking. Rather, it was to focus on ethnographic and historical evidence on land use and the fur trade. Indeed, my evidence was titled 'Past and Present Land Use of the Slavey Indians'. Yet, although the title never changed, the content did, for I found myself confronting an idea for which evidence was lacking.

Upon reading the data provided by the applicants' witnesses, I became convinced that something was fundamentally wrong with their work, for it did not jibe with my own recollections of the time I spent at Wrigley. These people were being miscast as impoverished, marginalized Canadians, for, to paraphrase what Dr Peter Usher stated about the Inuit, if these are poor people, they are the only ones who go to bed with stomachs filled with good meat provided from their own larders. It was a view that was further confirmed by the Dene, for they argued almost unanimously in opposition to the immediate construction of the pipeline. Their reason? It would interfere with their traditional land-based activities. In short, the Dene were presenting the view that their traditional way of life (as currently practised) could remain viable in the modern world. The problem, as they saw it, was that the means to ensure this end were not in their hands. As a solution they proposed the creation of an autonomous polity (consistent with a statement of principles summarized in the Dene Declaration) and economic tools for protection and development of their economy (based in large part on the fulfillment of government promises respecting the finalizing of an outstanding land claim that arose from disagreements concerning the terms of a treaty signed in 1921–2).

If one agreed that their way of life was dead or dying, the point of view presented by the Dene could make no sense, and, indeed, the applicants characterized their assertions as 'romantic' and 'politically motivated'. If, on the other hand, their assessment of their economy was taken to be valid, then their orientation could be understood as based on a realistic appraisal of the situation.

My testimony focused on determining which perspective was more appropriate and, although facts concerning these matters were used, did not present a story concerned with land use or economic history. In this respect, it represented my first attempt to grapple with how members of our society frame facts about Aboriginal peoples, for although one might argue that the assertions made by the applicants were merely 'politically motivated', they appropriated a way of looking at Aboriginal peoples that dominates contemporary Western thought (including theorizing in anthropology). My work indicated that there was little

factual basis for the assumptions made about the Dene as contemporary hunter-gatherers and sought to piece together an analysis that made better sense of the facts of cultural contact. It is a matter I have developed more fully elsewhere (Asch, 1979a, 1979b, 1982). However, it was also intended as a contribution to the process of the Berger Inquiry itself: independent factual evidence demonstrating that the contemporary way of life was not dying would help in understanding why the Dene did not want the pipeline built immediately and why they argued that, prior to its construction, a regime protective of their traditional way of life and controlled by them should be in place.

What follows is an edited and augmented version of my testimony at the Berger Inquiry, divided into three primary parts. The first focuses on economic history, establishing a theme about the course of development in the region. The second deals with the contemporary situation. This is followed by a final section evaluating solutions proposed by CAGPL studies in light of this evidence. Although the analysis was confined to the region of the Slavey, broadly speaking the findings are relevant to the Dene as a whole.

Economic History—Aboriginal Period

At first glance it may seem inappropriate to consider that the Dene had an economy at all during Aboriginal times; there was, after all, no 'marketplace'. However, if we define the term 'economy' in its most basic sense, as the production and circulation of goods, then it is clear that every society that survives in a material way from year to year must have an economy.

In the late pre-contact period the economy of the region was characterized by the dominance of small self-sufficient groups of approximately 20–30 related persons called by anthropologists 'local groups'. In order to maintain themselves, these groups harvested the many kinds of bush resources found in the region, including a wide variety of fish, small game animals, big game such

FIGURE 11.1. Slavey shaman (right), his son (left), and Dogrib boy (centre), Fort Rae, NWT, 1913. (© Canadian Museum of Civilization, photographer J.A. Mason, 1913, 26079)

as moose and woodland caribou, and a number of edible berries. As well, they relied on other resources in the environment, such as trees, which were important in constructing shelter, in transportation, and as fuel.

Given the nature of the terrain and the distribution of resources in the region, it is most likely that the local groups camped in winter near the shores of the larger lakes that dominate the region. Here, the small game and fish, the staples of the diet, could be found in most constant supply. Within these encampments, labour was organized along age and sex lines: men were primarily responsible for hunting big game and setting fishnets, and the women and children were responsible for the collection of small game. Women were also responsible for making clothing from local resources such as moose hide and rabbit skins.

The primary techniques used in collecting animal resources were snaring with babiche or sinew, and entrapment. Moose and other big-

game animals were hunted with bow and arrow, club, or spear when the prey were crossing water or open country. Fish were taken using fishnets made of woven willow bast or caribou babiche. Given this type of technology, the capture of large game most often required co-operative labour in hunting parties. Co-operation was also important for women's production tasks.

Transportation in the winter at this time relied primarily on human labour and was accomplished almost exclusively on foot. Yet, paradoxical as this may seem, the use of this form of transportation resulted in more group travel than in the later period when dog power was used. The reason for this is simple: without dog teams it would be easier to bring people to the game than the other way around. Hence, in winter the people moved around more than in later periods and, in fact, may have travelled throughout the region in search of game, returning only occasionally to the fish-lake base camp. In summer the people travelled primarily by shallow-drafted canoes, sometimes made of moose hide. Travel included an annual trip to one of the major lakes where an encampment of perhaps 200 persons would be formed, probably around the times of the fish runs. Before winter the people would return to their small local groups.

Within local groups, bush resources were distributed on the basis of reciprocity or mutual sharing. Generally speaking, all participated equally in the good fortune of the hunters and all suffered equally when their luck turned bad. Although the distribution system was basically informal, there was some formality concerning how certain animals were shared in that specific parts were reserved for the hunter and persons closely related to his or her immediate family. In this way, individual ability could be recognized, but not at the expense of the collective good. Thus, the whole membership of the local group, not each family or each individual, defined the self-sufficient unit.

There is little evidence available from historical or archaeological sources concerning the circulation of goods between local groups during this period. However, an examination of the productive base of the land indicates that the region is not highly varied as to kinds of resources but is somewhat variable from year to year as to the actual distribution of these resources. Hence, the primary problem of circulation probably concerned the creation of a balance in any year between local groups with resources surplus to their needs and those that did not have the minimum resources necessary for survival.

Theoretically, there are two ways in which this imbalance could be corrected: either surplus goods could be moved to people in need or people could move to areas in which a local surplus existed. Given the nature of the technology as well as the kinship system as reported by early European travellers, it would appear that the latter solution was the case. Thus, the principle of mutual sharing of resources extended to include all groups in the region. This was done through a kinship and marriage system that linked all the people in a region into a single social unit and conveyed reciprocal rights and obligations concerning the use of resources in the region to all.

In terms of inter-regional or inter-tribal exchange, the little archaeological and historical evidence available indicates that trade between groups did occur: copper as well as implements of European manufacture are found in the region prior to the arrival of the European traders. However, nothing of the mechanisms of this trade is known.

Economic History—Fur Trade Period

Direct involvement with the fur trade began in the last decade of the eighteenth century. Although contact was established as the result of the competition between the Hudson's Bay Company and the North West Company for hegemony in Western trade, virtually none of the intense rivalry between the two trading companies was transferred to the region. Here the North West Company maintained control in the fur trade until 1821 when, with the amalgamation of the two companies, the new HBC came into ascendancy. As a result, none of the disruptions in Native life that marked the period of competition in other parts of Canada appeared in the North, and, indeed, from the time of contact until roughly 1870 when the Bay lost its monopoly, the fur trade was marked by stability.

During the period of monopoly, the region was considered too remote to command much attention. Bay policy required that remote posts such as those in Dene territory must remain self-sufficient in food provisions. Further, because of the depletion of furs by intense earlier competition, the Bay developed a conservation policy. At least from 1821 until 1850 the HBC reduced trading in furs at all posts in North America, including those in this region. As well, supply lines at this time were maintained through the use of York boats and brigading from Winnipeg to the West, imposing severe restrictions on the amount of goods and furs that could be transported to and from the North.

FIGURE 11.2. Slavey Indian camp at Fort Simpson, NWT, 1934. (© Canadian Museum of Civilization, 80042)

The economy of the Native people changed little during this period from its Aboriginal strategy. It was still 'total' in that the people of the region, including Natives and Bay personnel, depended for their survival almost exclusively on local resources. This was achieved by Bay personnel through the exchange of trade goods for food and by the Natives through the continued use of a wide range of bush resources and the organization of the people into self-sufficient local groups. For the Native people, production, despite the new utensils and implements, was still primarily a collective activity: distribution of goods within and between local groups was still based on the principle of sharing. The only significant changes in Native economic life during this time were the adoption of certain trade items that made life a little easier and a shift in seasonal round to include both occasional trips to the trading posts for supplies at various times in the year and, especially later in the period, the occasional use of the trading posts rather than the major lakes as places for encampment during the summer.

With the sale of its territories in 1870 to the British Crown and thereby to Canada, the Bay lost its formal monopoly and with it an assured supply of furs at prices well below world market levels. In some areas of the Mackenzie region, such as Wrigley and Fort Norman, monopoly conditions continued to as late as perhaps 1900. In other parts of the region, such as Fort Simpson

Given such transportation and trading restrictions, goods available for trade at remote posts were limited in both kind and quantity. Of the goods available, the most important for the Indians probably were the new staples such as flour, tea, and sugar; metal utensils and implements; beads; blankets; tobacco and alcohol. To obtain these goods the Indians had to trade local resources. It would thus appear that production for the fur trade was not great and consisted mainly of supplying provisions rather than furs.

and upstream, the effect of free traders further south was soon felt. Thus, William Hardisty, chief factor at Fort Simpson, as early as 1875 suggested that, while the Indians at Fort Norman 'being in the centre of the District and far removed from the opposition . . . are still amenable to authority and generally work', the Natives in the Fort Simpson area 'would not deliver up their furs at the old prices.' One reason was 'the advent of free traders at Vermilion (in Alberta) and the exaggerated reports regarding them which have been carried all over the District'.

To meet this new competition, the Bay needed to provide more trade goods and to provide them more cheaply. The major stumbling block was the continued use of a transportation system that was costly, inefficient, and taxed to capacity. To solve this problem (and perhaps spurred on by the development of an independent steam transport system by the Roman Catholic missionaries), the Bay replaced the York boats with steam, first on the Athabasca in 1882 and then on the Mackenzie in 1885, and finally moved the major transshipment point to the North from Winnipeg to Edmonton after the completion of the rail link from Calgary to Edmonton in 1891. Between 1870 and 1890 transportation to the North was thus revolutionized.

Concomitantly, the Bay changed its strategy from one of monopoly in the collection of furs to the encouragement of competition. The control of the Company now was seen to be in terms of virtual monopoly in transportation and retail sales, where its directors believed they could maintain a high level of profit.

Competition and the new transportation system, as well as the Yukon gold rush of 1898 and the rise in fur prices during World War I, resulted in the complete transformation of the fur trade. The kinds of goods available changed greatly. Among the new items introduced by the turn of the century were the repeating rifle, the steel trap, wide varieties of Western clothing, dogs and dog teams, and chocolates and other luxury items. As well, the quantities of traditional exchange items

such as food staples, blankets, and metal utensils increased dramatically.

The new transportation system also meant that traders no longer depended on local resources for provisions. This new-found independence affected exchange relationships between traders and Indians. Natives still traded local resources, but whereas in the earlier period either provisions or furs could be used in exchange, now the Bay and the free traders alike manipulated exchange rates to encourage trade in furs. As early as 1871 the Bay limited the trade in percussion rifles to fur exchange, while allowing food and furs to be traded for common Indian guns. Late in the nineteenth century the Bay changed its standard of trade by doubling the exchange value of furs compared to provisions. The changing economic relationship was capped during the 1890s with the adoption of money as the medium of exchange and the concurrent demise of the old barter system.

As a result of these externally initiated developments in the fur trade, the Native economy in some areas had shifted by 1900 (and throughout the region by World War I) away from its virtual independence of trade goods to a situation where both trade goods and local subsistence resources were significant. Yet the internal organization of the economy did not change greatly. The primary economic unit remained the local group, which in most cases still wintered at fish lakes. Labour was still organized on the basis of age and sex; women and children were responsible for collecting small game, the men, for hunting, fishing, and now trapping.

Some changes in production resulted from the introduction of the rifle and the steel trap. Of these, perhaps the most significant was the new-found ability of individuals to maintain greater independence of others in their hunting and trapping pursuits. Yet, Aboriginal hunting techniques were still employed in hunting most game, including big-game animals, and co-operation therefore remained a significant component of production. As well, some changes occurred in the mobility of the people. The advent of the trapline, the year-round availability of provisions at trading posts, and the introduction of dog-team transport encouraged a more sedentary lifestyle to the extent that during the early twentieth century many families built permanent dwellings at fish lakes and along traplines. To obtain supplies and trade furs, the men now made at least two trips to the trading posts during winter, generally around Christmas and Easter. The women and children most often did not accompany the men to the posts but remained, as before, in the bush throughout the winter months. Summer travel was expanded by the introduction of motors on canoes and scows. The seasonal round now almost always included summer encampments at the trading posts.

Finally, the system of circulating goods among the people of the region remained virtually unchanged by the new fur trade conditions. Despite the increased individualization in production and the introduction of money into the economy, distribution both within and between local groups remained based on the principle of mutual sharing. Thus the main change in the distribution system of the region was the great increase in the amount of trade between the Native people and the traders.

Economic History—Recent Decades

The regional economy had been transformed by the new fur trade conditions from a 'total economy' to one that relied on both local subsistence and the use of externally produced goods that were exchanged for furs. However, this shift created no major changes in the internal dynamics of production and circulation within the Native economy. Nonetheless, as a result of this shift the standard of living was greatly raised. This must have made people feel quite wealthy. This rise in the standard of living, however, had an unexpected consequence: dependency. Now the stability and success of the economy were dependent in large measure both on external economic conditions, such as a high market price for furs in

relation to trade good prices, and, locally, on the availability of a productive surplus in one resource, furs. The latter problem was chronic, and after the influx of whites into the North during the 1920s, it almost led to the collapse of the economy. On the other hand, the first aspect appeared at the time to be insignificant, for the relationship between fur prices and trade good prices remained stable through two world wars and the Great Depression. Yet, ultimately, it was this factor and not fur production itself that led to the collapse of the fur trade economy when, beginning after World War II and lasting at least through the Korean War, there was a long depression in the value of furs and an astronomical rise in the prices of trade goods.

In the years immediately following World War II, Native peoples hoped that fur prices would soon rise again. In the meantime, most people, supported in part by the general introduction of family allowance and old age pension payments during the late 1940s, maintained their fur trade economy focus. By the 1950s it became apparent that the fur economy would never return, at least not without direct government intervention. Thus, for example, the Territorial Council in January 1956 unanimously passed a resolution that stated, in part:

Whereas the real income derived from fur trapping in the Northwest Territories is less than one third of its pre-war level . . . and whereas it is not possible for a person to live and to provide the minimum needs of his family at the present prices of fur . . . (be it resolved that) the Commissioner be requested to ask the Minister of Northern Affairs and National Resources to request the Government of Canada most strongly to give immediate consideration to the provision of assistance to the people of the Northwest Territories through the establishment of an appropriate measure of support for the price of fur; or, alternatively, to take all possible measures at the earliest date to stimulate the economic development of the Northwest Territories so that alternative means of employment and income can be provided for these people. (Council of the Northwest Territories, 1956)

The federal government also took a general position in favour of economic development. To this end, Jean Lesage, Minister of Northern Affairs and Natural Resources, in 1955 proclaimed a new education program for the Northwest Territories, recommending the construction of school facilities in smaller centres and a program of hostel construction in larger ones to facilitate universal education. This solution gained the approval of at least some of the band chiefs, for it seemed a way for the youth to overcome the problems of the contemporary economic situation.

By the early 1960s, grade schools had been constructed in virtually all communities in the region, and in most cases people moved into town where they would continue to receive benefits and could remain with their children. For the others, it was pointed out that:

Forgetful children should not forget that school is compulsory and that missing school for five consecutive or separate times is liable to punishment. Parents who fail to send their children to school without serious reason and notification to the teacher are liable to be fined and jailed. Moreover family allowance payments may be cancelled upon report made by the proper authorities. Mark well, children, that missing part of the day accounts for a day's absence, in so far as the punishments are concerned. Therefore, do your share for your sake and that of your family. (*The Catholic Voice*, 1957: 5)

Given the economic conditions, the threat of the loss of family allowances must have been quite an inducement to those unwilling to volunteer to send their children to school. Voluntarily or not, most people had moved into town within one year of the opening of a winter-term school.

The new circumstances had a profound effect on the internal organization of the regional economy. The movement of people away from residence at fish-lake encampments and the introduction of direct family allowance payments, old age pensions, and other cash benefits to the heads of nuclear families and to individuals completely undermined the economic rationale of the local group. Beginning no later than 1960, the nuclear-extended family, typically composed of an older married couple and their unmarried adult and younger children, became the primary self-sufficient economic unit.

While the overall economy still relied on both bush resources and trade goods, with the demise of fur itself as the means for obtaining trade goods, the internal organization of the economy was forced to shift into two virtually independent spheres of production and distribution: one for bush subsistence, the other for trade good subsistence.

Production and distribution for bush subsistence were little changed. Men were still responsible for hunting big game, fishing, and trapping; women, for the collection of small game and berries. However, the move into town meant that the men, who for the most part still retained their fish-lake hunting and trapping areas, had to travel long distances to obtain bush resources. On the other hand, permanent and enlarged local populations meant the eventual depletion of small game in the vicinity of communities and thus, ultimately, the virtual abandonment of winter collection activities by women.

Aside from the fact that the primary mutually sharing group was no longer the local group, the ideology of distribution in the bush resource sector changed little. Reciprocity still obtained in bush resource circulation both within the nuclear family and, where surpluses were available, between families that had co-resided within a single local group. Indeed, bush resources at times were shared within the community as a whole despite official counter-pressures against the ideology of reciprocity—for example, through government supervision of the distribution of game kept in community freezers.

The cash-trade goods subsistence sector also experienced pressures. In the past, furs alone had an exchange value sufficient for the trade good needs. With the collapse of the fur trade, people needed to obtain cash in addition to income received from trapping. In most cases, families relied on direct cash payments from the government to make up the difference: family allowances, old age pensions, and, in a few cases, welfare. In some families, some or all of the cash needed to live was generated by part- or full-time wage labour.

The cash-trade goods sector, regarding distribution, developed an ideology incorporating both Euro-Canadian and traditional Native features. On the one hand, the 'production', the cash itself, was not shared except to purchase those trade goods necessary to fill the subsistence needs of the nuclear family; any income generated by family members in excess of these needs was considered the private property of the income-earner, to be used individually on personal consumer items such as portable radios, record players, musical instruments, and amplifiers; for personal travel; or in some cases, to be buried as a useless thing. In rare instances, surplus money was lent (at no interest) to close relatives. It was never shared. On the other hand, traditional trade goods, especially food items, although now purchased with money rather than furs, were treated like bush resources and formed a significant part of the reciprocity system of distribution.

Movement into town also had a profound effect on mobility and travel. During the fur trade period women and children had remained fixed at fish-lake encampments throughout the winter, travelling extensively in summer. Now, aside from brief trips in summer, the women remained rooted throughout the year at the townsites. Here they resided, initially in houses that had been intended only for summer use,

and later, in some cases, in government-built dwellings. Further, the winter round for men had reversed itself in that, rather than venturing from the bush into town a few times during the season to obtain trade goods, they now travelled from town to the bush a few times a year to obtain bush supplies. Finally, the younger children remained in the local communities for the whole year, and as they grew older they went on to the major centres to continue their education: many never experienced living throughout the winter in the bush environment.

In sum, the collapse of the fur trade and the concomitant rise of governmental intervention in the economic and social life of the people did not produce a qualitative shift in the focus of the Native economy away from its reliance on both local subsistence and the use of trade goods, although in recent years the latter has become increasingly important. The past 40 years have been a period of marked change in the internal organization of the economy: production and circulation in the spheres of bush subsistence and cash-trade good subsistence became virtually independent of each other, creating what is known as a dual economy. Government policies introduced during the past 40 years have themselves created fundamental changes in those aspects of economic organization pertaining to the size and composition of the self-sufficient economic units, mobility and travel, and perhaps most importantly, contact with the bush on the part of the younger generation.

The contemporary Native economy has not solved the problem of dependency on external agencies. Indeed, the problem has deepened: direct government payments have replaced productive labour as the main resource for obtaining trade goods, yet these payments are seen by most people, Native and non-Native, as handouts to the poverty-stricken. In short, post-contact economic history is dominated by a single theme: the acceptance by Native peoples of immediate well-being in exchange for long-term economic dependence.

Economic History—Social Correlates

Changes in residence patterns or exchange relationships do not exist by themselves. The ideology about residence group formation exemplifies this. Slavey kinship structure is organized in a manner that unites residence with kin relationships. That is, the local group traditionally was formed around persons with strong and mutually reinforcing kin ties. Typically, these kinsmen were perceived to be related to each other in a manner that would discourage intermarriage among members. Solidarity, a sense of community, was established through a notion that persons who lived together were like what we would describe to be a 'family'. Regional bands were seen as groups of 'families' that intermarried frequently.

The Wrigley residents in the contemporary period are composed of members of three such former 'families', each of which traditionally resided in a separate locale during winter. Intermarriage frequently took place between these families, and they together formed the primary group within which the Wrigley regional band married.

The move into town created a single residence unit of what formerly was a regional band. What was its status? Were the three former bands amalgamated because they now lived together? Or were they to be considered three distinct entities that just happened to be permanently ensconced in the same locale? If the latter, intermarriage could continue, but at cost, since solidarity is based primarily on co-residence with kin. Without such mechanisms it might be difficult to maintain the peace when, as is inevitable in any social situation, friction arose between groups not perceived to be connected together. If, however, the first option were chosen, solidarity could be maintained through the creation of a new family structure, but the result would be the undermining of any possibility for intermarriage (for they would now all be considered members of a single family). In short, this could result in the inability of the group to reproduce itself.

While there was no conscious decision on this subject, the Wrigley Slavey generally opted for the first course, transforming their kinship relations in a manner that would promote the idea of Wrigley as a single family grouping. As well, they have tended to use such collective celebrations as drum dances (an event that brings together the whole community for group festivities at calendrical holidays such as Christmas) and feasts as a means to promote unity. They have used formal institutions such as the co-op to establish this idea.

Yet the move has had costs: the most important has been the effect on the reproduction of the social unit. The transformation of Wrigley into one family lessened the possibility of finding an acceptable marriage partner. As a result, very few marriages have taken place, and these have generally been with members of other regional bands, as far away as Fort Good Hope (some 650 kilometres to the north). As well, bickering continues, despite the assertion of solidarity, for when disagreement occurs it is easy still to remember the former separate status of each of the family groups. Social tension in Wrigley is therefore higher than it was when people lived in smaller family units.

In short, the contemporary period has produced social and political dislocations derived in the main from the imposition of strong external influences on the Dene and from their need, in attempting to maintain their way of life, to accept short-term solutions that have long-term negative impacts.

Contemporary Social and Economic Problems

Industry-sponsored studies, best represented by Gemini North Limited (1974), suggest that nine major problems face northerners today: (1) alcohol abuse, (2) poor housing, (3) high welfare, (4) health-related problems, (5) poor educational opportunities, (6) increasing crime rates, (7) social stress and tension as related particularly to the rise

BOX 11.1

Robert Clement at Fort Norman, 1976

I remember a few years ago, the people lived in their homes. They cut their own wood and hauled their own water. People were happier then, when they didn't have to depend on the government all of the time. We were happier then and we could do it again.

But look what has happened. Now the government gives the people everything, pays for the water and the fuel and the houses, the education. It gives the people everything, everything but one thing—the right to live their own lives. And that is the only thing that we really want, to control our lives, our own land.

of racism, (8) Native land claims settlement, and (9) poor recreational facilities.

I concur that these problems—except land claims settlement—exist, and they can be matched by many others. Yet, what is unmentioned is that these problems are surface manifestations of a pattern that has arisen out of the relationship between Native people and external agents—both governmental and business—during the past 30 years, a relationship best described as a massive intrusion of southern Canadian institutions, values, and powerful personnel into the ongoing social and economic processes of Native society. Many traditional Dene institutions and values have been put under tremendous strain, and this strain generates the surface problems.

Four examples of externally caused problems illustrate the strain on traditional institutions and values. The first two, education and welfare, are identified in the industry-sponsored studies. The latter two, wage employment and governmental insensitivity, are not mentioned as problems in these studies; indeed, wage employment is seen as a solution. The section concludes with some remarks concerning how Native people are working on both local and territorial levels to solve the problems we have presented them, an aspect of the contemporary situation conspicuously missing from the industry-sponsored reports.

One aspect of the education problem is the curriculum. The situation has improved some-

what from the period when the Alberta school curriculum was used, for today children are taught about their traditional culture as well as about contemporary southern Canadian society. Nonetheless, information about at least one aspect of their lives—their recent history—appears to be lacking both at the elementary school level and among recent high school graduates. Also, despite all the talk about respect for Native culture and courses concerning traditional crafts, it would appear that the elementary school curriculum stresses to teachers the position that Native culture is of the past and is today dead or dying, that children must learn that change is inevitable and that they should adapt to it:

> The North is experiencing increasingly rapid change. Clearly the learning program must do everything within its power to prepare people for change. In this sense the 'future orientation' of the curriculum is of prime concern. Children can enquire into the past, as well as the present, but the overall objective must be in terms of using this information to try and predict what might be. (Department of Education, n.d.: 258–9)

Many other problems are associated with the way in which education is organized, including the school year and compulsory attendance—issues of great importance today as children are still being forced from the bush and into the classroom.

The problem of welfare is not limited to the amount or pervasiveness of the payments themselves. Rather, it is importantly connected to whom they are given: to individual families. As noted, the traditional distribution system ensured that there was little wealth differentiation. This is still true of the distribution system related to the bush subsistence sector of the economy. On the other hand, the introduction of welfare payments in their present form has created the individualization of poverty and has helped to relieve the community of the traditional responsibility to help one another. The current form of the payments has undermined the values of the collective responsibility that is part of the reciprocal economy, and it has subtly led to the forced acceptance of the value, characteristic of our economy, of individual responsibility. In this sense, welfare represents a social intrusion that goes far beyond a mere question of dollars: like education, it creates a perfidious influence on the Native people to change their values.

The third problem area, wage labour, is closely related to the question of welfare. The introduction of permanent wage employment for only a small minority of people in the 1950s could have undermined the traditional value of economic equality by creating a class of rich and poor. However, during the 1950s and early 1960s, at least in Wrigley, there was little temptation to spend large amounts of money; luxury consumer items were rather scarce. As well, since jobs went to responsible family heads, the excess money was often used for socially useful activities, such as supporting children attending schools in other communities, or was not used at all. Now there are many well-paying seasonal jobs, especially in oil and gas exploration. Virtually all go to young men and, at least in the case of Wrigley, overwhelmingly to unmarried ones. Purchasing power has become concentrated in the hands of those with the fewest economic responsibilities. As a result, much of this income is spent on personal luxury items or on socially useless activities such as drinking parties.

(Indeed, it would appear that the problem of alcohol abuse may in part be generated by the excesses generated through wage labour.) In addition, payment to individuals has helped to create a distinction between the rich young men who work for wages and the seemingly poor young men who collect bush resources for the family. And yet, given the ways in which most wage-generated income is spent, the latter's activities are socially more useful both to the individual family and to the community.

In short, wage labour acts as a subtle influence to change values. It concentrates wealth in the hands of those who are least capable or willing to use it in socially productive ways. It can help to undermine respect for others who perform socially valuable labour. Under these circumstances, wage labour is often less of a solution than it is a problem.

The last in this litany of externally caused problems is government insensitivity. There are many examples of this in Wrigley. Promises made prior to the move concerned, among other things, housing, water, and wood delivery; the government apparently now says these promises either were never made or could not have been kept even if a government representative made them on behalf of his employer. There is also the Mackenzie Highway, which the people of Wrigley thought they had stopped, only to discover that it will now end there—the very circumstance they thought they had avoided by their agreement with the government (an agreement that derived from their own 'impact study' of the effects of the road ending at the neighbouring community of Fort Simpson).

The common theme connecting these problems is that they are largely the result of the intrusion of southern institutions and values. Native people in the last 30 years have been under ever-increasing pressure to abandon their traditional way of life, to replace it with institutions and values like ours. Despite our conscious and unconscious efforts to effect this end, this process has not been completely successful, and many aspects of the traditional ways of life survive and even flourish. Although the pressure cannot be discounted, it is being resisted in the sense that Native people are not succumbing; they are working to solve these problems and regain control over their lives.

This response dates back at least as far as the first intrusion into Native political autonomy at the time of the so-called treaty signings in the 1920s. However, it has only been in recent years, with the rise of territorial political organizations—the Indian Brotherhood of the Northwest Territories and the Metis Association, for example—that the response has generated political power. This culminated in the land claim and in political statements such as the Dene Declaration through which Native people hope to regain control over their economic, political, and social institutions. Thus, the land claim is not a problem, as the industry-sponsored studies suggest; it is an attempt to find a solution to a whole range of problems.

It is ironic but significant to note that among the strongest supporters of the land claim are the young and well-educated, the very individuals the industry-sponsored studies suggest are most alienated from the traditional way of life and most willing to embrace the Western one. An overwhelming majority of young people do not want to abandon their traditional lifestyle, and they see the land claim settlement as a way to protect themselves in future from what has happened to their society in the past. The most important point is that they are not sitting around waiting for us to solve their problems; they have arrived at a proposed direction for a solution themselves. The question is whether we will allow them to take that path and make it work.

On a local level, the co-op in Wrigley is an attempt to solve some problems. It is run by a Native board and operates so that many jobs are provided on a part-time basis, and preference is often given to heads of families. This provides equity in the distribution of income, ensures that money goes to responsible individuals, and

enables people to spend time pursuing bush collection activities. Where local people have some control over the internal organization of economic institutions, those institutions can be run to maintain traditional values such as mutual sharing even in the cash sector of the economy.

Conclusion

The proposals regarding the pipeline were strikingly similar to the bargain proposed by the fur traders: immediate material well-being in return for long-term economic dependency. In one respect, this new bargain was quite different. The fur trade deal created maximum material benefit for Native people with minimal changes in their traditional economic activities and organization; the 'new deal' required as a precondition the acquisition of the specialized skills necessary to obtain employment. In addition, the pipeline applicants anticipated the further erosion of the self-sufficient bush collection sector of the economy in favour of greater dependence on the cash-trade goods sector. According to the applicants, the desire of young Native men to have the relative 'security' of wage employment would foster the dependence.

Whether wage employment is secure anywhere in Canada, given our economic system, is an open question. Of concern here, however, is that the petroleum industry will not be secure in the North over a long period. That is, just as the fur trade's viability depended on the availability of furs and a high world market price for them, so the viability of petroleum development will depend on the availability of oil and a high world market price for it. But what happens when the resource gives out, or we in the south find a cheaper source of fuel? What happens if the world market price of petroleum products declines to a point where it is uneconomic to exploit and transmit northern oil and gas to southern markets? The petroleum corporations, just like the fur traders before them, will pull out. They must leave if the proposition becomes uneconomic and, of course, that day inevitably will come.

What will happen to Native northerners? The history of the fur trade provides the answer: there will be a general collapse in the cash-trade goods sector of the economy. Yet the projections of the CAGPL-sponsored studies suggested that within the next decade:

> The economy of the Native people will have been transformed from its present situation in which there are two viable but independent sectors: one concerned with bush resource collection and the other with cash-trade goods subsistence; to one which is almost totally dependent upon the cash-trade goods sector. . . . [and] a large segment of the Native community will consist of a highly trained labour force specializing in Petroleum exploration and related activities: a group unwilling or unable to use the bush as a means of obtaining subsistence.

The bargain the petroleum corporations were making is as follows: in return for reorganizing your labour force to suit our needs, we will provide you with employment for an indefinite period of time. As a result of our high wages, your people may well stop pursuing their traditional bush collection activities and therefore when we leave, as inevitably we must, there is a good possibility that you will be unable to sustain yourselves in your native land. It is against this type of proposition that Native people must protect themselves.

Yet, as the history of the fur trade shows, merely being participants in development will not accomplish even this dubious end. It is necessary that Native people have effective control over northern development, for only then can they decide which developments are in their own interests and provide safeguards to ensure that those aspects of their traditional economy they wish to maintain remain viable. A land settlement, should it follow the principles of the Dene Declaration, will provide this type of control.

Should a permit to begin construction of a pipeline be granted prior to a land settlement and the informed consent of all the Native northerners, it will undermine their attempts to regain control over the direction of their society, for the single largest decision about their future will have been made without their approval. Thus the granting of a permit prior to a land settlement will exacerbate the present situation and undermine the initiatives that Native people have undertaken to solve their problems.

My research leads me fully to support the position of the Native people that there must be no pipeline before all land settlements have been reached. It is the only reasonable protection against the complexity of problems both already known and as yet anticipated that must inevitably accompany a development scheme of this magnitude.

Epilogue 1995

In the spring of 1977 Mr Justice Berger issued his recommendations (Berger, 1977). Singular among these was his position that the proposed pipeline should be shelved for 10 years. Central in his decision was his acceptance of the view that the traditional economy of the Dene (and Inuit) could be maintained in contemporary times. The delay, in his view, was essential to provide time for the Native economy to be strengthened through controlled development. He recommended, among other things, the development of fur-processing facilities in the North and the infusion of the capital necessary to modernize the hunting-trapping sector of the Native economy.

Berger's vision was far-reaching, but it failed to gain the political support essential to its full acceptance by government and industry. Government acted on only one aspect of his recommendations and then only partially—the idea of shelving the project. Rather than agree to a full moratorium, government and industry merely kept quiet on the subject for a time. In 1980, industry proposed a smaller line that would carry oil from Norman Wells rather than gas from the High Arctic. Approval was given, although it was

BOX 11.2

Justice Thomas Berger, 1977

This process of cultural transformation has proceeded so far that in the North today many white people—and some native people, too—believe that native culture is dying. Yet the preponderance of evidence presented to this inquiry indicates beyond any doubt that the culture of the native people is still a vital force in their lives. It informs their view of themselves, of the world about them and of the dominant white society.

Euro-Canadian society has refused to take native culture seriously. European institutions, values and use of the land were seen as the basis of culture. Native institutions, values and language were rejected, ignored or misunderstood and—given the native people's use of the land—the Europeans had no difficulty in supposing that native people possessed no real culture at all. Education was perceived as the most effective instrument of cultural change; so, educational systems were introduced that were intended to provide the native people with a useful and meaningful cultural inheritance, since their own ancestors had left them none.

The assumptions implicit in all of this are several. Native religion had to be replaced; native customs had to be rejected; native uses of the land could not, once the fur trade had been superseded by the search for minerals, oil and gas, be regarded as socially important or economically significant.

—Thomas Berger, *Northern Frontier, Northern Homeland: The Report of the Mackenzie Valley Pipeline Inquiry* (1977)

agreed that the Native people would bear the highest cost and gain the fewest benefits; in a period of high oil prices and economic recession, it was seen to be in the national interest. Work on laying pipe along the route (which includes Wrigley) began in the winter of 1984.

More recent resource extraction projects on Dene lands have proceeded without even cursory reference to Berger's recommendations. By using 1990s technology, staking diamond claims in the Dogrib region has been among the most rapid in history. As with the Cree of James Bay, the Dogrib decision to negotiate a comprehensive claim in their region was made in the face of rapid development on their lands without opportunity for their intervention.

The inability of the Dogribs to control this recent wave of development on their land also stems from the failure of the 14-year-long Dene-Metis comprehensive claim negotiation process. The 1990 Dene National Assembly refused to ratify the agreement-in-principle that would have followed the government-imposed requirement of extinguishing their Aboriginal title and treaty rights to achieve a claim settlement. With the failure of the claim, government removed the moratorium on development that had been in place during negotiation and that had benefited (in the short term, at least) groups such as the Fort Good Hope Dene of the Sahtu region, who were able to seek petroleum exploration and development arrangements on their lands at more beneficial terms because their approval was necessary while the moratorium was in effect. Following from this experience, as well as observing the immediate effects of the 1984 Inuvialuit claim to the north, the two northern Dene regions elected to pursue regional claims as well. Essentially, two development options are available to Dene: settle a claim and co-operate in development activity, or, in the absence of a claims agreement, development will proceed without co-operation.

The other major avenue that Dene have investigated for controlling their lands and resources is the political sphere. They have participated in the process to reform the institutions of public government in the Northwest Territories, a process that has accelerated through the negotiation of the Inuit claim and its linkage with the establishment of the territory of Nunavut in the eastern Arctic. Dene are faced with the likelihood that they will not form a majority of the culturally diverse western Northwest Territories and have proposed measures designed to protect their political, economic, and cultural interests, such as residency requirements and double-majority votes on designated issues. However, most of these measures run contrary to the mainstream Canadian ideal of overt equality of treatment of all citizens within a region. The familiar Canadian alternative means of protecting ethnic minority rights is in geographical cultural enclaves, which can operate only in the specific instance of a region dominated by a single ethnic group, such as in Quebec and Nunavut. Thus, the Dene have undertaken the daunting task of promoting political arrangements unique in Canada, but not contrary to Canadian constitutional principles, against a backdrop of local and external interests that seek to establish structures familiar in the rest of Canada but that offer little protection for Dene interests.

However, two Dene regions argue that they have already negotiated a special relationship with the rest of Canada that guarantees protection of their interest: Treaties No. 8 and No. 11. Considerable research has been conducted and is ongoing to document the treaties as they were negotiated and to describe the nation-to-nation stature of the agreements. Through these treaties, Dene assert that their economic, land, political, and cultural rights were acknowledged in exchange for the promise of peaceful relations with non-Dene newcomers 'as long as the sun shines and the river flows', a solemn promise that they have upheld. In general, they seek recognition of the rights they maintain through the treaties as they were negotiated and the fulfillment of the Canadian sovereign's treaty promises.

What Dene experience indicates above all else is the essential appropriateness of the Dene demand for control over decision-making on their lands. What they wanted was accepted by Mr Justice Berger as reasonable. Yet within five years what they did not want started to take place while developments essential to their well-being remain shelved. Clearly, without local control, governments and other interests will have little incentive to pay attention to the legitimate, rationally founded arguments of the Dene themselves.

Epilogue 2002

It has now been 25 years since Volume I of the Berger Report was tabled in the House of Commons, recommending a 10-year moratorium on construction of the Mackenzie Valley Pipeline. One reason for this moratorium was to allow First Nations in the area of the proposed pipeline to settle outstanding land issues (often called 'land claims') with federal and territorial governments. Since then three comprehensive agreements have been reached: the Inuvialuit in 1984, the Gwich'in in 1992, and the Sahtu Dene and Metis in 1993. One 'land claim' along the Mackenzie Valley route remains unsettled: the Deh Cho.[1] Despite this claim remaining unsettled, there is renewed pressure on First Nations in the region to approve pipeline development. This pressure has three intermingling sources.

First is a recent sense of an energy crisis in North America. This is fuelled by high demand for oil and gas, increasing prices for these products, a dwindling supply of petroleum in the US, and a growing distrust of the reliability of foreign supplies. These circumstances have led to economic and political pressure on all governments in Canada to exploit non-renewable energy resources (Mitander, 2001: 1–2).

The second is competition between four potential pipeline routes proposed by petroleum companies in 1999 for delivering natural gas to southern markets. Two routes are being taken most seriously. One, along the Mackenzie Valley, is estimated to cost about $3 billion to build. The other, along the Alaska Highway, would cost $6.5 billion but might be constructed faster because it follows the highway. Both routes have often been referred to as 'stand-alone', meaning that one will be built, but not both. This competition has placed considerable pressure on the First Nations of both regions to approve proposals quickly (Crump, 2001: 2).

The third pressure arises out of the continued decline in demand and price for renewable resource products, especially for fur. Despite these declines, continuing to practice traditional hunting, fishing, and trapping is described by Elders and younger generations as being of prime importance. There are many reasons for this concern with the continuity of tradition. Most relevant here is the economic importance of wild foods to the local diet and the importance of the money brought in from trapping. As in the time of the Berger Inquiry, bought foods are expensive due to the high cost of shipping goods to remote areas, and little of it is fresh. Therefore, people depend on wild foods and on the money received in exchange for furs to purchase expensive goods—many of which are used for hunting and fishing. Despite this continued reliance on hunting, fishing, and trapping, there has been a recent rebirth of the message that trapping cannot provide sufficient income to meet the demand for imported goods and services (e.g., Barrera, 2001). One ramification of this drop in outside demand for renewable products is the pressure on First Nations governments to create jobs. The extraction and delivery of non-renewable resources such as oil, gas, and diamonds is seen by many (e.g., Antoine, 2001), but certainly not all, as an answer to the problem of the severe fluctuations and overall historic decline in the price of furs.

In June 2000 these pressures led the leaders of 26 First Nations in the Northwest Territories to come together in Fort Simpson to sign a Memorandum of Understanding (MOU). Deh Cho leaders were hesitant to sign because of concerns over a lack of consultation with Elders. Eventually they signed, but with the understanding that it did not commit them to building a pipeline. Rather, it was an agreement to investigate maximization of ownership by Native peoples in the resource industry and to draft a business plan. These leaders became known as the 'Aboriginal Pipeline Group'. Friction between the Deh Cho and other signatories was then created when the Premier of the Northwest Territories, Stephen Kakfwi, and other members of the Aboriginal Pipeline Group declared that they had a mandate to negotiate building the pipeline. The Deh Cho did not feel that this was what they had signed on to. They refused to sign the MOU of 15 October 2001 with the other members of the Aboriginal Pipeline Group and Imperial Oil, ExxonMobil, Shell Oil, and Conoco (known as the Mackenzie Valley Producers). This MOU agreed that the Aboriginal members (now the Mackenzie Valley Pipeline Corporation) would have one-third ownership of a proposed pipeline that would ship approximately one billion cubic feet of gas per day to southern markets. It is estimated that the Mackenzie Delta has 5.8 trillion cubic feet of sweet gas. The Mackenzie Valley Producers and the Mackenzie Valley Pipeline Corporation began the regulatory application process in January 2002. This process, along with the 'definition phase', is expected to take four years (Opportunities North, 2001).

Many members of the Deh Cho First Nation have now removed themselves from the Aboriginal Pipeline Group, and the Sahtu, now considering a proposal from Houston-based Arctic Resources that would allow for 100 per cent Aboriginal ownership of the pipeline, recently withdrew their signature.

The Deh Cho First Nation objects to signing any agreements to build a pipeline until they have the same assurances as the other First Nations who have settled on the basis of the Comprehensive Land Claims policy. It is their view that they do not need a process in which they are to 'claim' land that is already theirs and that they should not extinguish their treaty rights in what they consider to be 'land sales' (Nadli, 2001: 14). In their negotiations with government, they are foregrounding recognition of their political rights, such as the right to self-government. In contrast, negotiations between governments and the Inuvialuit, the Gwich'in, and the Sahtu Dene and Metis have resulted in an agreement whereby, for the extinguishment of certain treaty rights, the indigenous parties have private ownership over blocks of land. As a consequence, corporations must seek their approval for any development affecting these lands. The Deh Cho First Nation is seeking an interim resource development agreement with the governments that would give them a similar power to block such developments until a final agreement can be made. The federal government has been hesitant to negotiate such a deal outside of the terms of a regional, comprehensive land claim. As of this writing, this matter remains unresolved. As a consequence, given the crucial location of the Deh Cho region, the impasse has stalled movement towards an agreement to build a pipeline along the Mackenzie River Valley.

There are nonetheless, as noted above, economic and political opportunities that may well encourage all parties to resolve the outstanding issues by returning to negotiations.

Note

1. Deh Cho First Nation is a political body representing several Dene and Metis First Nations in southwestern NWT. Members include: Acho Dene Koe (Fort Liard), Deh Gah Gotie First Nation (Fort Providence), K'a'agee Tu First Nation (Kakisa), Katl'Odeeche First Nation (Hay River Reserve), Liidlii Kue First Nation (Fort Simpson), N'ah adehe First Nation (Nahanni Butte), Pehdzeh Ki First Nation (Wrigley), Sambaa K'e First Nation (Trout Lake), Ts'uehda First Nation (West Point), Tthe'K'ehdeli First Nation (Jean Marie River), Fort Liard Metis Nation, Fort Providence Metis Nation, and Fort Simpson Metis Nation.

References and Recommended Readings

Antoine, Jim (Minister of Aboriginal Affairs, Minister of Justice, Government of the NWT). 2001. 'The Emerging Aboriginal Business Community in the Northwest Territories', Speaking notes for AFN-NEXUS Conference, 17 July, Halifax.

Asch, Michael I. 1972. 'A Social Behavioral Approach to Music Analysis', Ph.D. dissertation, Columbia University.

———. 1975. 'Social Context and the Music Analysis of Slavey Drum Dance Songs', *Ethnomusicology* 19: 245–57.

———. 1979a. 'The Ecological Evolutionary Approach and the Concept of Mode of Production', in D. Turner and G.A. Smith, eds, *Challenging Anthropology*. Toronto: McGraw-Hill Ryerson.

———. 1979b. 'The Economics of Dene Self-Determination', in Turner and Smith, eds, *Challenging Anthropology*.

———. 1982. 'Dene Self-Determination and the Study of Hunter-Gatherers in the Modern World', in E.B. Leacock and R.B. Lee, eds, *Politics and History in Band Societies*. Cambridge: Cambridge University Press.

———. 1988. *Kinship and the Drum Dance in a Northern Dene Community*. Edmonton: Boreal Institute for Northern Studies. Discusses the social life of Wrigley in the late 1960s. Its focus is on the connections between the drum dance, kinship, and economics in the lives of these Dene people.

Barrera, Jorge. 2001. 'We can no longer make a living', *Inuvik Drum*, 18 Oct.

Berger, Mr Justice Thomas R. 1977. *Northern Frontier, Northern Homeland: The Report of the Mackenzie Valley Pipeline Inquiry*, 2 vols. Ottawa: Department of Supply and Services. A detailed account of the Dene and Inuit economy in the Mackenzie Valley. Berger describes the potential impact of the massive pipeline proposed by industry and makes recommendations on how to maintain a viable hunting-trapping way of life within a contemporary northern economy.

Brody, Hugh. 1981. *Maps and Dreams: Indians and the British Columbia Frontier*. Vancouver: Douglas & Mcintyre. This volume presents a concise portrait of how the Dene in northeastern BC are working to maintain a traditional way of life based on hunting and trapping in the face of those who would transform their lands to extract resources.

Catholic Voice, The. 1957. Monthly publication of the Sacred Heart Mission, Fort Simpson, Northwest Territories.

Council of the Northwest Territories. 1956. Legislative Acts. Yellowknife, NWT.

Crump, John. 2001. 'Return of the Pipeline', *Northern Perspectives* 27, 1: 1–3.

Department of Education, Government of the NWT. n.d. *Elementary Education in the Northwest Territories: A Handbook for Curriculum Development.* Yellowknife, NWT.

Gemini North Limited. 1974. *Social and Economic Impact of Proposed Arctic Gas Pipeline in Northern Canada.* Study prepared for Canadian Arctic Gas Pipeline Limited.

Helm, June. 1961. *The Lynx Point People: The Dynamics of a Northern Athapaskan Band.* National Museum of Canada Bulletin 176. Ottawa: National Museums of Canada. A summary of Slavey life in the 1950s, with discussion of social and cultural changes. Of particular interest is her discussion of Slavey culture and values and their attempts to incorporate a commercial fishing operation into their way of life.

———, ed. 1981. *Handbook of North American Indians,* vol. 6, *Subarctic.* Washington: Smithsonian Institution. Authoritative reference source on the ethnology, ethnohistory, and archaeology of the Mackenzie Valley Dene.

Honigmann, John. 1946. *Ethnology and Acculturation of the Fort Nelson Slavey.* Yale University Publications in Anthropology, 33. New Haven: Yale University Press. This is a general account of traditional culture and society and of the effects of contact with Western societies as analyzed from the perspective of the acculturation model. Honigmann emphasizes that in his view Slavey subsistence patterns result in a minimum of social and political complexity and in a high regard for individual autonomy.

Mitander, Victor. 2001. 'A Look Back at the Mackenzie Valley Pipeline Inquiry and the Alaska Highway Pipeline Inquiry: What Has Changed Since Berger and Lysyk Made their Recommendations', in *First Nation Rights and Interests and Northern Pipeline Development.* Materials prepared for a conference held in Calgary, 18–19 June. Vancouver: Pacific Business and Law Institute.

Nadli, Michael. 2001. 'Grand Chief Michael Nadli—The Deh Cho View', *Northern Perspectives* 27, 1: 14–15.

Opportunities North. 2001. 'Oil and Gas'. Available at: <www.nnsl.com/ops.html>.

Rushforth, E. Scott. 1986. 'The Bear Lake Indians', in R. Bruce Morrison and C. Roderick Wilson, eds, *Native Peoples: The Canadian Experience.* Toronto: McClelland & Stewart.

Usher, Peter J. 1972. *Fur Trade Posts of the Northwest Territories: 1870–1970.* Northern Science Research Group—14. Ottawa: Department of Indian Affairs and Northern Development.

———. 1976. 'Evaluating Country Food in the Northern Native Economy', *Arctic* 29, 2: 105–20.

Van Ginkle Associates Limited. 1975. *The Mackenzie: Effects of the Hydrocarbon Industry.* Study prepared for Canadian Arctic Gas Pipeline Limited.

Watkins, Melville, ed. 1977. *Dene Nation: The Colony Within.* Toronto: University of Toronto Press. The book is composed primarily of edited versions of the testimony presented by witnesses called by the Indian Brotherhood of the Northwest Territories at the Mackenzie Valley Pipeline Inquiry. It encapsulates the 'case' presented by the Dene at those hearings.

Wien, Eleanor F., and Henderson Sabrey. 1988. 'Use of Country Foods by Native Canadians in the Taiga', *Arctic Medical Research* 47, suppl. 1: 134–8.

Suggested Web Sites

Deh Cho First Nation: www.cancom.net/~dehchofn
This official site provides background information on each member community and some documents on issues that can be downloaded.

First Nations Information Project:
www.aboriginalcanada.com/firstnation/dirfnnwt.html
This site lists the languages of Yukon and the Northwest Territories. A directory lists the contact numbers of each First Nation in the NWT and Yukon.

Indian Claims Commission: www.indianclaims.ca
The ICC was set up in 1991 by the federal government in response to Assembly of First Nations concerns with the treaty process. The site provides a history of the treaty process in Canada as well as information on current claims and recommendations of the ICC.

Information North:
www.infonorth.org/profile/bin/showframes.pl
This site provides general information on NWT communities. Each community has a page with a map, brief history, current weather, population statistics, and treaty status.

CHAPTER 12

The Carrier and the Politics of History

ELIZABETH FURNISS

Introduction

The Carrier are a Northern Athapaskan-speaking people whose Aboriginal territory stretches across the central Interior of British Columbia from the Rocky Mountains in the east to the Coast Mountains in the west. This region, part of the vast Interior Plateau, is characterized by generally flat or rolling terrain. Thick forests of spruce, pine, and fir cover the ground, interspersed with numerous large and small lakes, streams, marshes, and meadows. This is the homeland of 20 Carrier First Nations, each having from one to several reserve villages.[1] Carrier people today are employed in a variety of occupations: they are hunters, fishers, trappers, traditional healers, hereditary chiefs, mothers and grandmothers, teachers, politicians, students, lawyers, loggers, and secretaries. Many Carrier people continue to speak their Aboriginal language, and cultural values and beliefs, spiritual concepts, and patterns of family and community organization continue to distinguish the Carrier from other Native nations and from non-Native society in Canada.

I first was introduced to Carrier people in 1985, when I was hired by the Nazko First Nation to conduct ethnographic research on the history of an ancient Aboriginal trade route. The trail, known to the Carrier as the Grease Trail and to non-Natives as the Alexander Mackenzie Heritage Trail, recently had become the focus of government-sponsored tourism development. Alexander Mackenzie's journey down the trail in 1793 was being celebrated as a landmark in Canadian history. In contrast, the Native heritage of the trail had been minimally represented, if not ignored, in the promotional materials. I was hired to produce a documentary video that would provide some balance to the interpretation of the trail's historical significance. It soon became apparent that the problem of interpretation of the trail's history was not simply one of the omission of Native content. My anthropological interpretation of the trail's Native heritage conflicted sharply with that produced by the trail developers. Somewhat to my surprise, my video sparked heated debates about which was the 'true' history of the trail. Through the events of that summer I became interested in the politics of history, especially as they relate to Native/non-Native relations in Canada, and this theme serves as a central theoretical framework for this chapter.

The Politics of History

History is defined here as a body of knowledge about the past. There is no one 'true' version of history; instead, each history is a subjective interpretation of the past. Consequently, many different histories exist, each shaped by the present cultural values, beliefs, and interests of the person creating the account. This does not mean that there are no facts of history. Events do occur. Where historical accounts vary is in which events of the past are highlighted and which are ignored, and in how the significance of these highlighted events is interpreted. The construction of historical accounts involves this process of selecting and interpreting the significance of past events, and this process is fundamentally mediated by the cultural context.

For example, history textbooks typically represent Canadian history as the 'discovery' of North America by individual explorers whose courage, perseverance, and faith enabled them to surmount overwhelming obstacles, often represented in terms of a harsh environment and 'hostile savages', to bring about ultimately the foundation of the nation of Canada. These histories celebrate some of the key values of contemporary Euro-Canadian culture: individualism, self-reliance, advancement through hard work, struggle, and self-sacrifice. The early explorers, however, did not achieve these feats alone. They relied heavily on the assistance provided not only by fellow countrymen and women, but also by Native people who served as guides, interpreters, and labourers. Nevertheless, this collective achievement is portrayed in individual, male terms; the figure of the explorer-hero embodies all of the cultural values that guide the contemporary lives of Euro-Canadians.

It is significant to look at the events that are not discussed in these textbook histories. These include the Canadian government's less than honourable treatment of Aboriginal peoples and, in regions such as BC, the systematic failure of governments to address the issue of Aboriginal title and rights. The phrase 'history is written by the victorious' is sometimes heard, and is relevant here. This refers to one of the most important political functions of official, government-sanctioned histories, which is to validate events of the past and to legitimate existing institutions and relations of authority within a state. Contentious issues in history often are erased from the historical record. Alternately, the image of the 'hostile savage' serves to rationalize Native–European violence as a natural and inevitable result of the progress of civilization; the image of the friendly Indians assisting the European explorers serves both to suggest Indian approval of the colonial project and to mask the fact that conflict and violence have permeated events in Canada through the past four centuries.

Histories, however, can function to challenge governmental authority and to draw attention to unresolved historical problems and injustices that occurred in the past. In the summer of 1993 the southern Carrier First Nations used the opportunity of the Mackenzie bicentennial celebrations being held in BC to critique popular conceptions of history. Carrier First Nations leaders were widely quoted by news media when they stated that to celebrate Mackenzie was to celebrate the start of 200 years of colonization and genocide of Aboriginal peoples.

All historical accounts, then, are shaped by the cultural context in which they are produced. The fact that all histories are relative does not mean that anthropology cannot contribute to the understanding of past events. On the contrary, it places anthropology in a unique position among the social sciences. It allows us to explore how different cultural contexts have shaped people's constructions of history, how these versions of history function to make sense of current social relations, and why, therefore, conflicting views of history often become the subject of intense debate.

The accounts of Native cultural history produced by anthropologists also are relative accounts. Anthropological accounts are shaped not only by the anthropologist's cultural situation, in most cases as a member of the dominant society, but also by his or her adherence to a particular theoretical tradition, which defines what questions are important to ask about cultural history. Consequently, it is important for anthropologists, when writing histories, to include some kind of commentary on the conditions, personal and professional, that have shaped the production of their own knowledge. For example, adherence to a particular school of thought, such as materialism, will result in an anthropologist posing different questions and interpreting data differently from an anthropologist using an idealist orientation.

My interests in anthropology, Native/Euro-Canadian relations, and the politics of history emerged from several different sources. I entered graduate studies in anthropology after receiving an undergraduate degree in the biological sciences. My primary reasons for turning to anthropology had to do with intellectual questions rather than ethnographic interests: I wanted to explore the basic question of why people in different cultures hold different beliefs, and why, under certain circumstances such as revitalization movements, people undergo rapid 'changes of mind'. After a summer living at Nazko and conducting research on the Grease Trail's history, and after completing my Master's degree, which was based on ethnographic research on a contemporary revitalization movement in the Secwepemc community of Alkali Lake, I then moved to a city in the central interior of BC. There I took the position of land claims researcher with the Cariboo Tribal Council, which at that time represented both Secwepemc and Carrier First Nations, and where I remained for four years. During this time, through developing friendships with Native people and through witnessing the realities of life in a frontier town, my eyes were opened to the dynamics of Native/non-Native relations, which, coming from a middle-class upbringing in a virtually homogeneous Euro-Canadian town on Vancouver Island, until then I had not experienced. I chose to return to graduate school and to transform my experience into an intellectual problem, namely, how was it that so many otherwise well-meaning non-Native people could hold such virulent attitudes towards Natives? My dissertation was an ethnography of Native/Euro-Canadian relations in an interior BC logging town and an analysis of contemporary colonialism, 'common-sense' racism, and Euro-Canadian historical consciousness, in which the politics of history remains paramount. I have continued pursuing these interests as a way also of contributing to a broader practical understanding of some of the problems Native people face in their relations with the majority Canadian society,

problems that have had tragic consequences for many Native people.

This chapter is centred on the theme of history, and it is relevant to an understanding of the Carrier people today for two reasons. First, history is important as an analytical device. It is both difficult and problematic to reconstruct a 'traditional' culture of the Carrier. Instead, their earlier culture is best understood in a historical framework. Through the eighteenth and nineteenth centuries the Carrier were introducing important changes in their culture and socio-political organization, and differences in these areas continue to distinguish different subgroups today. Culture, as a system of beliefs, values, and practices that characterizes a group and enables its survival in a particular setting, must be continually adaptive to social and ecological changes. Over millennia Native societies have been continually adjusting to such changes.

Earlier anthropologists were especially interested in studying the Carrier because of the opportunity they provide to explore the process of cultural change. The classic ethnographies of Morice (1893a, 1893b), Jenness (1943), and Goldman (1940, 1941, 1953) discuss Carrier culture and the manner in which different subgroups, over the last 200–300 years, have adopted the ideas of status hierarchies, clan organization, and potlatching through contact with Northwest Coast societies. Two recent ethnographies, by Antonia Mills (1994) and Jo-Anne Fiske and Betty Patrick (2000), have been written in the context of the Carrier peoples' contemporary struggles to gain recognition from the Canadian state of their enduring Aboriginal rights to land and self-government. Mills highlights cultural continuity as embodied in the ceremonial feast, a central political and legal institution among the Witsuwit'en.[2] Fiske and Patrick examine the conditions in which the *balhats*, or potlatch, became a central institution of political and legal authority among the Babine Lake Carrier, how this institution was undermined through the course of colonialism and the intrusion of the Canadian state, and how Babine Lake people are now looking to revitalize the *balhats* as a means of restoring modern forms of traditional justice and self-government. Using these and other works, in the first section of this paper I provide a brief sketch of nineteenth-century Carrier culture, its regional differences, and the innovations that people were introducing to their culture during this century.

History is important to this discussion for a second reason. History has become a key political resource in the Carrier's struggle to gain government recognition of their Aboriginal rights to land, resources, and self-government. Through these claims First Nations leaders are challenging the official histories promoted by governments and learned in school textbooks and in popular writings, and that exist as common-sense knowledge among the general public. These accounts typically portray Native societies of the past as 'primitive' groups of people who originally had no form of landownership or concept of property rights, and who now have lost their culture under the impact of European colonization. In contrast, Carrier leaders are seeking to show the legitimacy of pre-European contact forms of government and landownership, and also the existence of distinct Native cultures in the present. These different representations of Native culture and history are now being vigorously contested in courts, on blockades, and in the media. In the second part of this paper I focus on two examples of the contemporary politics of history: the Gitksan and Witsuwit'en land claims case, and the Nazko and Lhoosk'uz First Nations' protest over the development of the Mackenzie Grease Trail.

Carrier Culture and History in the Nineteenth Century

Sources of Information

This chapter relies on written accounts, rather than on primary research of Carrier oral traditions, to reconstruct the culture of the nineteenth-century Carrier. Oral traditions, such as the *kungax*

of the Witsuwit'en, contain a wealth of ethnohistoric information. Some of these traditions have served as primary sources of information for anthropologists. Thus, while oral traditions and anthropological perspectives to a degree are interwoven in the existing written literature, Carrier perspectives on their culture and history have yet to be fully represented.

The earliest written accounts of the Carrier can be found in the letters, diaries, and journals of explorers and fur traders. Alexander Mackenzie, in 1793, was the first European to enter Carrier territory. Both he and Simon Fraser, who explored the Fraser River in 1808, left journals of their explorations, and these journals contain valuable descriptions of Carrier life and customs. By 1807 the North West Company had established posts in the region, and the journals of the North West Company, and later the Hudson's Bay Company fort employees, contain notes on the local Carrier people. Records from Roman Catholic missions serve as additional sources of information.

The most comprehensive written accounts presently available on the nineteenth-century Carrier are found in the writings of the Oblate missionary Adrien Gabriel Morice. Morice arrived at Stuart Lake in 1885 and over the next 50 years published a wealth of ethnographic and linguistic studies. Comprehensive ethnographies are found in Jenness's study of the Witsuwit'en, or Bulkley River Carrier, based on fieldwork conducted in the 1920s, and in Goldman's publications on the Ulkatcho Carrier, based on fieldwork during the winter of 1935–6. In these and other studies (Duff, 1951; Hackler, 1958; Hudson, 1972, 1983; Kobrinsky, 1977), anthropologists have focused much of their attention on three main questions. How can we account for regional differences in Carrier culture? Why have some bands adopted ideas of status hierarchies, clans, and potlatching, while others have not? By tracing the adoption of these ideas by the different Carrier groups, what can we learn in general about how and why cultures change?

There have been two basic approaches to these questions. The materialist approach emphasizes the role of material and economic factors in shaping culture. The environment is believed to impose limitations on the forms of culture that may develop within it. Groups occupying similar environments develop similar technologies and strategies for subsistence, which in turn influence the patterns of social organization and the values and beliefs that develop. Because the technological and subsistence components of culture develop as adaptations to a particular ecological setting, they become the core features of that culture. These features tend to be stable over time, as long as ecological factors remain constant. Consequently, both cultural differences and cultural changes are explained in terms of the variation in economic or ecological factors. For example, diversity among the Carrier subgroups is explained in terms of the differential access that groups had to large, predictable salmon runs, which allowed a more sedentary lifestyle and the development of forms of socio-political hierarchy. A critically important assumption of the materialist approach is that humans have a universal drive to maximize their material wealth and that, given the opportunity, they will strive to exert control over and restrict others' access to valuable resources. This image of 'economic man' is a belief rooted in the cultural context of Western capitalism. To what extent these motives for human behaviour hold true in non-Western cultures is an important question that requires further study.

In contrast, the idealist approach emphasizes the role of ideas and values in shaping culture and cultural change. Culture is seen as the product of the creative activity of individuals, and culture changes when individuals consciously experiment with new ideas, social institutions, and traditions. However, in this approach individuals are less motivated by individual economic incentives than they are by social or cultural considerations. Second, the core features of a culture consist in the cluster of ideas, values, and beliefs, which then constrain how culture will change. If new traditions and practices are incompatible with existing values and beliefs, they will either be rejected or reformulated to fit into the cultural context.

One example of the different orientations of the materialist and idealist approaches lies in the question of the causes for the mobility of Native hunting societies in Canada. The materialist approach interprets mobility as a consequence of ecological factors, specifically the absence of sufficient resources in any one location to permit groups of people to stay in one place for extended periods. The assumption is that if people could develop a sedentary lifestyle, they would. However, the contemporary southern Carrier, although many are not engaged full-time in hunting, fishing, and trapping activities, continue to have a highly mobile lifestyle. People often are on the move, travelling between the bush, their homes on the reserves, and to the homes of family and friends on other reserves and in distant cities. The high value they continue to place on mobility indicates that social and perhaps symbolic factors are important in motivating people to travel. Idealist approaches would explore this by looking at the meaning and significance of travelling to the Carrier people, and by linking this to core ideas and values within the culture.

These two approaches, however, are not mutually exclusive, and materialist and idealist approaches are often used in conjunction. Both materialist and idealist theoretical orientations appear in the following discussion of the early Carrier, and each provides a useful although partial account of Carrier culture and society in the period of early European contact.

Who Are the Carrier?

At the time of first European contact the Carrier did not recognize a level of socio-political unity at the tribal level (by 'tribal' I mean a group generally defined on linguistic and cultural grounds). Nor did these bands have a name to designate the collective of Carrier-speakers. Instead, the most general and enduring level of social inclusion was the regional subgroup or band. Each band was a

Table 12.1. Carrier First Nations, 2002

Southern Carrier:	Ulkatcho, Cheslatta, Lhoosk'uz Dene, Nazko, Red Bluff
Central Carrier:	Lheidli T'enneh, Saik'uz (Stoney Creek), Nak'azdli, Tl'azt'en, Takla Lake, Nadleh Whuten, Stellat'en (Stellaquo), Wet'suwet'en First Nation, Yekooche
Northern Carrier:	Hagwilget, Moricetown, Nee-Tahi-Buhn, Skin-Tahi, Babine Lake, Burns Lake

territorial group consisting of closely related families that used the resources in a specific region. Each band was known to itself, and to others, by a name taken from the group's territory, with the added suffix *whoten*, sometimes abbreviated to *t'en*, meaning 'people of'.[3] For example, the Nazkot'en are the people of the Nazko River, or the river flowing from the south (*naz* = south, *koh* = river). In the mid-1800s there were approximately 14 bands; in 2002 there are 20 First Nations. These bands have been remarkably stable over time. Of the named bands that existed a century ago, most still exist.

The fact that the Carrier, at the time of European contact, had no common name and no sense of socio-political unity at the tribal level does not mean that bands were isolated. Rather, the different bands were closely interconnected through extensive bonds of kinship, through social and economic relations, and through ties of shared history, culture, and language. Nineteenth-century Carrier society was not a precisely bounded unit; rather, it was a society defined by a diffuse network of social relations that stretched across a wide territory. These networks were created and reinforced by frequent intermarriage between close and distant bands, by ties of reciprocal obligations among kin, and by frequent travel by individuals to visit relatives in other regions. In extreme circumstances, individuals from different bands might mobilize together for common political action, such as to launch a raid. In these cases, individuals were not motivated by a sense of obligation to an abstract 'tribal' identity, but to kinfolk who had been wronged and who now needed assistance. These cross-cutting networks of kin, and the constant movement and

interchange among people, created a situation in which ideas and knowledge were continually circulating. Viewing Carrier society as a diffuse network, rather than a homogeneous bounded unit, is critical to the later discussion of the way in which historical factors have contributed to regional cultural diversity.

The idea of the Carrier as a united linguistic and cultural collective was the creation of early fur traders, missionaries, and linguists. The name 'Carrier' has been used since the first European contact by Mackenzie in 1793. The term is believed to have originated with the Sekani, who referred to them as *aghelhne*, or 'the ones who pack'. This name was derived from a funeral ritual in which a widow carried with her the cremated remains of her spouse, which after a one-to two-year period were then ritually disposed. It is likely that the Sekani term referred only to bands with whom they had immediate social relations. In the early nineteenth century, observers listed only the central and southern bands in this category. By the end of the century the idea of the Carrier was extended to include all of the bands presently categorized. Thus it is by virtue of historical circumstance that the name Carrier came about. If early traders had arrived from the south, the Carrier might be known today as Yu'nahena, the name by which the Secwepemc knew the bands to the north. If the newcomers had arrived from the west, the Carrier might be known today as Akwilget, a name the Gitksan used specifically for the Witsuwit'en and their village Hagwilget.

The creation of new social categories is an important way of ordering social relations when previously isolated groups come into contact. It was critical for early traders, as a prerequisite for communication and business, to be able to identify the languages spoken by Native trappers. Thus the creation of the category 'Carrier', defined on linguistic and later cultural grounds, was a logical consequence of the nature of the European trader/Native trapper relationship. The term remains commonplace among anthropologists and linguists, who use it to refer to the basic linguistic and cultural similarities that existed, and continue to exist, among these bands.

With the influx of Europeans into their territories, the Carrier, like the traders and missionaries, were faced with the task of representing themselves to others by using social categories. In the course of developing relations with Europeans, the Carrier responded by representing themselves as *dakelh* (often recorded in fur trade and missionary records as 'Takully'). *Dakelh* is a contraction of *uda ukelh*, 'people who travel by water'. In the late 1980s in southern Carrier communities, the term *dakelh* was being used in everyday talk to refer generally to 'Indians'. As neighbouring Native groups such as the Secwepemc, Tsilhqot'in, and Nuxalk were included in this category, *dakelh* constituted a general pan-Indian identity that distinguished Native peoples from non-Natives. However, as of 2002 the term *Dakelh*, now capitalized, appears to be increasingly used in political discussions as a variant to 'Carrier', especially among the central and southern bands. In the central regions, the term *Yinkadinee*, 'people of the world', is often used instead of 'Carrier'. In short, the term 'Carrier' is quickly becoming an anthropological relic, and is used here only with caution and for the sake of convenience. The fluidity of terminology and the regional variation in names underscore the autonomous orientation of the different bands, the absence of an all-encompassing political identity, and a respect for diversity in perspective that I believe is a central value of Carrier culture.

Linguists and anthropologists have long perceived significant variation among the Carrier. In 1893 Morice, using linguistic and geographical criteria, divided them into three subgroups: lower, upper, and Babine. Some linguists classify Babine as a distinct language. Forms of socio-political organization also distinguish the different Carrier bands. While Morice's lower Carrier are organized into autonomous, flexible extended family groups of bilaterally related kin, the more northerly (Morice's upper and Babine) bands are organized into matrilineal clans whose hereditary chiefs exercise ownership over specific territories. I use a combination of linguistic, geographical, and ethnographic criteria to distinguish the Carrier into northern, central, and southern subgroups (Table 12.1). Today the 20 Carrier bands continue to display a high degree of political autonomy, as is evident in their being divided among three tribal councils, with some unaffiliated.

Geography, Climate, and Resources

Much of Carrier territory lies within the Interior Plateau, a region of flat or gently rolling terrain. The northern and western region is mountainous, particularly along the Bulkley River, which is flanked by the Hazelton Mountains to the west and the Skeena Mountains to the east and north. Summers are moderately warm and dry, with an average daytime temperature of 22° C, while winters are cold, with daytime temperatures occasionally dropping to −40° C.

Carrier territory is dominated by the sub-boreal spruce forest. White/Engelmann spruce, Douglas fir, and lodgepole pine are common, and willow and black cottonwood often are found along rivers. The mountainous regions, with their colder climate and heavier snowfall, are covered by spruce and subalpine fir interspersed with open meadows and grasslands.

The most important animals that the nineteenth-century Carrier used for subsistence were caribou, grizzly and black bears, beaver, and rabbits. Animals trapped chiefly for their fur included beaver, muskrats, wolves, black bears, martens, fishers, otters, wolverines, fox, lynx, coyotes, and mink. A variety of birds, including swans, geese, ducks, grouse, and loons, were also used for food. Numerous large and small lakes,

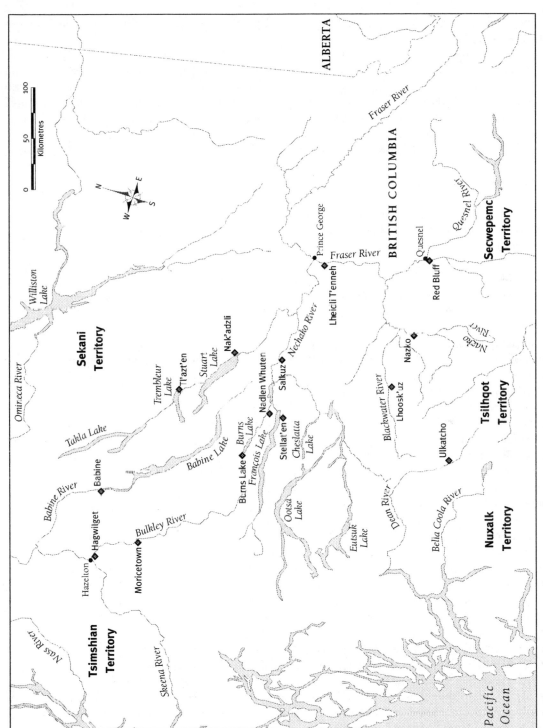

MAP 12.1. Carrier Territory and Contemporary First Nations

rivers, streams, and marshes are scattered over the landscape, and trout, whitefish, carp, and suckers were important components of the diet.

Salmon was particularly important. Much of the region is drained by the Fraser River and its tributaries, while to the north and west the Bulkley, Babine, and Dean rivers drain into the Pacific Ocean. Salmon ascend both of these systems to spawn. The sizes of the runs vary between watersheds, and each run varies also in regular cycles of between four to six years.

Subsistence Strategies and the Annual Round

All three Carrier subdivisions followed a similar pattern of seasonal activity. Throughout the year the most important economic unit was the family. Families moved through the region in regular patterns, harvesting, hunting, and fishing. With the exception of the summer months when people gathered for the salmon fishery, families tended to be widely dispersed. As a result of this mobile lifestyle, a complex network of trails connected villages, seasonal campsites, and hunting and fishing grounds. Trails also extended into the territories of neighbouring groups, with whom the Carrier carried on an active trade.

Some activities were predictable and gave structure to the seasonal round. In the summer, many families congregated at fishing stations to harvest and dry the salmon for winter. Salmon were harvested with weirs and traps, or with spear or net. A weir of woven sticks was erected partially or completely across a river to block the passage of fish. Large conical baskets, perhaps five to six metres in length and one and a half metres in diameter, were placed at the various openings of the weir. Traps often were set at night, and by morning could contain hundreds of fish. Salmon were gutted, split, and suspended on poles to dry over smouldering fires. The dried salmon were stored in underground pits or packed flat into bales and placed in elevated caches. The salmon-fishing season typically began in July and could extend into September or October. Many species of berries were collected during summer and dried into cakes to be stored.

In fall, families dispersed to distant regions to hunt. Hunting technology consisted of bow and arrow, spears, deadfalls, and snares. Various snare designs were used, each specific for the animal being sought. Snares for small animals were made of sinew; those for larger animals were made of strips of caribou hide.

A number of families might gather together for the caribou hunt. Fences kilometres long were constructed by attaching long poles horizontally to trees. These fences gradually converged to a small corral. Families worked together to drive the caribou along the fences and into the corral, where the caribou then were killed by waiting hunters. In the summer, hunters used smouldering fires to attract caribou, which were drawn to the smoke in their attempt to escape the torment of mosquitoes.

Meat from the fall hunt was dried for winter use, and skins were processed and sewn into robes and winter clothing. Through most of the year people travelled mainly on foot, packing their goods and supplies. Once snow fell people used snowshoes and toboggans. Canoes made of spruce bark or cottonwood also were used.

As the winter progressed and large animals became scarcer, attention shifted to ice fishing and snaring rabbits. People also made occasional trips back to the summer villages to retrieve stores of dried salmon. Winter camps were set up adjacent to good rabbit-snaring grounds and where the supply of firewood was plentiful. During winter families continued to camp on their own, occasionally joining other families if resources were plentiful. Some Ulkatcho families wintered with relatives among the Nuxalk (Bella Coola), while some Witsuwit'en joined the Gitksan village of Hazelton.

Late winter and early spring were the most difficult. Winter stores of food were almost gone, melting snow made travel difficult, and game was scarce. Families sustained themselves by ice fishing using net, spear, and set line. The inner bark of the hemlock was scraped, roasted, and its

FIGURE 12.1. Azel of Ulkatcho spinning sinew (c. 1922). Sinew is made from long tendons that run along the backbone of large animals. The material is split into fine strands, then several strands are twisted together by rolling between the palms. (© Canadian Museum of Civilization, photographer Harlan Ingersoll Smith, 1922, 55690)

fibres pounded into a pulp to form small dried cakes. These could later be softened with water and consumed. Black lichen, growing abundantly on the dead lower branches of pine trees, often was used as an emergency food. It was mixed with water and shaped into cakes, then roasted by the fire.

As spring progressed, families congregated along lakes and rivers, where nets, fences, and basket traps were used to harvest spawning trout and suckers. Plants such as wild parsnip were roasted, peeled, and eaten, and the bark of pine trees was cut and the sugar-rich sap scraped off and consumed. The roots of tiger lilies, which grow abundantly along rivers and streams, were roasted in underground pits. Waterfowl returned from the south and were snared, as were beaver, muskrats, and squirrels. Families dispersed and continued to hunt before gathering again at summer villages in July.

Regional Differences

The availability of salmon enabled each of the central and northern bands to establish two or more permanent villages situated near salmon-fishing stations. Both the northern and central bands relied on salmon as a principal source of food.

The rivers in the northwest, including the Bulkley and Babine, as well as Babine Lake, support the largest and most predictable salmon runs in Carrier territory. The watersheds of the Fraser, including Stuart, Trembleur, Francois, and Ootsa lakes, also support large runs, although the sizes vary substantially. When salmon were abundant the

FIGURE 12.2. Gaffing salmon at Moricetown on the Bulkley River (*c.* 1952). The harpoon has a detachable foreshaft attached with a leather thong. This prevents the fish from coming free or breaking the shaft when caught. (Courtesy of Royal British Columbia Museum, Victoria, PN3272)

Carrier in this central region gathered in permanent summer villages to fish; when salmon were scarce people travelled to adjacent bands, or across to Babine Lake, to acquire salmon from relatives or through trade.

Salmon in southern Carrier territory were much more unevenly distributed. Although major runs passed up the Fraser River, only moderate runs entered Blackwater River, along which most of the southern Carrier bands were centred. Significant runs entered Quesnel River, but they were subject to extreme fluctuations. As a result, the southern Carrier did not rely on salmon as a principal food source and followed a more mobile lifestyle than other Carrier.

Each Carrier band had one or several central gathering places. Although these may be called villages, people gathered here for only a small portion of the year. Further, villages had different significance among the northern and central bands as compared with the southern bands. Among the former, villages were places for gathering in the summer, harvesting salmon, organizing clan activities, and hosting potlatches. Among the southern bands, villages were more temporary. The Nazko, Quesnel, and Alexandria Carrier each had a village on the Fraser River, occupied briefly for salmon fishing. In the early nineteenth century the Ulkatcho Carrier, who had recently incorporated the traditions of clan organization and potlatching, had several villages: on the Dean River, at Qualcho Lake, and at Gatcho Lake. As potlatching became more important, so did the villages. By the late nineteenth century, due to dramatic population decline, only one of the villages, at Gatcho Lake, remained. In the 1930s the village was occupied only intermittently.

In short, the significance of villages differed from band to band. Periods of co-residence varied according to ecological factors, especially the availability of sufficient salmon to sustain large groups for long periods, and for cultural reasons. Unlike the Ulkatcho band, the more easterly southern Carrier bands had not incorporated the potlatch complex and had less cultural incentive to remain together in the villages.

Social and Political Organization

Bands were the most widespread and common group among the Carrier. Nevertheless, bands had no permanent political leaders, nor were they closely united in terms of political action. For day-to-day domestic activities, the individual family was the most important social unit. Among the southern Carrier, the family also was the most important political unit. The central and northern bands, however, had matrilineal clans, which served as their most significant political units. The following characterizations of the social and political organization of the nineteenth-century Carrier remain largely true today.

Southern Carrier families were highly autonomous, flexible, extended groups of bilaterally related kin. The Carrier term for the extended family was sadeku, all those individuals related through the grandfather. Because of the tendency for patrilocality—the wife joined the household of her husband—the core of the extended family group usually consisted of a group of brothers, their spouses and children, and married sons' wives and children. At any time, though, the household unit engaged in hunting or fishing might be as small as a nuclear family or as large as to contain three generations. The composition of households changed due to ecological factors, expanding in times of food abundance and splitting in times of shortage. Households changed composition for social reasons as well. Individuals might leave to defuse an interpersonal conflict, while others might leave to visit relatives or other sections of the country.

The extended family was led by the *detsah*, or headman, usually the oldest person in a line of siblings. He was considered the spokesman of the group, and he co-ordinated the tasks of hunting and fishing. In keeping with southern Carrier values of autonomy and egalitarianism, the headman's authority was informal. His continued leadership depended on his ability to make sound decisions and on the continued support of his relatives. The headmen, along with *duyunne*, shamans, were the most influential political figures in southern Carrier society.

Each extended family was associated with a particular hunting territory, although their rights to these territories were not exclusive and any band member could hunt wherever he wished. Rights to specific salmon- and trout-fishing stations, however, were considered family property. Individuals were expected to marry outside of the *sadekuka*, or descendants related through the line of great-grandfather, and marriages between the different bands, as well as with neighbouring Tsilhqot'in and Nuxalk, were common. As a result, each individual could trace a network of relatives through a wide territory. This created a network of kin who could be called upon to share food and access to hunting and fishing territories when needed.

In contrast, the most important political units among the northern and central Carrier bands were the matrilineal clans. The northern Carrier were divided into several clans, which were further divided into houses.[4] Membership in both clans and houses was determined through matrilineal descent. Each house was led by a hereditary chief who, on behalf of his house, exercised ownership and stewardship over specific hunting and fishing territories and controlled access to them. Only those families that could trace membership to the house were permitted to use these territories. The house chief was responsible also for settling disputes among families, providing help to destitute house members, and representing the interests of house members to other houses and clans.

The notions of social hierarchy and rank were expressed not only through the position of house chief but also through the ownership of titles and crests, which bestowed status to their holders. Each house owned a number of titles and crests. House crests were publicly displayed on totem poles, houses, and ceremonial regalia, and were tattooed on house members' chests and wrists. The crests represented animals, natural features, mythical beings, or manufactured objects, and were infused with spiritual power. The chief and most of the nobility of the house also owned at least one personal crest, which could be bought and sold.

The potlatch (or feast, as it is locally known) was a central institution in the social and political life of the northern Carrier. It provided the political vehicle for the public validation of chieftainship, for transferring and confirming property rights, and for conferring high status to individuals via titles and crests. It served a judicial role as a means of resolving disputes and enforcing the laws of the community. Through amassing and giving away goods, and thus the creation of a system of ongoing credit and debt, the potlatch served the economic function of the continuous redistribution of resources through the community. It served the social function of reaffirming the solidarity of kinship groups and for maintaining social networks based on reciprocity and alliance. Potlatching and house activities occurred primarily in the summer, when families were gathered together in villages for the salmon fishery.

In the nineteenth and early twentieth centuries the clan and potlatch-rank systems varied slightly among the central Carrier bands. Here clans were not subdivided into houses. While the Witsuwit'en and Babine Lake Carrier had five and four clans respectively, the central bands had various numbers of clans. The central bands no longer required clans to be exogamous; this became a matter of choice. As among the northern Carrier, the clans of the central bands were divided into nobility and commoners. The nobility owned titles associated with specific hunting and fishing territories, over which they controlled access.

Titles were inherited along matrilineal lines and were publicly validated through potlatching.

These regional differences among the Carrier are, in part, a product of local ecological adaptation. The availability of a rich, stable resource base, salmon, plus the fact that the best sites for salmon harvesting were restricted to a few key locations, enabled not only a more sedentary lifestyle, but also the development of a local elite, the clan and house leaders, who successfully exercised control of the means of production. The surplus in resources allowed for the creation of a system of ceremonial feasting, a central component of which was giving away large quantities of goods. However, while the environment enabled the development of socio-political hierarchy and potlatching, we can refine our understanding of Carrier cultural change by viewing these developments as a result also of historical factors. These developments are the products of the flow of ideas and practices from neighbouring nations and their creative adaptation into Carrier culture.

Carrier Cultural Change

How can we account for the existence of socio-political hierarchies and potlatching among some Carrier groups but not others? First, the northern bands are believed to have incorporated the ideas of social rank and status, and potlatch ceremonialism, through their contact with the neighbouring Gitksan, with whom they had close social and economic relations. In the early nineteenth century the Gitksan, a Tsimshian-speaking group of the upper Skeena River, held the lucrative position of middlemen in the Witsuwit'en trade with the coastal Tsimshian. The Witsuwit'en and Gitksan frequently intermarried and participated in each other's ceremonies. The five Witsuwit'en clans were linked with the four Gitksan clans for the purposes of regulating marriage and potlatching. From the Witsuwit'en and Babine Lake Carrier, the ideas of socio-political hierarchy and potlatching were picked up by Carrier bands to the east and south.

The existence of matrilineal clans does not necessarily lead to the development of social hierarchies, and the adoption of matrilineality may have been a separate phenomenon. The question of the antiquity of matrilineal clans among the Carrier and other Athapaskan groups is still debated. Dyen and Aberle (1974), based on their lexical reconstruction of proto-Athapaskan kinship terminology, believe that matrilineality is the ancient and original form of social organization among Northern Athapaskans. In contrast, Goldman (1941) and Steward (1960) believe that matrilineal clans were adopted by the Carrier at the same time as ideas of socio-political hierarchy and potlatching, and that bilateral organization was the original system among the Carrier. These latter ideas, which are based on material and ecological explanations, are explored in this section.

The question of exactly when ideas of social rank, status, and potlatching were adopted by the Carrier is difficult to answer, particularly when relying only on the scattered documentary sources left by early European observers rather than Carrier oral traditions. Steward, using a materialist approach, believes that the introduction of these ideas and practices among the Carrier occurred two to three decades before direct European contact. By the last two decades of the eighteenth century, Carrier bands were trading indirectly with European trading ships on the coast through Gitksan middlemen. The new source of wealth in furs was the trigger for the adoption of these new forms of social and political organization. When coupled with the abundance of salmon in northern Carrier territory, people now had sufficient resources to be able to host potlatches, which required a surplus of both foods and material goods to give away during the ceremonies. Along similar lines, Goldman believes that with the advent of the maritime fur trade, intermarriage intensified between the Carrier and the Gitksan as a way of solidifying trading relations. As the Carrier married into high-ranking families among the coastal nations, the ideas of social rank and clan organization were incorporated into Carrier

society. Now high-ranking families could claim exclusive control over trade with the high-ranking Gitksan families, and the emerging Carrier elite used this system to exert control over these valuable trade networks. Mills, as well as Fiske and Patrick, suggests that the feast system was incorporated at this time for judicial reasons, both as a forum for settling internal disputes and as a means to clarify territorial boundaries and resolve issues of inter-nation trespass.

The ideas of socio-political hierarchy, clan organization, and potlatching were adopted by the more southerly Ulkatchot'en as well as the Cheslatta. For reasons that remain unknown, the other bands to the east—the Lhoosk'uz, Nazko, and Quesnel (Red Bluff) Carrier—did not incorporate these traditions. As the Ulkatchot'en incorporated the idea of clans, however, the principles of clan membership were modified to fit in with the Ulkatcho emphasis on bilateral social organization.

This emphasis on bilaterality was reinforced by the close economic and social relations that the Ulkatcho Carrier had with the coastal Nuxalk. As among the Witsuwit'en and Gitksan, these relations intensified in the late eighteenth century with the inception of the maritime fur trade, when the Nuxalk assumed the role of middlemen in the southern Carrier trade with the European trading ships. While the Nuxalk lacked clans, their society, too, was organized around the principles of bilateral descent. In addition, the Nuxalk held to principles of social rank and status, which were demonstrated through individual ownership of crests. These crests were inherited along bilateral lines among the nobility of Nuxalk society, and the crests were validated through potlatch ceremonies.

The Ulkatchot'en, then, through their social relations with both the northern Carrier and the Nuxalk, were exposed to a wide variety of ideas about social organization, wealth, status, and principles of landownership. All these ideas were in a state of flux with the changes being introduced by the maritime fur trade. From this mélange of possibilities, the Ulkatchot'en adopted the ideas of clan organization, social rank, and potlatching, but remodelled these practices to suit their own needs and to fit into existing principles of social organization.

When clans were first introduced into Ulkatcho society in the early nineteenth century, they became associated with specific extended families. Clan affiliation was determined along bilateral rather than matrilineal lines: a child could choose to belong to his father's or mother's clan, or both. The extended family, now under the rubric of the clan, lived in the same village, where its members jointly hosted potlatches and shared common fishing and hunting territories, even though the boundaries of these territories were never sharply drawn. However, after a few generations the clans evolved to be primarily ceremonial organizations rather than landowning units, in contrast to the clans of the central and northern bands.

To strengthen their trade alliances with the Nuxalk, the Ulkatcho Carrier also incorporated the ideas of status and rank through ownership of personal titles and crests, which were validated through potlatches. However, like the clans, among the Ulkatcho Carrier the inheritance of these titles and crests occurred along bilateral lines, as among the Nuxalk, rather than along matrilineal lines, as among the northern Carrier.

In short, in incorporating clans, potlatches, and status distinctions through ownership of crests and titles, the Ulkatcho Carrier were not simply passive recipients of foreign cultural traditions. Instead, they actively modified these ideas while making changes to their own cultural practices. Clan organization and potlatches greatly declined in importance after the drastic reduction in population caused by the 1862–3 smallpox epidemic and after the sharp drop in fur prices in the 1930s, which left few individuals with sufficient wealth to host regular potlatches. Further, not all individuals were equally involved in the potlatch system. The idea of social hierarchy failed to take root in Ulkatcho society, partly due to its conflict with the fundamental Ulkatcho values of individualism and egalitarianism. However, in the last few years the Ulkatcho Carrier have begun to revive the clan system in their community, where they are remodelling the clans once again to fit the contemporary context.

Values and Beliefs

Despite differences in socio-political organization, a core set of values and beliefs that characterized nineteenth-century Carrier culture can be identified. The Carrier's survival as hunters, fishers, and gatherers depended on each individual having extensive knowledge of the land and its resources. Material technology was less important than the knowledge of how to construct and apply this technology efficiently. This knowledge consisted of a detailed understanding of animal habits, population cycles, climate, and topography. Knowledge was built up during an individual's lifetime in a number of ways. First, it was acquired through practical experience. As a child grew to adulthood he learned, through observation and through trial and error, the techniques of hunting, fishing, and trapping and the unique features of the animal populations, vegetation, and geography in his particular territory. Second, an individual's knowledge of the land and its resources was expanded through sharing information with other household members, with other families temporarily camped together, and with travellers encountered on the trails. As a result, Carrier culture placed strong emphasis on individual responsibility and autonomy, at the same time valuing the importance of communication and social co-operation.

While survival depended on practical knowledge, it was also important for people to live according to certain standards of conduct. The Carrier believed that all animate and inanimate objects in the world had a spirit. People's survival depended on their ability to maintain balanced relations with all the spirits in the land; if they did not, animals would not give themselves to hunters. Balanced relations were kept by living according to ethical standards and by performing rituals. These ethical concepts were encoded in oral traditions, which served as primary educational devices for children's moral training.

A person was expected to show respect for the foods and materials he or she used, to not waste any of these resources, and to perform rituals after a successful hunt. An individual was expected to be generous, to share meat from the hunt with other households and provide assistance when needed. The person was expected to be modest and not to boast of achievements or predict success in the future, whether for an upcoming hunt or the birth of a new child. Emphasis on individualism and autonomy was especially strong among the southern Carrier. No individual was believed to have the authority to tell another what to do; rather, each person was responsible for choosing his own course of action. Gossip and social exclusion served as effective mechanisms for social control. In extreme cases conflicts were resolved by household groups or camps splitting apart. If one lived by these values, the person would be fortunate in hunting and would enjoy good health. Misfortune or ill health was seen as the person's failure to live by these codes of behaviour or his breaking of a taboo.

Boys and girls might explicitly seek out direct contact with an animal spirit through the adolescent guardian spirit quest. These quests were an important component of the rites of passage to adulthood among the central Carrier. Among the Witsuwit'en and southern bands, however, the guardian spirit quest was optional. In any case, spirits came to individuals through dreams, providing knowledge of where to look for game or of future events. People with especially strong connections to animal spirits might become shamans, who had extraordinary healing powers.

The Impact of Colonialism

The Fur Trade

The Carrier were quick to become involved in the expanding land-based fur trade with Europeans. The first fur trade post to be established in BC was Fort McLeod, built in 1805 by the North West Company. The trade soon expanded into central Carrier territory with the building of Fort St James and Fort Fraser in 1806 and Fort George in 1807. In 1821 the North West Company merged with the Hudson's Bay Company. The same year saw the establishment of Fort Alexandria on the Fraser River in southern Carrier territory. It was built as the terminus of the newly established overland supply route from the Columbia River and collected furs from the Carrier, Tsilhqot'in, and Secwepemc. Fort Kilmaurs, on Babine Lake, was built the following year, drawing trade from both Carrier and Sekani trappers.

The forts were established in strategic locations, adjacent to Carrier villages and salmon-fishing stations. The transportation of goods and supplies from both the eastern and Columbia River posts was a slow and difficult process, and the forts were forced to rely on local foods—almost exclusively salmon—for survival. They obtained salmon either by directly harvesting the fish from the river or through trade from the local Carrier. The forts' reliance on local resources, access to which on occasion was strictly controlled by the Carrier, plus their well-established Aboriginal trading networks with coastal nations gave the Carrier a significant degree of control in their relationship with the traders and precluded them from becoming dependent on the forts for food or supplies. Two other forts, Fort Chilcotin (1829) and Fort Kluskus (1844), were constructed in southern Carrier territory in an effort to intercept the coastal trade; both failed in these efforts and were eventually closed.

The European fur trade instigated several changes in the economic and social organization of the Carrier. By the early twentieth century, southern Carrier families had extended their concept of family ownership of fishing sites to include rights to specific trapping areas. Individuals remained free to hunt anywhere in the band area. A similar process occurred among the central Carrier, where families began to exert control over trapping territories, thus weakening the system of clan-based landownership.

With the introduction of new technologies and goods, such as guns and ammunition, steel traps, axes, kettles, blankets, and cloth, the Carrier became inextricably linked to the economic system of the colonial society. The Carrier continued as active trappers through the late nineteenth century and well into the twentieth century. Through the trapline registration system, introduced in BC in the 1920s, individuals became the 'registered' owners of traplines, bringing Carrier practices more fully under the restrictive control of the provincial government. Nevertheless, trapping has played an important role in the Carrier economy to the present.

The Expansion of the Colonial Frontier

The gold rushes of the 1860s represented the second wave of expansion of resource industries into Carrier country. The Cariboo gold rush of 1858–64, followed by the Omineca rush five years later, brought thousands of miners into Carrier territory and resulted in the establishment of permanent transportation corridors. The free traders who arrived with the miners brought an end to the HBC monopoly over the fur trade. Next came colonial administrators, who sought to impose government authority by regulating mining claims and land pre-emptions and by keeping law and order on the new frontier. In the 1880s Indian agencies began to be established in the BC Interior, and Indian agents set out to regulate and restrict the lives of Native people according to the dictates of the Indian Act.

The 1860s also saw the decimation of the Carrier population by smallpox. The southern Carrier bands were especially hard hit. A band in the Bowron Lakes area was wiped out, while others were reduced to fractions of their former levels. As the gold rushes ended, a number of miners stayed in the region, pre-empted land, and established ranches and farms. Settlement in Carrier territory, however, remained sporadic until the construction of the Grand Trunk Pacific Railway between Edmonton and Prince Rupert in 1914. This triggered a land boom in central and northern Carrier regions, and settlers and land speculators pre-empted land and established small towns along the railway belt between Prince George and the Bulkley Valley. Economic development in northern BC remained minimal until after World War II, most of the settlers supporting themselves through small-scale logging, sawmilling, farming, and trapping.

Carrier Economic Changes

Although the Carrier had been employed in wage labour since the establishment of the fur trade posts, wage labour became a much more important component of the economy after the 1860s. Carriers found periodic work as ranch labourers and cowboys, as guides and packers along the goldfield trails, as workers in the coastal salmon canneries and the Interior sawmills, and as construction crews on the roads and railways being built in the region. Some families took up cattle ranching on a small scale and kept herds of horses that they used for packing supplies through the country.

By the early twentieth century the Carrier had developed a mixed economy based on hunting, fishing, trapping, seasonal wage work, and small-scale stock raising. They responded to disruptions in any one of these pursuits by shifting to other activities. For example, after the virtual collapse of the salmon fishery in 1913 and 1914, families turned to trapping and hunting. Wage work became scarce during the 1930s and again after World War II due to the mechanization of ranching and logging operations, causing families to shift once again to hunting and fishing. Government assistance programs, including old age pensions, family allowances, and social assistance, were made fully available in the 1940s and 1950s, and served as sources of income that augmented rather than replaced hunting and trapping.

Changes in Beliefs and Values

Religious colonization of the Carrier began with the establishment of two Roman Catholic missions, in 1867 near Williams Lake and in 1873 at

Stuart Lake. The goals of the missionaries were ultimately to bring about submission of the Carrier to the religious authority of the Church and to convert the Carrier to Catholicism and to a settled, agricultural existence. The establishment of two Indian residential schools, St Joseph's Mission near Williams Lake and Lejacq School at Fraser Lake, facilitated these plans. Children as young as five were sent to the schools, where they remained for 10 months of the year, and often until the age of 16. The intent of the residential school system was to remove children from their homes so as to block the transmission of cultural values and practices. At the schools the children were taught basic literary skills as well as cooking, sewing, farm labour, and a variety of trades. While the residential schools interfered with the transmission of culture to the younger generations, the schools nevertheless failed in their original goal, which was the assimilation of Native people into Canadian society.

The Carrier, in their typically pragmatic orientation to outside influences, nominally converted to Catholicism and welcomed the periodic visits by travelling missionaries while retaining many aspects of their own spiritual beliefs. By the early twentieth century the guardian spirit quest was no longer practised among the southern bands, although periods of ritual training still persisted for adolescent boys and girls. Many people today continue to believe in the power of dreams, and shamans occasionally are called upon to help individuals who are suffering from extraordinary illnesses. The relative isolation until recent times of the Carrier communities from the impacts of logging, mining, and settlement has facilitated the retention of their language, culture, and subsistence lifestyle.

Colonial Authority: Restriction of Aboriginal Rights

With the exception of small areas on Vancouver Island and in the northeastern corner of the province, governments did not sign treaties with the Native nations of BC. While settlers were encouraged to take up free tracts of land, after 1866 Native people were prohibited by law from pre-empting land, and the Carrier in the Bulkley Valley and Quesnel areas were powerless to prevent some of their homesteads, campsites, and graveyards from being pre-empted by settlers. The provincial government refused to address the issue of Aboriginal title. Instead, it sought to quell Native protests by establishing reserves, which for Carrier bands were allotted between 1871 and 1902. Final adjustments to the sizes of reserves were made through the 1916 federal/provincial Royal Commission on Indian Affairs.

By the turn of the century, Aboriginal hunting and fishing rights increasingly became subject to government regulation. The federal Fisheries Act outlawed the use of weirs, basket traps, and nets for salmon fishing on inland rivers. These regulations were enforced with vigour as the commercial salmon fisheries developed in the late nineteenth century, and particularly after the 1913 Hell's Gate slide, in which debris from constructing the Canadian National Railway filled the Fraser, almost completely blocking the salmon run. Federal fisheries officers destroyed weirs on Babine Lake in 1905 and 1906 but eventually reached a compromise with the seven Carrier bands on the Babine Lake, Stuart Lake, and Nechako River watersheds, in which the bands agreed instead to fish by net. On the Fraser, under the scrutiny of fisheries officers, some Carrier families switched to dip-netting salmon, a time-consuming and laborious method.

Expansion of the Forest Industry

Until the 1940s, settlement throughout most of Carrier territory was sparse. The Carrier remained in control of most of their territory despite government failure to negotiate Aboriginal title. This changed after World War II with expansion of the forest industry. By the 1960s small logging and sawmilling operations had become obsolete, and larger companies were supplying wood to the major pulp and sawmills. As the economy boomed, the population of non-Natives expanded.

Increased competition for work, plus the requirement for more highly skilled labour, led to gradual exclusion of Natives from the industry. As the industry expanded, clear-cutting pushed further into regions previously isolated. In the past the Carrier had been able to respond to downturns in the industrial economy, whether trapping or wage labour, by placing more emphasis on hunting and fishing. Now this backbone of their economy was threatened with the loss of the forests to logging. The historic failure of governments to recognize and address Aboriginal title now became critical. In the 1970s the Carrier began a new era of political struggle as they launched direct protests over the unresolved matter of Aboriginal title and rights. The question of history is at the centre of these debates.

The Politics of History: Two Contemporary Examples

Carrier bands today have adopted a variety of strategies to press for government recognition of Aboriginal rights and title. One is the use of the court system, with the rationale that legal recognition of Aboriginal title would force Canadian and provincial governments to negotiate land settlements. A second strategy is direct political action, including staging blockades and use of the media. The goal is to generate sufficient attention and public sympathy to pressure governments into direct negotiations.

The essence of Aboriginal claims is this: Native leaders argue that before European arrival each nation had its own system of landownership and government, through which resource use and social conduct were regulated. Natives assert that their rights to land and self-government have not been relinquished, but only suppressed, and that these rights persist today. They draw attention to the continuity of cultural traditions from past to present to demonstrate their continuing status as distinct societies within Canada.

These representations of culture and history, though, are subject to challenge. The common-sense belief of many non-Natives is that Native societies of the past were 'primitive' groups who had no form of landownership or concept of property rights. Many believe that Native people either have lost their culture under the impact of Western society, or that it survives in the form of arts and crafts, ceremonies and dances, and eco-spiritualism, all aspects of culture that non-Native Canadians can appreciate comfortably without having to consider the question of who owns the land. One recent example of these conflicting views of history is found in the Gitksan and Witsuwit'en land claims case.

The Gitksan and Witsuwit'en Land Claims Case

In 1984, 51 hereditary chiefs representing the houses of the Witsuwit'en and Gitksan peoples initiated legal action in the BC Supreme Court. Through this action the chiefs asked the court to recognize their past and ongoing ownership and jurisdiction over their traditional territories covering 54,000 square kilometres in northwestern BC. The court case, known as *Delgamuukw v. the Queen*, began in May 1987 and a decision was rendered in 1991. The case was appealed to the BC Court of Appeal and later to the Supreme Court of Canada, which brought forth its landmark decision in December of 1997.

The case was not only the longest Aboriginal title case heard in Canadian history, but was also unique with respect to the extensive historical evidence provided by the hereditary chiefs themselves. The core of this evidence consisted of Gitksan *adaawk* and Witsuwit'en *kungax*, oral histories documenting their ownership of land and resources in specific territories. Through this evidence and that provided by anthropologists and historians, the court was told of the Gitksan and Witsuwit'en clan and house systems, of the authority of the clan and house leaders, and of the critical role played by the potlatch in regulating and affirming political, social, and economic life. The Gitksan and Witsuwit'en argued that, despite the colonization of BC, they have not relinquished their Aboriginal title and that their traditional

BOX 12.1

Carrier Voices

The exclusion of Carrier voices from written historical literature has begun to be rectified. There are now a number of books written by Carrier authors portraying Carrier culture and history. Several children's books are available, such as *The Boy Who Snared the Sun* (1994) and *The Robin and the Song Sparrow* (1994) by Catherine Bird of Nak'azdli; *Atsoo and I* (1990) and *For Someone Special* (1990) by Laura Boyd of Nazko; and *Musdzi 'Udada'—The Owl Story* (1991) by Bernadette Rosetti. These have been produced to support language and cultural instruction in public schools. The Carrier Linguistics Committee (1970s–1980s) based at Fort St James and, more recently, the Yinka Dene Language Institute at Vanderhoof (1990–) have served key roles in documenting the Carrier language, training Carrier language teachers, and creating curriculum materials in Carrier language and culture. Their publications feature short stories, songs, poems, and discussions of plants and their uses as told by different Carrier contributors. A more comprehensive history is Lizette Hall's *The Carrier, My People* (1992),

based on information from her late father, Louis-Billy Prince of Nak'azdli. A genealogy of the historical figure Chief Kw'eh of Nak'azdli is documented in *Kw'eh Ts'u Haindene: Descendants of Kwah* (1979), written by Bernadette Rosetti, a great-granddaughter of Chief Kw'eh. A more widely available work is *The Spirit in the Land* (Gabriola Island, BC: Reflections, 1989), presenting background information on the *Delgamuukw* case as well as the opening statements of Witsuwit'en hereditary chief Gisday Wa and Gitksan hereditary chief Delgam Uukw to the BC Supreme Court. Finally, a number of collaborative publications are also available. *Stoney Creek Woman* (Vancouver: Tillacum, 1988) presents the life story of Sai'kuz elder Mary John Sr, while *Justa* (Vancouver: Tillacum, 1994) recounts the life of well-known Carrier political leader Justa Monk. *'Hang on to These Words': Johnny David's Delgamuukw Testimony*, edited by Antonia Mills, consists of the evidence provided to the court by Witsuwit'en Elder Johnny David (forthcoming, University of Toronto Press).

systems of law remain in effect in their territories and continue to order life in their communities.

In his controversial decision (McEachern, 1991), BC Supreme Court Chief Justice Alan McEachern put forth a fundamentally different view of history. The judge stated that the nineteenth-century Gitksan and Witsuwit'en were a 'primitive people without any form of writing, horses, or wheeled wagons'. According to the judge, they had only a rudimentary form of social organization, barely any degree of culture, and lived a marginal existence in which starvation was common and life was 'nasty, brutish and short'. McEachern concluded that the Gitksan and Witsuwit'en no longer have a

distinct Native culture because not all the people continue to hunt and trap and because many participate in wage labour, own automobiles, and consume store-bought food. Ultimately, the Court rejected the Gitksan and Witsuwit'en peoples' Aboriginal claim.

This view of history is rooted in a colonial ideology framed on the nineteenth-century theory of cultural evolution, which holds that all societies can be ranked on a scale of progressive evolution from 'primitive' to 'civilized'. Native societies are 'primitive' and occupy the lowest rungs of this scale, while European societies are 'civilized' and occupy the highest position. 'Primitive' societies, according to this theory, are not only weak, poorly organized, and precarious, but are inherently less worthy than 'civilized' societies. The implicit suggestion is that because 'civilization' is both inevitable and advantageous, the colonization of North America, the bringing of 'civilization' to the continent, and the domination of Native societies has been in Native peoples' best interests.

These views conflict sharply with those of contemporary anthropology. Native societies are no less highly evolved than European societies; rather, they have evolved differently, and have developed complex ways of adapting to their specific environments. For example, the changing nature of Carrier social organization in the late eighteenth and nineteenth centuries is not a sign of the indeterminate, unorganized state of 'primitive' societies, nor is it an indication that, through these changes, the Carrier 'lost' their 'traditional culture'. Instead, these modifications in social organization were adaptive strategies that enabled the Carrier to solidify trade relations and pursue their economic interests. The judge viewed Native culture to be static, defined by traits that existed in some mythical past but have now all but disappeared. In contrast, anthropology today emphasizes the dynamic nature of culture and the way people continually adapt their culture. For example, trappers now use trucks instead of snowshoes to get to traplines. To the judge, this was culture loss. However, while the form of transportation may have changed, its function remains. Modern vehicles enable Carriers to maintain their culture.

In short, not only does this view of history emerge from a cultural context of nineteenth-century European colonialism, it serves the political function of justifying and maintaining the status quo of Native–state relations in Canada. In his conclusion, Chief Justice McEachern, adhering to a belief in objective history, rejected the Gitksan and Witsuwit'en perspectives on their history as 'not literally true'. He failed to consider the possibility that there are many different perspectives on history, and he failed to consider how his own view of the Gitksan and Witsuwit'en

was shaped by a colonial ideology and by archaic beliefs about culture.

The Gitksan and Witsuwit'en chiefs appealed this ruling, and in 1997 the Supreme Court of Canada issued its decision. In a major reversal, the Supreme Court concluded that the oral histories of the Gitksan and Witsuwit'en peoples were in fact legitimate histories, and that Chief Justice McEachern erred in dismissing them as sources of evidence. The Court consequently ordered that the case be sent back to trial. In recognizing the legitimacy of Native historical traditions, the Court took a bold and long overdue step towards respecting the pluralism of historical ways of knowing and creating a framework for reconciliation between Aboriginal peoples and Canadian society. The Court also found that Aboriginal title has never been extinguished and persists in BC today. The Witsuwit'en are currently attempting to seek resolution of their claim by participating in the BC Treaty Commission process.

The Nazko and Lhoosk'uz Carrier and the Mackenzie Grease Trail

A second example of the importance of politics and history in contemporary Carrier life is in the Nazko and Lhoosk'uz Carrier's protest over development of the Mackenzie Grease Trail. This is an Aboriginal trade route, possibly thousands of years old, that runs over 300 kilometres between southern Carrier territory and Nuxalk villages on the Pacific coast. Southern Carrier people refer to it as the Grease Trail because of the large quantities of oolichan oil they obtained through trade with the Nuxalk. Alexander Mackenzie used it in 1793 to reach the Pacific. Mackenzie is celebrated as the first European to traverse North America north of Mexico and to thus establish symbolic claims to the territory that would become Canada. Many non-Natives today refer to it as the Mackenzie Trail, the Mackenzie Grease Trail, or the Alexander Mackenzie Heritage Trail.

The different names for this trail are symbolic of the debates that have since arisen over the trail's historic significance. In the early 1970s a national non-profit organization devoted to the preservation of natural areas for public use began efforts to have the route officially designated as a heritage trail. In 1982 the federal and provincial governments signed a formal agreement to develop and preserve the Alexander Mackenzie Heritage Trail. The trail is promoted as an important symbol of the birth of Canada.

In contrast, the thousands of years of the trail's Native history and its continued importance as a route linking the homesteads, fishing camps, and hunting and trapping territories of contemporary Carrier people have played a secondary role in the trail's promotional campaign. Given the depth of Native history in the region, the Carrier see Mackenzie's contribution to the historical significance of the trail as minor. While the trail has been promoted as a symbol of Canadian national identity, to the southern Carrier it has become a symbol of their struggle to maintain the integrity of their communities and to exert control over developments in their midst.

The concept of developing the trail as a heritage route arose in 1974. Spurred on by the dedicated efforts of two volunteer organizers, the trail development plan slowly took shape. Both the provincial and federal governments undertook feasibility studies. The location of the original trail travelled by Mackenzie was far from obvious, due to the many horse and wagon trails that crisscross the area. With close reference to Mackenzie's published journal, between 1978 and 1979 the 'official' trail was identified and cleared, and an informal plan was drafted for the development and interpretation of the historic sites along the route. A comprehensive hiker's trail guide entitled *In the Steps of Alexander Mackenzie* was published in 1981 by the non-profit organization.

The Nazko and Lhoosk'uz First Nations, however, knew little of these plans, and neither had been formally approached for input or approval. This was so even though the official trail crossed through eight of their reserves and through the entire territory over which the two First Nations recently had prepared a comprehensive claim.

'Native heritage sites', including historic villages and graveyards both on and off reserve land, were prominent features of the interpretive scheme. Yet no information had been provided to, or sought from, the local First Nations about how these heritage sites were to be identified, interpreted, or protected. In short, despite the need for the support of Carrier First Nations, there existed a complete lack of communication between the trail's developers and the local bands.

These events followed on the heels of the recent incursion of logging into southern Carrier territories. Up until the 1970s the Nazko and Lhoosk'uz people had remained largely sheltered from industrial developments and continued to live a hunting, fishing, and trapping lifestyle in homesteads dispersed along the Blackwater River. In 1974, however, logging began in the Nazko Valley, and roads began to be built in their hunting and trapping territories. The people erected a blockade and created sufficient media attention and political pressure to secure a short-term moratorium on logging. Eventually, however, logging proceeded, and clear-cutting the forests severely disrupted the economy and integrity of the communities. With this loss of control over their traditional lands fresh in their minds, the chiefs interpreted development of the Grease Trail as theft of their last remaining resource: their culture.

In 1979 the Nazko and Lhoosk'uz chiefs began a series of meetings with provincial and federal agencies in which the chiefs attempted to negotiate the terms of their participation in the trail's development. By virtue of their Aboriginal title and authority over reserve lands, they demanded to be included in decision-making equally with the provincial and federal governments. Second, they requested control over how Native heritage resources were defined, interpreted, and developed. After prolonged negotiations, however, these terms were refused. The First Nations were told they would have the same opportunity for input as other 'public interest groups'. When the chiefs informed the government agencies that no trespassing on reserves would be allowed unless an agreement was reached, the trail developers, in a classic example of the rewriting of history, began to reroute the official trail to bypass reserves. Although discussions between the agencies and the Carrier periodically occur, this conflict remains essentially unresolved and development of the trail continues without support from the Nazko and Lhoosk'uz First Nations.

Nevertheless, trail developers continue to use symbols of Native culture and history in promotional materials. In these representations, Native people alternately are erased from the landscape or assigned secondary roles that enhance the main plot line: celebration of the European 'discovery' and settlement of Canada. Mackenzie is portrayed as a courageous explorer of an uncharted land. When Natives do appear, they are either helpers or hostile savages who enhance the spectre of Mackenzie's heroism. Contemporary Native communities along the trail are either ignored or promoted as tourist attractions—the once hostile Indians are now friendly hosts willing to share their culture with visitors.

The history reproduced through the Mackenzie Grease Trail development is but one example of a pervasive genre of history—frontier history—found in school textbooks and bookstores and libraries across Canada. Frontier histories celebrate Canadian national identity while legitimating the colonization and domination of Native peoples. The image of early Canada as an empty wilderness heroically conquered by pioneering settlers serves to erase Native people—and the unresolved issue of Aboriginal title and rights—from historical consciousness. In the case of the Mackenzie Grease Trail, the presentation of contemporary Native people as friendly hosts allows tourists to appreciate the richness of Carrier culture without having to learn of the ongoing protests of the Nazko and Lhoosk'uz people and of the controversy that has surrounded the trail development since its inception.

Conclusion

Conflicts over historical representations have become almost commonplace in Native peoples' struggles with the Canadian state. These conflicts have given rise to renewed discussions among anthropologists about their moral obligations to the First Nations with whom they undertake research and to the consequences of advocacy work to the discipline. While the ability of anthropologists to resolve these on-the-ground conflicts is questionable, one of the main contributions that anthropology can make is to develop a better understanding of the cultural contexts in which different versions of history are created and contested. In order to understand the issues that concern Carrier and other First Nations today, we need to pay increasing attention to the subtle ways in which the ideas of history and images of Indians that permeate popular beliefs among the non-Native Canadian public reinforce the oppressive system of relationships that First Nations leaders are seeking to challenge.

Notes

1. I use the term 'First Nation' rather than the older term 'Indian band' to refer to the political groups defined by the Department of Indian and Northern Affairs. In addition, I use the terms 'Aboriginal' and 'Native' to refer to the Aboriginal people in Canada generally; I use 'Indian' when I wish to evoke non-Native perceptions of Aboriginal peoples in Canada.

2. An alternate spelling of Witsuwit'en is Wet'suwet'en. The term itself refers to Carrier bands in the Bulkley River area. Witsuwit'en is more commonly used today; however, some Carrier political organizations (the Office of the Wet'suwet'en Hereditary Chiefs, the Wet'suwet'en First Nation) continue to use the 'e' spelling.

3. In the following pages the words presented in italics are Carrier terms that have been written in the orthography developed by the Summer Institute of Linguistics (Antoine et al., 1974).

4. The term 'house' refers to a socio-political group that may or may not reside in the same dwelling.

Transactions of the Canadian Institute (1892–3). A detailed account of Carrier material culture, with emphasis on the central Carrier. Includes a list of Carrier bands and villages in the mid-1800s.

————. 1893b. 'Are the Carrier Sociology and Mythology Indigenous or Exotic?', *Proceedings and Transactions of the Royal Society of Canada for the Year 1892*, series 1, section 2, vol. 10.

————. 1978. *The History of the Northern Interior of British Columbia*. Smithers, BC: Interior Stationery. A readable overview, with many references to Carrier history, culture, and the Carrier's evolving relationship with European traders and missionaries. Based on Morice's experience as a missionary at Fort St James.

Steward, Julian. 1960. 'Carrier Acculturation: The Direct Historical Approach', in S. Diamond, ed., *Cultures in History: Essays in Honor of Paul Radin*. New York: Columbia University Press.

Tobey, Margaret L. 1981. 'The Carrier', in June Helm, ed., *Handbook of North American Indians*, vol. 6, *The Subarctic*. Washington: Smithsonian Institution. A summary of Carrier culture at the time of European contact, plus detailed bibliography.

Suggested Web Sites

Yinka Dene Language Institute:
www.cnc.bc.ca/yinkadene
A wide range of information on publications in Dakelh (Carrier) language, culture, and history.

Carrier Sekani Tribal Council: www.cstc.bc.ca
Extensive information on the Tribal Council's various activities.

References and Recommended Readings

Antoine, Franscesca, Catherine Bird, Agnes Isaac, Nelly Prince, Sally Sam, Richard Walker, and David B. Wilkinson. 1974. *Central Carrier Bilingual Dictionary*. Fort St James, BC: Carrier Linguistics Committee.

Duff, Wilson. 1951. 'Notes on Carrier Social Organization', *Anthropology in British Columbia* 2: 28–34.

Dyen, Isidore, and David F. Aberle. 1974. *Lexical Reconstruction: The Case of the Proto-Athapaskan Kinship System*. New York: Cambridge University Press.

Fiske, Jo-Anne, and Betty Patrick. 2000. *Cis Dideen Kat (When the Plumes Rise): The Way of the Lake Babine Nation*. Vancouver: University of British Columbia Press. A study of customary legal practices, with emphasis on the role of the potlatch as an institution of law and justice and on how community members are attempting to revitalize this institution as a means of restoring modern forms of traditional justice and self-government. Betty Patrick is Chief of the Lake Babine First Nation.

Gisday Wa and Delgamuukw. 1989. *The Spirit in the Land: The Opening Statement of the Gitksan and Wet'suwet'en Hereditary Chiefs in the Supreme Court of British Columbia, May 11, 1987*. Gabriola Island, BC: Reflections. An introduction to the history of the land claim and a summary of contemporary Gitksan and Witsuwit'en societies, their major institutions, and their systems of authority and landownership.

Goldman, Irving. 1940. 'The Alkatcho Carrier of British Columbia', in R. Linton, ed., *Acculturation in Seven American Indian Tribes*. New York: Appleton-Century. A summary of Goldman's ethnographic study of the Ulkatcho, focusing on social, political, and economic life.

———. 1941. 'The Alkatcho Carrier: Historical background of crest prerogatives', *American Anthropologist* 43, 3: 396–418. An analysis of the adoption of the clan and potlatch-rank systems among the Ulkatcho Carrier through their contact with the Nuxalk and northern Carrier.

———. 1953. 'The Alkatcho Carrier of British Columbia', manuscript. Victoria: Royal British Columbia Museum. A comprehensive ethnography of the Ulkatcho Carrier, based on fieldwork conducted in 1935–6. Focuses on social and economic life, religious beliefs, shamanism, and oral traditions.

Hackler, James. 1958. 'The Carrier Indians of Babine Lake: The Effects of the Fur Trade and the Catholic Church on their Social Organization', MA thesis, Jose State College.

Hudson, Douglas. 1972. 'The Historical Determinar Carrier Social Organization: A Study of North Athapaskan Matriliny', MA thesis, McMa University.

———. 1983. 'Traplines and Timber: Social Economic Change Among the Carrier Indians Northern British Columbia', Ph.D. dissertatic University of Alberta.

Jenness, Diamond. 1943. *The Carrier Indians of t Bulkley River: Their Social and Religious Life*. Washin ton: Bureau of American Ethnology, Smithsonia Institution. This is a detailed discussion o Witsuwit'en social and political organization, reli gious beliefs, and shamanism, based on three months of fieldwork in 1924–5.

Kew, J.E. Michael. 1974. 'Nazko and Kluskus: Social Conditions and Prospects for the Future', manuscript. Quesnel, BC: Nazko Band Office. A concise ethnographic summary of the Nazko and Lhoosk'uz Carrier, based on a year-long period of field research in the 1970s. Focuses on the social and economic impact of the proposed expansion of logging in Nazko and Lhoosk'uz territories. Available from the Special Collections Division of the University of British Columbia main library as part of the *Report on the Nazko and Kluskus Bands from the Nazko-Kluskus Study Team*.

Kobrinsky, Vernon. 1977. 'The Tsimshianization of the Carrier Indians', in J.W. Helmer, S. Van Dyke, and F. Kense, eds, *Problems in the Prehistory of the North American Subarctic: The Athapaskan Question*. Calgary: University of Calgary Archaeological Association.

McEachern, Allen. 1991. *Reasons for Judgment: Delgamuukw v. B.C.* Smithers, BC: British Columbia Supreme Court.

Mills, Antonia. 1994. *Eagle Down Is Our Law: Witsuwit'en Law, Feasts and Land Claims*. Vancouver: University of British Columbia Press. Mills was commissioned by the Gitksan and Witsuwit'en chiefs to present a report on the laws, feasts, and institutions of the Witsuwit'en for the *Delgamuukw* case. This is her report. It is based on two years of fieldwork and analysis of anthropological, historic, and linguistic data.

Morice, Adrien G. 1893a. 'Notes Archaeological, Industrial and Sociological on the Western Denes',

PART V

The Eastern Woodlands

CHAPTER 13

Farmers and Hunters of the Eastern Woodlands: A Regional Overview

MARY DRUKE BECKER

Environment

The portion of eastern Canada south of the boreal forest region forms a part, along with the northeastern United States, of the Eastern Woodlands culture area. The land is richly forested with both deciduous and coniferous trees. Lakes and rivers are scattered throughout the region; and First Nation territory has often been defined here by river drainage. The St Lawrence River, linking the Atlantic Ocean to the Great Lakes, was an important feature in both the social and physical landscapes of many of the people of the region.

The environment richly provided numerous resources useful to its indigenous inhabitants. The forests were home to a number of animals desired primarily for their meat and hides, but also for other purposes. These included deer, bear, moose, rabbit, beaver, otter, muskrat, fox, wolf, raccoon, skunk, bobcat, and numerous fowl. These were hunted with bows and arrows or spears, or caught in traps, round-ups, or deadfalls. Edible fruits, nuts, roots, and, in places, wild rice were harvested. Europeans have always recognized that staples of the region in historic times, particularly corn, beans, and squash, were cultivated. What has been appreciated only more recently is that many other vegetable products were not simply gathered; the plants were in one way or another tended. Aquatic resources, including salt and freshwater fish, sea mammals,

crustaceans, eels, and turtles, were also of major importance to most peoples in the region. Tools used for fishing were bone fish hooks, nets, harpoons, spears, and weirs. Animal skins and bones, wood and bark, clay, shell, stone, and other such items provided the raw materials from which people created the things necessary for life: clothing; shelter; utensils for building, hunting, fishing, gardening, and various domestic tasks; and objects that were used for ritual, decorative, or recreational purposes.

Social Organization

The Native people inhabiting the Canadian Woodlands during the historic period were primarily Algonquian and Iroquoian speakers. For the most part, Iroquoian-speaking people were more intensive farmers than Algonquian speakers, who relied more heavily on fishing, hunting, and gathering. Alliances and other friendly relations between Algonquian and Iroquoian peoples, when they occurred, often centred on trade, with corn and other agricultural produce going to Algonquians in return for meat, fish, and furs. Although the economic emphasis of each group was different, the economies of both were broadly based, so that Iroquoians also engaged in fishing, hunting, and gathering, while many Algonquians practised horticulture. In the warmer portions of the Eastern Woodlands, i.e., present-day New

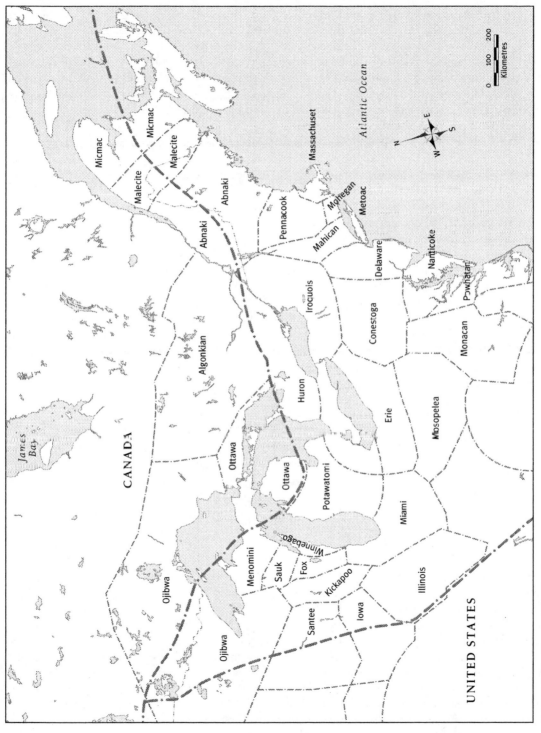

MAP 13.1. The Eastern Woodlands

England and the mid-Atlantic region of the US, where horticulture was more reliable, the contrast between the two groups was less marked. Regardless of the focus, the subsistence activities of Woodlands people were intensive, providing enriched economies.

Inter-village contact was common, and a complex system of trails linked villages to one another and to hunting areas. Generally, Algonquians were more likely to use water transportation than were Iroquoians. Their birchbark canoes were light and efficient, while Iroquoians used bulkier ones of elm bark. Water provided transportation for both peoples when they ranged significant distances from home for hunting, trading, negotiation, or warfare.

Among Algonquian speakers, differences existed between inland dwellers and maritime peoples such as the Mi'kmaq. The latter had a band organization similar to that found in the Subarctic in that it was based on principles of friendship and cognatic (bilateral kin-group) relations, while inland peoples were more oriented towards totemic descent groups, usually patrilineal. Nevertheless, the maritime people are considered to be more similar to Woodland cultural groups than to Subarctic ones largely because of the diverse, intensive nature of their subsistence activities. Iroquoians were, and many still are, organized socially on the basis of matrilineal kinship, and membership in a lineage or clan depends on the affiliation of one's mother.

Most differences among Algonquian groups result from variations in ecological adaptation. This is obviously the case with many maritime/inland contrasts. Most distinctions among Iroquoians, also, are tied to ecological adaptations. Others are primarily related to historic and other factors: the hunting practices of the Mohawk of Oka/Kanesatake more closely resemble those of their Algonquian-speaking Algonkin and Nipissing neighbours than they do those of other Mohawks.

A division of labour existed. Men were primarily responsible for hunting, fishing, warfare, councils, building, manufacturing implements for hunting and fishing, and, among those involved in horticulture, clearing the fields. Women were responsible for gathering and for planting, cultivating, and harvesting. They also participated in fishing, cleaned fish and game, cooked, cared for children, and made clothing and household utensils.

Political organization among inland Algonquians took the form of local chieftainships. In some cases, as among the Passamaquoddy and Maliseet, these chieftainships were patrilineally inherited. Among maritime people, leadership was band-based, usually with one leader per band. Some Algonquian local groups united to form national or confederate councils, as in the case of the Abenaki Confederacy, composed of Maliseet, Mi'kmaq, Passamaquoddy, and Penobscot. Iroquoians had local chieftainships, which in the case of the Six Nations (Mohawk, Oneida, Onondaga, Cayuga, Seneca, and Tuscarora) were based on both heredity and merit. Confederate structure is commonly associated with the Six Nations Iroquois, but it was also typical of other Iroquoians, such as the Huron.

History

When English and French explorers entered the region in the sixteenth century, Native people were thriving. Dire effects, however, followed contact with the strangers. Smallpox and other contagious illnesses for which people had no immunity cut back population drastically, as did warfare centring on the fur trade. We do not know how many entire groups, let alone families and individuals, were completely lost during the very early historic period.

Other changes also were forthcoming. For many Iroquoians and Algonquians the fur trade resulted in a specialization in trapping and trading and less reliance on traditional subsistence practices. For some Algonquians horticulture became somewhat more feasible because they no longer needed to break into small groups to search for food in times of scarcity and because,

FIGURE 13.1. (After Edward Chalfield) Nicholas Vincent Isawanhonhi, a Huron chief, holding a wampum belt, 1825. (Courtesy of the National Archives of Canada, C38948)

although horticulture was still less reliable than hunting in a relatively northern climate, there was now the security of an 'outside' source of supplies in the event of crop failure.

Through time a number of Woodlands people accepted Christianity. Many Natives were induced by missionary efforts in the seventeenth and eighteenth centuries to move to mission settlements. A number of communities and reserves in eastern Canada were formed in this way. Today, Christianity is found side by side with traditional religions in many Indian communities.

The map of Native people in eastern Canada has changed greatly during the historic period. Many groups were radically dispersed, some to points as distant as northern British Columbia or Mexico, as Euro-Canadian 'pioneers' settled in their land, or as warfare with other Natives also attempting to cope with new conditions necessitated that they flee. Others were annihilated. Some groups moved from their land in what is now the United States to French mission settlements or set up new communities when their own land was lost as a result of what were essentially European wars. Whatever their origins and however desperate their history, Woodlands Indians have survived to become an integral part of twenty-first-century Canada. The following chapters provide more detail concerning the culture and history of these people.

CHAPTER 14

Iroquois and Iroquoian in Canada

MARY DRUKE BECKER

Introduction

Iroquoian speakers, including the St Lawrence Iroquoian, Huron, Petun, and Neutral Indians, long inhabited what are now the provinces of Quebec and Ontario. According to their own oral histories, Iroquoians[1] have been on 'this island on a turtle's back' (the North American continent) since time immemorial. Their presence in Canada, however, was uneven during the historical period. By the twentieth century, except for some Huron and combined Huron and Petun (Wyandot/Wendat), there were no descendants of the Iroquoians living in what is now Canada who had been known to French missionaries and explorers in the sixteenth and seventeenth centuries. Today the Iroquoian population of Canada consists mainly of the Iroquois, the people of the Six Nations: Mohawk, Oneida, Onondaga, Cayuga, Seneca, and Tuscarora. These people moved to Canada from what is now New York state from the late seventeenth through the early nineteenth centuries.

This chapter presents an introduction to the historic Iroquois and Iroquoians and, especially, the modern Iroquois of Canada. The approach is based on the interpretive perspective advocated by Clifford Geertz. Interpretive anthropology assumes that a particular action can have many meanings even within a single culture, and certainly across cultures. For example, a simple action like 'blinking the right eyelid' (Geertz, 1973) could be an unintentional twitch, a wink,

or a pretended wink; it could be done to mimic or ridicule someone, or for any number of other reasons. For an interpretive anthropologist it is not enough simply to study behaviour, but to learn what that behaviour means or meant to the people involved. An interpretive anthropologist endeavours to determine which among the many meanings possible are attributed to particular actions.

As an anthropologist and student of Iroquoian and Iroquois history and culture for over 30 years, cognizant of the complexity, diversity, and multiplicity of interpretations, I will offer my analysis of the Iroquoian experience in what is now Canada. This necessitates 'translation' of behaviour, actions, and words—searching for the meanings behind them. I pursued my academic study of Iroquois culture via a fascination with the confederation of Six Nations known as the League of the Iroquois. My fieldwork in 1976–7 exposed me directly to the richness and complexities of Iroquois culture and grew into what has become a lifelong search to understand it. In the end, my analysis of the history and culture of the Iroquoian people of Canada is just one interpretation, informed and influenced by my theoretical anthropological training.

Interpretive Anthropology

The interpretation of cultural phenomena requires looking beyond the obvious to make sense of the complicated symbolic meanings involved in interaction. In studies of cross-cultural interaction, this requires that one describe the ways that diverse people interpret what they do and experience. Iroquois and Euro-Canadians often put different constructions on the same types of behaviour, a reality that has frequently caused mutual distrust, misunderstanding, and confusion. Understanding this can offer insight into the nature of their interactions.

Interpretive anthropology calls for an awareness of the cultural perspectives significant to the individuals involved in particular interactions, whether one is dealing with the past or the present. Through an analysis of sources, which when studying the past may include manuscripts, printed documents, graphics, and oral traditions, and in the present may encompass interviews, printed texts, and anthropological field notes based on observation of behaviour, among other things, the researcher must decide what was considered significant. Each source reflects the point of view of an individual. The object, then, is not merely to wade through all the separate points of view to find out what 'really' happened, but to take into account features of the interaction itself that point to the meaning attributed to them by the people involved. One must also be aware that in most cases the persons providing the documentation were themselves engaged in the interaction in some way. Their interpretations of it, therefore, entered into how they interacted and how they reported it.

Although materials used for analysis have limitations in and of themselves as sources of data, there are no limitations on the questions that may be addressed using their aid. A researcher is also free to compare data: the statements and observations made by the same person(s) at different times may be weighed for consistency and may be checked against data provided by others. An interpretive anthropologist must ultimately do 'fieldwork' among documents, observing and interpreting the interactions for which data are available, trying to understand both how the participants interpreted their interactions and the consequences of those interpretations.

The Historical Iroquoians of Canada

The first Iroquoian people of whom there is historical evidence are the St Lawrence (or Laurentian) Iroquoians, first mentioned by Jacques Cartier in 1534 and last by Jean François de la Rocque de Roberval in 1543. Their identity and fate have long been an enigma to scholars. Algonquian characteristics in their culture have led to speculation that they were 'Iroquoianized Algonquians'. Most researchers, however, tend to categorize them as Iroquoians, probably descendants of those whose culture developed prehistorically in the region from Middle Woodlands culture. Those associated with the village of Stadacona (near present-day Quebec City) lived in 7–10 villages along the river between Île aux Coudres and the Richelieu Rapids. The village of Hochelaga was on Montreal Island, as were two smaller settlements, apparently fishing camps. These villages were thriving when Cartier and Roberval travelled up the St Lawrence. But by the time Samuel de Champlain arrived in 1603, the St Lawrence Iroquoians had disappeared without a trace. Archaeological evidence suggests that they may have scattered, perhaps as the result of warfare, and settled among neighbouring Iroquoian or Algonquian people. However, evidence remains rare, and their fate is far from certain. The Iroquoian-speakers that Champlain mentioned are Huron. The Huron were to become the dominant Iroquoian group with whom the French had extensive contact until 1650, when they too dispersed following intense warfare with the Iroquois. The Huron were encompassed within the group of Iroquoian refugees called the Wyandots or Wendats.

The Huron were divided into five confederated tribal groupings—Attignawantan, Attigneenongnahac, Arendaronon, Tahontaenrat, and Ataronchronon. Meeting at least once a year to renew their alliance, they occupied a rich area of coniferous and deciduous forest west of Lake Simcoe and east of Georgian Bay. Other Iroquoian-speaking peoples with whom the French were familiar in Canada during the early seventeenth century were the Neutral, Wenro, and Petun.

The Neutral, so named by the French because of their tendency to remain neutral in the wars between the Huron and Iroquois, comprised five groups: Attiragenrega, Niagagarega, Antouaronon, Kakouagoga, and Ahondihronon, occupying from 28 to 40 villages lying south and east of Huronia. The relation of the groups is not known in detail, although evidence indicates that they formed a confederacy or shifting alliance. The Neutral disappeared as a cohesive group when, in 1647, the Seneca attacked one of their villages because its people had allowed a Seneca to be captured by the Petun in Neutral territory. Individuals may have found refuge among other Iroquoian people.

The Wenro are commonly associated with the Neutral and, at one time, were allied with them. Apparently, they were located close to Seneca country, in two villages near present-day Lewiston, New York. They moved to Huronia in 1638 because they felt threatened by the Iroquois. Having split with the Neutral, they were then without military support in their home base to defend themselves.

At the beginning of the seventeenth century, the Petun lived southwest of Huronia in what are now Ontario's Nottawasaga and Collingwood townships. The Petun were composed of two nations: the Wolves and the Deer. They were very similar to the Huron, especially the Attignawantan, except that they grew large amounts of tobacco, so much, in fact, that they have been called the Tobacco Nation. A number of Huron settled among the Petun in 1649. The combined Huron and Petun were eventually displaced in warfare against the Iroquois.

The Iroquoian-speaking peoples lived primarily in sedentary villages, which they moved every 10–12 years when conditions (e.g., soil exhaustion) warranted. In some cases, multiple village settlements developed. Two or three villages formed a cluster usually designated by a single name. Within a village, people lived in communal longhouses, averaging eight by 30 metres in size

and built of post frames covered by strips of bark. The arched roofs had holes that could be covered or uncovered as weather conditions permitted to allow release of smoke from the fires aligned down the centre of each house. Usually, two families shared a fire. Compartments formed of boards with supports suspended a distance from the ground lined both sides of the longhouse. Each family slept and stored clothing and goods in a compartment. Storage for dried foods and firewood was located at each end of the longhouse and under sleeping platforms. As Iroquois kinship was matrilineal and residence was matrilocal, each longhouse was inhabited by a group of related adult women, their spouses, and children.

Within villages, the main organizing units were matrilineally grouped women, who directed communal activities such as planting and gathering, and councils of peace chiefs and war chiefs, the former arbitrating internal disputes and making alliances, the latter deliberating on military actions. Decisions in council were generally made by consensus. No one was bound by a decision, however, although social pressure acted to induce acceptance of decisions made.

Age and gender were important determinants of economic activity. At least during the later historic period, the division of labour resulted in an association of men with forests and women with clearings, an association fundamental to the way Iroquoian people structured their world.

Women, aided by children, did most of the agricultural work and the gathering of fruits, other vegetable foods, and firewood. Women also made wooden utensils, pottery vessels, and clothing. Clothing consisted of moccasins for both sexes made of soft leather; breechcloths, complemented by leggings and mantles in winter, for males; and skirts, with leggings and mantles in winter, for females. All clothing was made of tanned animal skin (usually bear or deer). When European goods were introduced, cloth was gradually substituted for leather.

Iroquoian men were hunters, fishermen, councillors, and warriors. In spring, summer, and winter (primarily late winter and early spring), men went on hunting expeditions, using bows and arrows to kill large game, including deer, moose, bear, and mountain lion. More casual hunting, in late spring and early summer, focused on small game, e.g., otter and beaver. Fishing, by net, lance, and weir, was undertaken primarily in spring. Meat, fish, and some vegetable foods were commonly dried for storage. Men made hunting, fishing, and war tools, built homes and canoes, cleared new fields, and traded, negotiated, and warred with other nations. They had much greater contact with the world outside their villages than did women. However, Algonquian-speaking people sometimes wintered near Iroquois villages, giving women opportunities for contact with people outside their own village and nation.

There were, of course, variations on this cultural pattern. For example, although Hochelagans were characterized by the same subsistence and settlement patterns as other Iroquoians, Stadaconans were not. Corn was much less important, and fish much more so, to Stadaconans than to other Iroquoians and, hence, these people were less sedentary. Large numbers of Stadaconan men, women, and children travelled in summer to the Gaspé Peninsula to fish for mackerel. Others travelled east and north, toward Saguenay, to hunt white whale, seal, porpoise, and, possibly, walrus.

The Neutral and the Petun differed from the Huron in growing tobacco, which they traded extensively with their Algonquian neighbours. The Neutral followed different hunting practices from those of the Huron. They entrapped deer, several at a time, in enclosures established in an open space where they could be killed easily, while the Huron generally hunted one deer at a time. Furthermore, the Neutral apparently did not wear clothing as consistently as did the Huron. Two French missionaries, Daillon and Lalement, wrote that Neutral men sometimes did not wear breechcloths, although one mentioned that the women usually were clothed, at least from the waist to the knees. Lalement noted three ways in which the Neutral differed significantly from the

Huron, with whom he was more familiar. He categorized the Neutral as 'taller, stronger, and better proportioned' than the Huron. He remarked on a difference in burial customs, involving a longer mourning period among the Neutral, noting that the Huron brought bodies for burial immediately after death, while the Neutral waited until the 'very latest moment possible when decomposition has rendered them insupportable'. Lalement's third comment is blatantly ethnocentric:

> In going through the country, one finds nothing else but people who play the part of lunatics with all possible extravagances, and any liberties they choose, and who are suffered to do all that is pleasing to them, for fear of offending their demon. They take the embers from the fire and scatter them around; they speak and shatter what they encounter, as if they were raving,—although in reality, for the most part, they are as self-collected as those who do not play this character. But they conduct themselves in this way, in order to give, they say, this satisfaction to their special demon, who demands and exacts this of them,—that is to say, to him who speaks to them in dreams. (Thwaites, 1896–1901, 21: 187–231)

This behaviour, further discussed below, was not significantly different from that considered appropriate to dreaming among the Huron and Iroquois, although Lalement was struck by its prevalence among the Neutral.

Jesuit and Recollect missionaries left fairly rich records about Huron beliefs. These, of course, were of great interest to them. Lalemont's and other Jesuit reports reflect strongly their own cultural values. They provide what might be called a very 'thin' description. Intense anthropological analysis, the kind that Geertz has referred to as 'thick description', of these reports and other data has revealed that the Huron believed that the universe was inhabited by other-than-human beings as well as by humans. It was important to appease these beings, including those associated with animals, so that one's life would run smoothly. They believed that the dead went to a haven in the West, travelling there via the Milky Way. Every 10 years or so, the dead of a village were disinterred and brought by clan segments (groups of matrilineages—kin groups defined by being related through their mothers) to a large feast at which the bones were re-interred in an ossuary pit. Often this 'Feast of the Dead' coincided with the movement of a village to a new location. It served an integrative function, uniting village members both living and dead, and it allowed for the formal expression of personal grief. The Neutral had a similar ceremony.

The Huron had very sophisticated attitudes towards dreams, believing that they reflect a person's subconscious desires. Dreams were commonly analyzed by shamans, and every effort was made to fulfill them, symbolically if not literally. Each winter there was a three-day festival called *ononharioa* ('the upsetting of the brain'), in which villagers 'feigning madness' (to use a Jesuit description) recited their dreams and demanded fulfillment of them. French missionaries were amazed by this ceremony, often interpreting it as demonstrating the 'primitive' nature of the Huron. Psychoanalysts might view it as an effective cathartic practice, allowing for the expression of suppressed wishes. It certainly resulted in a redistribution of wealth. Many objects deemed necessary for fulfilling a dream were not returned.

Herbal medicines were used to cure some types of diseases; others, however, were thought to be caused either by other-than-human beings who had been upset or by sorcerers intent on causing harm. When such illnesses were diagnosed, ceremonies of supplication might be conducted to appease the angry beings, or incantations and extractions of foreign elements from the sick person's body might be undertaken if it was believed that a sorcerer was responsible.

Sorcery was considered a very real phenomenon, and the belief provided a valuable tool for social control. Leaders, for example, were discouraged from grasping too much power lest they be categorized as sorcerers. Sorcery also affected the Huron evaluation of Jesuit missionaries, who claimed to be power holders. Because spiritual power was respected, missionaries were valued and feared—feared especially because the power of the Jesuits to bring disease did not escape Huron attention. Disease ravaged the Huron and other Iroquoian peoples after contact. The Huron population decreased from about 20,000 to about 9,000 after smallpox epidemics in the 1630s. Although other factors were more directly responsible for their final disappearance, the effects of disease should not be underestimated.

It seems probable that the St Lawrence Iroquoians were destroyed primarily by disease and warfare and that the survivors took refuge among other groups, eventually losing their identity between 1543 and 1603. Their demise may have been precipitated by their attempts to play a dominant role as middlemen in the fur trade. The Stadaconans tried, for example, to keep Cartier's party from going to Hochelaga in 1535, telling the French that they might meet death if they did. One hypothesis is that the Stadaconans were destroyed by either the Hochelagans or the Algonquians in about 1580, and the Hochelagans were later attacked by the Mohawks.

By the early seventeenth century, the French trade had become important to other Iroquoians as well, affecting their relations with other Native peoples and often playing a role in their disappearance or dispersal. For example, the Huron were an important link between the French and people to the north and west. As trade concerns became increasingly important, nations of the Iroquois confederacy, particularly the Mohawk (who were already involved in the Dutch fur trade), became interested in the French trade. With the aid of guns and ammunition provided by Dutch traders, they waged war against the Huron, other Iroquoians, and the Algonquians in a push to widen their trade networks. Moreover, 'mourning wars' were waged, based on cultural incentives to

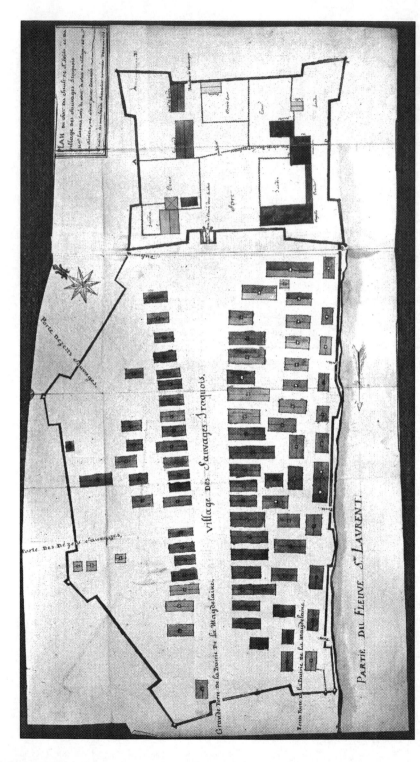

FIGURE 14.1. Plan du Fort de Sault de St Louis Villages des Iroquois (Kahnawake), mid-eighteenth century. (Ayer M.S. Map 211 in Ayer M.S. 299. Courtesy of the Edward E. Ayer Collection, The Newberry Library, Chicago)

replace those who died from disease and warfare. These have been correlated strongly with the incidence of disease among Iroquoian people (Brandão, 1997). In 1649, after a series of devastating defeats, the Huron abandoned their villages. The Wenro, who had taken refuge among the Huron in 1638, shared their fate. Many were killed or captured by Iroquois raiding parties; others took refuge with neighbouring tribes; some went to live among the Iroquois, who sought the refugees in an effort to increase their own numbers. A number of Huron, however, banded together for the severe winter of 1650 at Gahendoe (Christian) Island. Of these, about 300 settled under French protection at Île d'Orleans near Quebec City. They moved to the mainland six years later and their descendants, often referred to as the Huron of Lorette, remain there. Others took refuge among the Petun, who later were also displaced by the Iroquois. The combined Huron and Petun became known as Wyandots (the Huron name for themselves being 'Wendat') and settled at various sites in the Great Lakes region. Today many live on the Wyandotte Reservation in Oklahoma; others live near Sandwich, Ontario.

In 1647, warfare between the Iroquois and Neutral intensified, and by 1652 most Neutral had fled their villages. The last remnants identified historically were a group shown living south of Lake Erie on a map dated 1656. The Iroquois did not move into the territory vacated by the displaced Iroquoians; they used the area for hunting, trading, and travel during war. The first permanent Iroquois settlement in what is now Canada began in 1667 and was not directly related to the wars.

The People of the Extended Households

In the seventeenth century, the Iroquois inhabiting what is now New York state were a confederacy of five nations: Mohawk, Oneida, Onondaga, Cayuga, and Seneca. Their image of themselves was spatial—a longhouse with the Mohawk as the eastern door and the Seneca as the western. Their name for themselves was 'Kanonsionni' ('the League of the United [or Extended] Households'). Another Iroquoian-speaking nation, the Tuscarora, joined the confederacy after being driven from their homes in North Carolina in about 1713.

The nations of the Iroquois League were culturally similar to the other Iroquoians. They were primarily sedentary people, cultivating their staples of corn, beans, and squash. During the seventeenth and eighteenth centuries, the villages were composed of matrilineal longhouses. Matrilineages were grouped together to form clans, usually designated by the name of an animal. For example, the Bear, Wolf, and Turtle clans were present in all of the nations. Longhouses gave way, in the mid-eighteenth to early nineteenth centuries, to wooden frame houses occupied by extended families. Longhouses continue to be used for political and ceremonial functions.

The typical gender-based division of labour was in effect among the Iroquois. In later times, however, as game became scarcer, men became more involved in agriculture. The village was the primary focus of activity for women, older men, and children. Younger men often spent summers away from the village, joining war parties or attending councils. In late fall, early winter, and early spring, they were often away hunting. Women and children might accompany them on short expeditions. Fishing was done on rivers and streams in or near the village.

Like the Huron, the Iroquois saw their universe as composed of both human and other-than-human beings—from the smallest insects to beings such as Panther, the Thunderers, Grandmother Moon, and the Creator, whose power could be used for good or harmful purposes. Hence, many rituals and ceremonies, including those employed in the treatment of illness, were designed to appease these beings, to get them to use their power in helpful ways, or both. As an extension of this attitude, reciprocal alliances were a vital part of Iroquois interrelations. The Iroquois confederacy was itself an alliance of nations, and the Iroquois were proud of, and diligent in maintaining, the Covenant Chain alliance with the British and alliances with other Native people, the Dutch, and French. An Iroquoian symbol of the Covenant Chain was the linking of arms. Although Iroquois political practices were very similar to those of Canadian Iroquoians, their confederacy, designed to regulate matters between nations of the League and external affairs involving other nations, was much stronger than other confederacies among Iroquoian nations.

Chieftainships among the Iroquois during the seventeenth, eighteenth, and nineteenth centuries were hereditary (matrilineally). They remain so among some Iroquois groups. Primogeniture (being first-born) was not a feature of succession, merit being an important consideration in determining who among the descendants of a leader would take his or her place. The confederacy was, and is, led by a council of chiefs commonly called *sachems*. According to the Iroquois, the confederate council has been composed of 49 (some say 50) chieftainship positions since its foundation. Each chief is given the name of the person he succeeds when he takes office. Hence, the names of the current chiefs are those of the original founders of the confederacy. Although all positions may not be filled at any one time, the roll call of sachemship names is recited at each condolence council, where a deceased chief is mourned and a successor installed in his place. This roll call emphasizes the merging of the past with the present, as the recitation recapitulates the kinship basis of the confederacy. The matron of the lineage holding a vacant chieftainship selects a successor and presents him to the council for acceptance. Theoretically, the council may veto the matron's choice, but this rarely, if ever, happens.

Village chiefs, who may or may not also be confederate chiefs, also inherit their positions matrilineally. Most Iroquois communities now have elective councils as well as hereditary ones. The two types often vie with one another for recognition of legitimacy.

The League of the Iroquois allowed for local autonomy while providing a League-wide forum for airing problems and plans. This balanced structure permitted considerable diversity. Because a goal of unanimity in decision-making was actively sought, council negotiations were prolonged. The process of deliberation revealed highly valued positions. If neither side could persuade its opponents, discussions would be discontinued. Groups would often act independently. Occasionally, rifts between parties became strong, in some cases leading to the splintering of communities. Some modern Canadian communities were formed under such an impetus. Links were, however, usually maintained with the village of origin. Decision-making usually took place first within the appropriate council at the village level. For example, if the issue involved peace, it would be discussed by the council of peace chiefs; if war, by the council of war chiefs; if planting, by the council of women. If the members of the council were of one mind, and if the matter was of concern to the village as a whole, a general village council attended by all adult males would be held. Women's opinions were expressed by a male speaker. If unanimity was achieved at the village council and the issue affected other villages within the nation, a general council of these villages would be held, usually in the village where the matter was raised. Again, if all were in agreement, and if the matter involved the confederacy, a confederate council would be held. Steps in the process might be skipped, if appropriate. Although the same council and confederate structures are not in operation among all Iroquois people today, the process of decision-making, the emphasis on unanimity, and the resultant structuring of alternatives are features of both elected and hereditary councils.

At the time of European contact, the Iroquois had considerable inter-tribal contact. Those whose villages lay along the Mohawk River travelled extensively by water—even to Lake Erie and the St Lawrence River. The elm-bark canoe, their principal vehicle, was portaged overland from

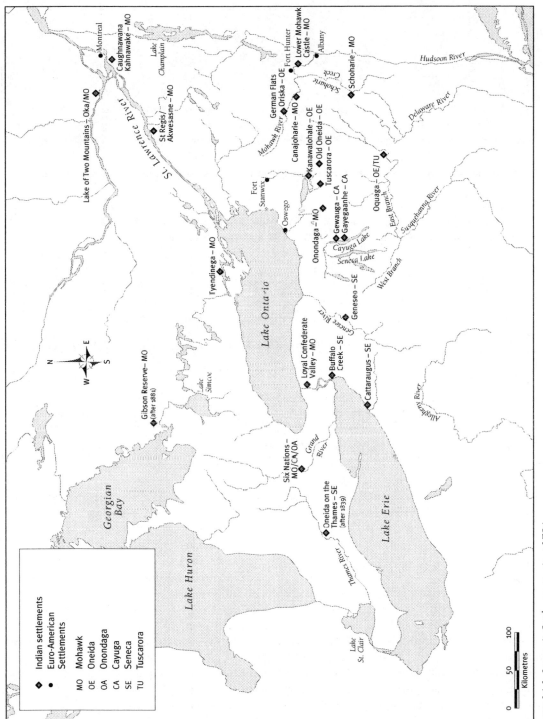

MAP 14.1. Iroquois Settlements, *circa* 1784

BOX 14.1

Trade, Sovereignty, and a Washing Machine

In 1988 Grand Chief Michael Kanentakeron Mitchell of the Mohawk Nation at Akwesasne crossed the international border via automobile into Canada at Cornwall, Ontario, with a washing machine and several common household items that he declared at customs. He was charged duty on these goods but refused to pay, asserting that the right of Native people to carry goods freely across this border had been established since pre-contact times by trading and social networks before the border itself existed. He proceeded into Canada to Tyendinega, where he gave the items to Natives of that settlement as a symbol of those networks. His next step was to sue the Minister of National Revenue, arguing that he did indeed have the right to bring goods across the international border without charge.

In 1998 the Federal Court of Canada ruled in favour of Chief Mitchell, and that ruling was upheld by the Federal Court of Appeal. The Canadian government failed to negotiate with the Mohawks to uphold Native rights. Instead, the case was appealed. It reached the Supreme Court of Canada in 1999. There, much of the Federal Court ruling was struck down, the argument being that insufficient evidence had been presented for trading networks extending back to time immemorial. The issue, of course, is not so much whether goods can be moved by Mohawks freely and openly over the border, but whether they have historical primacy over the border, rights to live independent of it. The Jay Treaty of 1794 speaks of these rights.

The ruling by the Supreme Court of Canada has been devastating, but of little surprise to many Natives, as well as non-Natives. Does the Supreme Court have a conflict of interest here, being biased in favour of the Minister of Revenue, a representative of the government of Canada? Are the Mohawk of Akwesasne a sovereign people that need not appear before magistrates of another nation to receive *recognition* of their rights? Do these rights exist? They are still asserted by the people of Akwesasne and by many Natives throughout Canada. How to deal with this ruling on their claims to these rights will be a challenge.

---

one body of water to another. Trails were used for warfare, hunting, and overland trade (in skins, wampum, corn, copper, and so on).

Iroquois Settlements in Canada

There are seven Iroquois settlements in Canada: Kahnawake/Caughnawaga, Kanesatake/Oka/Lake of Two Mountains, Gibson/Wahta, Akwesasne/St Regis, Six Nations/Grand River, Tyendinega, and Oneida on the Thames. A reserve of Mohawk descendants (Michel's Band) existed in Alberta until the members enfranchised in 1958, losing their Indian status. Some descendants now live in other Native settlements in western Canada.

Kahnawake, the oldest of the Iroquois reserves in what is now Canada, started in 1667 as a Jesuit mission settlement, primarily of Mohawk and Oneida. Located across the St Lawrence River from Montreal, the original settlement was called Kentake by the Indians, La Prairie by the French. The inhabitants moved the settlement further west on the south side of the St Lawrence three times between 1676 and 1716. Finally, they formed the settlement called by the French Mission Sault St Louis, and by the Iroquois Kahnawake ('at the rapids') after a Mohawk settlement in the Mohawk Valley (present-day Fonda, New York) from which some of the settlers had come.

From the beginning, contacts were maintained with Iroquois in what is now New York state. During winter, most of the people settled at Kahnawake dispersed, many to hunt near their former villages, which they visited and where they encouraged dissatisfied kinsmen and friends to join them in the northern settlement. Mohawk who hunted and traded along the St Lawrence were also encouraged by Indians and missionaries to settle at the Jesuit mission; hence, the settlement grew rapidly, causing much concern to people remaining in the Mohawk Valley.

During the nineteenth century, the traditional division of labour continued to some extent at Kahnawake, even after hunting and warfare ceased to be viable activities for males. In the late nineteenth century, men began working in high-steel construction in major cities. As time passed it became commonplace to return to Kahnawake from such places as Brooklyn, New York, on weekends or during longer breaks. High-steel work has been interpreted as a cultural substitute for the high-risk activity of warfare. Today, Kahnawake men are primarily high-steel workers, factory workers, employees of the reservation government, small businessmen, and small-scale farmers.

Kanesatake/Oka, too, began as a mission settlement. When Natives at La Prairie moved in 1676, some went to a Sulpician mission that finally settled on the north side of the St Lawrence River, near Montreal. The settlement, known in Algonquian as Oka and in Mohawk as Kanesatake, is occupied by Iroquoian- and Algonquian-speakers. It originally consisted of three tribal villages—Algonkin, Nipissing, and Iroquois—which were often seen as one village served by a single mission. Iroquois agricultural practices greatly influenced the Algonquians at Oka. In turn, the Algonquians influenced the hunting practices of the Iroquois. Beginning in the mid-nineteenth century, however, cutting and selling timber from the settlement began to replace hunting as an economic activity, particularly among the Iroquois. In using the land for this purpose, the Natives of Kanesatake/Oka met with resistance, which they

considered unjustified, from the Sulpician order, which also claimed the land. As a result, after 1881 some Iroquois moved to Gibson Reserve (Wahta), a land grant about 50 kilometres east of Georgian Bay, in an attempt to obtain a more secure land base.

Akwesasne/St Regis was originally a mission settlement called Akwesasne (Mohawk: 'where the partridge drums'), formed in the mid-eighteenth century. Accounts of its origin differ. Some maintain that conflict at Kahnawake led to the establishment of this spinoff settlement; others hold that the critical factor was overcrowding at Kahnawake, which disposed people to establish a new village. Akwesasne is now a reserve in Quebec, Ontario, and the state of New York. As a result of the Jay Treaty of 1794, which exempts Natives from some boundary considerations, many Mohawks consider the international border of interest only as it affects the source of treaty annuities. Agriculture and hunting were early means of subsistence at Akwesasne, but agriculture became the mainstay by the late nineteenth century. Today, small farms are less viable; hence, subsistence agriculture has been replaced by high-steel work, factory employment, small business enterprises, gaming, and employment by tribal governments on the reserve.

In the late eighteenth through mid-nineteenth centuries. Some Mohawk of Akwesasne, Kahnawake, and Kanesatake/Oka participated in the fur trade in western Canada, acting as guides and free trappers for the North West and Hudson's Bay companies. Some of them formed Michel's Band and settled not far from Edmonton; others formed small communities along the foothills of the Rocky Mountains. Both groups intermarried with non-Iroquois, principally Cree. Today, although some realize that they are descended also from Mohawk, most identify themselves as Cree.

Some Iroquois settlements were formed in Canada as a result of the American Revolution. Many Iroquois, viewing American settlers as a threat to their land and security, supported the British during the war. Moreover, many Iroquois held that it was the British rather than the Americans who were their true partners in the Covenant Chain. Despite promises from British officials, Indian interests were not protected during the peace negotiations. The 1783 treaty between the United States and Great Britain made no provisions for Indians: it divided land, including Native land, between the two nations. The Iroquois, who had been assured that they would be compensated, were determined to see that this promise was kept.

British officials in Canada were aghast at the outcome of the treaty and acknowledged their responsibility to appease the Indians and keep them as allies. In 1783, Frederick Haldimand, Governor-General in Canada, arranged for a land grant north of Lake Ontario at the Bay of Quinte. Many Iroquois, however, sought land nearer Iroquois country. Such land was found west of Lake Ontario on the Grand River and was purchased by the British Crown from the Mississauga Indians for the Mohawk and others of the Six Nations who had supported the British during the war or who otherwise desired to settle there. A grant for this land was given by Haldimand in October 1784. The British identified the villages at Bay of Quinte (Tyendinega) and Grand River (Six Nations) primarily as Mohawk, although the Six Nations settlement included a number of Onondaga, Cayuga, and Seneca, as well as some Tuscarora and Oneida. At that time the Indians at Six Nations identified themselves largely as Mohawk from the village of Canajoharie in the Mohawk River Valley and Mohawk and Oneida from the village of Oquaga in the Susquehanna River Valley.

At both settlements, agriculture was the primary economic activity, supplemented by hunting until the early nineteenth century when game became particularly scarce. At that point, work in neighbouring towns began to take the place of hunting in their economy.

Oneida on the Thames was formed in about 1839 as a result of the policy, adopted in the United States in the 1820s, of removing Indians west of the Mississippi River. Indians in what is now New York were among those pressured into moving and, while most resisted, some Iroquois wished to go. Most of the Oneida who left at that time settled near Green Bay in what is now Wisconsin. Some, however, came to Canada, where they continued farming and hunting.

Sorting the Winks and Twitches

In doing ethnohistorical research and ethnological work among the Iroquois of Canada, I have been impressed by common threads in the tapestry of intercultural relations between Indians and Euro-Canadians, particularly on a governmental level. Two themes are striking: first, that Euro-Canadian participation in Indian affairs has often been interpreted as assistance by the Euro-Canadians and as interference by the Indians; second, that the relationship existing between the two groups has also been variously interpreted: as alliance of sovereign peoples by the Indians, as dependence by Euro-Canadians.

The Natives of Kahnawake confronted a threat to their land in the 1760s, when the Jesuits claimed Sault St Louis as their own. One issue that brought the matter to a head was the question of revenues from settlement property leased to non-Indians. The Natives held that their ancestors had moved to the settlement with the understanding that the land, although held in trust by the Jesuits, was their own, in place of land left behind. The Jesuits, however, held that the settlement land was their property. The Natives sought help in resolving the matter. The Governor-General's ruling, based on a grant from Louis XIV dated 31 May 1680, maintained that the land had been granted to the Natives for as long as they inhabited it, and that it was to revert to the Crown if the Natives should leave the settlement. The Kahnawake Iroquois frequently refer to this ruling when defending their position of sovereignty over their land. They had used the assistance of their ally, the British government, in securing their land base and were satisfied with the outcome.

A similar case at Kanesatake/Oka, however, worked out differently. In the nineteenth century, members of the Roman Catholic order of Sulpicians insisted that the Natives did not have the right to cut timber on what the order claimed was Sulpician land. This claim was shocking to the Natives, who considered the land theirs. They requested that the government of Canada assist them. Although ruling after ruling has favoured the Sulpicians, on the basis of a 1717 grant, each judgement states that the Natives have rights to use and occupy the land. No formal provisions for implementing these rights have been made, the assumption being that the Sulpicians would provide for them. Subsequent Sulpician actions were far from satisfactory, however. Moreover, much land at Kanesatake/Oka was sold to Euro-Canadians by the Sulpicians, alienating the land from the Natives. Two efforts were made by the Canadian government to offer alternatives. One was that in 1881 land near Georgian Bay was purchased for the Iroquois as a reserve in place of Kanesatake/Oka. The land was far from the quality of land at Kanesatake/Oka, however. About one-third of the Natives moved to Gibson Reserve, although some later returned to Kanesatake/Oka. Those who remained became involved in farming, trapping, and the lumber industry. Today the Mohawks at Wahta own and operate the largest cranberry farm in Ontario.

The Iroquois remaining at Kanesatake/Oka pressed to secure their rights there. In 1945 Department of Indian Affairs officials took what they believed to be a final step in the matter when they purchased the original settlement from the Sulpicians for Native use. The motives of the officials were honourable. They wished to settle what had become a persistent problem. However, they overlooked one significant factor: the Indians were not party to the agreement. Given the dissatisfaction over the issue in the first place, this only served to cause further problems. In addition, the agreement did not make Kanesatake/Oka a reserve and, therefore, did not provide for securing the land to the Natives in the proper sense. In

this case, in which Natives sought control over land, the approach of the federal government emphasized the lack of control held by the people. We will see below what further implications this has had at Kanesatake/Oka. By excluding Indian participation in the decision-making, by acting *for* rather than with the Natives, the government of Canada before and after Confederation has opened many such decisions to uniform protests by Iroquois.

In a different example, a company was formed in 1832 to open the Grand River to navigation by dredging a canal. Investors were difficult to find, however, so Six Nations Reserve money ($160,000) held in trust by the federal government was invested with the permission of the Lieutenant-Governor of Upper Canada. This money was lost when the Grand River Navigation Company went bankrupt after rail transport developed. The Natives had opposed opening the river to navigation; moreover, their money was invested without their approval. Such interference has been highly resented. The Iroquois of Six Nations have appealed repeatedly to the government of Canada for compensation and have brought the case before the courts. Rulings, such as an 1894 Order-in-Council, recognize that the Iroquois are entitled to compensation. The question of who should provide it, the government of Britain or that of Canada, remains open; it is being pressed by the people of Six Nations. Both this case and that at Kanesatake seem to the Iroquois to confirm Canadian government action as interference rather than assistance.

Indian interpretation of the role of external government in Indian affairs is not always so uniform, however. In 1924, at the Six Nations Reserve, an elected council was approved and the hereditary council was locked out of the council house by members of the RCMP. The action was undertaken with the approval of people on the reserve who opposed extremes advocated by the hereditary council; it was categorized as gross interference by that council. While the elective council has remained in power, both continue to exist and provide counterbalances to one another. Although the Canadian government recognizes and negotiates with the elective council, 'the hereditary council is still important as a kind of standing committee for airing grievances and organizing resistance against Canadian regulation' (Shimony, 1961: 95).

The participation of external governmental bodies in internal Iroquois politics has not been uncommon in Canada. Elected and hereditary councils are also present at Oneida on the Thames. Generally, the two are rivals there. They are, however, superseded by a general council attended by all people of the reserve. Akwesasne/St Regis has three governmental bodies: elective councils on both the Canadian and US sides of the reserve, and a hereditary council representing the Mohawk as the eastern branch of the Iroquois confederacy. These three bodies are independent, mutually exclusive, and parallel systems, which co-operate in certain matters and compete in others for recognition by external parties. The elective councils are recognized as legitimate by both the Canadian and American governments; however, while neither government accepts the hereditary council as a valid governing body, neither can ignore it. Both systems maintain their independence from the governments of Canada and the US, preserving rights they perceive that they have as independent people. They have had to fight for these rights, though.

In their dealings with the government of Canada, the extent of Iroquois control over their resources has often been questioned. Issues involving land at Six Nations provide examples. The grant that the Native people at Grand River received from Haldimand in 1784 was not registered. This oversight led to 50 years of discord about the nature of the grant. No mention was made in the grant document of the land being held in trust; therefore, the Natives assumed that, as they had expected, the land had been given to them unconditionally, as they were valued British allies. When officials who had not been involved with the Iroquois during the American Revolution came to power, however, they interpreted the relationship as one of dependence rather than alliance. The Iroquois at Six Nations, however, continued to view the land as reimbursement for land and other property lost in the war. Moreover, they did not consider it full reimbursement, continuing to press for further compensation.

The Six Nations people became aware of the British interpretation after Mohawk leader Joseph Brant, with power of attorney from the chiefs, began leasing and selling land in the settlement to Euro-Canadians. When Brant requested that the sales be confirmed by the government for the protection of the purchasers, his request was refused because officials, notably John Graves Simcoe, Lieutenant-Governor of Upper Canada, believed that the land was held in trust for the Indians, not granted in fee simple. Brant resisted this interpretation, as did many other Indians of Six Nations. Brant argued that the land belonged to the Indians to do with as they chose, and that the sales were necessary to ensure a source of livelihood since hunting was no longer profitable and agriculture in the settlement needed improvement. Simcoe opposed Brant's arguments, citing the Royal Proclamation of 1763, which stated that no land could be purchased from Indians except through the Crown. However, Simcoe's superior, Lord Dorchester, favoured Brant's arguments, and eventually sales that Brant had made were 'registered and sealed', although new sales were forbidden. Brant continued to press the issue of unconditional control, and sales continued to be made until January 1841, when land at Six Nations was surrendered to the British Crown to be administered for the 'sole benefit' of the Indians. The land sales had not been supported by those Six Nations people who felt that steps should be taken to prevent sale of land in order to secure it for posterity. In maintaining this position, they approached the government for aid in preventing the land from being alienated. In response, the government increased its control over Six Nations affairs, a result that went far beyond what had been desired.

Such disputes over control of land are not wholly a thing of the past. In a more recent case, the control of the Mohawks of Kahnawake was challenged when Canada and the US undertook to build the St Lawrence Seaway. The Iroquois, angered that land given to their ancestors and confirmed as theirs in the dispute with the Jesuits would be taken from them and flooded, waged a legal battle. They were especially incensed because this seizure threatened their perception of sovereignty. Non-Natives, pressing for and securing a ruling of eminent domain, considered the expropriation of the land to be necessary for the greater good of the people of Canada and the US. For the Iroquois, the question was not simply one of what was good for the whole. Not only were they unconvinced that the development was a good thing, but also they were convinced that they were not being considered as part of the whole, that their interests were not being taken into account. This suspicion has been a nagging one for Natives in their intercultural relations with Euro-Canadians. So often it has appeared to them that their welfare as a people has been considered little, if at all, by Euro-Canadians wanting to accomplish something for themselves and making decisions with little or no input from Natives. The Seaway battle was lost by the Iroquois.

Conclusion

Interactions between Iroquois and Euro-Canadians have often been frustrating for both parties. The examples given demonstrate that the actions of Euro-Canadian governments in Indian affairs were seen differently by each party: generally, as interference by the Iroquois and as assistance by Euro-Canadians. The context of interaction between Iroquois and external governments has consistently been defined by the Iroquois as the need of independent allies to be mutually supportive and by the external government as the need to express goodwill to a semi-helpless people.

One sees the effect of layer upon layer of cultural and interpersonal misunderstanding and misinterpretation, complicated by changes among the actors and among the circumstances of action. Natives strive for control over their lives and land, although how this is done is at issue in disputes among themselves. Moreover, they feel that governments have a responsibility to act with them to protect their interest, this responsibility arising from the relations of the Iroquois as Euro-Canadian allies. Canadian governments, on the other hand, have interpreted the relationship between Natives and themselves as one of dependence of the Iroquois upon them, with government working for Natives for their benefit and protection. Underlying this is the assumption that, because of lack of education, lack of sophistication, and their general 'mode of life', Natives are open to being swindled and otherwise taken advantage of, and it is for their protection that certain policies are undertaken, even at times contrary to their wishes. The persistent misunderstandings have had yet another unfortunate result: they have created a mythology, on either side, that views the other as, at best, misguided and, at worst, mendacious. The resolution of existing conflicts and prevention of future ones must depend on participants in interactions accepting that the same types of behaviour can be variously interpreted: actions derive differing meanings from differing cultural perspectives.

The implications of the layering of different interpretations of cultural interaction resulted in violent confrontation at Kanesatake/Oka in 1990. Throughout the twentieth century, Native people of Kanesatake pressed for recognition of their rights over land there, without satisfaction. Frustration finally resulted in conflict at Kanesatake in the summer of 1990 as the town of Oka sought to expand a municipal golf course onto land claimed by the Natives. John Mohawk, a Seneca negotiator for the Iroquois confederacy, has interpreted the militancy that resulted as indicative of a 'loss of hope' that matters could be settled through negotiations. Barricades were constructed by Natives to keep workers from cutting trees for the expansion. Allying themselves with Mohawks of Kanesatake,

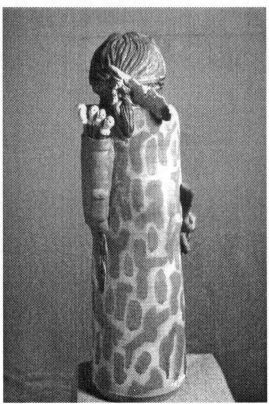

FIGURE 14.2. Sculpture of a Mohawk Warrior entitled 'Par for the Course', by Peter B. Jones. (Courtesy of the Woodland Cultural Centre)

Mohawks of Kahnawake barricaded the Mercier Bridge, blocking easy access to Montreal. A confrontation ensued between provincial police (Sûreté du Québec) and Natives. On 11 July 1990, as members of the Sûreté du Québec pushed their way past the barricades at Kanesatake with weapons drawn and onto land occupied by armed Mohawks, shots were fired and a police officer, Marcel Lemay, lay dead. It is unknown who fired the shots that killed Lemay. The Sûreté withdrew and a heated, armed, often racially tense standoff lasted throughout the summer while efforts towards negotiations were made.

Although numerous divisions were manifested among the people of Kanesatake, particularly over the involvement of the militant nativist Mohawks of what is known as the Warrior Society, there was a remarkable degree of consensus spanning political differences over the issues of autonomy, claim to the land, and assertion of control over their own affairs and resources. As in cases in the past, the support of allies was sought. A large number of other Natives were quick to show their support. The federal government of Canada was approached, as were the British Crown and the European Parliament. As with negotiations in the past, however, attempts to solve the problem were taken by the Canadian government *for* the Native people involved with limited consultation with them. The land under contention, for example, was purchased by the federal government so that expansion of the golf course is no longer in the hands of local politicians in Oka, as it had been. This has done little

---

BOX 14.2

Mohawks on the Border

A recent development at the international border that indicates that there may be some movement by governmental bodies in Canada and the US to recognize Natives as allies rather than as dependants is the collaboration of many law enforcement agencies in border patrol and investigation. These agencies include the Akwesasne Mohawk Police and the St Regis Tribal Police, both arms of the elective governments. The RCMP reports co-operation with both. Moreover, the federal Solicitor General of Canada and the Mohawk Council of Akwesasne announced a joint initiative 'to fight cross-border crime'. John Ashcroft, the Attorney General of the United States, in an address at the US Border Patrol-Native American Border Security Conference in January 2002, cited a successful multi-agency investigation, involving the tribal governments of Akwesasne, to fight a major smuggling operation. Concern over terrorism has heightened the attention of the governments of Canada and the United States to the border. These are interesting initiatives, although they are distant from the ideal of an autonomous Mohawk Border Patrol to control the flow of goods over the border that some Mohawks at Akwesasne have proposed. How long these efforts will continue, whether the relationship reflects one of alliance, rather than hierarchy, and to what extent the traditional Mohawk Nation Council will become involved, remain to be seen.

---

to address the issue of Native claims over this land, however. Non-Native Canadian interests were also divided. The issue of Quebec separatism following the defeat of the Meech Lake Accord for constitutional reform in Canada was just below the surface of negotiations. Claims of Native sovereignty took on new meaning for Canadians as relations of Québécois to the federal government began to be called into question. Ironically, many French-speaking citizens of Quebec failed to appreciate any similarity between their assertions for autonomy from the federal government and Native claims of sovereignty.

The confrontation continued for three and a half months, ending on 26 September when Natives behind the barricades, realizing that face-to-face combat was futile, walked out from behind them 'to go to their homes'. Arrests and legal battles ensued. The persistence of the people behind the barricades, however, put Kanesatake on the map, so to speak. It brought the complex issue of Native claims to sovereignty to the attention of Canadians and to many persons active in international arenas.

This may have been advantageous to all parties. There were acknowledgements in the speeches of Native leaders and Canadian officials after the crisis that they have been talking past one another and must take a careful look at the issue of sovereignty, which has been at the basis of many of the relations between Native and non-Native people in Canada for hundreds of years. It still remains to be seen whether this is merely rhetoric or represents a genuine recognition of the complexity of relations of Iroquoian people with the government of Canada. It is hoped that it is more than rhetoric and that reflection on these matters will bring parties 'in touch with the lives of strangers' who live next door.

Note

1. The terms 'Iroquoian' and 'Iroquois' can be confusing. 'Iroquoian' generally refers first to a language grouping including northern (discussed in this chapter) and southern Iroquoian-speakers (Cherokee), and then to the culture of the people speaking these

languages. 'Iroquois' refers to a specific group of Iroquoian-speakers, members of the Six Nations comprising the political confederacy known as the League of the Iroquois. Today these people often refer to themselves as the Haudenosaunee.

References and Recommended Readings

Bechard, Henri. 1976. *The Original Caughnawaga Indians.* Montreal: International Publishers. A history that focuses rather narrowly on the earliest settlers at Kahnawake, representing, however, a careful combing of the *Jesuit Relations.*

Blanchard, David S. 1980. *Kahnawake: A Historical Sketch.* Kahnawake: Kanien 'kehaka Raotitiohkwa Press. A brief, somewhat idealized history of Kahnawake, with good illustrations. Valuable as an introduction that provides some unconventional perspectives.

Brandão, José António. 1997. *'Your Fyre Shall Burn No More': Iroquois Policy toward New France and Its Native Allies to 1701.* Provides a detailed analysis of the Iroquoian wars.

Clifford, James, and George F. Marcus, eds. 1986. *Writing Culture: The Poetics and Politics of Ethnography.* Berkeley: University of California Press. This book offers advanced insight into interpretive anthropology, particularly in the field of ethnography.

Cruikshank, B.A. 1930. *The Coming of the Loyalist Mohawks to the Bay of Quinte.* Papers and Records of the Ontario Historical Society 26. Careful exploration of the initial settlement at Bay of Quinte (Tyendinega) referring especially to documents in the Ontario Historical Society.

Desrosiers, Leo Paul. 1947. *Iroquoisie.* Montreal: Les Études de l'Institut d'Histoire de l'Amérique Française. Very good study of the Iroquoians of Canada prior to 1646.

Geertz, Clifford. 1973. *The Interpretation of Cultures.* New York: Basic Books.

Johnston, Charles M., ed. 1964. *The Valley of the Six Nations: A Collection of Documents on the Indian Lands of the Grand River.* Toronto: University of Toronto Press. A valuable source book of transcriptions of documents pertaining to Six Nations/Grand River.

Morgan, Lewis Henry. 1972 [1851]. *League of the Ho-de-no-sau-nee or Iroquois.* Secaucus, NJ: The Citadel Press. Provides scholarly analysis and description of the League of the Iroquois by the 'father of American anthropology'. Also contains much information

about material culture. Although modern work has added much, often from a different perspective, Morgan's volume remains basic.

Quinn, David B. 1981. *Sources for the Ethnography of Northeastern North America to 1611.* Canadian Ethnology Service Paper No. 76. Ottawa: National Museum of Man Mercury Series. A discussion of sources of early material pertaining to the Indians and Eskimos of what is now Canada, including detailed summaries of the sources.

Shimony, Annemarie. 1994 [1961]. *Conservatism Among the Iroquois at the Six Nations Reserve.* Syracuse, NY: Syracuse University Press. Excellent, focused ethnography of Six Nations Reserve.

Speck, Frank G. 1923. 'Algonkian Influence Upon Iroquois Social Organization', *American Anthropologist* 25, 2: 219–27. Very good study of results of interactions of Algonquian- and Iroquoian-speaking people at Kanesatake/Lake of Two Mountains/Oka.

Thwaites, Reuben Gold, ed. 1896–1901. *Jesuit Relations and Allied Documents,* 73 vols. Cleveland: Burrows Brothers. A major source on the Iroquoians of Canada, written by Jesuits to their superiors in Paris and published as pamphlets to raise money for missions in New France. Much can be combed from them, if one realizes that the writers were Jesuits proselytizing among 'heathens'. (In French, with English translations.)

Tooker, Elisabeth. 1991 [1964]. *An Ethnography of the Huron Indians, 1615–1649.* Syracuse, NY: Syracuse University Press. A basic source of ethnographic information about the Hurons, making frequent comparisons between Huron and Iroquois cultural practices.

Trigger, Bruce G. 1969. *The Huron: Farmers of the North.* New York: Holt, Rinehart and Winston. An introductory volume about the history and culture of the Huron. Serves well as a quick and easy reference.

———. 1976. *The Children of Aataentsic: A History of the Huron People to 1660,* 2 vols. Montreal and Kingston: McGill-Queen's University Press. Provides extensive and detailed information on the Huron.

———, ed. *Handbook of North American Indians,* vol. 15, *Northeast.* Washington: Smithsonian Institution. An excellent, basic source of information about the history and culture of Indians of northeastern North America, including the Iroquois and Iroquoians of Canada. Contains articles written by major scholars.

York, Geoffry, and Loreen Pindera. 1991. *People of the Pines:The Warriors and the Legacy of Oka*. Toronto: Little, Brown & Company. A comprehensive description of the armed conflict at Oka/Kanesatake in 1990.

Suggested Web Sites

Iroquois Indian Musum: www.iroquoismuseum.org
Contains basic information about Iroquois archaeology, history, and culture with numerous links to other sites.

Six Nations Land Claims Office: www.snlandclaims.com
Contains information on the history of Six Nations land claims and contemporary legal initiatives.

Wampum Chronicles: www.wampumchronicles.com
Source of information, by Darren Bonaparte, a Mohawk individual, about Iroquois history and contemporary issues.

Wyandotte Nation of Kansas: www.wyandot.org
Provides extensive material pertaining to the Wyandots (Wendats).

CHAPTER 15

The Mi'kmaq:
A Maritime Woodland Group

VIRGINIA P. MILLER

Introduction

My training in cultural anthropology provided me with a very broad perspective on the study of people. In graduate school, I was influenced by the work of historical demographer Sherburne Cook, ethnohistorian Robert Heizer, and archaeologist Martin Baumhoff, all of whom took ecological approaches to the study of culture, and I became an ethnohistorian. When I moved to the Maritime provinces of Canada in the mid-1970s and wanted to familiarize myself with the Mi'kmaq there, I began looking for archaeological and ethnographic sources as well as reading historic source material in the Public Archives of Nova Scotia. I also visited reserves throughout the Maritime provinces to meet Mi'kmaq[1] people. Through all this, I learned how little anthropological work had been done on this large and complex group.

Why was this the case? Early anthropologists headed west to study the supposedly more colourful and exotic cultures of the Plains and the Northwest Coast. Few anthropologists, with the notable exceptions of Frank Speck and Wilson and Ruth Wallis, remained in the East to study the Mi'kmaq and other maritime groups. Apparently this neglect was due to the common opinion that, because of 500 years of contact with Europeans, the Mi'kmaq were essentially acculturated and no cultural information remained to be recorded. But in the last quarter of the twentieth century, the resurgence of Native pride and consciousness among virtually all Aboriginal peoples has refocused interest in eastern maritime peoples and other Native groups. Today, educated Mi'kmaq join with anthropologists, archaeologists, linguists, and other specialists to recover both cultural and historical material; here the integrative ethnohistoric method works well to enable reconstruction and reinterpretation of Mi'kmaq culture and culture history.

The path to reconstructing 'traditional' Mi'kmaq culture has not been entirely smooth, however. Several problems exist in the data available to ethnohistorians. One of these is that the Mi'kmaq were first contacted by fifteenth- and sixteenth-century European fisherman who were non-literate and so recorded no observations. Luckily, the contact they had with the Mi'kmaq was largely offshore, exchanging material culture items, and non-material culture changed little. Further, once written records began about 1600, they were written by male priests, adventurers, and traders; hence information on female aspects of culture is incomplete. But the seventeenth century reports are otherwise fairly complete, and were written by reasonably objective men whose accounts verify each other's work. What this chapter calls 'traditional' culture is really early seventeenth-century Mi'kmaq culture.

This account is written from a functional ecological perspective,[2] utilizing the methodology of ethnohistory. Sources include archival material, published primary sources, archaeological and linguistic material, and my own fieldwork and interview notes. A picture emerges of a way of life quite different from typical hunting and gathering cultures.

Traditional Culture

The language of the Mi'kmaq belongs to the Algonquian language family. It is closely related to that of the Maliseet, neighbours to the west, and to the Passamaquoddy of Maine. Long ago, the Mi'kmaq left the Great Lakes area—probably the source of the Algonquian language family—and migrated into what is now the eastern Maritime area of Canada. Here they developed their historic culture from the Woodland[3] tradition, already reflecting the coastal-inland pattern that was to characterize their movements in historic times.

A glance at the map reveals that the Mi'kmaq were a solidly maritime people: Nova Scotia is a peninsula connected to the mainland by a narrow isthmus; Prince Edward Island is an island in itself; and the parts of New Brunswick and Quebec occupied by the Mi'kmaq were coastal. Mi'kmaq also occupied the southern and western areas of Newfoundland. Many rivers and streams ran through Mi'kmaq territory, providing easy access to the sea.

In recent years, scholars have paid increasing attention to maritime hunting and gathering groups as it has become apparent that they are significantly different from their inland counterparts. Maritime groups not only have more species to draw on as food sources since they are able to utilize both land and sea resources, but the greater variety of resources available to them means increased flexibility in the event of the failure of any particular species. Abundant and relatively stable food supplies permit greater population densities, possibly resulting in the development of more complex cultures than among inland groups at corresponding latitudes. With the Mi'kmaq spending more than half the year on the coast, it

has been estimated that as much as 90 per cent of their diet came from the sea. Seventeenth-century accounts testify to the almost incredible abundance of food available during the annual runs of fish and eels and the seasonal migrations of birds. Equally important was the intimate knowledge Mi'kmaq had of their environment, allowing them to develop technology to exploit the food sources. Their use of both the bountiful sea and land resources may best be illustrated by an examination of their seasonal round.

In spring, Mi'kmaq settled in villages along the coast. Here they remained until fall, living in nuclear family units in conical birchbark wigwams erected and painted by the women with colourful designs; extended families might live together in large, rectangular, cabin-shaped birchbark structures. Summer village sites were chosen for their proximity to fresh water and marine food sources such as shellfish beds. Often a village was situated at the mouth of a river to permit easy travel by birchbark canoe to other coastal locations or inland locations. Good campsites were returned to year after year.

The Mi'kmaq diet consisted principally of products from the sea, with less reliance on land animals and plants. Food was never a problem from spring through fall. Oysters and clams were collected easily. With fish traps built across river and stream mouths, the Mi'kmaq took ample quantities of smelt, alewives, sturgeon, and salmon as these fish returned to fresh water to spawn. Large fish and lobsters were attracted at night with torches and were taken using bone-tipped harpoons. Coastal fish such as cod, plaice, skate, and striped bass could be caught with bone hooks and lines or taken by weirs constructed in bays, although ocean fish apparently did not play a significant part in the diet. Fish were prepared by the women, who cooked for the entire family. Fish were roasted whole on coals or between the prongs of a split stick over the fire. They might also be boiled in birchbark containers by dropping hot stones into the water. Women also preserved some fish for winter by smoking them.

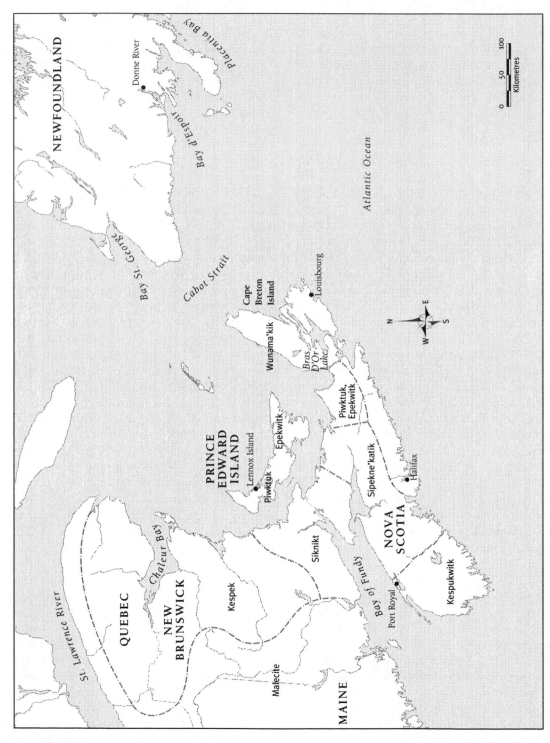

MAP 15.1. Mi'kmaq Political Units and Colonial Sites

wringing their necks. Eggs were an important food in the spring and gathered from nesting areas along the coast or from offshore islands. In summer, people ventured out in canoes to hunt small mammals, such as porpoises; from time to time they hunted small whales, and early sources tell us that they also ate beached whales. Seals found along the coast were clubbed.

Land animals, too, such as moose, beaver, bear, and caribou were hunted sporadically with bow and arrow, spear, or traps during the winter months when fish were not so readily available. In midsummer, strawberries began to ripen, followed by blueberries and cranberries. Women collected these as well as digging the groundnuts, which became suitable for use through late summer and fall. Dried berries and groundnuts were stored for winter.

In late summer, the Mi'kmaq began to move their camps inland, away from the impending harsh coastal winter storms. Men went ahead by canoe to choose and clear a winter campsite adjacent to a river or stream. Women had responsibility for transporting household goods using backpacks and tumplines before once again setting up camp,

FIGURE 15.1. Mrs Alexander Mitchell in Mi'kmaq ceremonial dress, Burnt Church Reserve, New Brunswick, twentieth century. (Courtesy of the New Brunswick Museum)

Birds, particularly ducks and geese, migrated in such numbers that they were easily snared, clubbed, or shot with bows and arrows. At night, torches were used to awaken and confuse sleeping birds, which fluttered around the torch while people knocked them down with sticks before this time covering their wigwams with birchbark, mats, and skins to fortify them against the approaching cold. When the fall eel runs began, great numbers were taken either in traps or with leisters. Eels, still today a favourite food, were roasted or boiled and eaten fresh, or smoked for the winter. The fall bird migrations once again provided an important food source.

As winter settled in, the hunters turned their attention to land animals. Despite the heavy reliance on fish and sea products, hunting was regarded as the most prestigious way of obtaining food, and all men aspired to be good hunters. The Mi'kmaq had their own breed of hunting dog, which they used to locate, track, and harass game. A good hunting dog was a valuable possession and its sacrifice for a feast bestowed great honour upon guests.

Moose were hunted with bow and arrow or taken with snares set across game paths. During the fall mating season, male moose could be lured within shooting range by the clever use of a birchbark moose call mimicking the call of a female, while the hunter poured water from a birchbark container into a pond in imitation of the sound of a female urinating. Winters with heavy snowfalls were the easiest times to take moose since deep snow slowed the animals' flight while hunters pursued swiftly and easily on snowshoes. Following a kill, the hunter marked the spot by breaking nearby tree branches, then returned to camp and dispatched the women to fetch the kill. Women prepared moose meat for eating, like other meat and fish, by roasting chunks on sticks placed near the fire or by stone-boiling in a birchbark container or wooden kettle. Large wooden kettles were fashioned from fallen trees by alternately burning and gouging out the centre of the tree. Because of their size and weight, wooden kettles were not portable; they remained on the spot where they were fashioned, thus often determining the location of campsites. Soups prepared by stone-boiling were the mainstay of the diet. According to early accounts, the soups were very fatty but quite nutritious and substantial, for they caused the Natives to 'live long and multiply much'. A delicacy was the roasted head of a young moose. Meat not consumed fresh was sliced thin by the women and smoked for future use. Finally, Mi'kmaq women pounded, then boiled, moose bones to yield 'moose butter', a fine, white grease

regarded as a great delicacy, which also served as a basic provision when the Natives were travelling or hunting. Animal bones were not given to the dogs or thrown into the fire for fear that the animal's spirit would take offence and warn others of its species against allowing themselves to be taken by hunters.

Traditionally, beaver were hunted year-round. During summer and fall, beaver were taken in deadfall traps or shot with bows and arrows as they fled a beaver house destroyed by a hunter. Winter hunting of beaver was more difficult, although it increased in response to the fur trade; traders preferred the heavier winter pelts. Early accounts have hunters locating a beaver lodge and banging on it, thereby frightening the beaver so they would flee under the ice to water's edge. There they would crouch silently until sniffed out by the dogs. Hunters would chop holes through the ice, grab the beavers by their tales to flip them out on the ice where they would be dispatched. In this way, all the beavers in a lodge might be killed.

Other land animals were taken as they were available, but particularly in winter. Fat bears preparing to hibernate in the fall were a favourite food; in winter, they were smoked out of hibernation and killed. Caribou were present in Mi'kmaq territory, but only in Newfoundland were they an important food, as in other locations they remained in remote or barren areas where they were difficult to track. Smaller animals such as muskrat and otter were taken, usually with deadfall traps.

The seal was important in the Mi'kmaq diet, and several species were taken. The Mi'kmaq took seals opportunistically year-round, but during the winter whelping season great numbers could be found and clubbed on the rocks and islands off the coast or on ice floes. Men probably left the inland camps in pairs or small groups to return to the coast for the seal hunt—not a great distance to travel by snowshoe, since the sea is never far away in the Maritimes. Both seal meat and the oil that the women rendered from seal fat were relished. The oil was stored in moose bladders, then drunk straight or served as a relish at feasts; it was also used as a body ointment and for hair grease. Following the seal whelping season, people relied for sustenance on their stored and cached foods in addition to hunting land animals, until early spring signalled the move back to the coast to begin the cycle once again.

The seasonal round described above represents a generalized situation; there was undoubtedly variation with the locale and the season. Although we may propose a general coastal-inland pattern of seasonal movement for the Mi'kmaq, they were never very far from the sea. It was possible for hunters to leave the inland camps in winter to venture to the coast for a week of seal hunting, or for everyone to leave temporarily to collect maple sap. Doubtless, families went off singly or in small groups temporarily to hunt or exploit a particular resource in another locale, or took off on junkets to visit relatives or friends in other settlements.

Social and Political Organization

A Grand Chief, or *sagamore*, presided over all the Mi'kmaq. Normally his residence was on Cape Breton Island, but in 1605, when the French settled Port Royal on the Bay of Fundy, the Grand Chief resided in that area. French accounts describe this individual, Membertou, as truly exceptional. A tall, majestic, bearded man, Membertou combined the capabilities of political leader, fearless warrior, and powerful shaman who merited the respect of all. Among the chiefly duties of Membertou was the calling of Grand Council meetings of all lower chiefs and respected men when a decision had to be made on matters affecting the entire nation.

Mi'kmaq territory traditionally was divided into seven political districts, each governed by a district chief. The names of these districts, as far as their meanings are known, reflect natural features:

- *Sipekne'katik* (Shubenacadie, in central Nova Scotia) means 'groundnut place'.
- *Wunama'kik* (Cape Breton Island, with the Mi'kmaq of Newfoundland being affiliated with this district) means 'foggy land'.
- *Piwktuk* (Pictou) means 'where explosions are made', while *Epekwitk* (Prince Edward Island) means 'lying in the water'. The district apparently was referred to by combining both names.
- *Eskikewa'kik* (east coast of mainland Nova Scotia) means 'skin dressers' territory'.
- *Kespek* (Gaspé) means 'the last land', in reference to it being the last district to join the confederacy.
- *Siknikt* (southeastern New Brunswick and west central Nova Scotia) does not have an easily translatable meaning.
- *Kespukwitk* (southwestern Nova Scotia) is also untranslatable.

Duties of the seven district chiefs included calling district council meetings as required, touring the district to meet and confer with lower chiefs, feasting visiting chiefs, and attending and participating in Grand Council meetings. An important function of the district chiefs was the annual reapportionment of hunting territories to family heads within the district; these hunting territories were reassigned as family sizes changed. Generosity and concern for others were qualities admired in chiefs, some of whom made it a point to dress poorly themselves while giving away their best possessions and furs to their followers as a way to cultivate love and respect.

Beneath the district chiefs were the local chiefs, whose territories were defined geographically, bounded by rivers or other natural features. Each of the local chiefs headed a group composed of his bilateral extended family and probably some unrelated individuals as well who chose to ally themselves with him. Group size was probably about 30–40 at a minimum, although reports exist of much larger groups; these larger groups may have been temporary aggregations made possible by a seasonal increase in food resources. Local chiefs were assisted in their leadership duties by local councils of male Elders.

Mi'kmaq society was ranked socially. Beneath the chiefs was a category that can best be termed 'commoners'. They included family members and other followers of the local chiefs, people who followed directives and who organized their daily lives along the lines of a sexual division of labour. Common men spent their time hunting, fishing, participating in raids, and manufacturing and repairing equipment for these activities. They constructed fish traps and weirs and made their own bows, arrows, spears, clubs, and all other wooden items, including cradleboards and long-stemmed pipes. They were also responsible for manufacturing birchbark canoes and snowshoe frames, although the women corded the snowshoes. If a man was a good hunter and warrior, with age he might accrue respect and prestige and receive the satisfaction of having some influence in the village council of Elders.

Some duties of Mi'kmaq women have already been mentioned; they transported household goods when moving camp, then set up and maintained camp. They brought home the kill and had responsibility for cooking food or for preserving it for winter by smoking or drying. They dressed the skins, made clothing and moccasins, and decorated some items with porcupine quills. Women collected plants and dug groundnuts for food and medicine. They manufactured household items such as birchbark containers and reed baskets and mats. And, of course, they bore and cared for the children. Like common men, common women might gain respect as they grew older, either as the wives of good hunters or warriors, or in recognition of their skills as an herbal curer, or for some other outstanding and valuable quality.

Slaves were at the bottom of the Mi'kmaq social order. Slaves were not commonly found in hunting and gathering societies; their presence is testimony to the abundant food resources in the maritime environment, for slaves did not contribute actively to the food supply, yet had to be fed nonetheless. Slaves were taken in war, though not all captives became slaves. Adult male captives were frequently killed on the field of battle,

but some were allowed to live and were taken home. A few of these may have been given to the women to torture, but others became assistants to the women around the camp and were forced to do menial chores such as fetching firewood or water. Female and young captives, however, were often adopted into the tribe and treated humanely despite their status as slaves. Slaves who tried to escape and were apprehended were put to death.

As in most hunting and gathering societies, kinship was traced bilaterally with perhaps a patrilocal emphasis in post-marital residence and a patrilineal emphasis in the inheritance of chiefly positions. The large, bilaterally extended families comprising the local groups of Mi'kmaq ensured that each nuclear family could call on a sizable group of closely knit kin in the event of misfortune. Similarly, the bilateral kin groups provided a large network of relatives to facilitate adoption of orphaned children.

That age differences were important to the Mi'kmaq was reflected in their kinship terminology: terms of address differentiated between older and younger brothers and between older and younger sisters. A single term was used to address both mother's brother and father's brother. Both parallel and cross-cousins were addressed with the same terms used for siblings, suggesting that the incest taboo extended to these relatives.

Life Cycle of Individuals

Large families were a source of joy and pride to the Mi'kmaq, who welcomed all children although they are said to have rejoiced more at the birth of a son than a daughter. If a woman became pregnant while she was nursing a child, she might induce an abortion, claiming that she could not nurse two children at the same time. However, the Mi'kmaq were not known to practise infanticide, perhaps another reflection of the ample food supply. Children of both sexes were indulged by all adults.

At an early age, both boys and girls began to learn the tasks later expected of them as adults. Girls learned female tasks by helping their mothers around camp, caring for younger children, gathering firewood and water, and bringing in and processing game. With their mothers, they also tanned skins and made clothing. Men's clothing included a loin cloth, leggings, cloaks, removable sleeves, and moccasins. Women's clothing was similar, though for more formal occasions elaborately decorated and coloured garments were worn. When women desired ornamentation, they pierced their ears and wore bracelets of shells and porcupine quills; men relied on face paint for special occasions such as feasts or raids. When girls reached puberty, it is likely that a puberty rite was held to observe the occasion, since the Mi'kmaq did practise menstrual seclusion for adult women, and, until the twentieth century, pubescent girls were sent to a designated older woman for instruction on how to conduct themselves as adults. Boys learned men's tasks from their fathers, making weapons and items necessary for hunting and fishing, and accompanying their fathers on the hunt. When a boy killed his first sizable game, usually a moose, his family held a feast to celebrate the boy's skills as a hunter.

When a boy reached young adulthood he began to look for a wife, most frequently in another village. After a young man found a girl who pleased him, he approached her father to ask for the girl's hand. If the father agreed and the girl was willing, the young man then spent a year in bride service, showing himself to be a good hunter and provider and generally a responsible adult. During this time, the prospective groom lived in the wigwam of his future in-laws, although sexual contact with his betrothed was prohibited. After a year, if the father approved of the young man's behaviour and abilities and the girl still agreed, a wedding feast was held featuring game brought in by the young man. Wedding speeches praised the groom and recited his genealogy. Following the wedding feast, the couple was free to move to the groom's village, to remain with the wife's parents, or to establish a new household. Family circumstances and personal inclinations influenced where the couple would live.

The arrival of children served to formalize the marriage; if a wife bore no children within the first few years of marriage, her husband was justified in divorcing her or in taking a second wife. Apparently adultery was rare. The Mi'kmaq practised levirate marriage: if a man died before his wife had borne a child, his widow was sometimes taken as a wife or a second wife by his brother or other close relative. (This practice is common in societies where marriage is regarded as a contract between groups rather than as an alliance between individuals.)

Polygyny was not uncommon among the Mi'kmaq, although normally only men who were exceptional hunters or chiefs would have more than one wife. Chiefs needed more than one wife simply because their hospitality duties required more than one woman to do the work of preparing for feasts and generally maintaining a relatively elaborate household. More than one wife also meant more children, and eventually more supporters for the chief.

Mi'kmaq men who had shown themselves to be good hunters and good family men were most respected. A brave warrior also commanded much respect and admiration among the Mi'kmaq, whose warring tendencies have not been greatly recognized in ethnographic accounts. The Mi'kmaq were enemies particularly of the New England Algonquian groups and the Mohawk, although they also fought the Maliseet and the Inuit from time to time. They travelled overland or canoed long distances to raid these groups and in turn were raided by them. Pallisaded villages close to the western boundary of Mi'kmaq territory in what is now New Brunswick testify further to the warlike nature of traditional Mi'kmaq society. The Mi'kmaq recognized some individuals as *ginaps*, war leaders.

Activities
The Mi'kmaq held feasts with dancing on numerous occasions, ranging from a son cutting his first

tooth, to a daughter's marriage, to funerals of family members. Outside the family circle, 'eat-all' feasts were held before a hunting party set out. At such feasts, all available food was consumed, indicating the optimism felt by hunters and non-hunters alike regarding the prospect of success. Raiding parties feasted before setting out. Men ate first at feasts, while women, children, and those not able to war ate afterward.

Waltes, a gambling game involving flipping marked bone discs on a wooden platter, was a favourite adult diversion. Storytelling served as a means of preserving tribal history and legends, for the amusement and education both of children and of adults. Young men pitted against each other their skills with bow and arrow and competed in feats of physical endurance. When weather permitted, young men of Cape Breton might undertake canoe trips to Newfoundland, stopping overnight on St Paul's Island.

Death and Burial

In pre-European times, Mi'kmaq men in particular lived very long lives; individuals over 100 years old were not uncommon. When a man knew his death was imminent, he would summon his family and friends and give his own funeral feast and oration. Guests would bring gifts of skins, weapons, and dogs and exchange gifts with the dying man as he disposed of his material property. Dogs were important at funerals because they were eaten at the funeral feast.

More commonly when an individual died without holding his own funeral feast, relatives and friends would begin a general weeping and wailing at the time of death; this might last several days, depending on the prominence of the deceased. If burial had to be postponed, the body was embalmed before being wrapped in skins or in birchbark painted red and black. It was then placed on a scaffold for up to a year. At an appropriate time when a good number of Mi'kmaq were gathered, the body was buried in the ground accompanied by gifts and personal possessions. Grave goods for men might include weapons,

skins, and sacrificed dogs. Ornaments and domestic items such as mats, bark containers, and spoons might be interred with women. A funeral feast with speeches in praise of the deceased was followed by dancing, completing the funeral rites. In some instances the property of the deceased, including his wigwam, dogs, and other items, might be burned. Mourning lasted about a year, during which time the bereaved painted their faces black and trimmed their hair short.

Beliefs and Religion

The Mi'kmaq worshipped the sun because they believed that the sun had created the earth and everything on it. Traditionally, it is said that the Mi'kmaq would face the sun at dawn and at sunset, with arms extended, and pray for the sun's blessing. The sun and the moon, both heavenly bodies, seem to have been regarded as manifestations of the Great Spirit, a concept shared with other Algonquian tribes. Souls of the dead ascended to the land of the dead by climbing the Milky Way. In the Mi'kmaq pantheon, there were a number of lesser deities beneath the Great Spirit; these were thought to be human in form, but to be immortal and to have supernatural powers, which they employed to assist mortals. Glooscap was the most prominent of these deities and seems to have served as an assistant to the Great Spirit. Glooscap spent time on earth during which he created natural features of the land inhabited by the Mi'kmaq. Some accounts say that Glooscap created animals. Glooscap also instructed the Mi'kmaq in the making of tools and weapons before he departed the earth, after foretelling the coming of Europeans and promising to return to help the Mi'kmaq in the event of war. On the lowest level of the Mi'kmaq pantheon were supernatural monsters and beasts, who harmed or destroyed people and consequently were feared and dreaded. 'Little people' were friendly beings helpful to mortals. They were thought to live in the woods.

Religion and spiritual beliefs thus permeated all aspects of life. The duties of religious leaders included predicting future events, directing hunters in the quest for game, and curing the sick. Shamans typically were men. Women who had passed menopause might become shamans, although this seems to have been rare. Shamans were powerful, ranking close behind chiefs. An individual combining shamanic abilities with chiefly qualities, as Membertou did, was regarded as particularly powerful.

Sweating was regarded as a means for adult males to cleanse and purify themselves. They periodically gathered in a wigwam around a shallow pit containing fire-heated stones. At intervals they poured water on the stones to make steam, before finally running out to jump into a nearby lake or roll in the snow. When they dressed, they were refreshed both physically and spiritually.

Some illnesses could be cured by the use of herbal medicines, but for a persistent illness, or for one with no apparent physical cause, the shaman was summoned. The shaman arrived in the sick person's wigwam bringing his medicine bag, his badge of office; it contained items such as curious stones or miniature weapons thought to be imbued with magical powers and therefore sacred. The shaman exorcised a malevolent being or supernaturally intruded object from the patient by singing and chanting to his spirits while dancing around the patient, pausing periodically to blow or suck on the affected body part in order to drive out the evil spirit causing the illness. After the ceremony, the shaman might announce that the patient was cured; if such was the case, the family rewarded him with furs and other gifts. A successful shaman might receive so many gifts for his services that he no longer hunted for his own food, thus becoming a full-time specialist. Doubtless, many part-time specialists existed as well. If, however, after the curing ceremony, a shaman realized the patient's case was hopeless, he would announce that death was imminent. Food, water, and general care were then withdrawn from the patient, and, if several days passed and the patient did not die, it is said that cold water was poured on his abdomen to induce the predicted death. It was due to this practice that the early French

priests saw their chance to discredit shamans and win converts to Catholicism. When Grand Chief Membertou lay near death in 1610 after a shaman's vain attempts to cure him of dysentery, the priests succeeded in curing him. The grateful Membertou then allowed himself and his followers to be baptized in the Catholic faith.

Acculturation

Adaptations that the Mi'kmaq had evolved over hundreds of years allowed them to flourish in this climatically harsh but food-rich environment. The complementary division of labour among male and female adults facilitated everyday life; the alliances and kinship networks brought about by marriages between bands and bilateral kin reckoning helped to bind the Mi'kmaq people together locally, while the Grand Chief, the Grand Council, and the system of political districts facilitated unified action of the Mi'kmaq people on political matters. The seasonal round permitted optimal utilization of resources. With frequent feasts and dances for a variety of occasions, regional and Grand Council meetings providing an opportunity for visiting friends and relatives, and other social activities and pastimes, even war raids, life must have been full and eventful. From the early accounts of the Mi'kmaq culture, one gets the impression that they had made an eminently satisfactory adjustment to life. Into this setting came the first Europeans.

It is very likely that the earliest Europeans were fishermen who preceded Columbus across the Atlantic. Undoubtedly they sometimes landed in search of fresh water or game, and also out of curiosity. That they came into contact with Mi'kmaq people and established trading practices at a very early date is borne out by an encounter of the French explorer Jacques Cartier with Mi'kmaq around the Bay of Chaleur in New Brunswick in 1534. Cartier's ship was hailed by a party of Mi'kmaq waving beaver skins on sticks in an effort to attract the Frenchmen's attention and have the opportunity to trade. Cartier reported that the Mi'kmaq were so eager to trade that they exchanged even the skins off their backs for French goods.

Contact and trade doubtless occurred during the sixteenth century throughout Mi'kmaq territory, but because the fishermen were for the most part illiterate, we have very few descriptions of the Mi'kmaq during this time. However, the fur trade in the eastern maritime area of Canada was sufficiently lucrative that Samuel de Champlain established a post at Port Royal in 1605 for the purpose of fur trading, and sources on Mi'kmaq culture increase after this. During the seventeenth century, trade intensified: hundreds of thousands of beaver, moose, and other skins were taken out of the area before the fur trade came to an end in the late eighteenth century.

To the dismay of the Natives, more than trade items came with the fur trade. Initially they welcomed Europeans and the goods they offered in exchange. Copper kettles and metal knives and axes were superior to the fragile pottery and stone-cutting tools the Mi'kmaq manufactured. As years of trade and contact with Europeans wore on, however, the Mi'kmaq found that both they and their culture were changing, and not in beneficial ways.

Probably the earliest disruptions in Native lifestyle began well before 1600. As the Mi'kmaq became caught up in the fur trade, they found that the trade demanded changes in their entire lifestyle and seasonal round. Trading ships were present only during the summer months. If the Mi'kmaq wanted to trade, they had to give up inland hunting and gathering and instead spend the time along the coast waiting for trading ships. This in turn drastically affected their winter diet; they were now unable to accumulate their normal summer food stores and were thus forced to rely during winter on whatever dried foods they received in trade and managed to save. Trade food items, an important commodity to the Mi'kmaq, emphasized dried vegetables such as corn, peas, and beans, ships' hardtack biscuits, and even prunes. Most of these were consumed as they were received, leaving only stores of hard-tack biscuit for the winter. Often the Mi'kmaq found themselves in a desperate situation before spring came.

In addition to dried foods, another trade item the Mi'kmaq learned to demand at an early date was alcohol, which affected their culture and population detrimentally. With the wine and brandy they received in trade, the men held drinking bouts during which fights broke out, sometimes leading to murder. Women, too, held drinking parties in the woods, separate from the men because the women feared the physical violence of drunken men. However, groups of women drinking in the woods served as a lure for sailors from the fishing ships, who found the inebriated women easy sexual prey. Thus, the value placed on female chastity and sexual fidelity was disappearing by the mid-seventeenth century, while the Mi'kmaq were incorporating offspring of mixed parentage.

The introduction of alcohol and the changes in diet, combined with exposure to unfamiliar European diseases, had an effect on the Mi'kmaq physically. Despite the lack of written records, there is no evidence that sizable epidemics of European diseases swept through the population before 1600. Instead, from their statements to Europeans in the early 1600s, most likely only local outbreaks of European maladies occurred. This nevertheless increased mortality rates. In addition, both Mi'kmaq and European observers noted the effects of dietary change on their general health: lung, chest, and intestinal disorders were increasingly common, especially in winter. Also related to the dietary change was a reduction in life expectancy. By the end of the seventeenth century, long-lived individuals were quite rare, and those were individuals who deliberately eschewed European foods in favour of a traditional diet.

A final consequence of changing lifestyle and changing diet was diminishing family size, observed as early as the seventeenth century. Large families and polygyny became less common after 1600. One reason for this was that, as Mi'kmaq men spent less time hunting and more time drinking and dissipating, they could not support more than one wife. Impotence resulting from the amount of alcohol consumed may also have been a contributing factor in reduced family size. Meanwhile, the miscellaneous accidents and injuries that had occurred in pre-contact times continued into post-contact times, but with greater effect, for they acted on a population with a diminishing birth rate. Children were more likely to die before reaching maturity, thus perpetuating the downward-spiralling trend in the population.

Nobody, much less the Mi'kmaq themselves, could foresee the great toll that these factors of changed diet, the introduction of alcohol, and European diseases would have on the population. But even before written records began for the eastern maritime area, shortly after 1600, it is apparent that the Aboriginal Mi'kmaq population had been heavily depleted. As a Jesuit priest in Nova Scotia summarized the situation in 1611: 'these countries . . . are very sparsely populated, especially those . . . which are near the sea; although Membertou assures us that in his youth he has seen *chimonutz*, that is to say, Savages, as thickly planted there as the hairs upon his head' (Thwaites, 1896, 1: 177). The Mi'kmaq population continued its decline for over 200 additional years until it reached its nadir somewhere around 1850, leaving a population of about 3,000. For the period between 1600 and 1850, the declining trend is particularly well documented in a rich assortment of published primary sources and unpublished archival material. Using materials from these sources, we will focus on Nova Scotia with some attention to the other provinces.

The French were the first to send permanent settlers to the area. French Acadians began to arrive shortly after the establishment of Port Royal, and they settled first in that vicinity, later extending their settlements along the Bay of Fundy and the isthmus of Chignecto, connecting Nova Scotia to New Brunswick.

After 1713, the French tried to strengthen their hold on Acadia by building a fortress at Louisbourg on Cape Breton Island. From Louisbourg, the French further cultivated friendship with the Mi'kmaq people, giving them gifts while inciting them to commit hostile acts against the English, who were themselves attempting to establish a foothold in Acadia. The French incitement was successful, and the seeds were sown for permanent mutual dislike and distrust between the Mi'kmaq and the English. Hostilities between the two were quite intense during the first half of the eighteenth century, escalating into a so-called 'Indian-English War' between 1722 and 1726, during which time the Mi'kmaq took great delight in harassing and seizing English ships and fishing boats. They even carried out an attack on Port Royal, which was then held by the English. The English countered by initiating a campaign of genocide against all Mi'kmaq, lasting over 50 years.

English attempts at genocide took various forms. They served poisoned food at a feast in 1712. They traded contaminated cloth in 1745, setting off an epidemic that caused the deaths of several hundred. They sent soldiers to roam Nova Scotia and destroy Mi'kmaq camps, murdering Natives without regard to sex or age. They even imported companies of Mohawks and New England Algonquians, traditional enemies of the Mi'kmaq, to track down and kill them. All these tactics cost the lives of uncalculated numbers.

Despite the open hostilities between the English and Mi'kmaq, it was the French, their friends and allies, who unwittingly brought the greatest harm to the Mi'kmaq. The French had settled Nova Scotia, and their close contact with the Mi'kmaq meant that any diseases contracted by them also spread to the Natives. Thus, in the early 1730s, Mi'kmaq around Louisbourg suffered a severe smallpox epidemic. In the years that followed, outbreaks of other European diseases also occurred among Mi'kmaq in the vicinity of Louisbourg. But the most disastrous epidemic came with the arrival of a French fleet in Halifax in 1746. All of mainland Nova Scotia had fallen into English hands, and this French fleet had been dispatched in an attempt to recapture the lost territory. Unfortunately, the huge fleet of 65 ships transporting more than 3,000 soldiers had encountered poor sailing conditions while crossing the Atlantic. Most of the ships had been sunk or otherwise dispersed, and the crossing had been greatly delayed. When the remnants of the fleet (roughly a dozen ships) reached Halifax, the men on board were suffering from a highly contagious fever, probably typhus, which had broken out at sea. While the fever caused the deaths of over 2,000 French soldiers, it wreaked even greater havoc among the Mi'kmaq, a large number of whom had gathered at the harbour to trade with the arriving Frenchmen. Contracting the fever, the Mi'kmaq in the area were decimated. The fever then spread rapidly through western Nova Scotia, an area especially densely populated in Aboriginal and early post-contact times. One reliable account of this epidemic estimated that it brought death to about 4,000 Natives, about one-third of the Mi'kmaq people of Nova Scotia.

This typhus epidemic of 1746 decimated the Mi'kmaq population in western Nova Scotia, but it really marked only the beginning of increasingly large numbers of Native deaths. The English genocide campaign, begun in the early 1700s, intensified after 1749, when the English established the city of Halifax in an attempt to maintain their control over mainland Nova Scotia. A testimony to the great numbers of the tribe is that when the English settlers arrived in Halifax three years after the great epidemic they still found numerous Mi'kmaq people. Probably these had moved here after the epidemic, since the Halifax area was reportedly a favourite hunting ground. Despite the ongoing genocide campaign in other parts of Nova Scotia, the newly arrived settlers found the Mi'kmaq around Halifax hospitable. One wrote home to England that 'when we first came here, the Indians, in a friendly manner, brought us lobsters and other fish in plenty, being satisfied for them by a bit of bread and some meat.'

Cordial relations were short-lived, however, possibly because the head of the new settlement,

Colonel Edward Cornwallis, seems to have been prejudiced against the Natives from the beginning. While admitting that he found the Mi'kmaq initially 'peaceable', he ordered his troops to clear a space 30 feet wide around the settlement and erect a fence; he then built a fort nearby. Perhaps because such actions were not lost on the Mi'kmaq and perhaps because of French incitement, several incidents occurred that seemed to Cornwallis to justify punitive action.

During the summer and early fall of 1749, some Mi'kmaq harassed an English settlement in eastern Nova Scotia and captured several ships. For the British, the last straw came at the end of September, when a party of men sent to cut wood for a government sawmill across the harbour from Halifax was attacked and five of them were murdered by Mi'kmaq. Cornwallis wasted no time: the very next day, 1 October 1749, he met with his Executive Council to discuss this hostile situation. Openly declaring war on the Mi'kmaq, Cornwallis felt, 'would be in some sort to own them a free people, whereas they ought to be looked on as Rebels to His Majesty's Government'. So the Executive Council decided to give orders to all Englishmen in the province 'to annoy, distress, and destroy the Indians everywhere'. At the same time, Cornwallis established two companies of volunteers to scour the entire province in search of Mi'kmaq. He placed a bounty of 10 guineas on every Mi'kmaq killed or taken prisoner; the following summer, the bounty was increased to £50. Despite the size of the bounty, only a very few payments were made, perhaps because, as one newspaper put it, of 'the care of the Indians in carrying off their dead'. The campaign had its effects on the Mi'kmaq people in numbers killed, but also in causing the population to shift its campsites and movements away from English settlements, for, again, as a settler put it, 'our soldiers take great pains to drive [the Mi'kmaq] away and clear the country of them.'

The campaign became so uncomfortable for the Mi'kmaq that several chiefs, including the

Grand Chief, came in to Halifax in 1752 with overtures of peace and concluded a peace treaty with the English. However, it was an uneasy peace as long as the French remained in Nova Scotia to incite the Natives against the English and as long as the Mi'kmaq themselves remained numerous and powerful enough to threaten the English. Four additional treaties were negotiated over the next quarter-century between the Mi'kmaq and the English, as both sides violated treaties.

Despite these treaties, the English campaign against the Mi'kmaq was pursued relentlessly. In 1756, the English renewed their bounty offer, and volunteer companies as well as individuals continued to hunt and kill Mi'kmaq wherever found. The following is one account of the massacre of a Mi'kmaq encampment in Nova Scotia in 1759:

> Intelligence had reached Annapolis . . . that a hostile . . . village existed on Green Point. . . . Major Rogers with his celebrated Rangers at once advanced in pursuit . . . they espied, through a spy glass, the object of their search. Here they encamped for the night, sleeping on the ground as was their custom. Leaving the men there, Rogers went in the morning, before daylight, to reconnoiter the village by moonlight. Arriving near the property of the late Sheriff Taylor, he surveyed the Indian settlement of wigwams with its rude inhabitants now engaged in festive entertainment, wholly unaware of the presence, almost in their midst, of a British soldier preparing for battle. After all was quiet, Rogers, joined by his men, attacked the sleeping encampment, killing the chief on the spot. Thus surprised and having no effective weapons of defense the Indians fled in disorder before the disciplined pursuers, who followed them along the shore. . . . Here most of them were slain, some being shot on the bank while others plunged into the waters and were drowned (in Clayton, 1966, 1: 7).

And this, of course, was only one such exploit perpetrated by one volunteer company. These companies did not keep records of how many Mi'kmaq they killed, but records reveal that the English employed such volunteer companies from at least 1744 to at least 1761, giving us some indication of a considerable number.

After 1780, pressure on Mi'kmaq lands intensified as increasing numbers of settlers poured into the area, clearing and fencing land. Many of these were United Empire Loyalists who chose to resettle in Canada rather than remain in the rebellious American colonies, and invariably they chose to settle in the most desirable locations. Often these lands were traditional Mi'kmaq hunting or fishing spots. Moreover, the settlers put increasing pressure on available game as they hunted moose as a replacement for beef cattle, which were not plentiful in Nova Scotia or New Brunswick at the time. As hunting and gathering opportunities declined and disappeared for the Natives and as the fur trade dropped off after 1780, Mi'kmaq people found themselves without food or goods to trade for food. The result, of course, was starvation, and great numbers, particularly in Nova Scotia, succumbed to starvation well into the nineteenth century.

Reports of Mi'kmaq suffering from hunger date from as early as 1775 in Nova Scotia, when some settlers in the western half of the province appealed to the government on behalf of 'several poor Indians, who from bad Success in hunting were in Great Distress'. A few years later, a bill to 'prevent the Destruction of Moose, Beaver, and Muskrat in the Indian hunting Ground' was introduced into the legislature, but it was defeated. Meanwhile, non-Native poachers in Cape Breton reportedly killed nearly 9,000 moose and caribou in the winter of 1789 alone. After 1790, when a series of unusually mild winters served to reduce further the number and quality of fur-bearing animals, accounts of outright starvation among the Indians became common. Even small game, such as birds and rabbits, was scarce, and numbers of Mi'kmaq began to congregate around white settlements for food. Settlers in one area of Nova Scotia complained in the fall of 1793 of large numbers of Mi'kmaq who not only begged food, but who had also become 'extremely troublesome' to the point of stealing and slaughtering settlers' stock for food.

The situation became so desperate that, as one settler put it in his petition of January 1794, 'a great many Mickmacks have died for want of victuals . . . notwithstanding the little they get from the superintendent . . . if they have not some more general relief they and their wives and children must in a few years all perish with cold and hunger in their own country.'

Finally, at the Indian Superintendent's urging, the Nova Scotia government established a committee in 1800 to study the Mi'kmaqs' situation and make recommendations for dealing with it. The only outcome of this committee was the establishment of a small sum set aside annually for relief of the Natives. At first £150, and then gradually increased until it reached £300 in the years just preceding Confederation, the sum was never sufficient to provide the food, clothing, and medical attention the Mi'kmaq people needed. The very first year that goods were distributed, the government agent in Antigonish reported that, while the Mi'kmaq in his jurisdiction were certainly in a miserable condition, some of them 'entirely naked', the goods allotted were insufficient for the needs of the overwhelming number who turned up for the distribution. And the suffering and deprivation went on at least until 1867, when the federal government assumed responsibility for the Natives.

But of course Mi'kmaq people were dying from causes other than simple starvation and exposure. The malnutrition and cold they suffered and the excessive consumption of alcohol by some Mi'kmaq contributed to lower resistance to diseases. During 1800 and 1801 there was a widespread epidemic of smallpox, possibly contracted from some recently arrived Scottish immigrants who landed at Pictou. Reports of the epidemic came in from all around the province. Mi'kmaq families fled to the woods from their usual haunts, hoping to avoid the smallpox, but

this movement had two bad consequences: it spread the disease to other Mi'kmaq and it prevented them from collecting relief supplies issued in the settlements. Both factors contributed to additional suffering. Smallpox was only the first well-documented European disease to affect the Mi'kmaq during the nineteenth century, and it recurred several times. As it recurred, all Mi'kmaq came to fear this disease greatly, in at least one instance refusing blankets that they thought had been in contact with smallpox patients. Since the early years of the century, the government provided inoculations against smallpox and encouraged the Natives to take them, but Mi'kmaq dislike and avoidance of vaccinations doubtless contributed to smallpox mortality.

Whooping cough, measles, typhus, typhoid fever, and numerous outbreaks of unspecified ailments labelled simply as 'sickness' all are recorded as causes of death among the Mi'kmaq during the first half of the nineteenth century. It appears that outbreaks of diseases occurred locally, and when white settlers in the vicinity were made aware of such an outbreak they notified the Indian Superintendent, who in turn called a doctor to attend the ailing Natives. An example of this procedure is provided by an epidemic of infectious hepatitis, which swept through Mi'kmaq camps around southern New Brunswick and mainland Nova Scotia in 1846 and 1847. Transmitted by frightened Mi'kmaq fleeing infected camps, the disease brought considerable suffering and painful deaths to 'a number' of them before medical doctors were summoned. Because of the 'threatened annihilation' of Mi'kmaq people living around Dartmouth, Nova Scotia, the government built a temporary hospital to isolate victims and bring the epidemic under control. But the conditions in which infectious hepatitis flourishes—poor hygiene, inadequate diet, substandard living conditions—testify once again to the mid-nineteenth-century living conditions of many Mi'kmaq and thus to their vulnerability to all manner of disease.

Infectious diseases such as these run their course in a relatively short time; lingering, wastat a constant low figure until the 1940s.

The pattern described for Nova Scotia generally was similar to that in New Brunswick. The Mi'kmaq of Prince Edward Island were entirely landless until 1870, when money was raised to purchase Lenox Island for them. Following Confederation in 1867, the federal government established reserves for the Natives, while the Newfoundland government in the early 1870s surveyed a reserve for Mi'kmaq families residing at Conne River. All the Mi'kmaq had a low profile through the later years of the nineteenth century and into the twentieth century. Many Mi'kmaq children were sent to be educated and acculturated at the residential school in Shubenacadie, Nova Scotia. Government monies did not provide well for Mi'kmaq families and they survived as best they could in a variety of economic activities. Some families sold baskets or porcupine quillwork to tourists; they also made butter tubs, coal pick handles, axe handles, baskets, and

FIGURE 15.2. Rita Joe, PC, CM, is a Nova Scotian Mi'kmaq Elder and a celebrated poet. She has been appointed a member of the Privy Council and has received the Order of Canada, among other honours and awards. (Courtesy David Mahoney)

ing diseases among the Mi'kmaq began to be reported about the middle of the nineteenth century. Tuberculosis, most prominent of these, may have been present since prehistoric times, but received first notice in 1841 when a settler reported in a letter to the Lieutenant-Governor of Nova Scotia that 'many [Mi'kmaq] have died off with consumption'. The frequency and intensity of this dread disease spread as deaths from tuberculosis caused Mi'kmaq of all ages and even entire families to disappear from the population. The incidence of tuberculosis peaked shortly after 1900, but its continued presence was largely responsible for keeping the Mi'kmaq population

hockey sticks to sell to local residents. Some men worked cutting wood for sawmills, or as labourers on the railroads and in the dockyards, or in fish and lobster canneries. Some acted as hunting guides. Others farmed while their wives were domestic workers. And doubtless some families camped on settlers' property, moving from place to place and picking up a living in a semi-traditional manner. World Wars I and II offered escape from unemployment or underemployment through enlistment in the armed forces, as did the Korean and Vietnam wars.

In 1969, the status Mi'kmaq of Nova Scotia created the Union of Nova Scotia Indians, while the New Brunswick Mi'kmaq formed the Union of New Brunswick Indians. Both began administering their own programs on the reserves. They also began documenting land claims, a process that paid off in part when the federal government agreed that part of Big Cove Reserve in New Brunswick had been taken over illegally in 1879, while the Wagmatcook Reserve in Nova Scotia was awarded $1.2 million for reserve lands illegally alienated. Another significant settlement came in 1993 when the Pictou Landing Reserve Natives in Nova Scotia were awarded $35 million in compensation from the federal government for failure to prevent a paper company's pulp waste pollution of their shoreline. The company's resulting cleanup of the water and shoreline has been favourably received by the reserve, which voted in 2002 to extend the lease in exchange for additional money and woodland donations. And the Acadia Mi'kmaq band in Yarmouth, Nova Scotia, received a $2 million settlement in 2002 for land illegally seized in 1871 by the federal government.

Mi'kmaq people have also had success in reclaiming traditional hunting and fishing rights, particularly as a result of the Supreme Court's *Marshall* decision in September 1999. Offering the final statement on a legal case begun in 1993, when Donald Marshall Jr was arrested and charged with fishing and selling eels without a licence during a closed season, the Supreme Court acquitted Marshall of the charges. The Court then went further to support and uphold the eighteenth-century treaty rights of the Mi'kmaq people with regard to commercial fishing and hunting, to provide them a moderate income from these resources. The *Marshall* decision triggered a continuing period of negotiations between individual reserves and the federal government to implement the decision. As a result, many reserves now own and operate fishing vessels and are developing a fishing industry to catch, process, and market fisheries resources. To carry out scientific research in monitoring and protecting ocean and land resources, the Unama'ki Institute of Natural Resources, established at a cost of $3.6 million, was opened at Eskasoni Reserve in

Cape Breton Island, Nova Scotia, in September 2002. In June 2002 the Mi'kmaq in Nova Scotia reached an agreement with the federal and provincial governments to negotiate the resolution of other treaty issues.

The Federation of Newfoundland Indians was formed in 1973 to work for recognition of the Natives living there, who had been virtually ignored by government when Newfoundland came into Confederation in 1949. Success came in 1984, when the federal government registered the Mi'kmaq people living at Conne River under the Indian Act. Since then, conditions have improved for these people and a land claim has been filed seeking compensation for the loss of traditional territory in southern Newfoundland. But in 2002 their fight continues for recognition of their treaty and Aboriginal rights, including applicability of the *Marshall* decision to the Newfoundland Mi'kmaq.

Since 1985, Bill C-31 has provided opportunity for some non-registered Natives, including Mi'kmaqs, to apply for registration under the Indian Act. But in 2003, some social problems still exist for the Mi'kmaq. The discrimination that existed in the judicial system in 1971 when Donald Marshall Jr was wrongfully convicted of murder and imprisoned for 11 years has been reduced. Other areas of concern include substance abuse and a high suicide rate. In New Brunswick, Big Cove Reserve has attempted to reduce a particularly high suicide rate by a combination of government-sponsored community programs and the revitalization of traditional cultural values.

Educational opportunities for the Mi'kmaq have improved significantly in the past 30 years, with many more attending universities and professional schools. There are Mi'kmaq teachers and researchers. Mi'kmaq science students find employment at the Unama'ki Institute of Natural Resources and elsewhere. There are Mi'kmaq nurses, and the first Mi'kmaq medical doctor has established a practice in Nova Scotia. A number of Mi'kmaq have become lawyers and chosen

BOX 15.1

The *Marshall* Decision

On 17 September 1999 the Supreme Court of Canada overturned two lower courts' convictions of Donald Marshall Jr on charges of fishing and selling eels without a licence and out of season. Their verdict confirmed that because of the eighteenth-century treaties the Mi'kmaq signed with the British government, the Mi'kmaq retained the right to fish for food and ceremonial purposes as well as for a 'moderate livelihood'. The verdict set off a state of panic in some parts of the Maritime provinces, where the general economy had been shaky for years and prospects for the fishery were uncertain even without Native participation.

The federal government seemed unprepared for the Court's decision and was slow to react, while the Mi'kmaq were jubilant and moved quickly to put boats in the water and exercise their right. Fall is a closed season for lobster-fishing in the Maritimes and many non-Native fishers were outraged when Natives hauled in catches. Shouting, shoving matches, and some violence escalated until the federal government requested the Mi'kmaq to take their traps out of the water until the situation could be clarified. Most complied, but fishers on several reserves refused and conflicts with some non-Native fishers continued violently to the point where the RCMP was called in to separate the groups. The seriousness of the situation caused 35 Atlantic First Nations chiefs to meet with the federal Minister of Fisheries and Oceans, Herb Dahliwal, in Halifax on 6 October 1999. Dahliwal appealed for calm and the chiefs agreed to a 30-day moratorium on lobster-fishing. Again, several reserves refused.

But through the violence, talks and negotiations continued among the federal government, Mi'kmaq chiefs and bands, and Native and non-Native fishers. In addition, a Parliamentary Standing Committee on Fisheries and Oceans began to study the situation. By December, the Committee recommended that the federal government buy back lobster licences from willing non-Native fishers for Native use and provide training for Natives wishing to enter the fishery. The government agreed, and also allocated money for fishing boats and gear for the Mi'kmaq.

By 2002 most Mi'kmaq reserves had negotiated agreements with the federal government and begun to take an active part in the lobster and other fisheries. Burnt Church Reserve in New Brunswick, scene of so much violence in 1999, was one of the last reserves to sign an agreement, in August of 2002. Both Natives and government officials hailed this agreement as symbolizing a healing between Natives and non-Natives in Atlantic Canada over the long-lasting fishing dispute.

A number of questions remain about the *Marshall* decision. For instance, while it affirms the Mi'kmaq treaty right to fish and hunt, does the right extend to harvesting forestry resources? In September 2002 this issue was tested in the New Brunswick Court of Appeal in the case of Mi'kmaq logger Joshua Bernard. But what about the Mi'kmaq in Newfoundland? As of September 2002, they have been denied the benefits of the *Marshall* decision.

careers to benefit their people. Economic development proceeds apace on reserves as malls, gas stations, theatres, and the like appear. Future economic prospects for Mi'kmaq people are brighter than ever.

Overall, the Mi'kmaq people are improving their lives through education, reclaiming treaty rights, and taking control of their resources and finances. Along with this has come considerable pride in being Mi'kmaq, as reflected in prefer-

BOX 15.2

Bernd Christmas, a Mi'kmaq Lawyer for the Twenty-First Century

Bernd Christmas is a fine example of a new generation of highly educated Mi'kmaq working to improve life for Aboriginal people today. Son of a German mother and a Canadian Forces father from the Membertou Reserve in Nova Scotia, Bernd travelled extensively while growing up. After graduating from Osgoode Hall Law School at York University and being called to the Ontario bar, he accepted a position as a corporate and commercial lawyer with a large Toronto firm. But Bernd's career track changed in 1995 when Membertou Chief Terrance Paul approached him with a request to provide legal assistance for the band. Bernd saw the invitation as a 'wonderful opportunity to do some good for my own people'. He returned to Membertou to become chief executive officer of the band as well as president and CEO of the Membertou Corporate Division based in Halifax. Recruiting Natives experienced in business, Christmas has been leading the struggle following the *Marshall* decision in 1999 to ensure that Aboriginal people benefit from major resource developments in the Maritimes. Some of the high-profile companies with which Christmas and his colleagues have negotiated contracts are Georgia Pacific, Clearwater Fine Foods, and Lockheed Martin. Christmas's approach of running Membertou Reserve 'like a business' has succeeded in reversing the reserve's financial position from almost $1 million of indebtedness six years ago to where today it makes a contribution of over $100 million to the economy. Early in 2002, the Membertou band passed a rigorous audit to achieve International Organization for Standardization (ISO) 9001:2000 certification, making it the first indigenous government in Canada to meet internationally recognized business standards. At the certification presentation ceremony, the Minister of Indian Affairs and Northern Development congratulated the band as 'a leading example among First Nations of what can be accomplished once the fundamentals of good governance are in place'. Clearly, Christmas has good reason to state that he and the whole 10,000-member community of Membertou are 'very, very proud of what has been accomplished'.

Bernd Christmas makes numerous contributions to the Mi'kmaq and others. He serves as negotiator for the Assembly of Nova Scotia Mi'kmaq Chiefs, and assists other bands and individuals on matters relating to economic development. He sits on the Board of Directors for the Canadian Council for Aboriginal Business and is one of three Canadian commissioners appointed to the International Commission for the Conservation of Tuna. He is on the Board of Directors for the Canadian Council for Aboriginal Business. And he is a member of the Board of Governors for the Nova Scotia Community College and the commissioner for the Cape Breton-Victoria Regional School Board.

ences for Native styles of grooming and attire and the number of powwows, dances, and other Native cultural events. In 2002, more than 26,000 registered Mi'kmaq people lived both on and off reserves in the five provinces. Despite intensive attempts at assimilation in the past 500 years, Mi'kmaq today remain a distinct group in Canadian society.

Notes

1. 'Mi'kmaq' is pronounced 'mig-maw', with the emphasis on the first syllable.

2. This approach expects that all parts of a culture normally interact harmoniously and pays particular attention to the culture's interface with the environment.

3. See the discussion in Chapter 13.

References and Recommended Readings

Clayton, Hazel Maud Snow. 1966. *Down Nova Scotia Way*. Digby, NS: privately printed.

Coates, Ken S. 2000. *The Marshall Decision and Native Rights*. Montreal and Kingston: McGill-Queen's University Press. Drawing on a variety of historical, anthropological, legal, and political science sources, this book describes in clear terms the background and major issues in the Mi'kmaq struggle for recognition of treaty and Aboriginal rights.

Denys, Nicholas. 1908 [1672]. *The Description and Natural History of the Coasts of North America*. Toronto: Champlain Society. The classic seventeenth-century account of Mi'kmaq culture. It also contains an early description of Mi'kmaq acculturation between 1634, the year of Denys's arrival in Acadia, and 1672, the year the book was published.

Hoffman, Bernard G. 1955. 'Historical Ethnography of the Micmac of the Sixteenth and Seventeenth Centuries', Ph.D. dissertation, University of California, Berkeley. Although not published, this is the best ethnography available. It uses the ethnohistoric method and is based on a thorough sifting of all archival materials.

Jackson, Doug. 1993. *'On the Country': The Micmac of Newfoundland*, ed. Gerald Penney. St John's: Harry Cuff. Provides a good historic overview of the Newfoundland Mi'kmaq.

Knockwood, Isabelle. 1992. *Out of the Depths*. Lockeport, NS: Roseway Publishing. A former student's account of the Indian residential school at Shubenacadie, Nova Scotia.

LeClercq, Chretien. 1910 [1691]. *New Relation of Gaspesia, with the Customs and Religion of the Gaspesian Indians*. Toronto: Champlain Society. Another of the classic seventeenth-century accounts, it is more complete than Denys, although parts of LeClercq may be based on Denys.

Lescarbot, Marc. 1911–14 [1609]. *The History of New France*. Toronto: Champlain Society. The earliest account of the Mi'kmaq. More complete than Denys.

Thwaites, Reuben Gold, ed. 1896. *The Jesuit Relations and Allied Documents*. Cleveland: Burrows Brothers. Especially vols 1–3, for 1610–16, as they contain Father Biard's early observations and speculations on the Mi'kmaq.

Suggested Web Sites

Big Cove Band: www.bigcoveband.com
Informative site that includes a broad variety of information on Big Cove Reserve in New Brunswick. Contains links to other Mi'kmaq sites.

Membertou Band: www.membertou.ca
Web site of a very progressive Nova Scotia reserve with information on Membertou Development Corporation.

Newfoundland Mi'kmaq: www.miawpukek.nf.ca
Helpful and broad-based community and government Web page.

Nova Scotia Museum: www.ednet.ns.ca/cgi-bin/redirnu/educ/museum/mikmaq
Site posts an extensive collection of Mi'kmaq portraits.

PART VI

The Plains

CHAPTER 16

Myths and Realities:
An Overview of the Plains

C. RODERICK WILSON

No Aboriginal people on earth have so captured the popular imagination as have the 'historic' Plains Indians. Frozen in mid-nineteenth century by strips of Hollywood celluloid, or for our grandparents by dime novels and Wild West shows, the Plains Indian has for millions become 'The Indian'. So much is this the case that Indians from culture areas thousands of miles distant at times feel compelled to don Plains-style feather headdresses and assorted other finery—so that others will recognize them as Indians.

Non-Indian devotees of Plains culture are found around the world. Black celebrants at Mardi Gras in New Orleans and throughout the Caribbean annually celebrate by means of elaborate costume, song, and dance an essentially mythic kinship with Plains Indians. European Boy Scouts devour both highly romanticized popular works and technical treatises on Plains (and Woodland) Indians, with some scrupulously following every possible detail in creating their own medicine bundles and actually becoming, in their own minds, members of their chosen tribe. Some North American hobbyists spend thousands of dollars and hours in perfecting historically accurate costumes and dances, and in performing them. A number of Canada's national myths have to do with events by which Plains Indians were incorporated into the Canadian state: the North-West Mounted Police protecting Canadian Indians from unscrupulous American whisky traders; the

Canadian Pacific Railway, the ribbon of steel that tied Canada together, being made possible by the pacification of the warriors of the Plains; the stark contrast in levels of violence on the Canadian and US frontiers. In myriad ways, both conscious and unconscious, the dominant Indian image, in Canada and the world, is that of the Plains Indian of about 1850.

What relationship, if any, exists between the popular image and the reality?

There are several ways to answer the question. One is to emphasize that the stereotype has virtually no relationship to the reality of the time that Indians have occupied the region. In the 12,000 or more years of its existence, the economic basis of Plains society changed substantially. The earliest known Plains dwellers appear to have relied mainly on spears to dispatch the large animals they hunted. Three major technological innovations transformed Plains hunting prior to the advent of European contact: the spear thrower, the bow and arrow, and the buffalo pound. Each brought new efficiencies to the hunt and in turn affected the life of the people. The real Plains Indians thus are part of a millennia-old pattern of dynamic change and development, of adjusting to major shifts in climate and environment, to altering frequencies of game population (including the extinction of major species such as the mammoth, mastodon, and ancient species of buffalo), and to new hunting tools that demanded new

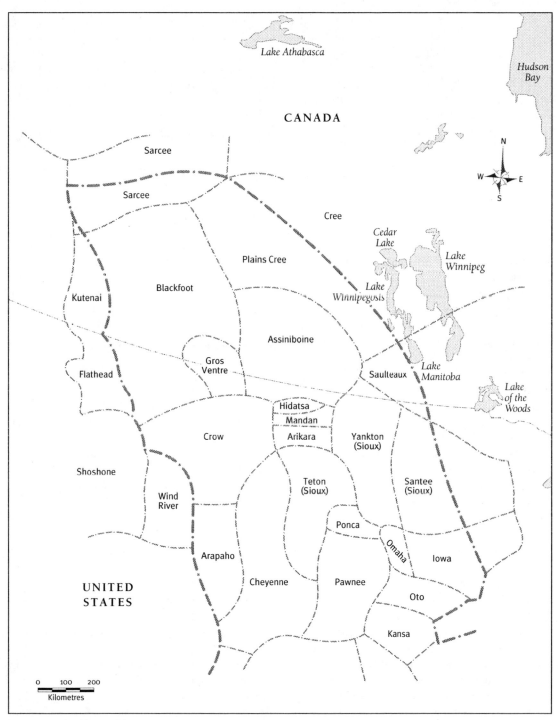

MAP 16.1. The Plains Culture Area

skills and new forms of social co-operation. The stereotype, in contrast, has no roots and does not speak to change. In fact, it denies change.

To further emphasize this point, it can be noted that the list of 'tribes' on the Canadian Plains during the 'classic' period is substantially different from what it was earlier. (1) Stoney (Assiniboine) people broke off from the Yankton Sioux and thereafter associated largely with the Cree. They lived in Minnesota 300 years ago at the edge of the parklands and Plains, hunting both deer and buffalo, and engaging in some horticulture. (2) Blackfoot, like the Cree and Saulteaux, speak an Algonquian language. They seem to have lived on the Plains for a very substantial period of time. (3) Although recent evidence indicates that Cree have lived in the parkland regions of the West for some time, the Plains Cree came into existence and moved onto the Plains through involvement in the fur trade. (4) Saulteaux, who refer to themselves as Bungi, could as well be called the Plains Ojibway. They also may have moved onto the Plains in early historic times. (5) Tsuu T'ina (Sarsi) are Athapaskan-speakers from the north who became buffalo hunters associated with the Blackfoot in recent times. Thus, of five tribes inhabiting the Canadian Plains in 1850, only one probably was not a newcomer. If one considers the Metis a tribe, the case is even stronger. Conversely, three tribes that in late prehistoric times lived in the Canadian part of the Plains, the Ktunaxa (Kutenai), Shoshone, and Atsina (Gros Ventre), had been displaced by 1850. Again, the stereotype gives no sense of the dynamic changes in the region. To put it more strongly, the 1850 Plains region was flooded with people (and peoples) compared to anything that had ever gone before.

Another indicator of the discrepancy between the stereotype and the tradition of Plains culture is the extent to which life changed as a result of the horse and gun. Each in turn increased the efficiency of the hunt. People not only could get more food and hides quickly, they could also carry bigger tipis and more goods, men could keep more women productively working and so were more likely to be polygynous, infant mortality dropped, and women at least were likely to live longer. Perhaps most significantly, high status now depended on having horses, creating a new impetus for raiding—and with the gun the level of violence increased dramatically. In addition, as Foster points out, life on the Plains was no longer entirely indigenous: the Europeans were also there. Although Plains life in 1850 was still grounded in the past, in many regards it was conspicuously different from anything that had gone before.

The stereotype, however, was not wholly invented. There were buffalo-hunting nomads who sought visions, counted coup, and ate pemmican. Dempsey writes graphically of Blackfoot in this period, and much of what he describes could also be said of other Plains tribes. Although Dempsey's portrait corresponds quite substantially with elements of the stereotype, major differences include: (1) as a generalization dealing with typical patterns, it allows for the fact that people's real behaviour is quite variable; (2) it recognizes that real Blackfoot had a past and that in many ways their present is markedly different from their life a century ago; and (3) in recognizing that today's changed Blackfoot are rooted in the life and values of the past, it implies that they have a future as a culture. (While Dempsey's view of identity is more trait-oriented than that of most younger scholars, even he sees a Blackfoot/ Aboriginal culture continuing into the future.) The implicit denial of an authentically Indian future is perhaps the most damning feature of the stereotype.

This discussion originated in a consideration of the popular stereotype of the Plains Indian. Part of our argument about the pervasiveness of this image is that it has affected also the perceptions of government officials and academics. Carter's chapter contains a thorough and depressing analysis of the extent to which the stereotype was one of the factors that effectively prevented Plains Cree and other Plains Indians from becoming productive

FIGURE 16.1. Assiniboine warrior. (Courtesy Saskatchewan Archives Board, R–A4945–1)

discussed these people. The personal example she provides is straightforward: her research of the facts dispelled the presuppositions with which she started. Some connections are not so easily traced, however. One of our unfinished tasks is to rethink not only our national and regional history, but also the disciplines themselves.

We conclude with the observation that the Plains stereotype has been, and continues to be, a factor in the Indian–government relationship in Canada. Although there are earlier treaties, the formal treaty-making process that created the modern reserve system is fundamentally a phenomenon of the Plains. That is where the numbered treaties started, and most treaty Indians still live in the Prairie provinces. The necessity of settling the Canadian Plains, of protecting them from a neighbour whose vision of manifest destiny conflicted with our own, and of tying the nascent nation together prompted the treaties. The treaties and reserves were also a product of the US Plains, a deliberate attempt to avoid the bloodshed and expense associated with the US frontier; such events as that of the Little Bighorn, where the Seventh Cavalry was routed by concentrated Indian forces, loomed large. It is no accident that Canadian reserves, generally, are both smaller and more scattered than are reservations in the US.

farmers in the late 1800s. Unfortunately, what she documents for these groups could easily be extended in both time and place.

Carter also mentions, almost in passing, that the Plains stereotype has affected the view of historians. She could have mentioned anthropologists as well, and any other academics who have

The treaties called for reserves. The government not only established reserves for the treaty

Indians but for thousands of non-treaty Indians who did not live on the Plains and with whom the government saw no necessity of signing treaties. But the reserve system, as legislated by the Indian Act, embodies an assumption that Indians are not competent to govern their own affairs, that land and money must be held by the government in trust for them. The Plains stereotype, it must be remembered, is in part a fusion of two conflicting stereotypes, both held by Europeans for centuries—the Indian as the uncivilized and barbaric savage and the Indian as the noble savage, the untutored child of nature. Noble he may be, but in the eyes of the law, a child. Most Canadians would be shocked to realize the domination that Indian agents legally exercised on reserves until recently, as well as the reluctance that is still frequently encountered among professional 'carers-for-Indians' to allow their 'noble charges' the simple dignity of running their own lives. The fact of the non-adult legal status of the Indian is central to most of the public controversies concerning Natives in recent years. Even the current attempt to revise substantially the Indian Act (as noted more extensively in Chapter 26), even though it incorporates numerous changes designed to 'give Indians greater self-determination', is fundamentally flawed by a process that brings in Natives for consultation after the process is designed. Look again at the last sentence. To speak of 'giving' anyone self-determination is at heart paternalistic.

The Plains stereotype does not alone explain the history and current conditions of Canadian Indians, but it certainly served, and continues to serve, to reinforce unfortunate tendencies towards paternalism.

CHAPTER 17

The Blackfoot Nation

HUGH A. DEMPSEY

Introduction

My own approach to Blackfoot research has undoubtedly been governed by the situation that brought me into contact with the tribes in the first place. In 1949, as a newspaper reporter, I began to cover Native political movements, during which time I met a girl from the Blood tribe whom I later married. As a result, I was constantly exposed to Blackfoot history and contemporary Indian-white relations as part of my life. The extension of my interests to writing Indian biographies arose when I began to question why such men as Crowfoot and Red Crow were such respected leaders. I soon discovered that biographies were excellent vehicles for relating Native history; the political and social events of the period became the background for the study, while the more personal aspects of a man's life provide a level of human interest that could not be gained in a formal history. Tragedy and triumph become more significant when related to a man's career.

I also learned that an event can be seen in different ways, depending on the experiences of the viewers. Prime Minister John A. Macdonald, for example, saw Crowfoot as a friend of the government for his actions in the North-West Rebellion of 1885. Crowfoot, however, was acting only on the best interests of his people. And if his actions helped the government, this was only a coincidence. One of my tasks, then, was to try to gain the Native insight into historical events when

virtually all writing on the subject had been done by white bureaucrats, reporters, and others. When this occurred, the results were often surprising.

For example, when Treaty No. 6 was being negotiated in 1876, Big Bear professed his fear of being hanged (so said the official transcript) and this immediately presented him as a man who intended to do evil. What Big Bear actually said, however, was that he did not want a rope around his neck. He was equating his situation to a wild horse that, once roped, lost its freedom.

In order to write Indian biographies, one is basically a historian, but one must be familiar with related fields of anthropology, political science, and even geography. At the same time, one is also an oral historian, gathering information from the Native people themselves. The information from these other disciplines is then interpreted from a historian's perspective.

The Ethnographic Blackfoot

Environment and Economy

Blackfoot territory during the historic period after 1750 was vast: it ranged from the North Saskatchewan River to the Missouri River and from the Rocky Mountains to the present Alberta–Saskatchewan boundary. Near the latter part of the nomadic era, the northern range shrank to the Battle River, as the Blackfoot withdrew in the face of Cree pressures and as the decreasing buffalo herds congregated farther south.

Blackfoot territory was primarily short-grass plains interspersed by coulees and streams bisecting it in an east-west direction. A number of these watercourses dried up completely during the summer. Lakes often were so alkaline that the water was virtually undrinkable. Most of the river areas and lakeshores were devoid of timber. When groves of trees were found, they became favourite wintering areas. The large mammals in Blackfoot country were the buffalo, grizzly bear, black bear, antelope, deer, elk, mountain sheep, and mountain goat. Of these, the Blackfoot were interested primarily in buffalo, calling its flesh *nitapiksisako*, 'real meat', implying that all other meat was inferior. Besides being used for food, the buffalo was the source of many articles of utilitarian and religious use, such as lodge covers, tools, clothing, drinking vessels, storage containers, expungers, and shields.

Lesser mammals were used as food only when buffalo was unavailable. These included porcupine, rabbit, and squirrel. Blackfoot rejected all fish as food; they considered them part of an evil Underwater World. Ducks, geese, partridge, and swans were sometimes eaten, and eggs were collected for food.

A wide variety of berries and edible roots were gathered by women: most prominent were the saskatoon or sarvice berry, chokeberry, bull berry, high and low bush cranberry, gooseberry, pin cherry, raspberry, strawberry, wild turnip, wild onion, bitter root, and camas root. Other plants had practical or medicinal uses: bearberry and the inner bark of the red willow were smoked, as was wild tobacco. Because of its bitter taste, the latter was mixed with herbs and, in later years, with commercial tobacco.

The weather in Blackfoot country was marked by hot dry summers and long cold winters, with warm chinook winds providing some respite during winter. Spring was often cool and wet, interrupted by late blizzards, while autumns were warm, dry, and pleasant; the term 'Indian summer' was most appropriate for the region. Spring and summer saw violent thunderstorms, to which

was attributed religious significance. The first thunderstorm of spring heralded a ritual of the medicine-pipe owners, while the thunder itself was considered to be a powerful deity. Death by lightning was not uncommon.

Under ideal conditions an abundance of food could be found by the Blackfoot; they could also starve during periods of drought or blizzards. If they went into their winter quarters and the buffalo remained far out on the Plains, if prairie fires drove the herds away, or if blizzards prevented hunters from leaving camp, hunger and privation would result. As nomads they could not store large quantities of food and thus were dependent on a regular supply of fresh meat. In autumn some meat was cut into long thin strips and sun-dried, but this provided emergency rations for relatively short periods of time. Other dried meat was pulverized and mixed with crushed, dried sarvice berries and hot fat, producing pemmican. This, too, provided a limited but important source of food in winter.

Buffalo were killed in various ways. For thousands of years Blackfoot used cliffs near streams as buffalo jumps. Those not killed by the fall were quickly dispatched. With the introduction of horses and guns, this method gradually fell into disuse and was abandoned during the mid-nineteenth century.

Another method of killing buffalo was the 'surround'. When hunters located a small herd they crept forward, sometimes disguising themselves as wolves or buffalo calves, and when close enough picked off animals on the fringe of the herd. If they were lucky the herd merely milled in a circle instead of running away, and the hunters might kill several animals before the buffalo took flight.

Perhaps the most thrilling way to kill buffalo was on horseback. When the Blackfoot acquired horses in the early 1700s they quickly learned how to ride among a herd at a full gallop, picking a fat cow and killing it with an arrow or lead ball. Specially trained horses were guided by knee pressure and often would press so close to the

FIGURE 17.1. Blackfoot warriors. (© Canadian Museum of Civilization, 73462)

quarry that the hunter's leg would touch the buffalo. So valued were these buffalo runners that they had no other duties to perform.

Smaller animals and birds were hunted on foot, young boys killing rabbits and partridges as part of their education. Young water birds were sometimes caught by teenage girls wading among the reeds. Picking berries and digging roots were entirely women's responsibility, although a teenage boy usually accompanied them to protect them in case of attack by a bear or other animal. Some of the berries were stewed or sun-dried for winter use.

Because of the movement of the buffalo and the seasonal availability of resources, the Blackfoot followed an annual cycle. In winter they gathered in small bands along wooded river bottoms, often near the foothills where they were within easy reach of the buffalo. There they stayed for weeks at a time, particularly when hunting was good. In such winter camps, tepees were strung out for miles among the protective cottonwoods of a river valley. Each band might have a separate camp, but they remained within a mile or two of another camp for mutual protection.

In spring people moved out into the prairies, sometimes in small family groups or bands, depending on the buffalo movements. Some would go deep into the foothills to cut new tepee poles or travois poles, while others went to trading posts or killed enough buffalo to make new lodge covers. By early summer they congregated in large camps, comprising whole tribes, so that the Sun Dance and other rituals could be held. When gathered in such large numbers they seldom remained in one spot for more than a week, as their horses soon grazed off all the nearby grass. After the ceremonies the people wandered off in small groups again, picking berries, drying meat, and making pemmican to sell to the trading posts. In early autumn they completed their fall trade and chose winter campsites. Often these were close to buffalo jumps, which provided a source of food as long as buffalo stayed in the area.

During all this, of course, there were small family groups wandering off to visit other tribes and young warriors raiding enemy horse herds, but the general practice was to follow the buffalo.

Social Organization

The Blackfoot Nation is made up of three tribes: the Blackfoot, or Siksik-a', meaning 'black foot' or 'black feet'; the Blood, or Kai-nai, meaning 'many chiefs'; and the Peigan, or Pi-kuni, meaning 'scabby robes'. The latter is further subdivided into the North and South Peigan. Allied to the nation, thus forming the Blackfoot Confederacy, were the Sarcees and the Gros Ventres, the latter separating and becoming an enemy in a dispute over stolen horses in 1861.

A number of myths explain how the Blackfoot tribal names came into existence. The most popular is that at one time they were an unnamed group beset by enemies on all sides. They agreed to divide into three groups—one to guard the northeast, another to protect the southeast, and a third the southwest. After some time someone from the northern tribe decided to visit the others. On his way he passed over a large area burned by prairie fire. When he reached the southeast camp, his moccasins were black with ashes. Entering the village, he asked a man who was the chief. 'I am', he said. Another person stopped and said, 'I am the chief', and soon the northerner was surrounded by several people, all claiming to be chiefs.

'I shall call your tribe "A-kainah", Many Chiefs', he said, 'for everyone here seems to be a chief.' Meanwhile, the Crees gave this tribe the name of Red People, for the ochre they spread on their clothes, and this was later translated as Blood People, or Bloods. Continuing the story, the Bloods looked at the visitor's moccasins and said, 'Very well, you have given our tribe a name, so we will reciprocate; your people shall be called "Siksika", Blackfoot.'

The man then went to the southwest tribe where their territory was rich in buffalo. The people had become lazy and the women had tanned their hides so badly that men walked about with pieces of dried flesh and hair on their robes. 'I shall call you "Apikuni", or badly dressed robes', he told them. Over time the word became corrupted to Peigan. Collectively these three tribes were called 'Sakoyitapix', 'the prairie people', or sometimes 'Nitsitapix', 'real people'.

Because the nation is divided between the US and Canada, a number of contradictions have arisen regarding spelling tribal names. For example, Canadians generally and those on the Peigan Reserve in southern Alberta use the term 'Peigan', while in the US it is spelled 'Piegan'. But most controversial has been the correctness of 'Blackfoot' or 'Blackfeet'. Some insist that one term is correct and the other wrong, but no evidence supports either thesis. The word 'sik-sik-a' is taken from two roots: 'Sik-si' from 'siksinum' or 'black', and 'ka' either from 'okat' (foot) or 'okats' (feet). When the chiefs signed a treaty with the Americans in 1855, the document identified the 'Blackfoot Nation' but was signed by four 'Blackfeet'; similarly, in the Canadian treaty the term 'Blackfoot Tribe' was used, but an adhesion to the document was signed by 'Blackfeet'. Today, most Canadians, anthropologists, and Natives in Canada use the term 'Blackfoot', while many Americans and Indians in the US use 'Blackfeet'. Therefore both terms appear to be acceptable.

The smallest political unit was the band, usually having an extended family as its nucleus. Bands with particularly good leaders or that were

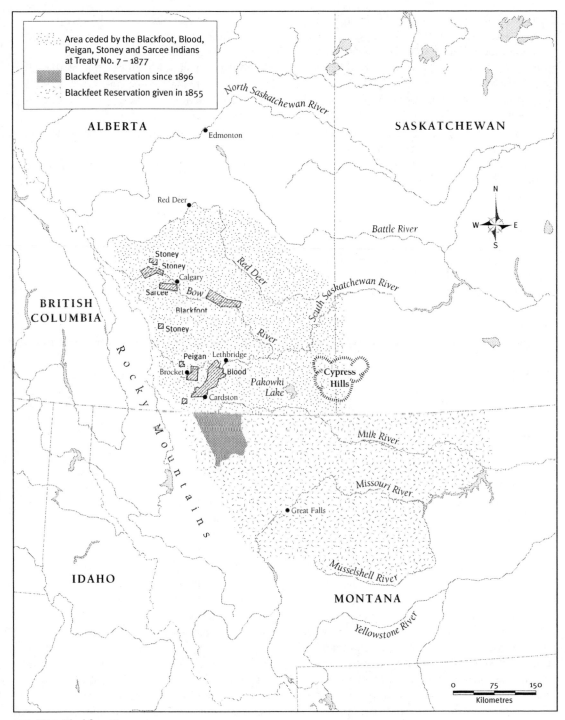

MAP 17.1. Blackfoot Reserves

constantly lucky in the hunt attracted people from other bands until they became too large to be economic. Others that experienced misfortune sometimes disappeared. For example, a band of Bloods called the Followers of the Buffalo kept growing in size because of wise leadership and every few years a group would break away, forming such new bands as Many Fat Horses, All Tall People, and Knife Owners. On the other hand, the Bear People lost their leading men in battle in 1872 and the survivors joined other bands.

Blackfoot bands received their names because of some distinctive feature or attribute of their members, or because of some incident. For example, when blizzards caused starvation among a band isolated in the foothills, its members were forced to subsist on fish. They became known as the Fish Eaters. Another band was named Gopher Eaters through a similar experience. Other names, like All Black Faces or All Short People, were purely descriptive. The names could change, if an old one became outdated or a new incident occurred. After settling on their reserve, the Followers of the Buffalo were renamed Camps in a Bunch while the Shooting Up band was renamed the Interfering band. The latter happened when a river changed course, leaving the band without water; joking friends said its members had interfered with the stream by taking all the water for tea.

A band was a self-contained unit small enough to find food yet large enough to protect itself. Nineteenth-century bands are estimated to have contained 20 to 30 families. Each band had a leader recognized as the political chief; another man was war chief. During normal times the political chief controlled the movements of the band, but should there be danger from enemy attack or other causes, the war chief immediately assumed control. The political chief took the role of chief magistrate, presiding at council meetings, giving instructions to the camp police, and settling disputes within the band. His police were members of one of the warrior societies.

When a boy reached his early teens he joined one of these societies made up of comrades his own age. Then, about once every five years, his society took over the membership of the group that was older than themselves and transferred their membership to a new cohort of younger persons. Those who were between, say, 20 and 25 years of age, or between 25 and 30, were most often chosen to act as camp police. They patrolled at night, acted as guardians during buffalo hunts, and protected the band while on the trail. They also carried out edicts of punishment decided by the chief. For example, a thief might be banished from the camp, or a man who went out alone to hunt buffalo and frightened the herds away might have his horse seized and riding gear destroyed.

When bands joined together to hunt or camp in winter, one leader was recognized as head chief; he presided at all council meetings. There was no single head chief of a tribe, but if an entire tribe was together, one man was chosen as the presiding authority over the camp. Yet if they should suddenly be faced with danger, the head chief would be replaced by a war chief, just as was done in smaller bands. For example, Red Crow was considered to be a great chief of the Bloods in mid-nineteenth century, but if the camp were threatened by an enemy, White Calf became war chief and had complete control over the warrior societies.

Council meetings were usually attended by the head chief, the war chief, and the heads of leading families. Decisions were made by consensus and the head chief seldom tried to give direct orders to councillors. He knew they were too independent to be intimidated and they could always withdraw from the camp if they disagreed with him. Instead, the head chief tried to win adherents through oratory; when he felt that he had enough support, he would announce his own intentions. If there was a dispute as to whether the camp should move north or south, the chief might present his arguments, gain support, and then say that he was going south. He did not order the others to follow, but he knew that they probably would go with him.

Religion

Religion pervaded almost every aspect of life. A woman beginning her quill working would pray; an old man awaking in the morning would sing a prayer of thanks; a person before eating placed a small morsel of food in the ground for the spirits.

The Blackfoot believed that their entire universe was inhabited by spirits, some good and some evil. One of the greatest was the Sun, who was head of a holy family consisting of his wife, the Moon, and their boy, the Morning Star. The thunder spirit also was a powerful deity, while even a lowly mouse had its supernatural role. A strangely twisted tree or an unusual rock formation was considered to be the manifestation of spiritual power and, as a result, passersby left offerings for good luck.

Often the most important spirits were those directly related to an individual's experiences. A teenage boy, for example, might go on a vision quest, looking for a spiritual helper. He would go to a secluded place—if he was particularly daring, to an area of great danger, such as a high precipice or a burial ground. Constructing a crude shelter, he lay down with a pipe beside him and fasted and prayed for four days. During that time he hoped that he would slip into a trance and that a spiritual helper would come. Sometimes it would be an animal in the form of a man, while at other times a creature itself might speak.

A famous leader, Red Crow, was hunting gophers with bow and arrow while still a boy. As he lay near a gopher hole he fell asleep and in his dream the gopher spirit came to him and promised to help him if he would go away and leave him in peace. 'When you go against an enemy,' advised the spirit, 'take a blade of grass and stick it in your hair. Then you'll never get hit' (Dempsey, 1980: 10). Red Crow followed this advice and although he was in 33 battles, he was never wounded.

As a result of their visions, young men wore amulets or ornaments in their hair or around their necks. Crowfoot kept an owl's head in his hair, while others could be seen wearing the skins of animals or other objects that represented their spirit helpers. Usually, each had specific songs and rituals performed by the owners. The objects themselves were unique to the individual; when he died they were buried with him.

Some men had visions of benefit to the whole tribe. As a rule, such people already were recognized as holy men and, as a result of their dreams, they created sacred pieces called 'medicine bundles'. This is a generic term for objects wrapped together and used for ritualistic purposes. Some medicine bundles contained war shirts decorated with scalps or weasel skins; others had animal skins, fossilized ammonites (known as 'buffalo stones'), or other parts of costumes. Perhaps most common was the medicine pipe, a long pipe stem decorated with eagle feathers. The pipe had no bowl, as it was not for smoking but for performing a dance to bring good luck to the tribe or to help someone who was sick. Medicine-pipe men—the owners of the pipes—led a distinctive lifestyle; they wore their hair in a certain way, painted their faces, carried the pipe on its own travois, and had many taboos. They possessed the spiritual power to keep evil spirits away from the tribe and to help those in need. Although they did not constitute a society, they would gather together periodically to open their pipe bundles, perform dances and rituals, and renew their vows. Every spring after the first thunderstorm, each medicine-pipe bundle was opened in response to the call the owner received from the thunder spirit.

Besides these revered medicine pipes, lesser pipes were individually owned. Most common was the black-covered medicine pipe, which was small enough to take to war and often was presented to a fledgling warrior by an older relative.

Medicine pipes and other medicine bundles originated in visions but, unlike personal amulets, could be transferred or sold. If a man wished to become a bundle owner, he went to someone who had such a bundle, offered to smoke with him, and announced that he wanted it. The owner could not refuse, so a price was arranged and a formal transfer ceremony took place.

The most ancient Blackfoot medicine bundle was the beaver bundle that, according to legends, was given to a hunter who camped by St Mary's Lake in what is now northern Montana. He was killing too many birds and animals, so one day when his wife went for water a Beaver Man came out of the lake and captured her. Later she led a procession from the lake to her husband's lodge; this group consisted of the Beaver Man, Sun, and Moon. The hunter was told that if he would stop killing game unnecessarily, his wife would be returned to him and he would be given a medicine bundle. Then, one by one, animal and bird skins were taken from the walls of his lodge and he was taught the songs and ceremonies for each. These were wrapped together with sweetgrass and face paint to make the beaver bundle.

Most medicine bundles contained a few standard items, such as braided sweetgrass used for incense and ochre to paint the user's face. The rest of the objects were worn or held during ceremonies, usually with each accompanied by its special song. The whole bundle was contained within a large rawhide case that hung on a tripod behind the owner's lodge in day and was placed above his bed at night. Incense was burned and prayers and songs were performed each morning and night.

Medicine bundles also were used by the various secret societies. Most common were the warrior societies, discussed earlier. Each member of a warrior society had his own bundle, which was simply a packet of paints and the costume he needed for his society's dances and ceremonies. A society had one or two leaders, each with a distinctive headdress and face paint. For example, a head man in the Raven Carriers society wore a coyote skin and had an eagle feather in his hair; while he danced, he carried a long red stick trimmed with cloth and feathers.

Although females did not normally take an active role in most societies, the Blackfoot were unique in that they had one society exclusively for women. It was called the 'Motoki', popularly translated as Old Women's Society, but, more accurately, it should be called the Sorority. Like the Longtime Medicine Pipe, some of the society rituals came to the Blackfoot from the Mandans in 1832, but they have been given a mythical origin relating to the actions of a white crow among a buffalo herd. The primary function of the Motoki was to acknowledge the importance of the buffalo to the Blackfoot people. In their rituals the women took the roles of buffalo killed by hunters and paid homage to the power of the buffalo spirit. The primary intention was to appease the spirits so that the tribe would have good luck in its future hunts. Among the costumes worn by the women were headdresses made of scalps from old buffalo bulls, worn by leaders of the society.

The Sun Dance

As can be seen, religion among the Blackfoot ranged from personal visions and a constant concern with the supernatural to more structured societies collectively performing rituals. The most complex ceremony, the Sun Dance, involved an entire tribe. This festival lasted for several days and had social and political overtones besides its purely religious function.

The term 'Sun Dance' is a misnomer, implying a simple dance to the Sun spirit rather than a series of religious ceremonies. The Blackfoot term for the Sun Dance, Okan, refers to the centre pole of the Sun Dance lodge—the most sacred object of the ritual.

The basic purpose of the Sun Dance was to allow everyone to reaffirm faith in the Sun spirit. Its nucleus consisted of constructing a lodge, presided over by a holy woman, where various dances and rituals were performed. The assembling of the entire tribe also became the occasion for secret societies to perform their dances or to exchange their memberships, for medicine-pipe bundles to be opened, for war exploits to be recounted, and for the self-torture ritual to be performed. None of these latter ceremonies was a part of the Sun Dance but, because they were performed at the same time, they were inextricably linked to the ritual.

The decision to hold a Sun Dance was made by a pure woman—i.e., a virgin or faithful wife—who had a male relative in danger of losing his life. A husband might be ill or a son may not have returned from a raid. The woman made a public vow that if the person's life was spared, she would sponsor a Sun Dance. Then, if her prayer was answered, she began preparations for the summer festival.

The sponsoring of a Sun Dance was expensive, so relatives and the extended family of the holy woman began to assemble blankets, horses, and other gifts to be given away. Others sought out a woman who had previously sponsored the ritual and made arrangements for her to transfer her medicine bundle, called the Natoas bundle, to the new sponsor.

The Sun Dance was held in July, as soon as the sarvice berries were ripe, for they were needed for sacramental purposes. A site was chosen by a warrior society in consultation with the chiefs—the location offering good protection against enemies, providing good grazing, and being close to the buffalo.

During the first several days while bands assembled, people enjoyed themselves gambling, horse racing, and visiting. The Motoki then held its ceremonies in the centre of the camp circle, building a lodge of travois and tepee covers that served as their home during the four-day ritual. On the last day, the women had a public dance and gave away gifts to visitors and friends.

By this time the grass near camp had been grazed over by the hundreds of horses, so a new campsite was chosen four or five miles away. There warrior societies, such as the All Brave Dogs, Pigeons, Horns, or Prairie Chickens, held their dances. At last the holy woman moved her lodge inside the camp circle, decorating its base with green boughs to signify that she was beginning her fast.

The main sacrament of the Sun Dance was the buffalo tongue. While fasting the holy woman was instructed by the former bundle owner how to cut tongues into thin strips and smoke-dry them over the fire. During the four days that the holy woman remained in her lodge, she could not touch water, even to wash, lest it rain. Instead, she wiped her face with a muskrat skin and prepared for the building of the main lodge. On the first day of her fast a huge sweat lodge was built just outside the northern edge of camp. This lodge was made of 50 willow sticks and was painted half black, for night, and half red, for day. Then 50 stones were heated in readiness for the sweat. This lodge symbolized the actions of Scar Face, a legendary Blackfoot who had visited the Sun spirit and had his scar removed in such a sweat lodge.

When the stones were ready, the holy woman and her teacher went to the lodge and sat beside it while their husbands went inside. While water was being placed on the stones and the men sweated in the steam, the holy woman painted a buffalo skull with symbols of the Sun, Moon, Morning Star, and Sun Dogs; later it was placed at the base of the Sun Dance pole. Women never entered a sweat lodge, so when the men came out the party returned to the holy woman's lodge to finish the fast.

These ceremonies were repeated for the next three days and each morning the participants moved to a new campsite. Finally, at the end of the fourth day, they arrived at the site of the Sun Dance ceremonies.

The following morning a warrior society left camp in search of a forked tree that would serve as the holy centre pole. When they found one they returned to camp as though they were scouts who had discovered any enemy camp. Then others in the society crept up to the tree. When it was cut down, they attacked it as a fallen enemy. The tree was taken back in triumph to camp, there to be laid on the ground in readiness for building the lodge. Others in the camp built the frame of the lodge, which was similar in shape to a circus tent. At last the holy woman ended her fast and went to the unfinished lodge where she prayed over the centre pole before it was raised in position.

Among some tribes that practised a Sun Dance, building the lodge involved little ceremony. For the Blackfoot, however, raising the pole was the highlight of the entire ritual. Guns were fired in the air, men gave war whoops, and everyone yelled joyously as the forked pole was fitted in place and rails from the outer walls were fastened to it. The happy mood continued as scores of people, young and old, collected green branches to place around the lodge as an outer wall. This part of the ceremony symbolized the beginning of new life, just as their faith in the Sun spirit was being renewed. Taboos were relaxed as young men lifted unmarried girls and sweethearts onto their horses as they went to collect greenery. By sunset the lodge had been completed and was ready to be sanctified. With the lodge completed, the work of the holy woman was finished and her fast was over. She provided a huge feast for the camp, and her family gave gifts to everyone who had helped. One particular symbol of opulence was the pathway between the holy woman's lodge and the Sun Dance lodge; when the woman travelled that route, it was carpeted with blankets and robes provided by her family. The farther the carpet of goods extended, the greater the prestige. After the ceremony, the blankets were given away.

That night, four warriors would build a small bower within the Sun Dance lodge and remain there all night, singing their holy songs. In the morning, men known as weather dancers lined up in two rows facing each other and, with faces elevated towards the sun, performed their ceremonial dance. Various warrior societies also performed public dances. The Sun Dance lodge was a holy place, so activities taking place there brought good luck.

A warrior might proclaim one of his war deeds and re-enact the entire episode in pantomime; if he lied or exaggerated, people believed that he would not live to see another summer. Young men who had made vows had skewers thrust through slits cut in their breasts and backs. The skewers in front were fastened to lines attached to the centre pole, while those at the back were used to suspend

a shield or buffalo skull. As he danced the young warrior thrust himself backward in order to tear the skewers free from his chest and then to wrest the obstruction from his back. This ritual is sometimes referred to as 'making a brave', implying that one did it to become a warrior. This is not true; the ordeal was suffered by a young man who had made a vow to the Sun for the good health or protection of someone in his family. It was an act of gratitude to the Sun spirit for an answered prayer.

The Sun Dance was in sharp contrast to more individualistic aspects of Blackfoot religion. The use of personal amulets and medicine bundles was a much older practice. Only with the acquisition of the horse and the availability of leisure time could the Blackfoot develop such a complex series of rituals as the Sun Dance.

Myths and Legends

To explain phenomena around them, Blackfoot created myths and legends, some based on spiritual experiences. Myths explained the origins of medicine bundles and painted tepee designs; they recounted the exploits of great warriors; they told of the origin of man himself.

The most common type of legend was related to a trickster-creator called Napi, Old Man. Napi was responsible for creating the world, making the first man and woman, creating life and death, and making all the flora and fauna in Blackfoot country. Yet Napi was not a god who was revered; rather, he was a supernatural personification of man, with all his wisdom and foolishness, bravery and cowardice, honesty and greed. Some tales caused listeners to double over in laughter as Napi is outwitted by an opponent or does something foolish.

There are many tales about Napi, such as those explaining why the bobcat has a flat face, why the skunk has a striped back, and how man became superior to buffalo. These stories were told partly for entertainment, but also to explain the world to young people, to allay their fears of strange phenomena, and to teach the customs and mores of the tribe. Through these stories children learned

BOX 17.1

Creation

This is an origin legend told to anthropologist George Bird Grinnell in the 1890s (Grinnell, 1913: 145–6). Old Man, or Napi, was the mythical trickster-creator of the Blackfoot.

In the beginning there was water everywhere; nothing else was to be seen. There was something floating on the water, and on this raft were Old Man and all the animals. Old Man wished to make land, and he told the beaver to dive down to the bottom of the water and to try to bring up a little mud. The beaver dived and was under the water for a long time, but he could not reach the bottom. Then the loon tried, and after him the otter, but the water was too deep for them. At last the muskrat was sent down, and he was gone for a long time; so long that they thought he must be drowned, but at last he came up and floated almost dead on the water, and when they pulled him up on the raft and looked at his paws, they found a little mud in them. When Old Man had dried this mud, he scattered it over the water and land was formed. This is the story told by the Blackfeet.

about good and evil, about the folly of greed, and about the importance of making wise decisions.

The Blackfoot were known for their extensive legends about stars. Most stars were said to have their origins on earth as Indians who had used their supernatural powers to join the Sky People. Even Blackfoot tepees pay homage to the stars; on the upper ears or flaps of most lodges are white circles depicting Ursa Major and the Pleiades. In fact, a Blackfoot painted tepee is rich in mythology; its main design is often the result of a vision. Another element of the design may relate to the Morning Star or to the butterfly, the spirit of sleep.

Stories about great warriors almost inevitably are rooted in supernatural feats. The Blackfoot believed that if a man performed some brave or important deed, he succeeded only because of the spiritual help he received. Crowfoot, head chief of the Blackfoot, was said to have received his power from the owl's head he wore in his hair; Red Old Man, a great warrior, had a mouse as his spiritual helper. When faced with a crisis these men often had visions or were led from danger by an animal or bird. A famous story deals with the warrior Low Horn, killed by Cree in the 1840s. According to tales, bullets could not kill him, and he died only when an elk antler was driven into his ear. The Cree then burned his body, but an ember exploded from the fire and turned into a grizzly bear that attacked the Cree. As they fled, a thundercloud overhead sent down lightning bolts to kill even more Cree. Later, the Blackfoot believe that Low Horn was reincarnated in a young boy who ultimately became a medicine man among the Bloods and died in 1899.

Warfare

The Blackfoot were in an almost constant state of warfare during the historic period. On one hand, they coveted the rich horse herds of the Crow, Shoshone, and Nez Perce to the south and southwest. To the north and east Cree and Assiniboine preyed on Blackfoot herds and also envied the heavy concentration of buffalo in Blackfoot hunting grounds. If war parties were not out raiding tribes to the south, they were being attacked from the north. To the southeast they sometimes came into contact with the Sioux.

Generally, Blackfoot went to war for booty or revenge. In the former case, a small war party might set out on foot, in expectation of capturing horses and returning in triumph. Killing an enemy was not their primary objective and scalping was not among the most heroic deeds. Rather, a warrior was praised for audacity and fearlessness in battle. Sleeps on Top was remembered because he rode into conflict armed only with a club and when he saw two mounted enemies he deliberately knocked one off the left side and the other off the right, just to show his bravery. Young warriors entering an enemy camp at night took the horses tethered to their owners' lodges, not just because they were the best animals, but to display their skill as raiders. Most Blackfoot went on raiding parties between ages 13 and 20. After then most were content to hunt and to breed horses, but others continued to go to war until they were old men. For them, wealth in horses was less important than the glory and excitement of war.

Revenge parties were entirely different. Usually a revenge party was formed after an enemy war party fell upon a helpless camp and killed people. Then grieving relatives called on fellow tribe members to form a huge war party, sometimes consisting of 200–300 men. If the killing had been done by Cree, Blackfoot made no attempt to seek out the actual murderers; they were satisfied to kill other Cree in revenge. Often, non-Natives did not understand that this practice also applied to them. If, for example, a whisky trader killed a Blackfoot, then the deceased man's relatives might kill the first non-Native they could find.

Less frequently, tribes were raided for trespassing on Blackfoot hunting grounds. Kutenais, Pend d'Oreilles, and Flatheads, who lived across the mountains, travelled to the prairies once or twice a year to hunt buffalo and usually sent scouts ahead to avoid conflict. If the Blackfoot learned of their presence, either a temporary peace treaty was made or the mountain tribe was forced to retreat. Similarly, frequent hunting parties of Cree and Metis (or Halfbreeds, as the Blackfoot called them) were deeply resented

because of their incursions. The Halfbreeds were particularly disliked because their huge, organized hunts resulted in the wholesale destruction of buffalo herds. As very little Blackfoot intermarriage with non-Natives occurred during the nomadic period, the Halfbreeds always were associated with the enemy Cree.

Family Life

When a child was born, it was named by its mother. If a girl, its name was sometimes based on the first thing the woman saw when the child was delivered: Sky Woman, Spider, or Kit Fox Woman. This might become the girl's official name, but more often a male member of the family, an uncle or grandfather, would select a name based on his own war experiences. Blackfoot believed that warriors must have had supernatural help to win a battle, so good luck was attached to names. This is why so many Blackfoot women had warlike names: Killed at Night, Double Gun Woman, Attacked Towards Camp, or Stabbed Twice. Others had names associated with the namer's spiritual helper: Elk Woman, Big Rabbit, Fisher Woman, or Yellow Squirrel.

Boys were given their first official name when a few days old. Most often an older member of the family would announce his right to choose the name, and, when he was ready, would perform a ceremony and go into a sweat lodge to sanctify his choice. The name chosen was based on the man's war or religious experiences but was recognized as a child's name, such as Shot Close, Little Child, or Berries. This name was used until the boy was old enough to earn an adult name on the warpath or in hunting.

Boys and girls played together until about five years old, at which time their formal education began. Girls learned to carry out simple chores, like collecting firewood and water or looking after younger children. The boys were taken in hand by an uncle or older brother and taught to use a bow and arrow, guard and round up horses, follow game trails, and become good riders. The first time a boy killed food for the lodge, such as a rabbit or partridge, the father announced the achievement throughout the camp and sponsored a feast for his comrades.

There were no special puberty rites among the Blackfoot. When a girl began her menstrual periods, she was taken away to a separate shelter. They believed that a woman at this time would bring bad luck if she stayed in the lodge with hunters. Her scent would be carried by the hunters and frighten game away.

When boys became 12 or 13, their comrades or older brothers often gave them derisive nicknames, like Lately Gone or Little Shine, to encourage them to go to war to earn adult names. On their first expeditions boys went as servants, making fires, cooking, repairing moccasins, and looking after camp. They did not take part in the actual raid and received no share of the plunder, but if they acquitted themselves well they might receive an adult name and be invited to go again. At this age, the name chosen would be one belonging to the family. Names were considered material possessions; when a person died, his name was the exclusive property of the extended family until it was taken by someone else. If a man had gained a particularly outstanding war record or had died under heroic circumstances, the name might be reserved until someone in the family performed a notable deed of valour. For example, a warrior named Crowfoot was killed while on a peace expedition to the Shoshone in 1828; because of the circumstances, his name was revered within the family. Not until the 1840s did a younger relative perform a deed of sufficient daring for him to take this name.

When a young man reached marriageable age he began a courtship, often meeting a girl on her way to get water or gather wood, or near her tepee at night. Clandestine meetings were discouraged by the girl's parents, as virginity was held in high esteem and had religious significance. A young man, particularly if he was handsome, might spend hours combing his hair or painting his face in a place where he was sure to be seen by the girl of his choice.

Marriage was arranged in a number of ways, depending on the wealth and social status of the participants. Most frequently, negotiations were held between the father of the girl and his prospective son-in-law or between the two male parents. Once an agreement was reached there was an exchange of gifts, with the groom and his family making a payment of about double the amount received. In some instances where the families were poor, the boy might agree to work for his father-in-law for a year, herding horses, hunting, and performing other duties. Usually, however, the bride moved to her husband's camp, her family providing her with a new tepee and furnishings. These were her property and, in the event of separation, she kept the lodge and all household utensils. Polygamy was common, the number of wives limited only by a man's wealth. Men commonly had two or three wives, while a chief at the treaty of 1877 was said to have had 10. Normally the first wife was the senior member of the female household and was referred to as the 'sits beside him' wife. She directed the duties of the lodge and accompanied her husband to feasts and ceremonies. It was not unusual for a man to marry sisters, with the belief that they could live together in harmony, while an older brother might marry the widows of a younger brother should that man die. Polyandry, the practice of a wife having more than one husband, did occur from time to time, but an overabundance of women due to male death in hunting and war made this infrequent.

If a woman proved to be lazy or unfaithful, a man could divorce her simply by sending her back to her parents and demanding repayment of the gifts. A woman also could leave her husband, but only on the grounds of extreme cruelty or neglect. Most often if a bride returned home she was promptly sent back to her husband so that the family would not suffer the humiliation of being accused of having raised an incompetent daughter.

In daily life there was a clear division of labour between men and women. Wives were responsible for pitching and striking tepees, packing, cooking, manufacturing and decorating most clothing, caring for infants, training girls, and general maintenance of the lodge. Men provided food, protected the camp, manufactured some objects related to religion and war, looked after horses, and carried out raids on enemy camps. Men painted exterior designs on lodges, although women were responsible for decorating liners, backrests, and parfleche bags. Women did virtually all of the beadworking and quillworking; men painted religious symbols on shields, robes, and rattles, and carved or produced instruments of war.

When a man was dying he was dressed in his best clothes and his personal possessions were placed around him. After he died the camp was abandoned, as the Blackfoot believed that his spirit would haunt the area before leaving for the sand hills. His lodge was sometimes sewn up and used as a death lodge; otherwise the body was placed in a tree or on a hill for burial. It was not buried underground, for the spirit had to be free to come and go. A man's horse might be killed to provide transportation when he finally left for the spirit world.

When a man died, women mourners cut off their hair, gashed their legs, sometimes cut off a joint of a finger, and wailed ritualistically in sorrow. Male mourners cut their hair and left camp, either on a raid or to visit another band. During mourning, men wore old clothing and lived simply, and women carried out their mournful wailing at frequent intervals for up to a year.

Blackfoot clothing was similar to that of other northern tribes. In fact, persons were known to walk into an enemy camp and not realize where they were until they heard a strange language being spoken. In 1810, fur trader Alexander Henry the Younger, when describing Blackfoot men, said:

Their dress consists of a leather shirt, trimmed with human hair and quill-work, and leggings of the same; shoes are of buffalo skin dressed

in the hair; and caps, a strip of buffalo or wolf skin about nine inches broad, tied around the head. Their necklace is a string of grizzly bear claws. A buffalo robe is thrown over all occasionally. Their ornaments are few —feathers, quill-work, and human hair, with red, white, and blue earth, constitute the whole apparatus. (Coues, 1897, 2: 525)

In 1833, when Prince Maximilian saw the Blackfoot on the Upper Missouri, he described women's clothing as consisting of a dress:

. . . coming down to their feet, bound round the waist with a girdle, and is often ornamented with many rows of elks' teeth, bright buttons, and glass beads. The dress wraps over the breast, and has short, wide sleeves, ornamented with a good deal of fringe. . . . The lower arm is bare. The hem of the dress is likewise trimmed with fringes and scalloped. The women ornament their best dresses, both on the hem and sleeves, with dyed porcupine quills and thin leather strips, with broad diversified stripes of sky-blue and white glass beads. (Maximilian, 1906: 249)

Of course, for everyday wear, both men and women had plain, unadorned clothing. The women, in particular, required such costumes when butchering or skinning buffalo. Children's clothing was virtually a miniaturization of adult costumes, though very young boys and girls went entirely naked in summer. However, the Blackfoot were extremely modest and even in the warmest weather a man would retain a breechcloth while a woman would simply unfasten the sides of her dress below the arms to create a cooling effect.

The average tepee used 12 to 14 buffalo skins and required as many as 23 poles of lodgepole pine. Tepees were erected upon a basic foundation of four poles tied together at the top, the others being laid against them. Tepees always faced east, both as a protection against the prevailing winds and for religious reasons, in order to face the rising sun. The ears of the lodge, which regulated the draught, were controlled by two poles fitted through eyelets cut into their upper corners.

Some wealthy men had lodges made of 30 buffalo skins. These were unique structures, used only by warriors who had performed greats feats of a dual nature, e.g., killing two enemies with a single shot. The lodges were made in two sections, each forming a single-horse travois load. Such a lodge had two entrances and two fireplaces, one of the latter being reserved for religious purposes. A tepee of this size was an obvious sign of opulence. Prior to the acquisition of the horse, lodges were much smaller, as they had to be dragged about on dog travois. The travois was made by tying two poles together near the end; this was placed at the pack animal's neck, with the poles dragging behind on either side. A net or rack between the poles behind the animal provided the means for carrying several hundred pounds of goods. The only other method of transporting goods was in packs carried by dogs, horses, women, and sometimes men. Blackfoot did not use canoes.

Although life was difficult for the nomadic Blackfoot, they enjoyed themselves whenever opportunity arose. Winter nights were spent telling stories—Napi tales to the children and war experiences and culture tales to adults. Some would be invited for an All Smoke Ritual, lasting from sunset to sunrise, each participant singing his or her own religious and personal songs in turn, taking breaks from time to time to smoke or eat. Some gathered to gamble, playing the hand game[1] for hours as they sang gambling songs. Young men rode around camp after sunset, singing songs beside the lodges of the wealthy in hope that they would be fed.

There were plenty of games for children— hide and seek, archery contests, races, throwing mud balls, or sliding down hills on sleds made of ribs. A popular game for young boys was to pretend that they were a war party. Two scouts would be sent ahead to see if they could find meat drying on a rack in camp. Then, on a signal, the boys raced forward and helped themselves. Often, the scouts were seen by their mothers; instead of getting dried meat, the boys received a severe clubbing from the owner of the lodge.

Besides sledding in winter, boys played a spin top game, whipping rocks on ice to make them spin and to knock their opponents out of a circle. Each pretended his rock was a warrior and the opponent an enemy; if he knocked the rock away, it became his prize. Another winter game was a contest to see who could throw a long stick, called a snow snake, the farthest. Properly hurled, the snake could slide for hundreds of metres along the crust of the snow.

Horse racing was popular with young and old. Some men trained horses used only for racing. Large amounts of goods and possessions might be bet on races. In some instances, the Blackfoot made a temporary peace with other tribes just to hold horse races.

A pastime of the women, besides shinny[2] and gambling, was to have working bees, which gave the opportunity to visit and tell stories. Sometimes they got together to make a new tepee for a friend or a prospective bride, while in other instances several quillworkers would bring their work to a lodge where they could visit and drink tea while working. In times of peace when buffalo were plentiful, life became pleasant. During these periods people took time out from their labours to play, gamble, sing, and visit.

Blackfoot History

Pre-Contact Period

Some controversy exists about the earliest hunting grounds of the Blackfoot. Considerable credence has been given to an account given by a Cree to explorer David Thompson in the winter of 1787–8. The Cree man, who had been adopted by the Peigans, claimed that the Blackfoot had lived in the woodlands near the Eagle Hills, in present-day Saskatchewan, and had wandered from there onto the Plains. Other information suggests that in the 1600s the Shoshone and perhaps the Crow were in possession of southern Alberta and that the foothills area was occupied by Kutenais. A smallpox epidemic in the early 1700s is said to have severely depleted the Kutenais and left the region vacant for Blackfoot to occupy.

There can be little doubt that Blackfoot were absent from southern Alberta and northern Montana in the 1600s, but this does not necessarily mean that they were a woodland people. At that time frequent fires kept the prairies free from trees right to the banks of the North Saskatchewan River. It is therefore probable that the Blackfoot occupied the region from the Bow River to the North Saskatchewan for countless generations before moving south. As a people without horses they could move only short distances at a time and did not require a vast hunting area. Furthermore, their culture is almost completely devoid of woodland traits, even though these characteristics have persisted among the Plains Cree, who are known to have a woodlands origin.

The Eagle Hills may well have been included in the Blackfoot hunting grounds, for this area was simply an extension of the Plains. The depletion of the southern tribes by smallpox coincided with the Blackfoot acquisition of horses and guns, and a southern movement became practical; even at that date the foothills were one of the finest hunting regions and offered the added advantages of mild winters and chinook winds.

Blackfoot did not see a white man until the mid-1700s, but they already knew about him and his inventions. When the first traders arrived on Hudson Bay in the late 1600s, they bartered metal objects, beads, and other goods to local Indians. These passed from tribe to tribe until they reached the Plains. Such utensils as knives, axes, and pots were bought by the Blackfoot from middlemen, usually Cree. One of the most important objects they obtained was the gun, for it was unknown to their enemies to the south. With it they were able to make the Shoshone and others flee in terror.

During this same period, between 1700 and 1725, the Blackfoot also obtained horses. These were descendants of those brought by the Spanish when they invaded Mexico in the 1500s. Over the years the animals had been acquired by southern tribes and were passed northward. David Thompson was told how the Shoshone first attacked Blackfoot using horses that 'they rode, swift as the Deer, on which they dashed at the Peeagans, and with their stone Pukamoggan (clubs) knocked them on the head' (Glover, 1962: 241–2). But the Blackfoot soon acquired horses as well, and by the time the first white man, Anthony Henday, visited them in 1754 they were skilled riders.

Fur Trade Period

By the late 1700s, the first trading posts of the British had been built within reach of the Blackfoot; by the 1790s, posts such as Fort Edmonton and Rocky Mountain House were located at the edge of their hunting grounds. Because their territory lacked good water routes and had few beaver or fur-bearing animals, traders had no reason to build forts south of the North Saskatchewan. As a result, the tribes were able to acquire European trade goods but were free of non-Native influences and were not obliged to alter their hunting and subsistence patterns as did some of their northern neighbours.

During this time the Sarcees, an offshoot of the woodland Beaver tribe, became allies of the Blackfoot, as did the warlike Gros Ventres from the south. The Blackfoot had good relations with the British, although the Gros Ventres proved to be intractable and ultimately destroyed a trading post before withdrawing to the southern part of their hunting grounds, in what is now eastern Montana.

In 1806 the Blackfoot had their first experience with white men travelling the Missouri River. The Lewis and Clark expedition was returning from the Pacific when they became involved in an altercation with the Peigans and killed a man. For the next quarter-century anyone coming up the river was considered to be an enemy. Not only were the Blackfoot incensed about the killing, they soon discovered that American fur-gathering methods were unacceptable. Whereas British companies established forts and encouraged Indians to hunt and trap, Americans operated independently, with trappers and mountain men invading Indian hunting grounds and doing the trapping themselves. Blackfoot believed that these men were thieves and treated them accordingly.

In 1831 hostilities virtually ceased when the American Fur Company finally made peace with the Blackfoot tribes and built Fort Piegan on the upper waters of the Missouri. From that time on the Blackfoot became keen traders who pitted American against British to get the best prices for their robes, furs, and dried meat.

The population of the Blackfoot tribes varied considerably during the nineteenth century, being affected primarily by smallpox epidemics in 1837 and 1869, and measles and scarlet fever epidemics in 1819 and 1864. In 1823 the populations were estimated to be 4,200 Blackfoot, 2,800 Blood, and 4,200 Peigan, but in 1841, just after the smallpox epidemic, it was reduced to 2,100 Blackfoot, 1,750 Blood, and 2,500 Peigan. The tribes made a rapid recovery, and in 1869, just before the next epidemic, there were 2,712 Blackfoot, 2,544 Blood, and 3,960 Peigan. After further losses in 1869–70, the tribes maintained a relatively stable population until they settled on reserves.

Treaties and Reserves

The American government made its first treaty with the Blackfoot in 1855. Consideration was being given to building a railroad across the Plains and clear title to Indian lands was required. In the treaty the Blackfoot surrendered the major part of the Montana plains in exchange for exclusive hunting grounds, annuity payments, and other benefits. Two additional treaties, although never ratified, were made in 1865 and 1869, and the vast reservation was cut down in size by executive orders of 1873 and 1874 and by agreements in 1888 and 1896. These pacts were made almost exclusively with the South Peigan tribe, as the Bloods, North Peigans, and Blackfoot considered themselves to be 'British' Indians.

Within a few years of the 1855 treaty, non-Natives began trickling into Montana Territory. First there were free traders, missionaries, and government officials. Then the discovery of gold along the mountains brought a flood of prospectors, merchants, and ranchers. The opening of steamboat navigation on the Missouri provided easy access as far upriver as Fort Benton.

This influx resulted in clashes between Indians and settlers, reaching such proportions by 1866 that Montanans were referring to a 'Blackfoot war'. The events culminated with an attack in January 1870 by the US cavalry, under command of Major Eugene Baker, upon a peaceful camp of Peigans. The soldiers, looking for Mountain Chief's camp where they expected to find a number of men wanted for murder, mistakenly attacked Heavy Runner's camp, killing 173 persons; the majority were women and children. This event became known as the Baker massacre.

The attack drove a number of camps to the Canadian side, but there Indians were exposed to the unlimited sale of whisky by American traders at such posts as Fort Whoop-Up, Standoff, and Slideout. Catholic missionary Constantine Scollen observed, 'The fiery water flowed as freely . . . as the streams running from the Rocky Mountains, and hundreds of poor Indians fell victims to the white man's craving for money, some poisoned, some frozen to death whilst in a state of intoxication, and many shot down by American bullets' (Morris, 1880: 248). The traders operated with impunity on the Canadian side because the territory had been recently transferred from British to Canadian jurisdiction and no means of maintaining law and order existed. Finally, in 1874, the North-West Mounted Police were sent west to stop the illegal traffic. The police established friendly relations with the Blackfoot, and in 1877 the Canadian government successfully negotiated Treaty No. 7, the Blackfoot Treaty, with the tribes that had chosen to live in Canadian territory. In the treaty Indians gave up all rights to their hunting grounds in exchange for reserves (in the US they are reservations), annuity payments, and other

---

BOX 17.2

Chief Crowfoot

In 1877, when the Blackfoot Nation agreed to sign a treaty with the Canadian government, the final acceptance speech was made by Crowfoot, chief of the Siksika Nation. He stated:

> While I speak, be kind and patient. I have to speak to my people, who are numerous, and who rely on me to follow that course which in the future will tend to their good. The plains are large and wide. We are children of the plains, it is our home, and the buffalo has been our food always. I hope you will look upon the Blackfeet, Bloods and Sarcees as your children now, and that you will be indulgent and charitable to them. They all expect me to speak now for them, and I trust the Great Spirit will put into their breasts to be a good people—into the minds of the men, women and children, and their future generations. The advice given me and my people has proved to be very good. If the Police had not come to the country, where would we be all now? Bad men and whiskey were killing us so fast that very few, indeed, of us would have been left to-day. The Police have protected us as the feathers of the bird protect it from the frosts of winter. I wish them all good, and trust that all our hearts will increase in goodness from this time forward. I am satisfied. I will sign the treaty. (Morris, 1880: 272)

---

benefits. Besides the Blood, Blackfoot, Peigan, and Sarcee Indians, their mortal enemies, the Stoneys, also signed the treaty.

By 1880 the buffalo herds had been virtually exterminated in Blackfoot territory as the result of extensive slaughter by white hide hunters and the increasing incursions of Crees and Halfbreeds from the north. The buffalo had been the staff of life for the Blackfoot. With its destruction they had no recourse but to go to the reserves. In Montana, the South Peigans went to the Blackfeet Indian Reservation, while in southern Alberta the Bloods settled on their reserve—the largest in Canada—south of Fort Macleod, the Peigans near Pincher Creek, and the Blackfoot east of Calgary.

Although each tribe developed along separate lines after that date, particularly where two countries and two administrations were involved, there were many similarities in their history. All were obliged to turn to farming and ranching as a means of livelihood; log houses replaced tepees; Catholic, Methodist, or Anglican missionaries built boarding schools and took children away from homes; and the ration house became the centre of reserve life. Both governments expected Indians to become self-supporting through farming within a few years, and when this did not happen the authorities turned to a welfare system to keep them fed and quiet. Few, if any, long-range programs were introduced, and for many Indians it was as though time were standing still. Many believed that governments were simply feeding them until they all died from such common diseases as tuberculosis, venereal disease, and scrofula.

The introduction of ranching in the 1890s improved the lot of many Indians, for they found parallels between hunting buffalo and raising cattle. However, when the agricultural industry became mechanized, capital was required, which the Indians did not have, and the problems of severe winters left many destitute and unable to cope with the demands of the dominant society. For the Indians the reserves became a haven from the avariciousness, discrimination, and hostility they experienced in neighbouring towns. In Canada, efforts were made between 1907 and

FIGURE 17.2. Anglican Mission, Blackfoot Reserve, c. 1900. Although teachers were dedicated, students faced massive cultural conflicts as well as the threat of tuberculosis because of the confined facilities. (Courtesy of the Glenbow Museum, NC 5–61)

1921 to force the Indians to surrender large parts of their reserves. The Peigans gave up almost a third of their reserve in 1909 and the Blackfoot ended up losing about half of their reserve. Only the Bloods resisted all attempts to give up parts of their reserve. In Montana the Blackfeet were allotted individual lands in 1907, and unclaimed areas were sold. In 1918 Indians were given permission to sell their allotments, and as a result the reservation became a checkerboard of Indian- and white-owned lands.

Recent Trends

Little progress was made on reserves until after World War II. Prior to that time, children were sent to residential schools and came out either to farm or to go on welfare. The Sun Dance contin-

ued to be the main ceremony, and warrior societies still met to hold dances and rituals. During the first half of the twentieth century the reserves became a mixture of the old and new. Elders still wore braids and spoke only Blackfoot, while young men dressed in modern clothes, participated in rodeos, and tried to find work on or near the reserve. Government policies discouraged anyone from getting an education beyond the age of 16. Some exceptional ones did become nurses and teachers, but most merely subsisted within the protection of their reserves. The mortality rate was high, particularly among infants, and the average life span was less than half the national norm. Although conditions were depressed and depressing, people still enjoyed family life, visiting, dancing, and participating in Indian events.

After World War II the governments of both countries began to provide more funds for better schools, improved health services, economic development, and the encouragement of self-reliance. In the 1960s the first graduates of integrated schools began to assume more significant roles. Most employees on the reserves were Indian, including band managers, welfare officers, public works staff, police, and teachers. With a better education some chose to leave reserves to work in nearby cities, although they usually returned after a few years. Attempts were made to introduce new industries to the reserves, but with only moderate success. Such businesses as a pencil factory, mobile-home plant, post-peeling plant, commercial potato industry, retail stores, moccasin factory, and other firms have been opened. Some existed for only a few months but others carried on successfully, employing dozens of people from the reserves.

Although opportunities for education and employment improved, many serious problems remained. The extension of liquor privileges to the Blackfoot during the 1960s caused a traumatic social upheaval, which, while levelling off at a later date, remains a serious problem. To this has been added a drug problem, which also has been calamitous, particularly among the young. Welfare and a lack of employment on the reserves continue as major difficulties. Yet many Blackfoot would prefer to put up with a welfare system and lack of employment, rather than leave their extended families and go to the alien world of the cities. While there has been a migration to nearby cities of Calgary, Lethbridge, and Great Falls, it is nowhere near the mass exodus that has taken place off other western reserves.

During this period, the Blackfoot assumed more responsibility for their own affairs and have taken over many jobs formerly performed by outsiders. One will find Native accountants, managers, police, teachers, social workers, road crews, and office staff carrying out their tasks diligently and efficiently. Members of tribal councils serve on many boards and committees, both on reserve

and off, for the benefit of their people. Still others have gained favourable reputations as artists, musicians, rodeo performers, and in other fields.

By the 1970s television began to make rapid inroads into Blackfoot life and culture. English replaced Blackfoot as the primary language in many households and oral traditions were abandoned. The Sun Dance almost died out on most reserves, while Indian Days flourished. Pan-Indianism began to replace tribalism as dances, songs, and even ceremonies were borrowed from other regions. However, a consciousness of their unique history and culture also resulted in the formation of museums, cultural centres, dancing clubs, and other activities designed to help preserve cultural elements. Even the Sun Dance regained strength as conscious efforts were made to interest young people in Native religion and culture.

Conclusion

It should be apparent from this chapter that the Blackfoot have been a proud and independent people. As long as there were buffalo to hunt they needed no outside help, but once their primary means of subsistence was gone they had to settle on reserves. After almost one and a half centuries of sedentary life, they have retained many parts of their culture, but other elements have been lost.

Since the 1980s there have been rapid changes in lifestyle. On one hand, the effects of higher education and professionalization are being felt on all reserves. Native lawyers, educators, administrators, and other professionals are directing their attention to their tribes. At the same time, the loss of language and culture has become so widespread that attempts are being made to stem the tide. Language courses are offered on all reserves and efforts are being made to interest young people in cultural programs. These have had only limited success as the pervasive influence of television has virtually eliminated the Blackfoot language from many homes.

As part of a political and cultural awareness, the Blackfoot tribe has officially changed its name to the Siksika Nation, while the Peigans are being called both the Peigan Nation and the Pikuni Nation, and the Bloods the Kainaiowa Nation. The term for the Blackfeet Indians of Montana has remained unchanged. The allied Sarcee tribe is now called the Tsuu T'ina Nation.

Although the economies of all reserves are still basically rural, attempts have been made to provide basic retail services to tribal members rather than relying on nearby towns. The Siksika tribal offices are located in a large structure that also includes a shopping mall. Among the Indian-run businesses there are a supermarket, cafeteria, furniture store, video store, video arcade, and laundromat. Included in the complex are a service station, chartered bank, and post office.

The Blood Reserve has an administration building and a small mall with a supermarket, cafeteria, and bank. By the early twenty-first century, the reserve also had six Native-run service stations. The Peigan Reserve has a store, service station, and craft shop, while the Indians in Montana are still served by white merchants in Browning—a town located on the reservation.

The establishment of Indian-owned businesses has resulted in a significant loss of trade on the part of nearby merchants and has caused some tension. However, the trend appears to be towards more such services as tribes attempt to find additional sources of income on their own reserves.

Similarly, efforts are being made to provide more educational facilities on reserves. Many students are still being educated in nearby integrated schools but all reserves now have their own facilities for teaching elementary and high school. The Blood Reserve, in particular, has placed considerable emphasis on Indian-run schools where language and culture courses are in the curriculum. In addition, the Bloods operate Red Crow College, affiliated with Lethbridge Junior College, while the Siksika have courses offered on the reserve by Mount Royal College of Calgary. Also, the University of Lethbridge has a Native Studies program especially directed towards Blood and Peigan Indians. Many Indians from the region are attending colleges, their numbers limited by a cutback of federal government spending.

In the economic and social spheres, the situation on most reserves has not greatly improved in recent years. Alcohol and drug offences continue to be a major social problem while unemployment remains in the 75–80 per cent range. Yet, some progress has been made through rehabilitation programs, and gradually intoxication is becoming less and less socially acceptable. Many social dances and meetings are now completely alcohol-free at the insistence of the sponsors.

All reserves are now close to being self-governing. No Indian Department or other federal officials reside on reserves and the bulk of employees, administrators, accountants, outside workers, etc. are Native. Decisions of tribal councils still must be approved by the government, but usually this is merely a formality. The reserves, in varying degrees, are also assuming responsibility for education, social welfare, and the administration of justice.

There can be no question that the future will continue to bring pressures that result in the loss of cultural practices. If, however, they are sometimes replaced with newer practices, such as those offered by pan-Indianism, a Native, if not traditional Blackfoot, identity will remain.

Self-government is moving ahead rapidly, perhaps too rapidly, as people are given powers and authority that may clash with traditional practices. For example, nepotism was an integral part of Blackfoot family life, but may be detrimental to tribal administration in the future. Also, people who were nomadic did not practise saving or engage in long-range planning, for theirs was a day-to-day existence. The change to the new order may therefore bring with it pain and hardship. Yet the Blackfoot are a highly intelligent and adaptable people who are still in the throes of transition. The setbacks are there, but the progress is as impressive as it is inevitable.

Notes

1. The hand game is a team game, usually with four to a side, that involves players guessing which hand or hands hold one or more markers.
2. 'Shinny' is a term applied to a number of team games involving sticks and a ball or puck. Thus, in Canada street or pond hockey is sometimes called shinny.

References and Recommended Readings

Coues, Elliott, ed. 1897. *New Light on the Early History of the Greater Northwest: the Manuscript Journals of Alexander Henry and of David Thompson, 1799–1814*, 2 vols. New York: Francis Harper.

Dempsey, H.A. 1972. *Crowfoot, Chief of the Blackfeet*. Norman: University of Oklahoma Press.

———. 1978. *Charcoal's World*. Saskatoon: Western Producer Prairie Books.

———. 1980. *Red Crow, Warrior Chief*. Saskatoon: Western Producer Prairie Books. Dempsey is best known for his biographies. Although dealing with individuals, they are placed in a historic and cultural context and so relate to wider, even contemporary issues. Red Crow, for instance, is portrayed as a political realist who adjusts to the reserve system but at no point loses his Indianness.

———. 1994. *The Amazing Death of Calf Shirt and Other Blackfoot Stories*. Calgary: Fifth House.

Ewers, J.C. 1958. *The Blackfeet: Raiders on the Northwestern Plains*. Norman: University of Oklahoma Press. This is the most important book on the Blackfoot in the pre-reserve period. Also of interest to students of change is Ewers's *The Horse in Blackfoot Indian Culture*, published in 1955 by the Smithsonian Institution, Washington, DC.

Glover, Richard, ed. 1962. *David Thompson's Narrative, 1784–1812*. Toronto: Champlain Society.

Grinnell, G.B. 1913. *Blackfeet Indian Stories*. New York: Charles Scribner's Sons.

———. 1962 [1892]. *Blackfoot Lodge Tales*. Lincoln: University of Nebraska Press. These are classics on traditional Blackfoot culture.

Hungry Wolf, Beverly. 1980. *Ways of My Grandmothers*. New York: W. Morrow. This contemporary Blackfoot writer is not to be confused with Adolf Hungry Wolf, a prolific German-born Californian writer often assumed to be Indian.

Long Lance, Buffalo Child. 1928. *Long Lance: The Autobiography of a Blackfoot Indian Chief*. New York: Cosmopolitan Book Corporation. In spite of the title, this is a fictionalized account of Blackfoot life by a mixed black-Indian-white journalist from North Carolina who worked among the Blackfoot.

Maximilian, A.P. 1906. *Travels in the Interior of North America*, in R.G. Thwaites, ed., *Early Western Travels*, vols 22–4.

Morris, Alexander. 1880. *The Treaties of Canada with the Indians of Manitoba, the North-West Territories, and Kee-Wa-Tin*. Toronto: Willing and Williamson.

Mountain Horse, Mike. 1979. *My People the Bloods*. Calgary: Glenbow Museum. Written during the 1930s, this is a fascinating Native viewpoint of history and culture by one of the first graduates of the local mission school system.

Wissler, Clark. 1910. 'Material Culture of the Blackfoot Indians', *Anthropological Papers of the American Museum of Natural History* 5, 1: 1–175.

———. 1912. 'Social Life of the Blackfoot Indians', *Anthropological Papers of the American Museum of Natural History* 7, 1: 1–64.

———. 1913. 'Societies and Dance Associations of the Blackfoot Indians', *Anthropological Papers of the American Museum of Natural History* 11, 4: 359–460.

———. 1918. 'The Sun Dance of the Blackfoot Indians', *Anthropological Papers of the American Museum of Natural History* 16, 3: 223–70. Intended for the specialist, these are the most comprehensive works on the Blackfoot.

Suggested Web Sites

Blackfoot tribe (Montana): www.blackfeetnation.com
    Official site of the Montana Pikuni, with everything from origin stories to local news, all to powwow music.

Blackfeet Tribal Business Council (Montana):
    tlc.wtp.net/blackfeet.htm
    This site is most useful for its connections to the Montana-Wyoming Tribal Leaders Council.

Blood Tribe Economic Development:
    www.telusplanet.net/public/btecdev
    More than the name implies, with wide-ranging updated information.

Treaty 7: www.treaty7.org
    Although not always current, this is a major site with good connecting links.

CHAPTER 18

The Plains Metis

JOHN E. FOSTER

Introduction

During the 1870s, Louis Riel, the noted Metis leader, estimated the Metis population of western Canada at more than 25 per cent of the total Native population (40,000 Indians; 15,000 Metis). Such relative numbers, in addition to events in the Red River Settlement at the time of the first Riel Rising ('The Transfer') in 1869–70 and during the Saskatchewan Rebellion 15 years later, denote historical prominence for the Metis. This historical prominence and their distinctiveness from the Indians elicit questions about the nature of their way of life and the historical factors responsible for their origins. Prior to the establishment of the fur trade the Metis[1] did not exist. Yet as the golden era of the fur trade waned on the western Plains, the Metis comprised over one quarter of the Native population. They were a startlingly successful socio-cultural adaptation to a particular socio-economic environment.

Until recently, studies into the origins and nature of Metis communities have tended to emphasize their 'mixed-blood' heritage and to view the Metis as a 'widespread' phenomenon in the fur trade, arising 'naturally' out of the social interaction between Indians and Europeans (Giraud, 1945). More recent works point to the view that, rather than being a widespread and natural phenomenon, the Metis as communities were an infrequent, if not unique, socio-cultural product of particular events and circumstances (Peterson, 1978). Yet as occasional as the appearance of new Metis communities may be in the historical record, in at least two instances—in the Great Lakes region and on the Canadian Plains—they flourished. Their appearance would appear to be related to alterations in the circumstances of the fur trade, which, for some participants, constituted new opportunities. Of the few Metis communities that arose during the nearly four-century history of the fur trade in Canada, perhaps the largest and most familiar is the Metis of the prairie-parkland in what is today the Canadian West.

The Disciplinary Context

The disciplinary basis of study in this chapter is historical rather than anthropological. The objective of historical study is an understanding of how the historical actors, in this instance the Plains Metis and their neighbours, perceived, understood, and acted upon their experiences. To obtain this understanding, the historian identifies relevant sequences of events in the context of particular circumstances. The patterns of behaviour that emerge are analyzed in terms of the logical associations that constitute explanation. Frequently, because of gaps in the historical record, the historical explanations that result are the 'best' case rather than the 'only' case possible.

The historian's sources of data are surviving documents. Historical analysis emphasizes the consistencies and inconsistencies found within a document and among related documents and evaluates them in terms of the historian's other experiences. The historian's analysis is not necessarily tied to a methodology that could be identified as belonging to a social science discipline. In historical analysis, empathy for the protagonists as much as rigorous logic should be reflected in sensitive and mature judgements that constitute historical explanations. In historical works of note, it is no accident that links of social class and/or ethnicity frequently tie the historian to his or her subject matter. Some historians would argue that a unicultural chain linking historical actors to recorder to historian provides a richness of experience that results in analysis and explanation capable of revealing the fullest range of complexities and the subtlest of distinctions involved in particular human experiences.

A quick perusal of scholarship bearing on the Metis in recent years demonstrates that, with notable exceptions, scholars in disciplines other than history have made the significant contributions to the field. Historians, essentially 'middle-class' and/or English-speaking, appear to have had difficulty in perceiving experiences of substance in the lives of the Metis. In part, the problem lies in the fact that the Plains Metis, with the exception of Louis Riel, have authored few of the documents that record their history. Most existing records were written by 'outsiders'. Yet the skilled historian should be capable of a document analysis that would guard against the biases inherent in such sources. The critical factor explaining the poverty of significant historical results is the historian's inability in this instance to draw upon the same wealth of personal experience in analyzing his subject matter. The socio-cultural distinctions between a twentieth-century historian in Canada and a British-born Hudson's Bay Company officer, during the period of modernization after 1820, are minimal in comparison with the distinctions between the same historian and a Metis buffalo hunter of that earlier era. This sense of the inadequacy of the historian's socio-cultural perspectives for analyzing the documents bearing on

the Metis has led some historians to search out new perspectives.

Some recent historical works have emphasized the benefits to historians to be derived from a quantification approach. Analysis of census documents, parish records, and 'Halfbreed Scrip' records have shown much in terms of Metis demography. The historical writings of Douglas Sprague and Gerhard Ens are useful examples. Others have turned to the findings and approaches of other disciplines to provide suggestions. In doing so they do not seek to abandon the strengths of their own disciplinary approach: rather, they seek new perspectives from which the contents of familiar documents can be analyzed to give forth understandings not apparent previously in historical analysis. It remains to be seen whether these perspectives will prove useful.

As with all study there is a personal dimension to the selection of subject matter. Experiences in my youth, expressed in the words of the dean of western Canadian historians, W.L. Morton, played a role: 'Teaching inspired by the historical experience of metropolitan Canada cannot but deceive, and deceive cruelly, children of the outlying sections. Their experience after school will contradict the instruction of the history class' (Morton, 1980). These explanations offered in the official histories did not seem to match the social reality I perceived in the surrounding community. The schoolyards of post-World War II western Canada reflected ethnocultural groups not evident in Canadian history texts. More frequently, where I expected historical explanation the official texts simply chose to ignore the subject. Where were the eastern Europeans, the Asians, and the Native peoples? Inevitably, my quest for explanations of the nature of my community led to an interest in 'beginnings'. This interest breached the barrier of the transfer and settlement to the pre-1870 world of peoples who were ancestral to a significant number of westerners today. And the historical explanations that have emerged since are not those that reading in the official histories would have predicted.

Origins

The origins of the Plains Metis are to be seen in the appearance of *les gens libres* (freemen) about the posts of the St Lawrence–Great Lakes trading system extended to the valleys of the Red, Assiniboine, and North Saskatchewan rivers in the closing quarter of the eighteenth century. Some *engages Canadien* (contracted servants) ended their employment in the interior rather than at Montreal. Coming together in two or three household bands, they supplied provisions and furs to the forts. Their survival and, in time, flourishing way of life required the active co-operation of the traders in the trading posts and, at the very least, the toleration of the Indian bands with whom they shared the prairie-parkland region. The explanation for the historical events and circumstances encouraging the appearance of these *gens libres* is to be found in part in fur trade experiences farther east in an earlier era.

When Western Europeans first contacted western hemisphere Indians with a view to trade rather than to settle, similar commercial systems marked their behaviour. From the coast of Brazil in the sixteenth century to the shores of Hudson Bay in the latter part of the seventeenth century similar trading systems announced the presence of Europeans. Coastal factories warehoused goods and furs for transshipment after Indian traders arrived from the interior to participate with their European counterparts in the ritual of exchange known as the fur trade. The French with Samuel de Champlain extended this coastal factory system up the St Lawrence to Quebec in 1608 and later, after the formation of alliances with members of the Huron Confederacy, to Montreal after 1641. The Huron were masterful traders, gathering furs from throughout the Great Lakes region and the Canadian Shield and transporting them to Montreal. French 'factory representatives', known as *coureurs de bois* ('woods runners'), journeyed sometimes illegally between Montreal and the Indian villages, facilitating trading contracts between particular Huron traders and particular Montreal merchants. In their role as brokers, they behaved in a manner that would win the approbation of their Indian hosts. They joined them in war; they shared their material good fortune; and they married women of the leading trading families, strengthening social ties to the band. The children of such unions, raised in Huron villages, grew to maturity as Huron. The very few raised in the colony of New France would grow to maturity as *Canadien*. There was little or no room for a Metis community to arise quickly in the coastal factory system of trade.

The identity of individuals performing the role of the Indian trader in the St Lawrence–Great Lakes trading system was irrevocably altered when Iroquois attacks in the winter of 1648–9 initiated the destruction of Huronia. In the aftermath, the French and the successors to the Huron, the Odawa, attempted to re-establish the coastal factory system. Social and political circumstances in the Great Lakes region would not permit it. The Iroquois, allied first to the Dutch and then to the English at New York, harassed the hunters on the Shield and the Indian traders journeying to and from Montreal. During the half-century following the destruction of Huronia, Indians ceased to perform the tasks of the Indian trader. The coastal factory system of trade gave way to the *en derouine* fur trade (itinerant peddling).

The essential difference between the coastal factory system and the *en derouine* fur trade saw Euro-Canadians[2] replace Indian traders in the task of trading furs from the hunting bands and transporting them to Montreal (Nute, 1966; Peterson, 1978). From a principal post in the Great Lakes area, such as Michilimackinac, under the command of a military officer appointed by the royal government in France, individual *bourgeois* (merchants) dispatched small parties of men *en derouine*, to trade with the hunting bands on their home grounds. These trading parties were led by a *commis* (clerk) whose success as a broker was essential to the success of the *en derouine* trade. Similar to the *coureur de bois* of a previous era, the *commis* found it useful to join his Indian suppliers on some of their war junkets, to share his material good fortune with them, and to take a country wife from among their womenfolk.

For those *commis* who succeeded in establishing enduring households, the country wife could be of critical importance. In addition to supplying vital social linkages to some of the bands, her economic skills could be essential in maintaining the *commis* in his broker role. In time, successful *commis* could emerge as *bourgeois*. The circumstances of the *bourgeois* appear to have been characterized by large households that occupied pivotal positions in the networks of extended families found throughout the Great Lakes region. In such extended families, many sons lived in much the same way as did Indian hunters and trappers: those sons most talented as commercial brokers, however, succeeded their fathers as *commis*. Daughters were sometimes given in marriage to *bourgeois* and *commis* in order to establish an alliance. The communities of Great Lakes Metis that arose out of this process survived Britain's conquest of New France by extending their kin ties to include British merchants who supplanted French and *Canadien bourgeoisie* after 1763. The appearance of American settlers—not traders—a half-century later would mark the demise of the Great Lakes Metis.

The *En Derouine* Trade in the West

A variety of factors, including distance and time, necessitated alterations in the *en derouine* fur trade to make it functional in the *pays de la mer de l'ouest*, the interior Plains over the height of land beyond the Lakehead. By 1680, the French had penetrated to the Lakehead; yet a hiatus of a half-century would follow before they would move farther west in strength. Historians have seen in La Verendrye's achievements the activities of a fur trader masquerading as an explorer and a colonizer (Morton, 1929). An equally legitimate interpretation would emphasize La Verendrye's solutions to the logistics problems. The supplies

of side pork and corn that sustained the fur brigades from Montreal could not supply the brigades beyond Kaministiquia and still contribute to the sustenance of brigades returning to Montreal. Wild rice (actually a grass), harvested by the Indians in the shallow areas of the lakes of the Canadian Shield west to Lake Winnipeg and traded at a series of provisioning posts marking the route westward, became the basis on which the St Lawrence–Great Lakes trading system expanded to the Great Plains.

The Seven Years' War caused a momentary retreat from the western lands before the British merchants, known as 'pedlars', returned with renewed vigour. In the violent and bloody competition that ensued among rival syndics of pedlars, the *en derouine* system was an effective tool. In time, the logic of monopoly inherent in the European end of the fur trade asserted its wisdom with the emergence, by the 1780s, of the North West Company to dominate the Montreal trade. Over the next four decades it would use the *en derouine* system as an effective competitive tool against the Hudson's Bay Company. In these circumstances, the *en derouine* system was also important as a means of solving the perennially critical problem of provisioning personnel.

The high profits of the North West Company rested on the annual labour-intensive canoe brigade carrying furs from the 'Eldorado' of the fur trade, the Athabasca country, to Grand Portage and later Fort William at the Lakehead, to be exchanged for trade goods canoed from Montreal. This brigade could not complete the round trip in the seasons of open water if it had to hunt or fish its way across a sizable portion of the continent. Caches of provisions in posts at strategic locations along its route of travel were essential to its success. In addition, many of the *engages* who paddled the canoes of this and the Saskatchewan and Red River brigades had to be fed during at least part of the winter months. It was for this reason that North West Company posts of the parkland region gave priority to provisions as well as to furs in their trading activities.

The problems and costs involved in provisioning personnel encouraged North West Company wintering partners (*bourgeois*) to supply small parties of men with goods to go *en derouine* with bands of Indians 'pounding' buffalo in the parkland during the winter months. (The 'pound' was an enclosure of wood and brush into which buffalo were driven and/or enticed to be killed. Where terrain permitted, the 'jump'—a cliff over which buffalo were driven—was used. With the advent of the horse the 'surround' was used with increasing frequency.) This practice, in addition to reducing demands on the posts' provisions, allowed the men to encourage the Indians to trade furs and surplus provisions at the fort of their employer.

The Emergence of the Plains Metis

By the 1780s some older *engages*, who had taken country wives from bands with whom they had wintered, chose to become free on the Plains and live out their lives primarily as buffalo hunters. As these men were frequently past their physical prime, and as they tended to have large families, who were provisioned at the expense of the post, the *bourgeois* would view positively such a cost-saving step. The usual practice of the fur companies was to give their *engages* their freedom at Montreal, far from where some of them might be tempted to initiate a competing trade. On the Upper Saskatchewan, however, the vast distances from the northwest to Montreal precluded all but the best-financed and -organized from adopting such a course of action.

The trading Indians, Cree and Assiniboine, who had carried furs to the Hudson's Bay Company posts on Hudson Bay, found themselves without a middleman role when the venerable old Company followed its new rival, the North West Company, into the interior after 1773. Previously, these bands had hunted buffalo in the parkland regions during the half-year they were not engaged in the annual journey to the coastal factories. With the end of their annual trading journeys they began to hunt buffalo year-round. During the late spring, summer, and early autumn they followed the herds from the parklands out onto the prairie. Their adaptation to year-round buffalo hunting was facilitated through the use of the horse, a superior means of hunting buffalo that had appeared a half-century earlier among the Blackfoot to the south and west. The horse would prove to be an innovation of significant consequence.

The Cree and Assiniboine bands who became year-round buffalo hunters became less dependent on European goods. Their appearance at the provisioning posts along the North Saskatchewan River became less frequent and more irregular. The fur trade could not be adequately provisioned by such suppliers. Freemen with their greater interest in European goods remained in relatively close contact with the provisioning post. Their importance to the North West Company was reflected in the higher prices they received and in the services extended to them that were not given in the Indian trade. In time the Hudson's Bay Company looked to the bands of *gens libres* for provisions. Mutual dependence tied the trader and the freeman hunter. Thus the households of the freemen proved admirably suited to fill the provisioning niche in the western fur trade. From their first appearance their behaviour distinguished them from the Indians. They pursued buffalo and beaver with an assiduity that the Indians believed to be unnecessary. The Cree of the region were tolerant of these newcomers with whom they had ties of kinship. They came to identify the freemen as *O-tee-paym-soo-wuk*, 'their-own-boss'. In time the newcomers would become the Plains Metis.

More by implication than by explication, an earlier generation of historians tended to see the Metis as products in large part of 'Indianized' or 'failed' Euro-Canadians. Influenced by the sense of rascality and outlawry associated with the *coureur de bois* of an earlier era, historians saw French-Canadian males who established Metis households as choosing the licentious freedom of

Indian ways rather than succeeding to the family and citizenship responsibilities of their own heritage (Saunders, 1939; Giraud, 1945).

Recent research, in contrast, would suggest that the choice of these men in 'going free' with their families in the interior was not a function of 'Indianization' or of a 'failed' Euro-Canadian; rather, it was the expression of a deep-rooted Euro-Canadian ethos of that era in the context of the western fur trade at the end of the eighteenth century (Moogk, 1976). To these men, work in the service of others was a temporary circumstance, tolerable only until one found the means of establishing himself as his own master, as a man of consequence. One behaviourial expression of this ethos, in the context of the St Lawrence–Great Lakes trading system on the western Plains at the end of the eighteenth century, was the freeman. Those *gens libres* who established enduring households that were succeeded by a later generation of buffalo hunters became the Metis. Thus, a significant dimension in the heritage of the Metis is an ethos that heavily influenced the lives of adult males whose cultural founts were pre-industrial France and Britain.

Another source contributing in some instances to the appearance of the Plains Metis were those active servants who did not leave their employment but established households in neighbouring Indian bands. Such 'house' Indian bands were a feature of the fur trade throughout its history. The households of servants in these bands were marked by frequent changes in personnel. Over half a century later an Anglican missionary described the household circumstances of these 'unskilled' servants in the fur trade:

The Hon. Company's servants seldom continue more than 3 years at the same post, and often only one. In the summer the whole of their time is occupied in voyaging upon the rivers, carrying out the furs which they had traded in the winter from the Indians; and returning with a new outfit for the trade of the ensuing year. . . . When a young voyager comes to his winter quarters, he finds he wants many things to fit him for this new existence which he has entered upon. He wants his leather coat, trowsers, mittens, duffle socks and shoes, all then must be made and kept in repair. He has not time to do this himself; he applies to an Indian who has got some daughters, or two or three wives. . . . thus the unfortunate voyager forms his connexion with the natives and raises an offspring. He may continue here two or three years, and enjoy the benefit of his helpmate. He goes off in the summer, returns in the autumn, and perhaps finds the same young woman given to another. This does not distract his mind, he forms another connexion as speedily as possible; by this time he believes he cannot get on without a woman. The next time he leaves his winter quarters, he perhaps is sent to a post 600 or 1000 miles from his former wives. . . . The same course is run until old age and grey hairs are upon him. (Cockran, 1975)

For these men the centre of their social world was the society of their workmates. Here they evaluated themselves in terms of how they felt they measured up to particular masculine virtues. It was in this society over half a century later that the demi-legendary Paulet ['Little' or 'Tiny'] Paul emerged:

[He was] a giant in stature and strength . . . with a voice like thunder and a manner as blustery and boisterous as March, eyes like an eagle and a pair of fists as heavy and once, at least, as deadly as cannon balls. . . . When the different brigades met at York Factory, and the question which could produce the best man, came to be mooted over a regal [*regale*] of Hudson's Bay rum, he was ever the first to strip to the waist and stand forth to claim that honour for the Blaireau ['Badgers', the name of the Saskatchewan York boat brigade]. . . . Such encounters, off hand at first no doubt, and having their inspiration in the rum keg, came to be a recognized institution of the trip. . . . [Michael Lambert] was the darling of the Taureaux ['Bulls', the name of the Red River York boat brigade]. . . . They liked Poulet [sic] because he was a hard man to beat, but they adored Michael because he could beat Poulet [sic]. . . . There was Jimmy Short, otherwise known as Checkam, who could put up an ugly fight. . . . He too had stood up for the honour of the Taureaux against Poulet [sic], but only to be knocked out. Still he had lived to tell the tale and that alone was an honour not to be despised. (Gunn, 1930)

The evidence is not conclusive about the extent to which these men and their households contributed to the Plains Metis tradition. In several instances, their descendants took treaty as Indians during the 1870s.

The Red River Metis

The confluence of the Assiniboine and Red rivers (downtown Winnipeg today) was the heart of the Red River Settlement, and the settlement itself played a major role in the history of the Plains Metis as possibly a majority of the Metis were found within its boundaries and hinterland. The heterogeneous nature of the settlement's population coloured Metis experience. The settlement divided at the junction of the two rivers with the Metis (numbering approximately 55 per cent of the population in 1835) and a few *Canadien* households occupying narrow river lots to the south and west of the fork. To the north, down the Red River toward Lake Winnipeg, lay the river-lot farms of the other Metis people in Red River, the 'Hudson Bay English' (30 per cent of the population, 1835), at Kildonan, the original Selkirk settlers (numbering 8 per cent, 1835), and at St Peters, the Indian village (Saulteaux and Swampy Cree numbering 7 per cent, 1835). Religion and language marked the basic division between 'French and Catholic' and 'British and Protestant' in Red River, although the two Metis

communities could make themselves understood in Cree or Saulteaux. Churches, schools, and the instruments of local government such as courts and the appointed Council of Assiniboia underlined distinctions between Red River and the circumstances of Metis living on the Saskatchewan.

The Metis hunting about the junction of the Red and Assiniboine rivers had welcomed the appearance of the Highland Scots crofters, the original Selkirk settlers, in the spring of 1812. Although these settlers were assisted by the agents of Lord Selkirk and the Hudson's Bay Company, the settlers were appreciated as a ready market for surplus buffalo meat and pemmican as well as for fish and water fowl. Yet the settlers' involvement in the competition between the North West Company and the Hudson's Bay Company polarized positions. The North West Company convinced the Metis that the settlers and the Hudson's Bay Company were usurping Metis lands. Almost inevitably, violence escalated to the Battle of Seven Oaks, 19 June 1816, when a party of Metis, commanded by the British-educated Metis son of a Nor'wester, Cuthbert Grant, killed more than 20 of a mixed party of settlers and Company servants, including the colony governor, Robert Semple. The legacy of this battle coloured relations between 'French and Catholic' and 'British and Protestant' for the next century.

The end of competition in the fur trade in 1820 witnessed the victory of the revitalized Hudson's Bay Company over the North West Company. Yet a majority of the officers in the new concern were former 'Nor'westers'. These Highland Scots merchant-adventurers based in Montreal had been more than able successors to the *Canadien* and French merchants, extending the St Lawrence–Great Lakes trading system to the Arctic and Pacific coasts. Their élan and esprit de corps had all but defeated the Hudson's Bay Company when their own shortcomings, a deficiency of system and regulation, made them vulnerable to the 'modern' managers who took control of the Hudson's Bay Company in 1810 (Rich, 1960). For these new men, effective

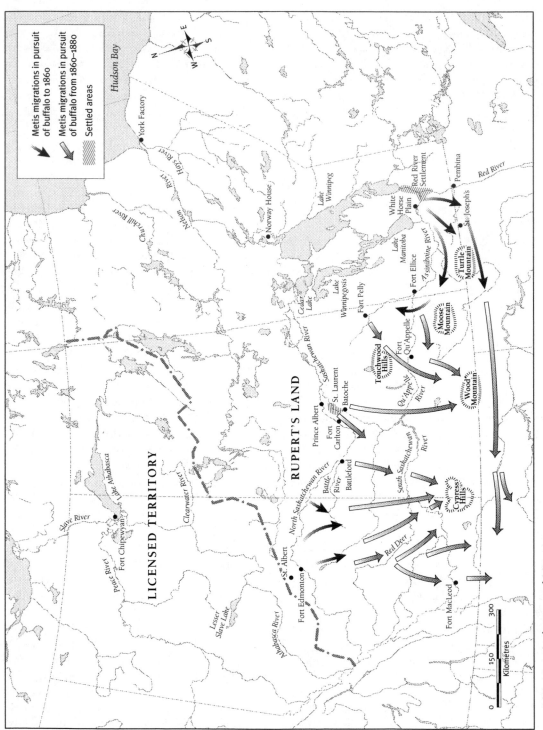

MAP 18.1. Metis Settlement and Migrations

management emphasized the efficiency of the process involved rather than the social interests of the participants. In the face of such management objectives the deficiencies of the pre-industrial ways and means of the Nor'westers were glaringly evident. They were defeated by the commercial superiority of modern management in the conduct of the fur trade.

The victory of the Hudson's Bay Company marked the dramatic beginning of a new era for the inhabitants of the old Northwest. The governor and committee of the Hudson's Bay Company, besides emphasizing modern business practices to control costs and maximize long-term profits, envisaged a settlement at the junction of the Red and Assiniboine rivers in harmony with the interests of the fur trade. Stimulated in part by the philanthropic efforts of Thomas Douglas, Earl of Selkirk, the settlement received support from the Company even before it passed into the hands of the Company in 1835. In a letter in 1822 to their principal officer in Rupert's Land, the governor and committee explained their reasons for encouraging a migration of Metis peoples to the Red River Settlement:

> It is both dangerous and expensive to support a numerous population of this description [Metis] in an uneducated and savage condition, and it would be impolitic and inexpedient to encourage and allow them to collect together in different parts of the country where they could not be under any proper superintendence. (Governor and Committee, 1938)

Throughout the 1820s, Metis families drifted into the settlement to squat for the most part with Company approval on river lots to the south and west of the forks. There they commenced the annual pattern of activities that would mark their way of life in Red River.

The Buffalo Hunt

Late in spring, most Metis left their river lots, some with small plots planted with root vegetables and barley, harnessed oxen or horses to their two-wheeled Red River carts, and set out south to the rendezvous point near Pembina, on the border with United States territory. Only the elderly, the sick, and the crippled remained at home. Many households, having a very skilled buffalo hunter or more than one hunter, hired *engages,* no doubt from among kinsmen, to drive additional carts and to participate in the processing.

At Pembina, a general assembly of the hunters met to select officers and promulgate basic rules. Images of the militia in New France and Lower Canada are suggested both in the selection of officers and in the promulgation of hunt rules. The first order of business was to choose 10 *capitaines* who in turn would each choose 10 *soldats*. The foremost of the *capitaines* was the hunt leader, variously styled as the 'War Chief' and *le President*. In addition, 10 guides were selected from among the hunters past their physical prime. No doubt the selection of the 10 captains and the 10 guides reflected the socio-political concerns of the Metis in terms of the major extended families in the community, but no documentary evidence has been found, as yet, to confirm such a pattern.

Social and political authority among the Metis was a function of an individual's achievements—his reputation—and it was characterized by limited powers, in terms of both duration and extent, authorized by the community. On the buffalo hunt each guide and each captain commanded for a day. In a cycle of 10 days all of the guides and captains would have command of the hunt. At dawn, the raising of the hunt flag above a guide's cart signalled his command for that day. With camp struck, carts packed, and livestock harnessed or herded, the hunt, in two or more lines of carts abreast, set out on a course determined by the guide-of-the-day. The captain-of-the-day positioned his soldiers ahead, abreast, and to the rear of the line of march. The soldiers sought buffalo, but they were also on guard against the Dakota (sometimes known as the Sioux), who claimed the resources of the lands on which the Metis frequently hunted. Two soldiers

FIGURE 18.1. Gabriel Dumont, buffalo hunter and military leader (c. 1880). (Courtesy Glenbow Archives, NA–1063–1)

launched the hunters forward into a crescendo of gunfire, stampeding buffalo, galloping horses, and exulting or cursing hunters. Clouds of dust, permeated with the smell of sweat and blood, would part momentarily to reveal possibly a downed rider lying lifeless or perhaps seeking assistance from those nearby. Others, surprisingly unaware of the chaos and confusion about them, closed with their prey. At the command *allez*, the individual hunter, astride his prized mount, had galloped forward. His horse then chose a target and closed with it. When nearly abreast of the buffalo the hunter in a single fluid motion lowered the barrel of his gun, fired his ball, and dropped a personal article, usually an article of clothing, to mark his kill. Instinctively his horse sidestepped the tumbling carcass and sought out another target while the hunter on his mount's back reloaded. Pouring a 'guesstimated' amount of gun powder from his powder horn into the barrel of his gun, the hunter then spat a lead ball, from those he carried in his mouth, into the barrel. The charge was rammed home with an abrupt smack of the butt on the saddle pommel or the hunter's thigh. Holding the gun upright until his mount closed with another quarry the hunter, again in a single fluid motion, lowered the barrel of his gun and fired.

In a matter of minutes the hunt for the day was over. The dust and noise receded to reveal hunters busy butchering their kill. From two to five buffalo would be killed by each hunter, depending on ability and particular circumstances. Later, when repeating rifles were introduced in the closing

always rode together: by riding away from each other at a gallop or toward each other they could signal the hunt as to whether buffalo or Dakota had been sighted. Whatever the quarry, the hunt flag was lowered, passing authority from the guide and captain-of-the-day to the hunt leader. At any hint of danger the carts were circled with shafts inward to corral the stock. If buffalo were sighted the hunters assembled in line abreast under the command of the hunt leader.

Slowly the line of hunters advanced. Severe sanctions in the rules of the hunt awaited any brash hunter who broke the line to rush the herd. At the quarter-mile mark the command *allez* years of the 1860s, kills of over 25 buffalo for one hunter would be recorded. Beginning with his last kill the hunter began butchering the carcasses in preparation for the women to dry the meat and manufacture pemmican. Cut into strips the meat was hung on racks to dry in the sun and over fires. When dried meat was pounded to flake into a coarse powder and an equal amount of melted fat was added, together with berries and other edibles in season, the resulting product was pemmican. Cooled and sewn into 90-pound buffalo-hide bags, pemmican could be transported and stored with ease. The Company's provisioning posts on the North Saskatchewan and the Red and Assiniboine rivers purchased pemmican and dried meat for their own needs, with the surplus being delivered to Norway House to provision the York boat brigades and for transshipment to northern posts to supplement the diet of fish.

Metis hunters and Plains Indians preferred the meat of the heifer or young cow. With the horse this target could be selected with much regularity. This practice contributed substantially to the demise of the buffalo.

The hunt remained a dangerous undertaking. In addition to the accidents associated with it there was the hostility of the Dakota. In most instances, violent confrontations were relatively short-lived and involved small numbers. In July 1851, however, the hunt from White Horse Plain, a Metis settlement a few miles to the west of Red River, came under sustained attack. They withstood the onslaught with only one dead and a few wounded while inflicting casualties that forced the Dakota to break off the action. On this occasion the Metis had corralled their stock behind the encircled carts while the women and children took positions behind them. The men charged forward the distance of a gunshot to scrape gun pits in the prairie sod. From these vantage points they kept the attacking Yankton Dakota from destroying their stock and thus, at the very least, leaving them stranded on the prairie. The *Canadien* priest who accompanied the hunt stood astride a cart, crucifix in one hand, tomahawk in

the other, exhorting his flock to persevere. The Metis victory at Grand Coteau confirmed in their own minds their paramountcy on the prairie west of Red River.

The return of the summer hunt to Red River saw 'recognized hunters' rather than individual hunters negotiate the sale of their pemmican and dried meat, at prices that remained low and varied little over the years. The recognized hunters appear to have been in many instances the heads of extended families with whom the Company sought influence. A smaller autumn hunt left the settlement late in October or early November to provision the Metis for the winter months. It was sufficient to sustain the leisurely round of visits among kinsmen, punctuated by celebrations associated with numerous weddings. During these months not a few Metis found themselves, over the years, increasingly attracted to the illicit trade in furs.

The summer hunt returned to Red River Settlement usually in time to harvest what insects, drought, or floods had allowed to survive on their small plots of cultivated land. To sustain their stock over winter each settler looked to the mile of land behind his river lot for hay. For some families this hay was insufficient. Each year they joined others waiting for the local Council of Assiniboia to declare the opening date for haying on the prairie lands beyond the hay privilege. Having spotted a likely area prior to the beginning of haying, the hunter and his family rushed to the area on the appointed date, claiming all the hay that he could encircle in a single day's cutting. The introduction of mechanical reapers in the late 1850s gave some farmers in Red River a notable advantage over Metis hunters.

The 'Free Trade' Controversy

Before 1820, in the shadow of the competing fur trade giants, a few enterprising traders, apparently linked to Great Lakes Metis families, had managed to establish small trading operations in the valley of the Red River. With the end of competition, the victorious Hudson's Bay Company, using a variety of successful carrot-and-stick techniques, stifled the illicit trade. Geographical isolation was the essential circumstance maintaining the Company's monopoly for the next two decades. Routes to outside markets, other than those of the Company, were either too difficult or too dangerous to sustain commercial links. Besides, the Company tied the Metis to their interests with a sinecure for their leader, Cuthbert Grant, entitled 'Warden of the Plains' and paying £300 per year. As a result, the Company took little interest in the exchange of furs between Indians and their Metis kinsmen, for most if not all the furs eventually found their way to the Company's warehouses. But with the end of geographical isolation, the Company viewed such exchanges in a far more negative light.

In 1844, Norman Kittson, a Canadian, opened a post for the American Fur Company at Pembina on the Red River, a few yards south of the international boundary. A knowledgeable trader, with kin ties to the Marion family that linked him to the Metis, Kittson would not fall victim to the Company's competition as his predecessors had. His post would become a beacon to enterprising young Metis who would see in its existence opportunities their fathers had known but which in recent years had seemed to recede before their grasp. In time, the Red River Metis leader, Cuthbert Grant, would lose his following, giving way to younger men who would challenge the Company's hegemony.

Within a decade of the end of the fur trade competition in 1820 the Hudson's Bay Company had slashed expenses, in part, by reducing its purchase of 'country provisions' and regularizing continuing purchases to the point where there was little variation in amount or price from year to year. Thus, by the 1830s the Metis found their market for pemmican and dried meat satiated. Between 1820 and 1840 the population of Metis doubled. At Red River in the same period the number of carts involved in the hunt grew from 540 to 1,210. As the Company dealt only with recognized hunters in purchasing the produce of

the hunt, it was increasingly difficult for young men to achieve this status and the social prestige and financial rewards it entailed. By the 1840s, opportunity for many young Metis males, as it was defined in terms of their own cultural traditions, was shrinking. No doubt many Metis regarded the construction of Kittson's post as a godsend.

From the time of their first appearance on the western Plains in the latter quarter of the eighteenth century the *gens libres* had traded furs with Indian kinsmen. While such exchanges acknowledged socio-economic ties between kinsmen, there could be, as well, a commercial dimension to the transactions. Both Indians and freemen in the period before 1820 were aware that the trading companies paid higher prices to freemen than to Indians to encourage further the freemen's demonstrated diligence in pursuing both provisions and furs. In some circumstances this price difference could be exploited by Indians through their freemen kinsmen. In these occasional trading activities the freeman kept alive the image of the *commis* conducting an *en derouine* trade. This image was a cultural legacy to which the Metis of the Red River region could turn when the promised rewards of the buffalo hunt became increasingly difficult to realize and when Kittson's post seemed to provide a means to return to the entrepreneurial ways of the past

The Hudson's Bay Company's opposition to the free traders culminated in the Sayer trial of 1849. Guillaume Sayer and three other Metis were accused of trading furs in violation of the Company's charter. A committee of 10 Metis, probably headed by Louis Riel *père*, assembled an armed mob of 300 Metis to surround the courthouse and give expression to their views. The trial proceeded with Sayer being found guilty, largely on the basis of his son's testimony. The Company's chief factor at Red River, John Ballenden, satisfied with a legal victory in the courts of Rupert's Land in support of the Company's charter, addressed the court, requesting additional charges against Sayer be dropped and punishment suspended. When the court agreed, a French-speaking member of the jury, misconstruing developments, rushed to the courthouse door to cry *'le commerce est libre.'* His words were greeted with a *feu de joie*, much self-congratulatory back-slapping, and general merriment. Before their eyes the Company's officers saw legal victory dissolve into commercial defeat. Henceforth, the Company would have to meet the challenge of the free traders through appropriate business techniques and not with the legal canons of its charter. The Metis in turn felt they had successfully asserted their hinterland interests in the face of the agents of the London metropolis who, in defining new opportunities for themselves, seemed to deny it to those residing in the region.

The Metis victory at the Sayer trial was expressed in the 1850s with the appearance of successful free traders such as Pascal Breland and Louis Goulet. Besides strengthening the settlement's commercial ties with St Paul in Minnesota Territory, they extended business links southwest towards the Missouri, west towards the Qu' Appelle Valley, and north towards the North Saskatchewan River.

The Buffalo Robe Trade

Years earlier, in the decade after 1800, American fur traders on the lower reaches of the Missouri River identified buffalo robes, cow pelts taken between the middle of November and the middle of March, as a marketable product in the growing cities of northeastern North America. While there was no market in Europe, North Americans valued buffalo robes as sleigh throws and bedcovers and sometimes as a raw material for the manufacture of winter boots and coats. From a few hundred robes a year before 1820 the market expanded to more than 100,000 robes a year a half-century later. After 1850 the heads of several extended families among the Metis emerged as traders (*bourgeois*) whose networks of hunters and their families, *hivernants* (winterers), chose to winter on the prairie at wooded oases such as Moose Mountain, Wood Mountain, and, in time, the

Cypress Hills, rather than return to river lots at Red River or St-Albert in the Saskatchewan country. By the 1870s encampments such as Tail Creek and Buffalo Lake south of Fort Edmonton numbered several hundred *hivernants*.

As the nineteenth century advanced eastern institutions other than buffalo robe buyers became aware of opportunities in a land previously thought fit only for nomadic hunters and fur traders. Their agents soon put in an appearance. Roman Catholic and Protestant missionaries who earlier had been in Red River now jostled each other on the upper reaches of North Saskatchewan River and beyond. Canadian settlers appeared, as yet in small numbers, in Red River and, as Overlanders, traversed the Plains to cross the Rocky Mountains into British Columbia. Members of the British gentry sought adventure as tourists in the wilds of the fur trade West. Government-sponsored expeditions led by John Palliser and H.Y. Hind gathered data on hinterland resources that the outside world avidly sought. Interests other than the fur trade were preparing their assault on the resources of the Northwest. In Red River the closing years of the 1860s were marked by the failure of farm and hunt, necessitating the importation of relief supplies from Canada and the United States. Such events raised questions about future opportunities for the Metis.

The Transfer and the Aftermath

The transfer in 1870 of the Hudson's Bay Company's territories to the control of a recently created country, the Dominion of Canada, marked the loss of the Northwest's last vestige of independence from the modern world. This conquest, which had been evolving over the previous half-century, would be consolidated in the next decade and a half. In Red River in 1869, Louis Riel's defiance of the Canadian Lieutenant-Governor-designate, William McDougall, and his establishment of a provisional government marked the assertive action of a community determined to secure its interests in the new order. Not a few Metis traders opposed Riel out of fear that his actions would disrupt the robe trade. Yet others saw Riel's provisional government as assurance of and opportunity for the future. Riel and the Metis behind him did not limit their political frame of reference to themselves. They saw the other communities of the old Northwest, together with the Metis, as having legitimate corporate interests that the Canadians would have to recognize if the old inhabitants were to survive as communities and to prosper in the new order. In 1870, negotiations with representatives of Riel's provisional government culminated with the Canadian government passing the Manitoba Act (styled the Manitoba 'Treaty' by Riel and the Metis). In this legislation, Riel and his government believed they had determined the political and constitutional structure necessary for the corporate survival of the old communities. The Canadians, for their part, felt they had granted in a more formal fashion what they believed they had always been prepared to grant: the rights, privileges, and responsibilities of individual citizenship (Morton, 1956a). In the Canadian pantheon of truisms, opportunity was primarily a function of individual merit and not corporate privilege. The Canadians believed that, in terms of equity, circumstances demanded a period of wardship for the Indians through the treaty system before full citizenship could be extended. For the Halfbreeds, including the Metis, the problem of equity was supposedly acknowledged in the provision in the Manitoba Act for 1.4 million acres to be reserved for the children of 'Halfbreed heads of families'.

The year 1874 witnessed the departure of the last hunt from the Red River Settlement. In the same year the trickle of Metis migrating westward became a flood. The Manitoba Treaty had not achieved what Riel and his followers felt they had successfully negotiated with the Canadians. A number of the migrants journeyed southwestward to Dakota Territory, creating the temporary large settlement of St Joseph before continuing westward to Montana Territory. More journeyed

westward to the Qu'Appelle Valley and the environs of Fort Ellice and Fort Pelly. Many continued northward to the valley of the South Saskatchewan, a couple of days' journey south of Prince Albert, to establish the parish of St Laurent with the tiny village of Batoche in its midst A few traders, such as Louis Goulet, journeyed westward to the Metis indigenous to the Saskatchewan country. For many Metis in Red River the exodus westward was the pursuit of opportunity in the robe trade. But for others the migration was fundamentally a flight from what the future appeared to hold in Manitoba and a search for an opportunity to establish a base from which the objectives of the Manitoba Treaty could be retrieved from failure.

Much has been written on the Saskatchewan Rebellion of 1885. In the historical literature there has been a tendency to find fault with the actions of the Canadian government, seeing them as provoking the violent responses of some Indians and Metis who had legitimate grievances (Stanley, 1963, 1964). A more recent revisionist work has presented evidence to question both the culpability of the government and the 'blamelessness' of Metis actions (Flanagan, 1983). Were the Metis not to a major extent the authors of their own misfortune in placing themselves under the leadership of the erratic Louis Riel? Writings on Indian motives in the Rebellion generally suggest that, while they acted independently of the Metis, they aspired to ends similar to those expressed by the Metis at the time of the transfer of HBC lands to Canada, which the Metis believed they had enshrined in the Manitoba Act (Tobias, 1983). More recent work indicates that most Indian leaders were committed to achieving their ends through negotiation (Strongchild and Waiser, 1997). The fundamental aspiration of both Metis and Indians in 1885 was to be recognized as corporate entities and to be guaranteed a relevant role in the future of the West. For the Canadians, with their emphasis on individual rights and responsibilities, such corporate aspirations constituted unfair privilege. The defeat of the Metis on the battlefield at Batoche on 12 May 1885 ended for a half-century their collective purposeful pursuit of this objective.

Dispersal, frequently to the fringes of the dominant society, marked the fate of many if not most Metis following the Rebellion. Some in the area of Winnipeg chose to emphasize things 'French' and 'Catholic' in their heritage as a means of retaining a distinct identity and defining a corporate role for themselves in the settlers' West. Others sought strengthened ties with kinsmen on the Indian reserves. Research to determine with some precision who among the Metis did what after 1885 has been initiated only fairly recently. It would appear that little of permanent benefit accrued to the Metis from the government's program of Halfbreed scrip. The expression 'the road allowance people', referring to Native families living in rough cabins on Crown lands, reflects the fate of many.

The New Order

The dominant ethnic element among the settlers who surged onto the prairie lands in the 15-year period from 1896 to 1911 was Ontarian. They saw property ownership as a fundamental value, and they believed it should be widely dispersed throughout society. Universal adult male suffrage was the political means by which governments were disciplined to act as agents of this community. Others, such as Americans and those of the British Isles, held very similar views and found opportunities to act on them in the Canadian West. In time these traditions would blend to create distinct western Canadian views. A series of Halfbreed scrip land grants were made between 1870 and 1900 to facilitate Metis adjustment to this new order.

The conditions and terms under which land was made available to the Metis varied during the period scrip was granted. In many instances, the 240-acre land grants were sold to speculators who were able thus to establish large blocks of homestead lands for their own speculative purposes. In many other instances, when terms permitted, the Metis took money scrip entitling them to $240. A suggestion of ignorance or irresponsibility on the part of the Metis is often associated with the decision to take money scrip (see Box 18.1).

It was not, however, until Marquis wheat became widely available to western farmers after 1900 that grain farming offered a reasonable chance of success. Without the certainty of grain harvests from year to year, the agricultural future of the West was limited to livestock. In the years prior to 1900 the agricultural response of the Metis, which emphasized livestock and mobility, could be viewed as effective as that of any ethnic group. When it is remembered that the Metis were eligible as well for homestead entry, then the decision to take money scrip can be considered an effective adaptive response rather than evidence of ignorance or irresponsibility.

At the moment our impression of Metis agricultural practices after 1885 highlights a home base near a prairie lake or slough with small plots of land planted to grains and root vegetables. The produce of the gardens was supplemented by gathering the eggs of waterfowl or hunting and snaring birds and animals found in the vicinity. Livestock—a few cattle and horses—were moved as pasturage and other factors dictated. In such circumstances, particularly when the home base was protected by a homestead entry and open range was still available, it made sense to take money scrip rather than acquire more land. With capital to purchase the requirements of semi-nomadic agriculture—such as wagons, harness, portable stoves, and tents—survival was enhanced. When it is noted that the value of fur shipped from Edmonton remained greater than agricultural produce until after 1900, then the survival value of Metis agriculture is readily apparent. They could continue to harvest furs as they had done during the era of the buffalo hunt. Only later, when Crown lands filled with homesteaders and grain farming could be conducted with some certainty of success, did the decision to take money scrip rather than land scrip appear to be a mistake.

BOX 18.1

Metis Scrip and Ethnicity

Metis scrip, literally provisional certificates entitling the bearer to a certain amount of land federally owned and surveyed in Manitoba and the North-West Territories, was first issued to the Metis in Manitoba in 1876 and extended to Metis in the North-West Territories in 1885. Scrip was issued to adults and children who could document that they were of Indian-European ancestry and had been born in British or Canadian territory. The program was designed to provide the Metis of the North-West Territories with access to land and was ostensibly granted in extinguishment of Metis claims to Indian title. There are unsettled legal issues, such as whether scrip really extinguished Metis Aboriginal title and whether there was fraud involved in buying scrip. Nevertheless, this massive administrative program constituted the governmental roots of a modern Metis ethnicity when the occupational bases of Metis ethnicity were disappearing on the Plains. The various scrip commissions that held hearings in the North-West Territories from the 1880s to the 1920s not only created a massive administrative, statistical, and genealogical archive, but they named and defined an ethnicity or identity to which the Metis ascribed in order to receive its benefits.

While Metis communities and individuals in the nineteenth century had a wide variety of cultural and economic affiliations with vague ethnic boundaries, the scrip program demanded distinct and absolute ethnic boundaries. By the time scrip and treaty commissioners travelled to northern Alberta to negotiate Treaty No. 8 in 1899, they found few differences between the Indian and Metis populations, who were much intermarried. They offered the Metis of the region the choice of entering treaty or taking scrip. Once they chose, they were bound by their decision. At times some members of a family became treaty Indians while others were granted scrip and enumerated as Metis. In a sense, a type of person came into being at the same time that the 'Metis Scrip' category was being invented. Scrip and treaty administrative practices that defined and counted collective identities in an all-or-nothing manner enabled/forced people to see or organize themselves in light of these categories. As late as the 1990s the Metis National Council used the taking of scrip as one of the markers in determining membership in the Metis Nation.

—Gerhard Ens, Department of History and Classics, University of Alberta

An essential problem for the Metis early in the twentieth century was their lack of access to capital to enable them to complete the transition to sedentary agriculture with an emphasis on grain. They lacked social connections that might have unlocked some financial doors; they lacked expertise in Canadian political ways that might have opened others. Finally, they emerged from the period of the Halfbreed scrip grants without ownership of significant amounts of land. Many Metis communities were doomed to exist as islands of enduring poverty that did not accom-

pany their settler neighbours into the 'good life' following the pioneering era. With the end of open land, with the establishment of the viability of settled farming, and with the loss of an institutional basis for expressing their corporate identity, large numbers of Plains Metis were dispersed northward and westward into the region of the boreal forest to join kindred peoples to eke out difficult lives on the fringes of settlement.

With the onset of the Great Depression in 1929, efforts were rekindled to resurrect *la nation Metisse*. A notable example in Alberta saw an

FIGURE 18.2. Frank Moberly, guide, near Jasper, Alberta (c. 1920). The Moberlys and other Metis residents of the Jasper region were evicted when it became a national park. In the 1970s their descendants gained a land settlement north of Jasper. (Courtesy Glenbow Archives, NA–3187–7)

Food, clothing, shelter, and medical treatment were dominant concerns in the agitation of Dion, Brady, and Norris. Questions of cultural survival were viewed as irrelevant when questions of physical survival were uppermost. In December 1934, the Metis Association of Alberta succeeded in having the provincial government establish a Royal Commission 'To Investigate the Conditions of the Half-Breeds of Alberta' under Justice A.F. Ewing. The result of the Ewing Commission's hearings was the Metis Betterment Act, 1938.

The question can be asked whether this Act was an improvement over the Manitoba Act of 1870. The Metis Betterment Act established eight Metis colonies at different locations in northern Alberta. In imitation of the federal government and its views of Indian reserves, the colonies were to constitute a protected environment in which the Metis could be instructed in 'the intricacies of modern society'. It was hoped that within a few years the success of the legislation was to be reflected in the disappearance of the colonies and the assimilation of the Metis into western Canadian society. The Metis would become fully participating individuals in the life of the dominant society. A similar view was expressed by many if not all the leaders of the Metis community.

The 1960s witnessed an upsurge in activity among the Metis in western Canada. In 1961 court action was launched against the province of

enfranchised Indian, Joseph Dion, the son of an Indian agent, Jim Brady, and the son of an early Edmonton businessman, Malcolm Norris, acknowledge their Native heritages by identifying their personal interests with those of the Metis people. The result was the creation of the Metis Association of Alberta. In 1938 the Saskatchewan Metis Society came into existence.

Alberta for its refusal to pay royalties on resources, particularly oil and gas, removed from Metis settlements. In 1965 the Metis of northwestern Ontario formed an organization that would become known as the Ontario Metis Aboriginal Association. In 1967 the Saskatchewan Metis Society amalgamated with the Metis Association of Saskatchewan, while in the same year the Manitoba Metis Federation united the Metis of that province who could trace their organizational roots to 1887 and the formation of l'Union National Metisse Saint Joseph du Manitoba.

In the 1970s organizational growth continued in northeastern British Columbia and in the Northwest Territories. At the national level the Metis associations of the three Prairie provinces would form the Native Council of Canada. In 1981 they would leave the NCC to form the Metis National Council (MNC).

At the national level the MNC continued to press for federal responsibility that would lead to constitutional recognition, self-government, and a land base. At a series of first ministers' conferences during the 1980s the MNC believed it had accomplished its initial objectives, with the Metis Nation Accord to be included in the Charlottetown Accord, but the Canadian electorate's resounding defeat of the constitutional referendum in 1992 and its savaging of two of the three mainline parties in the federal election of 1993 appear to have ended constitutional reform for a period of time. Other strategies, if not altered objectives, may suggest themselves in the wake of an apparently angry, awakening electorate targeting what they define as 'special interests' and a professional middle class that appears to have profited handsomely by brokering these special interests. For the angry electorate, national and provincial institutional leadership has betrayed the traditions of fairness and opportunity for the individual taxpaying citizen. Special interests have become 'citizens plus' at the expense of others. This altered perception of special interests could well prove to be the greatest challenge for Metis leadership at both the national and provincial levels.

At the provincial level a significant effort emphasized Metis participation in government action directed at the educational and social problems experienced by many Metis. In Alberta a series of 'framework agreements' between the provincial government and the Metis Nation of Alberta (MNA—formerly the Metis Association) aspires to promote joint planning and joint action on the part of the parties involved. To this end a joint committee, involving senior provincial government and MNA officials and co-chaired by individuals of each interest, is responsible for strategic planning and monitors the progress of the various subcommittees. While the provincial government may be simply seeking more effective delivery for its programs at a time when increased hostility towards government performance is being expressed by many in the electorate, the MNA sees in these agreements the experiences that will eventually lead to constitutional recognition, self-government, and a land base.

The task for Metis organizations in the 1990s is to convince an increasingly negative electorate, nursing its own sense of betrayal and victimization, that such aspirations for the Metis constitute fairness rather than privilege.

Epilogue: The Metis since 1985

The beginning of the twenty-first century has seen the continuation of several issues confronting the Metis since the mid-1980s. The most compelling are Metis identity (see Box 18.2), Metis Aboriginal rights (particularly the inherent right to hunt and fish), and a continuation of their land rights battle. These concerns have coalesced in several court cases that have propelled and altered definitions of Metis as well as the parameters of the organizations that represent them.

For many years, Metis have been working to reformulate their identity—both in terms of changing the public's perception and changing their perception of themselves. The role Metis pressure groups have played making these changes is considerable, through programs of

BOX 18.2

Metis Identity:
The Historic Metis Nation and the Other Metis

In the 1991 Canadian census, 139,000 people identified themselves as Metis. But this figure is problematic, because it does not distinguish between the different groups that have taken on the identity of Metis in various parts of Canada. At the most basic level, Metis simply means people who are part Indian, but historic, geographic, and legalistic issues began to complicate the issue after 1985 and the repatriation of the Canadian Constitution.

Today, 'Metis' is most commonly taken to refer to the western or Red River Metis population, the group derived from the Red River colony of the seventeenth and eighteenth centuries, when separate groups of French, Scottish, and English 'half-breed' populations began evolving. These separate populations are now amalgamated into a single entity known as 'Metis' or the 'Historic Metis Nation' as their representative organization, the Metis National Council (MNC), refers to them. In September 2002, the MNC defined Metis as meaning 'a person who self identifies as Metis, is of historic Metis Nation ancestry, is distinct from other Aboriginal peoples and is accepted by the Metis Nation'. Historic Metis Nation ancestry generally means being able to trace ancestry back to Red River in the 1800s. The geographic area of the historic Metis Nation would most likely be limited to Manitoba, Saskatchewan, Alberta, Montana, and North Dakota, although some populations in Ontario and British Columbia also lay claim to membership in this group.

However, this definition ignores other populations in Canada and the United States that also have laid claim to the term 'Metis'—groups with separate characteristics and local histories not specifically tied to the Red River Metis. Such groups would include the Grande Cache Metis of northern Alberta, some groups in the Northwest Territories, as well as groups living in northern Ontario, Labrador, and the Maritimes. Recently, several groups in the United States have begun using the term as well. Some Canadian courts have muddied the waters further by insisting that Metis claiming an Aboriginal right to hunt and fish must also live a 'distinct Aboriginal lifestyle' in order to be considered Metis.

The diversity found among different Metis populations is yet to be acknowledged by the Canadian government. For example, although the term 'Metis' encompasses a wide variety of peoples, with complex and varied identities, neither the census nor the Canadian Constitution recognizes the Metis as anything other than a single, holistic Aboriginal group.

—Joe Sawchuk, Native Studies Department,
Brandon University

cultural awareness and negotiations with the government. The most obvious example is recognition of the Metis as one of Canada's Aboriginal peoples under section 35(2) of the Constitution Act, 1982. This was a direct result of lobbying, particularly by the Native Council of Canada and some of the more active provincial organizations, such as the Association of Metis and Non-Status Indians of Saskatchewan. However, the constitutional definition has set the stage for conflict between different groups of Metis and their allies. The first was splitting a long-standing political union between Metis and non-status Indians. The second was a growing separation between the western or 'historic' Metis (the descendants of the Metis population that had its origins in the Red

River area of southern Manitoba) and other Metis populations in Ontario, Labrador, and elsewhere, who also claim constitutional recognition.

By the 1990s, the Metis National Council was postulating the idea of a historic Metis Nation. In their view it was limited to people descended from Red River Metis, distinct from other mixed-blood populations, and it alone was entitled to use the name 'Metis'. The interests of Metis not part of this historic Metis Nation are served by the Congress of Aboriginal Peoples (CAP) at the national level, and by various regional organizations at the provincial and territorial levels. Among those CAP claims to represent are 'Bush Cree/Metis'; 'Bay Metis', in northern Ontario; and Gwitchin Metis, in the northern Mackenzie area.

Ontario offers an interesting example of the diversity of Metis identity. There are at least two groups of 'Metis' in the province, with very different ideas of Metis identity. The Metis Nation of Ontario identifies with the traditional Red River Metis. The Ontario Metis Aboriginal Association (OMAA) represents the 'Metis Indians' of northern Ontario. They are Metis historically centred around Sault Ste Marie, with a history and traditions separate from the Red River Metis. This split between the 'Metis Nation' from the Prairie provinces and other groups claiming a Metis identity in the rest of Canada has also been noted by the Royal Commission on Aboriginal Peoples (RCAP). The RCAP recommends that the government recognize all of these groups for purposes of nation-to-nation negotiations and as Metis for that purpose.

Currently, an issue generating great interest is the recognition of Metis Aboriginal rights, especially hunting and fishing rights. There have been court cases recently in Saskatchewan, Manitoba, and Ontario involving Metis Aboriginal rights. Generally, it would appear that provincial courts are beginning to accept the idea that Metis may have an inherent but limited right to hunt and fish for subsistence. However, in order to be eligible for hunting and fishing rights, several courts have held that the Metis in question should also 'live an Aboriginal lifestyle' (Andersen, 2000: 96; Isaac,

1999: 316). The rationale for this distinction is not clear, since status Indians are not required to meet such a stipulation to claim their Aboriginal rights. These cases also have implications for identity. In R. v Powley (2000, 1999), Ontario courts not only recognized an inherent right to hunt and fish for subsistence, but postulated a definition for Metis entitled to these rights. Because these Metis were from Sault Ste Marie, the definition had no reference to receiving scrip or being part of the historic Metis Nation. This court also dispensed with the requirement that Metis live an Aboriginal lifestyle to have Aboriginal rights. Because of the general direction of these cases, some provinces, such as Manitoba, are developing policies and/or memoranda of understanding to be signed between the Metis provincial organizations and the government regarding Metis co-management structures for natural resources.

The other important issue is land claims. There are at least two large land claims before the courts. The first was filed by the Manitoba Metis Federation in 1981 and was based on challenges to the Manitoba Act of 1870, specifically that various federal and provincial statutes and Orders-in-Council enacted during the 1870s and 1880s were unconstitutional because they had the effect of depriving the Metis of land to which they were entitled under the Manitoba Act, 1870 (*Manitoba Metis Federation v. A.G. Canada*, 1988; *Dumont v. A.G. Canada*, 1990). Although this case has languished for years, it is expected to be back before the courts soon. The second involves land in northwest Saskatchewan, with the Metis of that region claiming that their Aboriginal title to lands and resources was not extinguished by the 1906 scrip distribution. It was filed by the Metis Nation of Saskatchewan in 1994, but it is not clear when this case will come to court. There are many more potential claims. It is estimated that the western Metis organizations have enough evidence to pursue claims involving more than 2.4 million hectares of land across all three Prairie provinces.

The term 'Metis' has undergone many changes since the 1880s and early 1920s, both in terms of ethnic boundaries and in geographic location. It continues to change. While the term may originally have been limited to the historic Metis Nation, questions of identity and constitutional, legal, and organizational issues have now expanded the concept far beyond the Plains.

Notes

1. The term 'Metis' designates those communities the historical actors saw as distinct from both Indian and Euro-Canadian communities in the fur trade era. The term 'Metis' was and is the labelling term used by some Metis communities to identify themselves.
2. Although these people were mostly *Canadien*, they did not remain exclusively so. In later years their numbers included non-French Europeans and even a few non-local Indians.

References and Recommended Readings

Andersen, Chris. 2000. 'The Formalization of Metis Identities in Canadian Provincial Courts', in Ron F. Laliberte, Priscilla Settee, et al., eds, *Expressions in Canadian Native Studies*. Saskatoon: University of Saskatchewan Extension Press.

Brown, J.S.H. 1980. *Strangers in Blood: Fur Trade Families in Indian Country*. Vancouver: University of British Columbia Press. An excellent study of nineteenth-century fur trade officers' families, suggesting the concept of patrilocality to explain why children of these families did not become Metis.

Campbell, Marjorie. 1973. *The North West Company*. Toronto: Macmillan.

Cockran, William. 1975. 'To the Secretary of the Church Mission Society from Rev. W. Cockran, Red River Settlement, July 25, 1833', in L.G. Thomas, ed., *The Prairie West to 1905*. Toronto: Oxford University Press.

Ens, Gerhard. 1988. 'Dispossession or Adaptation: Migration and Persistence of the Red River Metis, 1835–1890', *Historical Papers*. Ottawa: Canadian Historical Association. A challenge to those who would see the Metis essentially as victims.

Flanagan, Thomas. 1983. *Riel and the Rebellion: 1885 Reconsidered*. Saskatoon: Western Producer. A controversial revisionist work on the causes of the 1885 Rebellion.

———. 1992. *Louis Riel*. Ottawa: Canadian Historical Association, Booklet 50. A brief survey by the current leading authority on Riel.

Foster, John E. 1983. 'The Metis: The People and the Term', in A.S. Lussier, ed., *Louis Riel and the Metis*. Winnipeg: Pemmican.

———. 1994. 'Wintering, the Outsider Adult Male and the Ethnogenesis of the Western Plains Metis', *Prairie Forum* 19, 1. The question of origins is examined.

Giraud, Marcel. 1945. *Le Metis Canadien*. Paris: l'Institut d'Ethnologie. Translated by George Woodcock as *The Metis in the Canadian West*. Edmonton: University of Alberta Press, 2 vols, 1986. The fundamental study on the Plains Metis.

Governor and Committee of the Hudson's Bay Company. 1938. 'To George Simpson from the Governor and Committee, London, February 27, 1822', in E.E. Rich, ed., *Journal of Occurrences in the Athabaska Department by George Simpson 1820 and 1821, and Report*. Toronto: Champlain Society.

Gunn, J.J. 1930 'The Tripmen of Assiniboia', in *Echoes of the Red*. Toronto: Macmillan.

Hargraves, J.J. 1871. *Red River*. Montreal: Printed for the author by John Lovell. The son of a Hudson's Bay Company chief factor, the author had a familiarity with Red River and the fur trade West unrivalled by any other non-resident. His description of the buffalo hunt complements that of Alexander Ross (below).

Innis, H.A. 1975. *The Fur Trade in Canada*. Toronto: University of Toronto Press. The classic statement of the staple trade thesis in terms of the fur trade.

Isaac, Thomas. 1999. *Aboriginal Law: Cases, Materials and Commentary*, 2nd edn. Saskatoon: Purich.

MacLeod, M.A., and W.L. Morton. 1963. *Cuthbert Grant of Grantown: Warden of the Plains of Red River*. Toronto: McClelland & Stewart. This study of the first prominent leader among the Plains Metis is a useful depiction of the Red River Metis at mid-century.

Metis National Council. 1993. 'Abridged Version of the Metis National Council's Report to the Royal Commission on Aboriginal Peoples', *The Metis Nation* 2, 2: 1–32. Ottawa: Metis National Council. A sophisticated expression of a Metis perspective on their history and current issues and circumstances.

Moogk, P.N. 1976. 'In the Darkness of a Basement: Craftsmen's Associations in Early French Canada', *Canadian Historical Review* 57, 4: 399–439.

Morton, A.S. 1928. 'La Verendrye: Commandant, Fur Trader and Explorer', *Canadian Historical Review* 9, 4: 284–98.

Morton, W.L. 1956a. 'Introduction', in W.L. Morton, ed., *Alexander Begg's Red River Journal and other Documents Relating to the Red River Resistance of 1869–70*. Toronto: Champlain Society. This is the best scholarly history of the transfer of HBC lands to Canada.

———. 1956b. 'Introduction', in E.E. Rich, ed., *London Correspondence Inward from Eden Colvile, 1849–1854*. London: Hudson's Bay Record Society. The best scholarly history of the Red River Settlement from 1840 to 1855.

———. 1980. 'Clio in Canada: The Interpretation of Canadian History', in, A.B. McKillop, ed., *Contexts of Canada's Past: Selected Essays of W.L. Morton*. Toronto: Macmillan.

Nicks, Trudy. 1980. 'The Iroquois and the Fur Trade in Western Canada', in C.M. Judd and A.J. Ray, eds, *Old Trails and New Directions: Papers of the Third North American Fur Trade Conference*. Toronto: University of Toronto Press.

Nute, G.L. 1966. *The Voyageur*. St Paul: Minnesota Historical Society.

Peterson, Jacqueline. 1978. 'Prelude to Red River: A Social Portrait of the Great Lakes Metis', *Ethnohistory* 25, 1: 41–67. A seminal article in the study of the Metis, it is fundamental to any scholarship on the subject.

Ray, A.J. 1974. *Indians in the Fur Trade: Their Role as Hunters, Trappers, and Middlemen in the Lands Southwest of Hudson Bay, 1660–1870*. Toronto: University of Toronto Press. The first, and still essential, study to delineate an Indian history in the fur trade West

Rich, E.E. 1960. *The History of the Hudson's Bay Company*. London: Hudson's Bay Record Society.

Ross, Alexander. 1972 [1856]. *The Red River Settlement: Its Rise, Progress, and Present State*. Edmonton: Hurtig. Ross was a former fur trader who retired to the Red River Settlement with his Okanagan wife and their children. This folk history account contains the most useful description of a buffalo hunt in the primary sources.

Royal Commission on Aboriginal Peoples (RCAP). 1996. *Report of the Royal Commission on Aboriginal Peoples*, 5 vols. Ottawa: Government of Canada.

Saunders, R.M. 1939. 'The Emergence of the *Coureur de bois* as a Social Type', *Canadian Historical Association Annual Papers*.

Sawchuk, Joe, Patricia Sawchuk, and Theresa Ferguson. 1981. *Metis Land Rights in Alberta: A Political History*. Edmonton: Metis Association of Alberta. The most useful survey of Metis history in the twentieth century with a focus on Alberta.

Sprague, Douglas. 1988. *Canada and the Metis, 1869–1885*. Waterloo, Ont.: Wilfrid Laurier University Press. For many readers a history of 'victims' and 'oppressors'.

Sprenger, Herman. 1972. 'The Metis Nation: Buffalo Hunting vs. Agriculture in the Red River Settlement (circa 1810–1870)', *Western Canadian Journal of Anthropology* 3, 1: 158–70. An excellent challenge to the view that the hunting ways of the Metis were inappropriate in the context of agricultural opportunities at Red River.

Stanley, G.F.G. 1963. *The Birth of Western Canada: A History of the Riel Rebellions*. Toronto: University of Toronto Press.

———. 1964. *Louis Riel*. Toronto: Ryerson.

———, et al., eds. 1985. *The Collected Writings of Louis Riel/Les Ecrits complets de Louis Riel*, 5 vols. Edmonton: University of Alberta Press. Of essential importance for the period of the transfer and the Rebellion.

Strongchild, Blair, and Bill Waiser. 1997. *Loyal till Death: Indians and the North-West Rebellion*. Calgary: Fifth House. Documents the Indian strategy of maintaining the peace during the Rebellion and subsequent federal attempts to link them to the Rebellion.

Tobias, J.L. 1983. 'Canada's Subjugation of the Plains Cree, 1879–1885', *Canadian Historical Review* 64, 3: 519–48.

Van Kirk, Sylvia. 1980. *'Many Tender Ties': Women in Fur Trade Society in Western Canada, 1670–1870*. Winnipeg: Watson and Dwyer. The definitive historical study of women in the fur trade.

Suggested Web Sites

The Metis National Council: www.Metisnation.ca/
MNC is the organization of the Metis Nation, those descended from Red River Metis. The site links to member organizations in Ontario, Manitoba, Saskatchewan, Alberta, and BC.

Congress of Aboriginal Peoples: www.abo-peoples.org/
CAP is a national organization representing off-reserve Indians, Inuit, and Metis. It represents Metis not served by MNC, including the Alberta Metis settlements, Bush Cree Metis, 'Bay Metis' in northern Ontario, Gwitchin Metis, and Labrador Metis.

The Other Metis: www.otherMetis.net/

  While this site promises information on Metis everywhere, it is particularly dedicated to those 'not represented by the better known Canadian Prairie Metis
  organizations and their national organization, the
  Metis National Council'.

Metis Scrip Records Online:

  www.archives.ca/02/02010507_e.html

  National Archives of Canada searchable database of
  scrip records. This Archivia Net site has over 15,000
  digitized scrip applications, primarily from
  Manitoba. To search records by either name or locality, use the above address and then search under
  Record Group 15.

Court Cases Cited

R. v. Powley (2000), O.J. No. 99 (Ont. Sup. Ct.)

R. v. Powley (1999), C.N.L.R. 153 (Ont. Prov. Ct.)

Dumont v. A.G. Canada, [1990] 2 C.N.L.R. 19 (S.C.C.)

Manitoba Metis Fed. v. A.G.Canada, [1988] 3 C.N.L.R. 39
  (Man. C.A.)

CHAPTER 19

'We Must Farm To Enable Us To Live': The Plains Cree and Agriculture to 1900

SARAH CARTER

Introduction

This chapter explores the topic of agriculture on Plains Cree reserves in the late nineteenth century, addressing the question of why farming failed to form the basis of a viable economy in these communities by 1900. The answer to this question is complex, but has little to do with the prevailing explanation that Plains people had no inclination or ability to farm. The Plains Cree made sustained, determined efforts to establish an economy based on agriculture, but they faced many obstacles. There were environmental and technological challenges shared by all farmers at this time. Aboriginal farmers laboured under particular disadvantages because of their unique relationship with the federal government that ought to have assisted them in this enterprise but ultimately functioned to undermine their efforts. A 'peasant' farming policy imposed from 1889 to 1896 was especially damaging to Plains Cree agriculture. It is also argued in this chapter that non-Aboriginal people have persistently found it useful to insist that Aboriginal people and agriculture were incompatible, despite obvious evidence to the contrary. It was a convenient myth to sustain because it could be claimed that people who did not farm were not in need of much land and that economic underdevelopment of the reserves was due to the indifference and neglect, not of the government, but of Aboriginal people.

Early in September 1879, at Fort Carlton, North-West Territories, Plains Cree chiefs Ahtahkakoop, Mistawasis, and Kitowehaw, with five councillors, met with Edgar Dewdney, the recently appointed Commissioner of Indian Affairs. The chiefs were frustrated that promises of agricultural assistance, made to them three years earlier in Treaty No. 6, were 'not carried out in their spirit' (Anon., 1879: 26). They stated that they intended to live by the cultivation of the soil, as 'the buffalo were our only dependence before the transfer of the country, and this and other wild animals are disappearing, and we must farm to enable us to live.' They insisted that government had not fulfilled its part of the treaty in assisting them to make a living by agriculture and that what had been given them made a mockery of the promises made in 1876. This was by no means the first effort of these chiefs to place their concerns before government officials, and there were similar expressions of dissatisfaction and disappointment throughout Manitoba and the North-West Territories.[1]

Such evidence of the strong commitment of the Plains Cree to agriculture seemed startling to me when I set out to explore why agriculture failed to provide a living for residents of arable Indian reserves in western Canada. The standard explanation, one firmly embedded in the non-Aboriginal prairie mentality, seemed compelling: that Aboriginal people of the Plains never had any inclination to settle down and farm despite concerted government efforts and assistance. I originally approached the topic with the argument in mind that agriculture was the wrong policy, for the wrong people, at the wrong time. Before I was too far along in my research, however, I found that there was little evidence of agriculture floundering because of the apathy and indifference of Aboriginal people, although it was certainly the case that this view was consistently maintained and promoted by the Department of Indian Affairs and later by many historians. Yet from the time of the treaties of the 1870s and well before, Aboriginal people were anxious to explore agriculture as an alternate economy when they began to realize the buffalo were failing them. It was not government negotiators but the Aboriginal spokesmen who insisted that terms be included in the treaties that would permit agricultural development. Aboriginal people of the western Plains were among the earliest and largest groups to attempt agriculture west of the Red River Settlement. Like most other 'sodbusters', Aboriginal farmers were inclined to become commercial farmers specializing in grain. The fact that they did not had to do with government policy and intent, not with Aboriginal choice and inability.

My topic and approach are the product of a number of influences, including the work of 'new' social historians who, beginning in the 1960s, argued that history should be not only the study of elites but of ordinary people as well, and of the day-to-day as well as the dramatic events. The new social history stressed that non-elites— ethnic minorities, women, the working class, and non-literate peoples—sought in various ways to transcend the limitations placed on them and were not hopeless victims of forces beyond their control but rather coped creatively with changing conditions. While Arthur J. Ray, Sylvia Van Kirk, and John Milloy cast Native people in a central role as active participants in the history of the pre-1870 West, the same could not be said of the more modern era. In the dominant narrative histories of the West in the post-1870 era, Aboriginal people all but disappeared after they made treaties and settled on reserves. The story of the establishment of the rural core of the prairie West was inevitably told from the point of view of the new arrivals, with little mention of the host society, and generally a record of positive achievement was stressed and the casualties of development were downplayed. Studies of late nineteenth-century imperialisms, which increasingly drew regions into a transcontinental network, provided context for understanding that what happened in western Canada was not unique, but was part of a global pattern of Western expansion.

Aboriginal Adaptations to the Northern Plains

The Plains culture that evolved over centuries in western Canada seemed far removed from the sedentary lifestyle of farms, fields, and fences that began to alter forever the prairie landscape in the late nineteenth century. The Plains Cree, the northernmost people of the Great Plains of North America and one of the last Aboriginal groups to adopt Plains culture, developed a lifestyle that was well suited to the predominantly flat, treeless landscape and to the northern Plains climate of extremes and uncertainties. Particular habits of movement and dispersal suited the limited and specialized nature of the resources of the northern Plains. The Natives exploited the seasonal diversity of their environment by practising mobility. Plains people moved their settlements from habitat to habitat, depending on where they expected to find the greatest natural food supply. All aspects of life hinged on this mobility; their tepees, for example, were easily taken apart and moved, and their other property was kept to a strict minimum so that they would be unencumbered. As homesteaders were later to learn, basic necessities such as good soil, water, game, and fuel rarely came together in many Plains areas, and this combined with the great variability and uncertainty of the climate to make mobility central to the survival of the indigenous peoples of

FIGURE 19.1. Cree camp near Saskatoon, *c.* 1900. (Courtesy Saskatchewan Archives Board, R–B1016)

the Plains. Many of the earliest homesteaders on the Plains found that they could not stay put either, certainly not at first; they sought off-farm jobs, especially during the 'start-up' years, or they were obliged to try several localities in their search for basic necessities. External inputs in the way of seed-grain relief, subsidies, or rations were often necessary as the resources of a fixed locality could not always sustain the inhabitants.

The buffalo was the foundation of the Plains economy, providing people not only with a crucial source of protein and vitamins but with many other necessities, including shelter, clothing, containers, and tools. Aboriginal life on the Plains followed a pattern of concentration and dispersal that to a great extent paralleled that of the buffalo. But Plains people were not solely hunters of buffalo. To rely on one staple resource alone was risky in the Plains environment, as there were periodic shortages of buffalo, and it was mainly the gathering and preserving work of women, based on their intimate understanding of the Plains environment, that varied the subsistence base and contributed to 'risk reduction', a role the immigrant women to the Plains would also acquire. Mid-

summer camp movements were determined not only by the buffalo but by considerations such as the ripeness and location of saskatoon berries, the prairie turnip, and other fruits and tubers. Many of the foodstuffs women gathered were dried, pounded, or otherwise preserved and stored for the scarce times of winter. Women fished, snared small game, caught prairie chickens and migratory birds, and gathered their eggs. A high degree of mobility was essential for people effectively to draw on the varied resources of the Plains.

Nineteenth-century European observers tended to see the Great Plains as a timeless land, as a place without history, its people unaffected by any outside forces and leaving no mark of their presence upon the land. Captain William Butler, who described the Plains in 1870 as a great ocean of grass, wrote that 'This ocean has no past—time has been nought to it; and men have come and gone, leaving behind them no track, no vestige of their presence' (Butler, 1968: 317–18). European observers saw Plains people as living at the mercy of natural forces and failed to appreciate the sophisticated adaptations to the environment and the many ways in which resources were altered, managed, and controlled. Methods such as the buffalo pound, like the Huron enclosures and Beothuk drivelines for capturing deer, have been described as a form of animal management. There is evidence that people of the northern Plains were concerned with keeping up buffalo herd numbers as they periodically burned the grasslands in the autumn to keep forage levels high. This burning increased yields, encouraged spring grass growth earlier, and induced buffalo into favoured areas of fresh, young grass. Fire was used to influence buffalo movement—to direct a herd to a kill site and to keep buffalo away from fur trade posts so that Europeans could not provision themselves. Fire was also used to protect valuable stands of timber.

Well before the treaties of the 1870s some Plains people, particularly the Cree and Saulteaux, had begun to raise small crops and to keep cattle to smooth out the seasonal scarcities that were increasing as the buffalo receded westward. As the homesteaders were later to learn, however, especially those who attempted farming before the development of dry-land farming techniques and early-maturing varieties of grain, yields from cultivated plants were highly unpredictable, and a more flexible economy that combined agriculture with hunting and gathering was the most feasible until the disappearance of the buffalo in the late 1870s. Agriculture was a far more ancient and indigenous tradition on the Plains than the horse culture, which was a much more fleeting episode. Cree were acquainted with cultivated plant food and techniques of agriculture through several of their contacts, most notably the Mandan, Arikara, and Hidatsa, who maintained a flourishing agricultural economy on the upper Missouri. There is evidence of an agricultural village on the banks of the Red River near the present-day town of Lockport, Manitoba, that dates from between AD 1300 and AD 1500 (Putt, 1991: 64). Blackfoot were found by the earliest of European fur traders to be growing tobacco.

Aboriginal people of the Plains were not as 'passive' as the landscape; their world was not static and timeless. The archaeological and historical records suggest that on the Plains learning new ways took place regularly, that there was much adaptation and borrowing among people, and that changes occurred constantly. The Plains Cree, for example, had a history of making dramatic adjustments to new economic and ecological circumstances, modifying the ways in which they obtained their livelihood. With the establishment of fur trade posts on Hudson Bay after 1670, the Cree, along with their allies the Assiniboine, quickly seized the opportunity to function as middlemen to the trade. With the expansion of European fur trade posts inland in the late eighteenth century, the Cree took advantage of a new economic opportunity and worked as provisioners of buffalo meat to the trading companies. They showed themselves to be remarkably flexible in rapidly adjusting to the rewards and demands of different environments—the forest, parklands, and Plains. The branch that became the Plains Cree readily adopted many of the characteristics, techniques, and traits of Plains buffalo and horse culture. Aboriginal people such as the Cree were accustomed to making dramatic adjustments to new ecological and economic circumstances, and there is no inherent reason to believe that they could not have made adjustments to the new order of the post-1870 era by becoming full participants in the agricultural economy. The fact that they did not was due not to their own choice; rather, there was a refusal to let them do so as they were denied access to the opportunities and resources that would have allowed them a more independent existence.

While Aboriginal people of the Plains required assistance and instruction to establish a farming economy, they had certain advantages that new arrivals did not enjoy. They had an intimate knowledge of the resources and climate of the West. They were much better informed on rainfall and frost patterns, on the availability of water and timber, and on soil varieties. They had experience with locusts, fires, and droughts. Aboriginal farmers might have had a better chance than many of the settlers from the humid East. Many of these never could accept the discomforts and conditions, and they departed, and even for those who remained acclimatization could take several years. Settlers from elsewhere might well have benefited from the knowledge Aboriginal people of the Plains had to offer. One settler in Saskatchewan, who had previously worked as a trader, consulted an Aboriginal friend named South Wind when he wanted to locate his homestead in the 1880s, and learned, for example, how to use fire to protect stands of timber and how to replenish the hay swamps. He later found local legislation regarding fire to be a 'positive evil' and wrote that 'our legislators should have had old South Wind at their Councils.'[2] Accounts of such consultation are, however, very rare.

As early as the 1850s European travellers to the Plains reported that the Cree were concerned about the scarcity of buffalo, that many were anxious to try agriculture and wanted assistance in the way of instruction and technology. They were well aware that the buffalo hunt was no longer going to sustain them. With the demise of the fur trade, agriculture appeared to be the only option. During the treaty negotiations of the 1870s Plains people sought government aid to make the transition to an agricultural economy. In return for their offer of an opportunity for peaceful expansion, Aboriginal people asked that they be given the instruction and technology that would allow them to farm. Aboriginal spokesmen did not see any inherent conflict between their distinctive identity and active participation in an agricultural economy. Circumstances obliged them to cease living as their ancestors had done, but they did not therefore cease to be Aboriginals. Like the Natives of the older provinces of Canada, they were in favour of agriculture, resource development, and education that would assist them to survive, but they did not, for example, intend to abandon their religious ceremonies and beliefs. Euro-Canadian observers consistently insisted on seeing Plains people as hunters, gatherers, and warriors incapable of adopting agriculture.

A Crop of Broken Promises: The 1870s

The main focus of this study are those people of the Treaty No. 4 district of southeastern Saskatchewan who settled on reserves in the Touchwood Hills, File Hills, and along the Qu'Appelle River. Most were Plains Cree, collectively known as the *mamihkiyiniwak*, the Downstream People, although Assiniboine, mixed Cree-Assiniboine (Young Dogs), and Saulteaux also settled here and were intermingled with Plains Cree bands. Although these people form the main focus, evidence was also drawn from the Treaty No. 6 district, settled primarily by Plains Cree known as the Upstream People. In the later 1870s, the earliest years of Indian reserve settlement in present-day Saskatchewan, farming proved nearly impossible despite concerted efforts. For some bands, farming was never to be successful because of the nature of the reserve site itself. Other bands received high-quality agricultural land that was later to excite the envy of other settlers. The earliest instructions to surveyors were that care should be taken to ensure reserve lands 'should not interfere with the possible requirements of future settlement, or of land for railway purposes.' At that time what was seen as the 'fertile belt', and the proposed route for the Canadian Pacific Railway, ran northwest along the Assiniboine and North Saskatchewan rivers. Land further south was considered arid and unlikely ever to be wanted by settlers, so many reserves, such as those along the Qu'Appelle River, were surveyed there. But when the CPR route was changed in 1881 and rerouted through the south, many of these reserves were located near or on the railway route, in the midst of what was hoped would become the settlement belt and the heart of a prosperous agricultural economy.

Farming in the 1870s proved to be nearly impossible because the implements and livestock promised in the treaties were inadequate. Ten families, for example, were to share one plough. Bands varied in size, numbering between 17 and 50 families, but regardless of size, each was offered

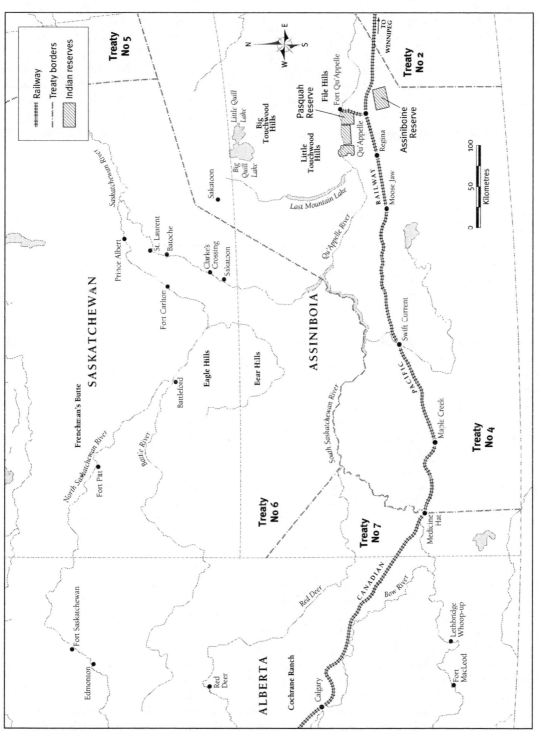

MAP 19.1. Saskatchewan and Assiniboia Districts, *circa* 1900

only one yoke of oxen, one bull, and four cows. To earn a living from the soil, a yoke of oxen was required by every farming family. As one Plains Cree chief pointed out in 1879, it was perfectly ridiculous to expect them to get on with so few oxen, that every farmer in the Northwest, however poor, had his own yoke of oxen, that 'We are new at this kind of work, but even white men cannot get on with so few oxen' (Anon., 1879: 28). In addition to the overall inadequacy of the agricultural assistance promised in the treaties, government officials were reluctant and tentative about distributing what was promised. The people prepared to farm expected their supply of implements, cattle, and seed immediately, but officials were determined to adhere strictly to the exact wording of the treaty, which stated that implements, cattle, and seed would be given to 'any band . . . now actually cultivating the soil, or who shall hereafter settle on these reserves and commence to break up the land.' Aboriginal people could not settle until the surveys were complete, and in some cases this took many years. They could not cultivate until they had implements to break the land, yet these were not to be distributed until they were settled and cultivating. Government officials shared the belief that the distribution even of those items promised in the treaties could 'encourage idleness', and there was concern that the implements and cattle would not be used for the purposes for which they were intended.

There were also problems with the quality and distribution of seed grain. In the earliest years the seed arrived in a damaged state and was received in midsummer when the season was far too advanced for planting. Acres sometimes lay idle because there was no seed available, and more land might have been broken had there been seed to sow. It was also learned after a number of years that people cultivating the reserves had to be supplied with some provisions in the spring during ploughing and sowing. The people of Treaty No. 6 had successfully bargained for this during their negotiations, but no such promise had been made

to the people of Treaty No. 4. Although David Laird, Lieutenant-Governor and Indian superintendent for the North-West Superintendency, recommended in 1877 that some provisions be distributed in the spring to Treaty No. 4 bands, this request was struck from the estimates in Ottawa. It proved impossible for more than a few to remain on their reserves and cultivate as the others were obliged to hunt and gather provisions for the group to survive. Once seeding was finished, and sometimes even before, many residents of the reserves were out on the Plains, leaving behind only a few to tend the crops.

Aboriginal farmers were hampered in their earliest efforts by the kind of ploughs they were issued. By the late 1870s, Manitoba farmers had learned that American ploughs, especially the John Deere, with its chilled-steel mouldboard, were far superior for western conditions than the Ontario models. The Indian Department, however, continued until 1882 to purchase only Canadian-manufactured ploughs, which proved to be unsatisfactory. There were problems keeping in good repair the implements and wagons that were distributed, as they frequently broke down, crippling operations. Wooden parts were sometimes replaced by the farmer, but the breakage of metal parts was much more serious, as reserve farmers did not have access to blacksmiths, who were also required to point, or sharpen, ploughshares. Other equipment and livestock supplied by contractors under the terms of the treaties were clearly inferior, and Aboriginal people simply refused to accept some of it. An 1878 commission of investigation found Winnipeg Indian commissioner J.A.N. Provencher guilty of fraud in the awarding of contracts and it was discovered, among other things, that it was standard practice to furnish the Indian Department with 'the most inferior articles' (Titley, 1997). In 1879 one observer described the carts and wagons supplied to but refused by Treaty No. 6 people near Fort Carlton as 'the poorest description of Red River carts, which have been used by freighters up to this point, and are really unfit for further use;

while the wagons are literally falling to pieces.' The axes, 'miserably small', were also refused (Anon., 1879: 29).

Perhaps the most scandalous example of corruption was in the cattle sent to a great many reserves in the late 1870s. They received wild Montana cattle, which were unaccustomed to work and could not be hitched to the plough. The milk cows given out were of the same description. The Fort Carlton bands were astounded when these cattle were brought to them from Montana, when tame cattle could have been purchased at Prince Albert or Red River. Most of them died over the first winter of 1878–9. Some choked themselves when tied in stables; others could not be fed because they did not take to the food. As one Plains Cree chief stated, 'We know why these Montana cattle were given us; because they were cheaper, and the Government, thinking us a simple people, thought we would take them' (ibid., 28). He was correct. It became clear during the 1878 investigation that individuals in Winnipeg had profited by purchasing these creatures from Montana at about half the rate that they actually charged the Indian Department.

Aboriginal farmers laboured under other disadvantages as well. In these earliest years there were no grist mills located near reserves, and the wheat they raised was of no use to them without milling facilities. With the disappearance of the buffalo, the main source for all their apparel also vanished. They lacked clothing and footwear, which one official described as the greatest drawback to their work. To cover their feet they cut up old leather lodges, but these too rapidly diminished. Often hungry, weak, and ill, people could not work no matter how willing.

There was little progress in agriculture in the years immediately following the treaties of the 1870s. Early on, government officials insisted that this had to do with the indifference and apathy of Aboriginal people, who willfully rejected an agricultural way of life and inflexibly and stubbornly insisted on pursuing hunting and gathering. Through idleness they were creating their own

problems. An explanation that belittled and deprecated the abilities of Aboriginal farmers absolved the government of any responsibility in the matter, and it was to be the favoured explanation of department officials well into the twentieth century. During these initial years of government parsimony, indifference, and outright corruption an opportunity was lost. Many of those who wished to farm found it impossible and became disheartened and discouraged. Had the government shown a genuine interest, some steps towards the creation of an agricultural economy might have been taken during the years before 1878–9, when the food crisis, brought on by the total disappearance of the buffalo, became severe. There was much distress, suffering, and death throughout the Northwest by 1878, although reports of starvation were systematically denied by government officials and the western press, as such news could damage the reputation of the region as a prospective home for thousands of immigrants. Once again, Aboriginal people were portrayed as chronic complainers with imaginary grievances, and they were blamed for having 'not made the usual effort to help themselves'.[3]

The other legacy of the years immediately following the treaties was the sense of betrayal felt by Aboriginal people who had expected government assistance in the difficult transition to an agricultural economy. As Chief Ahtahkakoop stated in 1879, 'On the transfer of the country we were told that the Queen would do us all the good in the world, and that the Indians would see her bounty. With this message came presents of tobacco, and I took it at once; and I pray now that the bounty then promised may be extended to us.' Three years after the treaty the chief was convinced that the 'policy of the Government has been directed to its own advantage, and the Indians have not been considered so much.' These chiefs had made several representations to government authorities, 'but they were as if they were thrown into water' (ibid.).

Chief Pasquah, from the Pasquah Reserve in southeastern Saskatchewan, had presented Joseph

Cauchon, Lieutenant-Governor of Manitoba, with similar grievances and concerns a year earlier.[4] His people, though willing to farm and diversify their subsistence base, had no cattle to break and work the land, no seed to sow, and no provisions to sustain them while at work. Aboriginal people had reason to feel that they had been deceived and led along a path that ended in betrayal, that their treatment constituted a breach of faith. They were getting the clear impression that the treaties were made simply as a means of getting peaceable possession of the country without any regard to their welfare. As Aboriginal spokesmen grasped every opportunity to implore the government to assist them to make a living by agriculture, department officials increasingly reacted by blaming the Natives for their misfortunes and portraying them as troublemakers and chronic complainers, incapable of telling the truth.

The Home Farm Experiment

In the wake of alarming reports from the Northwest of destitution and starvation, an ambitious plan to both feed and instruct Aboriginal people in farming was hastily contrived in Ottawa in the fall and winter of 1878–9. A squad of farm instructors, mainly from Ontario, was sent west in the summer of 1879. They were to establish 'home farms' at 15 sites in the Northwest: six in the Treaty No. 4 district and nine in the Treaty No. 6 district. At these farms, located on or near the reserves, the instructors were to raise large quantities of provisions to support not only themselves, their families, and employees but also the neighbouring Aboriginal population. Their farms were to serve as 'model farms' for Aboriginal observers, and in addition the instructors were to visit the reserve farmers from time to time to assist them in breaking, seeding, and harvesting and in building their houses, barns, and root houses. At two 'supply farms' in the Treaty No. 7 district large quantities of produce were to be raised, but the farmers at these sites were not given the additional responsibility of instructing Aboriginal farmers.

The home farm plan was hastily and poorly conceived in Ottawa by people without any knowledge of Aboriginal people or of the region's soil and climate. The men chosen as instructors were unfamiliar with conditions of life in the West and knew nothing about Aboriginal people. They had to be provided with both guides and interpreters. As one Aboriginal spokesman stated, it only made sense that a farm instructor be a man 'from the country, who understands the language, and with whom I could speak face to face, without an interpreter' (ibid., 2g). The official rationale for not choosing local people was that 'strangers' were likely to carry out their duties more efficiently, would not have their favourites, and would treat all fairly and alike. It is also clear, however, that the position of farm instructor was a patronage appointment, and all were chosen by Sir John A. Macdonald, the Canadian Prime Minister, from a list furnished by Laurence Vankoughnet, deputy superintendent-general of Indian Affairs. In addition, the tasks assigned the instructors were beyond the resources and capabilities of any individual, however well acquainted he might be with conditions in the Northwest. It soon proved that the instructors had great difficulty establishing even the most modest farms. The government found itself responsible for the support of instructors, their families, and employees, who ran farms with such dismal returns that they contributed almost nothing to the expense of running them. It was also soon discovered that the farmers simply could not attend both to their own farms and to assisting on reserve farms. The instructors seldom visited the reserves and lacked even basic knowledge about the people they were to instruct. The program turned out to be an administrative nightmare. Difficulties with personnel arose early, and the program was characterized by resignations and dismissals. The instructors were angered by government decisions to charge them for the board of themselves and family, and also to charge them for food they consumed that they had raised themselves.

BOX 19.1

Ahtahkakoop, Mistawasis, and Kitowehaw, 1879

On 2 September 1879 a meeting took place at Fort Carlton between Indian Commissioner Edgar Dewdney and Treaty No. 6 Plains Cree leaders Ahtahkakoop, Mistawasis, and Kitowehaw. A 'special correspondent' from the *Montreal Gazette* also attended and reported on the meeting in an article published in that paper on 29 September. The Hudson's Bay Company interpreter translated the words of the Plains Cree leaders beginning with Ahtahkakoop:

> We waited for you, and we see you now; we wonder if our word met you. We have often been talking of the promises we got and when we saw that they were not carried out in their spirit, we made representations to the Minister, but they were as if they were thrown into the water. We are very glad to meet you now, as you come with full authority to act. We will not touch on anything, but the promises which have not been fulfilled. . . . The cattle we got from Government all died; they were brought from Montana, and we protested that they would not do. . . . They were like the wild fowl, we saw them here, and then they disappeared; some, when tied in stables, choked themselves; some could not be fed, and to catch them was a fight, so wild were they. . . .

Mistawasis then came forward and said:

> I will tell you, as we understood the treaty made with Governor Morris. We understood from him that he was coming into the country to help us to live, and we were told how we were to get a living, and we put ourselves at work at once to

settle down. . . . We expected that we would have had good cattle, but those brought were so poor that it was a mockery of the promises to give us cattle with little else than skin and bone. . . . Government is too slow in helping the Indians if they are going to help us at all. The fall before we saw [Lieutenant-] Governor [David] Laird, and wished him to give us more ample assistance in the way of farm implements and seeds. He said his powers were limited, but he would write to the Government, and let us know. To all these representations we received no answer. The country is getting so poor that it is for us either death by starvation, and such aid as will enable us to live. The buffalo was our only dependence before the transfer of the country, and this and other wild animals are disappearing, and we must farm to enable us to live. . . .

Ketawayo [Kitowehaw]:

> Every farmer, however poor, at Prince Albert has his yoke of oxen and we have tried and find that we cannot do with so few. We are new at this kind of work, but even white men cannot get on with so few oxen. . . . We know why these Montana cattle were given us; because they were cheaper, and the Government, thinking us a simple people, thought we would take them. The cattle have all died. . . . Hitherto everything we have asked has been promised to be represented to the Government, but we have never got any answer, and we want now an answer. . . .

—Anonymous, 1879

Beset with all of these difficulties, the home farm program floundered. In the House of Commons, government critics hammered away at the plan. They claimed that the instructors were incompetent carpetbaggers, but the central criticism was that there should be no such expenditure on the Aboriginal people of the Northwest, as this was encouraging idleness when they should be made to rely solely on their own resources. One member of Parliament argued that the program was an enormous waste of money because efforts to 'civilize Indians' were inevitably doomed to failure.[5] Government defenders of the program argued that the essential problem lay with Aboriginal people, who were 'idlers by nature, and uncivilized'. In the opinion of Prime Minister Macdonald they were not suited to agriculture, as they 'have not the ox-like quality of the Anglo-Saxon; they will not put their neck to the yoke.'[6]

There were many vocal critics of the home farm program in the Northwest as well. Non-Aboriginal residents viewed the program as unfair, because too much was being done to equip Aboriginal people to farm, more than was available to the true 'homesteaders', upon whom it was felt the prosperity of the region depended. The home farm program ingrained the idea that Aboriginal farmers were being lavishly provided with farm equipment and other assistance that was 'conducive to the destruction of self-reliance, and calculated to give them a false impression of what the Government owed them.' In the wake of the food crisis in the Northwest the government had begun to provide modest rations to reserve residents. Indeed, some of the farm instructors found much of their time taken up issuing relief in the form of 'musty and rusty' salt pork in exchange for assigned work. Many non-Native residents were critical of the distribution of rations, which they saw as a reward for idleness and as unfair because it gave Aboriginal farmers an advantage over other struggling farmers.

The home farm program had a very brief life in its original form. By 1884 the department had officially retired the policy, which had already undergone much modification. Farm instructors remained and their numbers increased, but their own farms were to consist of no more than a few acres and they were to concentrate on instruction. New recruits were no longer brought from Ontario at great expense, but were men from the Northwest.

The Pioneer Experience: Agriculture in the 1880s

All who attempted farming on the Plains in the 1880s experienced frustration and failure. Crops during this decade were damaged year after year by drought and early frosts. Prairie fires became a serious hazard, consuming haystacks as well as houses, stables, and fences, and hampering the abilities of farmers not only to winter cattle but to carry out the whole cycle of farming operations. There was a high rate of homestead cancellation, and many of the community experiments of ethnic, religious, working-class, and aristocratic groups did not survive the decade.

A major difference between the Aboriginal farmer and his neighbours was that while new-comers had the option to leave and try their luck elsewhere, reserve residents had little choice but to persevere, as under the Indian Act they were excluded from taking homesteads. Aboriginal farmers could not obtain loans because they were not regarded as the actual owners of any property, however extensive and valuable their improvements might be, and they had difficulty obtaining credit from merchants. Because of many of the technicalities and prohibitions of the Indian Act, Natives were prevented from doing business or transacting even the most ordinary daily affair. They were deprived of the right to do what they chose with nearly everything they acquired by their own personal industry. People who came under the Indian Act were prevented by a permit system from selling, exchanging, bartering, or giving away any produce grown on their reserves without the permission of department officials. A pass system, imposed initially

FIGURE 19.2. Native farmers, c. 1906–10. (Courtesy Archives of Manitoba, Edmund Morris Collection, G11–510)

during the 1885 Rebellion but continued well into the twentieth century, controlled and confined the movements of people off their reserves. Those who wished to leave the reserve were obliged to acquire a pass from the farm instructor or Indian agent declaring the length of and reason for absence. The most recent arrivals to the country had far more rights, privileges, and freedom than the original inhabitants.

Despite these restrictions and the drought, frost, and prairie fires of these years, reserve farmers in some localities made significant advances in the 1880s. Several of the problems that had hampered reserve farming in the past had to some extent been ameliorated. Through a 'cattle on loan' policy, for example, many bands had considerably increased their numbers of work oxen, cows, steers, heifers, and bulls. Under this system the department 'loaned' a cow to an individual who was to raise a heifer, either of which had to be returned to the Indian agent. The animal

became the property of the individual, although the agent's permission was required to sell or slaughter. Reserve farmers also had increased access to grist mills in the 1880s as the department initiated a program of granting bonuses to individuals who would establish mills in the Northwest. Recipients of the bonus were obliged to charge Aboriginal customers a little less than ordinary customers for a 10-year period. The department also displayed greater concern to supply the services of blacksmiths, which bolstered agricultural operations.

Reserve farmers began to acquire some of the up-to-date machinery necessary to facilitate their operations. Mowers and rakes were the most common purchases. Some reserves were fortunate in their abundant hay supplies, and a number of bands sold hay on contract to other reserves, to settlers, and to the North-West Mounted Police. Selling hay was one of the very few opportunities for outside employment available to reserve residents. These machines were purchased with their own earnings or through pooled annuities. They were not purchased for them by the department. Agents and farm instructors in the 1880s felt that access to mowers and rakes was essential for all bands, not only those that sold hay. As stock increased on the reserves, mowers and rakes were necessary to provide enough hay. Reapers and self-binders were also acquired during this period. The self-binder lessened the danger of being caught by frost during a protracted harvest and it also reduced the waste experienced in binding with short straw. Such machinery permitted farmers to cultivate larger areas. By the late 1880s on some reserves in the districts of Treaty No. 4 and Treaty No. 6, farmers were beginning to see some significant results of their labour, and they had produce that they wished to sell: predominantly cattle, grain, and hay.

Like other prairie women of this period, Aboriginal women helped in the fields during peak seasons such as haying and harvest, but otherwise the business of grain farming was predominantly a male activity. Women continued to harvest wild resources such as berries, wild rhubarb, prairie turnip, and birch sap, and they hunted rabbits, gophers, and ducks. Because of increased settlement, the pass system, and calls for the restriction of Aboriginal hunting rights, these opportunities became increasingly constricted. Aboriginal women were eager to learn new skills and to adopt new technology. By the late 1880s the wives of many farm instructors acquired the title of 'instructress' and they, as well as the wives of missionaries, taught skills such as milking, butter-making, bread-making, and knitting. Women adapted readily to these activities, but a chronic shortage of raw materials made it difficult to apply what they had learned. While the women knew how to make loaf bread, for example, they did not have the proper ovens, yeast, or baking tins, so they continued to make bannock, despite government attempts to abolish it from the diet as it required more flour than loaf bread. They seldom had yarn with which to knit.

There were no buttons for the dresses the women made. They were often short of milk pans, although they made their own using birchbark. One instructress reported in 1891 that the greatest drawback was 'their extreme poverty, their lack of almost every article of domestic comfort in their houses, and no material to work upon'.[7] They lacked basic necessities such as soap, towels, wash basins, and wash pails, and had no means with which to acquire these.

The log dwellings on reserves in this era and well into the twentieth century were invariably described as 'huts' or 'shacks' that were one storey and one room. The roofs were constructed with logs or poles over which rows of straw or grass were laid. They were chinked inside and out with a mixture of mud and hay and had clay stoves but no flooring, and tanned hide was used for window covering. It was impossible to apply lessons of 'housewifery' in such shacks. In publications of the Department of Indian Affairs, however, Aboriginal women were often depicted as poor housekeepers who willfully ignored instruction in modern methods. They were blamed for the poor living and health conditions on the reserves. Explanations that stressed the incapacity of Aboriginal women to change, like those that disparaged the farming abilities of the men, absolved the government of any responsibility for the poverty of the reserves.

The Pressure of Competition

As Aboriginal farmers acquired the technology required by western conditions and as they began to increase their acreages and their herds, they also began to pose a threat as competitors in the marketplace. By the late 1880s, farmers in parts of the Northwest were complaining loudly about 'unfair' competition from Aboriginal people. It was widely believed that government assistance gave Aboriginal farmers an unfair advantage. Non-Aboriginal settlers had the misconception that reserve farmers were lavishly provided with livestock, equipment, government labour, and rations, and did not have to worry about the price at which their products were sold. There was absolutely no appreciation of the disadvantages they laboured under, or of how government regulation and Canadian laws acted to stymie their efforts. Editorials in the *Fort Macleod Gazette* regularly lamented 'Indian competition', which was injuring the 'true' settlers of the country. If the Siksika (Blackfoot), Kainai (Blood), Pikuni (Peigan), and Tsuu T'ina (Sarcee) were 'cut loose' from the treaty, support could be given to their industries, according to the *Gazette*, but it was 'pretty hard to ask the people of the country to contribute toward the support of a lot of idle paupers, and then allow them to use this very support for the purpose of taking the bread out of the settler's month [*sic*].'[8]

It was argued in the *Gazette* throughout the 1880s and 1890s that Aboriginal people should not be permitted to compete with the settlers in the sale of hay, potatoes, or grain. Any evidence that they were successful in securing contracts was used as proof that they had underbid non-Natives. There was no consideration that their product might be superior, as was certainly the case with the hay purchased by the North-West Mounted Police, who often noted in their reports that the best hay was bought from reserve farmers.[9] In a letter to the editor in July 1895, one local resident claimed that 'it is altogether unfair to allow these Indians to enter into competition with white men who, even with hard work, find it difficult to make both ends meet and provide for their families.' Evidence of unfair competition was used by the editors of the *Gazette* to bolster their larger campaign of the later 1880s to have Aboriginal people moved to one big reserve, an 'Indian territory' out of the way of the Euro-Canadian settlements. It was argued that Indian policy had been a failure as Aboriginal people 'had not made a single step toward becoming self-supporting.'[10] There was apparently no recognition of the fact that it was impossible to become self-supporting to any degree unless they were allowed to sell their products.

Concerns about unfair 'Indian competition' were echoed in other parts of the Northwest as well. The residents of Battleford and district were particularly strident in their objections to the competition of the Plains Cree in the grain, hay, and wood markets. Here, as well as in the district of southern Alberta, there was concern that reserve residents not become successful stock-raisers as the supply of cattle to the Indian Department for rations was a vital source of revenue for many settlers. On 13 October 1888 the editor of the *Saskatchewan Herald* of Battleford denounced any plan to 'set the Indians up as cattle breeders, encouraging them to supply the beef that is now put in by white contractors'.

Here, as in other districts, Aboriginal farmers were in competition with new settlers for hay land. Because of the predominantly dry years of the 1880s hay was very scarce some seasons. Off-reserve areas where reserve farmers had customarily cut hay became the subject of heated disputes. Non-Aboriginal residents of the Battleford district successfully petitioned the Minister of the Interior in 1889 to limit the hay land available to Aboriginal farmers off the reserves, despite the fact that the Battleford agent had warned that there would be no alternative but to decrease stock on the reserves. Many influential people in the West had a direct interest in the continuation of rations and in seeing that Aboriginal people were not self-supporting. Large operations like the W.F. Cochrane Ranch in southern Alberta found a sizable market for their beef on the neighbouring reserves. In his correspondence to department officials he naturally objected to any reduction in rations, arguing that this meant that their lives, as well as their property and cattle operation, would be in danger.[11]

The Peasant Farming Policy, 1889–97

In 1889, Hayter Reed, Commissioner of Indian Affairs in Regina, announced that a new 'approved system of farming' was to be applied to Indian reserves in western Canada. Reserve farmers were to reduce their area under cultivation to a single acre of wheat and a garden of roots and vegetables. Along with a cow or two, this would sufficiently provide for a farmer and his family. They were to use rudimentary implements alone: to broadcast seed by hand, harvest with scythes, bind by hand with straw, thresh with flails, and grind their grain with hand mills. They were to manufacture at home any items they required, such as harrows, hayforks, carts, and yokes. This policy complemented government intentions to subdivide the reserves into small holdings of 40 acres each. Publicly, the subdivision of the reserves and the peasant farming policy were justified as an approach intended to render reserve residents self-supporting. Individual tenure, it was claimed, would implant a spirit of self-reliance and individualism, thus eroding 'tribalism'. Hayter Reed argued that the use of labour-saving machinery might be necessary and suitable for settlers, but Indians first had to experience farming with crude and simple implements. To do otherwise defied immutable laws of evolution and would be an 'unnatural leap'. In Reed's view, Aboriginal people had not reached the stage at which they were in a position to compete with white settlers.[12] Another argument forwarded against the use of labour-saving machinery was that rudimentary implements afforded useful employment for all.

Clearly, however, there were other reasons for the peasant farming formula and for allotment in severalty, reasons that were understood and appreciated by non-Aboriginal settlers. The *Saskatchewan Herald* (20 August 1887) applauded the policy for the Aboriginal farmer:

Thrown thus on himself and left to work his farm without the aid of expensive machinery, he will content himself with raising just what he needs himself, and thus, while meeting the Government's intention of becoming self-sustaining, they at the same time would come into competition with the white settler only to the extent of their own labour, and thus

remove all grounds for the complaint being made in some quarters against Government aided Indians entering into competition with white settlers.

This was a policy of deliberate arrested development. The allotment of land in severalty was viewed by officials, as well as by Prime Minister Macdonald himself, as a means of defining surplus land that might be sold (Tyler, 1979: 114). Severalty would confine people within circumscribed boundaries, and their 'surplus' land could be defined and sold. Arrested development was a certain means of ensuring that much reserve land would appear to be vacant and unused.

Despite the protests of Aboriginal farmers, Indian agents, farm instructors, and inspectors of the agencies, the peasant farming policy was implemented on Plains reserves beginning in 1889. Officials were not to authorize the purchase, hire, or use of any machinery. Even if people had purchased machinery before the policy was adopted they were still to use hand implements. Farmers with larger holdings were to use the labour of others rather than revert to the use of machinery, or they were to restrict their acreages to what they could handle with hand implements alone. Officials in the field were dismayed by the policy that robbed the farmers of any potential source of revenue. They argued that the seasons in the Northwest were simply too short for the use of hand implements, which meant a loss in yield at harvest time and resulted in a much reduced supply of hay. Agent W.S. Grant of the Assiniboine Reserve protested that 'the seasons in this country are too short to harvest any quantity of grain, without much waste, with only old fashioned, and hand implements to do the work with.' In his view the amount of grain lost in his agency through harvesting with hand implements would be of sufficient quantity to pay for a binder in two years.[13]

Aboriginal farmers were profoundly discouraged by the new rules. It was widely reported that many refused to work with the hand implements and gave up farming altogether. One farmer from

Moose Mountain declared he would let his grain stand and never plough another acre, while another gave up his oxen, his wheat, and the reserve.[14] Other aspects of the program, such as the home manufactures idea, were unrealistic and unworkable. Homemade wooden forks, for example, were simply not strong enough for loading hay, grain, or manure. They were to make their own lanterns, but agents protested that people could not look after their cattle at night without proper lanterns. At headquarters in Ottawa it proved impossible even to acquire some of the old-fashioned implements, such as hand mills, destined for the Aboriginal farmers. But Reed was not sympathetic to or moved by the objections and complaints, and he refused to give in to the 'whims of Farmers and Indians'. He advised that losing some of the crop or growing less grain was preferable to the use of machinery. If grain was being lost, the solution was for farmers to confine their acreage to what they could handle. Department employees were not to convene or be present at meetings with Aboriginal farmers, as this would give 'an exaggerated importance' to their requests for machinery. They risked dismissal if they refused to comply with peasant farming policy.

Effects of the Restrictive Policy

The policy of deliberate discouragement of reserve agriculture worked well. By the mid-1890s, per capita acreage under cultivation had fallen to about half of the 1889 level and many serious farmers had given up farming altogether. In 1899 a resident of Prince Albert, William Miller Sr, wrote to the Minister of the Interior that in passing through the Duck Lake and Carlton reserves, he noted 'no less than five fields [which can] be seen from the trail now without a bushel of grain sown in them . . . that previously used to be an example to the settlers around.'[15] Peasant farming, severalty, and measures such as the permit system combined to undermine and atrophy agricultural development on reserves. The

Canadian government acted not to promote the agriculture of the indigenous population but to provide an optimum environment for the immigrant settler. Whatever Canada did for its 'wards' was subordinate to the interests of the non-Aboriginal population. Government policy was determined by the need to maintain the viability of the immigrant community.

Aboriginal people protested policies that affected them adversely, as they had from the 1870s. They raised objections to government officials, petitioned the House of Commons, sent letters to newspapers, and visited Ottawa. But the outlets for protest were increasingly restricted. Grievances related to instructors and agents rarely went further. Agency inspectors were, as mentioned, not allowed to hold audiences with reserve residents. The published reports of agents and inspectors were to divulge only that 'which it was desired the public should believe'.[16] Visiting officials such as the Governor-General, who were usually accompanied by journalists, were taken only to select agencies that would leave the best impression. Department officials, particularly those in the central office, shared the view that Aboriginal people were chronic complainers not to be believed and a people who would go to extraordinary lengths to avoid diligent work.

Hayter Reed and the peasant farming formula were disposed of the year after Wilfrid Laurier and the Liberals came to power in 1896, but the damaging legacy of the policy was to be felt for years to come. Laurier was fortunate in coming to power just at a time when a constellation of factors, including rising world wheat prices, increased rainfall on the Prairies, innovations in dry-land farming techniques, and massive immigration allowed a wheat economy to prosper in western Canada. Aboriginal farmers, however, had little place in this new age of prosperity. By the turn of the century agriculture did not form the basis of a stable reserve economy, and after that date the likelihood faded even further as the new administrators of Indian Affairs promoted land surrenders that further limited the agricultural capacity of

---

BOX 19.2

The Permit System

Edward Ahenakew used a fictional character named 'Old Keyam' to convey the Plains Cree experience of life on a prairie reserve in the early twentieth century. In this passage he describes the aggravations of the permit system that discouraged interest in farming and the cattle industry:

> This may be 'kindly supervision' but it is most wretchedly humbling to many a worthy fellow to have to go, with assumed indifference, to ask or beg for a permit to sell one load of hay that he has cut himself, on his own reserve, with his own horses and implements. I say again, it may be right for some, but that is no reason why those who try to get on, and who do get on, should have to undergo this humiliation. . . .
>
> For myself, I think that I would rather starve than go to beg for such a trifling thing as a permit to sell one load of hay, while I am trying to make every hour of good weather count. To sell ten loads might be different. From the standpoint of the Government it may seem good, a kind of drill or discipline. But who on earth wants this when he is busy in a hurry, and needs food for himself? I have seen with my own eyes, Indians wasting a day, even two days, trying to get a permit to sell, when they are short of food. The Agent cannot always be at home, the clerk may be away, or busy, and the Indian must wait,

though he may have to drive to the Agency from another reserve. . . .

> As for our cattle—there again, they are not ours. A white man, owning cattle and having no ready money, draws up a plan for himself which includes selling. An Indian may have more cattle than that white man has, but do you think that he can plan in the same way? No. He is told that the commissioner has said that no cattle are to be sold until the fall. It is useless to plan under this system, yet planning is what successful work requires. . . .
>
> Old Keyam paused to let his words sink in, and before he could continue, a young man spoke. 'I have something to add to that. Sure, we all like the farm instructor. He's good-natured, teases us, doesn't mind when we tease him. Well, we were branding cattle last week, and he asked in his joking way what we thought ID [the brand of the Indian Department] meant. Old Knife was there, and he's smart. He gave quite a speech about it, said that it stood for our chief source of light in the darkness, a sort of half-moon—only the outward curve with its full true light shone towards Ottawa in the east, the other part to the west, and that it was hollow, not giving much light, and double barred at that. Whoever planned that brand, he said, knew the whole business well.'

—Ahenakew (1973: 148–50)

---

reserves. The fact that there was 'vacant' and 'idle' land on many reserves, to a great extent the result of the peasant farming years, conveniently played into the hands of those who argued that Aboriginal people had land far in excess of their needs and capabilities. Government policy was

that it was in the best interests of all concerned to encourage reserve residents to divest themselves of land they held 'beyond their possible requirements', and the policy received widespread support in the western press and from farmers and townspeople. Residents of towns near Indian reserves regularly submitted petitions claiming that these tracts retarded the development and progress of their districts. Such pressure resulted in the alienation of many thousands of acres of reserve land, often the best land, in the years shortly after the turn of the century. The economic viability of reserve communities was deliberately eroded by the dominant society, mainly through government policies.

Conclusion

In the post-treaty era to 1900 the Plains Cree were resolved to establish a new economy based on agriculture. They faced many impediments and frustrations in these efforts. Implements and livestock promised under treaty were inadequate, and government officials proved reluctant to distribute these. These officials insisted that people were to be settled on their reserves *and cultivating* in advance of their receiving the implements and cattle promised to them, although that which had been promised was necessary for cultivation. Seed grain arrived too late or in a damaged state and wild Montana cattle were distributed instead of domestic oxen. Workers on reserves lacked proper clothing and footwear, and they were weak because of hunger and illness. Many reserves were distant from markets and transportation and there were no milling facilities in the earliest years of reserve life.

The government attempted to address some of these problems and the food crisis in the Northwest through a 'home farm' policy that was hastily devised and implemented in 1879. The plan was to have farm instructors establish model farms, raise large quantities of food for rations, and teach agriculture. It was a poorly conceived policy as these tasks were beyond the capabilities of the men appointed, most of whom had no acquaintance with Aboriginal people or with conditions in the Northwest. This policy was shelved by 1884, but farm instructors remained on many reserves, indicating an important measure of

government commitment to the establishment of farming at that time, and some advances in agriculture were made in the mid- to late 1880s. But environmental conditions were grim for all farmers at that time. There were early frosts, and drought and prairie fires caused enormous damage. Aboriginal farmers laboured under particular disadvantages. Because of the prohibitions of the Indian Act they could not expand their land base or try their luck elsewhere by taking out homesteads, and they could not take out loans or transact their own business affairs.

Despite all of the challenges of the 1880s, Plains Cree farmers in some localities made significant advances, raising a surplus for sale and acquiring necessary machinery by the end of that decade. Non-Aboriginal residents of the West expressed concern about this success and the threat of competition in the limited markets. In 1889, in response to these concerns, the government introduced a 'peasant' farming policy. Reserve farmers were to cultivate no more than an acre or two using only rudimentary hand implements. The central argument of this chapter is that this policy, combined with the other disadvantages and conditions that beset Plains Cree farmers, impaired the establishment of a viable economy.

Epilogue

Aboriginal farmers, who lost the opportunity to participate in commercial agriculture in the 1890s, did not regain any ground in the early twentieth century. Cree historians Edward Ahenakew and Joe Dion both describe a pattern in their communities of an initial interest in agriculture and stock-raising that was atrophied because of the weight of regulation and supervision. They fell further behind in technology as well as training, as they did not have access to either the formal or informal agricultural education programs of the wider farming community. The reserves remained pockets of rural poverty.

Twentieth-century visitors to reserves often found Aboriginal people living in the midst of farmland that was not cultivated at all, was leased to non-Natives, or was worked with obsolete methods and technology. It was generally concluded that they were a people who had been unable to adapt to farming, who stubbornly clung to the past, and who were impervious to 'progressive' influences despite years of government assistance and encouragement. The initial enthusiasm of many for agriculture and the policies of deliberate discouragement have been obscured and forgotten.

A 1966 survey of the social, educational, and economic conditions of the Aboriginal people of Canada, headed by anthropologist Harry B. Hawthorn, found that some of the most depressed reserve communities in the country were in agricultural districts of the Prairies where there appeared to be land for livestock or crops. Investigators described what few farms there were as marginal or sub-marginal, or the land was leased to neighbouring non-Aboriginal farmers, or farming had been abandoned altogether. Although in recent decades there has been some expansion of agricultural and livestock industries, many of the old obstacles remain, including some of the limitations of the Indian Act. The process of settling outstanding treaty land entitlements in Saskatchewan will eventually expand reserve holdings for economic development, but here, too, old obstacles remain. Members of the non-Aboriginal public continually question the Office of the Treaty Commissioner about the wisdom of such measures, insisting that 'Prairie Indians were never farmers, only hunters and warriors. Why should they get land for farming now? They . . . will only waste good farmland.'[17] Such attitudes remain deeply embedded, and collective amnesia continues, as it remains important to deny that Aboriginal people could ever make proper use of such a valuable commodity as land.

Notes

1. 'North-West Territories' was the form used until 1912, when it became the present 'Northwest Territories'.
2. National Archives of Canada (NAC), Saskatchewan Homesteading Experiences, MG 30 C 16, vol. 3, 790.
3. *Saskatchewan Herald* (Battleford), 26 Apr. 1879.
4. NAC, RG 10, vol. 3665, file 10094, interpreter to Joseph Cauchon, 1 June 1878.
5. *House of Commons Debates*, 1884, 2: 1105 (Philipe Casgrain).
6. Ibid., 1107 (John A. Macdonald).
7. NAC, RG 10, vol. 3845, file 73406–7, T.P. Wadsworth to Hayter Reed, 17 Feb. 1891.
8. *Macleod Gazette*, 16 Aug. 1887.
9. Annual Report of Commissioner L.W Herchmer for 1889, in *The New West: Being the Official Reports to Parliament of the Activities of the Royal [sic] North-West Mounted Police Force from 1888–89* (Toronto: Coles Publishing Company, 1973), 6.
10. *Macleod Gazette*, 7 Dec. 1886.
11. NAC, Hayter Reed Papers, W.F. Cochrane to L. Vankoughnet, 6 Sept. 1893, file W.F. Cochrane.
12. NAC, RG 10, vol. 3964, file 148285, Hayter Reed to A. Forget, 24 Aug. 1896.
13. Ibid., W.S. Grant to Reed, 1 Oct. 1896.
14. Ibid., J.J. Campbell to Reed, 8 Oct. 1896, and Grant to Reed, 1 Oct. 1896.
15. NAC, RG 10, vol. 3993, file 187812, William Miller Sr, to the Minister of the Interior, 21 July 1899.
16. NAC, RG 10, Deputy-Superintendent letterbooks, vol. 1115, Reed to J. Wilson, 3 Aug. 1894.
17. Peggy Brezinski, Review of Carter, *Lost Harvests*, *Anthropologica* 34 (1992): 267.

References and Recommended Readings

Ahenakew, Edward. 1973. *Voices of the Plains Cree*, ed. Ruth M. Buck. Toronto: McClelland & Stewart. Through his fictional character Old Keyam, Ahenakew (1885–1961) presents a vivid portrait of life on prairie reserves, especially of the crippling effects of government policies and regulations.

Anonymous. 1879. *Chronicles By the Way: A Series of Letters Addressed to the Montreal Gazette Descriptive of a Trip Through Manitoba and the North-West*. Montreal: Montreal Gazette Printing Co.

Butler, William F. 1968 [1872]. *The Great Lone Land*. Edmonton: Hurtig.

Carter, Sarah. 1999. *Aboriginal People and Colonizers of Western Canada to 1900*. Toronto: University of Toronto Press. A historiographical overview of the wealth of interdisciplinary scholarship of the last three decades on the history of the Canadian prairie West with an emphasis on the multiplicity of perspectives that exist.

————. 1990. *Lost Harvests: Prairie Indian Reserve Farmers and Government Policy*. Montreal and Kingston: McGill-Queen's University Press. An analysis of agriculture on prairie reserves from the treaties to World War I.

Christensen, Deanna. 2000. *Ahtahkakoop: The Epic Account of a Plains Cree Head Chief, His People, and Their Struggle for Survival 1816–1896*. Shell Lake, Sask.: Ahtahkakoop Publishing. A comprehensive biography of a prominent Plains Cree leader, as well as a rich account of the culture, society, and economy during an era of rapid change. There is a great deal of emphasis on reserve agriculture.

Dion, Joseph. 1979. *My Tribe the Crees*, ed. Hugh Dempsey. Calgary: Glenbow-Alberta Institute. An account of the early years of settlement at Onion Lake and Kehiwin.

Dyck, Noel. 1991. *What is the Indian 'Problem?': Tutelage and Resistance in Canadian Indian Administration*. St John's: Institute of Social and Economic Research, Social and Economic Studies No. 46. A critical examination of past and present relations between Aboriginal people and governments in Canada, with emphasis on prairie Canada.

Elias, Peter Douglas. 1988. *The Dakota of the Canadian Northwest: Lessons for Survival*. Winnipeg: University of Manitoba Press. A detailed analysis of the different economic strategies adopted by the Dakota, including the farming bands at Oak River, Birdtail, Oak Lake, Standing Buffalo, and White Cap.

Hawthorn, H.B., ed. 1966. *A Survey of Contemporary Indians of Canada: Economic, Political, Educational Needs and Policies*. Ottawa: Indian Affairs Branch.

Lux, Maureen. 2001. *Medicine That Walks: Disease, Medicine and Canadian Plains Native People, 1880–1940*. Toronto: University of Toronto Press. An account of the diseases that afflicted Aboriginal people that, along with poverty, malnutrition, and overcrowding, dramatically reduced their numbers. Lux analyzes how non-Aboriginal specialists theorized the impact of these diseases and also explores the persistence of Aboriginal healing practices.

Milloy, John S. 1988. *The Plains Cree: Trade, Diplomacy and War, 1790–1870*. Winnipeg: University of Manitoba Press. An analysis of the complex trade and military patterns of the branch of the Cree that became a Plains people. Milloy argues that the Plains Cree culture flourished in the era to 1870 and was not undermined by their contact with European fur traders.

Putt, Neal. 1991. *Place Where the Spirit Lives: Stories from the Archaeology and History of Manitoba*. Winnipeg: Pemmican.

Ray, Arthur J. 1974. *Indians in the Fur Trade: Their Role as Hunters, Trappers, and Middlemen in the Lands Southwest of Hudson Bay, 1660–1870*. Toronto: University of Toronto Press. The first and most significant revision of fur trade history, placing the emphasis on the role of Aboriginal people. Ray explored how the Cree and Assiniboine were involved, the extent to which they shaped the trade, and the effects of the fur trade on these societies.

Sluman, Norma, and Jean Goodwill. 1982. *John Tootoosis: Biography of a Cree Leader*. Ottawa: Golden Dog Press. Tootoosis, from Poundmaker Reserve in Saskatchewan, gives an account of the obstacles facing reserve farmers, of government efforts to effect land surrenders, and strategies adopted to circumvent them.

Titley, E. Brian. 1997. 'Unsteady Debut: J.-A.-N. Provencher and the Beginnings of Indian Administration in Manitoba,' *Prairie Forum* 22, 1: 21–46.

Tobias, John L. 1983. 'Canada's Subjugation of the Plains Cree, 1879–1885', *Canadian Historical Review* 64, 3: 519–48. An important revisionist analysis of Plains Cree actions and strategies in the immediate post-treaty years.

Tyler, Kenneth J. 1979. 'A Tax-Eating Proposition: The History of the Passpasschase Indian Reserve', MA thesis, University of Alberta.

Van Kirk, Sylvia. 1980. *'Many Tender Ties': Women in Fur Trade Society in Western Canada, 1670–1870*. Winnipeg: Watson and Dwyer.

Suggested Web Sites

Aboriginal Claims in Canada:
   www.ualberta.ca/~esimpson/claims/indianact.html
   An index to other sources and a guide to and text of
   various claims and treaties.

Annual Reports of the Department of Indian Affairs:
   www.nlc-bnc.ca/2/23/index-e.html
   The complete annual reports for the years 1864–1990.
National Aboriginal Document Database:
   www.landclaimsdocs.com/index.html
   A vast array of on-line documents including treaties,
   statutes, court decisions, and government policies.

PART VII
_____

The Plateau

CHAPTER 20

The Plateau:
A Regional Overview

DOUGLAS HUDSON and MARIANNE IGNACE

The Region and Its People

The Canadian portion of the Plateau culture area is essentially the same region as that defined locally in British Columbia as 'the southern Interior'. This area is bounded on the west by the Coast Range and on the east by the Rockies, and comprises a series of interconnected plateaus and north–south valleys that extend south into the United States. With a history of extreme glaciation, the Interior is now environmentally diverse and includes seven biogeoclimatic zones ranging from sagebrush deserts to sub-boreal spruce forests. The resources of the Fraser and Columbia River watersheds are of key importance to the Aboriginal nations and communities of the Plateau.

The Plateau is also linguistically diverse. At the core of the Canadian Plateau are Interior Salish language communities—Okanagan, Thompson or Nlaka'pamux, Shuswap or Secwepemc, and Lillooet or St'at'imx [St'at'imc]. The suffix -mx, also spelled -emc, -imx, or -imc, means 'people'. In the southern Plateau, in what is now the US, are other Interior Salish and Sahaptin-speakers. At the northern end of the Plateau, transitional to the Subarctic culture area, are the Athapaskan-speaking Ts'ilqot'in (Chilcotin) and Southern Carrier, who are linked both linguistically and culturally to their northern neighbours of the Western Subarctic, and likely represent a south-ward movement of Athapaskan-speaking groups.

Another Athapaskan-speaking group, the Nicola, was located in the Nicola Valley but merged with Okanagan and Nlaka'pamux communities in the 1800s. Another language, an isolate, is the Ktunaxa or Kutenai of southeastern BC and north-ern Idaho and Montana.

The inclusion of the Athapaskan-speaking Ts'ilqot'in and Carrier in the Plateau can be seen as problematic. As noted in Chapter 1, all such defi-nitions are to some extent arbitrary. In this case, early overviews of Plateau cultures included the Ts'ilqot'in and Carrier, and sometimes even the Sekani. However, if one emphasizes linguistic and cultural affiliations, all of these groups would be more appropriately included in the Subarctic. This is especially true of the Sekani, whose traditional territories lie outside of the Fraser and Columbia River drainages. The Ts'ilqot'in and Carrier (espe-cially the Southern Carrier around Quesnel) could, however, be seen as occupying an inter-mediate position between the Plateau and the Sub-arctic. Although earlier editions of this book included the Carrier and Ts'ilqot'in in the Plateau, we do not. Thus our description focuses on the Salishan-speaking groups of the Plateau. An over-view of the shifting boundaries of the Plateau is found in Walker (1998: 1–7).

Over time, due to disease, displacement, migration, and population growth, populations shifted and territorial boundaries were modified. A number of historic population shifts are directly

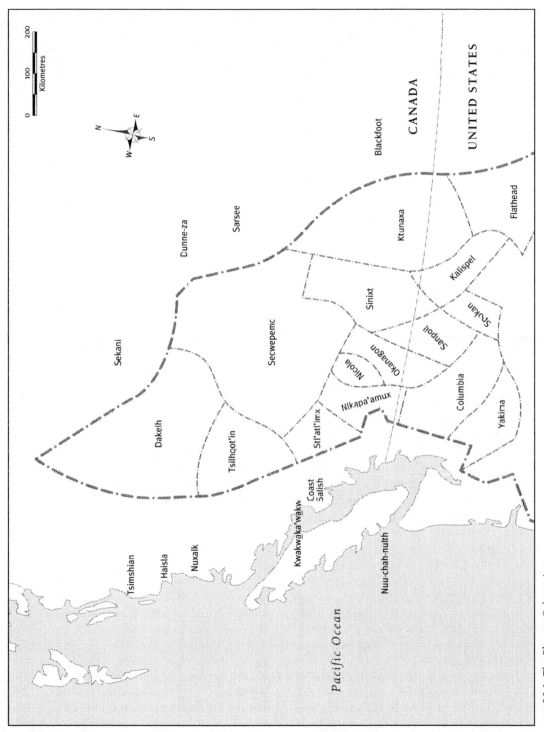

MAP 20.1. The Plateau Culture Area

Table 20.1. Plateau Language Groups

Language Family	Language (Current/Past Spelling)	Subgrouping
Salish (Interior)	St'at'imx/Lillooet	Fraser River
		Lower
	Nlaka'pamux/	Upper
	Thompson	Lower
	Secwepemc/Shuswap	Fraser River
		Canyon (Chilcotin R.)
		Lake (Shuswap L.)
		North Thompson
		Bonaparte
		Kamloops
	Nsilc/	Okanagan
	Okanagan-Colville	Similkameen
		South Okanagan
		Sinixt/Lakes
Ktunaxa/Kutenai	Ktunaxa/Kutenai	Upper
		Lower
Athapaskan	Nicola	
	(Dakelh/Carrier)	Southern
		Ulgatcho
	(Ts'ilqotin/Chilcotin)	

related to European-introduced epidemics. Smallpox destroyed up to half the Sanpoil in 1782–3, swept through the southern Plateau in both 1800 and 1832, and caused the extinction of a Carrier band in the Ootsa Lake region in 1837. The most devastating smallpox epidemic occurred in the early 1860s; the overall Aboriginal population of BC was reduced by anywhere from one-third to two-thirds, and among the Secwepemc alone seven bands along the Fraser River were virtually wiped out. Ts'ilqot'in bands moved eastward to occupy land formerly held by Secwepemc; in turn, the southern Carrier moved southward into former Ts'ilqot'in territory. By the 1800s the Nicola were absorbed by the Nlaka'pamux (Thompson), while during the early twentieth century, many of the remaining Lakes Okanagan moved to the US. In face of their band being eliminated by the Department of Indian Affairs, others married and/or settled among neighbouring Okanagan bands in Canada. The Aboriginal nations of the Canadian Plateau, along with their languages and subgroupings, are indicated in Table 20.1.

Plateau Cultural Patterns

The societies of the Plateau region show a high degree of cultural diversity, making it difficult to identify typical Plateau cultural patterns. One of the key features characterizing the Plateau is the availability of abundant runs of salmon. This feature can be used as a basis on which to identify a common cultural pattern that distinguished Plateau groups from their neighbours. Other dominant features of Plateau culture in the 1800s were: the establishment of semi-permanent winter or summer villages; the existence of kinship

FIGURE 20.1. Plateau Indian fishing for salmon on the Fraser River, Lillooet, BC, *c.* 1952. (Courtesy of the British Columbia Archives, HP 68625)

groups within each band that exercised steward-ship over resources within the Aboriginal nation and regulated access to them by ways of kinship and affinal ties; and connections to the larger groups or, in a secondary sense, through inter-nation ties by way of kinship and marriage.

Plateau groups gained access to salmon through two major river systems: the Fraser and Columbia. The quantities and species of salmon, however, varied greatly among communities on the Plateau, depending on where they were situ-ated. In addition, salmon runs fluctuate cyclically. While most Aboriginal groups on the lower Fraser had access to all five species of salmon, communi-ties situated on the upriver watersheds depended on chinook, coho, and sockeye salmon. The size of individual sockeye runs could vary tremen-dously from year to year. For example, a recent four-year cycle of sockeye runs in the Stuart Lake watershed was estimated at 589,600, 35,500, 26,800, and 24,500. Plateau groups coped with these regular fluctuations in salmon availability through a system of access to resources based on consanguinal and affinal ties whereby, in order to obtain resources in off years, families would fish and hunt with relatives and in-laws from areas within and outside their language group. Moreover, inter-group trade in dried salmon in exchange for other foods and goods was a crucial feature of Plateau society. Dried sides of salmon were a currency among Plateau nations, and when the fur-trading companies set up posts among Plateau nations during the early nineteenth cen-tury, dried salmon obtained from the Plateau groups became the staple protein for the traders. Other Plateau groups that had fewer salmon resources relied more on game and freshwater fish. In addition to protein resources, a variety of plants played a significant role in subsistence activities and trade. Indeed, a distinguishing fea-ture of Plateau culture was the reliance on root plants, including camas and bitterroot on the southern Plateau, and yellow avalanche lily, spring beauty, and balsam root on the northern Plateau. Plateau peoples harvested root plants through

methods and regimes that are similar to tech-niques used in horticulture, thus blurring the dis-tinction between hunting and gathering or foraging peoples as opposed to horticulturists.

Plateau groups followed a similar annual round of subsistence activities. In spring, people gathered at upland lakes to catch runs of trout as they were preparing to spawn in creeks running out of these lakes. During mid- to late spring, numerous green vegetables, as well as lodgepole pine cambium, were harvested. In late spring and early summer, people dug large quantities of edi-ble roots, some of which were steamed in under-ground pits and then dried for winter. During the summer, families congregated along the major rivers to trap, spear, or net salmon and dry it for the winter months. One particularly important fishing location for the Lillooet was and is the confluence of the Bridge and Fraser rivers, north of the town of Lillooet. Many different species of berries were collected and dried for winter use. In fall, families dispersed to the mountain regions to hunt large game and to prepare dry meat for win-ter. Deer were the most important large-game ani-mals hunted in the southern Plateau; before the twentieth century, elk and caribou were also key large-game animals in the northern Plateau. The caribou range has since shrunk due to a warming trend, and moose have now become plentiful and an important source of meat in northern regions. In the winter, those groups that had access to abundant salmon resources congregated in semi-permanent villages, where stores of dried salmon sustained them through the cold months. During the winter, as people used their stored provisions, they supplemented their diet with fish caught through ice fishing and with small game caught by snaring.

Trade was also important to the Plateau econ-omy. Networks linked the St'at'imx and Nlaka-'pamux with coastal groups, who in turn acted as intermediaries with adjacent Interior communi-ties. Trade items from the southern Plateau entered the Interior of BC via the Okanagan and Similkameen peoples, and Plains items worked their way into the Plateau through the Ktunaxa and Okanagan.

In the 1800s, Plateau groups recognized several different levels of social organization. The most important social group, in terms of day-to-day domestic activities, was the extended family, which hunted, fished, and gathered materials necessary for survival. Groups of related families that used a common territory constituted a band, which was named after the territory it occupied. Each band had from one to several villages that were occupied in the winter months. Among Plateau groups, chiefship operated mainly at the level of such large villages or clusters of interconnected small villages. Village chiefs were appointed by a council of Elders and/or community members, although in some cases there was a tendency for chiefship to be passed on from father to son. Autonomous villages within an Aboriginal nation were linked to one another through a common language and a sense of common history and custom, and especially through ties of kinship and exchange, which further served to provide mutual access for kin and in-laws to the resource-gathering locations of the diverse groups. Despite the relative economic and political autonomy of villages or bands, each Aboriginal nation had a sense of common identity and joint ownership of the resources of the entire tribe. Thus, according to oral histories and written ethnographic information from the early 1900s, the hunting grounds, plant-gathering areas, and most fishing areas were considered 'tribal property'. It was only in the Lillooet area that some productive fishing rocks were considered to be owned or stewarded by particular families.

Kinship among the Plateau groups was primarily reckoned along bilateral lines—that is, it was traced through both the father's and mother's sides. The prohibition of marriage to close kin, usually extended at least to second cousins, meant that many people were compelled to marry outside of their village group, and often outside of their band. Bilateral kinship, a tendency towards group exogamy, and the ethic of sharing and providing assistance to kin resulted in the creation of a network of relatives throughout the region who could be called upon to provide food, assistance, and access to hunting and fishing grounds when resources in one's own territory were scarce. Indeed, resource use and access along the entire Plateau were characterized by an inter-group and inter-nation system of primary access through immediate ties of kinship and socialization, and a supplementary system of secondary access through ties of affinity and parents' or grandparents' connections to places and groups. This brings up the third defining feature of Plateau groups: the existence within each band of kinship groups that exercised particular stewardship rights over valuable resources, with those groups most dependent on the rich salmon resources having the most formally developed and restrictive systems. Plateau societies have not remained static over time, however, and over the centuries there may well have been fluctuations in the degree to which specific ownership rights were exercised by kinship groups. The discussion here relates to Plateau cultures during the nineteenth century.

Among the St'at'imc, the most productive salmon-fishing sites were controlled—in the sense of first access and caretakership—by specific families or heads of families. Although the Plateau groups differed in the type of kinship groups that developed to restrict access to the resources, most included some dimension of restrictive, exclusive control. On this basis Plateau groups can be distinguished from Subarctic cultures.

Plateau cultures varied also as a result of their interaction with neighbouring nations. In particular, the arrival of the horse on the Canadian Plateau during the early to mid-1700s revolutionized trade routes, travel, and some aspects of material culture. During the early 1800s, as a result of the intensification of social and trade relations between the Interior and coastal nations, the traditions of clan organization, social classes recognizing a nobility, and potlatch ceremonialism began to spread from the Northwest Coast

FIGURE 20.2. Ktunaxa Indian family, *c.* 1914. Note the influences of neighbouring Plains groups in dress and tepee styles. (Courtesy of the British Columbia Archives, HP 73839)

societies to the southern Carrier, Ts'ilqot'in, and Secwepemc. These groups simultaneously incorporated and modified these traditions. Clans, for example, became bilateral in order to fit the system of social organization operating in the new settings. Although the ethnographic information is limited, it appears that each dominant family within a band became associated with a clan, and by the mid-1800s northern Secwepemc families along the Fraser River were attempting to exercise ownership rights to fishing stations in the name of their clan, with other Secwepemc communities continuing to insist on the joint tribal ownership and stewardship of resources. The clan system never became fully entrenched among the Secwepemc and other Plateau groups, though, and it began to disappear after the rapid popula-

tion decline brought about by the 1862 smallpox epidemic. In the southern Plateau, the Ktunaxa were greatly influenced by their associations with the Plains nations. They regularly travelled across the Rocky Mountains to hunt for buffalo, and much of their technology, such as tepee and dress styles, as well as their sun dance ceremonialism, bears the Plains cultural influence.

Origins

To a nation composed mainly of immigrants, questions of origins and 'first arrivals' seem important. Many non-Natives, for example, enjoy studying their personal family history and tracing their roots back generations to different countries of origin. Archaeologists share these concerns with 'first arrivals' and seek to answer questions regarding the origins of Native peoples in North America. To indigenous peoples, however, these questions are irrelevant; indigenous peoples have always been here. Plateau Indians explain origins in terms of how the earth was transformed by ancestral beings and how people separated from the rest of nature, receiving mortality as the price for guaranteed salmon runs, sunlight, and other things. Archaeological and indigenous approaches to the issue of origins are rooted in different cultural perspectives on the past; both address the reality that Aboriginal people have occupied the Plateau for a long, long time.

Like other Interior Salish, the Okanagan narrate stories about their origin and the actions of the Creator, or Old One. Specific features of the landscape, though, are attributed to the actions of Coyote, a character whose wanderings resulted, among other events, in the introduction of salmon to the Columbia River system. Narratives about Coyote point to his responsibility for the absence of salmon in the Similkameen River. In those accounts, Coyote was denied a woman he sought from the Similkameen people, and in retaliation he dammed the mouth of the Similkameen, forever blocking the passage of salmon. The presence today of kokanee, a landlocked salmon, in the Similkameen suggests that salmon once did ascend its waterways to spawn, but a rock slide at some unknown time forever eliminated the runs. The Coyote story is in many ways a lesson about knowing the land. The contrast between indigenous and non-Native interpretations of the significance of landscape symbolizes the different cultural approaches that the two cultures use to conceptualize and narrate history.

Colonial Political Economy

The colonial presence in the Plateau is relatively recent. It was not until the first decade of the 1800s that trading posts were established in the northern Plateau, although European trade goods had become part of the material culture by the late 1700s. From the northern Interior posts the traders explored further south, Simon Fraser reaching the mouth of the Fraser River in 1808 and David Thompson the mouth of the Columbia in 1811. Through these explorations the fur trade gradually expanded into the Plateau and by 1821 a string of trading posts had been set up. The fur trade relied heavily on Indian participation. The forts depended on Natives not only as suppliers of furs, but also as providers of salmon, on which the forts based their subsistence. Natives also served important roles as messengers and labourers. While the fur trade did initiate some changes in technology and land tenure, its overall effect on Plateau cultures was minor and Native/trader relations were relatively balanced.

This tenuous equilibrium was shattered with a series of gold rushes in the British Columbia Interior during the 1850s and 1860s. The Cariboo gold rush alone drew thousands of miners northward into St'at'imx, Secwepemc, and—to a lesser extent—Okanagan territories. At the same time the smallpox epidemic of 1862 struck the Plateau region, wiping out entire bands and causing dramatic depopulation among the Native groups, who had no natural immunity to the disease. Natives were soon outnumbered by miners and displaced from their hunting grounds, and hydraulic mining practices damaged or destroyed a number of valuable salmon spawning beds. The major gold rushes ended by the 1870s, and in their wake came colonial administrators and settlers.

The central and southern Plateau contained rich agricultural lands. By the 1880s much of the cultivatable land had been pre-empted. As farms and ranches were established and fences erected, Plateau groups lost access to some of their hunting territories and fishing stations. The 1860 Land Ordinance prohibited the pre-emption of Indian villages and fields, but even this minimal protection of Native rights was ineffectual. Due to the lax administration of the times, a number of settlers were able to pre-empt Native homesteads and cultivated fields. After 1866 the land

FIGURE 20.3. These Ts'ilqotin men in Lillooet, BC, may have been employed as ranch hands in the surrounding area. (Courtesy of the British Columbia Archives, HP 90320)

rights extended to settlers were denied to Indians. While non-Natives could apply for free grants of land, Indians were prohibited from using the pre-emption system at all. The failure of governments to recognize Aboriginal rights to hunting or fishing grounds, and their failure to negotiate treaties to formally acquire Indian lands, further exacerbated Indian/settler land conflicts. Small reserves were established in the late 1800s, but the issue of Aboriginal title continued to be ignored by governments.

By the 1880s Indian agents had arrived and were attempting to implement the terms of the Indian Act. Government control over Indian fishing, hunting, and trapping was extended in the following decades. Fishing by means of nets, weirs, and basket traps was outlawed by federal fisheries regulations, hunting was restricted, and trapping was brought under government control. BC Native leaders continued to lobby for government recognition of Aboriginal title, and their campaign gained momentum in the 1910s and

1920s. In response, in 1927 the federal government passed legislation to make it illegal for Indians to collect or donate money for the purpose of pursuing land claims.

Plateau groups responded in a variety of ways to these forces of change. Many Natives took advantage of the economic opportunities created by the colonial economies and played an important role in the gold rushes, working as miners, guides, and freighters. As the agriculture industry developed, Natives took jobs as cowboys, farm labourers, and migrant harvesters. As well, many families incorporated small-scale cattle- and horse-raising into their round of economic activity, sold their stock on the local market, and successfully competed with non-Native ranchers. Natives also played significant roles in the transportation industry, hauling supplies by team and wagon into the Interior. Native labourers cut ties and timbers and freighted supplies during the construction of railways in the 1880s and the early 1900s. Ironically, these railways also signalled the end of Native employment in small-scale freighting; further, the railways undermined Native rights by enabling non-Native settlement and the expansion of resource industries into previously isolated regions.

The colonial economy had varying impacts in different regions of the Plateau. Secwepemc and Okanagan territories were settled early, and these groups responded by developing a mixed economy in which wage labour and stock-raising existed alongside trapping, hunting, and fishing. Other groups that occupied lands more marginal to non-Native interests were able to maintain a measure of control over their lands, continuing to follow a subsistence lifestyle based primarily on hunting, fishing, and trapping. With the rapid growth of logging, mining, and hydroelectric projects in the twentieth century, the lifestyle and cultures of all of these groups changed significantly.

Contemporary Issues: Resource Conflicts

A number of resource conflicts in the Plateau emerged as significant issues in the 1980s and 1990s. North of the town of Lytton, at the confluence of the Fraser and Thompson rivers, the Stein Valley became a focal point for conflicts between the Nlaka'pamux and forestry companies. The Stein Valley is an area of much cultural significance, with pictographs, camps, trails, and other sites of historical and cultural importance to the Nlaka'pamux. The conflict was resolved by turning the Stein Valley into a park that highlights these heritage values.

Fraser River fisheries and water flows also emerged as significant issues in the late twentieth century. The Fraser River system, at the heart of the Canadian Plateau, is heavily industrialized, and a number of bands have raised more general concerns about deteriorating fisheries because of water pollution. A related issue is the twinning of rail lines along the Fraser and Thompson rivers and the possible damage this might cause to salmon habitat. Further, many of the areas slated for expansion along the river valleys run through

Indian reserves, many of which contain villages, cemeteries, and fishing stations. In response to this crisis, Indian bands from the lower Fraser Valley to the headwaters of the Thompson River formed an organization, the Alliance of Tribal Councils, to oppose what has become known as the CN Twin Tracking project. The Alliance unites people from different languages and traditional political jurisdictions. The main concerns of the Alliance centred on potential loss of reserve lands, cemeteries, and heritage sites, increased rail traffic, reduced access to traditional fishing sites, and potential loss of spawning habitats in upriver regions. In the late 1980s the Alliance of Tribal Councils (now known as the Alliance of Tribal Nations) initiated court action to prevent construction of the second rail line.

Part of the concern is that events of 1913 might be repeated. Railway construction along a stretch of the Fraser River known as Hell's Gate resulted in tonnes of rock being blasted into the river, obstructing the passage of migrating salmon. Salmon runs in the Fraser River system were almost eliminated. To many Interior Indian groups, it was a time of great deprivation.

Contemporary Social Issues

One of the most important issues discussed among Canadian Aboriginal peoples in recent years has been the impact of the Indian residential school system. Indian residential schools were a joint venture of the federal government and various religious denominations. They existed for over a century, the last ones closing only in the 1970s. The Kamloops Indian Residential School on the Kamloops Indian Reserve in the southern Secwepemc Nation at one point was the largest such school in Canada. Native children were removed from their homes and were raised in these church-run boarding schools, where they were taught Christian beliefs and morality as well as agricultural, commercial, and domestic skills, and were denied the right to speak their Native language. The explicit goal of the schools was to remove children from the cultural environment of their families so as to prevent the transmission of Aboriginal cultural knowledge, values, and beliefs.

Native people in the Plateau region are now examining the long-term psychological and social consequences to their communities of the residential schools' assimilation program. Many Native leaders today link the residential school experience to a range of social problems faced by many reserve communities, and, of course, to the loss of their Aboriginal languages.

A number of Plateau communities have taken steps to address these issues by developing their own social programs and systems of justice rather than turning to outside governmental agencies for assistance. In 1980 the Spallumcheen First Nation became the first Indian band in BC to sign a child welfare agreement with the province. In an effort to stem the apprehension of children from the community by provincial human resources workers, the Spallumcheen band council persuaded the provincial government to recognize its authority and responsibility for providing for the care of its own children and for the support and treatment of families in crisis.

For many Plateau communities, though, the outstanding issue is an affirmation of Aboriginal title and rights. A number of court cases have served to raise the issue of Aboriginal rights and traditional hunting and fishing activities. In 1995, a group of Secwepemc people, in company with Aboriginal supporters from other parts of Canada, held a sun dance, not a traditional Plateau ceremony, on ranchland at Gustafsen Lake. The group argued that the land was a sacred place and insisted on its Aboriginal rights to the land. After a standoff of 31 days, the BC government forcibly evicted them and charges were laid, resulting in the conviction of some of the participants. In the 1990s, the provincial and federal governments embarked on a treaty negotiation process, but many of the Plateau groups refused to participate, arguing that the conditions of treaty negotiation

and resolution imposed by the governments, which included extinction of Aboriginal title, are contradictory to Aboriginal rights and interests. The *Delgamuukw* decision of 1997 provided a reference point for the recognition of Aboriginal title in Canadian law and also for the need to accommodate Aboriginal interests in industrial activities. As an expression of their Aboriginal rights, the Westbank band carried out logging within its traditional territory without permits from the provincial government. The Penticton band in the Okanagan erected blockades along a road leading to a ski resort to publicize their concern about such uses of traditional territories. Similar actions have been taken by members of other communities in the Lillooet and Kamloops areas to protest the expansion of ski resort facilities on traditional lands or to challenge the BC provincial government's jurisdiction over fee simple title in light of a priori Aboriginal title.

In recent years, the Sinixt, a group of Okanagan people whose traditional territory is in the Arrow Lakes area, have struggled to have their continuing existence and Aboriginal territories recognized. After the last recognized band member in Canada died, the Canadian Department of Indian Affairs during the 1950s declared the Sinixt to be 'extinct' (most Sinixt had earlier been expelled to the Okanagan-Colville reservation in Washington state, while others had moved into Okanagan Lake bands). But road construction in 1987 revealed burials and a village site. Individuals who identified themselves as Sinixt set up a blockade in 1989 to halt further development of the road and sought to re-establish the Sinixt presence in their Arrow Lakes homeland.

Reference

Walker, Deward, ed. 1998. *Handbook of North American Indians*, vol. 12, *Plateau*. Washington: Smithsonian Institution.

CHAPTER 21

The Okanagan

DOUGLAS HUDSON

Introduction

This chapter describes the Aboriginal cultures of the Okanagan Valley of south-central British Columbia, home to the Okanagan people. 'Okanagan' originally referred not to people, but to a place. Meaning 'head of the river', in reference to the farthest point that salmon could ascend in the Okanagan system, it indicated a spot near a traditionally important fishing site, Okanagan Falls. The people called themselves *skiluxw*, 'people', although nowadays they also call themselves Okanagan.

Fieldwork: A Personal Perspective

My fieldwork in anthropology has involved working with a number of BC groups. My first research—as a student at the University of Victoria—was on indigenous place names in the Saanich Peninsula, near Victoria. It was a brief project, involving Coast Salish place names and narratives, and emphasized to me the importance of the land being imbued with cultural meanings through place names and stories about topographical features. The research was an extension of a course in linguistic fieldwork, and the role of language in defining and expressing world views remains an important element of my interests. Later, I lived for a year with a Dakelh band in northern BC, carrying out ethnographic research for my Ph.D. My focus was on social organization, resource use, and social and economic change.

After a stint of teaching at the University of British Columbia, I did a year's ethnographic work with Okanagan and Similkameen communities on the Okanagan Indian Curriculum Project. I have also worked on landownership and occupancy studies with the Nisga'a and Taku River Tlingit in northwestern BC and on resource use with Sekani and Dunne-za in northeast BC. Most recently I worked with Stl'atl'imx communities in a project involving ethnographic fieldwork, archival research, archaeological projects, and traditional land use.

Involvement with these communities and their histories has caused me to rethink some issues in anthropology and to appreciate the different ways in which communities seek to maintain traditions and control of traditional lands—and the ways anthropology itself is in a dialectical relationship with these different histories. For example, I cite my work on the Okanagan Indian Curriculum Project.

Okanagan people were dealing with educational problems. One was that their history had been reduced to meaninglessness in a region that eulogized the first non-Aboriginal settlers. For years, settler society had denied an Indian history in presenting its own. Another pressing issue was ensuring that an Okanagan voice be developed, that Okanagan views of Okanagan culture and relations with Canadian society be articulated. A writing centre in Penticton, the En'owkin Centre (discussed later), grew out of those needs.

The picture that emerged from my studies relied on fieldwork, early accounts by fur traders

Table 21.1. Okanagan-Similkameen Bands

Band Names	Band Membership (1986)
Okanagan (also known as Head of the Lake)	960
Westbank	262
Penticton	445
Osoyoos (or Inkameep)	199
Lower Similkameen	237
Upper Similkameen	34

and ethnographer James Teit,[1] and work by other anthropologists and historians. The early accounts emphasized the importance of salmon runs in the Okanagan economy. In the contemporary picture, though, the salmon no longer come. Years of commercial fishing, irrigation agriculture, flood control, hydroelectric power, and dams had severely reduced Columbia River salmon runs. A very significant part of the material basis of Okanagan culture disappeared. Since 1954 no salmon have spawned past Vaseux Lake in the south Okanagan. The lament for, and anger about, the assault on salmon is an important element of contemporary writing by Aboriginal Okanagan authors (see Roche and McHutchison, 1998).

In my opinion anthropological research will increasingly involve debates between the intellectual requirements of the discipline and the practical needs of indigenous people who draw on anthropologists. The aims of anthropology as a discipline are perhaps not enough to justify research, especially to the Native communities being researched, and one of the tasks of anthropologists will be to integrate academic and practical anthropology, merging theoretical problems with practical problems defined by Aboriginal people. In BC, the research landscape is increasingly defined by legal actions over exercises of Aboriginal rights (especially with respect to resource use) and the 1997 *Delgamuukw* decision

by the Supreme Court of Canada. That decision meant that Aboriginal interests in the land and its resources had to be addressed. The following comments, then, are my interpretation of Okanagan culture; they do not represent or appropriate the voice of the Okanagan. To organize the material, I have developed a model of economic, social, and ceremonial frameworks of activities. These activities impose and create meaning on the land, and each provides an entry point into the larger cultural picture. The categories are heuristic devices; they are not necessarily the ways in which Okanagan people see their relationships to the land or to each other.

The Region

The Okanagan people lived and live in southern BC. Okanagan territory also extended into Washington state. The international border effectively cuts across Okanagan lands and communities. While this chapter focuses on the Canadian Okanagan, the watershed extends into the United States and includes the Similkameen and Methow rivers. Okanagan people with distinct dialects inhabit these areas. Very closely related are the languages of two other groups, perhaps actually better thought of as dialects of Okanagan-Colville: Colville in the Colville Valley in Washington, and Lakes (or Sinixt) in the area of the upper Columbia River, Arrow Lakes, and Slocan Lake in BC. These dialects comprise the Okanagan-Colville language group. Currently in Canada there are Okanagan communities in the Okanagan Valley, the Similkameen Valley, and in the upper part of the Nicola Valley. Table 21.1 lists these Okanagan communities or bands.

Early Descriptions

Okanagan peoples are first mentioned in early fur trade records. One of the earliest descriptions was by the American fur trader Alexander Ross (1986: 311–12), who in 1811 wrote:

> The Oakinackens[2] inhabit a very large tract of country, the boundary of which may be said to commence at the Priest's Rapid on the south. From thence, embracing a space of upwards of one hundred miles in breadth, it runs almost due north until it reaches the She Whaps,[3] making a distance of more than five hundred miles in length. Within this line the nation branches into twelve tribes, under different names. These form, as it were, so many states belonging to the same union, and are governed by petty chiefs who are, in a manner, independent; nonetheless, all are ready to unite against a common enemy. These tribes, beginning at the southern boundary and taking each according to its locality, may be classed as follows: Skamoynumachs, Kewaughtchenunaughs, Pisscows, Incomecanetook, Tsillane, Intietook, Buttle-muleemauck, or Meathow, Inspellum, Sinpohellechach, Sinwhoyelp-petook, Samilkameigh,[4] and Oakinacken, which is nearly in the center. All these tribes, or the great Oakinacken nation, speak the same language, but often differ a good deal from one another as to accent.

This description indicates that there was a named set of communities known as Okanagan when the first traders arrived. Each of the named groupings was identified with a watershed. Today, there are several Okanagan communities in the Okanagan and Similkameen valleys, some on reserves adjacent to urban centres in a region that is undergoing substantial population increase. There is also a significant off-reserve population (see Table 21.1). The reserves were established from the 1860s to the 1880s, and today occupy strategically important locations.

Okanagan Society as Network

As a researcher working with seven bands, I was quickly introduced to the myriad connections between communities in the Okanagan. Going to rodeos became a key fieldwork activity; that is where the people were! (A fieldworker in the 1800s would have gone salmon fishing for the same reason.) Around those events webs of connections emerged. Okanagan people interacted with each other and with neighbouring groups on the basis of social rules and traditions in a variety of activities. Three main settings, or frameworks, for interaction can be identified: (1) economic activities, (2) social and political activities, and (3) religious and ceremonial activities. These are analytic categories; in life they were not mutually exclusive. Thus, salmon fishing was an economic activity in that fish were caught and processed; it was a social activity because the people assembled were also engaged in any number of informal activities; and it had ceremonial aspects in that a ritual specialist conducted ceremonies to celebrate the return of the salmon.

Okanagan people moved extensively throughout the region to participate in various economic, social, and ceremonial activities, utilizing a network of relatives and friends. This system ensured that people and food were redistributed, an important feature in a land characterized by seasonal and local variations in resources. It also ensured that the key fishing sites were available to numbers of people. Ultimately any speaker of the Okanagan-Colville language could be considered a potential friend. This network was a major feature of Okanagan society. To understand how it worked—and continues to operate—we need to examine its economic, social, and ceremonial basis.

Okanagan Society: Economic Activities

The traditional economic basis of Okanagan society centred on a few key locations where resources could be harvested by relatively large numbers of people at specific times of the year. The most important of these were the salmon-fishing sites in the Columbia River system, including the Okanagan. The annual subsistence cycle involved extensive movement in the summer and fall and a more sedentary life during winter, a season of important ceremonies.

Fishing

Most Plateau groups had direct access to productive fishing sites. Trout, kokanee, sturgeon (in Okanagan Lake), suckers, and other fish were taken. In late summer and fall salmon ascended rivers in the Columbia River watershed to spawn in small tributaries. The canyons through which they passed became important fishing places. The restricted number of canyons meant that people gathered at them. Two of the most important sites for the Okanagan were Okanagan Falls in the southern Okanagan, and Kettle Falls, on the Columbia River. An 1865 account by Charles Wilson, a member of the Northwest Boundary Commission, outlines their importance, and the kinds of fishing technologies used:

> At the Okinagan River a weir, constructed of slight willow wands, was found, which extended right across the stream and at one end had an enclosure into which several openings were left; the remainder of the weir, being nearly, if not quite, impassable, all salmon passing up the river found their way into a sort of 'cul-de-sac', where the Indians were busily engaged in spearing them. At Kettle Falls on the Columbia and Great Falls on the Spokane, salmon are caught in a large wicker basket, suspended from the rocks at one end of the falls, and projecting slightly into the water. At the foot of the rock there is an eddy, and the water coming down with less force at this point, the salmon here make their

chief effort to leap the falls, the greater number, however, fail to clear the rock, many leap right into the basket, whilst others strike their noses against the rock and fall back helplessly into the trap below. (Wilson, 1865: 297)

Salmon fishing was controlled by a salmon chief, who directed the construction of the traps and weirs and performed a ceremony to mark the capture of the first salmon. The First Salmon Ceremony symbolized the community's dependence on salmon and the need to maintain a proper relationship with it. Under the guidance of the salmon chief, the first salmon caught was cooked and distributed to members of the assembled community. Its bones were returned to the river to maintain the cycle. The salmon chief also had general supervisory powers, as the following observation from the above source in 1865 indicates:

> One blow from their practised hands settles the account of each fish, which is then thrown out on the rocks and carried to the general heap, from which they are portioned out to the different families every evening by a man known as the 'salmon chief'.

Prohibitions underscored the practical and symbolic importance of salmon. Swimming was banned upriver from the weir, and menstruating women and recent widows and widowers could not come near the weir or eat salmon. These reflected Okanagan conceptions of pollution and purity, a cultural logic that highlighted the importance of salmon and injected into resource-use activities notions of gender and changes in status.

Information about salmon was also included in stories about Coyote, a male transformer figure who brought salmon up the Columbia River. The stories usually emphasized Coyote's greed as he sought food and women. An account of why there are no salmon in the Similkameen River system involves Coyote going to the river and having his advances turned down by the women there. In frustration, Coyote erected a rock barrier near

---

BOX 21.1

Coyote, Salmon, and Dams

An Okanagan story about Coyote was brought into court hearings by a recent application to reactivate a dam originally built in 1920 at Enloe Falls, Washington, for hydroelectric power. The proposal included construction of fish ladders to enable salmon and steelhead on the Similkameen River to pass above the dam. The Similkameen and the Okanagan Nation Alliance in BC opposed the fish ladders, and brought in the Coyote account to explain why there never have been salmon in the Similkameen River above the falls.

Coyote travelled to the Similkameen and Okanagan, looking for a wife. The Similkameen, known as the mountain sheep people, rejected Coyote's advances, so he created the falls, which became a barrier to fish migration. The people in the Okanagan Valley welcomed Coyote, and in return he brought salmon there.

In 2000, the US Federal Energy Regulatory Commission rescinded a 1996 licence for hydroelectric power granted to Okanogan County, noting that no provisions had been made for fish ladders as required under the US Endangered Species Act. The issue was still a topic of discussion in 2001, as a report on the status of the dam stated: 'Based on the Coyote legend, the Canadian Indian Tribes firmly believe salmon never went up the Similkameen River. The tribes adamantly oppose fish passage up the Similkameen, and have put forth a great deal of effort to make their oral history and opinion heard on this subject' (quote from Minutes of the Regular Meeting of the Okanogan County Public Utility District Board of Commissioners Held in Okanogan, 19 June 2001, from: http://www.okanoganpud.org).

---

the mouth of the river to prevent salmon from ascending. So the Coyote story serves as an ecological (and moral) story about the absence of salmon in one watershed. The rock barrier exists; the Coyote story is an Okanagan way of giving meaning to landscape features. To obtain salmon, Similkameen people went to Okanagan Falls, to other places on the Okanagan River, or to groups on the Fraser River system to the west.

The wanderings of Coyote are also reflected in the ways that the Okanagan people describe features of the landscape. Distinctive rock formations, for example, are referred to as Coyote's fishing place or parts of his anatomy. Most of these formations carry no special markings, and their meanings and association with Coyote are embedded in oral traditions. They provide reference points for Okanagan relationships with the land, mapping out the territory but also serving as places that evoke stories with moral or ecological lessons.

As to division of labour, men built the weirs, often to the accompaniment of special songs to ensure success, but the processing of fish fell to the women. While a weir potentially could collect thousands of fish, the availability of women's labour to cut and dry salmon provided a limit on the number that would be taken. Each family tried to obtain enough salmon to last the winter; some obtained a surplus that could be traded to neighbouring villages for other commodities. As people from miles around gathered at major sites, these aggregations became highly interactive scenes. They played games (like *lehal*, 'stick game'), raced horses or on foot, traded, visited, and looked around for potential mates. Depending on circumstances, these gatherings could last from June into October.

While salmon were the most important fish in the Plateau, others also had their place. Kokanee (landlocked salmon) were taken at numerous creeks throughout the Okanagan watershed. The Similkameen supported abundant trout, Dolly Varden, and greyling. In spring, suckers were caught in traps as they migrated from lakes to streams. White sturgeon were caught in the major lakes and streams. Ling cod, 'devil fish', were taken in winter with hand lines.

Gathering

Roots, berries, and other plant parts were collected in season from spring to fall for food, drinks, and medicine. Bitterroot (*spitlem*), one of the most important plant foods, was gathered by women in April and May in upland areas in the Okanagan and Similkameen watersheds. For example, the traditional bitterroot digging grounds of the Penticton people are located up Shingle Creek, west of Penticton (Turner, 1978: 27), a place I once visited in April to see what was involved. The roots are small, dug with a special digging stick of hardened wood, then dried and stored for winter use as a vegetable. April is called *spitlemtem*, 'bitterroot month'. A First Roots Ceremony was held in the southern Okanagan to celebrate the gift of new food and highlight the passage from winter to spring. Like fishing, harvesting bitterroot provided an opportunity for people to get together to socialize, tell stories, and exchange goods after the winter months.

The types of plant foods available to particular groups varied, but most villages had access to bitterroot in April and May, saskatoon berries in July, wild potatoes (*sxʷinqʼwinum*) in May–June at high elevations, wild onions in June–July, black moss (*skawlip*), and a variety of other plants and berries.

A description from the early 1800s in the Okanagan region describes in a general way the cooking of plants (Ross, 1986):

Roots and vegetables of every description are cooked during the summer by means of furnaces in the open air; they are then baked on stones, formed into small cakes, and dried in the sun, after which the whole is carefully laid by for winter use.

The use of moss by the Southern Okanagan was highlighted by Ross:

On the pines of this country there is a dark brown moss which collects or grows about the branches. This moss is carefully gathered every autumn, when it has the appearance of dirty, coarse wool. It is soaked in water, pressed hard together, and then cooked in an oven or furnace, from which it comes forth in large sheets like slate, but supple and pliable, resembling pieces of tarpaulin, black as ink, and tasteless; and when cut with a knife it has a spotted or marbled appearance, owing to the small number of sprigs of wood, bark, or other extraneous substances unavoidably collected with the moss in taking it from the trees. This cake, when dried in the sun, becomes as hard as flint, and must always be soaked in water before use. It is generally eaten with the raw fat of animals, as we use bread and butter. It is viscous and clammy in the mouth, with but little taste. Thus prepared, it will keep for years, is much liked by the natives, and sometimes eaten by whites. It is called squillape. (Ibid., 342)

In the southern part of the Okanagan, particularly in the state of Washington, camas was an important resource and productive areas attracted people from considerable distances.

The account below indicates the complex relationship between plants, people, and ceremonies. Written in the 1930s by an Okanagan woman, Mourning Dove, it mentions going to make camp on a mountain in the southern Okanagan, Mount Baldy (*Pak-kum-kin*, white top) at a place where there was the frame of an old sweat lodge. This was an area used to collect herbs. Mourning Dove recounts being taught at this spot about the proper uses of herbs and the association between men and women and male and female plants (Mourning Dove, 1990a: 86–7):

> Several different plants were used for love charms, but the rarest and strongest grew only in the high mountains on the edge of snowbanks, glaciers, or alpine springs. They were sought when in full bloom. In the forests at lower elevations, the favorite plants were red and yellow columbine. None of the plants of the low country were thought to be as powerful as those near the timberline. No herb was ever taken until the person had been thoroughly cleansed by three successive days of using the sweat lodge or taking icy baths. Clean clothing was put on after every bath. During the purification treatment, wild rose leaves and fir-bough tips were used to rub the body to remove all impurities and the human smells so repulsive to the spirits of the plants. Plants were dug only at the first light of sun or just after sunset. The body or its shadow could never block the sun from the herbs. Both sun and herbs were greeted by a song of individual invention and paid with offerings of buckskin, cloth, horsehair, beads, or, recently, coins.

Hunting

Okanagan country contained large and small game animals that were hunted or trapped. Animals hunted included deer, elk, bighorn sheep, and bear. Smaller game used for food included rabbits, marmot, and beaver. There were four great annual hunts: in spring, for deer and sheep; in late fall, for deer, sheep, elk, and bear; in mid-winter, for deer; and late in winter, for sheep. Noted hunters directed collective activities. Success in hunting was seen as the outcome of knowledge and adherence to proper ritual. For example, hunts might be preceded by purification in a sweat lodge.

Division of Labour

Men and women worked together in economic endeavours in a complementary way. In general,

men built weirs and hunted while women processed resources and gathered plant foods. Stored food belonged to women, giving them effective control over the household economy and the exchange of food. Both sexes were essential in functioning households.

Networks

The very nature of Okanagan social organization linked local production groups in various kinds of exchange. For example, the Ashnola area of the Similkameen watershed was an important mountain sheep habitat. The Ashnola people invited not only neighbouring Similkameen bands but also other Okanagan people as well as Nlaka'pamux (Thompson) and Nicola people to the hunt. Osoyoos (Nk'mip) people went as far south as Kettle Falls to dig camas bulbs, and traded bitterroot, hemp, and blankets to the Nlaka'pamux and Secwepemc (Shuswap) for salmon. Trading networks linked Okanagan people to the coast and the Plains, as items made their way along a vast network flowing east and west, north and south. Keremeos people, in the Similkameen, referred to a place where Blackfoot came to trade. Based on fieldwork in the 1930s, Walters (1938. 74) noted that the Southern Okanagan people went up the Methow River and crossed the Cascade Mountains to trade wild hemp (used as twine in fishnets) for seashells. Other descriptions of Inkamip trade are found in Walters (1938: 77):

> Their trade relations are predominately to the north. They go up the Okanogan River beyond Lake Okanogan, about two miles from Enderby, to trade for salmon with the Shuswap. . . . The Inkamip go in August, taking about four days on horses. Since the white traders came, the Shuswap have planted potatoes for which the Inkamip also trade. The Inkamip go to the mouth of the Kamloops to trade with the Thompsons every August. They go from Lake Osoyoos to the Similkameen River, up the river on the eastside by Princeton to the head of the river, and cross to

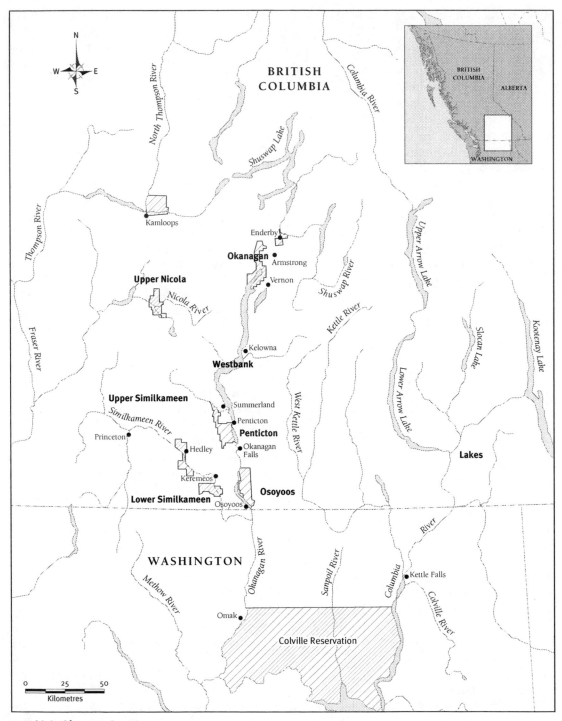

MAP 21.1. Okanagan Locations

the Kamloops River. They take raw hemp, gathered in Similkameen country . . . .tanned deerskins and dried huckleberries, and bring back only salmon. . . . The Inkamip dig camas at Kettle Falls and trade for fish there.

Another example of the connections between groups is found in a description by Mourning Dove (1990a: 99–100) of groups associated with Kettle Falls:

> Our camp was close to the Colvile on the west, beside our Okanagan distant relatives from Osoyoos. The west side was called La-chin (Woven kettle or Bucket) because of the many depressions made by whirlpools there. The east side was known as Scalm-achin (Dug Ground) because the ground was rough with boulders and looked as though nature had dug it out in places. Tribes generally camped in specific areas, and Colvile hospitality saw to it that no visitor ever left without a full load of dried salmon. The Colvile camped on both sides of the falls to oversee the fishing. The east side encampment included Kalispel, Spokan, Coeur d'Alene, and Flathead, while on the west side were the Okanagan, Sanpoil, Squant, and Wenatchi.

Horses became part of Plateau culture by the mid-1700s. One impact was to expand the use of traditional resources. A recurrent theme in photographs from the late 1800s and early 1900s is the use of horses to pack supplies in and food out of highland hunting and gathering areas. A second impact was to shift trade patterns. Okanagan Falls and Kettle Falls were the most important salmon-fishing sites (and therefore the biggest trade centres) in the Okanagan region. After horses became common, trade shifted from longer water routes to overland routes, following open plateaus. In this cross-country trade between the Okanagan and the Colville, the Similkameen Valley became more important: 'The great trade route to the north was now across country from Colvile to Okanagan River; then it branched off, about half

of the volume of trade going up the Similkameen to the Thompson, and the rest passing on to Oka-nagan Lake' (Teit, 1930).

Okanagan Society: Social and Political Activities

The basic residential unit of Okanagan society was the village, a cluster of houses containing related people who used the area's resources in common. Villages were occupied primarily during winter; the rest of the year was spent at seasonal hunting, fishing, and gathering camps. Villages were located in protected valleys, and people referred to themselves as occupants of a particular winter village. The actual placement of the village depended on the availability of firewood, and a village might move up or down a valley as wood supplies were depleted.

Houses were either built over a circular excavation of two or three feet and covered with poles and turf or made from tule reed mats. Some of the latter resembled tepees, while others, housing several families, were oblong in shape.

A village contained several special-use structures in addition to its dwellings. A short distance from the houses, small huts were constructed for menstruating women or girls entering puberty. Here they stayed, away from direct interaction with the main camp, as this period in one's life was considered potentially powerful, with possible detrimental impacts on resources. There were special prohibitions on eating deer meat or salmon, for example. Several sweat lodges might also be in evidence, with separate lodges for men and women. Food was stored in raised caches or pits dug into sandy ridges.

Village Organization

Local village autonomy was a feature of Plateau culture. While villages were linked through linguistic and social ties, each retained its independence. For the Okanagan, several house groups, perhaps scattered in contiguous settlements, were seen as a community under the direction of a

FIGURE 21.1. Alexander Kwikweitêsket, head of the Lake band of the Okanagan. He is wearing a beaded chief's bonnet set with tail feathers of the golden eagle and hung with strips of twisted ermine skin. The robe is made of twisted hare (winter white coat). Photo by V. Vincent, 1910. (Courtesy of the Royal British Columbia Museum, PN 6586)

will. Because extensive kinship ties linked most members of the community, a chief was also a person who had a large number of relatives upon whom he could call for assistance and support. The chief's status and knowledge were important in maintaining community relations and ensuring that economic and ceremonial tasks were carried out for the benefit of the whole community. Chieftainship could be inherited; the Okanagan placed great emphasis on the order of birth, and the first-born son of a chief was a prime candidate to be named successor. A council of Elders drawn from the community advised the chief and helped choose his successor.

If the community consisted of more than one settlement, each residential cluster also had a headman who took on some of the tasks of chief. A headman had responsibility to direct the group in successful hunting by his dream power, a power that came from a guardian spirit quest and knowledge of animals. Further, each house group in a settlement had a 'house leader'—usually the eldest male—who represented the house group in dealings with the rest of the community. In parts of the southern Okanagan

chief. The chief, usually male, derived his power from his status as a 'worthy' man as a consequence of his family's high status, his knowledge of village affairs, and his ability to merit the respect of others. A chief was followed because of his attributes and did not have power to force people to do his the chief did not give directions himself but worked through a spokesperson. However, the informality of daily living and the required seasonal movements militated against formalizing power, as individuals could relocate to other communities where there were kin.

There also were other positions referred to as chiefs, and these functioned in a variety of capacities. A salmon chief directed the construction and operation of a fish weir, and a shaman directed activities during winter dances and healing ceremonies. Thus, it may be appropriate to view chieftainship not as single fixed position, but to see chiefs and headmen as managers of a series of specific activities—economic, social, political, and ceremonial—for which they had the required knowledge, ability, and respect.

The essence of the Okanagan political system is evident in the observations made by a fur trader in the early 1800s, although it appears that the powers of the chief are overstated at the end:

> The government, or ruling power among the Oakinackens (Sinkaietk) is simple yet effective, and is little more than an ideal system of control. The chieftainship descends from father to son: it is, however, merely a nominal superiority in most cases. Their general maxim is, that Indians were born to be free, and that no man has natural right to the obedience of another, except he be rich in horses and has many wives; yet it is wonderful how well the government works for the general good, and without any coercive power to back the will of the chief, he is seldom disobeyed: the people submit without a murmur. (Quoted in Walters, 1938: 94)

That chieftainship was to some extent inherited raises the question of whether, or to what extent, social classes existed. The Okanagan did not have a rigorous division into a high and low class. Rather, there were families whose members were considered to be of high status and morality, while other families had 'lost their history'. In other words, gaining authority was partly based on prestige, which in turn reflected proper conduct, and was partly based on institutional factors, such as being an eldest son. Those who had no history had lost, through accident or poor choice, the respect of the community and thus lacked relatives who would attest to their character and rights to particular positions. In a sense they had lost their place in the kinship system. They were part of the community, but without the respect that they might otherwise have enjoyed.

Ownership

Okanagan communities were kinship-based, and all rights of ownership and access to resources must be seen in this light. Property could be corporeal or incorporeal. Corporeal property refers to tangibles like land and material objects. The group—family, village, or band—owned resource areas in the sense that its members reproduced rights of access and control over them. Others could participate, but only with permission. Chiefs managed, and in that sense owned resource areas, but the extensive ties that linked Okanagan people created a social universe of friends, relatives, neighbours, and trading partners. Thus, in a sense, the region and its resources were potentially but conditionally accessible by all Okanagan collectively, with local resources controlled by various kinship and residential groups.

Incorporeal property, such as guardian spirits, songs, and dances, was owned by individuals, in that they alone had the right to perform a particular dance or song. However, there was also a social, or group, aspect to this ownership. Names were seen as the property of families, and particular names were inherited or transmitted within kin groups. Possessors of particular names, though, could confer them on others if compensated—although again the names stayed within particular families. Special songs and dances might also be transferred from a parent to a child.

Social Units

Although the nuclear family—the husband-wife pair and their unmarried children—existed in traditional Okanagan society, it was economically and socially merged into the extended family that was the basic social unit and the primary unit of production and consumption. A household was usually an extended family and might consist of two brothers and their wives and children, or of an older couple with their married children, or of 'cousins' living with their families. A wealthy man of high status might establish a polygynous family (multiple wives), but this was not widespread.

The kindred (all one's relatives traced through the families of both parents) were important to the Okanagan. Kin provided security and protection; in neighbouring villages there would usually be at least one member of one's kindred or people who could be considered *chichops*, 'relatives'. Another category of kin was the *kalh*, the descendants of a particular grandparent or great-grandparent. For example, two people descended from someone named Quinisco would consider themselves *kalhquinisco*, with special obligations of mutual respect and support. Membership in a *kalh* is traced through male and female lines, but does not have any corporate functions.

Kinship Terms

Okanagan kinship terms were organized on different principles from those of English. Some examples of these follow. (1) Different terms were used by male and female speakers. Therefore, the sex of the speaker was important. Males and females defined social relations in different ways, as reflected in the use of kinship terms. Not all terms differed, however—just those for very close kin. (2) Different terms were used for older and younger siblings, indicating that age was important (recall that the eldest son was most likely to inherit his father's position). (3) Sibling terms were extended to cover children of parents' siblings (people whom an English-speaker would call 'cousin' were called 'brother' and 'sister'). This reflects the social basis of kinship terms in all societies; in Okanagan society one's parents' siblings' children are in the same kindred as oneself and therefore called by a term reflecting common membership in a social group and best translated as 'person of my generation in my social group'. A detailed list of Okanagan kinship terms is found in Mattina and Jack (1990: 163–5).

The determination of potential mates was another aspect of Okanagan kinship. Genealogies

were the topics of extended conversations. As one person commented, 'First and second cousins are *skuit*, just like your own brother and sister. You can't marry them. Perhaps you can marry a third cousin'. That marriages were arranged helped to ensure that they took place between families of similar social standing. The parents initiated the proceedings with a series of small exchanges, some of which predated the actual marriage, while others continued for years after. These economic exchanges gave the marriage stability by emphasizing that marriage was the concern of the group.

Life Cycle

All cultures recognize to some extent the passage of individuals from one status to another. Referred to as a life cycle, these passages often involve a social or ceremonial recognition of physiological changes (such as puberty) and social changes (such as going from unmarried to married status). The Okanagan life cycle emphasized several key events and periods in life, starting with birth. The emphasis was on being guided into, and becoming, a knowledgeable member of Okanagan society.

Birth

The birth of a child received special recognition. One of the earliest descriptions of an Okanagan birth ceremony states:

> After childbirth, the women have to live apart for about thirty days, frequently washing themselves, and, before joining the others, they have to wash all their clothes and undergo general purification. A small lodge is erected about ten or twelve paces from the large or family one, and in this the woman lives during the period of her seclusion, which is kept with great strictness, notwithstanding the close proximity of her friends and relations. When the time of childbirth is felt to be approaching, the woman goes out and plucks a sprig of the wild rose, which she places upright in the ground of the lodge and fixes

her eyes upon it during the pangs of labour, which, it is believed, are alleviated by this ceremony. The rattles of the rattlesnake are also frequently used as a medicine to procure ease in the same cases. (Wilson, 1865: 294)

Following their seclusion, mother and child were welcomed back into the community by the Elders. In some cases a few relatives and close friends gave an informal feast. For the next few years the baby was carried in a cradle. The infant received a temporary name during the first year, then an ancestral name was conferred, usually by a grandparent. The name had to be purchased if a person using it was still alive. The name could come from either the mother's or the father's side. Boys often received names of animals, and girls received names of plants.

Childhood

In childhood boys and girls gradually learned the distinctions between male and female roles. Education was largely informal, through observation, oral history, and comments from Elders. Tales were used to teach children, and to remind adults, about the importance of proper conduct. Parts of the physical landscape were used as reference points for information, where events were associated with natural rock formations or other features. As noted earlier, these were often tied into narratives about the activities of Coyote. These culturally defined places on the landscape served as aids in understanding Okanagan cultural history, topography, and ecology. To learn about the travels of Coyote (and the places where Coyote stopped or transformed parts of the landscape) is to learn about the territory.

Boys learned to hunt and fight. Their first animal kill went to the Elders for redistribution, thus reinforcing the power of the group over the individual. Similarly, girls learned skills needed to perform successfully as adults—the techniques of gathering and root-digging, for example. Children's play emulated tasks and roles to be performed later as adults. For example, they might play with miniature fish weirs. Adults required children to take early morning swims in icy water and sweats in lodges to build their character and prepare them for the change from childhood to adulthood, which was signalled by puberty and the guardian spirit quest.

Guardian Spirit Quest

The transition from childhood to adulthood was an important event for males and females. Just prior to the onset of puberty, boys went into the countryside to obtain a guardian spirit, which came in a vision. This quest sought the transfer of power from the natural to the social world, and, if successful, a boy had a spirit helper for the rest of his life. Boys prepared for the quest by fasting, sweating, and physical exercise.

After preparation, a boy went to an isolated area and sought for four days the vision of a guardian spirit. In one account, a boy dove to the bottom of a lake every day for three days without achieving a vision. On the fourth day, a human figure appeared, announcing that it was a particular animal, and from that day on the boy would be able to draw on its power in times of need. This power, which was called *sumix*, had to be sought and obtained prior to or at puberty. After puberty it was felt the search would prove more difficult or fruitless. Not all of those who sought a guardian spirit found one and those who obtained one did not necessarily become fully aware of its power until later in life. Thus the quest of a guardian spirit, whose assistance was essential to adult success, came just at the point when boys faced manhood.

Girls also received instruction at puberty, going to a special place of retreat. These places often were the tops of large, flat rock formations that even today are marked by a circle of rocks placed around each girl in her vigil. Each rock represented a lesson learned from an Elder.

Marriage

In traditional Okanagan culture, parents arranged the marriages of their children, initiating a series of exchanges. An early exchange might feature the parents of the boy giving fish and meat (symbolic of male activities) to the parents of the girl, who in turn gave roots and berries. After marriage, a couple usually lived in the village of the husband, although the social network provided for other residential options. The last such arranged marriage recounted to me was about 1920.

It was during adulthood that the power of a personal supernatural began to be revealed, requiring a person to 'dance out the power' at a winter ceremony. This is further discussed in the section on ceremonies. It seems that social maturation was paralleled by spiritual maturation. Thus marriage and participation in winter ceremonies marked the complete transition to adult status in Okanagan society.

Death

The deceased were buried in talus slopes, rock slides. Special belongings, perhaps copper pendants or dentalia,[5] were also interred. Death brought an obvious end to a person's direct participation in society, but names borne by the deceased remained in the extended family or kindred and were transferred to descendants. The birth of children who were given ancestral names maintained the family over generations; the use of previous names reinforced a world view in which the past merged with the present in a common social sphere.

Male-Female Relations

Children were born into well-defined male and female roles; by the onset of puberty, they had a good notion of their place in society. While the kinship system emphasized the importance of tracing relatives through both the father's and the mother's sides, a tendency to stress male relations existed. This 'patrilateral bias' was reflected in residence patterns, the political system, and elsewhere. Women, however, did control food, giving them some economic power. Decision-making also involved the voices of both men and women. The relationship between males and females in

Okanagan society was expressed as being similar to two fir trees growing up beside each other: one, a male tree; the other, a female.

Okanagan Society: The Ceremonial Framework of Action

The tension between individual rights and collective responsibilities ran as a constant theme through Okanagan society. This is perhaps best expressed in concepts and ceremonies where power (*sumix*) is in focus. Through the spirit quest an individual acquired power, but the community, probably through a shaman, guided the individual to use that power to benefit the community.

Although spiritual power was a dominant aspect of many Okanagan ceremonies, secular ceremonies also occurred. The following types of ceremonies can be identified. (1) Renewal ceremonies (such as the first-root and first-salmon ceremonies) emphasized the continuation of important food resources. (2) Redistributive ceremonies were secular and included naming ceremonies and a more elaborate distribution often called the potlatch in anthropological literature. Perhaps 'potlatch' is a term best reserved for the formal exchange ceremonies among Northwest Coast groups; while the Okanagan redistributed goods and food at a number of social occasions, none are actually called potlatches. It also appears that those Okanagan who recalled potlatching saw it as something peripheral to traditional Okanagan culture but part of the culture of the Nlaka'pamux and Secwepemc. (3) Power ceremonies, including the Winter Dance and the Medicine Dance, focused on spiritual matters.

Winter Dance

The most important Okanagan ceremony, one in which spiritual power was a key element, was the Winter Dance, held when people gathered in their winter villages. According to the Okanagan view of the world, the power that one acquired through the guardian spirit quest required dancing or else the possessor would get ill or even die.

Power itself was not equally distributed. Only males obtained it, and it had two levels: power that could be used to protect oneself, and power that could be used to help—or hurt—others. Not everyone had this second curing power, and some used it to harm people; sickness, for example, might be attributed to natural causes or to the direct actions of a malevolent shaman. The distinctions between the two main types of spiritual power are reflected in the Okanagan terms *chuchuin* and *sumix*. *Chuchuin* ('voice' or 'whisper') meant that a voice came to a person during the guardian spirit quest, giving him a supernatural helper. But that person had no real *sumix*, or power, merely a spirit helper. *Sumix* came when a person was older—usually when one's hair turned white.

Different animals conferred different kinds of power. Most power was seen to come from grizzly bear, cougar, blue jay, rattlesnake, and eagle—all of which gave the possessor the power to cure. Blue jay also gave power to find drowned or lost people.

To perform at a Winter Dance required several steps. A neophyte had a power dream in which the guardian spirit required a dance. He then sought the service of a ritual expert (shaman, or medicine man) as master of ceremonies. A central post was erected in the dance lodge, and, in some cases, the lodge was ceremonially swept to purify it. The neophyte then danced before the assembled group and distributed gifts. Other people then expressed their power in dance.

The vocabulary of the ceremonies and formal gatherings differed from everyday speech. It was called 'High Okanagan', a language of leaders and those with specialized knowledge, in contrast to the language of everyday life.[6] When I was doing fieldwork in 1980, there was concern that only a few individuals still knew the specialized vocabulary of ceremonies and specialized knowledge. This emphasized to me the value of narratives and the coding of information. With a loss of language goes a loss of a number of levels of knowledge and ways of knowing. Not everyone was schooled in the 'High Okanagan' language. So the loss of a few key people meant the loss of the equivalent of a narrative library, a class of Okanagan intellectuals whose specialized knowledge, coded in specific linguistic categories and terms, was pivotal to Okanagan culture. The role of storytellers in this society was more important than most non-Natives would think.

Summary

Okanagan society and culture required a successful and efficient technology and a flexible and workable social system that enabled people to gather in great numbers at appropriate times, yet facilitated the movement of people between different areas and villages. Traditional Okanagan society was held together in a variety of ways. Through a multitude of social ties, primarily based in kinship, most Okanagan were linked and could enlist aid from people in numerous places. Collaborative activities, such as deer-hunting and salmon-fishing, facilitated inter-group exchanges. Participation in ceremonies involving large groups of people reinforced mutual systems of meaning and identity.

Post-Contact Change in Okanagan Life

The earliest changes in Okanagan life associated with European contact were in their fashion profound, but at first they were incorporated into ongoing patterns with relatively little disruption. The fur trade did not threaten Indian ways of organizing social relations, of using the land, or of developing power. The most disruptive events of the mid-1800s were the diseases that left devastation and demoralization in their wake. For example, in 1883, 13 Inkameep people died at Osoyoos from smallpox, which had initially been contracted at the town of Hope, on the lower Fraser River, by an Inkamip woman, and had been brought inland (Department of Indian Affairs, 1883: 50–1).

Until the 1860s the Okanagan Valley represented a means of getting somewhere else—a route for shipping furs and trade goods to distant markets or a passageway to beckoning goldfields. The 1860s brought prospectors and ranchers, both representing a new kind of claim on lands traditionally used by the Okanagan. A customs post to mark the US–Canada border was established at Osoyoos in 1862; a trading post and store were opened in 1866 at Penticton; and more land became pre-empted by ranchers and settlers in the 1860s and 1870s. The pressure grew on the BC and Canadian governments to restrict the landholdings of Indians. What had been Okanagan territory became plots of land owned by Euro-Canadians. Other parcels of land were surveyed as Indian reserves, a process that took years to complete because of conflicts between the BC government and Ottawa.

Economic Changes

As the Okanagan region became incorporated into an expanding Canadian society, Indian labour became more important for economic activities dominated by non-Indians. These included ranching, farming, logging, sawmilling, and other activities.

It is significant that the Okanagan were quick to engage in economic activity on an ownership basis. Freighting and ranching were two such enterprises in which Okanagan Indians were conspicuously active. However, Okanagan cattlemen raised stock on common rangelands open to all ranchers (called a commonage) south of Vernon only until access was curtailed, largely due to pressures from non-Indian ranchers. Similarly, Similkameen cattlemen drove stock from Keremeos to Princeton for seasonal grazing until their use of 'free range' was also curtailed. Some Okanagan reserves were large enough that some cattle could still be raised, but they could never become fully competitive with non-Indian ranchers. In other words, attempts by the Okanagan to compete in the larger economy were systematically thwarted.

While some traditional economic activities remain important for many Okanagan, fundamental changes have taken place. Many of the key fishing places are no longer viable. Both Okanagan Falls and Kettle Falls have been lost to dams, the latter by construction in the 1930s of Grand Coulee Dam in Washington. The number of salmon reaching the Okanagan system diminished following construction of a series of dams on the Columbia. Traditional fishing technologies have also been lost. Weirs and fish traps were banned by the Canadian government around 1900 and were destroyed by fisheries wardens throughout the Okanagan. Urbanization and the rerouting of streams have further diminished fish production and harvesting (see Cannings and Durance, 1998, for an overview of specific changes).

Religious Changes

The continuation of winter dances, guardian spirit quests, and other activities associated with spirit power was anathema to the missionaries who moved into the Okanagan Valley in the late nineteenth century. Adherents of spirit power were at one time forbidden to attend churches and winter ceremonies were condemned. Given the Okanagan belief that power had to be danced out, the result of banning spirit dances was predictable. Without the traditional form of releasing power, people were felt to have fallen ill or died because of pent-up pressures. Few guardian spirit quests have been carried out for decades, although the belief still persists that power exists as a force beyond human control. The guardian spirit quest was a culturally recognized means of transferring power from the natural and supernatural worlds to the human world, where it became, in a way, social. A balance between power possessed by humans (as spirit power) and untapped power in the natural and supernatural worlds existed. But that balance has been broken by the suppression of spirit dances, and an overabundance of such power is felt to exist outside of human control. In recent years, there has been a resurgence of winter dances and of practices generally that foster a uniquely Okanagan identity.

Social and Political Changes

During the late nineteenth century the economic, political, and social activities of the Okanagan Indians and the Euro-Canadian immigrants became intertwined, with a myriad of reciprocal exchanges. For example, an 1870s account by a settler at Keremeos (Allison, 1991: 39) points to early economic ties:

> The Indian women used to gather and dry Saskatoons, so I did the same and when they brought me trout which they caught by the hundreds in baskets they set in the One Mile Creek, I paid for them with butter and then dried and smoked the trout.

Other early writers point to close relations between Indians and non-Indians in the Okanagan, although ignoring the issue of fundamental differences of political power. A description of Penticton in the 1920s reads:

> At that time we, of the town, lived much closer to our Indian neighbours than we do now. We knew each other by name, stopped to chat on the street and we played together. We depended on hay cut on the reserve or winter pasture for our horses. We bought wood and buckskin gloves from them. (Sismey, 1976: 19)

The Euro-Canadian settlers and their descendants have since created their own version of Okanagan history, one that talks about the material exchanges but sets aside the early social relations between Indians and non-Indians. The result has been a certain fabrication of social distance between the groups, one readily accepted by more recent immigrants to the Okanagan who know little or nothing of early settler history aside from the official versions.

While informal relations between Okanagan and immigrant neighbours were generally mutually beneficial, formal relations were characterized by changes over which the Okanagan had little control and to which they frequently objected. The traditional system of leadership was altered by the imposition of external political frameworks. First, Catholic missionaries introduced the Durieu system in BC Indian villages about 1875. This system called for Indian church leaders in each village under the supervision of the local priest. Each village had a church chief with captains under his command. Although the ideal was to appoint already established chiefs, the church chiefs were appointed by the priest and were directed to enforce his commands concerning morality and conduct. According to Knight (1978: 247), the influence of this system seems to have largely declined by the late 1890s, but recollections of it remained with Okanagan Elders in the 1980s.

A second major change occurred when the Department of Indian Affairs established a system of elected chiefs and councillors to run band affairs. Most of the chiefs elected in this fashion were male, but in 1953 the first woman was elected[7]—to the Penticton Indian band council. All Okanagan bands now elect chiefs and councillors.

After Euro-Canadian penetration of the Okanagan, much of the responsibility for social services shifted to non-Okanagan institutions, and it became difficult to retain many cultural practices. The residential schools played an important part in undermining the teaching of traditional culture. Children began to spend most of the year in a residential school, such as at Kamloops, at some distance from their home villages. Forbidden to speak their languages and separated from siblings, the children became isolated from the teachings of their parents and Elders. Older Okanagan people retain the experiences of residential school life: cooking, washing clothes, splitting firewood, growing crops, and instruction in a foreign language (English). Perhaps with the best of intentions, the residential schools operated on the premise that the Indian child should be separated from his or her own traditions and family for most of the year.

In the 1870s, frustrated with government inaction on Indian land claims and faced with increasing alienation of Indian lands by settlers and ranchers, some Okanagan and Secwepemc people argued for a co-operative political venture. Through armed force and, possibly, an association with Chief Joseph and the Nez Perce, then fighting the US government, a resolution to outstanding grievances would be forced. A meeting at the head of Okanagan Lake in 1877 resulted in the formation of a Secwepemc–Okanagan Confederacy. No armed resistance came, however, and the nascent confederation was effectively broken up by the Indian Reserve Commission and priests, who made agreements with individual bands and split the movement.

Okanagan involvement in political movements continued throughout the twentieth century. In 1916, several BC bands formed an organization called the Allied Tribes of BC. This organization included the Okanagan. At that time, however, no resolution of land claims issues was possible.

In the late 1960s, Okanagan people were involved in the formation of the Union of BC Indian Chiefs. In the 1970s, a majority of the bands in the Okanagan Valley formed the Okanagan Indian Tribal Council, with an office in Penticton. This in turn became part of the Central Interior Indian Tribal Councils, representing Interior bands and tribal organizations. The political picture is more complex today; in the 1980s and 1990s a number of umbrella organizations emerged. The Okanagan communities have formed a political organization called the Okanagan Nation. The present president of the Union of BC Indian Chiefs, an important political organization that draws significant support from Interior First Nations communities, is a former chief of the Penticton band. Okanagan women were also prominent in the development of Aboriginal women's movements in the 1960s and 1970s.

Indian reserves were surveyed in the 1860s in the Okanagan and Similkameen. Correspondence by surveyors in 1866 points to surveys done in 1865 and earlier that were apparently deemed too extensive. At any rate, three reserves in the Okanagan were roughly laid out in 1865. As a portent of events to come, the surveyor at the time, helped by a major landholding settler in the valley, wrote that the reserve boundaries were established without the aid of survey instruments. The report also criticized the generosity of the reserves, noting that the size of one was 'more than double the amount necessary to serve the Indians settled on the Okanagan' (British Columbia, 1875: 34–6).

The governments of BC and Canada argued for decades about the sizes of BC reserves and struck a commission in 1912 to settle the issue. It held meetings with Indians, chambers of commerce, and other interested parties, and presented a four-volume report in 1916, confirming the boundaries of some reserves, adding to others, and, most importantly, reducing some. In the Okanagan, of 146,428 acres of reserve land, the commission cut off 18,537 acres and added 2,600 acres.

To the federal and provincial governments, the issue of reserves was settled. To the Indians, the process by which reserves were diminished was seen as questionable, and bands began research to substantiate claims that alienation of land occurred without the band's permission and that compensation was due. In the 1980s the federal and provincial governments agreed to settle the issue of alienated or 'cut-off' lands, as they were known, and several bands have received compensation. In 1981, for example, the Penticton band received 4,880 hectares of land and $13 million to resolve their losses.

Also in recent years, there has been an attempt by one Plateau group adjacent to the Okanagan, the Sinixt, or Arrow Lakes people, to have their existence recognized. The Sinixt used the resources of the Arrow Lakes and moved in a north-south pattern between what is now Canada and the United States. Many of the Arrow Lakes people were incorporated into the Colville Indian Reservation in Washington, while others married into the Okanagan. But in 1956 the Canadian Department of Indian Affairs declared that the

Arrow Lakes band was extinct after the last band member recognized by the Canadian government died.[8] Road construction in 1987 revealed burials and a village site. In 1989, a blockade was set up to halt further development of the road, and individuals who identified themselves as Sinixt sought to re-establish the Sinixt presence in the Arrow Lakes region, an issue that is ongoing (Pryce, 1999).

The current economic basis of Okanagan communities reflects participation in the larger economic system. Some Okanagan reserves have recreational complexes catering to tourists, others have residential housing developments on land leased from bands, and one band has extensive vineyard operations.

Contemporary Resource-Use Conflicts

Like other indigenous groups in BC, Okanagan bands have been involved in land and resource-use issues that have gained prominence in the 1990s and 2000s. Water levels are an issue throughout the Okanagan, especially to the Osoyoos band at its southern, downstream, end, as irrigation plays an important role in their economy. Disputes over recreational uses of the Okanagan watershed, especially ski resorts, have resulted in road blockades, notably in areas where access is through Indian reserves. In 1994, the Penticton band erected blockades along a road leading to a ski resort to publicize their concern about such uses of traditional territories.

In 2000 the Westbank band started logging in areas outside of their reserves but within their asserted traditional territory, and in doing so invoked a response from the province. The issue of Aboriginal rights as highlighted by the *Delgamuukw* decision became a key issue in the dispute. Part of the reason for Westbank's initiative was their frustration with the treaty process and the lack of agreements while resources in their traditional territory were being harvested by non-Okanagan interests, specifically logging companies that had timber-cutting licences from the province. Years earlier, in 1971, for example, Okanagan fishing rights were contested in the

courts. The issue was whether or not traditional fishing rights could be exercised in a particular creek without having to seek permission from fisheries officers. At that time there was not a *Delgamuukw* decision to reach for, and in the absence of explicit treaties the judge ruled that Okanagan Indian fishing had to be subject to government fisheries regulation. In 2000, the 1997 *Delgamuukw* decision could be appealed to as one of the bases of Aboriginal activities. I say 'one', because a consistent theme runs through the conflicts—that Okanagan rights are rights that flow from Okanagan culture and are not rights conferred by government edicts. The Osoyoos band has more recently sought to reduce the timber-harvesting levels of a large forestry company on Osoyoos traditional territory. Both examples show that there are parallel processes developing: first, the reassertion of Aboriginal activities that are direct continuations of visible Aboriginal activities (such as fishing), and second, the recontextualization and extension of traditional practices in a way that affirms an Aboriginal right to use traditional lands. Thus, logging is seen as both an extension of Aboriginal uses of the forest and its resources and an assertion of the right to use and manage traditional lands and resources in ways that serve the economic interests of contemporary communities.

Economic options, though, have been circumscribed by industrial transformations of the landscape. The damming of the Columbia River reduced salmon runs to the Okanagan and flooded parts of Sinixt territory. The impacts on Columbia River Indian tribes in the US have been described by Watkins (2000). For the Okanagan people, the rehabilitation of salmon spawning areas is a key current issue. Many of the runs were lost or reduced not only because of Columbia River dams, but also because of extensive irrigation and water diversion projects in the Okanagan Valley itself (Cannings and Durance, 1998). A whole generation of Okanagan people has grown up without direct access to what was once a crucial economic and cultural resource.

BOX 21.2

Spotted Lake

Spotted Lake, *klikuk*, is a heavily mineralized small lake about 9 km west of Osoyoos, in the south Okanagan. The lake's name is derived from its appearance: mineralized circles dot the lake. It is one of the most sacred of Okanagan sites and traditionally was used for spiritual and medicinal purposes, particularly by women. Plans in 2000 by its owners to export its mineral-rich mud for commercial uses raised protests by the Okanagan Nation Alliance (ONA).

The history of Aboriginal attempts to gain control of the lake date to early in the twentieth century. In 1917 the Okanagan attempted without success to secure reserve status for Spotted Lake. Then, in 1980, they successfully opposed plans to develop a health spa at the lake. Finally, in 2000 came the proposal to export 10,000 tonnes of mineral mud for cosmetic products. Again, the ONA asked the federal government to purchase the land for a reserve.

In October 2001 the federal government and the Okanagan purchased 22 hectares of land surrounding Spotted Lake. The negotiations involved the Minister of Indian Affairs and Northern Development, Chief Clarence Louie of the Osoyoos Indian band, Chief Dan Wilson of the Okanagan band, and ONA representatives. Spotted Lake is to be under the stewardship of the seven bands in the ONA—Osoyoos, Upper Similkameen, Lower Similkameen, Okanagan, Penticton, Westbank, and Upper Nicola. Pauline Terbasket, executive director of ONA and a member of the Lower Similkameen band, stated: 'I have always been aware of this lake, and protecting our homeland is a testament to our children. Being Okanagan is being from this place. It is part of who I am—my connection, my customs and my roots as an Okanagan woman are here' (Johnson, 2001).

Education

In the past decade, a number of bands and tribal councils have moved towards administering their own educational programs that now include indigenous language and culture components. The issue of representations of Okanagan culture and history also became important. To deal with this, the En'owkin Centre was established by the six bands of the Okanagan Tribal Council in 1981 in Penticton. The En'owkin Centre developed out of the Okanagan Indian Curriculum Project, and its transformation from research-focused activities to the writing of curriculum material flowed from Okanagan people themselves.

An important element of the En'owkin Centre is its international school of writing, established to assist First Nations writers. They face issues of 'voice', of cultural representation, and of developing literary styles. Views from within Okanagan culture are being published out of En'owkin. The term 'En'owkin' itself is a statement about reclaiming voice. But as one of the writers, Jeanette Armstrong, explained (in Jensen, 1995: 282–99), it refers more to a conflict resolution approach, a dialectic process of putting opposite views forward, of looking at the other side. Another goal of the En'owkin process is decolonization, of bringing representation home. Okanagan people see James Teit's classic writings, which are the basic ethnographies in the Plateau, as giving short shrift to Okanagan culture. The Nlaka'pamux were at the centre of Teit's writings, and other Plateau groups such as the Okanagan were seen as variations of a basic underlying Nlaka'pamux cultural pattern. In more recent years, a picture of Okanagan culture from within has emerged, for example in the recent Okanagan publication *We Get Our Living Like Milk from the Land* (Armstrong et al., 1995).

Conclusion

Like other Aboriginal groups in BC, the Okanagan are positioning themselves in the larger Canadian society in terms of Aboriginal rights, a situation that is directed increasingly by litigation. Two factors have changed the legal landscape somewhat. One is the BC Treaty Process, in which most Okanagan bands have not participated. The other is the *Delgamuukw* decision, noted above.

Okanagan lands have become key elements in the regional economy. Reserve lands are strategically located along major transportation corridors, adjacent to urban centres that consume recreational activities and require housing. Lands outside the reserves, which I have been calling traditional territories, are the same areas on which urban centres are being built or resource-harvesting activities like logging are taking place.

The picture in the Okanagan is one of both accommodation and conflict. Aboriginal communities have had to go to court for the return of alienated reserve lands, and some are still engaged in research to document the loss of reserve lands. In traditional territories there is conflict over uses of the land, particularly with respect to large-scale logging by major corporations and the uses of highlands for commercial activities such as ski resorts. Paralleling the confrontational process is one that emphasizes the voice of Okanagan Aboriginal peoples, represented in writings that deal with colonialism, culture change, and continuity. An example is Okanagan author Jeanette Armstrong, whose novels *Slash* and *Enwhisteetkwa* speak of Okanagan culture in current times. She raises the issues of the environmental degradation of Okanagan land and of retaining Okanagan autonomy within an expanding industrial state (see Jensen, 1995; Lutz, 1995). Some of her ideas are reflected in the following comments:

The Okanagan word for 'our place on the land' and 'our language' is the same. We think of our language as the language of the land. This means that the land has taught us our language. The way we survived is to speak the language that the land offered us as its teachings. To know all the plants, animals, seasons, and geography is to construct language for them.

We also refer to the land and our bodies with the same root syllable. This means that the flesh that is our body is pieces of the land come to us through the things that the land is. The soil, the water, the air, and all the other life forms contributed parts to be our flesh. We are our land/place. Not to know and to celebrate this is to be without language and without land. It is to be displaced.

The Okanagan word we have for extended family is translated as 'sharing one skin'. The concept refers to blood ties within community and the instinct to protect our individual selves extended to all who share the same skin. I know how powerful the solidarity is of peoples bound together by land, blood, and love. This is the largest threat to those interests wanting to secure control of lands and resources that have been passed on in a healthy condition from generation to generation of families.

Land bonding is not possible in the kind of economy surrounding us, because land must be seen as real estate to be 'used' and parted with if necessary. I see the separation is accelerated by the concept that 'wilderness' needs to be tamed by 'development' and that this is used to justify displacement of peoples and unwanted species. I know what it feels like to be an endangered species on my land, to see the land dying with us. It is my body that is being torn, deforested, and poisoned by 'development'. Every fish, plant, insect, bird, and animal that disappears is part of me dying. I know all their names, and I touch them with my spirit. I feel it every day, as my grandmother and my father did. (Armstrong, 2001)

Views for the Future

As the Okanagan region continues to be 'developed', issues concerning traditional Okanagan land will increasingly be contested. Access to the traditional material basis of Okanagan culture will diminish, continuing a process that started decades ago. The degree of economic integration of Okanagan communities into the nation-state will likely be an issue, perhaps highlighting differences between Okanagan Aboriginal communities that have reserve lands near urban centres and those in less urbanized regions.

I see a revitalization of Okanagan culture on another level. Writers in the En'owkin Centre will continue to stimulate a renewed interest in Okanagan culture and ideas about relations to the land and to nature. These writings will likely challenge the general direction of growth and land use in the Okanagan Valley, and will play an increasing role in political discourse about environmental issues and Aboriginal landownership and stewardship. Part of this process involves bringing back into the discourse writings by earlier Okanagan writers such as Mourning Dove. The stories of Coyote may yet again inform people about prior ecological relationships to the land.

It is difficult to predict what will happen with Aboriginal rights. Although the *Delgamuukw* decision places Aboriginal rights at the forefront of resource-use issues, each community has to prove its specific rights to traditional territories and demonstrate Aboriginal use and occupancy. As a result, litigation will likely continue to frame Aboriginal rights in ways that pit narrative histories against documentary histories. So far, the BC Treaty Process has not shown that it can bring completion to key issues of landownership and rights in a way that bridges Aboriginal and state notions of landownership and control. That the majority of Okanagan communities have yet to enter the treaty process

suggests the future will bring continued conflicts over Aboriginal entitlement.

Notes

1. A resident of the town of Spences Bridge from the late 1800s, James Teit was engaged by Franz Boas to write on Plateau cultures. His writings form the starting point for studies of Secwepemc, Stl'atl'imx, Nlaka'pamux, and Okanagan. He lived in the area for decades, was married to a Nlaka'pamux woman, and was active in Aboriginal political organizations.
2. Okanagan.
3. Shuswap, now Secwepemc.
4. Similkameen.
5. Cylindrical seashells used to make necklaces, etc. Prestigious trade items, their presence here is indicative of extensive trade networks.
6. An Elder expressed the difference as being equivalent to that between a high school graduate and a Ph.D. He said this knowing I was working on my Ph.D.
7. By way of context, no Indians could vote in federal elections until 1960.
8. For example, a standard reference book (Duff, 1964) lists the Lakes, or Arrow Lake Tribe, as extinct.

References and Recommended Readings

Allison, Susan. 1991. *A Pioneer Gentlewoman in British Columbia: The Recollections of Susan Allison*, ed. Margaret Ormsby. Vancouver: University of British Columbia Press.

Armstrong, Jeanette. 1982. *Enwhisteetkwa: Walk on Water*. Penticton, BC: Okanagan Tribal Council.

———. 1985. *Slash*. Penticton, BC: Theytus Books.

———. 2001. *Sharing One Skin: Okanagan Community*. Okanogan, Wash.: Columbia River Bioregional Project.

Armstrong, Jeanette, Delphine Derickson, Lee Maracle, and Greg Young-Ing, eds. 1995. *We Get Our Living Like Milk from the Land*. Penticton, BC: Theytus Books. An Okanagan perspective on Okanagan land, history, and culture.

British Columbia. 1875. *Papers Connected With the Indian Land Question, 1850–1875*. Victoria: Wolfenden.

Cannings, Richard J., and Eva Durance. 1998. 'Human Use of Natural Resources in the South Okanagan and Lower Similkameen Valleys', in I.M. Smith and G.G.E. Scudder, eds, *Assessment of Species Diversity in the Montane Cordillera Ecozone*. Burlington, Ont.: Ecological Monitoring and Assessment Network.

Carstens, Peter. 1991. *The Queen's People: A Study of Hegemony, Coercion, and Accommodation among the Okanagan of Canada*. Toronto: University of Toronto Press. A critical study of the social and political history of a contemporary northern Okanagan community.

Cline, Walter, et al. 1938. *The Sinkaiek or Southern Okanagan of Washington*, ed. L. Spier. General Series in Anthropology, vol. 6. Manasha, Wis.: G. Banta. A collection of articles on the Okanagan Indians of Washington state, based on research conducted in the 1930s.

Department of Indian Affairs. *Annual Report of the Department of Indian Affairs for 1883*. Canada, Sessional Papers.

Duff, Wilson. 1964. *The Indian History of British Columbia*, Anthropology in British Columbia, Memoir No. 5. Victoria: Provincial Museum of British Columbia.

Jensen, Derrick. 1995. *Listening to the Land: Conversations about Nature, Culture, and Eros*. San Francisco: Sierra Club.

Johnson, Wendy. 2001. 'Spotted Lake Returns to Okanagan First Nations for Safekeeping', *Oliver Chronicle*, 29 Oct.

Kennedy, Dorothy, and Randy Bouchard. 1998. 'Northern Okanagan, Lakes, and Colville', in Deward Walker, ed., *Handbook of North American Indians*, vol. 12, *Plateau*. Washington: Smithsonian Institution. A detailed overview of Okanagan culture, with additional information on Lakes and Colville.

Knight, Rolf. 1978. *Indians at Work*. Vancouver: New Star Books.

Lutz, Hartmut, ed. 1991. *Contemporary Challenges: Conversations with Canadian Native Authors*. Saskatoon: Fifth House.

Mattina, Anthony, and Clara Jack. 1990. 'Okanagan Communication and Language', in J. Webber and the En'owkin Centre, eds, *Okanagan Sources*. Penticton, BC: Theytus Books.

Mourning Dove. 1990a. *Mourning Dove: A Salishan Autobiography*, ed. Jay Miller. Lincoln: University of Nebraska Press.

———. 1990b [1933]. *Coyote Stories*. Lincoln: University of Nebraska Press. Mourning Dove is the pen name of Christine Quintasket, an Okanagan author whose writings first appeared in the 1920s. She is important in the development of Okanagan literature.

Ray, Verne. 1939. *Cultural Relations in the Plateau of Northwestern America*. Publications of the Frederick Webb Hodge Anniversary Publication Fund, vol. III. Los Angeles: Southwest Museum. A classic overview of the basic elements of Plateau culture.

Robinson, Harry. 1989. *Write It on Your Heart: The Epic World of an Okanagan Storyteller*, ed. Wendy Wickwire. Vancouver: Talonbooks/Theytus.

———. 1992. *Nature Power: In the Spirit of an Okanagan Storyteller*, ed. Wendy Wickwire. Vancouver: Douglas & McIntyre. Two collections of stories of Okanagan culture and history based on interviews with an Okanagan storyteller.

Roche, Judith, and Meg McHutchison, eds. 1998. *First Fish, First People: Salmon Tales of the North Pacific Rim*. Vancouver: University of British Columbia Press.

Ross, Alexander. 1986. *Adventures of the First Settlers on the Columbia River, 1810–1813*. Lincoln: University of Nebraska Press.

Sismey, Eric. 1976. 'Okanagan Days', Okanagan Historical Society, *40th Report*. Vernon, BC.

Spencer, Robert, Jesse Jennings, et al. 1977. *The Native Americans*. New York: Harper and Row. This volume contains an overview of the Sanpoil and Nespelem of the southern US plateau; useful for comparative purposes.

Teit, James, and Franz Boas. 1930. 'The Okanagan', in *The Salishan Tribes of the Western Plateaus*. Bureau of American Ethnology, 45th Annual Report. A classic account of Okanagan and Plateau culture, although with an overemphasis on Nlaka'pamux (Thompson) culture.

Turner, Nancy. 1978. *Plant Foods of British Columbia Indians, Part 2, Interior Peoples*. Victoria: British Columbia Provincial Museum.

———, Randy Bouchard, and Dorothy Kennedy. 1980. *Ethnobotany of the Okanagan-Colville Indians of British Columbia and Washington*. Victoria: Occasional Papers of the BC Provincial Museum, No. 21. An account of Okanagan plant use, with extensive ethnographic information.

Walters, L. 1938. 'Social Structure', in W. Cline et al., *The Sinkaietk or Southern Okanagan of Washington*, ed. L. Spier. General Series in Anthropology, vol. 6. Manasha, Wis.: G. Banta.

Watkins, Marilyn. 2000. 'Effects of Grand Coulee Dam on Native Americans in the United States', in *Dams and Development*, Grand Coulee Dam, Annex 9. The Report of the World Commission on Dams. London: Earthscan.

Webber, Jean, and the En'owkin Centre. 1990. *Okanagan Sources*. Penticton, BC: Theytus Books. A collection of articles on Okanagan culture and history by Okanagan community writers, anthropologists, historians, and others.

Wilson, Charles. 1865. *Report on the Tribes Inhabiting the Country in the Vicinity of the 49th Parallel*. Transactions of the Ethnological Society, London, New Series, vol. 4.

Suggested Web Sites

Okanagan Nation Alliance: www.syilx.org
    The official ONA Web site, representing the seven communities of the Okanagan Nation; includes a map of traditional Okanagan territory.

Living Landscapes: www.royal.okanagan.bc.ca
    Information on the natural and human history of the Okanagan, part of a project sponsored by the Royal Museum of BC.

Center for Columbia River History: www.ccrh.org
    Information on the natural and human history of the Columbia River, with some Canadian data.

CHAPTER 22

The Secwepemc:
Traditional Resource Use and Rights to Land

MARIANNE IGNACE and RON IGNACE

Introduction

In late spring 1997, Marianne Ignace and two of her young children accompanied Secwepemc[1] Elder Nellie Taylor from their home on the Skeetchestn Reserve in the Secwepemc Nation into the sagebrush hills between Ashcroft and Cache Creek, BC, to harvest *llekw'pin*, bitterroot. A member of the purslane family, it has been culturally and nutritionally important to the Secwepemc and other Plateau peoples for thousands of years. Its starchy taproots, harvested when the plant bursts into bright pink flowers, were widely used in a variety of dishes. Secwepemc still savour *scpet'am*, a pudding made from bitterroot, salmon eggs, saskatoon berries, and other wild fruits and roots. It can be termed one of our 'national dishes'. Since *llekw'pin* has always been restricted to certain soils and habitats in the southern interior dry belt, the root was an important trade item among Secwepemc communities, and between them and other Aboriginal Nations.

MARIANNE IGNACE: *After parking our car, I began digging for the precious roots with a small pickaxe, delivering my harvest to Nellie, who cleaned off the dirt and peeled the dark red skin off the shrimp-like roots. Nellie, in turn, sat with our seven-year old daughter, showing her the difference between 'male' and 'female' plants, telling her about going digging llekw'pin with her grandmother long ago. Soon a rancher pulled up in his truck, telling us to get*

off his land and asking what we were doing on his property with a pickaxe? I explained what we were doing. He had recently bought the ranch and did not know that it was situated on llekw'pin harvesting grounds. He reluctantly tolerated us, this time.

Both co-authors have experienced such situations, with landowners telling us not to 'trespass' to get to Secwepemc fishing grounds or hunting areas, and with 'private property' signs and barb-wire fences indicating the incompatibility of traditional resource pursuits (fishing, hunting, and plant harvesting) with settler land tenure. During the last 20 years, we have seen some of our most productive soapberry gathering sites turned into logging roads, tourist interpretation centres, and housing subdivisions. Our Elders' oral histories abound with memories of settlers trying to evict them from places where they had hunted, fished, gathered plants, camped, and travelled for generations. Federal fisheries policies and provincial game regulations have criminalized traditional fishing and hunting activities across Canada.

This paper focuses on the traditional resource management and harvesting regimes of the Secwepemc and how this way of life has been affected during the past 100 years. As Secwepemc, we view using the traditional resources of our land, *Secwepemcul'ecw*, as our collective *right*, deriving from our *Aboriginal title*. Encroachment on these rights and practices through government policies and resource development has severely

FIGURE 22.1. The late Nellie Taylor scraping a buckskin before tanning it, October 1987. (Courtesy Marianne Ignace)

challenged our ability to exercise our rights. Over generations, the combined effect of changes to the landscape produced by resource development, of government land policies and fish and game policies, and of the assimilation policies of the Canadian government, has been to challenge the transmission of traditional knowledge about the land. It has endangered the knowledge systems, the connections between our world view and practices. As we will show, much of that connection involves our language, Secwepemctsin, which is endangered. As Secwepemc people struggle to carry out resource harvesting, we face the connected challenges of endangered rights, endangered landscapes and biodiversity, endangered knowledge systems, and an endangered language.

As authors, we come to this topic in ways that

connect indigenous peoples, anthropology, social research, law, and politics. As co-authors, we use the term 'we' when referring to the Secwepemc, because of our separate and joint connections to them through birth and marriage and as parents of Secwepemc children. At times, we choose to use the voice of one or the other.

MARIANNE IGNACE: *I grew up in a Plattdeutsch-speaking area of northwestern Germany, where a different identity and language were associated with low social class and where cultural and linguistic differences were denied by the dominant society. Anthropology has provided a way to account for, and put into perspective, the experiences of peoples that have a long connection with their landscape and who have become marginalized. Coming to Canada in the mid-1970s, I already appreciated the value of collaborative research in and with Aboriginal communities in piecing together Elders' knowledge, often embedded in language, and interpreting it with their help and for the benefit of younger generations. From the 1980s, being expert witness in court cases involving the Haida and Secwepemc Nations has further shaped my work. It involved translating what Aboriginal bearers of knowledge and storytellers saw and experienced, in a language that also satisfied anthropological models and the court system. That research led to Ron and me establishing a post-secondary research and education institution, Secwepemc Education Institute, where, with academics and Elders, we train our own people in social research skills and allow them to receive their own academic credentials while staying close to their communities.*

RON IGNACE: *I am Secwepemc on both sides of my family. Being raised by my great-grandparents, Edward and Julienne Eneas, is what most shaped my identity. They were born in the 1870s, and followed a seasonal round of hunting, gathering, and fishing, mixed with ranching and agriculture, until near their death in the early 1960s. My great-grandfather was also chief during my early childhood, and my great-grandmother was the sister and niece of previous chiefs appointed by Secwepemc tradition, who took an active role in the Aboriginal rights movement during the early twentieth century. Their handed-down memories shaped my thinking. Unlike most of my age-mates, I was raised in our language, Secwepemctsin. After time spent at the Kamloops Indian Residential School, followed by menial labour and Vancouver's skid row, I set out to study anthropology and sociology at the University of British Columbia. Upon completing my Master's degree, my community, Skeetchestn, induced me to become elected chief. They have re-elected me 10 times at this point (2002). Since the late 1980s, I have also served as chairman of the Shuswap Nation Tribal Council and as president of the Secwepemc Cultural Education Society. As part of my effort to write about the economic and cultural history of the Secwepemc, I am completing a Ph.D. in anthropology.*

What brought each of us to anthropology was the search for connections among indigenous peoples and the quest for answers about how, historically, colonization took its shape. The voices of other indigenous peoples that we hear in some anthropologists' writings have stimulated us to explain history, culture, and the underlying meanings that people give to their lives, which have too often been silenced.

We have collaborated on academic and applied research regarding Secwepemc land tenure, oral histories, political history, language, and ethnobotany. Our home, family, and lives are not separated from 'the field' where we conduct research. Instead, our work pushes us to consciously consider, incorporate, and write about our lives, and the lives of our relatives, Elders, and friends. Anthropological research provides a way for us to piece together the 'broken cup' of Secwepemc cultural knowledge, practices, and meanings. It also provides a way to transmit that knowledge to younger generations and those who were deprived of all but pieces of that puzzle, not as academic knowledge, but to make sense of their Secwepemc past. We thus draw on anthropological research methods, knowledge, and theory. We also question anthropological models, as our consideration of Secwepemc plant gathering shows.

In addition, as providers for our family and community members, we have practised hunting, fishing, and plant gathering according to Secwepemc traditions. In other words, our anthropological training has influenced the way we research, write about, and perceive the Secwepemc. Our life as or among Secwepemc people has also influenced our anthropology.

To explore Secwepemc traditional and contemporary resource use, we will begin by explaining our ancestor's system of resource use and management when their control of the land was unimpeded. We can construct this with the help of archaeological data, nineteenth-century ethno-historical data, and ethnographic information, some of which was recorded by James A. Teit, but current and remembered practices allow us to throw further light on these data. Resource use and management, however, is more than technology and practices. There is a cognitive dimension comprising the world view, beliefs, and spiritual and social connections underlying the practices. We find that this cognitive dimension can best be understood by self-reflexively examining what one of us (Ron Ignace) knows about such connections and what the oral histories of Elders and contemporaries who hunted, fished, and gathered plants reveal about its role in their/our lives.

The second part of this chapter will examine how the processes of colonization, dispossession, and coercive tutelage have had impacts on our ability to harvest our resources and maintain control over our lands. We will thus discuss the processes of history that affected this, along with the human, social, and economic impacts on the Secwepemc.

Lastly, we will discuss contemporary Secwepemc use and control of traditional resources, including how they have become the topic of litigation, political negotiation, and practical management regimes.

Coyote's Work: Secwepemc Culture and the Seasonal Round

Secwepemc means 'spread-out people'. 'Shuswap', widely used in the ethnographic literature and in common language to refer to us, is an anglicization of the word 'Secwepemc', produced by explorers who struggled to hear some of the sounds of our language. The Secwepemc are the largest Interior Salish-speaking Aboriginal Nation in Canada. Our territory encompasses some 180,000 square kilometres in the south-central area of what is now British Columbia, stretching from near the Alberta border west of Jasper to the plateau west of the Fraser River, and southeast to the Arrow Lakes and the Columbia River. Secwepemc territory is bordered by, and overlaps, that of 10 other nations, including the Salish St'at'imc, Nlaka'pamux, and Okanagan, and non-Salish Tsilhqot'in, Carrier, Sekani, Cree, Blackfoot, Stony, and Ktunaxa. Secwepemcul'ecw, our

homeland, is traversed and characterized by the two major rivers of the BC Plateau, the Fraser and the Thompson. Most Secwepemc communities are and were located along these rivers and their main tributaries, although the resource use areas encompassed all our territory (see Map. 22.1).

Ancient Culture: Archaeology and Oral History

The oldest archaeological evidence of human occupation in Secwepemc territory is the remains of a boy who died in a flash flood at Gore Creek, east of Kamloops, some 8,300 years ago. Only a few years ago, his remains were repatriated to Secwepemc homeland after having been stored in a museum for decades. Until recently, archaeologists assumed that the Interior of BC was under a thick layer of ice until some 11,500 years ago. Recent finds of fossilized kokanee, a land-locked salmon, on the shores of Kamloops Lake (dated at 18,000 to 15,500 BP) demonstrate that parts of the Interior formed a warm, ice-free area and that human occupation may have been possible much earlier than previously thought. Following deglaciation, salmon runs established themselves in the Fraser and Thompson watersheds by or before 6,000 years ago. We don't know with certainty when Secwepemc people began to harvest these salmon. Archaeological data conservatively suggest that the historic configuration of salmon fishing and root harvesting, with winter residence in underground dwellings, took shape by around 4,000 to 3,500 years ago.

Stspetékwll, ancient oral traditions, throw a different, but perhaps complementary, light on our origins and history. Old One, the Creator, provided humans with the arts and customs that distinguish them from animals by giving them diverse languages and showing them how to fish and to make baskets and other implements. Ancient myths also detail the travels of Tlii7sa and his brothers, and other 'transformers', who travelled the ancient landscape of ice, fire, floods, and dangerous animals and monsters, defeated them, and left their marks throughout the land. Most of all, Old One sent Coyote, *sk'elep*, to finish the

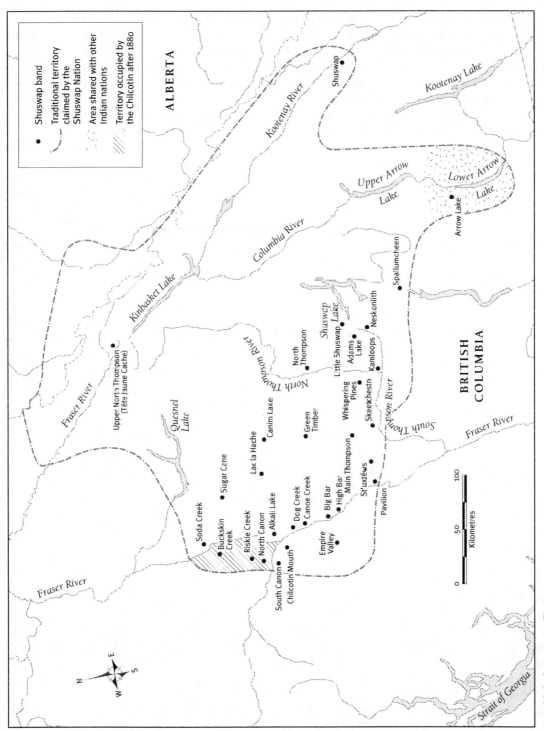

MAP 22.1. Secwepemc Territory

work of turning the land into Secwepemc land. Sk'elep broke the fishing weir of two medicine women downstream from the Secwepemc, thus enabling salmon to travel upriver into the mid-Fraser and Thompson watersheds. By impregnating the women, he connected the Secwepemc through kinship with our Nlaka'pamux neighbours on the Fraser to the south.

Stspetékwll have moral and social dimensions. The deeds of Coyote, the trickster, challenge and affirm our values of what is appropriate behaviour and how we are socially and spiritually connected to nature and to others. In addition, they represent the indigenous idiom that parallels and throws light on events of geology and ancient history, cast, however, in the language of poetry between whose lines we have to read the science. As archaeologist Knut Fladmark (1986: 12) notes:

> We should turn to the ancient oral histories to add real life and texture to our conception of prehistory. Seen with mutual tolerance for each other's different world-views, the broad themes of native traditional folklore and modern archaeology are compatible, strengthening and complementing each other to brighten our understanding of B.C.'s ancient past.

The Traditional Seasonal Round

Secwepemcul'ecw is subdivided geographically, the people referring to one another as follows. Tk'emlupsemc are the 'people of the confluence' (of the North and South Thompson rivers). Sextsinemc, 'people of the shore' (of the main Thompson River), are near the Bonaparte and Hat Creek rivers to the west. Set'emc, 'people of the mid-Fraser River', live along the big river (the Fraser). The St'emcul'ecwemc, 'people of St'emculecw' or possibly 'people of cleared land', are upstream near Williams Lake. Styetemc, 'inland people', live among the lakes and plateaus between the Fraser and North Thompson rivers. Tqéqeltkemc 'people of the upper reaches', live on the mid and upper North Thompson, although a group of them, the Kenpesq'et (Kinbasket),

moved to the Upper Columbia near Ktunaxa territory during the 1800s or earlier. Sexqeltkemc, 'upstream people', are on the South Thompson and eastward towards the head of Okanagan Lake. Within these divisions, there were further subgroups, centred around main villages. Each of these main villages had a chief, *kukwpi7*, appointed by custom. Disease in the mid-1800s reduced the 30 main villages to 17.

Secwepemcul'ecw is enormously varied in topography, climate, flora, and fauna. There are nine biogeoclimatic zones. There is the interior Douglas fir zone, the wetter cedar and hemlock forests of the highland plateaus, and the dry bunchgrass, ponderosa pine, and sagebrush slopes of the interior dry belt. There are montane parklands, subalpine fir and spruce forests, lodgepole pine forests, subalpine meadows, and alpine tundras.

The annual subsistence cycle began in spring, when families gathered at highland lakes as soon as the ice broke, to net cutthroat and rainbow trout at their outlets as they prepared to spawn. These fisheries brought together large numbers of Secwepemc from different villages, facilitating social and political gatherings. April and May saw young shoots of balsamroot, fireweed, and cow parsnip harvested. People later moved to choice harvesting areas at mid or higher elevations to dig large quantities of edible bulbs and roots, including balsamroot, avalanche lily, and spring beauties, as well as bitterroot, wild onions, biscuit root, Mariposa lily, yellowbells, chocolate tips, and tiger lily. Vast amounts were dried and stored for winter or, in some cases, prepared through a mixture of sun curing, pit-cooking, and drying. In late May, families stripped the sweet cambium of lodgepole pines. From early July to early September, numerous species of berries, including saskatoons, soapberries, three species of blueberries, huckleberries, raspberries, strawberries, blackcaps, choke cherries, gooseberries, and currents ripened at mid to higher elevations.

As early as February, Secwepemc fished for steelhead in the Thompson River by drifting downriver in canoes at night and spearing fish attracted by their pitch torches. During late spring, the first runs of Chinook or spring salmon travel up the Fraser and Thompson rivers into their tributaries. While these salmon continue to run throughout the summer, in summer and early fall sockeye salmon return to their spawning grounds in tributaries of the mid-Fraser and Thompson river system. Although sockeye runs show great fluctuation in their four-year cycles, the different runs provided enormous quantities of food. Mid- to late fall brought runs of coho salmon. In the murky waters of the Fraser, the preferred method was dip-netting, while fishing in the clear waters of the Thompson involved harpooning, gaffing, and spearing, as well as set nets and gill nets. Before the early twentieth century, weirs and dams were an effective way to fish selectively for large numbers of salmon of a particular run.

More bulbs and roots, including chocolate lily or rice root as well as silverweed, whose stringy but fleshy roots are called 'Indian spaghetti', were also harvested during this time. Late spring to early September also marked the time when Secwepemc replenished their repositories of medicinal plants, gathered especially at mid and higher elevations. The period from August to October, when deer were fat and the fawns had matured, was the main hunting season. Task groups of related men, their parents, wives, and children would travel to base camps in or below the montane parklands. As the men hunted mule deer, caribou, and elk higher up, the women and children lived at the base camp and set snares to trap small game. They deboned and dried the game brought in by hunters. Since early in the twentieth century, moose have replaced caribou and elk in much of Secwepemc territory. During the fall hunt, family groups would harvest black tree lichen in the Douglas fir zone, then pit-cook and dry it for winter use. Hunting also occurred throughout the year as necessary, as when families gathered for a funeral or had run out of meat.

From spring to late fall, Secwepemc thus travelled to and from resource-producing locations, sometimes hundreds of kilometres from their winter villages. They camped for weeks at a time, harvested foods, and prepared them for winter, but living in camps was *as significant* a part of the way of life. Winter food was stored in cache pits near villages, but also in pits along the way to resource locations and near camps or processing locations for use next season. When horses arrived during the 1750s, they soon replaced much travel on foot or by canoe, although dugout cottonwood canoes and birchbark canoes, as well as rafts, continued to be used on the rivers and lakes.

In late October or early November, during the 'entering month' when bears retired into their dens, people moved into their underground pit houses for the winter, living on preserved foods. Most of the winter villages, and thus the contemporary communities, were at or near the Fraser and Thompson valleys. Teit estimated the Secwepemc population at some 9,000 in 1850, when numerous diseases had already taken their toll. Some villages, especially those at Keatley Creek and Kelly Lake near the Fraser River, and at Clearwater on the North Thompson, had well over 100 pithouses. Other sites consisted of two to four pithouses. The first traders who arrived among the Secwepemc in 1811 noted more than 2,000 people living at the confluence of North and South Thompson.

Fishing, hunting, and gathering involve intricate skills. They enact(ed) and transmit(ted) cultural and social principles of the division of labour by age, sex, and experience, and the social cohesion, role relationships, and economic efficiency resulting from these. As to fishing, in general (although with exceptions) men caught fish and women processed them. Older men, unable to spear fish, helped with butchering and showing younger people how to fish. Experts in making fishing gear, they passed these skills on to the younger generation. Older women supervised the gutting, filleting, and slicing of fish for drying, and tended the smoke fires and drying racks. By working alongside them, observing and copying, and sometimes being gently corrected, children and teenagers learned the important skills of slicing fish properly, hanging them, building the proper kind of fire, etc. Learning and teaching took place by example rather than overt instruction.

Resource Management

Although Teit referred to specific 'hunting grounds' associated with each of the seven Shuswap divisions, he stressed that they conceived of their land as 'tribal property':

> All the land and hunting grounds were looked upon as tribal property all parts of which were open to every member of the tribe. Of course, every band had its common recognized hunting, trapping and fishing places, but members of other bands were allowed to use them whenever they desired. . . . Fishing places were also tribal property, including salmon-stations. . . . At the lakes every one had the privilege of trapping trout and erecting weirs. (Teit, 1909: 572; cf. Boas, 1890: 638)

Teit also added that 'berry patches were tribal property, but picking was under tribal control. All the large and valuable berrying spots were looked after by the chief of the band in whose district they were situated' (ibid., 573). 'Tribal control' here means control by the band or community since chiefship existed only at the band level. Of root-digging grounds, Teit noted that they were 'common tribal property. Some people of the northern Fraser River bands laid a claim on the root-digging grounds of Quesnel Lake, where very large lily-roots grow, but these claims were not recognized by the rest of the tribe' (ibid., 582). Likewise, the chiefs of the Interior reiterated this tribal (or national) sense of land tenure to Sir Wilfrid Laurier in 1910 (see below).

The collective and joint sense of ownership of Secwepemc territory and its resources continues to exist, despite the federal government's attempt to instill a sense of private property through the Indian Act and schooling. Secwepemc Elders still reveal a strong sense of their territory and its resources being owned collectively by all. In 1985, when the Skeetchestn chief and council were developing a fishing bylaw, they had recommended that all non-Skeetchestn persons had to get a permit to fish in their waters. The Elders would not approve the bylaw unless it recognized that all Secwepemc had the right to fish there without a permit. They maintained that, as Secwepemc, they had the right to fish anywhere in Secwepemc territory. Non-Secwepemc Aboriginals had to get a permit, but it must be free. Non-Secwepemc are allowed to assist their Secwepemc spouses or families in fishing, or to provide for them if their Secwepemc spouse or children are unable to do so. Should they abuse this privilege, it could be revoked. On the other hand, non-Aboriginal people were required to buy a permit and were restricted to fly-fishing. The bylaw also requires that all users of the fishing grounds keep the grounds clean and treat the fish and the place with respect. Once amended in this fashion, the band passed the bylaw. It is still in force and has not been contested.

Within Secwepemcul'ecw, the tribal land providing equal access to resources, local regions are seen as being stewarded by people from local communities. Elders thus describe band territories as 'belonging' to the Tk'emlupsemc, or the people from Skeetchestn. Band territories are usually marked by considerable overlap. Particular communities, led by their chiefs and caretakers (see below), are thus collective stewards over particular tracts of Secwepemcul'ecw. Members of all other communities within the nation are welcome at the resource-producing locations, including fishing grounds, of other communities. Elders from all parts of Secwepemcul'ecw remember that in the past, people from all parts of Secwepemcul'ecw would come to prolific fishing grounds such as the mouth of Deadman's Creek and High Bar, Gang Ranch, and Soda Creek on the Fraser.

Access to the resources of the nation and to a particular band was provided by kinship, descent, relations of affinity, residence, and socialization. Since residence patterns were usually patrilocal, most individuals took their primary sense of belonging to a nation and community from their father's side. In addition, a person had access to the territory of the other parent, even where that other parent was from another nation. If the other parent was from another community within the nation, an individual would get to know the hunting, fishing, and gathering areas near that community while visiting relatives and would be invited to share the harvest.

Access to other nations' territories was thus enabled by virtue of maintaining kinship ties with people from there. This gave individuals secondary affiliations with any number of other nations and communities, resulting from the out-marriage of parents, grandparents, and other ancestors. As long as kinship ties with such people were kept active, a person was welcome to fish, hunt, gather, and live in these territories. This principle of mutual access to resources by virtue of kinship and descent was common to all first peoples of the Plateau and provided a crucial means of sharing and distributing resources. Teit also noted for the Thompson (Nlaka'pamux) people that:

> Among the Spence's Bridge and Nicola Bands any member of the Shuswap and Okanagan tribes who was related to them by blood was allowed full access to their hunting-grounds, the same as one of themselves . . . . If, however, a person who was not related to a Thompson Indian were caught hunting trapping or gathering bark or roots, within the recognized limits of the tribal territory, he was liable to forfeit his life. (Teit 1900: 293)

Another way of accessing resources was through relations of affinity. A woman usually moved in with her husband's people upon marriage, but it was also customary for the new couple to live with her parents for a time, explaining the term for son-in-law, snek'llcw, 'someone who changes house'. Since a strong prohibition to marrying blood relatives existed, many people from smaller villages married outside their community. Demographic and genealogical records dating to the early 1800s show that patrilocal residence was normative, with about a third of marriages involving spouses (mostly women) from other villages.

A non-Secwepemc person married into a Secwepemc community was welcome to accompany his/her in-laws to help provide for the family. Likewise, a Secwepemc person who married a Secwepemc from another community would accompany his/her in-laws on hunting, fishing and gathering trips. For example, if a woman from Skeetchestn married a man from Alkali Lake, he would participate in the harvesting activities of Skeetchestn and become familiar with the resources there, thus providing for his family.

Resource management was thus accomplished through a system of collective ownership, sharing between communities and nations, and the stewardship of particular resources. Teit's ethnographic work notes 'hunting chiefs'. Our oral histories refer to the stewards over particular resources, such as game, fish, or plants, as yucwmin'men, 'caretakers'. It was their job to monitor the ripening of berries and the state of root patches, salmon runs, and game habitat and occurrence, and to let the people of their village know where and when these resources were ready or whether runs or harvests might fall short. In addition, particular individuals were also tacitly put in charge of maintaining trails to community hunting, fishing, camping, and plant-gathering areas.

Resource caretakership involves a complex set of (or dialectic relation between) resource-gathering practices and a system of knowledge and beliefs. Ethnobiologists refer to this as traditional ecological knowledge and wisdom (TEKW). At the core of the cognitive dimension of Secwepemc TEKW is our ancestors' and the present generation's relationship with the land, maintained through 'storied knowledge' about the land, intimately connected to our language. All landforms and geographical features are named. These names contain roots referring to the specific nature of that place and lexical suffixes that indicate the shape or form of the place, derived from the shapes of the human body. Thus, a sidehill is *ck'emenk*, 'coming together at an angle' of a belly-shape. *Pet'memnus* is an area surrounded by wooded hills where one emerges from the woods into an open meadow (*pet'*, to emerge from the woods; *men*, instrumental; *us*, face. The additional *m* identifies the word as a place name).

In addition to the named landforms, place names commemorate the landscape. By way of ellipses and allusions, where the word merely hints at something, they can refer to the shape of landforms, natural phenomena, or animals or plants that are prominent in a location. They also commemorate past events, the oral history connected to the landscape. A subalpine area in Wells Gray Park is named *kélentem*, 'he was chased', after a group of Cree invaders. A ridge on the Adams Plateau where people meditated during spirit guardian quests is called *smetúsem* (*s*, nominalizer; *met*, to sit/live, *us*, face, *em*, intransitive action). Pavilion Lake is *np'etkwe7ten*, 'fart in the water place' (*n*, inside; *p'e*, to fart; *etkwe*, water; *ten*, place), in memory of Coyote killing a powerful skunk here.

In referring to places, Secwepemc speakers employ a complex system of deictics, pointing words. They refer to landscape features as being close to the speaker, close to the listener, or away from both; absent or present; visible or invisible; coming this way or going that way; this side of the river or on the opposite side; and upstream or downstream.

Secwepemc TEKW includes the relationship with all living things on the land. The act of hunting involves far more than volition and action on part of the hunter. An animal that is killed through fishing or hunting 'gives itself up', *kecmentsut*, but only if the person approaches that animal with a clean mind and body. Many stories about animals that give themselves up to be hunted during times of bereavement, or when people are in need, are handed down among Secwepemc people.

Because the animal has given itself, respect must be shown to the species and its environment. This includes a range of practices combining ritual/spiritual and practical aspects, such as ensuring physical and spiritual cleanliness before hunting through sweat bathing. The Elders do not allow fish guts to be thrown into the river, nor will they allow anyone even to spit into the river, to keep the fishing grounds clean, lest the fish stop running. Fish, of course, are known for their sense of smell, and fish guts will cause them to avoid the shore, where they can be caught. The same kind of rationale is behind women not hunting or accompanying hunters when menstruating. Respecting the harvested animal or plant also includes thanking it, not in public ceremony, but by a quiet prayer of thanks and an offering. Secwepemc raised in this tradition still make an offering of tobacco, sometimes a coin, sometimes a small food offering.

In the Secwepemc cognitive system that connects the land, living things, and humans, there are consequences for not following these norms, for not respecting the animals who give themselves. When fishers are unsuccessful despite their known skills, the reasons are not construed to be unspecified 'bad luck' or lack of skill (given that they have been trained and have learned), but are related to lack of respect. The offences to animals that prevent success in hunting or fishing can also be situated in the realm of social offences against other people, especially of not sharing.

Nellie Taylor often told of how she and her partner, Cecilia Peters, went to Hi-Hium Lake to fish trout. Two young men had set up camp and were roasting the fish they had caught without offering any to the Elders. 'After that, the fish just quit running for them. They never caught any more', she remarked wryly. By violating the norm of sharing (especially with Elders), they had acted inappropriately and had brought about supernatural sanction of their behaviour in that the fish stopped running for them.

The knowledge and consciousness of the spiritual and social context of harvesting were

BOX 22.1

Scwicw—Yellow Avalanche Lily

Root crops and bulbs contributed much to Secwepemc diets well into the 1900s. Elders such as Bill Arnouse and Ike Willard report that their families harvested several hundred pounds each season. Extended family groups would harvest *scwicw* and other roots in late spring. Adults rolled back the grassy top soil and extracted the roots, about 30–40 cm below the surface. In so doing, they loosened the soil, and young children would replant immature bulbs. Children would also pick the corms (the propagating part) off the bulbs and replant them. Caretakers of the *scwicw* would burn harvesting patches in early spring, in multi-year cycles. Within about two years, a burnt patch yielded large bulbs. Experiments with plant-harvesting strategies have shown that such techniques enhance crops rather than diminish them.

There is also indication that Secwepemc caretakership and management of *scwicw* went one step further: to transplanting them in a new habitat. The most prolific sites are meadows above the South Thompson River near the villages of Neskonlith and

Adams Lake, about 600 metres above sea level. This area is an unusual habitat for *Erythronium grandiflorum*, which in all other locations throughout western Canada grows in subalpine meadows at around 1,500 metres.

According to Secwepemc and St'at'imc traditions, grizzly bears inspired Interior Salish people to develop processing techniques for *scwicw*. As the stories go, hunters observed grizzlies digging *scwicw*. Instead of immediately eating them, they left them exposed to the sun for some days, then returned to eat them. Chemical analysis reveals that freshly harvested bulbs contain an indigestible starch. Sun curing converts the inedible starch into fructose and edible starches. Further human intervention through pit cooking produces a balanced combination of edible starch to satisfy hunger and fructose to satisfy the palate. Similar chemical conversions through the combination of sun curing and pit cooking (as opposed to boiling or roasting) exist for roots that contain the starch inulin, such as balsamroot and wild onion.

transmitted through stories that illustrated what happened to Coyote when he showed disrespect. Storied knowledge also involves the many anecdotes and stories about what happened to specific individuals that are part of the living memory of the community. A heartfelt sense of connection to the land, and the stories of the land, was also expressed in Secwepemc songs.

Practical Management Regimes

Secwepemc resource use entailed sophisticated strategies of plant propagation and habitat management developed over some 3,500 years. One of many examples involves the management and harvesting strategies around yellow avalanche lily (see Box 22.1). These included landscape burning

to enrich the soil, replanting corms to ensure new growth, reseeding dug-up patches, and loosening soil with root-diggers. Lily patches managed in this way tended to produce plentiful harvests year after year. Burning, pruning, and cyclical harvesting also increased and sustained the yield of berry crops like saskatoons, soapberries, and blueberries. As Elder Mary Thomas observed, these strategies made Secwepemc plant management regimes 'just like a garden'. That is, they were closely akin to horticulture, although involving 'wild' plants rather than cultigens. Indeed, when Hudson's Bay Company traders introduced Secwepemc to domesticated plants (potatoes, onions, carrots, and grains) in the nineteenth century, they quickly incorporated gardening into their seasonal round. The word they coined for gardening is *kw'en'llq*, 'to try out plants'.

Secwepemc History— the Nineteenth Century

The nineteenth century brought pervasive change. Fur traders and explorers made exploratory trips on the Fraser and Columbia rivers in the early 1800s and established trading posts by the 1820s, notably Thompson River Post at Tk'emlups (Kamloops) in the heartland of the southern Secwepemc. Although the trade in furs fluctuated and was deemed infeasible, Thompson River Post, operated by the HBC, continued to play a major role in the interior trade until the early 1860s. The bunchgrass hills surrounding the post provided welcome pasture for brigade horses; more importantly, the Secwepemc and neighbouring groups provided quantities of dried and fresh salmon, which became the staple of the traders. HBC records show that 12,000–20,000 salmon were bought annually from 1822 to the late 1850s.[2] The invasion of gold-seekers into the interior in 1858 precipitated a smallpox epidemic which, during 1862–3, killed from one-third to two-thirds of the population, wiping out most Secwepemc on the west banks of the Fraser River near Chilcotin Canyon.

During the early 1860s, the BC colonial governor, James Douglas, arranged several reserves at Tk'emlups and in the Shuswap Lakes area, under a policy whereby reserves were to be allotted as 'severally pointed out by the Indians themselves'. Further reserves were proposed or mentioned. However, after his retirement, the colonial government rescinded them. Also, a land ordinance forbade Indians from pre-empting (claiming a homestead) or purchasing land. The 1860s also saw the arrival of Oblate missionaries at Tk'emlups and near Williams Lake.

While BC was a colony (1858–71), government policy did not explicitly interfere with Native fishing and hunting. Officials did, however, use the nomadic lifestyle of the Shuswap as an argument against them, claiming that in making a living by fishing and hunting they did not 'really' utilize the land and therefore had no 'real' rights to it. For example, BC colonial gold commissioner Phillip Henry Nind noted of the North Thompson Shuswap in 1865:

> These Indians do nothing more with their land than cultivate a few small patches of potatoes here and there; they are a vagrant people who live by fishing, hunting and bartering skins; and the cultivation of their ground contributes no more to their livelihood than a few days digging of wild roots. (British Columbia, 1875: 29)

These remarks foreshadow those of BC Commissioner of Lands and Works Joseph Trutch throughout the ensuing years. In 1865, Trutch wrote:

> I am satisfied from my own observation that the claims of Indians over tracts of land, on which they assume to exercise ownership, but of which they make no real use, operate very materially to prevent settlement and cultivation, in many instances besides that to which attention has been directed by Mr. Nind, and I should advise that these claims should be as soon as practicable enquired into and defined. (Ibid., 30)

Under the racist and parsimonious land policies of Trutch, reserves previously laid out by Douglas were drastically reduced or entirely eliminated. Secwepemc land title was not recognized by the institutions of the new government. In addition, the Secwepemc were prohibited from pre-empting or buying lands outside of their small reserves while large numbers of settlers were allowed to obtain, virtually free of charge, title to most of the arable land.

After British Columbia entered Confederation in 1871, the provincial and federal governments took several years to propose Indian reserves in the province. During this time, Secwepemc chiefs were considering warfare against the new government. When word of this leaked out, the governments quickly launched a Joint Reserve Commission to allocate reserves throughout BC, but with no per capita formula, as had been done in the treaty areas. The land eventually reserved for the remaining 17 Secwepemc communities amounted to about 1 per cent of Secwepemc Aboriginal territory.

The Secwepemc people, led by their chiefs, played a prominent role in the early twentieth-century Aboriginal rights movement. Through trips to Ottawa and London, and through petitions and memorials to the federal government, they tried to address our peoples' grievances regarding lands and the loss of hunting, fishing, and plant-gathering resources.

Secwepemc Traditional Resource Use, 1880s–1970s

In their presentation to Prime Minister Laurier when he visited their territory in 1910, in similar petitions from that time, and in their testimony before the McKenna McBride Commission in 1913, Secwepemc chiefs complained about the loss of land and resources. Chief Andre of the North Thompson people, in his eighties at the time, said to the commissioners:

> You know how poor I am, just like as if I was tied up—therefore I am kind of poor. It seems as though I cannot help myself to better myself, like as if I were afraid all the time. Everything seems to be locked up now, different from what it used to be a long time ago. It used to be that everything was open to me, a long time ago. That is what I want. I want to be more free, so that I can get along better. I want to know whoever is the Chief that is going to help me on that point, to help me on what is good.

Joe Tomma, chief of Skeetchestn (Deadman's Creek), spoke to the Commission on 29 Oct. 1913:

> The grievance of all the Indians in B.C. [is] that the white man has kind of spoilt us and

locked us in. The white men have taken all the land and claimed all the water rights, and stopped us from hunting, fishing, etc.

On 25 October 1915 Chief Francois Silpahan, Little Shuswap band, declared:

> It is not on our reserve only that our hard feelings commence; it is for lands outside the reserves where the whitemen have stopped us. They stopped us from getting deer and birds, stopped us fishing. That is what we have told the Government in Ottawa. . . . When the Indians were here a very long time ago, and able to look for their own food all over, the Indians used to increase, and they used to have good living.

As late as 1876, I.W. Powell, Indian Superintendent for BC, expressed the necessity to preserve Indian fishing in the following terms:

> There is not, of course, the same necessity to set aside extensive grants of agricultural land for Coast Indians; *but their rights to fishing stations and hunting grounds should not be interfered with, and they should receive every assurance of perfect freedom from future encroachments of every description.* (Department of Indian Affairs, *Annual Report*, 1876: 32; emphasis added)

It is notable that Powell addressed the Aboriginal fishery as a right, which should be free from encroachment.

Fishing Restrictions

Until the mid- to late 1870s, the colonial and subsequent provincial governments did not interfere with Aboriginal fishing, especially for salmon. Indeed, the instructions on BC reserves, issued in 1874, noted that 'Great care should be taken that the Indians . . . should not be disturbed in the enjoyment of their customary fishing grounds' (British Columbia, 1875: 131). Indian Superintendent Powell spoke of Indian fishing as a 'right'.

BOX 22.2

Memorial to Sir Wilfrid Laurier

Presented at Kamloops by the chiefs of the Shuswap, Okanagan, and Thompson tribes by Chief Louis of Kamloops. Written by their secretary, James Teit.

We take this opportunity of your visiting Kamloops to speak a few words to you. We welcome you here, and we are glad we have met you in our country. We want you to be interested in us, and to understand more fully the conditions under which we live. . . .

When the *seme7uw'i*, the Whites, first came among us there were only Indians here. They found the people of each tribe supreme in their own territory, and having tribal boundaries known and recognized by all. The country of each tribe was just the same as a very large farm or ranch (belonging to all the people of the tribe) from which they gathered their food and clothing, etc., fish which they got in plenty for food, grass and vegetation on which their horses grazed and their game lived, and much of which furnished materials for manufactures, etc., stone which furnished pipes, utensils, and tools, etc., trees which furnished firewood, materials for houses and utensils, plants, roots, seeds, nuts and berries which grew abundantly and were gathered in their season just the same as the crops on a ranch . . . and all the people had equal rights of access to everything they required. You will see the ranch of each tribe was the same as its life, and without it the people could not have lived.

They [the government officials sent by Douglas] said that a very large reservation would be staked off for us (southern interior tribes) and the tribal lands outside of this reservation the government would buy from us for white settlement. They let us think this would be done soon, and meanwhile, until this reserve was set apart, and our lands settled for, they assured us that we would have perfect freedom of traveling and camping and the same liberties as from time immemorial to hunt, fish, and gather our food supplies wherever we desired; also that all trails, land, water, timber etc., would be as free of access to us as formerly. Our Chiefs were agreeable to these propositions, so we waited for treaties to be made, and everything settled.

—Excerpted from the original in
Ignace and Ignace (1999)

Soon after, however, with competition for salmon from commercial fishing, especially on the lower Fraser River, the federal Fisheries Department began imposing restrictions on Indian fishing, asserting that Indian weirs and traps, as well as nets, were detrimental to the salmon. Antoine Gregoire, a Secwepemc from Adams Lake, was called in 1877 to give testimony as to Secwepemc fishing methods. He swore that:

[the Shuswap] know, and say, that if the young fish are destroyed, the shoals returning from the sea will be proportionally diminished. That the Indians, with this fact in view, are careful not to destroy, wantonly or wastefully, the mature fish, or to impede their passage to the spawning beds. That the barriers they construct in rivers are only to retard the passage of the fish, to enable the Indians to obtain their necessary winter supply, and that these temporary obstructions are thrown open, as necessary, to give passage to the ascending fish. (Department of Indian Affairs, RG 10 Series, 24 Sept. 1877)

FIGURE 22.2. Chief Ron Ignace and his son, Joe Thomas Ignace, gaffing sockeye salmon, 2002. (Courtesy Marianne Ignace)

The near destruction of many of the Fraser and Thompson River salmon runs, due to a massive landslide at Hell's Gate on the Fraser in 1913–14 caused by CN Railway construction, further precipitated fisheries regulations. In the 1910s, the Upper Adams sockeye run, once rivalling the famous Lower Adams run, was wiped out by the construction of a log slide. Aboriginal fishers, last users of the resource, were singled out by wardens. Oral histories from this time noted fish wardens destroying weirs and fish traps and impeding fishing activity. On the North Thompson at Barriere River, a weir across the river had since time immemorial ensured a good salmon supply. The late Ida William, as affirmed by her older sister Josephine Wenlock, remembered that:

There used to be lots of people go in there and fish up there, but since the warden start bother the people . . . . They spoil everything,

break all, they had some kind of little bridge where they sit down and fish, the game warden, fish warden supposed to come over and knock everything down, let it go in the water. This fish warden come around, get smart to the Indians, my mom used to say, 'Geez, he's awful.' This fish warden, two old ladies took him and threw him in the water. That fish warden come around, get smart to Indians, and after that kinda closed everything for Indians. They can't go out and get some fish from where they used to fish. If you want to fish in the river, you have to get a licence or something like that.

A decade after the Barriere River weir was destroyed because of the preposterous claim that it diminished the runs, the Barriere spawning grounds were all but wiped out by construction of a hydroelectric power dam by local non-Natives.

Many other memories during the first half of the twentieth century, and even into the 1980s, are about fish wardens, who in rural areas also doubled up as provincial game wardens, imposing closures, destroying fishing gear, fishing platforms, and weirs, and confiscating fish.

Into the 1950s, Secwepemc carried out their traditional seasonal round of subsistence. Garden crops, however, supplemented indigenous foods. Like Aboriginal peoples elsewhere, Secwepemc of the late nineteenth and early twentieth centuries realized the usefulness of gardening, farming, and ranching. They were not conceived of as incompatible or qualitatively different activities, but as complementary ways of making a livelihood. However, the Department of Indian Affairs' 'peasant farming policy' extended to the Interior of BC. Around 1900, the Department of Indian Affairs divided the arable areas of reserves into location tickets consisting of small acreages, and supplied the Indians with hand implements and seed in order to farm. The Secwepemc, for whom farming and gardening were similar to traditional plant management regimes, easily adapted to growing orchards, grain crops for their horses and cattle, and garden crops for their families, and were eager to grow surplus crops for cash. The Indian Act, however, prevented them from getting their goods to market without going through the bureaucracy of the Department of Indian Affairs. Moreover, during the early twentieth century, transport unions began to monopolize the transportation of goods and excluded Native people from membership in their unions. At the same time, water rights were diverted away from reserves, making it increasingly impossible to irrigate crops in the dry southern Interior.

During the first half of the twentieth century many of our ancestors found seasonal employment as cowboys and ranch hands on ranches, integrating these activities into the seasonal round. Groups of Secwepemc families camped out on the margins of large settler-owned ranches such as Hat Creek, Douglas Lake, and Gang Ranch. While men engaged in farm labour, women and children gathered wild plants. Families also hunted and fished.

From the turn of the century to the 1950s, Ron Ignace's great-grandparents, Julienne and Edward Eneas, like all of the 15 or so interrelated extended families of the Skeetchestn band, maintained a 10-acre location ticket on their reserve. There they grew garden crops and kept a few cows, horses, and chickens. After planting the garden in early May, the family (Julienne and Edward, their adult son and daughter, and the latter's large families) spent two weeks or longer at Xixyum Lake catching hundreds of pounds of rainbow trout, which they dried and packed home. They were joined there by families from Skeetchestn, St'uxtews (Bonaparte), Tk'emlups, and Pellteq't (Clinton). Until fall, they followed the traditional seasonal round throughout a 100-mile radius. As they travelled to camping, fishing, and gathering areas by horse and buggy, Julienne often packed along the family's chickens in a gunnysack, while other families took their milk cows along. At this time, most Secwepemc still relied almost entirely on country foods and gardening produce.

Elder Ida Matthew narrates her family's mixed economy during the 1930s:

> Long time ago, my father, and Se7 and
>   Maryen were all camping together
> at Tsqeltqéqen.
> My father was clearing land at Genier's.
> My mother and Maryen were picking goose-
>   berries
> around the rocks, and they picked any other
>   kinds of berries.
> And when they finished work, my father and
>   them, and Se7 and them
> filled the gopher holes until they were full
>   of water.
> When the gophers came out, they clubbed
>   them,
> then they took them out, and we ate them.
> And maybe some of them, my mother
>   would dry.
> And all the things they gathered, they dried. . . .

And my mother was trapping groundhogs.
We were helping my mother pick whatever
    berries there were.
I remember we had a lot to eat,
when my mom and them picked, and when
    they hunted,
and when they trapped gophers. We always
    ate meat.
And my dad, he was setting the net in the
    river while he worked at Genier's.
He put a net in the river. He would spear
    whatever [fish] there was.
I don't remember what are all the kinds of
    fish called.
But I remember they were good to eat.
That's all.[3]

Despite the Department of Indian Affairs' attempts to instill and enforce a sense of private property and the nuclear family, economic production was done by co-operative labour within large extended family groups.

As noted earlier, the increasing restrictions placed on using the land by new fee-simple title-holders[4] severely curtailed the ability of the people to follow their traditional seasonal round. The settlers and ranchers continually tried to oust families from what they saw as their lands. One Secwepemc Elder remembered such an incident at what had become Six Mile Ranch, situated on the grassy slopes south of Kamloops Lake. This area was called the 'breadbasket' by Skeetchestn Elders: even in times of scarcity in severe winters, deer could be found there. Families used to camp at Six Mile and hunt and gather there. By the 1950s, however, landowners and their fences made this difficult:

Them *seme7s*, white people, used to kick us out of there. [Long before that] they kicked us out from Savona, where we *used* to camp, lot of people used to camp. You know the thing was, we used the place until they fenced it all along in there [during Trans Canada Highway construction in the late 1950]. We used to go down by M's there. Dad would park the old

wagon. We'd walk down the rest of the way. . . . We'd go down there, maybe camp the night, and then from there, dad would hobble the horses, and we'd camp. . . . They always ask us, 'Why did we give up our rights?' We had no choice; we were chased out. We were told we were trespassing.

Another Elder remembered:

[In the 1950s] I had a car, so I'd take my brother and my dad, take them out there to go hunt, and we already had to open gates to get to hunt. So we had to open farmers' gates. So I told my dad, 'Why should we not use our land to hunt in?' I said, 'I'll go knock on [the farmer's] door and let him know that we are hunting on our land here.' So I go down there and knock on his door, and [he said], 'Go ahead, let your brother and dad hunt.' He calls it his field now, but that was all our hunting areas. So there, we are slowly getting fenced out. Fences are really getting us. (Translated from Secwepemctsin by the authors).

Since the 1951 revisions to the Indian Act, 'provincial laws of general application' came to apply to Indians on reserves, and the provincial Department of Fish and Game began prosecuting Indians hunting off reserve. Evading game wardens thus became an ongoing aspect of hunting. As Skeetchestn hunter Terry Deneault remembered, during the 1960s and 1970s the '*seme7s* [white people] didn't allow us to hunt, so just like the deer, we used to have to hide away.' Other Secwepemc who hunted then noted that the nature of hunting changed. Hunters often carried out clandestine hunting trips, quickly making a kill and taking the carcass home before the game warden could catch them. This had an impact on people's ability to learn the ritual practices and the many storied discourses surrounding hunting. One person remembered about this time:

In the sixties to the seventies, [game wardens] were pretty nasty. They were always on our case about hunting out of season. They were after us because we used to hunt all year long, because we needed to take care of our families. . . . They really enjoyed chasing us around. They were always trying to catch us. . . . At the same time you had to get the deer. So you found them real quick, shoot them, clean them, skinned them, gutted them and run, and you're back out of there. . . . I think that's eroded our culture with hunting and fishing. When I was hunting here in the sixties with my uncles and in the seventies with my brothers, we never took time to even say a prayer after we shot a deer. It was like, 'Get that thing done and let's get out of here!' I find now, when I go hunting with my family members . . . when we catch the deer or moose, we'll take the time to say the appropriate prayer and thank-you's, and take time to teach the children how to properly take care of the animal, what they should be watching for, how they should be doing it, so then the knowledge begins to be passed on in the proper manner. That did not really happen here in the late sixties and seventies. There was only one purpose, that was to get a deer and to get out of there as quick as you could.

Enforced attendance at residential school for virtually all Secwepemc children between about 1930 and 1970 also had consequences for the transmission of skills, knowledge, and the spiritual connections related to resource pursuits. Children would spend only a few weeks at home during July and August, thus having little chance to engage in resource harvesting with their elders.

Changes to the Environment

In the Interior of BC, cattle grazing has produced severe impacts on forests and grasslands. As noted earlier, ranching has been a facet of Secwepemc economics for a century. Early in the twentieth century, however, provincial grazing permits allocated virtually all non fee-simple lands in the interior of BC as private grazing leases to non-Aboriginal ranchers. As foresters concur, cattle ranching has wreaked havoc with many indigenous plant species. For decades, cows have browsed on and trampled root plants like spring beauties or 'Indian potatoes', bitterroot, yellow avalanche lily, and others. The habitats of these plants have been further reduced by the spread of non-indigenous species such as dandelion, mullein, introduced grasses, thistle, and knapweed.

Since the 1960s, logging activity has intensified, resulting in a continuous patchwork of cut blocks throughout the plateaus and mountains of the area. While the succession of growth in clear-cuts supports the regeneration of some berry species and supports continuing habitat for ungulates, logging has had a devastating impact on numerous food and medicinal plants whose habitats are wetlands or moist areas, which were drained and eroded through logging activity. A vast network of logging roads, some established on the ancient horse and foot trails used by Secwepemc hunters, now extends throughout the region. Other roads criss-cross them and have destroyed the old trails.

In recent decades, urban development put further pressures on people's ability to use traditional resources. The urban and suburban population of the south-central Interior, centred around Kamloops, increased tenfold. Sprawling subdivisions now stand where families used to camp, gather berries, and hunt. Competition from sport hunters and fishers has increased. Secwepemc hunters, in general, are reluctant to hunt during the fall hunting season, as the forests become populated with sport hunters.

Secwepemc plant harvesting has declined notably in recent decades. Some families continue to gather large quantities of berries, including blueberries, huckleberries, chokecherries, and especially soapberries, highly valued as the main ingredient for a beverage and whipped up into 'Indian ice cream'. The vicious cycle of the effects described above, including habitat loss, knowledge loss, the availability of market foods, and threats from settlers, have resulted in root crops and green vegetables being replaced in the diets of younger people. In recent years, however, younger generations of Secwepemc have begun recapturing the knowledge and skills to harvest these plants. Some have reintegrated them into their diets.[5]

Legal Issues

Aboriginal fishing for food and ceremonial purposes has been recognized as an Aboriginal right in law since the 1990 Supreme Court of Canada *Sparrow* decision, supported by section 35 of the Constitution Act, 1982. *Sparrow*, however, has not improved Secwepemc ability to catch fish. Commercial overfishing on the coast, as well as environmental conditions, caused Pacific salmon stocks to reach all-time historic lows. As last users of the resource, the Secwepemc have had few fish available. Declining fish stocks, in turn, resulted in charges being pressed against numerous Secwepemc fishers. In 1994, Daniel Gaspard of the St'uxtews band was criminally charged for selling about a dozen salmon. As noted earlier, the trade in *scwik'* (dried sides of salmon) is an ancient activity among Interior Aboriginal peoples. The judge, however, could not (or would not) grasp the traditional rules of access to the fishery and trade in fish, and chose to accept expert evidence presented by the Crown that, unsupported by data, denied the existence of the St'uxtewsemc, denied the importance of fishing, and asserted that Secwepemc trade in fish was insignificant, involving 'exchanges like trades of desserts at church picnics'.[6] Daniel Gaspard was eventually acquitted on appeal.

In another case (*R. v. Deneault and R. v. Lebourdais*), fishers from two Secwepemc communities were criminally charged as they returned from the Secwepemc fishing grounds at High Bar on the Fraser. The Crown asserted that the Secwepemc Aboriginal right to fish did not extend to all fishing grounds within the nation but only to stations near one's own reserve, in complete conflict with traditional protocols of access. Upon Marianne Ignace's presentation of anthropological expert evidence for the defence, as well as Elders' and witnesses' testimony, the Crown dropped the charges.

Given the *Delgamuukw* decision, some Secwepemc communities have engaged in court action over specific tracts of land scheduled to be logged or to be developed into resorts or golf courses. They argue Aboriginal title to the land, supported by past and ongoing traditional use of the land. The Six Mile land dispute involved the Skeetchestn band's opposition to real estate development, including a golf course, resort hotel, and housing, on what had become fee-simple land as well as on a parcel of Crown land on Kamloops Lake. The Skeetchestn band, as steward within the Secwepemc Nation over this area, argued that its inherent title to this land and its fundamental economic interest in the land were being violated by impending development. The band sought to have its Aboriginal title registered on par with the developer's title, thus questioning the provincial land registry system. In the end, a settlement was negotiated. The province compensated the band for loss of hunting areas, created some protected areas involving heritage and spiritual sites, supported alternate economic opportunities through eco-tourism, and agreed to put the Secwepemc Nation's Aboriginal rights and title in abeyance.

On the political level involving the Secwepemc as an Aboriginal nation, the legacy of having suffered the 'divide-and-conquer' strategies imposed by federal and provincial governments—including splitting our nation into several agencies and the legal status that bands as 'First Nations' versus Aboriginal nations enjoy—has made joint action difficult.[7] In the last two decades, the Secwepemc have been represented through a variety of tribal councils, including the Shuswap Nation Tribal Council representing nine southern bands and the Cariboo Tribal Council, which includes four northern bands. One band is in the Lillooet Tribal Council and another is aligned with Ktunaxa Nation in the Ktunaxa-Kinbasket Tribal Council. The remaining communities are independent. While the Cariboo Tribal Council, the Ktunaxa-Kinbasket Tribal

Council, and the Esk'et (Alkali Lake) First Nation joined the troubled BC treaty process, the Shuswap Nation Tribal Council did not join it because of the enormous debt load taken on by First Nations in the process of negotiations and the continuing stipulation that treaties must *extinguish* Aboriginal title.

What the Future Holds

In light of over a century of shrinking access to resources and government policies that criminalize traditional resource activity, why do Secwepemc continue to fish, hunt, and gather and to insist that they are inextinguishable *rights*?

Throughout the period we described, our chiefs, Elders, and community members have continued to exercise, and to insist on, our rights. The 'Memorial to Laurier', other forms of court testimony, and oral histories all bear witness to that. Secwepemc people continue to see hunting, fishing, and plant harvesting as activities that express who we are. Most of us who pursue hunting or fishing do so on weekends, but that does not mean that, economically and culturally, its significance has waned. In many Secwepemc households, game and fish constitute an important part of the diet. The cycles of redistributing game, fish, and wild plants allow us to maintain our ancient values of sharing. As one younger Secwepemc observed:

> It's still a very important part of our diet yet. The people still rely on it this every day, [to feed] big families. It's a necessity, as a matter of fact. Most people, they look at it as a part of not only our diet, but as a traditional thing we've done for many years, and we continue to do them, it's our right there, and we're going to hang onto it.

In times of life-crisis a people's deepest values are immanent. So it is with Secwepemc traditional resource use. When a person has died, during the four days of the wake and at the feast following the interment, relatives and friends of the bereaved family prepare salmon, trout, deer meat, and moose meat, all from animals who gave themselves up, taking pity on those in grief. Hunters, without needing requests or instructions, go out to hunt in honour of the deceased and to comfort the family. They bring back food, and stories of animals that turned up at unusual places, giving themselves for the occasion, or that carried messages from the deceased, witnessing the power of those who have departed.

Conclusion

And this brings us back to the beginning. Sadly, the trip to gather *llekw'pin* in 1997 was Nellie Taylor's last. Until weeks before her death in July 1998, she asked for the plant medicines that sustained her for so many years, although the 'White man's disease' (lupus) that ravaged her body had no final Secwepemc remedy. However, in the months before she died, she took comfort in eating *llekw'pin*, soapberries and other berries, Indian rhubarb, and root plants, drinking teas, and continuing to speak Secwepemctsin. We know that she took comfort in the feast of country foods that honoured her, where one last plateful was sent to her through the fire. As survivors, we also take comfort in her teachings, which validate our rights, our knowledge, and our practices of traditional resource use.

Acknowledgements
This paper represents a portion of our collaborative research in and with Secwepemc communities since the mid-1980s. In 1990–3, 1994–7, and 1999–2002, some of our work was funded by the Social Sciences and Humanities Research Council of Canada through various Strategic Research Grants in which we collaborated with Dr Nancy Turner (University of Victoria) and Dr Hari Sharma (Simon Fraser University). Other parts of our research were supported by the Shuswap Nation Tribal Council and by the Skeetchestn and North Thompson bands. We would like to thank

the many Secwepemc Elders, relatives, friends, and colleagues who have shared their knowledge with us. *Yiri7 re skukwstsetselp*! This paper is dedicated to the memory of Nellie Taylor.

Notes

1. We use the practical orthography for writing Secwepemctsin developed by linguist Aert Kuipers and Secwepemctsin speakers in the 1970s and 1980s. It enables one to represent all six vowels and 43 consonants on a standard keyboard, but some sounds need explanation. A 'c' is a hissed sound made by putting the tongue against the roof of the mouth, as in the German 'ich'. An 'r' is made in the same position in the mouth, but is voiced. The 'll' (equivalent to the linguist's 'barred l') is a kind of hissed 'hl' sound. The 'q' is a uvular stop or 'throat k', and the 'x' is produced in the same part of the throat, but with friction, like the German 'ach'. The 'g' is a hummed throat sound made in the pharynx, a bit further back in the throat than the French 'r'. Letters followed by an apostrophe indicate glottalized sounds, plosives, made with a catch in the throat. The "t'" actually sounds like a popped 'tl'. Finally, the '7' denotes a glottal stop, or a 'catch in the throat', and can occur in the middle or at the end of a word. For a detailed description, see Ignace (1988).

2. For details on the extent of fishing for the Hudson's Bay Company post, see Archibald McDonald Dispatch to HBC Governor George Simpson, 1827, John McLeod's Journal, Thompson River Post (TRP), 1822–3; Archibald McDonald Journal, TRP, 1826–7, and diary of trip with G. Simpson; John Tod Journal, TRP, 1841–3; Paul Fraser, TRP, 1850–2, 1854–5; William Manson, TRP Journal 1860–4; John Moffat, TRP Journal; John Tait, TRP Correspondence 1873–5. All of the above are situated at the Kamloops Museum and Archives, as well as in the Hudson's Bay Company Archives at the Manitoba Provincial Archives.

3. This narrative is part of a larger body of Secwepemc texts recorded, transcribed, and translated by Marianne Ignace, Ron Ignace, and Mona Jules. To reflect the way of speaking in the Secwepemc language, and the poetry of their speech, these narratives are rendered in verse form.

4. Fee simple is the ordinary form of landholding in Canada.

5. Of importance in this endeavour has been our collaborative ethnobotany research since 1990, which has involved more than 40 Secwepemc Elders from all of our communities, as well as ourselves, Dr Nancy Turner (University of Victoria), Dr Harriet Kuehnlein (McGill University), and Secwepemc and non-Aboriginal research assistants. This multidisciplinary work has led to numerous publications and to courses in ethnobotany through Secwepemc Education Institute, in collaboration with Simon Fraser University. In these courses, we have convened Elders and younger Secwepemc to teach, learn, and practise plant harvesting and processing techniques, and to share the traditional knowledge behind these practices. Many of our students and Elders in turn have reintegrated traditional plant harvesting and processing, including pit cooking, into activities in their own communities.

6. The Crown's anthropological expert witness in *R. v. Gaspard, R. v. Lebourdais,* and *R. v. Deneault,* was Sheila Robertson, a geographer who has acted widely in this capacity for the Crown, most notoriously in *Delgamuukw v. R.* See Culhane (1998) for a scathing critique of Robertson's evidence.

7. We use the term 'Aboriginal nation' as 'a sizeable body of Aboriginal people with a shared sense of national identity that constitutes the predominant population in a certain territory or collection of territories. Aboriginal Nations usually contain numerous First Nation communities within the same nation' (RCAP, 1996, vol. 1: xiv). By contrast, the term 'First Nation' by and large is a euphemism for an Indian band under the Indian Act, reflecting merely a single community rather than the larger political, linguistic, and cultural entity.

References and Recommended Readings

Anastasio, Angelo. 1972. 'The Southern Plateau: An Ecological Analysis of Intergroup Relations', *Northwest Anthropological Research Notes* 6, 2: 109–229. This article notes that communities and nations on the Columbia Plateau maintained relations through sharing resources. This was facilitated through kinship-based protocols of access.

Boas, Franz. 1891. 'The Shuswap', in *Second General Report on the Indians of British Columbia*, Sixtieth Annual Report of the British Association for the Advancement of Science for 1890, London.

British Columbia. 1875. *Papers Connected to the Indian Land Question, 1850–1875*. Victoria: Wolfenden Government Printer.

Canada. 1913–16. Royal Commission on Indian Affairs for B.C., Kamloops Agency 1913, Transcript of Testimony. Vancouver: Union of BC Indian Chiefs.

———. 1997. *Report of the Royal Commission on Aboriginal Peoples*, 5 vols. Ottawa.

Culhane, Dara. 1998. *The Pleasure of the Crown*. Vancouver: Talonbooks.

Dawson, George Mercer. 1891. 'Notes on the Shuswap People of B.C.', *Transactions of the Royal Society of Canada* Section II, Part 1: 3–44. A significant early report on the Secwepemc, written by the head of the geological survey of Canada, an avid amateur ethnographer.

———. 1892. 'Notes on the Shuswap People of British Columbia', *Proceedings and Transactions of the Royal Society of Canada for the Year 1891*, series 1, vol. 9.

Fladmark, Knut. 1986. *B.C. Prehistory*. Ottawa: Canadian Museum of Civilization.

Hayden, Brian, ed. 1992. *A Complex Culture of the British Columbia Plateau*. Vancouver: University of British Columbia Press. This book, based on data collected in the early 1970s, presents articles on St'at'imc (Fraser River Lillooet) resource use. Since the Upper St'at'imc are closely connected to the Western Secwepemc, they are of interest. Articles by Steven Romanoff, Michael Kew, and Randy Bouchard with Dorothy Kennedy are especially relevant to our discussion of fishing and resource use among the Secwepemc.

Ignace, Marianne. 1998. 'The Shuswap (Secwepemc)', in Deward E. Walker, ed., *Handbook of North American Indians*, vol. 12, *The Plateau*. Washington: Smithsonian Institution. Summarizes and evaluates early ethnographic information and provides a history since the early 1800s. It also throws light on Secwepemc place names and names for groups as rendered in multiple orthographies.

———. 1999. 'Guardian Spirit Questing in the 90s: A Mother's View', in Peter Murphy, George Nicholas, and Marianne Ignace, eds, *Coyote U: Stories from Secwepemc Education Institute*. Penticton, BC: Theytus Press. Written from a personal perspective, this essay details the difficulties contemporary Secwepemc parents and teenagers face in following traditional practices like guardian spirit questing.

——— and Ron Ignace. 1999. 'The Memorial to Sir Wilfrid Laurier: A Commentary', in Murphy, Nicholas, and Ignace, eds, *Coyote U*. This is the text of the Memorial, with historic and cultural commentary.

Peacock, Sandra, and Nancy J. Turner. 1998. 'Just Like a Garden: Traditional Plant Resource Management and Biodiversity Conservation on the B.C. Plateau', in P. Minnis and W. Elisens, eds, *Biodiversity and Native North America*. Norman: University of Oklahoma Press. This article discusses the detailed plant management and propagation regimes of the Secwepemc and other Interior peoples.

Teit, James. 1900. *The Thompson Indians of British Columbia*. New York: American Museum of Natural History, Memoir No. 2.

———. 1909. *The Shuswap*. Memoir of the American Museum of Natural History. New York. This is the most detailed source on nineteenth-century and pre-contact Secwepemc culture. It should be read in conjunction with his *The Thompson Indians, The Lillooet*, and *The Salishan Tribes of the Western Plateau*.

Turner, Nancy J., Marianne Ignace, and Ron Ignace. 2000. 'Traditional Ecological Knowledge and Wisdom of Aboriginal Peoples of British Columbia', *Ecological Applications* 10, 5: 1275–87. This article summarizes some of our TEKW research, particularly on Secwepemc root-plant gathering and management.

Walker, Deward E., ed. 1998. *Handbook of North American Indians*, vol. 12, *The Plateau*. Washington: Smithsonian Institution. The volume features encyclopedic coverage on all Canadian and US Plateau peoples.

Suggested Web Sites

Secwepemc Cultural Education Society: www.secwepemc.org
SCES is the umbrella organization for the presentation of Secwepemc culture, heritage, and language. It includes links to their post-secondary programs.

Shuswap Nation Tribal Council: www.secwepemc.org/sntc.html
This is the umbrella political organization for the Secwepemc.

Cariboo Tribal Council: www.caribootribal.org
This council represents most northern Secwepemc bands.

School District No. 73: www.sd73.bc.ca
School District 73 is in partnership with the Secwepemc Nation.

PART VIII

The Northwest Coast

CHAPTER 23

The Northwest Coast: A Regional Overview

MARGARET SEGUIN ANDERSON

The Aboriginal cultures of the Pacific coast of Canada developed in a rich natural environment. Villages and seasonal camps in sheltered harbours close to rich salmon spawning routes allowed access to shores and shoals that also yielded halibut, cod, herring, oolichan, shellfish, and marine mammals in abundance. Unique localized resources were recognized and exploited by each tribe, and even by each village, but frequent contacts between neighbouring groups along the coast stimulated sharing of ideas, techniques, and institutions throughout the area, creating the patterns that outsiders have designated as Northwest Coast culture. This cultural complexity developed *in situ* over several millennia. By about 2,000 years ago the cultures of the region had developed most of the features that were associated with Northwest Coast culture at the time of contact.

The evolution of knowledge, tools, and techniques permitted an effective adaptation to the maritime zone; the Aboriginal patterns of such items as halibut hooks have never been bettered. The permanent villages of large red-cedar plank houses located in protected sites throughout the area were built by skilled carpenters and embellished with carvings that have received recognition as masterworks of a great artistic tradition. Well-built canoes 60 feet and more in length carried the people to their fishing sites, to collecting territories for shellfish, berries, bark, and roots, to hunting areas for land and sea animals, and to other villages for purposes such as trade, weddings, feasts, and occasionally raiding. A few trails, such as the famous grease trails in the North, penetrated the thick rain forests that barred movement past the beach rocks up the steep mountain slopes that plunged into the fjords.

Cultures along the entire Northwest Coast display a number of common cultural features: permanent winter villages; elaborate ceremonial activities, including property distributions; sophisticated traditions of rhetoric; and even similarities in the sound systems of the languages throughout the region. For example, even though there are four distinct and apparently unrelated language families represented along the BC portion of the Northwest Coast (Haida, Tsimshianic, Wakashan, and Salishan), all of them share the fairly unusual features of glottalized consonants, a uvular series of stops, and lateral fricatives; neighbouring Northwest Coast nations in Alaska and Washington state display the same features. Archaeologists have found evidence of trade dating back thousands of years, including obsidian that can be traced hundreds of miles to a few source deposits. The evidence is strong that this is an area in which there has been intensive cultural interaction for thousands of years. In fact, these cultures evolved as trading nations, and their distinctive cultures could not have developed without trade.

Salmon has been for thousands of years the staple food and cultural foundation of all the

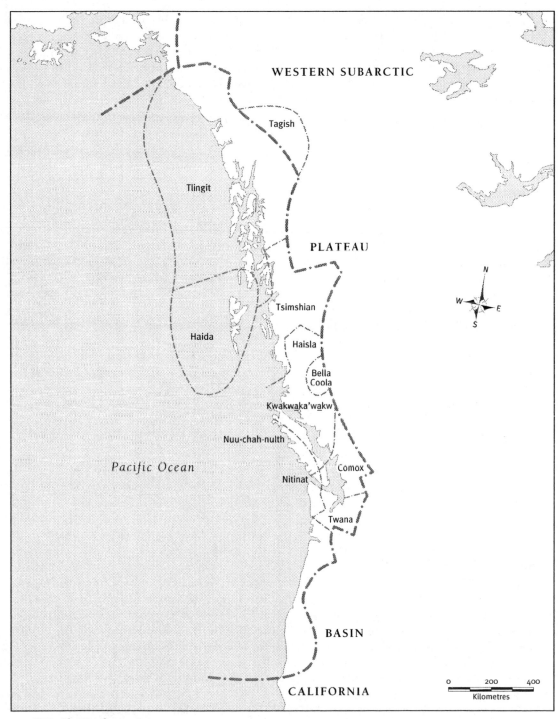

WESTERN SUBARCTIC

Tagish

Tlingit

PLATEAU

Tsimshian

Haida

Haisla

Bella
Coola

Kwakwaka'wakw

Nuu-chah-nulth

Pacific Ocean

Comox

Nitinat

Twana

BASIN

N
W   E
S

0   200   400
Kilometres

CALIFORNIA

MAP 23.1. The Northwest Coast

groups on the Northwest Coast, and also of their neighbours in the adjacent Interior. Coastal cultures had access to an array of resources and the number of runs that they could intercept meant that their salmon stocks very rarely failed them; the Interior groups, on the other hand, were reliant on fewer stocks upriver, close to the spawning grounds, and these were subject to huge fluctuations and frequent failures. The development of the technology to dry, store, and transport salmon (and its essential condiment, oil from fish or sea mammals) was the prerequisite allowing for the development of the complex cultures of this entire region. This technology provided the base on which the coastal groups built elaborate cultures founded on wealth accrued through the harvest and trade of food from the productive territories owned by extended groups of kin. While there was extensive use of the other plant and animal resources, the most important resource, and the foundation of the distinctive culture of the Northwest Coast, was salmon. It is no wonder that the people of this entire region have been dubbed 'salmon people'. The per capita consumption of salmon by the Northwest Coast peoples reached 220 kilograms of fresh, edible salmon each year (Newell, 1997: 29).

Huge quantities of salmon, fish oil, berries, and other products were normally preserved and traded by coastal and Interior groups each year. Here is an account of one Interior group's smokehouses:

An inspector visiting Babine Lake and the headwaters of the Skeena River in 1904 gives an interesting description of the operations of the Indians: 'The banks of the Babine river have a lovely appearance at this place and a most wonderful sight met our eyes when we beheld the immense array of dried salmon. On either side there were no less than 16 houses 30 x 27 x 8 feet filled with salmon from the top down so low that one had to stoop to get into them, and also an immense quantity of racks, filled up outside. If the latter had stood

close together they would have covered acres and acres of ground, and though it was impossible to form an estimate, we judged it to be nearly three-quarters of a million fish at those two barricades, all killed before they had spawned, and though the whole tribe had been working for six weeks and a half it was a wonder that so much salmon could be massed together in that time.' It was estimated that each Indian family used about one thousand salmon per year; a total for the Indian population of that district alone of about one million fish. Fish was the principal food of the multitude of dogs. Salmon were used as an article of commerce and formed a sort of legal tender, ten salmon being equivalent to a dollar. Dried salmon were sold to miners, merchants, and packers operating dog sleighs. It has been estimated that the average consumption of fish by Indians in British Columbia amounted to about twenty million pounds per year: about seventeen and one-half million pounds of salmon, three million pounds of halibut, and one-quarter million pounds of sturgeon, herring, trout and other fish as well as eighty thousand gallons of fish oil valued at $4,885,000 in 1879, and at $3,257,000 in 1885. (Carrothers, 1941: 5–6 n. 2)

Two years after this scene was described, the government forced the destruction of the weirs at Babine, despite warnings by their own agents that this would cause starvation in the Interior. The large number of fish taken by Aboriginal people had become an issue as soon as canneries appeared on the coast, and a campaign to wrest fish from Aboriginal fisheries was mounted through political manoeuvring and media hysteria such as the following headline story from a Victoria newspaper of a century ago:

Indians Wiping Out Sockeye
A report in detail concerning the manner in which Indians at the headwaters of the Skeena and other northern rivers are striking

at the very root of the life of the salmon-fishing industry in British Columbia, one of the greatest sources of the people's wealth, has been received. . . . no less than 2,000,000 salmon . . . were killed in the Indian traps this year. That number of fish, if canned, would make about 142,857 cases. (Newell, 1997: 91)

In fact, the Aboriginal fisheries were not a danger to the stocks; long-standing Aboriginal fisheries management practices ensured that there would be sufficient escapement for spawning, even in years of scarcity and looming famine. But the campaign to appropriate salmon and other resources for commercial exploitation impacted the coastal nations heavily.

The large quantity of salmon observed at Babine Lake in 1904 was needed by communities in the Interior for their winter food supply; it was the staple food and the largest source of calories—the core of a diet that was supplemented by other local foods and oil-rich seafoods traded from the coast. This supply was not always reliable, however; each salmon run has a four-year cycle in which abundance varies 1,000 per cent and more from the dominant year to the low year in the cycle. Babine Lake is a terminal fishery, and the stocks available there are limited to those that spawn in the lake and its source creeks. If these stocks were in a low-cycle year; or if a landslide blocked an important part of the river system during the period when the juvenile fish for a given run were moving out to sea; or if extremely high water—or water that is too warm, too cold, or too loaded with silt—causes high mortality among the returning spawners; or if any of a number of other crucial variables is unfavourable, then the numbers could be so reduced that the Babine Lake runs were a small fraction of their normal abundance and the local people would be unable to dry sufficient salmon for their needs. In such a situation, fish for trade, on which other Interior groups depended, was unavailable from the Babine. The same scenario applied to Interior

groups who relied on salmon from the upper reaches of the Fraser watershed, including the Nechako. In some years other Interior groups had surplus available for trade. The long-established trade networks within the Interior were crucial to the survival of all the communities in the region, and the area near the divide between the watersheds of the Skeena and Fraser was central to this. However, occasionally there was a year when none of the Interior groups had sufficient fish to supply their needs and trade to other communities for the essential winter supply. When this occurred, the coastal groups could reap huge profits by trading dried salmon for valuable furs, moose and caribou hides, wild sheep or mountain goat wool and horns, obsidian, copper, amber, jade, slaves, and other valuable goods. This opportunistic profit was facilitated by the fact that Interior and coastal traders made regular trading trips and coastal traders were constantly aware of the state of the fish runs on which various Interior groups relied. Dried eulachon, oils from eulachon and other vertebrates, and foods preserved in oil were staples of the regular trading excursions, but traders also offered smoked seal meat, dried halibut, half-dried salmon and (full-dried) salmon *wooks*, smoked cockles, seaweed, dentalia shells, and manufactured items such as rattles and kerfed boxes so perfectly constructed of single cedar planks bent to shape and pegged at the corner and bottom that the resulting box could hold water—or grease!

When Europeans entered the region they benefited from the Aboriginal trade and tried without success to take control of it. When the first Europeans arrived at Fraser Lake to establish Fort Fraser, they anticipated being able to purchase their winter supply of dried salmon from the Aboriginal traders there; however, there was a shortage that year due to a failure of the Stuart River run and they had to turn to other sources of supply. When the runs that Interior people relied on were inadequate to supply all the communities, there was no choice but to turn to coastal groups for salmon and other seafoods.

FIGURE 23.1. Of all the Northwest Coast populations, the Haida were the most devastated by diseases introduced by Europeans. Ninstints on Anthony Island was already abandoned by 1901 as a result of population depletion from epidemics, the forest beginning to reclaim the site. (Courtesy of the Royal British Columbia Museum, PN 837)

In addition to filling the demand caused by shortfalls in the Interior in poor years, coastal traders regularly supplied Interior groups with fish and sea mammal oils and other coastal products. Salmon dried in the Interior is oil-poor because the fish have depleted their stores of fat during their lengthy migration upriver. For example, it is more than 1,100 kilometres up the Fraser to the spawning grounds in the northern Interior. These lean fish dry and store exceptionally well but lack nutrients needed to sustain people during the cold Subarctic winters. Interior game is also extremely lean and nutritionally inadequate for winter survival—it is literally possible to starve on a diet of such lean meats. Coastal salmon, on the other hand, is richer in oil, and even when caught in the river mouths or lower river courses (as most Aboriginal fisheries were), the product was relatively rich. This meant that it would not dry as well or last as long in storage, but it was more nutritious in calories and essential nutrients. A supply of nutrient-rich oils from the coast formed an essential component of the Interior Aboriginal winter diet. The river corridors and grease trails were busy every year supplying this need, and traffic intensified in times of scarcity in the Interior.

The trade between the coast and Interior has gone on for millennia, and it was an essential factor in the cultural development of Interior peoples, who sustained relatively densely settled populations and complex cultural practices more common among agriculturalists while living as hunter-gatherers. Trade with these Interior communities was a key part of the context in which coastal cultures developed and flourished, elaborating their distinctive emphasis on ownership of territories and resources validated and dramatized through art, ceremony, and lavish distributions of wealth obtained through trade.

The complex cultural pattern of the Northwest Coast was developed only after salmon became established in the rivers, and the peoples of this region recognize and affirm the importance of these fish. People spoke of salmon respectfully, treated them with care as the source of well-being

and wealth, and saw themselves as people whose entire lives were intertwined with the salmon. The territories of the coastal nations yielded abundant harvests of many types of foods and materials used to manufacture such items as boxes, bowls, canoes, luxury goods, and tools. But the key resource, and the foundation of the wealth of the entire region, was salmon.

Ownership of the territories was vested in local corporate groups of kin; control of territories and access to resources was gained by inheritance of a ranked name/title among all the groups, and in some could also be obtained through marriage, as a gift, or as a prize of war. Inherited differences of rank associated with economic and supernatural privileges were substantial among all the groups. Chiefs had the power to allocate resources, command labour, make alliances, and even to take the life of a slave.

Shamans used both an extensive natural pharmacopoeia and supernatural abilities to cure illness. The natural remedies were potent, and the social cohesiveness created for a patient by the dramatic shamanic performances healed illness of the spirit as well.

The religious beliefs of all the groups emphasized contact with supernatural beings who controlled wealth, health, and life itself. Humans endeavoured to establish relationships with supernatural powers through ceremonial activities, notably ritual purifications, feasts, potlatches, and winter dance ceremonies. Ritual occasions drew on the power of the artistic traditions to create lavish events in which setting, costume, oral literature, drama, song, and dance expressed the profound spirituality that pervaded the cultures. Gift-giving feasts called potlatches manifested the wealth and power of the great chiefs, who had the ability to mediate with the supernatural powers. Winter ceremonial dances, often lasting months at a time, represented the supernatural forces that created order, brought wealth, and ensured the continuity of the group.

The intrusion of Europeans into the Northwest Coast brought few changes for the first 100 years from initial contact in the late eighteenth century. The early explorers traded iron tools and other European goods for furs, foods, and Native artifacts, but did not seek to alter the pattern of Native cultures—indeed, the traders were heavily reliant on the indigenous people for their own provisions as well as for furs. The first European goods obtained were integrated into the traditional cultures as prestige items and useful tools in Native technologies. But the explorers set the stage for more radical changes by demonstrating the potential profit to be made from the furs traded by the coastal Natives, especially the fur of the sea otter, which could be sold for huge profits in China. A very busy maritime fur trade was quickly established, reaching its greatest magnitude in the decades around the turn of the nineteenth century. The early nineteenth century saw the establishment of permanent trading posts along the coast, but the sea otter population was depleted by the 1830s. The trade shifted to other furs, many obtained from Interior groups, and the coast chiefs reaped large profits as shrewd middlemen. Though the profits of the trade were high, the cost was also great. A number of Old World diseases were introduced, taking a huge toll among the Native population. Smallpox, measles, venereal diseases, tuberculosis, and influenza swept through whole tribes, sometimes reducing the population to a small fraction of its former level. Unscrupulous traders anxious to obtain scarce furs traded alcohol and firearms, which made hostilities between traditional enemy groups much more lethal.

Even greater changes occurred as missionaries, adventurers, gold miners, and settlers entered the area in large numbers in the mid-nineteenth century. Many of the intruders had an exaggerated sense of the glories of 'civilization' and little understanding or tolerance for the complex cultures of Native people. Rights in land were not acknowledged, and resources were appropriated without apology. British Columbia entered Confederation in 1871, which placed the Native population under the existing accretion of statutes relating to Indians, which in 1876 became the Indian Act, and small reserves were provided for each local group. In most cases the allocation was unilateral, involving little consultation and no agreement by the Native group. Though Native title had not been extinguished by any treaties or agreements (except for a few groups in the southern part of Vancouver Island), the province refused to enter negotiations to do so. A few groups pressed their claims repeatedly, notably the Nisga'a in the North. In 1973, the Nisga'a case was finally heard by the Supreme Court of Canada. Although the decision was split, the federal government was forced by the narrowness of this decision, and by the implications of the case presented around the same time by the James Bay Cree, to recognize a continuing Native title. The *Delgamuukw* decision in 1997 clarified crucial questions, affirming that Aboriginal title, where it can be established in fact, is a living right that must be reconciled with Crown sovereignty. Most of the First Nations of BC have spent over a decade attempting to negotiate treaties based on Aboriginal claims to their traditional lands through the BC treaty process. The province is quite inflexible, however, and the process may prove extremely lengthy.

The extravagance of potlatches during the nineteenth century was often viewed with astonishment and dismay by outsiders, particularly those bent on fitting Native people into the mould of Victorian civilization. The disruption of traditional, established rank relationships among chiefs and the huge surplus of wealth that entered Native economies during the fur trade are now thought to have created stresses and imbalances in the traditional system, leading to lavish competitive potlatching as a way of re-establishing social order. Late in the nineteenth century the potlatch was outlawed by the Canadian government, causing it to go underground and curtailing the scale of the events. Masks and paraphernalia associated with the potlatches and winter ceremonials were confiscated and fines and prison confinement were sometimes levied in an attempt to enforce the law. Despite almost universal conversion to various Christian denominations, the traditional functions of the feasts were continued by many groups through this period, and, with the dropping of the prohibition during the 1950s, the feasts and dances are once again public celebrations in many Native communities.

Native languages were vigorously suppressed by the agents of Dominion authority as well. Until the 1940s and even later in some areas, standard policy in many schools was to administer corporal punishment to pupils who spoke in their Native tongues. Inevitably, the policy succeeded, to the extent that there are now very few Native speakers under age 30 in any Northwest Coast language. Official policies and public attitudes have reversed, but unless the language programs now offered in schools are given much higher priority the languages will not long survive.

As the fur trade declined in significance and the economy of BC began to focus on the lumber industry and the commercial fishery, Native people on the coast continued to fish, hunt, trap, and engage in other traditional activities, but they also entered the new industries in substantial numbers. Native men fished commercially during the salmon runs while Native women worked long hours in the canneries scattered along the coast, to which entire families moved for several months of the year. The economic cycle of the developing resource industries was frequently boom/bust; labour shortages during the boom periods made entry into wage labour both easy and attractive for Natives, who comprised a large proportion of the population of the province. The centralization of many industries and the rapid expansion of the immigrant settler population have pushed Natives out and decreased the significance of their participation in all industries.

The absolute number of Indians in BC fell during most of the nineteenth century, reaching a low point of under 25,000 in 1929. Though the Indian population is now greater than it was before initial contact, it comprises less than 3 per cent of the population of the province. There are close to 200 bands in BC, most with memberships under 500 persons. The greatest proportion of the population is along the coast, as it was in Aboriginal times. About 60 per cent of registered Indians reside on reserves, which are the smallest in area per capita of any province. Each band is governed autonomously, with funding for some programs provided through the federal Department of Indian Affairs. In the last two decades, tribal associations have been formed in a number of areas on the coast, bringing together tribal or regional associations of bands to lobby and to provide a link in the administrative chain as the federal government attempts to devolve service delivery to local communities. Economic development, improved facilities and educational opportunities, and the settlement of the land claims remain the primary focuses, as they have been for the past several decades.

References

Carrothers, W.A. 1941. *The British Columbia Fisheries*, Political Economy Series 10. Toronto: University of Toronto Press.

Newell, D. 1997. *Tangled Webs of History: Indians and the Law in Canada's Pacific Coast Fisheries*. Toronto: University of Toronto Press.

CHAPTER 24

Understanding Tsimshian Potlatch

MARGARET SEGUIN ANDERSON

Introduction

This chapter will focus on the Tsimshian feasts, which, with the feasts of the other Northwest Coast groups, are referred to as 'potlatch'.[1] Gift-giving feasts were widespread on the Northwest Coast at the time of contact and were sometimes very elaborate and lengthy during the nineteenth century. They continue to be an important focus and in the past two decades have increased in frequency and prominence. Although there have been numerous descriptions and analyses of such feasts, none seemed to provide an integrated account that 'made sense' of either the traditional or current Tsimshian feasts that I read about and saw. In particular, the literature gives little insight into the symbolic value of the actual events to the Tsimshian.

Accounts of traditional Tsimshian feasts have emphasized their importance in structuring social and economic relations, but have given little insight into the significance of details of the feasts, displays, and orations involved, into the logic or pattern of the symbols as selected and ordered in time and space, or into connections with the symbolic value of elements in other aspects of Tsimshian culture. I refer to these aspects of the feasts when I speak of the symbolic value of the actual events to the Tsimshian. I will attempt here to interpret Tsimshian feasts by tracing connections between elements found in the feasts and other aspects of the culture. I focus on the relationships among Tsimshian belief in reincarnation, traditional attitudes towards other realms of power—including spirits, animals, and supernatural beings—and, most significantly, the relationship between an individual and his father's clan. The appreciation of these relationships makes the traditional potlatch of the Tsimshian understandable not only as a means of perpetuating a social structure but also as a viable economic system. Furthermore, the shape of the modern feast system and the significance of its continuity for over 200 years are clarified when seen in this context.

A Personal Note

The reader of an ethnographic essay may not always be aware that it is an intensely personal account, not an impersonal presentation of objective 'facts'. It is sometimes equally difficult for an author to convey effectively the extent to which her background, interests, and the history of her particular research effort have shaped the final presentation. The following personal information seems relevant here. I am not Tsimshian. I am a linguist by training. I taught in a department of anthropology for 19 years and then became the first chair of First Nations Studies at the newly established University of Northern British Columbia. There I was able to help create a space in the curriculum for First Nations to develop an indigenous scholarship, including language courses on languages of the region (Haida, Tsimshian, Nisga'a, Gitksan, Haisla, Wetsuwet'en,

Carrier, Ts'ilqot'in, and Cree). I began work on Tsimshian culture in the village of Hartley Bay, at the invitation of members of the community, to work with a local language program, and six years later married a man from the community. I am presently a Professor at UNBC, living and working in Prince Rupert (and my husband is still fishing commercially). I am working with language programs among the Tsimshian, Nisga'a, and Gitksan, as well as co-ordinating a regional cohort of UNBC's Master's program in First Nations Studies.

As a linguist, I am concerned always with language, and most particularly with *meaning* in language; as a linguist who taught for many years in an anthropology department, I am concerned with meaningfulness of *cultural* phenomena. My approach to understanding the feast system starts from the assumption that the Tsimshian are not just 'doing something' in the feasts, but that they are also 'saying something'. Trying to understand how the Tsimshian interpret the messages of feasts implies building a Tsimshian 'cultural philology'. One way to do this is to 'deconstruct' meaning from context and exegesis, and then to 'reconstruct' an enriched interpretation. Successive layers of such an interpretation act to focus understanding of the parts and the whole. Each fragment of information provides part of the interpretation for the others. This sort of approach is sometimes referred to as *hermeneutic*. It is an instance of a trend in the social sciences that Geertz describes: 'many social scientists have turned away from the laws and instances ideal of explanation toward a cases and interpretation one, looking less for the sort of thing that connects planets and pendulums and more for the sort that connects chrysanthemums and swords' (1983: 19).

Constantly probing for meaning in the activities of anyone is occasionally disconcerting. The difficulties have been ameliorated in my work in Hartley Bay because the feast system is viewed as important and interesting there, and because I first met people in the village while I was working on their language program. Though I am not Tsimshian, being in a Tsimshian village feels comfortable, intellectually and practically. Perhaps, as a woman, I felt more at home in a place where women are relatively potent than I did in 'my own' milieu at the university in the 1970s, where the power structure was generally overwhelmingly male. The immediate past president of the Tsimshian Tribal Council is a woman, Deborah Jeffrey, who was recently named to a national panel on Aboriginal education. The CEO of the Wilp Wilxo'oskwhl Nisga'a is also a woman, Deanna Nyce, with whom I have worked for 10 years developing programs and co-authoring several papers. In every Aboriginal community in this region, women hold positions of responsibility in education and social services and maintain strong roles in family and community activities. Tsimshian traditional practices that fostered strong women matriarchs are being undermined steadily, however. Residence in nuclear families, band membership rules that recognized links through males only for several generations, submersion as minorities in urban communities, and the imposition of education and religious institutions that denigrated matrilineal descent and succession have led to a lack of understanding of these institutions among many Tsimshian people, eroding the foundation of this aspect of the culture.

The research for this work included five years of intermittent residence in Hartley Bay over 15 years. During the time I sought an understanding of the nature of current feasts in that community and discussed oral traditions with many elders, a number of whom have died in this time. I have also assembled recollections of activities in the community over the past 70 years. Textual material collected in Hartley Bay by William Beynon has provided some independent documentation from the 1940s and 1950s. Texts and descriptions of feasting traditions from other areas, especially Garfield's ethnographic work at Port Simpson, have been consulted and discussed with community members, but most of the materials from other locales are considered foreign; similarities are seen as interesting, but do not compel integration.

The interpretation that follows is intensely local, in that the material from Hartley Bay vastly outweighs that from other communities and sources. Paradoxically, much of the locally derived interpretations should prove to hold in their general contours for other Tsimshian groups, as well as for the linguistically related Gitksan and Nisga'a. The material reveals patterns grounded in conventions of discourse and linguistic structure that were shared by all speakers of the Tsimshianic languages. These patterns comprised the process by which Tsimshian people defined 'otherness' and 'us-ness'. They were productive of unique practices and the existing context in each locale, but I hope that the patterns themselves express some of the shared understandings that constitute the unique genius of Tsimshian culture.

The Context of the Study: The Tsimshian

Traditional Tsimshian chiefs conducted themselves with the formality and concern for protocol now associated with international diplomacy. Each territory was held to be a world apart, distinct in history, custom, and law; to enter the territory of another village (or even of another lineage segment) was to enter a foreign land. The inhabitants of each domain figured as reciprocal, symbolic 'others', providing an important component of a view of the universe as a place of many worlds. The people of each village emphasized the foreignness of outsiders by epithets (both polite and pejorative) and by descriptions of the exotic practices of each. Actual and classificatory kinship relationships penetrated the insularity of each village. Knowledge of other groups was often intimate and detailed. Ideas, customs, and objects moved easily between groups, but adoption of foreign customs was framed by the premise that, once adopted, the customs were no longer foreign; they were placed within the local meaning system. If a chief received a privilege such as a dance from a neighbouring chief, the privilege and the story of its acquisition became a part of

the interpretative context for his own group—part of their story. If the other group understood it differently, that was the natural result of the foreignness. As long as each chief had a legitimate claim to use the privilege, interpretations were correct for respective worlds, and this would be affirmed at performances. The external form was shared, as was the understanding that allowed the local interpretations to coexist. Foreigners might be seen as capricious, and potentially dangerous, but not as wrong in being foreign.

Generalizations became broader as distance increased, and all the groups beyond the Northern Kwakiutl were merged as *didoo* ('people down south'). Details of shared kinship and history were known, but had to be constantly revitalized in order to continue to hold force in structuring interactions.

People who arrived late on the coast, and who seemed to live in ships rather than houses, became known as *'amsiwah*, or 'driftwood people'; their peculiarities became known far and wide, most notably the absence of women among them. The Tsimshian have come to know a great deal about the *'amsiwah*, of course, and we have become a very significant 'other' group for them; yet only occasionally have we *'amsiwah* understood the Tsimshian in the context of the local meaning systems in which they continue to live.

The Tsimshianic Groups

The Tsimshianic-speaking peoples occupied territories along the Nass and Skeena rivers and their tributaries and estuaries, extending to the islands and coast to the south. There were four major linguistic divisions: the Nisga'a on the Nass; the Gitksan on the upper Skeena, above the canyon at Kitselas; the Coast Tsimshian on the lower reaches of the Skeena and the adjacent coast; and the Southern Tsimshian, who extended Tsimshian culture as far south as modern-day Klemtu.

The four Tsimshianic divisions were united by closely related languages. Boundaries between the divisions were marked by the linguistic patterns themselves, by distinctive ecological contexts in

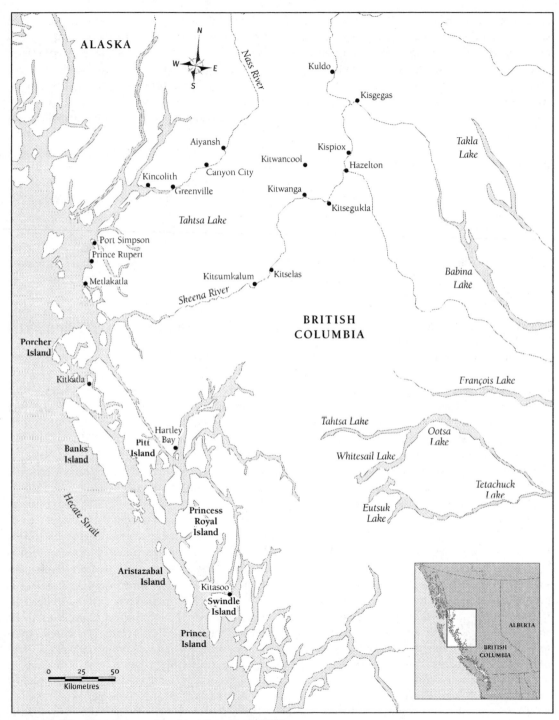

MAP 24.1. Tsimshian Communities (data from Duff, 1959)

each division's territories and the annual cycles attuned to those contexts, by different emphases in ritual activities, and by the political context and relationships to foreign groups maintained by each. The boundaries were bridged by long-established travel and trade relations, intermarriage, feasting exchanges between certain chiefs, and occasional conflict.

There were up to four exogamous clans in each village, designated by the primary totemic crests of each: blackfish and grizzly bear, raven and frog, eagle and beaver, and wolf and bear.[2] A clan might include several distinct lines that traced origin to separate ancestors whose exploits were recounted in the lineage history; these lines maintained mutual exogamy but did not consider themselves directly related, and they sometimes hosted each other at feasts and in various ways interacted as mutual 'others'. The local segments of these lineages were the groups that held territories and feasted as units. Depending on the size of the local segment there might be one or more houses headed by chiefs who had inherited names carrying economic and ritual privileges. The chiefs had established relative ranks, which determined their right to precedence in political interactions.

The territories belonging to a local segment of a clan were administered by the chiefs, each of whom inherited control over a specific territory with the name of his maternal uncle. Women also held names of high rank, inherited from their own mothers and maternal aunts, but it was unusual for a woman to hold a territory-controlling name, though she might hold the privilege of managing certain resources such as berry-picking grounds. Generally, each clan represented in a village had control over sites for each type of available resources in the area, but one local lineage segment often held the highest-ranked names and controlled the bulk of the territory.

Large red-cedar plank dwellings housed each of the local lineage segments; if the group was large and several chiefs were of high rank there might be several such houses for a segment. The residents of each house were usually a group of men closely related through their mothers, with their wives, children, dependants, and slaves; such a group was the unit of production and consumption. The man bearing the highest-ranked name was deemed to be the owner of the house, but he took counsel with the holders of the other ranked names in making decisions about matters that bore implications for the power and prestige of the house. Matters of mutual interest, such as defence, were discussed with the chiefs of the other houses in the village as well. Succession to the highest-ranked names was a matter of concern to chiefs in other villages, and was validated by guests assembled from a wide area. Individuals who did not hold high-ranked names associated with territories could join one of the houses to which they were related.

All changes in social relationships were declared and legitimated by property distributions and feasts. The major focus of feasting among Tsimshian groups was the cycle that began with the death of a chief and culminated with the installation of his heir, who was generally the eldest son of his eldest sister. The cycle generally included a memorial feast, the feasts associated with the erection of a memorial pole and the building of a new house, and the final feast of name assumption. When the deceased was the head of a local lineage, guests were generally invited from all groups with which political relationships were maintained. The prestige of the local lineage and the maintenance of its economic and political power were dependent on the success of events, including distribution of sufficient wealth to demonstrate control over territories.

Chiefs were responsible for relationships with other villages and with foreign tribes such as the Haida, Tlingit, and Haisla. They also bore responsibility for keeping their group in balance with the supernatural beings who controlled the continuation of food and wealth. Each lineage had inherited relationships to supernatural beings encountered by the original holders of their names. Animal species such as bear, salmon, seal, and mountain goat were governed by their own chiefs, who demanded proper respect. Named locations were also occupied by powerful supernatural beings who controlled the continuation of the wealth of an area and the safety and success of those who visited. Accounts of ancestral interactions with supernatural beings were an integral part of the assumption of a ranked name. Such events were depicted by the crests that were carved and painted on houses, poles, and specific household goods of each chief; some powers might also be dramatized in performances, which involved masks, costumes, songs, and dances exclusively owned by the lineage. Some of these crest privileges were common to all members of a lineage; others were restricted to those holding a particular, highly ranked name.

Winter ceremonial performances and dances brought supernatural powers into the Tsimshian worlds. The old Tsimshian form of winter ceremonial was the *halayt*, which was firmly integrated into the rank structure. Chiefs controlled supernatural power for the people, manifesting their abilities in dramatizations of a special set of names. A series of four winter ceremonial dances had apparently been entering the Tsimshian system via the Northern Kwakiutl connections at Kitimat and Bella Bella in the late pre-contact period. Two of these were open to all ranks, but two were restricted to particular chiefs.

Another form of relationship with supernatural power was the province of the ritual specialists known as shamans, some of whom were also chiefs. Shamans practised several sorts of healing based on the Tsimshian understandings of the nature of illness. Part of the responsibility was to combat the effects of witchcraft, which was surreptitiously practised by disaffected individuals.

The material culture of the Tsimshian was a magnificent manifestation of this intricate, coherent, symbolic vision. The privilege of owning and displaying many treasures was restricted to those with sufficient rank to respect them properly by distributing property; other items were limited to those with supernatural powers, such as shamans

and members of secret societies. The large houses were carved and painted with designs representing the crests of the house owner, fronted with complex poles erected in honour of past chiefs. Everyday objects such as clothing, baskets, canoes, fish hooks, and storage boxes were finely made, frequently displaying complex symbolic decoration. The sculptural style of Tsimshian carvers has been acclaimed, and their creations were sought by other groups during traditional times as avidly as by modern collectors.

The relationships of the Tsimshian to the land, to their neighbours, to supernatural beings, and even to themselves were ultimately radically transformed by the intrusion of Europeans and Euro-Canadians. Initial contacts with explorers and maritime traders did not undermine the traditional patterns; the goods received in trade were incorporated into cultures as useful items in traditional technologies or as prestige items in the system of crest privileges. But sea otter furs proved to be tremendously valuable and led to the rapid development of a maritime trade. The sea otter was brought to the edge of extinction within five decades. The trade shifted to land furs, which the Tsimshian acquired by direct trapping and by controlling the trade of Interior groups, reaping large profits as middlemen.

A land-based trading post was established by the Hudson's Bay Company in Tsimshian territory at the mouth of the Nass River in 1831 and moved in 1834 to Fort Simpson. The chiefs who controlled the trade became even wealthier, and the nineteenth century was probably the period of greatest opulence for the Tsimshian. Huge amounts of wealth entered the Native economy and a ready supply of iron tools allowed the carvers to reach even higher standards and greater productivity. At the same time, established relationships of rank were destabilized by new aggregations around the trading post, which brought together chiefs who had not previously had stable political relationships through the feast system. There were extraordinary mortality rates because of diseases such as smallpox, measles,

FIGURE 24.1. Metlakatla, BC, showing the eastern portion of Metlakatla with cannery buildings on the left. (Courtesy of the British Columbia Archives, HP 55799)

influenza, and venereal infections. Frequent deaths encouraged the promotion of multiple claims as names became vacant, leading to some competitive potlatching.

Other influences entered the area. In 1857 a lay preacher for the Church Missionary Society named William Duncan came to Fort Simpson. He began by learning the language of the Coast Tsimshian; he was ultimately to convert most of the Coast Tsimshian people and to build a new community with them at Metlakatla, a traditional Coast Tsimshian site. Metlakatla was a great success, and nearby groups actively sought missionization.

Duncan fought the *halayt*, but awarded various badges and the insignia of new power that replaced it. Church activities, hymn singing, participation in brass bands, sports days, village offices, and clubs were all enthusiastically embraced by the Tsimshian who joined Duncan. Shamanic healing was denounced, but Duncan made available substitute services, and the use of traditional medicines not accompanied by ritual

performance was not prohibited. Duncan did not forbid the telling of stories, and he was of the opinion that several demonstrated knowledge of the Flood and other biblical events. Property distributions for display were denounced, but Duncan himself obliged the same rank system by granting positions of authority to chiefs in the new community structure and by collecting property and redistributing some of it through the chiefs. Duncan did assign English-type last names, which were transmitted patrilineally, but did not forbid the remembrance and transmission of Tsimshian names, nor apparently of feasts at which they were bestowed, as long as the format included Christian prayers and distribution of presents only as payments. The chiefs also had leading roles as public speakers and as Duncan's counsellors. Duncan's intransigence was difficult for many of the church workers who came to work with him, but it was quite consonant with the behaviour the Tsimshian expected of a chief. A Christian Tsimshian social pattern was forged from the desire of the Tsimshian to retain their territories and power and from Duncan's visionary Christianity.

Duncan stayed at Metlakatla for 25 years, drawing increasing numbers to the village and the Christian Tsimshian life. Duncan became hugely influential because of his great success, but he never lost his intransigence in the face of what he saw as error. This led him into difficulties with authorities in the church; in 1887 he left to start a New Metlakatla in Alaska, with over 800 Tsimshian people. The land to which they moved was far from traditional territories they had continued to use for hunting or fishing, and many firm converts chose to remain in BC. Old Metlakatla reverted to a small village, and the populations of other villages were restored.

During the late nineteenth century the Tsimshian saw an influx of gold seekers, adventurers, and a few settlers. By then the Aboriginal nations were no longer treated as sovereign. When British Columbia entered Confederation, small reserves were allocated to each village, and the Tsimshian groups came under the provisions of the Indian Act without ever having signed treaties; none of the groups have abandoned claims to their traditional territories. The Nisga'a pressed their Aboriginal claim with tenacity, leading the government at one point to pass a law forbidding the raising of funds to finance such activities. The Nisga'a claim was finally heard by the Supreme Court of Canada. Despite an ambiguous decision issued in 1973, the case was one of the major factors that set the stage for serious negotiations between the federal and provincial governments and the First Nations of British Columbia. The current British Columbia treaty process has roots in these events, and the Nisga'a finally achieved a treaty including land, cash compensation, and extensive self-government powers.

The Tsimshianic languages were used during initial missionization but were suppressed by later missionaries, educators, and administrators. Southern Tsimshian is now extinct. There are few speakers of the other Tsimshianic languages under the age of 30. Official suppression of the languages has been abandoned, but they are unlikely to continue as living systems unless they are given substantial artificial support. While positive steps have been initiated, the revitalization of these languages is not yet a policy priority and few resources have been allocated.

The Tsimshian participated actively in the development of the modern economy of their homeland. Their success in the commercial fishery is particularly notable, but the Tsimshian people also made contributions in areas such as logging, transportation, and commerce.

The Symbolic Structure of the Traditional Tsimshian *Yaawk*

The preceding section has established a context. In this section I weave threads between some traditional Tsimshian religious premises and symbolic association and the traditional *yaawk* as the central Tsimshian social institution. The model of symbolic analysis has its roots in philology, as discussed above. Because of constraints on length, three sections of the argument are presented in précis; the fourth section is presented in greater detail to illustrate the sort of evidence available.

i. The Tsimshian local matriclan, which was the functioning feast group, was a *waap* (house). A house is symbolically a box, a container. Persons were not *in a waap*, they *were* the *waap*.

The matrilineage is imaged as a house, which is a container motif, like a box containing preserved food and/or wealth. The participants in a feast are assigned places within the house. The feast 'empties' the house. Houses are much like persons; built by father's clan, named at a potlatch after the building, and carved and painted with the crests of the lineage (Garfield, 1939: 276). In fact, the significant 'members' of the lineage are not particular individuals but the 'social persons' of the ranked names. Individuals are required to carry

---

BOX 24.1

First Nations Language Revitalization

The 28 First Nations languages indigenous to BC represent six distinct language families. All are seriously endangered, and some languages have already been extirpated. The federal and provincial governments have spent well over $3 billion building and maintaining beautiful museums such as the Canadian Museum of Civilization and the Royal British Columbia Museum to store and display artifacts from Aboriginal cultures. During 2002, funding for First Nations language retention and revitalization programs in BC from all sources amounted to less than one-tenth of 1 per cent of that. The Assembly of First Nations is seeking support from government for new legislation that would provide protection and support for the languages of the First Nations, including official language status and stable funding for documentation, development of curricula, and a range of language learning programs. There have been some positive initiatives spearheaded by local First Nations. They include immersion schools, such as that at Gitwangak. Language and culture adult immersion programs are offered through the Secwepemc Cultural Education Society (SCES). A new First Nations Developmental Term Certificate program for language teachers has been approved by the BC College of Teachers. University courses in 14 languages are offered for credit by the University of Northern British Columbia, and in six languages through the SCES program partnership with Simon Fraser University. Despite all of these efforts, however, the erosion of indigenous languages seems inexorable, and will only be reversed through a determined—and well-funded—long-term struggle.

---

the names, but the structure of the lineage is the structure of the names. From this perspective individuals are indeed contained, *in* a name. This interpretation of the significance of containers is quite different from that in work developed from a psychoanalytic perspective (Dundes, 1979; Fleisher, 1981), which suggested that the potlatch on the Northwest Coast was a manifestation of 'anal erotic character traits'.

The Tsimshian see themselves as forming the container, rather than as inside of it; their concern is not with excretion per se, but with the restoration of real beings to their proper worlds and with the preparation of an 'empty container' to receive new wealth.

ii. A *waap* includes individuals who were more or less 'real'. A 'real' person (*Sm'ooygit*, 'chief') held a high name, passed to him/her matrilineally; each name was associated with an origin story, crests, songs, dances, and economic powers. Becoming 'real' depended on lifelong participation in the property distributions at *yaawk*. Relations between groups, whether human villages or different species, were mediated by their respective real people.

That *Sm'ooygit* literally translated as 'real person' has often been noted. 'Reality' in this sense means 'exemplary', but this is not an absolute quality. It should be seen as a cline: slaves are outside the cline; commoners are less real than chiefs; chiefs can be ranked from less to more real. Real animals can appear in human form in the human world. Occasions are also more and less real; real occasions are those in which real beings interact, altering the world. Real people were those who had been 'shown to the people' and 'pushed up' since childhood; who had 'fed the people' by giving feasts and distributing property; who had 'put on

FIGURE 24.2. High-ranking Gitksan women dressed in ceremonial regalia that includes frontlets, Chilkat blankets, and dance aprons, 1910. (Courtesy of the Royal British Columbia Museum, PN 3929)

the affairs of the local clan. Relations between local clans were arranged by the highest-ranking persons in the village, in consultation with advisers and with the consent of the ranking name-holders from the other local clans. Consent was given by participating in public feasts and ceremonies at which decisions, particularly concerning successions to names, were announced. Relations with other Tsimshian groups, including trade, marriage, and settlement of disagreements, were similarly channelled through the real people, usually the highest-ranked name-holder(s). Relations with non-Tsimshian, including notably the Nisga'a and the Gitksan (speakers of Tsimshianic languages, but not called Tsimshian), Haida, Tlingit, and northern Kwakiutl groups, were essentially 'royal affairs'. These interactions were particularly delicate, even potentially violent if mishandled. Apparently the early missionaries and traders were also thought to be 'real'. Collison (1915: 9) mentions that 'in the spring (April) of 1860, Mr. Duncan first visited the Nass River. He was well received at the lower villages, where several of the chiefs feasted him and gave him presents of furs.'

a name' entitling them to social and economic prerogatives; who 'could talk to people'; and those whose conduct, particularly on 'real' occasions, affected the entire lineage.

Communication and negotiation within and among human groups was channelled through these real people. Decisions within a *waap* were made by the ranking name-holder with the support and advice of his councillors. If there were several houses in a local clan, the ranking members of each, led by the highest-ranking name-holder, managed

Since the real people were responsible for dealing with other groups for the entire constituency (house, lineage, village), their conduct was important to the group. Failure of any sort was an indication that standards were not being maintained. Failure in fishing or hunting demonstrated that real people among the animals were not prepared to acknowledge the claims of the human group. A wound or an accident signalled a loss of prestige and potency—if relations with other powers were correct then the accident would not have occurred. Generally, when an accident happened to a real person, distributions of property served to inform other real beings that any defect had been remedied and were a part of a cure, along with increased self-discipline. The person was said to 'wash' by making these distributions. Failure to be treated appropriately at a feast (being called later than appropriate, or given less than proper in relation to others) also had to be answered—otherwise it was evident that the individual or group belonged to the level accorded them, and the prestige of the person slighted was actually diminished. Since such a loss of power would affect the individual's influence with all other real beings and reflect on *all* members of the lineage, demands for rightful recognition were not mere self-aggrandizement.

Individuals with more reality were more potent. Relations with beings in all worlds were required, and these were mediated by the real beings. Interaction of a real being entailed simultaneous effects on the less real beings under his sway—for example, if the chief of the spring salmon willingly entered a river where fishermen were waiting, so would his tribe.

iii. In addition to the Tsimshian tribes and other human groups they were acquainted with, Tsimshian recognized other societies. Each animal species had its own village, with 'real people', commoners, and slaves, similar to Tsimshian villages. Food animals came to the Tsimshian by the animals' own consent, directed by their chiefs. There were also villages for human ghosts, with similar social structure. However, spirits of both animals and humans were subject to reincarnation. Actions taken on animal bodies in human villages influenced the animals in their own villages. Complete, respectful consumption of animal bodies was required to ensure the health of the animals. Proper reincarnation

among humans was dependent on human feasting. The consequences of actions in one domain could be observed in the others. Real animals in their villages were aware of actions taken by humans; human shamans were especially adept at perceiving other worlds.

Whether we interpret them as literal or metaphoric statements, their myths indicate that traditional Tsimshian did not view the universe anthropocentrically: they were aware of parallel worlds, some inhabited by animal people and some by supernatural powers, as exemplified in the story of 'The Prince Who Was Taken Away by the Salmon People' (Boas, 1916: 192 et seq.), which also shows the way in which actions in one world had consequences in the others. The story tells us that a young prince who had taken a bit of dried salmon from his mother's box to feed a slave during a famine was taken by the salmon to their village. The salmon village had houses carved with figures of spring salmon, the largest inhabited by the old chief of the spring salmon, who had been ill with palsy for two years:

> The sick chief ordered his attendants to spread mats at one side of a large fire. They did so. Then the Prince went and seated himself on the mats which had been spread for him by the chief's attendants. As soon as he was seated on a mat, behold! An old woman came to his side, who touched him, and said, 'My dear Prince!' Then she questioned him. 'Do you know who brought you here?' The prince replied, 'No' — 'The Spring Salmon have brought you here, for their chief has been sick with palsy for over two years. When you unfolded the salmon the other day, the chief got a little better because you did so.'

Though the other worlds were very like the world of the Tsimshian, there were also clear refractions of structure. In their domain, animals perceived themselves as human and perceived humans as powers or foreigners (never, apparently, as food animals). The salmon come to the world of the Tsimshian to fish for their own salmon, which are to us the leaves of the cottonwood tree, and while there, their salmon bodies are food in turn for the Tsimshian. As long as the proper respect was shown to the salmon caught, as long as the fish was completely consumed (and any bones, etc. burned afterwards, or returned to the water), the salmon would return.

Each world (each village) was as 'real' as the others. Relations between each village/world were the particular responsibility of the real people and the real beings, and also shamans, who were especially adept at discerning the state of affairs of other worlds and at negotiating with them, frequently being given tokens of supernatural power from other worlds. A real person who put on a high name was connected to other worlds through the tokens of contacts with real beings made by his predecessors in that name—tokens such as songs, dances, crests, and power. These treasures and potent connections were maintained in perpetuity by the feast system.

Among these other worlds were villages of ghosts. Although the details of the traditional understanding of reincarnation are no longer clear, the concept is still firmly held in Hartley Bay, and evidence from the Gitksan suggests that in Aboriginal times the parallel to the worlds of the animal people was close. That is, a baa'lx (person reincarnated) also preferred to come back to a person who is generous at feasts.

iv. Tsimshian saw symbolic associations between fathers, foreigners, animals, and the supernatural. A father contributed food to his wife and children, members of a waap different from his own, as animals fed their bodies to humans, who lived in a world other than their own. Just as the real animal remained in its own village, the reality of a father remained a part of his own waap. Members of father's clan had special ritual duties to a child and were paid by the child's matriclan for these duties at feasts.

Though the significant category of kinship relations for Tsimshian was the matrilineal clan to which an individual belonged, the ksi'waatk ('where you come from', your father's side) was extremely significant in an individual's life as well. The name given to a child was supposed to have been selected from a set of names belonging to the matrilineage, but it should also have reference to the side of the father. Throughout life, services were performed by 'father's side,' or 'father's sisters,' including the naming of the child, piercing of ears, birthing, mourning, and all medical treatment. Services such as house-building and pole- and canoe-carving were also to be purchased from the father's clan. In turn, an individual returned respect to the father's side—'paying' when a crest of the father's side was displayed, giving food to a member of the father's clan who returned blankets or other goods to the giver, being supported by a member of the father's side in some dances, and paying for the many services provided. By a careful comparative analysis of kin terminologies from Tsimshian, Haida, and Tlingit, Dunn (1984: 5) established several symbolic associations:

> From the Tsimshian perspective a set of binary opposition serves to set the Haida and the Tlingit apart. . . . The Haida are symbolic male, while the Tlingit are symbolic female. The Haida are elder, the Tlingit younger. The Haida are animal, supernatural, and unfamiliar, while the Tlingit are human and 'known,' i.e. related. For the Tsimshian the Haida are 'father' while the Tlingit are 'little sister.'

The association of fathers with supernaturals, animals, and foreigners (Haida especially) allowed the Tsimshian to maintain reciprocal relations with supernaturals and animals in their own world through feasts and payments made to the father's side. Powers, good relations with animal real people, and success were gifts from the supernatural—first received from a supernatural father, then passed on matrilineally. The father/benefactor is inevitably located by the end of the story in a different world/village than the child/receiver, who has a token of the gift embodied in a name, story episode, song, dance, crest object, etc. (There are few Tsimshian tales of human males marrying supernatural women, and none that I know of resulted in children, and in a matrilineal system, children of such a union would not, of course, be Tsimshian anyway.) The continued potency of the gift from the supernatural father was contingent on a continued relationship with the benefactor in the other world.

The establishment of payments and services also allowed for clear delineation of rights in persons, despite mixed residence patterns. Since any service performed by a member of a person's father's lineage was promptly and publicly paid for by members of the mother's lineage, there was a clear statement of group affiliation. Each residence unit necessarily included members of other clans, but even a long-term resident belonging to another clan was an outsider, while a visitor from an allied house/clan from a distant village was immediately accorded a place fitting his/her status.

The traditional feast system was central as the context for keeping and building relations of power. The names were an incarnation of powers that were socially manipulable. One interesting possibility is that the guests at a *yaawk* might have been receiving food and gifts in an inversion of the bestowal of gifts by non-human real beings, in fact, instead of those beings. Gifts from the non-human real beings included food, wealth, and crests. Since gifts must be publicly acknowledged, and eventually the giver should become a receiver, by their participation in feasts the hosts (real human beings) keep relations of power and dependence valid with the other real beings (represented by real human beings who were guests, instead of real beings from other worlds).

As animal food had to be consumed for animals in their villages to be reincarnated and healthy, humans had to 'eat' the wealth held in a lineage for more wealth to return. This was particularly important at death, which was the centre of Tsimshian feast activity. By feasting, in which one's

father's clan received wealth, the integrity of power in other worlds was ensured and future wealth for the clan was possible. Wealth was returned to enable future wealth, as animal food was consumed to ensure future reincarnated animals. One effect of the feast, then, was to return substance accumulated in a *waap* to the fathers, reuniting the fathers' substance with their own reality, which is part of their own matrilineal *waap*.

Payments for services and gifts were given throughout life to members of one's clan. The great potlatches were generally given at the time of assumption of a name at the death of one's predecessor (usually mother's brother). Contributions to this endeavour were collected from all members of one's group. The guests were persons of sufficient reality from other clans in the same village, other Tsimshian villages, and foreign groups. Property was distributed according to the rank of the guests as payment for specific services performed (burial, putting on a name, carving a pole, etc.) and for validating the *yaawk* by attending. The clan was in fact emptying its wealth to its fathers, since the services were performed by the members of father's clan, and since classificatory kinship terminology made brothers and sisters of clan members, so that each of the guests was *ksi'waatk* to the host or his siblings, all of whom contributed to the feast. By giving to fathers the clan is simultaneously giving to the supernatural animals with whom fathers are symbolically associated, thus restoring their (supernatural animals') worlds by reuniting substance with reality.

If the *yaawk* centred on emptying a clan after the death of a name-holder, it simultaneously was involved with the filling of the name by the incarnation of a new name-holder, who had the responsibility to 'bury' his predecessor in the name and was thus generally the host of the event. It is by understanding this that we can understand why the clan had to be emptied. Just as a hunter had to be clean—to fast and purge himself—before hoping to encounter animals, a new name-holder came to the supernatural full of things acquired by his predecessor through his connection to the same supernatural, holding part of the substance of the supernatural that had never been restored.

If the term 'incarnation' for the elevation of the new name-holder is taken seriously, it may be useful to see the assumption of the name as the final stage in the reincarnation that was begun at birth. The services of naming performed by the father's clan make it likely that this is appropriate, as does the comparison with the closely related Gitksan, who make it explicit that a person should take the name of his/her *baa'lx*. If this was indeed the final step in reincarnation, it is interesting to recall the story of 'The Princess Who Rejected Her Cousin' (Boas, 1916: 185 et seq.). The relevant material is too long for quotation, but a general summary with a few quotations is necessary to show its significance for the argument to be developed (my summary notes are in square brackets):

A very long time ago there was a great village with many people. They had only one chief. There was also his sister. They were the only two chiefs in the large town. The chief also had a beautiful daughter, and the chief's sister had a fine son . . . they expected that these two would soon marry . . . the girl rejected the proposal . . . but the young prince loved her very much, and still she refused him . . . the princess wanted to make a fool of her cousin . . . [she led him on, and asked him to show his love, first by cutting his cheeks, and by cutting off his hair—which was dishonourable as a mark of a slave. He did as she wished, but then she rejected him and mocked him] . . . 'Tell him that I do not want to marry a bad-looking person like him, ugly as he is;' and she gave him the nickname Mountain with Two Rock Slides, as he had a scar down each cheek . . . the prince was so ashamed and left his village with a companion . . . he came to a narrow trail and went along it, finally meeting an old woman in a hut who knew him and his story. She told him

he would come to the house of Chief Pestilence, and told him how to behave so that Chief Pestilence would make him beautiful. The prince did as she told him and became as beautiful as a supernatural being . . . when he came back his companion was just bones, but he took him to Chief Pestilence and he was also made beautiful . . . they returned to their own village . . . the princess wanted to marry him . . . he then mocked her . . . she went with a companion . . . they met a man who asked them which way they intended to go, and the princess told him they were going to see Chief Pestilence . . . She passed by him, and did not look at him, for she was ashamed to let anyone look at her . . . [They got to Chief Pestilence's house, but with no counsel such as the young man had received, she went to all the maimed people in the house who called her, and was maimed and bruised . . . they eventually returned to their own village, where the princess lay in bed, and finally died.]

This story may be interpreted as a story of two types of death and reincarnation, one proper and the other socially censured. If the relationship between the prince and the princess is remembered, it will be apparent that the young man who 'went away' (died) had behaved properly in life, and we may assume that the old woman whom he encountered on his path represented his father's clan aiding him in the other world. The young woman, on the other hand, had humiliated the prince, *the son of her father's sister* (who was the person who would ordinarily help at the burial, mourn, and participate in a mortuary feast as a guest). She met with no helpful guide on her travels; she did encounter a man, who may have been a representative of her father's side, but he offered no counsel because she was too ashamed to talk to him. If this interpretation is accurate, it establishes the central symbolic nexus or rationale for the feasting of the Coast Tsimshian, which primarily centred on the mortuary feast and the elevation of an heir: *to make it possible for the lineage members to be rein-carnated properly.*

Several expressions and customs in current use are clarified in the context of this interpretation. First, people who are more real are *ksi'waatk* to a wider group of people. 'Big' people thus provide services to and receive gifts and payments from more people. This was apparently also true in the past; Boas indicated rules for the 'support' of dancers (1916: 512) that show a much wider group of people treated a person with a big name as *ksi'waatk*. In certain dances it was (and is) necessary for onlookers to hold up dancers. Each dancer is supported by a noble who is of the same clan as the father of the dancer—so that during an encounter with the supernatural in this world, one is supported by one's *ksi'waatk*, who also supported one in such an encounter in other worlds, helping one to be properly restored to this world. The more real a person, the more potent was the connection with supernatural.

Another example of a current usage that is both clarified in this context and contributes to an understanding of the traditional symbolism is that if a person makes a gift of food to another and then eats from the gift, it is said that 'You'll get sores.' The process of 'incarnation' may have been continuous, requiring constant good relations with supernaturals. This would explain the emphasis put on 'washing' if a real person had an accident or made a mistake, and the expectation that real people should be physically without defect. One washed away shame by distributing property, usually to *ksi'waatk*. The vilest insult that could be hurled by a traditional Tsimshian was that a person was *wah'a'yin*, or 'his scabs don't heal' (the literal translation is 'without healing'). In English texts this is glossed as 'without origin' or 'having no relatives'. These two glosses may imply that such a person had no *ksi'waatk* to provide treatment for injuries in return for payment, and, perhaps in the light of the argument above, that there was also no supernatural connection to give potency to the person's name—that, in fact, the person was not real.

The Tsimshian knew that they were real and that their villages were real. No place was at the centre of the Tsimshian universe, but all places are equally centres. The Tsimshian also knew that they had a duty to partake of the gifts received from other worlds and to return gifts to those worlds through their fathers, who connected them to those other worlds.

Modern Feasts

Although one of the most significant functions of the inter-tribal feasts was the protection of territories, the real threat to Tsimshian territorial sovereignty after the middle of the nineteenth century did not come from other Tsimshian or Native groups but from the encroachment of white resource appropriation and settlement and the failure of the province to acknowledge the validity of the original ownership. The set of 'others' to be considered in the world has shifted so that the most significant rival is Canadian society at large. The patterns of asserting claims vis-à-vis the new power remained within the Tsimshian tradition. Councils of chiefs drew from all tribes, forming organizations to press land claims and other crucial issues. One of the most significant organizations was the Native Brotherhood of British Columbia, which held its first meeting in Port Simpson on 15 December 1931. Delegations from Masset, Hartley Bay, Kitkatla, Port Essington, and Metlakatla attended. By 1936 the efforts of such active organizers as Chief Heber Clifton of Hartley Bay and Chief Edward Gamble of Kitkatla had brought in branches from Vanarsdale, Klemtu, Bella Bella, Kitamat, Kispiox, Kitwanga, Skeena Crossing, and Hazelton.

The Local Context: The Gitga'ata

The modern Tsimshian village of Hartley Bay is located at the entrance of the Douglas Channel in the southern portion of Tsimshian territory. The village was established in 1887 by a small group of people who had their traditional territories in the same general region, centring on their winter village, about 12 miles north of the present village.

From the 1860s to the 1880s the Gitga'ata joined the mission village of Metlakatla, probably residing there in the winter and travelling to their own territories for the balance of the annual cycle. When Duncan left Metlakatla to begin his community again in Alaska, the founders of Hartley Bay established a new permanent village in their own territories. This village was strict, as Duncan might have wished. From the beginning the community defined itself as a progressive, Christian, Tsimshian village, with equal emphasis on each aspect of the definition. A council of chiefs wielded a firm hand over all aspects of daily life in Hartley Bay during its early decades, and all of Duncan's rules were enforced until the middle of the twentieth century, when curfews and Sunday work prohibitions were relaxed.

The first reserves for the village were allocated in 1889, with additional allocations by the Royal Commission on Indian Affairs in 1916. The chiefs at Hartley Bay steadfastly refused to participate in the process, insisting instead on a settlement of their title to their entire traditional territory, which the Commission would not discuss. At the present time the village of Hartley Bay is engaged in the land claims process with the other Coast and Southern Tsimshian villages.

Feasting was apparently continued without interruption. Recollections of Elders from Hartley Bay indicate a firmly ensconced modern feast tradition early in this century. The feasts were of the sort considered respectable by Duncan; they still begin with prayers. The feasts given were solemn at funerals and had a lighter tone when the occasion was not so serious. The person who was to inherit a name generally 'buried' his uncle, including sponsoring the memorial feast and paying the members of the father's side who had prepared the body and supplied the coffin. Marriages were arranged by families, in some cases as late as the 1960s, and generally they still maintain clan exogamy or include a clan-adoption process to maintain the formal structure of exogamy.

Traditionally, the names within a clan were ranked; the relative rank was displayed most prominently at feasts, when guests were seated in positions according to rank. The convention of recognizing the highest-ranked chief in the strongest clan in a tribe as the chief of the village was shared by all the Coast Tsimshian villages and is followed at Hartley Bay at the present time; the hereditary chief of the Gitga'ata is Wah'modm, the highest name of the Blackfish. The same individual also holds another high Blackfish name, Nta'Wi'Waab. This individual, John Clifton, is the hereditary chief of the Gitga'ata. The chief of the Eagle clan at Hartley Bay until his death in 1982 was Louis Clifton, John Clifton's eldest brother. (Traditionally, of course, brothers would not have been in different clans; John Clifton was taken by the Blackfish clan during the life of his father, but also retains his Eagle name.) Louis Clifton was succeeded in his Eagle name by his sister's son, Charles Robinson, and on his death the name went to his nephew, Ernest Hill Jr. The holder of the highest-ranked Raven name in that Gitga'ata lineage is Heber Clifton, who currently resides in Prince Rupert. His younger brother, Chief William Clifton, is the highest-ranked resident Raven chief. Both of these men are sons of the late Louis Clifton. There is not an active Wolf clan at Hartley Bay, the group died out and in married Wolf clan people have been adopted as Blackfish. Within each clan there is a recognition that lesser names were also traditionally ranked among themselves, but little regular use is now made of these relative rankings.

The interpretation of traditional feasts offered above was that they were a mode of discourse, a way of creating messages and expressing the social order to members of the group and to other groups. The organization of the feast discourse conforms to conventions of discourse structure observed in some conversations at the present time in Hartley Bay. Very briefly, the convention is that the event (conversation or feast) cannot end until consensus is reached and expressed. In the conversations to which it applies, this means that

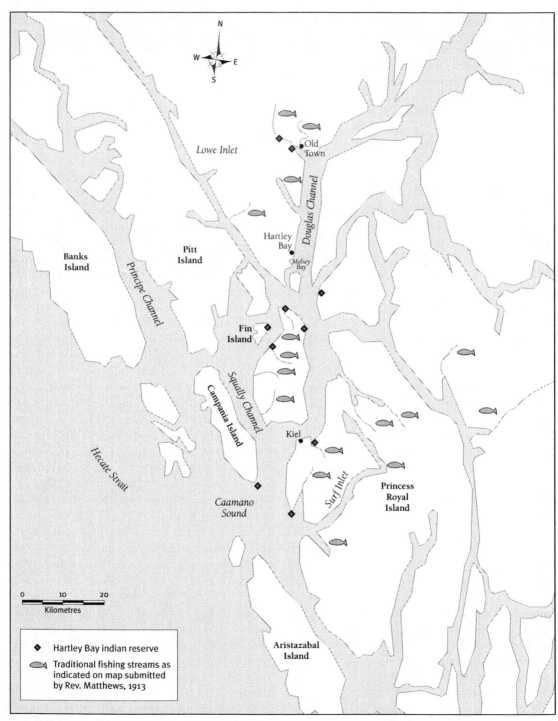

MAP 24.2. Fishing Sites in the Territory of the Gitga'ata

a listener can subtly compel modifications in a statement by declining to provide a supportive closure to the conversation; in feasts, it means that the appropriate guest must be present and participate for the feast to fulfill its function.

The discourse convention includes the understanding that it is inappropriate to hold discussions with persons who do not have a proper authority to speak on a matter. It was manifested in the dealings of the Gitga'ata with the Royal Commission on Indian Affairs, which visited Hartley Bay in 1913. 'The Indians were asked to give testimony as to the character of the reserve, population, etc., but they flatly refused to do so' (Campbell, 1984: 27). Eventually, a request for lands was submitted by a missionary in the village.

The current feasts at Hartley Bay continue to function as discourses, following the traditional patterns. However, the discourse currently gains interpretation in the historical and structural context in which the Tsimshian are now placed.

A Unique Feast

The Raven Feast of Chief Billy Clifton, on 2 January 1980, was in many ways typical of current feasts at Hartley Bay, but in a few respects it was a unique event. The feast was hosted by Billy Clifton, who was ranked as the highest resident chief of the Raven clan in Hartley Bay. The most unusual feature of this event was the adoption by Mr Clifton of his uncle, Chief John Clifton, as a member of the Raven clan.

Ordinary feasts are based on a well-understood pattern in which the guests ratify the acts of hosts. Their presence is an acknowledgement of the right of the host clan to present their claims. Implicit in the Raven feast of Chief Billy Clifton was a violation of these expectations. It was not an ordinary right of the Ravens to take a member of the Eagle or Blackfish clan as a member (and Chief John Clifton was already a member of both of these clans). This adoption was extraordinary and required explicit affirmation to be successful.

The process of adopting Chief John Clifton and putting a Raven name on him was marked by several modifications of ordinary feast procedures. The primary orator for the Raven clan, Ernest Hill Sr, delivered a prologue speech, which 'made sense' of the adoption. He addressed the concerns of the Ravens, indicating that the new Raven would help their clan, and he made explicit claim that the adoption would make all the clans work together and was good for the entire village, including the Blackfish and Eagles.

The adoption allows Ravens to put claims on John Clifton, thus potentially infringing on the exclusive claims of the Eagles and the Blackfish. In ordinary feasts, the clan of the father is asked to put the name on the individual. The namers are then paid off, which gives the father's clan restitution for the service, as well as for raising the child. The adoption of Chief John Clifton as a Raven, and the putting on of his Raven name, was performed by members of both the Eagle and Blackfish clans. They thus showed that they were willing to share rights in him with the Ravens. The involvement of both clans in this adoption makes it clear that the namers are *ksi'waatk*, not only in the sense of the father's clan but in the more general sense of 'where you come from'. Chief John Clifton was being taken from both the Eagle and Blackfish clans, and members of both ratified the adoption by participating.

This feast, then, presented a new kind of claim couched in a traditional form; a 'new tradition' has been forged. This new tradition celebrates the unity among members of the village and it is incarnate in the person of the chief who participates in all three clans. Symbolically, three have become one, and low has become high. I have couched the process in these terms deliberately because I would argue that the symbolism is distinctly Christian, not as a replacement of traditional symbols but as an interpretation of them. Christian symbols are the sensible interpreters of traditional Tsimshian symbols in this village, which has never wavered from the Christian Tsimshian course set when the people came back from Metlakatla.

The new structure has appeal at this time, particularly for members of the Hartley Bay community who were not tightly integrated into the traditional rank hierarchy. The privilege of names has been extended to most members of the village, but the stock of ranked names is running out. Chief John Clifton is perhaps the only member of the community who could have creatively reformed symbolic structures in this way. The political context of the village now is a united one, confronting the next round in the struggle to retain their territories not from rival chiefs but from a non-Tsimshian government. This feast may be a manifestation of the context within one village, in which a chief and the united people are 'One Step Higher', which is the English translation of the Raven name given to Chief John Clifton.

Current Issues and Future Challenges

In this new millennium, the community of Hartley Bay faces many of the issues confronting other First Nations: effective governance, access to economic opportunities and management of resources in their territories, local control over education, and the urgent concerns of ensuring cultural and linguistic vitality for future generations. In the area of governance, Hartley Bay is exploring forms of internal and external political organization that will meet the aspirations of the community. At present the community still relies on a chief and council system for internal governance, elected under the 'band-custom' provisions of the Indian Act. No adequate mechanism has been developed to involve members of the band who are not resident on-reserve in community governance, though several recent court decisions have deemed it illegal to exclude non-reserve band members from participation in elections; this is a focus of considerable tension at present. The growing proportion of members resident off-reserve due to the addition of members under Bill C-31 has added pressure. However, a number of local factors are also involved, including a shrinking absolute number of on-reserve residents due

to increasingly constricted economic opportunities; whereas the Hartley Bay School had 78 children enrolled in grades K–10 in the late 1970s, in 2002 there are fewer than 50 children in the school. At the level of the Tsimshian Tribal Council there has been a move to involve the hereditary chiefs in decision-making and to represent through them the unity of the Tsimshian Nation in negotiations with governments. This has not been effected consistently at this point; one of the difficulties has been that the long-term suppression of the feast system has made identification of the currently entitled name-holders difficult in some communities, and the traditions of generosity, respect, and authority that underpinned the system have been considerably eroded. Since the Tsimshian system was repressed for so long there is a great deal of 'straightening out' to be done. Band membership rules relied on patrilineal descent for several generations, and there are now many situations in which none of the matrilineally descended members of a house are resident in its home community. In some cases there have been wholesale adoptions, some legitimated by feasts and others self-styled and clearly illegitimate. Some ambitious and unscrupulous people are rumoured to have 'gotten a name from a tombstone'—a reference to attempts by interlopers to usurp the rights of succession. The Gitksan and Nisga'a have organized processes to empower the hereditary chiefs to address such violations, but the Coast Tsimshian have not yet found a means to address this and it is causing serious disruption in some communities.

Shifting management priorities and the downward spiral of employment and income in both the forestry industry and the fisheries have been difficult to combat. For example, Area Six, the fisheries management area closest to Hartley Bay, has been almost entirely closed to commercial fishing in recent years, which local people attribute to favouritism towards sports fishing interests from Kitamat and fly-in lodges. This has made it uneconomic for fishing vessel owners to reside in the community. At the same time there is pressure to decrease the number of days for commercial fishing in nearby areas such as the mouth of the Skeena River. One reason is that while there are large available stocks of some species such as sockeye (millions of these fish return to the Skeena River each year), other stocks that migrate at the same time are small (some runs number under 2,000), and the current technology available to the commercial industry makes it expensive to harvest selectively. It is ironic that a century ago the federal government destroyed weirs and traps that had been used for millennia on the grounds that they were a threat to conservation. These same technologies are now being touted as remedies to the problems confronting the mixed-stock fisheries. However, individuals and groups with extensive investment in the current fishing industry are deeply concerned about the impact of such schemes on their futures. Commercial fishers have also suffered through several rounds of government 'solutions' that have cut back the privileges of fishing licences (commercial licence holders used to be able to fish the entire coast, but now must purchase three separate area licences to do so; they used to be able to switch from trolling to gill-netting and now can use only a single gear type on a licence). The Aboriginal Fishing Strategy and community rather than individual licences are being used to reorient harvesting away from the current industrial mode. Hartley Bay received a community licence for harvesting herring roe-on-kelp several years ago, and this is one of the economic projects that offers some potential; the Tsimshian Tribal Council employs fisheries guardians and trained community members in fisheries management, but none of them have achieved a real role in the management process. The future of this key economic sector is likely to be very turbulent. Two Tsimshian communities have accepted commercial salmon aquaculture operations in their territories, though vocal segments of these communities are vehemently opposed to this industry on the grounds that it is a danger to wild stocks and pollutes shellfish beds in the area. Meanwhile, prices paid for sockeye salmon—the 'money fish' of the commercial fishery—have dropped from over $5 per pound in the mid-nineties to $1 per pound in 2002. The Allied Tsimshian Tribes have filed suit claiming an Aboriginal right to a commercial fishery, and at the same time, environmental organizations are seeking to partner with Tsimshian communities to help them build sustainable futures in their territories—or to manipulate First Nations as their puppet spokespersons to take control of the coast, rename it the 'Great Bear Rainforest', and close it to all commercial activities. Which interpretation one accepts depends in large part on prior assumptions. The pressures on communities are intense.

Logging reserve lands and developing a tourism business at a former village site are other current projects that Hartley Bay is pursuing to establish a more diversified economy. The Tsimshian Tribal Council is working on issues such as land rights, management of fisheries and forestry in their territories, repatriation of Tsimshian cultural objects from museums, and the development of educational programs, including Tsimshian language and cultural programs. Social control within the communities has broken down drastically—with unemployment rates up to 90 per cent, high school graduation rates below 30 per cent, and bleak opportunities for progress at the treaty table, the rates of substance abuse, family violence, and suicide have multiplied. The greatest certainty as the Tsimshian community moves into the twenty-first century is that many of the issues they confront will remain unsettled for a long time.

Conclusion

This chapter has focused on the Tsimshian feast complex. The interpretation presented offers some insights into the meaning system that gave coherence to the traditional Tsimshian feasts and to the adaptations that have been made in changing circumstances over the past century. The Tsimshian people continue to seek a future in which they can maintain their identity and

BOX 24.2

Looking for Justice

In 1997 the Supreme Court of Canada issued its decision in the *Delgamuukw* case, named after a Gitksan Sm'oogit who was one of the plaintiffs. The Court clarified a number of issues in this ruling (quotes here are from the majority opinion).

1. *Where it can be established in fact, Aboriginal title is a living right protected by the Canadian Constitution and must be reconciled with Crown sovereignty.*
   'Aboriginal title encompasses the right to exclusive use and occupation of the land held pursuant to that title for a variety of purposes, which need not be aspects of those aboriginal practices, customs and traditions which are integral to distinctive aboriginal cultures. . . . Section 91(24) of the *Constitution Act, 1867* (the federal power to legislate in respect of Indians) carries with it the jurisdiction to legislate in relation to aboriginal title, and by implication, the jurisdiction to extinguish it. . . . A provincial law of general application cannot extinguish aboriginal rights.'

2. *Oral histories are admissible in court and must be given independent weight.*
   'The factual findings made at trial could not stand because the trial judge's treatment of the various kinds of oral histories did not satisfy the principles laid down in *R. v. Van der Peet*. The oral histories were used in an attempt to establish occupation and use of the disputed territory which is an essential requirement for aboriginal title. The trial judge refused to admit or gave no independent weight to these oral histories and then concluded that the appellants had not demonstrated the requisite degree of occupation for "ownership". Had the oral histories been

correctly assessed, the conclusions on these issues of fact might have been very different.'

3. *Aboriginal rights may be infringed, but not without consultation and compensation.*
   'Constitutionally recognized aboriginal rights are not absolute and may be infringed by the federal and provincial governments if the infringement (1) furthers a compelling and substantial legislative objective and (2) is consistent with the special fiduciary relationship between the Crown and the aboriginal peoples. The development of agriculture, forestry, mining, hydroelectric power, general economic development, protection of the environment or endangered species, and the building of infrastructure and the settlement of foreign populations to support those aims, are objectives consistent with this purpose. Three aspects of aboriginal title are relevant to the second part of the test. First, the right to exclusive use and occupation of land is relevant to the degree of scrutiny of the infringing measure or action. Second, the right to choose to what uses land can be put, subject to the ultimate limit that those uses cannot destroy the ability of the land to sustain future generations of aboriginal peoples, suggests that the fiduciary relationship between the Crown and aboriginal peoples may be satisfied by the involvement of aboriginal peoples in decisions taken with respect to their lands. There is always a duty of consultation and, in most cases, the duty will be significantly deeper than mere consultation. And third, lands held pursuant to aboriginal title have an inescapable economic component which suggests that compensation is relevant to the question of justification as well. Fair compensation will ordinarily be required when aboriginal title is infringed.'

The *Delgamuukw* case and other recent court decisions, such as the reaffirmation of the treaty right of Mi'kmaq Indians to a 'moderate livelihood' from their resources, have been widely discussed and it has been anticipated that these judgements would lead to a breakthrough at last in the treaty-making process in BC. Five years after the *Delgamuukw* decision there has been no real progress at the treaty table, and the newly elected provincial government recently insisted on a province-wide referendum on the treaty making process that was condemned by Aboriginal leaders. The questions in this referendum were simplistic and biased. The government has declared that the results of the referendum vindicate its positions. In the summer of 2002, a Tsimshian group is in court to try to force consultation on logging plans on their traditional territories, and there are protests and 'illegal' roadside sales of salmon at Gitwangak, apparently in hopes that there will be arrests that can move the issue into the courts. Other BC First Nations are also looking to the courts for justice. There is widespread frustration that court decisions are being ignored by the provincial government.

manage their own affairs on the lands where their culture developed over several thousand years, and where it can continue to flourish.

Notes

1. This chapter summarizes my monographs on feasts. My field research was supported by grants from the Contract Ethnology Program of the National Museum of Man and the Social Sciences and Humanities Research Council of Canada. While aspects of the interpretation presented here have been discussed with members of the community of Hartley Bay and a copy has been submitted to the band council of the village, the interpretation, and any errors, are my responsibility. Spellings of Tsimshian terms follow the system in Dunn's *Practical Dictionary of the Coast Tsimshian Language*. Original spellings are retained in quotations from other authors.

2. Nisga'a educator Dr Bert McKay (d. 2003) noted that crest animals are those that can eat the same food as do humans (personal communication). This seems to be an apt observation for all except the frog, but frog is a complex symbol everywhere on the Northwest Coast.

References and Recommended Readings

Adams, John W. 1973. *The Gitksan Potlatch: Population Flux, Resource Ownership and Reciprocity*. Montreal: Holt, Rinehart and Winston. A cultural ecological analysis based on 1960s fieldwork. Adams argues that the Gitksan redistributed people to territories and resources by assigning individuals to groups through the feast system. The description of current feasts is detailed.

Anderson, Margaret Seguin, and Marjorie Halpin. 2000. *Potlatch at Gitsegukla: The 1945 Field Notebooks of William Beynon*. Vancouver: University of British Columbia Press. In 1945 there was a 10-day cycle of feasts, *halayt* performances, and totem-pole raisings attended by William Beynon in his role as a Laxkibu Sm'oogyit. His field notebooks are the best account of feasting during the twentieth century, shaped by his insider perspective and knowledge of the language and culture. Anderson and Halpin provide a lengthy introduction.

Barbeau, Marius. 1929. *Totem Poles of the Gitksan, Upper Skeena River, British Columbia*. Ottawa: National Museum of Canada, Anthropological Series No. 12, Bulletin 61. Along with *Totem Poles* (1951), this is one of Barbeau's longer and more enduring contributions.

Berger, Thomas R. 1981. 'The Nisga'a Land Case', in Berger, *Fragile Freedoms: Human Rights and Dissent in Canada*. Toronto: Clarke, Irwin. A clear presentation of the struggle for recognition of the Nisga'a claim to hereditary lands. Berger represented the Nisga'a before the Supreme Court; though the panel split, the case helped set the stage for serious land claims negotiations in Canada.

Boas, Franz. 1916. *Tsimshian Mythology*. Washington: Bureau of American Ethnology, Thirty-first Annual Report. A rich collection by the Tsimshian Henry W. Tate. Boas provides extensive annotation and a description of traditional cultures based on information in the myths.

Campbell, Ken. 1984. 'Hartley Bay: A History', in M. Seguin, ed., *The Tsimshian: Images of the Past, Views for the Present*. Vancouver: University of British Columbia Press.

Duff, Wilson. 1959. *Histories, Territories and Laws of the Kitwancool*. Victoria: British Columbia Provincial Museum, Anthropology in BC, Memoir No. 4. A record of the information considered significant by the people of a Gitksan village, significant because of the collaboration involved in producing it as well as for the information presented.

Dundes, Alan. 1979. 'Heads or Tails: A Psychoanalytical Study of the Potlatch', *Journal of Psychological Anthropology* 2, 4: 395–424.

Dunn, John Asher. 1984. 'International Matrimoieties: The North Pacific Maritime Province of the North Pacific Coast', in Seguin, ed., *The Tsimshian*.

Emmons, George T. 1907. *The Chilkat Blanket*. Memoirs of the American Museum of Natural History, vol. 3, Anthropology, vol. 2, Dec.

Fleisher, Mark. 1979. 'The Potlatch: A Symbolic and Psychoanalytical View', *Current Anthropology* 22, 1: 69–71.

Geertz, Clifford. 1980. 'Blurred Genres', *American Scholar* 49, 2: 165–79.

Garfield, Viola. 1939. *Tsimshian Clan and Society*. Seattle: University of Washington Press. An extremely valuable discussion of traditional and developing social organization by an important contributor to the area.

Robinson, Will, and Walter Wright. 1962. *Men of Medeek*. Kitamat, BC: Northern Sentinel Press. House history from a Tsimshian Sm'oogyit who died in 1949; considerable material of interest in understanding world view and social organization.

Seguin, Margaret, ed. 1984. *The Tsimshian: Images of the Past, Views for the Present*. Vancouver: University of British Columbia Press. A collection of recent scholarship from diverse perspectives focused on a single group; includes material on feasts, shamanism, history, and culture change.

Usher, Jean. 1973. *William Duncan of Metlakatla: A Victorian Missionary in British Columbia*. Ottawa: National Museum of Canada, Publications in History 5. A scholarly analysis of the activities of this intriguing missionary.

Suggested Web Sites

Gitxsan Chiefs: www.gitxsan.com
Information on treaty talks, the *Delgamuukw* case, natural resource issues, and even a Gitxsan chat group.

Nisga'a Lisims Government: www.nisgaalisims.ca
Official site, links to community and cultural topics, government programs, and treaty and legislative issues.

Tsimshian Tribal Council:
www.tsimshian-nation.com/home.htm
Excellent information from the Tsimshian Tribal Council and treaty office on resource issues and the Ts'msyen Sm'algyax Authority, including a link to the 'talking dictionary'.

UBC's Museum of Anthropology: www.moa.ubc.ca
The museum is famous for its collections of Northwest Coast material. Visit the 'Prelude to the Study of a Totem Pole', which Marjorie Halpin developed to help understand totem poles. The site explores the form and meaning of a totem pole from Gitanyow, and is both scholarly and elegant.

CHAPTER 25

From Kwakiutl to Kwakwaka'wakw

PETER MACNAIR

Introduction

This chapter is based on ethnographic fieldwork among the Kwakwaka'wakw of British Columbia and on the study of published anthropological and archival records and material culture in museum collections. As a museum ethnologist, I have, since 1966, spent several years in Kwakwaka'wakw villages, working with the community, to record traditional technologies and practices as they continue today based on ancient ways dating back to time immemorial. This overview of traditional Kwakwaka'wakw society looks at the history of the name, the land and territory of these people, the impact of Euro-Canadian contact, material culture, social organization, and ceremonies, notably the potlatch, which encompassed all aspects of life.

The History of the Name

Of the more than 20 independent First Nations that occupy the Northwest Coast of North America, the Kwakwaka'wakw (formerly known as the Kwakiutl) are the most extensively described in the published and archival ethnographic literature. The anglicized spelling 'Kwakiutl' was introduced by the pioneering ethnographer Franz Boas in his seminal work, *The Social Organization and the Secret Societies of the Kwakiutl Indians* (1897), and it remained the standard rendering for more than 80 years. For example, authors Edward S. Curtis (1915),

Clellan S. Ford (1941), Helen Codere (1950), Audrey Hawthorn (1967), James P. Spradley (1969), and Aldona Jonaitis (1991) all have used the term 'Kwakiutl' in a generic sense, applying it to the entire group.

The word 'Kwakiutl' was used by scholars to define a confederation of about two dozen village groups that speak the same language and occupy northern Vancouver Island and adjacent areas of the British Columbia mainland. Over the years, the word has been spelled in a variety of ways: Kwawkewlth, Kwagyol, Kwagiulth, Kwagutl, and Qua-colth, to cite a few. All are attempts at transcribing the Native word 'Kwagu'ł', whose exact meaning remains obscure despite attempts by Native speakers, anthropologists, and linguists to provide a translation.

The term 'Kwagu'ł', in any of its variations, is actually the proper name of a single village group, now known as the Fort Rupert tribe. The other village groups all have their own names: for example the Ławits'is (Angry Ones) of Kalugwis village on Turnour Island, the Dzawada'enuxw (People of the Eulachon Place) of Gwa'yi village in Kingcome Inlet, the Kwikwasut'inexw (People of the Other Side) of Gwa'yasdams village on Gilford Island, and the Da'naxda'xw (the Sandstone Ones), now of T'sadzis'nukwaame' on Harbledown Island.

These other groups have long objected to the designation Kwakiutl as not applying to them. Around 1980, a group of Old People ('Old People' being an honorific English-language term preferred by many in the community to 'elder') suggested adopting the word 'Kwakwa̱ka'wakw' as an alternative because it means 'those who speak Kwak'wala', and the dialect spoken by the majority of the village groups (and understood by all) is Kwak'wala. The adoption of the term Kwakwa̱ka'wakw was promoted by the U'mista Cultural Centre at Alert Bay, the most populous of the Kwak'wala-speaking villages, and in 1981 it entered the literature in several language books published by the centre. Now, the term is in common use in the print, radio, and television media and in most scholarly publications. Usage is not, however, universal; in the Northwest Coast volume of the *Handbook of North American Indians*, the Smithsonian Institution retains the descriptor 'Kwakiutl' while providing a detailed history of the term (Suttles, 1990: 366).

The Homeland

The Kwakwa̱ka'wakw comprise about 20 village groups, or 'tribes' as they were called by Franz Boas. Each village functioned relatively independently of the others, although there were many social and ceremonial occasions that brought the people together.

The territory claimed by the Kwakwa̱ka'wakw includes the east coast of Vancouver Island north from Campbell River to Cape Scott and from there around to the exposed western side of the island south to Cape Cook. As well, they occupy the BC mainland and adjacent islands north from Discovery Passage to Smith Sound. Dense coniferous forests, where red cedar, hemlock, Douglas fir, and spruce dominate, fill the mountainous landscape, and deciduous trees such as red alder and cottonwood flourish in the river bottoms. The evergreens sweep to the water's very edge, denying a safe landing to canoe-borne travellers over much of the shore.

Scattered along the shoreline are expansive sheltered beaches covered with broken white clamshells, marking areas of long use and habitation. Some of the sites are large permanent winter villages, identified by shell middens up to six metres deep, while others are smaller seasonal campsites. Archaeologists are only beginning to analyze Kwakwa̱ka'wakw sites in any systematic way, but radiocarbon dates indicate human occupancy in the territory for at least 8,000 years. This does not imply that the Kwakwa̱ka'wakw themselves have been present continuously for that long period, but it does clearly indicate that humans have lived in the area for millennia.

The Kwakwaka'wakw have lived continuously in some winter villages—for example, 'Ya̱lis (Alert Bay on Cormorant Island) and 'Tsax̱is (Fort Rupert on Vancouver Island)—for more than 150 years, having moved from traditional sites for economic advantage. Other villages such as Hega̱ms (Hopetown village on Watson Island) have been the home of one extended family since time immemorial. Many of the traditional winter villages were occupied until the 1960s, when the federal government closed the village schools and families were removed to more centrally located reserves.

In the late nineteenth century, 10 to 20 large communal houses lined the shore of a winter village, just above high tide. Measuring about 20 by 20 metres, each dwelling housed an extended family of around 25 people. The crests of the lineage were painted on the house front and, inside, carved house posts and other architectural details bore witness to the family's history. The houses were constructed of two parallel roof beams supported on each end by a lintel, each of which in turn was held up by two house posts. The walls were made of large cedar planks placed vertically. When the family moved to fishing and gathering sites during the yearly round, they would lash the house planks between two canoes, creating a platform for transporting household goods. At the seasonal camps, the planks were then installed around permanent house frames or used to erect lean-to structures.

These seasonal campsites offered families access to specific shellfish, marine, and land plant resources, and were occupied for days or weeks at

FIGURE 25.1. Early in the twentieth century most Kwakwa̱ka̱'wakw lived in cedar plank houses and followed a traditional lifestyle. The village of Blunden Harbour welcome figures were erected on the beach front. These served to welcome guests invited to witness ceremonial occasions and attend potlatches. Photo by C.F. Newcombe, 1901. (Courtesy of the Royal British Columbia Museum, PN 258)

a time. Each family moved throughout a large territory as they exploited resource areas reserved exclusively for their own use, visiting several sites between March and October to gather and preserve food for sustenance during the long winter months. They went from berry-gathering patches to clam beds to halibut-fishing stations, and to the broad rivers and small streams where Pacific salmon returned from the ocean, in regular cycles, to spawn.

In times past, travel was mainly by water, although foot trails cut across strategic peninsulas and penetrated the Coast Mountains to the Interior Plateau. Dugout canoes, ranging in length from three metres to 20, were the main means of transport. Every Kwakwa̱ka̱'wakw was a skilled paddler, familiar with the rhythm of the tides and the vagaries of weather.

The change of seasons along the coast from fall to winter is dramatic: southeasterly storms bring abundant rain and gale-force winds, the days are short, the nights long. Winter, when people were sequestered in their home villages, was the time to hold dramatic ceremonies marking significant events such as marriages, the naming of children, transferring privileges, and memorializing the dead.

Material Culture

The material culture of the Northwest Coast First Nations is known for its large plank houses, totem poles, spectacular masks, and ocean-going canoes carved from giant logs. The Kwakwaka'wakw versions of these are unique, reflecting a deep understanding of their environment and its potential to feed, house, and clothe them. This rich material culture was based on wood, and of all the trees that grow on the North Pacific coast, the western red cedar (*Thuja plicata*) and yellow cedar (*Chamaecyparis nootkatensis*) are the most significant, providing the raw materials for everything from clothing to massive buildings. Light, strong, straight grained, and pungent with decay-resisting oils, the wood is easily worked by a skilled carpenter or carver. Planks as wide as two metres and more than 10 metres in length were split from cedar logs by the careful use of a number of yew wood wedges tapped successively with a stone hammer. Such planks were treasured heirlooms.

In addition to serving as the walls of houses, cedar planks are used to construct many types of containers in the shape of boxes. To form a four-sided box, three kerfs are cut nearly through from opposite sides of a board, which is then steam-heated to soften the wood enough to bend at each kerf to a 90-degree angle; the join is pegged with small wood dowels or 'sewn' together with cedar root through drilled holes. A plank bottom is attached by the same means and, if required, a tight-fitting lid is fashioned. In their roughest form, the bent-wood boxes were used for temporary storage of food or gear, but most boxes were carefully crafted and painstakingly decorated with engraved geometric designs, or carved and/or painted with representations of crest figures. They were used to store food such as dried or smoked fish, shellfish, berries, fruits, and roots. Still others were 'boxes of treasures' in which ceremonial regalia were respectfully stored. Infants were bound into slat cradles that were versions of the boxes, and the dead were placed in rectangular wooden chests that functioned as coffins. The bent-wood boxes could be so skilfully constructed that they were watertight and thus functioned as water buckets, cooking boxes, and containers for other liquids such as eulachon grease, a prized condiment.

While every Kwakwaka'wakw had basic carpentry skills, specialists tackled the monumental carving tasks. Canoe-makers served long, demanding apprenticeships before they could successfully create the balanced, flowing lines of a cedar log canoe. By steaming the hollowed-out and shaped log, the canoe-maker could add as much as 70 centimetres to the beam. But greater skills were needed even before the spreading took place, for the canoe-maker had to know in advance how the dimensions of his craft would shift during the spreading process and had to allow for these in the carved form before it was steamed.

Other artisans achieved renown as carvers and painters, producing an array of ceremonial objects such as masks, rattles, and huge feast dishes from the wood of red cedar, yellow cedar, alder, and yew trees. Each village had several artists who often worked together on major projects such as carving totem poles or large masks. Apprentices to the established master carvers were invariably sons or nephews, and, as a result, village substyles developed within the general art form. The general Kwakwaka'wakw style, in both the sculptural and two-dimensional painting traditions, is clearly distinct from that of other Northwest Coast groups. It is based on a simpler archaic style known as Old Wakashan, which was practised at the time of European contact. In the last quarter of the nineteenth century, the Kwakwaka'wakw art form evolved into a distinctively flamboyant one, incorporating complex carved planes and elaborate painted detail. This trend towards complexity in the art was helped along by the availability of iron tools, which made carving easier and faster. Iron was known to the people of the Northwest Coast before the time of European contact; indeed, during his voyage of 1778, Captain James Cook noted that both iron and stone blades were in use. However, as metals became more available through the burgeoning trade, shell, stone, and bone blades were replaced with steel or copper. Significantly, however, though the material changed, the forms of the ancient tools were retained; today, elbow adzes, D-adzes, chisels, and straight- and curved-blade knives are still the preferred tools of Native carvers.

In addition to the wood of the cedar, the Kwakwaka'wakw used its bark, roots, and young branches. In the spring, they cut strips of bark up to eight metres long from cedar trees and then used small flexible bone spatulas to split away the smooth inner layer from the rough outer bark. They gathered bark from both red and yellow cedar, though they preferred the bark of the yellow cedar for the manufacture of the clothing worn in early times. The inner bark of yellow cedar required laborious preparation to produce soft fibre for capes, skirts, and blankets. Using whalebone beaters, women would pound the flat strips of bark until the fibres began to separate and shred, imparting a supple softness. The prepared strands were then woven on a single-bar loom.

The inner bark of red cedar was also split into thin strips of even width and then woven, using a checker-weave technique, into mats of many sizes and shapes. Some mats were coverings on which food was served, some functioned as sleeping mats, some provided extra insulation on walls or served as room partitions. Mats were also used to cover canoes to protect the delicate craft from a hot summer sun that threatened to split their thin sides.

The long young branches (called withes) and roots of the cedar and spruce provided material with which to 'stitch' planks together through drilled holes, to weave mesh burden baskets, and to twist into ropes. Every object had an ingenious and well-defined function. For instance, open-work baskets made from tough cedar root allowed the shellfish to drain while they were gathered; once the basket was filled, it was vigorously plunged in and out of the sea to clean the sand and grit from the outer surface of the shells.

Food and the Seasonal Round

The sea dominated the daily routine and yearly round of the Kwakwaka'wakw. The ocean provided the bulk of their protein-rich diet: fish, clams, cockles, abalone, and mussels were significant foodstuffs and other bivalves, univalves, and crustaceans were taken when needed. Such land mammals as deer and elk and a variety of fowl, including ducks, geese, and grouse, were also important sources of food. Of the many sea mammals available, only seals were a significant source of food; they did not hunt whales.

Just as the cedar tree dominated the material culture, salmon was the mainstay of their diet. Five species of Pacific salmon spawn in the streams and rivers of Vancouver Island and the adjacent mainland, returning from the open ocean to their home rivers from spring through November to spawn in their millions. Various techniques were employed to secure the fish, such as traps, weirs, nets, and harpoons. Most such fisheries were near the mouths of rivers or a short distance upstream. Oil content differs considerably among the five salmon species, and those with the most oil—spring, sockeye, and coho—are favoured for fresh consumption. Pink and, most importantly, dog salmon are preferred for preservation because they have a lower fat content and so lend themselves well to smoking and drying. In early times, extended families would cure literally thousands of dog salmon in smokehouses; thus preserved, the fish would keep in a cool, dry environment for several months.

Halibut was nearly as important as salmon, and still other fish such as lingcod, flounder, herring, and rockfish offered welcome variety. A small ocean-run smelt, the eulachon, which returns in early spring to spawn in two major rivers in Kwakwaka'wakw territory, was netted by the tonne. From the eulachon, a highly prized oil was rendered for use as a condiment, greatly enhancing the flavour of dried salmon. The oil was traded widely with other groups and was presented to noble guests at special feasts.

The Kwakwaka'wakw did not practise agriculture, but they did supplement their diet by taking advantage of a wide variety of plant foods. Family groups owned resource areas where they systematically gathered clover, cinquefoil, and other roots; they also owned berry patches where they picked salmon berries, thimbleberries, and, most importantly, salal berries. Berries were enjoyed fresh and were also preserved to make them available year-round; berry cakes were made by mashing the berries and sun-drying the mixture in flat, square sheets. The cambium layer of the hemlock tree, scraped and processed into cakes, offered a form of starch, as did the bulbs of the blue camas traded from Coast Salish neighbours to the south. Spring brought a variety of young plant shoots, providing a welcome change from winter's fare.

Everything considered, the Kwakwaka'wakw lived in an area relatively abundant in food. Successful exploitation of the environment depended on an intimate knowledge of its potential and its seasonal variations, as well as on sophisticated technology and physical labour with which to harvest and preserve available foods. Popular accounts suggest that the people of the Northwest Coast occupied a paradise where food-getting was a simple and assured matter, but a careful examination of Native reports indicates that this was not the case. Every day of the year saw a good portion of the population at work on some aspect of the food quest. Also, rationing was a concern of every household, because long and fierce winter storms prevented travel by canoe for days on end. And although clams and other shellfish were usually available at door-front, some winter villages contained more than 500 people, so an immediate resource could be quickly overharvested, causing future hardship. In the villages of the Da'naxda'xw and Dzawada'enuxw tribes,

which were located on rivers flowing from the Interior Plateau, harsh, ice-bound winters were not unusual. Stories of privation and even starvation are part of the histories of the Kwakwaka'wakw and other Northwest Coast peoples; life was not easy and was far from assured.

Early Contact

The Spanish and British exploratory voyages of 1774 and 1778 in the Pacific Northwest led to a busy trade in the highly valued fur of the sea otter, attracting a host of British, European, Russian, and American vessels. The first direct European contact for most Kwakwaka'wakw occurred in 1792 when Captain George Vancouver circumnavigated the island that now bears his name.

Vancouver's landing at the 'Namgis village he called Cheslakees was indeed eventful; a reasonable description of its inhabitants and their lifeways survives both in his journal and that of his staff botanist, Archibald Menzies. The English mapmakers were surprised to discover goods of European manufacture in the hands of these Kwak'wala speakers whose village was located on a high terrace above the mouth of the Nimpkish River. The 'Namgis had muskets of Spanish manufacture that they handled with confident ease, and they had a good supply of iron. Menzies noticed that they had a pewter basin, on the bottom of which was engraved the name of a French ship that only three months earlier had put into Friendly Cove on the central west coast of Vancouver Island. This was proof that the 'Namgis communicated by land, across Vancouver Island, with the Mowachaht of Yuquot (or Friendly Cove) and with their chief, Maquinna, who figured prominently in the records of British and Spanish voyages.

At the time of their first contacts with Europeans, the Kwakwaka'wakw probably numbered as many as 8,000. A large village, such as the one Vancouver described, housed about 500 individuals. This is a large population for the land area occupied, considering they were not agricultural-ists. The Kwakwaka'wakw generally responded favourably to the presence of white people in the early contact period. They welcomed the trade goods and, though some aspects of the new-comers' technology were superior, the First Nations people remained very much in control.

This situation began to change as the sea otter population dwindled. The maritime fur trade was just about exhausted by 1825, but it was replaced by a land-based trade, spearheaded by the Hudson's Bay Company. By 1849, the HBC had established Fort Rupert on northern Vancouver Island, almost at the centre of the Kwakwaka-'wakw world. Profound changes rapidly fol-lowed—some positive, but others horrifyingly tragic. The wide, shallow, sandy, protected har-bour was chosen by the HBC as the site for the fort because of its proximity to a coal seam that serv-iced the needs of steam-powered vessels, which were increasingly important to Britain's maritime ascendancy in the Pacific. Although it was an ancient village site, by the mid-1800s it was used only seasonally by two Kwakwaka'wakw village groups. About two years after the fort was estab-lished, four closely related groups moved their winter residences to the site. The leading and highest ranking of these four was the Kwagu'ł (this name now describes all four groups).

Because of their proximity to the fort, the Kwagu'ł quickly became middlemen in the land-based fur trade. As their riches grew, so did their prestige, and, in effect, Fort Rupert became the ceremonial centre of the Kwakwaka'wakw. Theat-rical performances became more elaborate as privileges were acquired through intermarriage with Heiltsuk, Oweekeno, Haida, Tlingit, and Tsimshian neighbours to the north. The Old Wakashan art style became more flamboyant as both the two-dimensional and, to an extent, the sculptural art styles of these northern groups were incorporated by the Kwakwaka'wakw.

In 1860 the First Nations were still very much masters of the territory that was to become British Columbia, though the population was in decline due to the devastating effects of tubercu-losis, venereal disease, alcohol, and guns. Tragedy and terror marked the year 1862 when smallpox was introduced at Fort Victoria; within two years, the epidemic killed more than one-third of the Native population of what is now BC. Still, the Kwakwaka'wakw endured.

Social Organization, Ceremony, and the Potlatch

In 1886 when the young anthropologist Franz Boas first visited BC to study the Kwakwa-ka'wakw, their traditional lifeways were still intact, and what was not currently practised was well remembered by older people. Two years later, when Boas arrived in Fort Rupert, he fortuitously met village resident George Hunt, who was fluent in both Kwak'wala and English. Hunt was unique: born of a high-ranking Tongass-Tlingit mother and an English father who was employed by the HBC, he was not Kwakwaka'wakw, but he was, in many regards, culturally a Kwagu'ł. Furthermore, his status and integration into the community had increased when he married a Kwakwaka'wakw woman and claimed, through his Tlingit mother (who came from a matrilineal society), a number of northern privileges that were, in turn, passed to his children.

Hunt interpreted for and advised Boas as he attempted to learn about and describe Kwakwaka-'wakw society. Boas struggled to define the essen-tial functioning social unit in anthropological terms, eventually discarding the terms 'gens', 'clan', and 'sib' and applying the Kwak'wala term 'na'mima, which he anglicized as 'numaym' (here-after spelled 'namima'). The accepted translation of this term is 'one kind', though many contemporary Kwak'wala speakers prefer 'brothers'. 'Namima' implies an extended lineage group, all of whom are descended from a single mythic ancestor.

Each namima has its own origin story about its mythic ancestor. For example, one namima of the 'Namgis tribe, which now resides at Alert Bay, is descended from a Salmon and a Thunderbird, who occupied the mouth of the Nimpkish River at a time when the world was young and animals could change at will into human form and back again.

The monster fish swam ashore, transformed into a man, and began to build a house. Alone, he was able to insert the four house posts into the ground, but he could not lift the two massive roof beams to their place atop the house posts. He sat at the river's edge, lamenting this fact, when suddenly he felt a presence; turning, he discovered a Thunderbird on a boulder in the river. The bird readily agreed to assist him and, grasping a beam in his talons, flew into the sky and put it into place. The Man-Transformed-from-Salmon thanked the bird and indicated that he wished the bird were a man as well. 'Oh, but I am', the Thunderbird replied, throwing back his beaked headdress to reveal a human face. Then the bird removed his headdress and his feathered cape and threw them into the sky, where they returned to the middle heavens, the dwelling place of Thunderbird. Together, the two became the founders of a 'Namgis namima; ever since, their descendants have had the right to display these images on house-front paintings, carved house posts, ceremonial settees, dance blankets, and masks used in elaborate theatrical tableaux, re-enacting the adventures of these mythical forebears.

Several namima constituted a village group, or 'tribe' as Boas termed such units. Each namima within a village functioned more or less independently, exclusively owning defined resource areas that only they could exploit. In routine daily activities, individual people identified primarily with their extended families, but as a tribe they recognized a common origin and stood united in defence of their tribal territories. Inheritance of positions within a namima was based on primogeniture and rank. The head chief was considered to be the direct descendant of the group's mythic ancestor. Lesser chiefs, usually brothers of the head chief, their families, and attached commoners completed the namima. The head chief made all the decisions, economic and ceremonial. He determined when and where the group should move according to the annual cycle, directing forays for gathering clams, fishing for halibut and salmon, and harvesting roots and berries. The ceremonial privileges of the namima were jealously guarded by the head chief and the transfer of prerogatives through marriage, by way of either the male or the female line, was arranged by him.

The ranking system was complex and extended beyond the namima: the namima were ranked within the tribe, and the tribes were ranked as well. This system applied only to the positions within the potlatch system; it did not apply in a broader political context. There was a first-ranking chief of the first-ranking namima of the first-ranking tribe, under whom the remaining potlatch positions were ranged. However, not all members of one tribe were positioned above all of those in the next ranking tribe. For example, the first-ranking chief of the first-ranking namima of the third-ranking tribe might occupy a higher position than that of the fifth-ranking chief of the fourth-ranking namima of the second-ranking tribe. In practice, the ranking system did not function strictly according to the theoretical model, because an individual's fortunes were always a factor. In the late nineteenth century the system was threatened when, due to deaths by disease, positions became vacant simply because no rightful heir existed. In part because of the declining population, upstarts began to claim positions not normally available to them and were able to force their suits through their acquired wealth. During the 1880s, individuals of lower status began to enter the white man's economic system, earning money in the growing fishing and lumber industries in order to gain the wherewithal to attempt access to vacant positions.

The institution that governed the ranking system, and indeed all society, was the *potlatch*, a

Chinook term that means 'to give'. (Chinook was the lingua franca developed by traders and Native people on the Northwest Coast.) The actual word may derive from the Nuu-chah-nulth word *pach'itl*. The potlatch encompassed all aspects of culture: linguistic, social, political, ritual, ceremonial, legal, and artistic. Its purposes were to legitimize marriages and privileges acquired through them, to name children, to transfer privileges from one generation to the next, to confirm the assumption of a new position, and to memorialize the dead. Guests from other namima or tribes gathered to witness these transfers, as they could be confirmed only through such public events. Following the display of dances, recounting of ancestral histories, and bestowal of names, the assembled guests were feasted and then paid with goods, notably woollen trade blankets but also china, enamelware, storage trunks, furniture, bolts of cloth, even ceremonial regalia such as dance blankets, aprons, and headdresses. By accepting these gifts, the guests, or witnesses, validated the claims of their host and confirmed his status.

Certain jealously guarded potlatch privileges were on display at all times, but others were revealed only in ceremonial contexts. An example of the former would be a house belonging to a namima member. It would have a name, possibly a crest design painted on the facade, house posts generally carved to represent mythic ancestral figures, and other architectural details designated as inherited prerogatives. These details would always be evident to the casual observer; they were part of the permanent villagescape.

On the other hand, most potlatch privileges were shown only at special times of the year. Primarily, these are dance dramas that incorporate a highly developed stagecraft. The Kwakwaka'wakw have two distinct dance cycles, the *T'seka* (Red Cedar Bark Dance) and the *Tɬa'sala* (Chief's Dance). Of these, the *T'seka* is more important, because it incorporates the *Hamatsa* (Cannibal Dance), which has come to characterize the Kwakwaka'wakw winter ceremony.

Rigorous training is required prior to the first public appearance of the *Hamatsa* dancer. The individual selected for initiation spends up to three months in relative seclusion, attended only by members of the *Hamatsa* society. During this period, he learns songs and dance movements specifically created for him. At one time, ritual bathing and fasting were part of the initiation and enhanced contact with the cannibal spirit.

Once the *Hamatsa* initiate is trained, guests are invited to witness his first performance. His entry into the dance house is preceded by the sound of whistles that represent the cries of various spirits. The initiate, who is inhabited by the spirit of a man-eating monster, appears on the floor of the dance house in a frenzy, hungering for human flesh. Attendants guard him yet are often unable to restrain his frenzy as he suddenly darts into the audience to attack an onlooker. He might actually bite an individual, drawing blood. The movements of his hands, face, and feet act out the words of his song, most of which described his hunger for and consumption of human flesh. As the dance progresses, the initiate is gradually tamed and brought back to a state of normality by the calming gestures of designated participants. Eventually, he leaves the dance floor, to be replaced by performers wearing bird-like masks representing the mythical attendants of the cannibal spirit.

There are many variations in *Hamatsa* performances, and each represents an individual privilege. A dancer might enter the house holding a corpse in his outstretched arms. In the most dramatic enactments, a number of veteran *Hamatsa* might rush onto the dance floor and appear to devour the corpse. The performances are marvellous theatre; those bitten by the *Hamatsa* have agreed to be so 'mutilated' beforehand and are paid handsomely for their willing participation. While it is possible that, in the distant past, morsels from desiccated human corpses were swallowed, the usual practice was to substitute animal flesh.

Similar stagecraft was evident in the many dances that followed the *Hamatsa* performance.

FIGURE 25.2. Potlatch at Alert Bay. Guests are assembled to hear the words of the speaker, who is recording the privileges and claims of his chief. When the speeches are concluded sacks of flour will be distributed to the assembled guests. Photo by W.M. Halliday, *c.* 1910. (Courtesy of the Royal British Columbia Museum, PN 10067)

In one, a singing woman climbed into a box that was then placed in the fire. As the box was consumed by the flames, her voice gradually faded away, and, eventually, her charred bones were raked from the coals. Four days later she reappeared, unaffected by her ordeal. Unknown to the audience, however, the box had no bottom; once inside, the singing woman lifted a trap door concealed in the earthen floor of the dance house. She crouched in an excavated chamber and sang through a tube that carried her voice to the edge of the fire, giving the appearance that she was still in the box. After the guests had left the house, she was retrieved from her hiding place and later presented alive and unhurt at a suitably dramatic moment.

Other ingenious props were also used to impress the viewers: masks suddenly opened to reveal an entirely different creature, giant mechanical frogs hopped around the floor, flocks of birds flew around the dance house, puppets emerged from unexpected places. Knowledgeable observers expected such dramatic surprises and delighted in them. However, uninformed onlookers such as government and church officials were often unaware of the stagecraft involved and objected to aspects of the *Hamatsa* performance that involved the apparent consumption of human flesh.

In fact, this supposed 'cannibalism' was one of three major objections to traditional Kwakwaka'wakw lifeways expressed by early government and religious authorities, who petitioned the federal government to legislate against the 'heathen' practice of 'cannibalism'. They garnered support for this position through publishing lurid reports in the popular press.

The second concern expressed by authorities related to the traditional form of Kwakwaka'wakw marriage. Often such unions were arranged when the intended bride and groom were still infants or when the bride was considerably younger than her husband-to-be. Advantageous unions were sought by both families, though it was the bride who brought privileges, as her dowry, in the form of dances, songs, and names. These privileges were held by the groom's family for eventual bestowal on the children born to the couple. The groom's family was required to make payment for these prerogatives: in the historic period, the principal unit of payment was a woollen blanket, commonly a Hudson's Bay blanket. In earlier times, cedar-bark blankets, boxes, and canoes were the standard payments. The authorities, however, regarded such transactions as the buying and selling of women. The fact that such arranged marriages were central to the social fabric of the Kwakwaka'wakw was entirely lost on those who sought to control the destinies of their charges and who applied pressure on the Canadian government to curb the 'heathen' practice.

The final concern of early missionaries and Indian agents had to do with the great and ostentatious displays of wealth that accompanied any formal Kwakwaka'wakw event. At a potlatch, as many as 10,000 blankets were given away. This was an incredible amount of wealth for any individual to amass in the nineteenth century, especially a Native person. The potlatch host appeared to be impoverished at the end of his great display of gift-giving. In a material sense, he was. Elderly people today recount how, as children, they returned to their houses to find them devoid of all but the most essential possessions. Virtually everything—furniture, clothing, utensils—had been given away. Such actions were contrary to the way of life that the authorities were trying to force upon the First Nations of BC. They looked upon the Indians as an emerging peasantry who should lead quiet, industrious lives in nuclear family units, contributing to the Canadian economy as docile labourers.

From the Kwakwaka'wakw point of view, giving away possessions was not impoverishment; it was the only way of validating transfers of privileges between generations and of gaining prestige. To give away wealth was to be wealthy. Not only did the individual rise in stature through such actions, so did the entire namima, for the extended family worked, often for years, to amass the goods and food required for distribution at a large potlatch.

However, the authorities were unable to appreciate the reality and validity of the Kwakwaka'wakw way, and so, through a series of legal actions, they began to undermine the basic structures of Northwest Coast traditional society. In 1884, federal legislation banned the potlatch and its attendant dances; and, in time, charges were brought against individuals who continued to engage in ancestral ceremonies. The bitter culmination of more than three decades of pressure by a series of local Indian agents occurred in 1921 when more than 20 high-ranking Kwakwaka'wakw nobles and chiefs were found guilty of contravening the law against the potlatch and were sentenced to terms of up to six months in prison.

In spite of persecution, the Kwakwaka'wakw held on to their traditions by practising them in secret. People would slip away to remote villages to conduct clandestine potlatches; for protection, they posted sentries to warn of approaching police patrol boats. One ingenious chief went from one household to another in Alert Bay distributing goods while whispering the traditional business he was conducting to senior members of each family. When accosted by the Indian agent, he explained that he was giving away Christmas presents. So the potlatch tradition was maintained, although in a reduced form.

Few individuals or institutions outside the First Nations communities offered much support for the old ways, and indeed, the Kwakwaka-'wakw themselves were divided as to whether their traditional practices should be retained or not. By 1950, three generations of anthropologists had made their reputations studying the Kwakwaka'wakw, and major museums in North America and Europe were filled with treasures that had once been the property of families and the objects of their fierce pride.

The anti-potlatch legislation almost achieved what it had been intended to do; it certainly tore away much of the traditional social fabric of the Kwakwaka'wakw people. Nonetheless, determined men and women continued to speak their language, in spite of being forbidden to do so while being forced to attend residential schools in their youth. The training of young men as *Hamatsa* continued in remote villages, though the initiation was not as prolonged or as rigorous as it had been in the past. Marriages, while not arranged in the traditional sense, were still marked by the transfer of privileges brought as a dowry by the bride.

In 1951 the Indian Act was rewritten, and the section banning the potlatch was quietly omitted. It was not formally repealed (which would have at least implicitly recognized the potlatch and the negative effects of the previous legislation), as BC First Nations would have preferred. Soon afterward, outside agencies began to provide some encouragement for traditional lifeways. Notably, this came as support from the Museum of Anthropology at the University of British Columbia and from the British Columbia Provincial Museum (now the Royal British Columbia Museum). Both institutions employed the Kwakwaka'wakw carver Chief Mungo Martin, who spent the last dozen years of his life restoring old totem poles and carving new ones for the museums, as well as teaching apprentice carvers.

In addition, he built a ceremonial bighouse on the grounds of the Provincial Museum, carved new masks for use, and dedicated the house with a formal presentation of some of his dance privileges that culminated in the distribution of potlatch gifts. Finally, potlatching was again public and acceptable.

One consequence of renewed potlatch activity by the Kwakwaka'wakw was a resurgence of public interest in traditional artifacts. Collectors and art dealers moved in, and within a few years most of the regalia that had survived earlier collecting expeditions was gone. While there was concern in the 1950s that the carving tradition was seriously threatened, apprentices to Mungo Martin, notably Henry Hunt, Doug Cranmer, and Tony Hunt, ensured that the Kwakwaka'wakw art form was not lost. In the remote villages, Willie Seaweed, Charlie G. Walkus, Charlie George, and Tom Willie continued to carve through the late 1960s to the early 1970s. The Royal British Columbia Museum commissioned some of these carvers to produce masks, rattles, dance screens, and other potlatch regalia. Eventually, a collection of nearly 200 items was amassed and the museum made these available for use in local ceremonies, a practice that was eventually phased out because individual Kwakwaka'wakw were increasingly commissioning a new generation of artists to create ceremonial regalia.

Some of the concerns the Old People had expressed about the survival of traditional Kwakwaka'wakw culture were resolved; others were not. The potlatch, assailed for more than 70 years by civil and religious authorities, had been made legal by 1951. The last old practitioners, men and women, reaffirmed it and guided it through to the 1980s. With their passing, a new generation embraced the potlatch in the 1990s, modifying some aspects of the surviving format and seeking to reintroduce ancient practices they had heard or read of but never witnessed.

The creation of new art, in tandem with the potlatch, has grown and flourished. By the year 2000, more than 50 accomplished artists were

BOX 25.1

The Importance of Language

Language is an integral part of Kwakwaka'wakw culture. The greatest fear expressed by the Old People was that there would be no singers available to continue the tradition. Singers are crucial to the potlatch, chanting mourning dirges, feast songs, and songs that direct, through words and rhythm, the movements of dancers.

Among a handful of old song masters who were determined to pass on the knowledge was Chief Tom Willie, whose repertoire exceeded 400 songs, many of which he had recorded for museum archives. He encouraged young people, most of whom had little exposure to the Kwak'wala language, to learn and practise songs at weekly sessions. He was adamant that they learn formally, providing translations of words and phrases, relating them to nuances of the dance, and insisting on exact pronunciation.

They also learned the theoretical structure of songs, the four levels of voice required, and the complex, often syncopated, beat patterns. In time some of them composed songs, creating tunes, crafting the lyrics in English, and then taking the verses to a fluent bilingual speaker who translated the words to the Owikeeno language (closely related to Kwak'wala), which Tom Willie insisted was more melodic and better suited for songs than Kwak'wala. Inspired by the success of Tom Willie's students, other groups began to memorize songs, primarily by listening to tapes.

Orators also play key roles at a potlatch. The namima chief of times past relied on three functionaries: an orator who spoke on behalf of the chief, an inviter who formally summoned guests to the event, and a record-keeper who kept an account of the names and positions of all namima members. Nowadays one man fills all three roles. The oratory of the potlatch is replete with words, grammatical forms, and pronunciations that are now archaic. Many of these are being lost.

Although most potlatch business is still conducted in Kwak'wala, it will take a focused effort by the entire community to keep the language alive. Consideration has been given to conducting parts of all business and public meetings in Kwak'wala.

---

working in the Kwakwaka'wakw style, achieving success in the commercial art market as well as satisfying all the ceremonial needs of a potlatch host by creating totem poles, masks, rattles, Chilkat weavings, button blankets, and other regalia. For some families, their treasure boxes are now as full of regalia, or more so, as were those of their grandparents. In the past 15 years, new ceremonial *gukwdzi*, traditional ceremonial 'bighouses'—which can accommodate more than a thousand guests at a potlatch—have been built in Campbell River, Fort Rupert, Alert Bay, Gwa'yi (Kingcome village), and Tsadsisnukwomi (New Vancouver on Harbledown Island), while other communities such as Comox and Gwa'yasdams (Gilford village) have expanded and refurbished older bighouses. In the same period, more than 40 memorial poles and grave monuments have been erected. It is indeed a tribute to the commitment of present-day Kwakwaka'wakw and a strong reassurance of the future that these striking monuments have again come to dominate villagescapes.

Personal Experience among the Kwakwaka'wakw

In 1966, as a young representative of the British Columbia Provincial Museum, my own introduction to the 'Namgis village at Alert Bay was made easy because I was accompanied by the late Helen

Hunt, the wife of carver Henry Hunt and the confidant of Chief Mungo Martin, whom she served as an adviser and interpreter. The occasion of our visit was the dedication of a new traditional ceremonial house. Men and women who had known 'Dr Boas', and some of the children of his associate, George Hunt, participated in the event. We saw old men dance the *Hamatsa*; they had been trained as rigorously in their art as were those dancers described in the works published 70 years earlier by Boas and Hunt. Descendants of the singing woman who was 'burned' in the fire (as described earlier) were present and remembered the event. At the same time, children from the nearby residential school were herded into the dance house to witness events that were almost as unfamiliar to them as they were to their non-Native teachers.

During that first visit to Alert Bay, Mrs Hunt not only introduced me to the potlatch but also quite literally introduced me into the community. She found a place for me to stay and presented me to people. This was, however, merely a particular instance of her self-appointed task of teaching me, formally trained in anthropology and museology, how to be a real ethnologist.

When Mrs Hunt introduced me to the host and sponsor of the potlatch, I asked for permission to photograph the event. He not only granted the request but also asked if I would tape record it. From this significantly collaborative beginning, the Royal British Columbia Museum now has an inventory of 100 or so contemporary potlatches, from 1966 to the present, recorded on film and tape and accompanied by detailed notes. This is an invaluable scientific and artistic collection, accessible to outsiders with the permission of the hosts of the potlatches. It has also served as the means by which the museum has been able to train young Kwakwaka'wakw in the techniques of recording and analyzing cultural events, a practice that has assumed greater importance as the people have taken on the task of cultural education in their own community and to the larger outside community.

In the early days, I was frequently challenged by young Kwakwaka'wakw men and women about my intentions; many thought that I was foolish to waste my time with old people and irrelevant lifeways. But as time passed, the reality, validity, and significance of displaying one's mythic origins from a magic past and the logic of confirming this history through an attendant potlatch were recognized by that younger generation. Perhaps one of my most treasured experiences came while I was cruising through Blackfish Sound on a modern seine boat owned by a successful Kwakwaka'wakw fisherman. 'You know', he said, 'when I first met you, I thought your interest in the Old People was irrelevant, and I thought they were foolish to spend so much time and effort in their old age to get money and gifts together to give away. But now that I have given a potlatch, I can say that I felt much better giving away $10,000 than ever I would have if I took that money and spent it on myself. The Old People are right.'

Conclusion

For millennia, the Kwakwaka'wakw lived in close harmony with the seasons, travelling throughout the year to make use of the resources of land and sea by means of a well-developed technology and hard labour. Their rich material culture was based on wood, primarily cedar, and their main food source was salmon. Their complex social organization, ranking system, and ceremonial dance rituals, together with every other aspect of their culture, centred on the potlatch, which involved a payment of goods and food to assembled guests who were gathered to witness a host's claim to ancestral rights and hereditary position. After Europeans and Americans began arriving in their territory, the Kwakwaka'wakw slowly lost control to colonial administrators, but even when the potlatch was outlawed, they continued to keep their culture alive in secret.

Certainly, the glorious past can never be regained, but the Kwakwaka'wakw are working hard to see that their culture continues. The

BOX 25.2

A Heritage of Life on the Sea

The traditional economy of the Kwakwaka'wakw was based on the bountiful resources of the ocean. In Kwakwaka'wakw territory the sea predominates, and on a winter's day it merges in a grey continuum to include forest and sky. Until early in the twentieth century, great, buoyant, seaworthy cedar canoes were the means of transport through the myriad waterways between Vancouver Island and the mainland. By about 1910 fish boats, powered by gas engines, were replacing the ancient craft, though a few large canoes survived. In 1939 a crew paddled a canoe 18 metres in length from Alert Bay to Vancouver, a distance of about 300 kilometres. After that, knowledge of canoe-building was lost until about 1985, when the established totem-pole carvers began to address the challenge. Within a decade, many canoes were built and long journeys were undertaken: from Waglisla (Bella Bella) to Vancouver, Waglisla to Seattle, Prince Rupert to Vancouver, and Owikeeno to Victoria.

At the turn of the century, many Kwakwaka'wakw combined their sea-going heritage with new economic realities by establishing themselves as successful commercial fishermen. The late Chief Harry Assu of Cape Mudge once told me that his father, Billy, landed 400,000 salmon over a four-month season in 1921.

Since then, ocean resources have diminished dramatically. In the early 1990s the Kwakwaka'wakw fishing fleet, which was the mainstay of their communities, numbered dozens of seine boats, gill netters, and trollers. There was also a food fishery that supplied the five species of salmon in quantities sufficient to last each family for a year. In the fishing season of 2000, the entire seine fleet was allowed only one 24-hour opening for the Fraser River sockeye run, yielding insufficient revenue to cover the costly upkeep of a commercial boat.

Contemporary Kwakwaka'wakw feel that, despite the benefit of generations of intimate knowledge of the salmon's life cycle, their experience and advice are largely being dismissed by authorities. Ownership and management of traditional resources remain unresolved because, with one exception, modern-day treaties with BC First Nations have not been signed. The present situation does not bode well for the future of the fishing industry on the Pacific coast.

U'mista Cultural Centre in Alert Bay has published 12 language books with accompanying audio tapes to help Kwak'wala survive. Through language and cultural programs run by them in their own cultural centres and in public and alternative schools, today's young Kwakwaka'wakw are being offered an insight into a world that was in many ways denied their parents and grandparents. A privileged few of us can capture some sense of what it was like through discussions with the Old People who are still living and who remember those times. The sensitive reader can discover in printed passages some of the power of the oratory and the richness of the language, and some of the ingenious technical and artistic accomplishments of the Kwakwaka'wakw.

Like all First Nations in BC, the Kwakwaka'wakw face many political, economic, and social issues in their dealings with all levels of government. High on the agenda are land claims, ownership and management of traditional resources (particularly forestry and fishing), and dealing with the legacy of abuse of residential schools. It is a tribute to the tenacity and spirit of the Kwakwaka'wakw that they were able to retain the potlatch that is so central to their culture and are working to preserve their language and art. Whether they can regain control of the resources that sustained them for millennia is another matter.

References and Recommended Readings

Assu, Harry. 1989. *Assu of Cape Mudge: Recollections of a Coastal Indian Chief*. Vancouver: University of British Columbia Press.

Barnett, H.G. 1938. 'The Nature of the Potlatch', *American Anthropologist* 40: 349–58. This short article remains one of the most simply yet clearly stated definitions of the potlatch.

Boas, Franz. 1897. *The Social Organization and Secret Societies of the Kwakiutl Indians*. United States National Museum Report for 1895, Washington. Boas's first major descriptive work on Kwakwaka'wakw society, the potlatch, and ceremonial dances. Many masks are illustrated and their use briefly described.

———. 1909. *The Kwakiutl of Vancouver Island*. Memoir of the American Museum of Natural History No. 8. New York. A comprehensive description of Kwakwaka'wakw technology and industries such as weaving and woodworking.

———. 1966. *Kwakiutl Ethnography*, ed. Helen Codere. Chicago: University of Chicago Press. Boas's most comprehensive statement on the Kwakwaka'wakw, incorporating an incomplete manuscript and selections from published works, arranged and edited by one of Boas's foremost students.

Codere, Helen. 1950. *Fighting with Property*. Monograph of the American Ethnological Society. New York.

Curtis, E.S. 1915. *The Kwakiutl. The North American Indians*, vol. 10. Norwood, Conn. A well-organized work on the Kwakwaka'wakw, including comprehensive descriptions of various winter ceremonies and their mythological bases.

Ford, C.S. 1941. *Smoke From Their Fires: The Life of a Kwakiutl Chief*. New Haven: Yale University Press. An amusing, insightful biography of Kwakwaka'wakw Chief Charles Nowell, whose life spanned two eras and two cultures.

Hawthorn, Audrey. 1979. *Kwakiutl Art*. Vancouver: Douglas & McIntyre. This profusely illustrated work features ceremonial items.

Holm, Bill. 1983. *Smoky Top: The Art and Times of Willie Seaweed*. Vancouver: Douglas & McIntyre. The personal artistic style of the greatest twentieth-century Kwakwaka'wakw artist is analyzed, with insightful views into his role as singer, dancer, and leader at winter ceremonies and potlatches.

Jacknis, Ira. 2002. *The Storage Box of Tradition: Kwakiutl Art, Anthropologists, and Museums, 1881–1981*. Washington: Smithsonian Institution. The role of anthropologists and museums in the acquisition, interpretation, exhibition, and promotion of Kwakwaka'wakw art and material culture from 1881 to 1981 is studied comprehensively.

Jonaitis, Aldona. 1991. *Chiefly Feasts: The Enduring Kwakiutl Potlatch*. Vancouver: Douglas & McIntyre. A richly illustrated catalogue of seminal exhibits from the American Museum of Natural History collection. It includes essays on potlatch and museum issues by Gloria Cranmer Webster, Wayne Suttles, Ira Jacknis, Aldona Jonaitis, and Douglas Cole.

Joseph, Robert. 'Behind the Mask', in Peter Macnair, Robert Joseph, and Bruce Grenville, eds, *Down From the Shimmering Sky: Masks of the Northwest Coast*. Vancouver: Douglas & McIntyre. Chief Joseph writes eloquently about his childhood and adult experiences as a masked dancer.

Macnair, Peter L., Alan Hoover, and Kevin Neary. 1980. *The Legacy: Continuing Traditions of Northwest Coast Indian Art*. Victoria: British Columbia Provincial Museum. Reprint, Vancouver: Douglas & McIntyre. An introduction to the art and material culture of Northwest Coast First Nations.

Spradley, James P. 1969. *Guests Never Leave Hungry: The Autobiography of James Sewid, a Kwakiutl Indian*. Seattle: University of Washington Press.

Suttles, Wayne. 1990. 'Introduction to Northwest Coast', in Wayne Suttles, ed., *Handbook of North American Indians*, vol. 7, *Northwest Coast*. Washington: Smithsonian Institution.

Suggested Web Sites

U'mista News:
www.schoolnet.ca/aboriginal/umistweb/index-e.html
Source of current, culturally relevant stories, with links to other activities of the U'mista Cultural Society.

Royal British Columbia Museum: www.rbcm.gov.bc.ca
A major repository of artifacts, totem poles, photographs, and assorted other sources of information on both traditional and contemporary regional Aboriginal life.

PART IX

Conclusion

CHAPTER 26

Taking Stock:
Legacies and Prospects

C. RODERICK WILSON and R. BRUCE MORRISON

In the early twenty-first century, what can be said about the place of Inuit, Metis, and First Nations people? In answering the question, we will briefly review where we have been, consider the contours of current life, and give some thought to what lies ahead.

In the early decades of the last century it was generally believed that Native people were dying, both literally and culturally. In earlier centuries disease had swept through most populations on the continent, laying waste whole communities. By 1900 the worst killers, particularly smallpox, were abating, but Native populations generally continued to decline through the 1920s. In both Canada and the United States the so-called Indian wars were over. Indians and Metis, defeated militarily, seemed literally to be at 'the end of the trail', as a popular painting of the period expressed it.

Reserves were established across southern Canada, and, under the authority of the Indian Act, agents decided which Natives were Indians and controlled where Indians could live and travel, what crops they could plant, to whom they could sell their produce, whether or not they could butcher their own animals for their own consumption, and a myriad of other details of daily life. The Act explicitly prohibited various activities, such as alcohol consumption and voting, taken for granted by ordinary Canadians. It also outlawed participation in ceremonies that were central to many Indians—the Sun Dance of the Plains and the potlatch of the Northwest Coast. This is analogous to passing a Catholic Act to regulate the lives of Canadian Catholics that prohibits them from attending Mass, or passing a Baptist Act banning baptism.

To put it simply, Indians were now administered as a colonized people. The common assumption was that those who managed to survive physically would in time become members of Canadian society virtually indistinguishable from others. To that end the Act provided that any Indians acquiring an education, economic independence, or a non-Indian husband would automatically cease to be Indian. They obviously now had the means to participate in society as Canadians and, it was assumed, had already become separated from their natal communities.

The Metis, whether Red River Metis or simply Natives who for one reason or another did not have legal status as Indians, were generally left to whatever fate they might find. Various schemes designed to extinguish any Aboriginal claim were introduced; these usually took the form of scrip entitling the bearer to land. Many Metis did not receive scrip, and most who did were not in a position to take advantage of its potential (for a number of cultural, technological, and economic reasons). As a result, most Metis have had no special status; legally, many were seen as squatters on Crown land. Until the Constitution Act was passed in 1982, Alberta was the exception, having passed in 1938 a Metis Betterment Act establishing 'colonies' on the model of the federal reserves. Although the Act provides a significant opportunity for some Alberta Metis to find land that is legally secure, this protection entails a substantial loss of local control and subjection to an external bureaucratic structure. Other provinces also have developed programs specifically to alleviate social problems associated with the Metis. On the one hand, these programs are mute testimony to the unrealistic nature of the federal government's assumptions about the circumstances under which it considers itself to have fulfilled its obligations to Canadian Natives. On the other hand, the provincial agencies administering these programs tend to put their clients into a limited version of the same kind of dependent, controlled status as the federal government has historically placed status Indians.

Although the Inuit have a long history of contact with outsiders, the harshness of their environment and the lack of resources that would bring significant numbers of Euro-Canadians to the Arctic have until very recently inhibited the development of a colonial administration. That changed in the early 1950s as the government felt it necessary for national security purposes to create a northern presence and because, on humanitarian grounds, it felt obligated to provide educational and health services. In the late 1950s the trend further accelerated when for many Inuit both the caribou and the fish failed and people starved. One consequence of increased services was an increased governmental presence that is colonial in character. The nature of this colonialism is illustrated by an event: in late 1984, as Inuit heard of widespread famine in Ethiopia, they responded with great generosity—famine and sharing are things they know about. The town of Spence Bay, in addition to money collected from individuals, sent the entire surplus from the town budget, some $48,000. Their gift was disallowed on the grounds that all expenditures by the town in excess of $200 need government approval. One of the ironies of this case is that by then the centre of colonial control for northern settlements was no longer Ottawa but Yellowknife.

As each chapter has indicated, however, Canada's Aboriginal peoples have, by and large, survived their colonial experiences. Admittedly, there have been substantial losses, both demographic and cultural, but Canadian Native societies have demonstrated the capacity and will to make major accommodative changes to their new circumstances, to attempt to change some of those circumstances, and to maintain their separate identities. Given the desperate conditions of many of these societies 100 or even 50 years ago and the strength of the social forces working for their assimilation, their continued presence as functioning societies is a considerable feat.

Some 'Hard' Data

How many Natives have survived a century or more of colonialism and what are their characteristics? Let us start by making a few demographic generalizations, based on the 2001 census. First, they are a young population; the median age is 24.7 years (as opposed to 37.7 for the general population). Another way of saying the same thing is that they are growing rapidly, with a birth rate about 1.5 times the national average (although a few decades ago it was four times the average). Only 4 per cent are seniors (65 or older) compared to 13 per cent in the general population.

Second, they are disproportionately a northern and rural population. Aboriginal people constitute 85 per cent of the population in Nunavut, 51 per cent in the Northwest Territories, 23 per cent in Yukon Territory, 14 per cent in Saskatchewan and Manitoba, around 5 per cent in Alberta and BC, and less than 2 per cent in Ontario and those provinces to the east. But at the same time, Ontario has more Aboriginal people than any other province or territory. Perhaps we should rephrase the first sentence of this paragraph: Aboriginal people still are spread more evenly across the whole country than is the general population.

Table 26.1. Urban Aboriginal Populations, 2001

City	Number	Percentage of Population
Winnipeg	55,755	8.4
Edmonton	40,930	4.4
Vancouver	36,860	1.9
Calgary	21,915	2.3
Toronto	20,300	0.4
Saskatoon	20,275	9.1
Regina	15,685	8.3
Ottawa-Hull	13,485	1.3
Prince Albert	11,640	29.2
Montreal	11,085	0.3

Source: Statistics Canada (2003).

Third, they are a surprisingly urban population: 49 per cent live in areas loosely defined as urban, while 25 per cent live in 10 metropolitan areas. Table 26.1 indicates the 10 largest urban concentrations of Aboriginal peoples. At the same time, urbanization among indigenous people is to a surprising extent a western phenomenon. The numbers of Aboriginal people in Toronto, Ottawa, and Montreal are far lower than one might expect, given their prominence nationally. Prince Albert and Montreal have roughly the same number of Aboriginal inhabitants—but Montreal is 100 times as large! It is clearly a far different thing to be one of 11,000 Natives in Montreal than to be one in Prince Albert. The sense of community and the distance physically and socially from one's home community are likely to be very different. In addition, status Indians moving to the city are moving into an administrative limbo: the federal government has historically seen its responsibility as having to do with reserves, while provincial and municipal governments have tended to see the federal government as being entirely responsible for all Native people. Only belatedly is this problem being specifically addressed by all three levels of government.

Now, let us look at some more specifics. According to Indian and Northern Affairs Canada (INAC—formerly and sometimes still known as the Department of Indian Affairs and Northern Development [DIAND]), as of 2001 there were 690,101 Indians in Canada. This apparently straightforward statistic, however, becomes amazingly complicated upon scrutiny. Like other statistics published by Indian Affairs, it refers only to those registered as Indians by the federal government—status Indians and Inuit. This population of 'Indians' may vary significantly, both in total numbers and in other ways, from populations defined by other criteria. In the Canadian census, for instance, people are allowed to self-designate themselves with regard to ethnicity. In 2001 Statistics Canada came up with 558,175 registered Indians. In the 1991 and 1981 censuses, the INAC and Statistics Canada numbers varied by 10 and 13 per cent, but in different directions! With regard to its 1996 figures, Statistics Canada noted that they were low because 77 Indian reserves and communities had 'incomplete enumerations'. While the INAC count is based on precise criteria as to who exactly is legally an Indian, and that is a question of importance, the point is that there are other legitimate terms in which one can phrase the question of who is an Indian.

The term 'non-status Indian' designates individuals who may think of themselves as Indian and so be regarded by others, but who are excluded from government lists. In government statistics they are usually lumped together with Metis people, both being 'unofficial' Indians (at one time both groups frequently were referred to as 'half-breeds'; this may or may not have been appropriate in particular instances). In the 2001 census, some 292,000 Canadians designated themselves as Metis, up significantly from 204,000 people in 1996, 135,000 in 1991, and 98,000 in 1981. A 43 per cent increase in five years is far beyond any natural increase (the non-Aboriginal population of Canada grew by 3.4 per cent in the same period). Clearly, a far higher percentage of the population who could claim Metis status are now doing so. This is nevertheless a very low number that probably indicates more about the unsatisfactory nature of the census question or about the current usefulness of the term than about how many people it could properly be applied to. By way of contrast, note that the Metis and Non-status Indian Association in the single province of Ontario 20 years ago claimed a membership of over 200,000. Depending on the criteria employed, estimates of the non-status and Metis population for the country as a whole range from a low of some 400,000 to over two million. The largest Metis populations are found in Alberta, Manitoba, and Ontario.

The Inuit have been administered, and counted, separately from Indians. Because their bureaucratic history has been briefer and less subject to efforts to exclude community members from official lists, there is less disagreement about how many there are. INAC counted 55,700 in 2001, up from 36,215 in 1991 and 25,370 in 1981. This contrasts with Statistics Canada's list of 45,070 in 2001.

The federal government has kept count only of status Indians and Inuit. The Constitution recognizes Indians (undefined), Inuit, and Metis as Aboriginal people. Accordingly, we can only state that they number somewhere between one and three million.

As Table 26.2 indicates, Ontario has the largest status Indian population in the country, followed by British Columbia. One thing the table does not show is what proportion of the provincial population is Indian. For Ontario and all provinces to the east, the proportion is low, at about 1 per cent. The proportion in BC and Alberta is higher, at around 3 per cent, and higher yet in Saskatchewan and Manitoba, at about 10 per cent. It is highest in the North as a whole, at about 25 per cent. As noted earlier, if we were to look at the proportion of Aboriginal people instead of registered Indians, the relationships remain roughly constant, but the numbers change and the contrasts heighten.

BC stands out for its high number of bands. Yukon (at 484 people per band) has the smallest average band size, followed by the NWT at 584. BC has the smallest average band size of any province (667) and Alberta (at 1,993) has the largest. While the NWT and Yukon have the fewest people living 'off-reserve', they also have few people actually living on reserves because few were ever established (which brings to notice the non-comparability of many statistics). While the category 'off-reserve' is not quite the same as urban, the statistics in this column are indicative of the extensive and ongoing urbanization of Canada's Indian population. The national average of 43 per cent living off-reserve is up dramatically from 29 per cent two decades ago. Even the NWT, at 29 per cent living off-reserve being the least urban region, exhibits a major shift from its 7 per cent figure of two decades ago.

A somewhat different perspective on residential patterns is provided by another set of INAC statistics involving the characterization of

Table 26.2. Status Indian Residence by Region, 2001

Region or Prov.	Number of Bands	Population (% of Nat.)	On-Reserve (% of Prov.)	Crown Land (% of Prov.)	Off-Reserve (% of Prov.)
Atlantic	31	26,991 (3.9%)	17,390 (64.4%)	22 (0.1%)	9,579 (35.5%)
Quebec	39	64,404 (9.3%)	43,569 (67.6%)	1,288 (2.0%)	19,547 30.4%)
Ontario	126	157,062 (22.7%)	78,170 (49.8%)	1,500 (1.0%)	77,392 (49.3%)
Manitoba	62	109,788 (15.9%)	69,960 (63.7%)	1,729 (1.6%)	40,099 (36.5%)
Sask.	70	108,801 (15.8%)	53,501 (49.2%)	1,839 (1.7%)	53,461 (49.1%)
Alberta	44	87,703 (12.7%)	55,361 (63.1%)	2,685 (3.1%)	29,657 (33.8%)
BC	198	112,305 (16.3%)	56,455 (41.4%)	440 (0.4%)	55,410 (49.3%)
Yukon	16	7,751 (1.1%)	476 (6.1%)	3,432 (44.3%)	3,843 (49.6%)
NWT	26	15,296 (2.2%)	239 (1.6%)	10,632 (69.5%)	4,425 (28.9%)
Canada	612	690,101	373,121 (54.1%)	23,567 (3.4%)	293,413 (42.5%)

Source: INAC (2002).

communities as urban, rural, remote, or 'special access'. Using these criteria, the Atlantic region, Alberta, and Saskatchewan have their status Indian populations most concentrated in urban and rural areas (at over 90 per cent), while the most remote is Manitoba (at almost 50 per cent), followed by Yukon and NWT.

As noted above, Canada's Native population is younger than the non-Native population and is growing at a faster rate. Among the general population, 19 per cent are under 15 years old; the corresponding figure for Aboriginals is 33 per cent. Such differences have consequences. The present Indian population (and that of Aboriginals generally) is characterized by an unusually large number of young, economically dependent people. This has created a high demand for educational and social services. In the coming decades, however, as this group matures, they will generate new demands for employment opportunities, frequently in regions now having few jobs. A second consequence is more internal to the Indian community. What kinds of pressures for change are created by a situation in which, quite suddenly, the majority of the population is very young but very few are elderly?

While a population that is growing instead of dying suggests a social turnaround of more than simply demographic consequence, it does not mean that all is well for Canadian Indians.

Although mortality rates continue to drop, they are still high; for people under 45 they are typically three times the national average. The death rate for children under one year of age declined dramatically in recent decades, but it is still twice the national average. Violent deaths generally are three times the national average and among the young may be 10 times the national rate. Suicides among young Indian adults are very high; for those aged 15–24 the rate is six times the national average. Conversely, middle-aged and elderly Indians have suicide rates close to or below those of the general population. Further, non-Indians are about three times more likely to die from cancer or diseases of the circulatory system than are Indians. Indians are thus at higher risk in many, but not all, categories of mortality.

The most clearly disproportionate statistics involve incarceration in provincial prisons (which involve sentences of less than two years). In 1996 Natives constituted 2.7 per cent of Canadians, but 16 per cent of those in provincial custody. The Prairie provinces had the most disproportionate numbers: in Manitoba, where 8 per cent of the population is Native, 61 per cent of the prison population was Native; in Saskatchewan the numbers were 8 per cent and 76 per cent; in Alberta they were 4 per cent and 34 per cent.

Such statistics could be cited almost endlessly, but it is necessary to ask questions about what they mean. Usually they are presented much as they have been here, with an explicit contrast between Indian and non-Indian. It seems obvious that Indians are in most respects severely disadvantaged in comparison to other Canadians. Unfortunately, the data frequently do not allow for meaningful comparison, because in critical ways the populations being compared are so different. To take a specific example where there has been little change in recent decades: nationally there are about four deaths by fire per 100,000 people each year, while the corresponding figure for Indians is about 30. What weight, however, should be given the fact that most Indian communities are in rural or remote regions? As noted above, in some regions of the country a very large number of Natives live in areas of difficult access. Would the incidence of death by fire in correspondingly remote non-Native communities be any lower? Perhaps, but we do not know, so we are left comparing apples and oranges. Thus, although the data do not really provide a sound basis for social action, agencies must act on the available information. While presumably no one argues that there should be a fire hydrant next to each trapper's cabin, the argument is frequently made that all Canadians should have the same level of social services. This noble ideal, ostensibly redressing apparently scandalous social inequity, fails to take account of the diverse real-world conditions in which people live and often becomes a rationale either for moving Indians to places where there are fire hydrants or for bringing urban amenities, through industrial development, to rural and remote people. Neither solution is necessarily beneficial. That is, 'comparative' statistics can buttress arguments for providing services that Native communities desire, or they can be used to justify programs that would undercut their social or economic foundations (note the chapters by Asch and Feit for recent examples). In other words, the attempt to create equal living conditions for Indians, buttressed by non-comparable data, confuses general equality with specific identity and results in socially undesirable consequences.

There are other interpretive problems. Hospitalization rates for tuberculosis among Indians and Inuit have recently been two and three times the national average. Does this result from lack of reasonable health care? How relevant are the isolated living conditions of many of these people? What of the general antipathy towards treatment that isolates the victim from family, community, and even treatment that is culturally relevant? How significant is the Aboriginal genetic predisposition to tuberculosis? In spite of the high current rate, perhaps the situation overall is better viewed as a prime example of something the government has done right: the Inuit rate of tuberculosis infection is only about 8 per cent of what it was 40 years ago, and the Indian rate is less than 20 per cent of what it was 40 years ago.

Indians are much less likely than other Canadians to have a legally sanctioned marriage. This in some part reflects the failure of the government to recognize traditional forms of marriage. More importantly, it indicates the impact of legislation on choices about legal marriage. Unmarried mothers receive much higher welfare payments than do separated or divorced mothers. Until 1985 the Indian Act, section 12(1)b, stripped Indian status from women, and from the children of women, who married men who were not legally Indian. For decades many Indian women found it not in their interest to be formally married. This may well have implications for family stability and social attitudes, but the statistics cannot reasonably be interpreted simply as they might be for non-Indian populations.

As a last example, consider that although the 'sixties scoop' of Native children by social services workers is long over, there are still five times as many Indian children as non-Indian in the 'care' of the government. While the Indian population has almost doubled in the last 25 years, the percentage of Indian children being taken into care has also doubled. In the same period, the number of adoptions of Indian children has grown by a factor of five, while the proportion being adopted by non-Indians has grown from about 50 per cent to about 80 per cent; put another way, eight times as many Indian children are now lost to the Indian community as formerly. This has been explained largely on the basis that these children are now living in better material and social conditions. That claim would of course be difficult to substantiate in many cases, but even if it were true, would the pattern be justified? By what standards does one judge—is the number of toilets per household an appropriate measure? Does a *community* have a right to its children even where parental care undeniably has broken down?

Finally, to return to an earlier point, however inadequately the INAC statistics indicate conditions for Aboriginal people generally, and however misleading they may be when interpreted out of their cultural and social context, the fact that these statistics have been generated about one segment only of the Canadian population, in order to facilitate their administration, is in itself a dramatic statement about the nature of the relationship.

Renewal

Optimism is increasing in many Native communities today. That is not to say that all is well. Even the average non-Indian is aware of at least some aspects of the negative statistical profile as it is generally presented: inadequate housing, over-representation in prisons, high mortality rates, etc. Nevertheless, the negative picture is much less than the whole story. The main story has to do with the renewed vitality of Native society.

The reader will remember that reference has been made from time to time throughout this book to the impact of images and ideas on our thinking. A dominant image in Canadian thinking is that Native people are best considered as part of the past: their social structures and economies are antiquated; they may have a legitimate or even honoured place in history, but their traditions are a hindrance to them and the country; that they might have a viable future as Natives is almost unthinkable. This pervasive stereotype, when reinforced by the generally held negative statistical profile of contemporary Native people, has profoundly damaging consequences. These negative effects may be seen at work in the general population, in school textbooks, among planners, and at times among Native peoples themselves.

To counter the notion that Native society is moribund, we have two observations. Several chapters, particularly those dealing with people living in more remote parts of the country, have demonstrated that changes in the lifeways of Indian peoples have been substantially less than has commonly been supposed. A second observation is that, although traditional behaviours may have been substantially modified, there are important continuities in meaning, purpose, and function—that is, although social behaviour has changed, the cultural rules generating behaviour have not. Our assessment of these findings is that the Native community, even in those areas where there is less continuity with the past, is experiencing renewal.

Renewal, as used here, takes many forms and includes all aspects of life—economic, social, political, educational, and religious. Most of all, it has to do with identity. For increasing numbers of Canada's Aboriginal people, to be Native (whether Inuit, Metis, or Indian) is to have pride, in the sense of self-esteem. One of the most important areas of Native renewal is growing success in controlling alcohol abuse. This combats the dominance of the image of the drunken Indian in Euro-Canadian society. More importantly, it is a fact that largely through their own efforts this major social problem is being controlled. The point is best made by reviewing some specific cases.

Alkali Lake in central BC is home to about 400 people. Some 25 years ago the chief and his wife felt almost alone in being sober and were desperate to do something to alleviate the terrible problems they saw associated with drinking. They had no particular expertise or resources. Starting with one person, a band councillor in whom they saw potential, they worked on him, even to the extent of following him into the bar and just sitting there as he drank. In time he responded to their intensive attention (shaming is a powerful traditional technique of inducing socially approved behaviour), and they turned to others. After four years they had recruited only a handful of non-drinkers, but it was a start. The chief learned to exert other kinds of pressure, also. People who committed alcohol-related offences on the reserve were presented with the options of choosing to enter treatment or of being dealt with by the law. He learned that bootleggers could be charged under the Indian Act, and went himself with the RCMP to collect evidence to convict the five bootleggers on the reserve, one of whom was his mother. Minimal fines were levied, but the point was clear that he

meant business and that subsequent charges would be made under the Criminal Code. Welfare and family allowance checks were converted into groceries and clothing before people could drink them. As these efforts took hold, other areas of life changed. A number of families pooled their resources to start a grocery store. Several families pooled their funds to buy a house in town for their high school students to use. A piggery and a co-operative farm were started. Seeing the positive changes, DIAND provided funds to start a sawmill. In short, the entire social and economic fabric of the community was revitalized. Although at this point in time the economic aspects of the case described, written in 1985, seem overly optimistic due to the cessation of short-term DIAND funding, this does nothing to diminish the almost miraculous social transformation that was accomplished. Nor does it diminish the continuing impact that the 'Alkali Lake story' has had on other Native communities seeking to find sobriety.

An urban community in Ontario suffered economic hardship as local industries closed. Many turned to alcohol; suicide attempts rose to an astronomical 17 per month. In this instance, there were trained personnel at a treatment centre for alcohol abuse, but they lacked sufficient staff to provide services to the community at large or to address directly the high suicide rate. The centre workers were able, however, to mobilize the community to draw on its own resources to effect a major turnaround, primarily through forming numerous small groups to provide mutual social support.

On a more formal level, the groundbreaking work of the Nechi Institute at Edmonton is noteworthy. They created a new model for addictions counselling and treatment in the 1970s. It was one of the first formally constituted programs of its kind to be conceived and operated by Native people. The central purpose of the Institute was to train addictions counsellors, but the diverse group of people who participated in the program during the early years began working in many other fields, especially health care, education,

BOX 26.1

Wally Awasis:
Adaptation and Transformation in Vancouver

In 1985, addicted to alcohol and drugs on Vancouver's Skid Row, a 27-year-old Plains Cree residential school survivor made a desperate decision. Wallace James Awasis (originally from Thunderchild, Saskatchewan) voluntarily had himself committed to the Round Lake Treatment Centre near Vernon, BC. There, Elders such as Alden Pompana (Lakota) introduced Wally to Plains-style ways: drumming and singing, sweat lodge, powwow, and Sun Dance. They taught him that 'culture is healing'. An Aboriginal person can be healed (emotionally, spiritually, psychologically, and perhaps even physically) using the values, pride, ceremonies, rituals, and knowledge inherent in Aboriginal cultures. A person can be whole, strong, and free from addictions and suffering (the legacy of colonialism) by what anthropologist Anthony Wallace termed 'revitalization' and Onondaga scholar David R. Newhouse describes as 're-traditionalization'. Wally speaks about it as 'getting back our pride, our identity, and our self-esteem'. He tells urban Indians, 'You don't have to lose your culture just because Mother Earth is buried under concrete.'

When Wally returned from Round Lake in 1985, he could not find a way or a place in Vancouver to maintain his sobriety and his commitment to Native spirituality. Courageously, with three of his brothers (who were also in recovery), he formed the Arrows To Freedom drum group as a vehicle for cultural and spiritual healing. Over the years, Wally, Kenny, Dale, and Duncan Awasis, together or individually, established not only the ATF drum group, but a myriad of related ceremonials (such as sweat lodges), events (such as powwows and Native Family Nights), cultural programs and workshops (through school boards, friendship centres, and other outlets), and alcohol and drug treatment programs (such as their Alcoholics Anonymous-based 'Red Road Warriors Support Group'). The work of this family has been seminal, and has completely altered the Aboriginal subculture of Vancouver by giving members of the many Native nations residing there Plains-style options to hope and empowerment—adaptive strategies for survival, recovery, and renewal in an intertribal urban environment.

Today, Duncan and Dale continue their healing work on the Prairies. Kenny drums and sings with his own drum group, Thunderchild, and organizes cultural events all over the Lower Mainland of BC. In 1999, Wally incorporated ATF as the Arrows To Freedom Cultural Healing Society. He continues to teach that 'You can succeed in modern-day society as a Native person. You don't *have* to lose your identity. You still can be proud of who you are and live in the whiteman's culture, side by side with your own culture, and you can blend them together and take the good from the both.' As well as his cultural work, Wally is also completing a degree in the Native Indian Teacher Education Program at UBC. As he has often told me, 'I got ahold of both worlds.'

—Lindy-Lou Flynn. Ph.D. candidate, Department of Anthropology, University of Alberta

social work, and business development. Nechi's mission, although always focused on addictions counselling, quickly involved a broad range of community development activities. This broad range reflects Nechi's ideal of basing its work on traditional values and traditional knowledge. That is, the holistic perspective Nechi adopted saw addictions as symptoms of a much larger

FIGURE 26.1. Wally, Raven, and Thunder Eagle Awasis take the Arrows To Freedom drum into Carnegie Hall at Hastings and Main, the heart of Skid Row in the Downtown Eastside of Vancouver. ATF established Native Family Night here in 1986. 'The Carnegie' is an alcohol- and drug-free community centre for people of this most destitute urban neighbourhood in Canada. In the words of Kenny Awasis, 'This is where the people needed it the most . . . so that they could come in one day a week out their lives and share a little bit about these ways' of drumming, singing, dancing, and spirituality, to help them in their own recovery. (Courtesy Lindy-Lou Flynn)

picture. Nechi's work in developing formal training models based on Native traditional knowledge was a truly innovative idea in the 1970s. It is now part of the predominant treatment and intervention paradigm.

Conclusions to be drawn from these examples include: (1) although we can discuss alcoholism and its treatment as isolated matters, in the real world, for both the individual and the community, life demonstrates interconnectedness; (2) although Nechi and other organizations may work closely with non-Native organizations such as Alcoholics Anonymous, the active leadership of local Native people is imperative; (3) although professional expertise may be useful when available, it is probably more important that plans be locally devised and implemented; and (4) it may be that for many problems—particularly if they are chronic—technical answers are less important than social ones, for resolution will likely involve concepts such as respect, dignity, and control. To put these comments another way, the examples cited illustrate the attempts of Canadian Native people to create an appropriate Native milieu for themselves.

The reader will not be surprised to learn that there are also increasing numbers of Native-run businesses. So much is this the case that some of the major banks now have Native financial services divisions. There are also Native-owned trust companies. These moves represent explicit, self-interested decisions to invest resources in Native communities and Native people because they are recognized as having profit-generating potential. As a banker noted when the trend started, 'The thing that held native people back has been lack of capital and no structure for capital formation. . . . They're starting to hire the kind of talent that's necessary to do it. When you put together the people, resources, land and dollars, you get an explosive situation. I think this will be one of the big stories in finance and development' (O'Malley, 1980).

The Sawridge band near Slave Lake, Alberta, is a prime example of the trend. It opened the first Native-owned hotel in Canada in 1973. It

has since enlarged the hotel, opened another in Jasper, and built a shopping centre in Slave Lake. The band is fortunate in having modest oil revenues to initiate these ventures and also in having capable management. While traditional government development structures often discouraged responsible management, many contemporary leaders recognize it as a key to achieving their goals.

It is also clear that Native leaders recognize the importance of linkages between sectors: economic development is not solely economic in its purposes or effects. In Saskatchewan the Meadow Lake Tribal Council (MLTC) was created to pool the resources of nine reserves and to implement a broad range of development activities. They successfully took over a school system, partly to promote their long-range plans for developing local leadership. Their lumbering operation, NorSask, in 2001 continued to lead the industry in percentage return on assets, return on equity, and return on capital employed. From 20 years of transformative successes, MLTC has learned: (1) the road to prosperity is through healthy people leading healthy lives; (2) it is imperative to get the best advisers and technicians you can, and to listen to them; (3) petty differences must be put aside for the common good; and (4) corporate business growth is the vital ingredient in vibrant community development.

Where is this leading? Most recently it led to Nicaragua. Contigo International, MLTC's nongovernmental organization, is taking its integrated approach to economic and social development to the Miskito Indians of eastern Nicaragua. Based on their own experience, they will help them harvest 400,000 hectares of pine forest and develop specific projects for each of the 14 villages involved.

The contemporary projects we have mentioned contrast sharply with the historic past in which reserve economies usually had little impact on regional economies except as a raison d'être for government services. A good example of the new potential has occurred on the Huron reserve near

BOX 26.2

Iisaak

Iisaak. Among the Nuu-chah-nulth people of Vancouver Island, the word (pronounced E-sock) means 'respect'. These days it also refers to Iisaak Forest Resources, a forest services company jointly owned by the Nuu-chah-nulth (51 per cent) and Weyerhaeuser (49 per cent). The reference, of course, is to the philosophy of the company, rooted in traditional values. Another key concept is *hishuk-ish ts'awalk*, 'everything is one'. That is, the company seeks to respect the limits of what is extracted from the forest and the interconnectedness of all things.

Iisaak operates in the Clayoquot Sound area. In part it owes its existence to the massive civil disobedience that took place there in 1993, with the arrest of over 800 people for blockading logging operations. They were protesting the 'business as usual' clear-cut logging of one of the last stands of old-growth forest on the coast, in an area of exceptional natural beauty. As it happens, the protests were within an area the Nuu-chah-nulth First Nations had claimed as traditional territory in 1980. This claim had been accepted for negotiation by the federal government. Various attempts were made throughout the 1980s to reconcile the competing interests of Aboriginals, environmentalists, forest companies, governments, and local communities. The failure of these attempts led to the well-known blockade.

Eventually, in 1999 Iisaak was created as a partnership between the Nuu-chah-nulth and MacMillan Bloedel (later bought out by Weyerhaeuser). Later in the year agreements were also signed with an environmentalist consortium and then with a local association of displaced non-Native forest workers.

Iisaak manages a forest of some 88,000 hectares. It is obviously concerned with sustainability, but it also pursues collaborative approaches involving all local communities, value-added products, and the utilization of techniques fostering biodiversity, forest complexity, and quality of product. At the level of specifics, in 2000 Iisaak harvested some 22,000 cubic metres. The average size of an opening created by felling trees was only 0.2 hectares, no new roads were made, and 50 kilometres of old logging roads were deactivated.

Iisaak is very much still a project in progress, but the prospects are encouraging. Its forest was certified in 2001 by the Forest Stewardship Council, an international non-governmental certification body stressing 'best practices' policies and high conservation value forests. Later in the year it received the prestigious Gift to the Earth award from the World Wildlife Foundation. Iisaak not only is showing respect, it is receiving it.

Quebec City. Under the leadership of Chief Max Gros Louis, 14 businesses were organized. The band is now the largest employer in the area and sells its products to Canadian Tire, Eaton's, and foreign markets. When the companies were organized 52 families were on welfare. Now all able-bodied persons, as well as 125 Euro-Canadians, are employed.

Educational innovation was alluded to above in the context of economic change; it needs to be considered in its own right. One of the most significant changes of the past three decades is the growth of band-controlled schools and school systems. This is not an automatic panacea, but it has been of vital importance in restoring a sense of community and personal identity that goes far beyond learning the 'three R's'. That schools can teach both computer programming and traditional languages, that functionally monolingual students (and they still exist) learn to read French or English better if they are first literate in their own language, that children have the inherent right to appropriate role models in their schools: these are ideas that need to be accepted widely and to be pondered at length. The residential schools of the past may indeed not have been intentionally villainous, but we all, and especially Native people, are still paying for the psychological and social havoc they created.

That the number of Native students in the post-secondary educational systems has increased exponentially in recent years is in part an aspect of generalized Native renewal. That the growth is so impressive is also a function of the base being so low; in absolute terms the numbers are still small. That there are now some Native medical doctors in Canada is a matter of pride, but also of shame in that there are so few. Nevertheless, students in these and other programs are important. It is critical that Native communities have functioning in them educated people, including professionals (the current ratio of Native medical doctors to the total Native population in Canada is less than 1:30,000; for the general population it is about 1:500). It is also of importance to the national community that some of them enter mainstream Canadian society and be seen to be competent there.

There have always been Native intellectuals. There have been Native academics, including anthropologists, but their numbers have been few. One also needs to remember that some of the early Native anthropologists were not called that, but rather were referred to as informants. That, hopefully, has changed. Among the changes is the number of Native people, trained in anthropology and other disciplines, who are using that training to analyze productively aspects of their own situations. As anthropologists we find this especially exciting because, while there are difficulties in studying one's own society and culture (partly because one of the universal features of culture is the creation of generally accepted fictions), the insights of an insider are nevertheless frequently of a nature virtually inaccessible to an outsider.

The Canadian Journal of Native Education is a good source of some of this material, much of it done by graduate students.

We will in no way do it justice, but we must mention at this point not merely academic writing, important though it is, but writing of all sorts—life stories, poetry, plays, songs, novels, and an opera.

And now, in 2002, we have *Atananarjuat (The Fast Runner)*, medal winner at Cannes and at or near the top of everyone's list of the best film of the year—not the best Aboriginal film, but the best film. Natives have been experiencing a virtual explosion in the arts, and it has been going on for decades. In music the sales of tapes and CDs for powwow and other traditional forms, and for both cross-over and mainstream forms by groups that are explicitly Aboriginal and by people who seem only incidentally Aboriginal, are doing very well. And we can make similar observations for acting, painting, carving, dancing, and other arts, both within Aboriginal communities and across the nation and the world. It is all significant simply because it is there; Native people are expressing their joys and sorrows through the arts as do other people who have the resources.

It is risky to single out individuals, but sometimes it is useful. Tom Jackson is not the only Native in the entertainment industry whose name and face are instantly recognizable to most non-Native Canadians. That there are a growing number of other high-profile Aboriginal performers is significant. Also significant is Jackson's 'Huron Carol', an annual tour of musical artists that, among other things, has raised millions of dollars for food banks. In 1996 he went on to organize 'Dreamcatcher Tour', creatively addressing suicide and other social issues. Community responsibility and other traditional values are still alive.

A final point in this section is that economic development, operas, and alcohol treatment centres are important not only in their own right, and as examples of a general renewal, but are inextricably linked with renewal as a spiritual phenomenon. Anthropologists have analyzed the series of

Indian attempts early in the colonial era to regain control of their lives by religio-political means as a series of revitalization movements. The Longhouse religion of the Iroquois, the Ghost Dance of the Sioux, the Native American Church, and the Shakers of the west coast are historic examples still current. Recent movements are more diffuse, so we have spoken only of renewal, but there are linkages. North American Natives have consistently responded to crises essentially as spiritual problems, the specific workings out of which are related to a core of meaning.

Traditional religious forms have long been repressed in much of Canada, but they often merely went underground. Increasingly, the meaning of these forms is being rediscovered or more openly acknowledged. Some of the momentum is legislative (the 'Potlatch Law' was dropped in 1951; Elders may now conduct services in federal prisons), but the larger factor is a resurgent nativism. Traditional ceremonies such as the sweat, pipe, fast, and Sun Dance are now widely practised. It is important to note that this is not merely the repetition of something that the grandfathers did, but a revival or even a reinvention of living traditions. For many Native people it is also true that Christianity has become at least part of their spiritual identity.

Today, as in the past, activities that are primarily ceremonial are an important part of Native calendars. Possibly the best example is the former Ecumenical Conference at Morley, Alberta, annually drawing thousands of participants from across the continent. On a smaller scale, Native people attend personal or regional rites in growing numbers.

The outcomes of this renewed spiritual heritage are many. They include such diverse and related activities on the west coast as constructing longhouses, erecting totem poles, carving ceremonial regalia, making prints and paintings, taking potlatch names, and joining traditional societies. They include such varied 'political' acts as Chief Robert Smallboy leading his band into the wilderness to escape contamination by Euro-Canadian

society, the American Indian Movement occupying DIAND offices in the 1970s, and traditional chiefs lobbying the British House of Lords to prevent the patriation of the Canadian Constitution. They include economic acts as apparently separate as remote James Bay Cree hunters accepting as gift the lives of moose that give themselves to the hunters, and Metis architect Doug Cardinal successfully winning an international competition to design a new building for the National Museum of Civilization in Ottawa.

The formation of Canada constituted a massive, sustained shock to Aboriginal society. Contrary to Euro-Canadian expectations, Native people have survived. It is yet too early to say that they are everywhere flourishing, and they are still threatened, but the evidence of renewed vigour is there for those who will see it.

We noted that although the Indian and Inuit populations continue to experience rapid growth, it is the Metis population that has experienced the most explosive growth—43 per cent in five years. Most of that growth is not due to Metis children being born, but rather results from adults who formerly did not report themselves as Metis deciding to do so. In this connection we would note that the census also provides opportunity for people who do not identify themselves as Aboriginal to nevertheless declare themselves as having Aboriginal ancestry. Some 344,000 non-Aboriginal Canadians in 2001 chose to do so. We suggest that this is, at least in part, a sign that they think of being Aboriginal as a good thing. Native renewal is first of all a good thing for Native people. That it is good for the whole country is worth thinking about.

The Need for Structural Change

In spite of the positive signs of renewal in Canada's Native communities, for these developments to come to fruition there must be basic change in the structural arrangements whereby Aboriginal peoples are governed as part of Canadian society. The failures of the past and the present are not merely the result of such factors as inadequate health-care services, inappropriate textbooks, or restricted access to capital, important though these matters are. While failures of health, education, and economic growth must be addressed in their own right, and while it is important to be aware that Native people are experiencing some success in resolving these social problems, it is essential to recognize that the subordinate legal status of Native peoples will continue to manifest itself in various forms of social malaise if the status quo is maintained. To a greater or lesser extent Native problems are rooted in the fundamental fact of Canadian Native history and contemporary life, that is, they are subjugated peoples without control over the defining facts of their lives.

Native people are quite aware of their colonial status, although all might not put it in these terms. The various forms of renewal—artistic expression, religious rites, political activism, even Native businesses—have in common a strong sense of identity, in being Native as opposed to being Euro-Canadian. Hence, Native leaders have a long tradition of attempting to create conditions whereby Native communities can function as polities within Canada, or, in the current phrase, can achieve some form of self-government.

The facts of life on the reserves have changed considerably in recent decades, but the fundamental nature of the Indian–government relationship has changed not one whit. Indians have been granted the right to vote and to drink, agents no longer live on the reserves, and many bands have control over expenditures; many harsh and arbitrary features of the reserve system have been moderated. 'Consultation' and 'development' have become bywords of the new era. Unfortunately, it is still possible to argue that nothing has been altered: assimilation (first officially repudiated in 1946) remains the overall goal, and Ottawa, however benign its intentions and practices, retains ultimate power.

At the time of writing, Bill C-7, The First Nations Governance Act, is under consideration.

The minister, Robert Nault, describes it as 'the first time in Canadian history that First Nations people have had a direct voice in the development of legislative changes to the Indian Act . . . to shape legislation which would provide . . . more modern community law-making and . . . to design their own community codes on leadership selection, financial management, and accountability' (www.fng.gc.ca/fnga_e.asp).

There is much about Bill C-7 that is commendable. It provides opportunity for reserve communities not only to define much of the bureaucratic detail of their communities (things that Ottawa should never have been involved in) but to shape the form and substance of their governance. Nevertheless, across the country and at all levels, the bill is widely opposed.

The Indian Act was last rewritten in 1951. A number of the previous Act's most odious features were repealed at that time. Among other changes, the clause making the potlatch and Sun Dance illegal was dropped. While in a sense this was a victory for all Native people, it is more significant that the change was unilateral: there was no consultation, no apology, no compensation, and no return of confiscated property. The changes were made and Indian people found out about the changes after the fact, just like the rest of us.

Indian Affairs was reorganized in 1964 to provide increased responsibility to personnel working at the community level. Much the same impetus that gave rise to this reorganization led to the commissioning of a landmark investigation by anthropologists to analyze data collected nationally on the educational, social, and economic conditions of Indians and on this basis to make policy recommendations. Commonly called the Hawthorn Report, its release in 1966–7 touched the national consciousness with its detailed inventory of the disadvantaged conditions of most Indians. Amid promises from Ottawa of increased consultation, the reserves were almost flooded with community and economic development workers. Two facts are relevant: (1) government action to correct long-standing problems resulted from studies by non-Indian academics, not as a result of the needs themselves or of the petitions of Native people; and (2) while DIAND sent many fine people to work on various projects, many failed because the local community did not have the power to make key decisions. Such failures left some communities worse off than before.

Shortly thereafter, the now infamous 1969 White Paper on Indian Policy was released. At the stroke of a pen it proposed to abrogate federal responsibility for Indians. That this occurred during a period when DIAND was trumpeting its new, consultative approach is more than ironic. Appearances to the contrary, the White Paper was actually well-intentioned, but was based on assimilationist assumptions. Three characteristics of its chief promoters (Prime Minister Pierre Trudeau and Indian Affairs Minister Jean Chrétien) stand out as symptomatic of general problems in Indian–government relations: (1) they had no understanding of Indian culture or history; (2) their genuine concern for the rights of individuals left no place for the concept of group rights; and (3) as politicians they tended to judge questions of Indian rights from the perspective of their dominant concern—how alternative responses would affect the struggle to keep Quebec in Confederation. The proposals were totally and emphatically rejected by Indians, primarily through the activity of provincial and national Indian associations. This in a sense marked their coming of age as bodies created by Indians in response to the necessity of acting corporately when attempting to negotiate with the government. Nevertheless, it took a sustained, national effort to block a government initiative that was disastrously ill-conceived.

In 1974 the government established the Office of Native Claims. Typical of its work was resolving a claim by Treaty No. 7 Indians that they had never received the annual funds for ammunition stipulated by the treaty. A simple contractual obligation a century old could be settled only through the creation of a special agency by the government.

When writing the first version of this chapter in 1985, we stated, 'At this moment the government continues to propose, as it has for several years, immanent change in section 12(1)b of the Indian Act, which strips Indian status from women who marry non-status men. While the present legislation clearly produces inequity, whatever change is made in this clause merely changes the formula whereby winners and losers in the "Indian game" are determined. It will not address the basic problem of Ottawa's defining who can be an Indian.' When rewriting this paragraph in 1994, we saw no reason to change that assessment, nor is there now. The legislation, Bill C-31, was passed in 1985. It has had enormous impact; some 110,000 people (about 17 per cent of the registered population) have received status as Indians under this change to the Indian Act. For many, being reinstated has been a profoundly significant event; for many others, it has meant that not much has changed. The legislation, for many Indians, continues to be very controversial, partly because of perceived continued inequities and a federal failure to provide funding, but primarily because, while the result may in the end be that bands will have control over their membership, the process itself was not negotiated but imposed unilaterally by Parliament.

The courts, while generally protecting treaty rights, have not held them sacrosanct. In a series of cases concerning hunting rights (starting with *Regina v. White and Bob*, two BC Indians accused of hunting deer on a reserve contrary to provincial game regulations), the courts have held that treaties take precedence over provincial law. However, in *Regina v. Sikyea* (where a Treaty No. 11 Indian shot a goose for subsistence purposes out of season), the court ruled that the federal Migratory Birds Convention Act unilaterally invalidated that aspect of the treaties. This is quite consistent with the nature of a parliamentary democracy, wherein any government 'promise' is subject to change by a simple majority vote. The decision is, of course, contrary to the Indian view that a treaty can be changed only by mutual consent and that the necessity of mutual consent further implies that Indians exist and have rights independent of any Act of Parliament.

Here again, however, recent events force some amendment of the argument. In a case involving the Musqueam of BC, *R. v. Sparrow* (1990), the Supreme Court decided that federal regulations on fishing did not apply to the Musqueam because their right to fish was, in the language of the Constitution Act, an 'existing aboriginal right'. This was the first time the court addressed the issue of what the language of section 35(1) of the Act actually meant. It was a significant and historic reversal of much of the trend noted above. However, as Asch and Macklem (1991) note, the judgement was made not on the basis of inherent Aboriginal rights but of contingent rights, of rights ultimately deriving from the action of the state.

With this thumbnail sketch of the last half-century in mind, one can see why First Nations people and leaders are more than a little skeptical about offers of consultation. Historically, federal offers of consultation have not meant much. In this case, the bill was already framed when the call for consultation went out. Is consultation after the fact worth bothering with? For Chief Matthew Coon Come and the Assembly of First Nations, it seems to have been an easy call.

A Basis for Change

George Manuel, Indian elder statesman, developed the concept of the Fourth World in a seminal book of that title. The idea refers to tribal peoples who have become incorporated into modern nation-states, but it rejects the notions associated with the Third World concept. An image that Manuel uses to express his central idea is the Two Row Wampum Belt, an Iroquois record of an early treaty in which two parallel rows run the whole length of the belt. It symbolizes the continued, undiminished existence of two independent yet intimately connected realities. It represents his vision of what Canada must become if Aboriginal peoples are to participate fully in the nation.

Manuel's vision is at odds with the picture of Indian–government relations elucidated above. Perhaps the clearest expression of the assimilationist-unilateralist position was articulated by then Prime Minister Trudeau: 'we won't recognize aboriginal rights. . . . It's inconceivable . . . that in a given society one section of the society have a treaty with the other section of the society' (1969: 331). Fortunately for Canada's Native people, their own efforts, rulings by the courts, and public opinion have shifted the political realities.

Historically, intense lobbying by Native organizations, particularly in response to the 1969 White Paper and around the Constitution Act of 1982, has been central in reducing the federal drive for accelerated assimilation and in enlarging the non-Native constituency that believes new legislative alternatives for Native governance are possible.

Recent court decisions have had a profound effect on government policy. British colonial policy, most clearly enunciated in the Royal Proclamation of 1763, recognized Aboriginal rights; this eventually led to treaties and the reserve system. The government's theory was that treaties extinguished Aboriginal title; one consequence was the view that even reserves were owned by the Crown and held 'at the good will of the sovereign' in trust for her Indian wards. Court decisions involving Aboriginal rights tended to be incredibly ethnocentric by modern standards, reserving full rights to those Natives who, by European standards, were civilized.

The 1973 Supreme Court judgement in the Nisga'a case (*Calder v. Attorney General*) was a turning point. Since they had never signed a treaty, the Nisga'a claimed still to possess Aboriginal rights. They also used anthropological testimony to demonstrate that they had exercised a sophisticated form of land tenure prior to European contact and subsequently. Although the Nisga'a lost the case on a technicality, all six judges giving substantive decisions recognized that the Nisga'a had possessed rights of a kind that the Court could recognize; they split evenly on the question of whether these rights persisted. The Prime Minister was forced to acknowledge that perhaps Aboriginal peoples had more rights than he had thought.

Subsequent initial judgements in cases involving James Bay Cree and Dene claims reinforced the idea of continuing rights. In the Dene case the claimants were signatories to a treaty (No. 11), but the universal testimony of those then present was that it had not been presented as something that would lessen, let alone terminate, their rights. Court recognition, or near recognition, of persisting Aboriginal rights encouraged the government, and Native groups, to negotiate agreements rather than risk all in court, where neither side could be sure of winning. The court decisions allowed Natives negotiating comprehensive agreements (the Inuit, Dene, and James Bay Cree) to press for recognition of continuing decision-making rights, not mere public consultation.

The Mackenzie Valley Pipeline Inquiry and the 1977 report by Justice Berger are noteworthy not only because they showed that an eminent jurist thought the Dene had continuing social and political rights and because ordinary Dene successfully communicated their views to the Inquiry and to the public, but because the Inquiry demonstrated widespread public support for the notion of treating the Dene fairly, i.e., of recognizing continuing Aboriginal rights. This and similar cases also deeply involved anthropologists and other scientists in such support roles as gathering and analyzing data and refuting the assimilationist arguments of the developers. In fact, the demands for solid evidence regarding such matters as historic and contemporary land-use patterns have led to the development of more sophisticated research techniques.

The 1982 decision of the Supreme Court in favour of the Musqueam band of Vancouver was another turning point. It recognized that: (1) Aboriginal title still exists; (2) bands own reserve land; (3) verbal promises by federal officials are legally binding; and (4) DIAND must transact Indian business only with the permission of the band council and in its best interest.

The *Sparrow* case, as noted above, while in several regards a significant step in recognizing the continuing nature of Aboriginal rights, makes those rights contingent on state action and hence lessens the likelihood of government or judicial recognition of inherent rights to self-government.

The 1997 *Delgamuukw* decision has been mentioned by several of our authors, notably Anderson. It was clearly a gain for Aboriginal peoples, establishing that Aboriginal title continues and that oral history relating to ownership must be given equal weight with documentary history by the courts. One of the ironies here is that the ruling was made by way of overturning a lower court decision that was couched in what most anthropologists would regard as ethnocentric language disparaging societies that had not developed writing and a 'civilized' way of life. Developing satisfactory ways of evaluating oral history (as we already do written history) will not be easy, but the Court has at least opened the door.

Important though the *Delgamuukw* affirmation of oral history was, its greater importance is with respect to Aboriginal title. It affirms that Aboriginal title is inalienable except to the Crown, is communal, includes the right of both traditional and modern forms of economic exploitation, and is protected by the Constitution. On the other hand, *Delgamuukw* also affirmed that Aboriginal title is not absolute, but may be infringed upon by both federal and provincial governments if there are 'compelling and substantial reasons' to do so and if the special fiduciary (trustee) relationship between the Crown and Aboriginal peoples is maintained. As is always the case, it will take time to sort out the practical implications of all this, but it is clearly part of a long-term trend of the courts being forced to spell out the ongoing nature of Aboriginal rights to governments that, to varying degrees, had tended to assume that they would go away.

Reference was made above to the testimony of Treaty No. 11 signers, that they had not understood the treaty to involve a transfer of land title, regardless of the written text. The logic of that testimony has now had some 20 years to develop, and literally scores of land claims cases involving treaty are coming before the courts, for, of course, the oral history in the earlier treaty areas is of the same nature: the treaties were seen as establishing a reciprocal relationship with the Crown, not as 'selling land'. Parenthetically, one might comment that it is hard to imagine that a person knowing a Native community in any kind of depth could imagine them knowingly agreeing to a transfer of land title. In any case, Indians in treaty areas are anticipating that the courts will recognize that they have some continuing rights in their traditional lands outside of the reserves.

Towards Self-Government

What, then, are the practical prospects for Native self-government in Canada? The Inuit of the former eastern Northwest Territories achieved self-governance in 1999. By virtue of geographic and historic vagaries, they remain a substantial majority in their region, and so Nunavut (Our Land) became a reality, and perhaps eventually will become a province, without the necessity of special constitutional arrangements integrating them as Aboriginals. Thus Nunavut will be both an ordinary territory, or province, and an essentially Inuit domain.

The same likely will be the case soon for Inuit residing in northern Quebec. For the past few decades they have been uniquely administered, with both the federal and provincial governments claiming jurisdiction. Provincially, at least in recent years, the politics of Quebec sovereignty within the nation as a widely supported goal has led many people to realize that new forms of Aboriginal administrative autonomy, perhaps leading to self-government, are both understandable and, possibly, inevitable. In 1999 the Nunavik Political Accord, setting that part of Quebec

north of 55 degrees on the road to self-government, was signed by Inuit, provincial, and federal officials. Detailed negotiations continue, with 2004 as a possible date for establishing Nunavik as a new polity within Quebec and Canada..

That there will be a parallel Dene realm in the western NWT (Denendeh) seems unlikely. Negotiations that might have led to this have failed. What is now being offered to the Dene communities is a form of legislated, municipal/administrative self-government. Some regions are working towards this within the framework of the comprehensive claims process, others on the basis of treaty rights. In both cases the federal government insists, as it does elsewhere, that as a basis for settlement the Dene must agree to the extinguishment of all remaining Aboriginal rights, including the inherent right to self-government.

The Inuit and Indians of Newfoundland and Labrador have been treated much as Metis, with no particular rights. Before Newfoundland joined Canada in 1949 they were considered to be ordinary citizens of the colony. Since Confederation the federal government has extended Aboriginal status to them only from the mid-1980s.

The Constitution Act, 1982, section 35, states that 'The existing aboriginal and treaty rights of the aboriginal peoples of Canada are hereby recognized and affirmed', and 'In this Act, "aboriginal peoples of Canada" includes the Indian, Inuit and Metis peoples of Canada.' What these clauses will come to mean for Natives outside the NWT is not at all clear, although with the *Sparrow* case a beginning has been made. It is possible to read them in a way that would not, for instance, benefit Aboriginal people in Newfoundland.

In any case, some forms of self-government are being developed across the country without recourse to the Constitution. As noted earlier many Natives see the process of renewal as being, in a broad sense, a path to self-government. That is, through various means of self-help, by running their own schools, health facilities, businesses, and the like, they are actively taking increased control over their own destinies, regardless of external support or opposition. For status Indians, however, despite the extent of internal renewal generated, there remain the formal, unilateral mechanisms of federal power, even under the current proposed changes to the Indian Act. As previously noted, although renewal is requisite to dignity, sustained renewal requires an end to dependence.

British Columbia is a special case because almost none of it was covered by treaty. Not until after 1973 did any of its governments recognize the need for treaties. A treaty process has been instituted to remedy both this deficiency and to move ahead into significant self-government, but not yet with much success. The one resolved case is that of the Nisga'a, and it has become controversial. Following the 1973 Supreme Court decision, serious negotiations did not occur until 1991 and an agreement did not emerge until 1998 (111 years after Nisga'a chiefs first petitioned for recognition of their land rights). It was formally signed in May 1999. The agreement allowed the Nisga'a to retain 1,992 square kilometres of their traditional land (note that most media reports had it that they were given the land!), it compensated them for lost land and revenues, and it recognized them as a distinct polity within BC. The least one can say about the aftermath is that it was filled with political rhetoric, most of it premised on the dubious proposition that in a democracy everyone should have a say even in government-to-government negotiations.

In Alberta at this writing, the Lubicon Cree First Nation seems to be nearing agreement with the federal government on a reserve, 'only' 60 years after it was first promised to them, and an economic, social, and political package that would allow them to move forward. The question then will become whether agreement will be forthcoming with the province, which must, at a minimum, provide the land.

It is worth noting at this juncture that the failure of governments to honour agreements is not merely a feature of some distant past; current examples can still be found. For instance, on 16 December 2002, officials of the Pimicikamak Cree First Nation and provincial officials gathered at Cross Lake in northern Manitoba to turn sod, cut a ribbon, and celebrate the initiation of a 15-month action plan to implement aspects of the Northern Flood Agreement (NFA). The NFA had been signed on the same day 25 years earlier, to help the Pimicikamak and neighbouring Aboriginal communities adjust to a major hydroelectric dam, which has dramatically impacted the local ecosystem. It has never been implemented. Provincial officials have decided to honour the Agreement and work with the Pimicikamak partly, we think, because it makes good economic and social sense, but they did not decide to do so without extensive political pressure from church-based organizations. The federal government and Manitoba Hydro, also signatories to the NFA, were not present and still are not involved.

Nevertheless, in spite of far more failures than we would like to see, the federal government has publicly committed itself to proceeding towards self-government and is working on a piecemeal basis to that end. Substantive negotiations are painfully slow—at the present rate the process will take a century or more—and the government continues to resist the idea of an inherent right to self-government. But a start has been made. In the meantime, numerous bands are taking control of at least part of their system, on the basis that they must do what they can.

In 1969, when the White Paper was presented, it would have seemed ludicrous to suggest that in 35 years some Canadian Native people would have achieved meaningful self-government and that for many the possibility could seriously be discussed. The Two Row Wampum Belt may yet become a meaningful symbol of the Canadian experience.

References and Recommended Readings

Akiwenzie-Damm, Kateri. 1998. *Residential School Update*. First Nations Health Secretariat. Ottawa: Assembly of First Nations. Broad coverage of perhaps the most critical Aboriginal social issue of our time.

Asch, Michael, ed. 1997. *Aboriginal and Treaty Rights in Canada: Essays on Law, Equality, and Respect for Difference*. Vancouver: University of British Columbia Press. A collection of essays exploring a number of contemporary legal issues as they impact Canadian Native peoples. It is in effect a plea for broader, more anthropological rulings from courts.

—— and Patrick Macklem. 1991.'Aboriginal rights and Canadian sovereignty: an essay on *R. v. Sparrow*', *Alberta Law Review* 29: 498–517.

Dickason, Olive P. 2002. *Canada's First Nations: A History of Founding Peoples from Earliest Times*, 3rd edn. Toronto: Oxford University Press. Currently the standard text, taking a very broad perspective and touching on most contemporary issues.

Dyck, Noel. 1991. *What is the 'Indian Problem': Tutelage and Resistance in Canadian Indian Administration*. St John's: ISER Books, Institute of Social and Economic Research, Memorial University of Newfoundland. A careful analysis of the fundamental contradictions in Canada's Indian policy, with thoughtful recommendations for the future.

Francis, Daniel. 1992. *The Imaginary Indian: The Image of the Indian in Canadian Culture*. Vancouver: Arsenal Pulp Press. An exploration of the roots of our images about Native people and the current realities flowing from those ideas.

Frideres, James S., and Rene R. Gadacz. 2001. *Aboriginal Peoples in Canada: Contemporary Conflicts*, 6th edn. Scarborough, Ont.: Prentice-Hall. A historical and sociological analysis of the legal, demographic, and social status of Canadian Native people.

Goddard, John. 1991. *Last Stand of the Lubicon Cree*. Vancouver: Douglas & McIntyre. A detailed account of Canada's best-known case of failure to come to agreement on a land claims settlement. In a sense it is now dated, but then, nothing much has changed since it was written.

INAC. 2002. *Registered Indian Population by Sex and Residence, 2001*. Ottawa: Minister of Public Works and Government Services Canada.

Lobo, Susan, and Steve Talbot. 2001. *Native American Voices: A Reader*, 2nd edn. Upper Saddle River, NJ: Prentice-Hall. Although largely American in content, this very broad-ranging book by Aboriginal authors does present Canadian and joint perspectives as well.

Long, David, and Olive P. Dickason. 2000. *Visions of the Heart: Canadian Aboriginal Issues*, 2nd edn. Toronto:

Harcourt Brace. Covers a broad range of issues with insight, and often written in a powerful voice.

McFarlane, Peter. 1993. *Brotherhood to Nationhood: George Manuel and the Making of the Modern Indian Movement*. Toronto: Between the Lines. A study of the life of George Manuel and his impact on the Canadian Indian movement.

McKee, Christopher. 2000. *Treaty Talks in British Columbia: Negotiating a Mutually Beneficial Future*, 2nd edn. Vancouver: University of British Columbia Press. Historically, BC has been the most intransigent province with respect to treaties. This volume analyzes the current complexities.

Malloy, Tom. 2000. *The World Is Our Witness: The Historic Journey of the Nisga'a into Canada*. Calgary: Fifth House. Broad coverage of the first modern treaty in BC and a focal point for recent debate.

Manuel, George, and Michael Posluns. 1974. *The Fourth World: An Indian Reality*. Don Mills, Ont.: Collier-Macmillan. A profound, simple, and influential combination of political philosophy and personal narrative. Essential reading for the serious student and a marvellous starting point for the novice.

Newhouse, David R. 2000. 'From the Tribal to the Modern: The Development of Modern Aboriginal Societies', in Ron F. Laliberte et al., eds, *Expressions in Canadian Native Studies*. Saskatoon: University of Saskatchewan Extension Press.

O'Malley, Martin. 'Without reservation', *Canadian Business* (Apr.): 37–41.

Perpetual, Jeanne, and Sylvia Vance. 1993. *Writing the Circle: Native Women of Western Canada—An Anthology*. Edmonton: NeWest. Over 50 Indian and Metis women write about their lives, to great effect.

Ross, Rupert. 1996. *Returning to the Teachings: Exploring Aboriginal Justice*. Toronto: Penguin Books Canada. Ross displays more cultural understanding than anyone else writing on this difficult subject.

Royal Commission on Aboriginal Peoples (RCAP). 1996. *Report of the Royal Commission on Aboriginal Peoples*, 5 vols. Ottawa: Government of Canada. The most thorough analysis and recommendations concerning Aboriginal conditions in Canada.

Statistics Canada. 2003. *Aboriginal Peoples of Canada: A Demographic Profile*. Ottawa: Minister of Public Works and Government Services Canada.

Tennant, Paul. 1990. *Aboriginal Peoples and Politics: The Indian Land Question in British Columbia, 1849–1989*.

Vancouver: University of British Columbia Press. A detailed political history of the treatment of Indian lands in a complex jurisdiction.

Tester, Frank James, and Peter Kulchyski. 1994. *Tammarnit (Mistakes): Inuit Relocation in the Eastern Arctic, 1939–63*. Vancouver: University of British Columbia Press. A broad examination of the evolution of Canadian Aboriginal policy in the North during the formative stage of the modern era.

Trudeau, P.E. 1969. 'Remarks on aboriginal and treaty rights', in P.A. Cumming and N.H. Mickenberg, eds., *Native Rights in Canada*, 2nd edn. Toronto: General Publishing, 1972.

Waldram, James B. 1988. *As Long as the Rivers Run: Hydroelectric Development and Native Communities in Western Canada*. Winnipeg: University of Manitoba Press. Modern economic development projects are examined in the context of the historic relationship between the Crown and the colonized.

Weaver, S.M. 1981. *Making Canadian Indian Policy: The Hidden Agenda 1968–1970*. Toronto: University of Toronto Press. The definitive study of how the 1969 White Paper came to be; reveals the government's internal debate over policy formation.

Wiebe, Rudy, and Yvonne Johnson. 1996. *Stolen Life: The Journey of a Cree Woman*. Toronto: Knopf Canada. A moving, in-depth anlalysis of a single case involving our 'justice' systems.

Suggested Web Sites

Aboriginal Canada Portal: www.aboriginalcanada.gc.ca
Currently claiming 7,500 links to and 15,000 pages on Aboriginal organizations, specific Aboriginal communities, and federal, provincial, and local programs for Aboriginal people.

Assembly of First Nations: www.afn.ca
Site for Canada's national association of status Indians.

Indian and Northern Affairs Canada: www.inac.gc.ca
An extensive government site including legislation, publications, news, and history.

Native Law Centre of Canada: www.usask.ca/nativelaw
Legal briefs, pleadings, and opinions; books and monographs; and current news about the Canadian Aboriginal legal scene.

GLOSSARY

Aboriginal: Pertaining to the original inhabitants of a particular territory and their contemporary descendants. In Canada, the First Nations, Inuit, and Metis peoples.

acculturation: The process of learning a second or subsequent culture.

affinal: Related by marriage.

allotment by severalty: A form of landholding in which single pieces of land are owned by individuals, as opposed to various forms of communal ownership.

Amerindian: A person indigenous to North or South America.

assimilation: The process whereby an individual or group no longer identifies with their primary culture and becomes part of another group.

autochthonous: Aboriginal, indigenous.

babiche: Thin, dehaired strips of rawhide used in the manufacture of various artifacts, such as snowshoes and fish nets.

bast: The inner bark of trees, or fibre obtained therefrom.

bola: A hunting instrument or weapon consisting of two or three stone or metal balls joined by thongs; when successfully hurled, it entangles the legs of its prey.

bilocal residence: Post-marital residence with or near the family of either the wife or husband.

clan: A kin group whose members believe themselves to be descended from a common ancestor so distant in time that not all connecting links can be specified.

cognatic: Descent rules and groups formed by the operation of such rules, in which descent is reckoned through both male and female links, most commonly in the form of either **bilateral** descent (reckoned through equal affiliation with the relatives of one's father and mother) or of **ambilineal** descent (reckoned through either female or male links).

consanguine: A 'blood' relative.

cosmology: A 'map' of the social and natural world for a culture that explains what kinds of beings there are, where they are, and how they interact.

cultural broker: Someone who acts as an intermediary between two cultures, usually helping members of the subordinate culture learn to operate in a dominant culture.

culture: The set of learned behaviors, beliefs, values, and attitudes characteristic of a social group.

economic man: The idea that human behaviour can be explained by economic self-interest.

ecotone: A transitional zone between two ecological communities.

endogamy: Marriage within one's social group.

epistemology: The philosophical study of the grounds of knowing, especially with regard to the limits and validity of knowledge.

ethnography: 1. The fieldwork method of cultural anthropology in which a specific group is intensively studied through participation in their daily lives. 2. A study reporting the results of such fieldwork.

ethnology: The theoretical method of cultural anthropology; the study of human behaviour generally through cross-cultural comparisons.

exogamy: Marriage outside of one's social group, typically a clan or lineage.

extended family: A social group consisting of near relatives in addition to the central conjugal unit and their offspring.

factor: A person who carries on business transactions for another; specifically, a senior field rank in the Hudson's Bay Company.

fee simple: Land that is owned and may be passed on to heirs without restrictions, i.e., the ordinary form of landholding in Canada.

fiduciary: A relationship that involves one party (such as DIAND) acting as trustee for another (such as the various Indian bands).

Fourth World: A concept developed by George Manuel to describe the internal colonialization of indigenous peoples within nation-states formed by settler societies; includes Aboriginal people around the world who have been incorporated into contemporary states.

gentrian: Pertaining to any of a number of colourful birds with limited ability to fly, particularly the turkey.

hermeneutics: The perspective that explains human behaviour by understanding actions as parts of systems of meaning.

horticulture: Food production from temporary fields using human labour and relatively simple tools.

household: The social group living together as a domestic unit.

hunting and gathering: Refers to subsistence by means of hunting and fishing and by collecting vegetal material in a way that involves less tending of plants than actual gardening; also called foraging.

idealism: The perspective that explains human behaviour primarily by recourse to non-material factors such as values and beliefs.

indigenous people: The original inhabitants of a particular territory and their contemporary descendants. In Canada, the First Nations, Inuit, and Metis peoples.

kindred: The totality of one's relatives, counting bilaterally.

leister: A barbed, three-pronged fish spear.

lineage: A set of kin whose members trace descent from a common ancestor through known links, usually forming a matrilineage (with female links) or a patrilineage (with male links).

market economy: A system of exchange in which goods are moved through the mechanism of buying and selling them for money.

materialism: The perspective that explains human behaviour primarily by recourse to the material conditions of life, such as economic advantage.

matrilineal: Having descent through the female line; children of both sexes are assigned membership in the kin group of the mother.

matrilocal: Post-marital residence with the family of the wife's mother.

Native people: The original inhabitants of a particular territory and their contemporary descendants. In Canada, the First Nations, Inuit, and Metis peoples.

nuclear family: A domestic group consisting of a wife, husband, and their unmarried children.

ontology: The branch of philosophy concerned with the nature and essential properties of being.

ossuary: A place where bones of the dead are deposited.

pan-Indian: 1. Something characteristic of Indian peoples in general. 2. The modern trend for Indian peoples to borrow cultural traits from each other and so, in at least some ways, become more alike.

participant observation: Learning by doing; the primary field method of anthropology, whereby living within a community provides the primary means for learning about it.

patrilineal: Descent through the male line; children belong to the father's kin group.

patrilocal: A couple living with or near the husband's father.

patronym: 1. Loosely, a surname passed down patrilineally. 2. Strictly, a child taking a name formed from the father's name plus a prefix or suffix, as in *Johnson*, son of John.

polygyny: That form of plural marriage (**polygamy**) in which one man marries two or more women.

potlatch: Major ceremonial feast found on the Northwest Coast and to a lesser extent in the intermontane West. For a time outlawed by the Indian Act.

primogeniture: The pattern whereby the eldest child, or the eldest son, inherits particular rights.

reciprocity: A system of exchange in which gifts are given to people who then have an obligation to offer other gifts.

resistance: In anthropology, the notion that Aboriginal responses to external forces are partially shaped by the desire for and necessity of opposition.

shaman: A religio-medical practitioner whose powers to heal, find game, and/or divine the future come from spiritual helpers.

sinodont: A term applied by Turner to a dental pattern encompassing the prehistoric and contemporary peoples of China, northeastern Asia, and the New World.

structuralism: A perspective that attempts to discover orderly patterns common to languages, myths, kinship systems, and other aspects of culture.

totem: Derived from an Ojibway word referring to relatives, the term has primary reference to animist notions linking contemporary kinship groups to animals, natural objects, or natural phenomena from whom various rights and obligations are derived through descent.

unilineal: Pertaining to descent traced exclusively through either the father's or the mother's line.

usufruct: Literally, to use the fruit; the right to make use of and to benefit from that which is not, strictly speaking, owned. Typically this might entail the right to hunt, fish, trap, or otherwise harvest the resources on a tract of land.

value: A conception of the desirable or the valuable; by extension, the moral and aesthetic aspects of culture.

weir: A fence-like structure placed across a stream or inlet; in conjunction with fish traps, it facilitates the efficient harvesting of fish.

world view: The overall framework through which a person views life; how people think the world is. An opposition is frequently posited between sacred and secular world views.

Treaty No. 8

ARTICLES OF A TREATY made and concluded at the several dates mentioned therein, in the year of Our Lord one thousand eight hundred and ninety-nine, between Her Most Gracious Majesty the Queen of Great Britain and Ireland, by Her Commissioners the Honourable David Laird, of Winnipeg, Manitoba, Indian Commissioner for the said Province and the North West Territories, James Andrew Joseph McKenna, of Ottawa, Ontario, Esquire, and the Honourable James Hamilton Ross, of Regina, in the North West Territories, of the one part; and the Cree, Beaver, Chipewyan, and other Indians, inhabitants of the territory within the limits hereinafter defined and described, by their Chiefs and Headmen, hereunto subscribed, of the other part:

WHEREAS, the Indians inhabiting the territory hereinafter defined have pursuant to notice given by the Honourable Superintendent General of Indian Affairs in the year 1898, been convened to meet a Commission representing Her Majesty's Government of the Dominion of Canada at certain places in the said territory in this present year 1899, to deliberate upon certain matters of interest to Her Most Gracious Majesty, of the one part, and the said Indians of the other.

AND WHEREAS the said Indians have been notified and informed by Her Majesty's said Commission that it is Her desire to open for settlement, immigration, trade, travel, mining, lumbering, and such other purposes as to Her Majesty may seem meet, a tract of country bounded and described as hereinafter mentioned, and to obtain the consent thereto of Her Indian subjects inhabiting the said tract, and to make a treaty and arrange with them, so that there may be peace and good will between them and Her Majesty's other subjects, and that Her Indian people may know and be assured of what allowances they are to count upon and receive from Her Majesty's bounty and benevolence.

AND WHEREAS the Indians of the said tract, duly convened in council at the respective points named hereunder, and being requested by Her Majesty's Commissioners to name certain Chiefs and Headmen who should be authorized on their behalf to conduct such negotiations and sign any treaty to be founded thereon, and to become responsible to Her Majesty for the faithful performance by their respective bands of such obligations as shall be assumed by them, the said Indians have therefore acknowledged for that purpose the several Chiefs and Headmen who have subscribed hereto.

AND WHEREAS the said Commissioners have proceeded to negotiate a treaty with the Cree, Beaver, Chipewyan and other Indians, inhabiting the district hereinafter defined and described, and the same has been agreed upon and concluded by the respective Bands at the dates mentioned hereunder, the said Indians DO HEREBY CEDE, RELEASE, SURRENDER AND YIELD UP to the Government of the Dominion of Canada, for Her Majesty the Queen and Her successors for ever all their rights, titles and privileges whatsoever, to the lands included within the following limits, that is to say:

Commencing at the source of the main branch of the RED DEER RIVER in Alberta, thence due west to the central range of the Rocky Mountains, thence north-westerly along said range to the point where it intersects the 60th parallel of north latitude, thence east along said parallel to the point where it intersects Hay River, thence north-easterly down said river to the south shore of Great Slave Lake, thence along the said shore north-easterly (and including such rights to the islands in said lake as the Indians mentioned in the treaty may possess) and thence easterly and north-easterly along the south shores of Christie's Bay and McLeod's Bay to old Fort Reliance near the mouth of Lockhart's River, thence south easterly in a straight line to and including Black Lake, thence south-westerly up the stream from Cree Lake, thence including said Lake, south-westerly along the height of land between the Athabasca and Churchill Rivers to where it intersects the northern boundary of Treaty Six, and along the said boundary easterly, northerly and south-westerly, to the place of commencement.

AND ALSO the said Indian rights, titles and privileges whatsoever to all other lands wherever situated in the North-West Territories, British Columbia, or in any other portion of the Dominion of Canada.

TO HAVE AND TO HOLD the same to Her Majesty the Queen and Her successors for ever.

And Her Majesty the Queen HEREBY AGREES with the said Indians that they shall have right to pursue their usual vocations of hunting, trapping and fishing throughout the tract surrendered as heretofore described, subject to such regulations as may from time to time be made by the Government of the country, acting under the authority of Her Majesty, and saving and excepting such tracts as may be required or taken up from time to time for settlement, mining, lumbering trading or other purposes.

And Her Majesty the Queen hereby agrees and undertakes to lay aside reserves for such bands as desire reserves, the same not to exceed in all one square mile for each family of five for such number of families as may elect to reside on reserves, or in that proportion for larger or smaller families; and for such families or individual Indians as may prefer to live apart from band reserves, Her Majesty undertakes to provide land in severalty to the extent of 160 acres to each Indian, the land to be conveyed with a proviso as to non-alienation without the consent of the Governor-General in Council of Canada, the selection of such reserves, and lands in severalty, to be made in the manner following, namely, the Superintendent General of Indian Affairs shall depute and send a suitable person to determine and set apart such reserves and lands, after consulting with the Indians concerned as to the locality which may be found suitable and open for selection.

Provided, however, that Her Majesty reserves the right to deal with any settlers within the bounds of any lands reserved for any band as She may see fit; and also that the aforesaid reserves of land or any interest therein, may be sold or otherwise disposed of by Her Majesty's Government for the use and benefit of the said Indians entitled thereto, with their consent first had and obtained.

It is further agreed between Her Majesty and Her said Indian subjects that such portions of the reserves and lands above indicated as may at any time be required for public works, buildings, railways, or roads of whatsoever nature may be appropriated for that purpose by Her Majesty's Government of the Dominion of Canada, due compensation being made to the Indians for the value of any improvements thereon, and an equivalent in land, money or other consideration for the area of the reserve so appropriated.

And with a view to show the satisfaction of Her Majesty with the behaviour and good conduct of Her Indians, and in extinguishment of all their past claims, She hereby, through Her Commissioners, agrees to make each Chief a present of thirty-two dollars in cash, to each Headman twenty-two dollars, and to every other Indian of whatever age, of the families represented at the time and place of payment, twelve dollars.

Her Majesty also agrees that next year, and annually afterwards for ever, She will cause to be paid to the said Indians in cash, at suitable places and dates, of which the said Indians shall be duly notified, to each Chief twenty-five dollars, each Headman, not to exceed four to a large Band and two to a small Band, fifteen dollars, and to every other Indian of Whatever age, five dollars, the same, unless there be some exceptional reason, to be paid only to heads of families for those belonging thereto.

FURTHER, Her Majesty agrees that each Chief, after signing the treaty, shall receive a silver medal and a suitable flag, and next year, and every third year thereafter, each chief and Headman shall receive a suitable suit of clothing.

FURTHER, Her Majesty agrees to pay the salaries of such teachers to instruct the children of said Indians as to Her Majesty's Government of Canada may seem advisable.

FURTHER, Her Majesty agrees to supply each Chief of a Band that selects a reserve, for the use of that Band, ten axes, five hand-saws, five augers, one grindstone and the necessary files and whetstones.

FURTHER, Her Majesty agrees that each Band that elects to take a reserve and cultivate the soil, shall, as soon as convenient after such reserve is set aside and settled upon, and the Band has signified its choice and is prepared to break up the soil, receive two hoes, one spade, one scythe, and two hay forks for every family so settled, and for every three families one plough and one harrow, and to the Chief, for the use of his Band, two horses or a yoke of oxen, and for each Band, potatoes, barley, oats and wheat (if such seed be suited to the locality of the reserve), to plant the land actually broken up, and provisions for one month in the spring for several years while planting such seeds; and to every family one cow, and every Chief one bull, and one mowing machine and one reaper for the use of his Band when it is ready for them; for such families as prefer to raise stock instead of cultivating the soil, every family of five persons two cows, and every Chief two bulls and two mowing machines when ready for their use, and a like proportion for smaller or larger families. The aforesaid articles, machines and cattle to be given once for all for the encouragement of agriculture and stock raising; and for such bands as prefer to continue hunting and fishing, as much ammunition and twine for making nets annually, as will amount in value to one dollar per head of the families so engaged in hunting and fishing.

And the undersigned Cree, Beaver, Chipewyan and other Indian Chiefs and Headmen on their own behalf and on behalf of all the Indians whom they represent, DO HEREBY SOLEMNLY PROMISE and engage to strictly observe this Treaty, and also to conduct and behave themselves as good and loyal subjects of Her Majesty the Queen.

THEY PROMISE AND ENGAGE that they will, in all respects, obey and abide by the law; that they will maintain peace between each other and between themselves and other tribes of Indians, and between themselves and others of Her Majesty's subjects, whether Indians, Half-breeds or Whites, this year inhabiting and hereafter to inhabit any part of the said ceded territory; and that they will not molest the person or property of any inhabitant of such ceded tract, or of any other district or country, or interfere with or trouble any person passing or travelling through the said tract, or any part thereof, and that they will assist the officers of Her Majesty in bringing to justice and punishment any Indian offending against the stipulations of this Treaty, or infringing the law in force in the country so ceded.

IN WITNESS WHEREOF Her majesty's said commissioners and the Cree Chief and Headmen of Lesser Slave Lake and the adjacent territory HAVE HEREUNTO SET THEIR HANDS at Lesser Slave Lake, on the twenty-first day of June in the year herein first above written.

Signed by the parties hereto, in the presence of the undersigned witnesses, the same having been first explained to the Indians by Albert Tate and Samuel Cunningham, Interpreters.

Father A. LACOMBE as advisor of the Commission.

GEO. HOLMES
E. GROUARD O.M.I.
W.G. WHITE
JAMES WALKER
J. ARTHUR COTE
A.E. SNYDER Insp. N.W.M.P.
H.B. ROUND
HARRISON S. YOUNG
J.F. PRUD'HOMME
J.W. MARTIN
C. MAIR
H.A. CONROY
PIERRE DESCHAMBEAULT
J.H. PICARD
RICHARD SECORD
M. McCAULEY
DAVID LAIRD, Treaty Commissioner
J.A.J. McKENNA, Treaty Commissioner
J.H. ROSS, Treaty Commissioner
KEE NOO SHAY OO X* Chief
MOOSTOOS X Headman

FELIX GIROUX X do
WEE CHEE WAY SIS X do
CHARLES NEE SUE TA SIS X do
CAPTAIN X, Headman from Sturgeon Lake (*his mark)

In witness whereof the Chairman of Her Majesty's Commissioners and the Headman of the Indians of Peace River Landing and the adjacent territory, in behalf of himself and the Indians whom here presents have hereunto set their hands at the said Peace River Landing on the first Day of July in the year of Our Lord one thousand eight hundred and ninety-nine.

Signed by the parties hereto, in the presence of the undersigned witnesses, the same having been first explained to the Indians by Father A. Lacombe and John Boucher, Interpreters.

A. LACOMBE, as advisor to the Commission
E. GROUARD O.M.I. Ev. d'Ibora
GEO. HOLMES
HENRY McCORRISTER
K.F. ANDERSON Sgt. N.W.M. Police
PIERRE DESCHAMBEAULT
H.A. CONROY
T.A. BRICK
HARRISON S. YOUNG
J.W. MARTIN
DAVID CURRY
DAVID LAIRD
Chairman of Indian Treaty Commissioners
DUNCAN X TASTAOOTS Headman of Cree's

In witness whereof the Chairman of Her Majesty's Commissioners and the Chief and Headman of the Beaver and Headman of the Crees & other Indians of Vermillion and the adjacent territory, in behalf of themselves and the Indians whom they represent have hereunto set their hands at Vermillion on the eighth day of July in the year of our Lord one thousand eight hundred and ninety-nine.

Signed by the parties hereto in the presence of the undersigned witnesses, the same having been first explained to the Indians by Father A. Lacombe and John Bourassa, Interpreter.

A. LACOMBE, as advisor of the Commission
E. GROUARD O.M.I. Ev. d'Ibora

MALCOLM SCOTT
F.D. WILSON H.B. Co.
H.A. CONROY
PIERRE DESCHAMBEAULT
HARRISON S. YOUNG
J.W. MARTIN
A.P. CLARKE
CHAS. H. STUART WADE
K.S. ANDERSON Sgt. N.W.M. Police
DAVID LAIRD, Chairman of Indian Treaty Comrs
AMBROSE X TETE NOIRE, Chief, Beaver Indians
PIERROT X FOURNIER, Headman of Beaver Indians
KUIS KUIS KOW CA POOHOO X,
Headman of Cree Indians.

In witness whereof the Chairman of Her Majesty's Treaty Commissioners and the Chief and Headman of the Chipewyan Indians of Fond du Lac (Lake Athabasca) and the adjacent territory in behalf of themselves and the Indians whom they represent have hereunto set their hands at the said Fond du Lac on the twenty-fifth and twenty-seventh days of July in the year of Our Lord one thousand eight hundred and ninety-nine.

Signed by the parties hereto in the presence of the undersigned witnesses, the same having been first explained to the Indians by Pierre Deschambeault Rev. Father Douceur and Louis Robillard, Interpreters.

G. BREYNAT O.M.I.
HARRISON S. YOUNG
PIERRE DESCHAMBEAULT
WILLIAM HENRY BURKE
BATHURST F. COOPER
GERMAIN MERCREDI
LOUIS X. ROBBILLIARD
Witness H.S. YOUNG
K.S. ANDERSON Sgt.N.W.M.P.
DAVID LAIRD, Chairman of Indian Treaty Commissioners
LAURENT X DZIEDDIN, Headman
TOUSSAINT X Headman
(The number accepting treaty being larger then at first expected, a Chief was allowed, who signed the treaty on the 27th July before the same witnesses to signatures of the Commissioner and Headmen on the 25th.)

MAURICE X PICHE Chief of Band

The Beaver Indians of Dunvegan having met on this sixth day of July on this present year 1899 Her Majesty's Commissioners the Honourable James Hamilton Ross and James Andrew Joseph McKenna Esquire and having had explained to them the terms of the Treaty unto which the Chief and Headmen of the Indians of Lesser Slave Lake and adjacent country set their hands on the twenty-first day of June in the year herein first above written do join in the cession made by the said Treaty and agree to adhere to the terms thereof in consideration of the undertakings made therein.

In witness whereof Her Majesty's said Commissioners and the Headmen of the said Beaver Indians have hereunto set their hands at Dunvegan on this sixth day of July in the year herein first above written.

Signed by the parties thereto in the presence of the undersigned witnesses, after the same had been read and explained to the Indians By the Reverend Joseph Le Treste and Peter Gunn, interpreters.

A.F SNYDER Insp. N.W.M.P..
J. LE TRESTE
PETER GUNN
F.J. FITZGERALD
J.H. ROSS
J.A.J. McKENNA
Commissioners

NATOOSES X Headman

The Chipewyan Indians of Athabasca River, Birch River, Peace River, Slave River and Gull River, and the Cree Indians of Gull River and Deep Lake having met at Fort Chipewyan on this thirteenth day of July in this present year 1899 Her Majesty's Commissioners the Honourable James Hamilton Ross and James Andrew Joseph McKenna Esquire and having had explained to them the terms of the Treaty unto which the Chief and Headmen of the Indians of Lesser Slave Lake and adjacent country set their hands on the twenty-first day of June in the Year herein first above written do join in the cession made by the said Treaty and agree to adhere to the terms thereof in consideration of the undertakings made therein.

In witness whereof Her Majesty's said Commissioners and the Chiefs and Headmen of the said Chipewyan and Cree Indians have hereunto set their hands at Fort Chipewyan on this thirteenth day of July in the year herein above first written.

Signed by the parties thereto in the presence of the undersigned witnesses after the same had been read and explained to the Indians by Peter Mercredi, Chipewyan Interpreter and George Drever, Cree Interpreter.

A.E. SNYDER Insp. N.W.M.P..
P. MERCREDI
GEO. DREVER
L.M. LE DOUSSAL
A. DE CHAMBEUIL O.M.I.
H.B ROUND
GABRIEL BREYNAT O.M.I.
COLIN FRASER
F.J. FITZGERALD
B.F. COOPER
H.W. McLAREN
J.H. ROSS
J.A.J. McKENNA
Treaty Commissioners

ALEX X LAVIOLETTE, Chipewyan Chief

JULIEN X RATFAT
SEPT. HEEZELI
Chipewyan Headmen

JUSTIN X MARTIN, Cree Chief
ANT. X TACCARROO
THOMAS X GIBBOTT
Cree Headmen

The Chipewyan Indians of Slave River and the country thereabouts having met at Smith's Landing on this seventeenth day of July in this present year 1899 Her Majesty's Commissioners the Honourable James Hamilton Ross and James Andrew Joseph McKenna Esquire and having had explained to them the terms of the Treaty unto which the Chief and Headmen of the Indians of Lesser Slave Lake and adjacent country, set their hands on the twenty-first day of June, in the year herein first above written do join in the cession made by the said Treaty and agree to adhere to the terms thereof in consideration of the undertakings made therein.

In witness whereof Her Majesty's said Commissioners and the Chief and Headmen of the said Chipewyan Indians have hereunto set their hands at Smith's Landing on this seventeenth day of July in the year herein first above written.

Signed by the parties thereto in the presence of the undersigned witnesses after the same had been read and explained to the Indians by John Trindle Interpreter

A.E. SNYDER Insp. N.W.M.P..
H.B. ROUND
J.H. REID
JAS. HALY
JOHN TRINDLE
F.J. FITZGERALD
WM. McCLELLAND
JOHN SUTHERLAND
J.H. ROSS
J.A.J. McKENNA
Treaty Commissioners

PIERRE X SQUIRREL Chief
MICHAEL X MAMDRILLE Headman
WILLIAM X KISCORRAY ditto

The Chipewyan and Cree Indians of Fort McMurray and the country thereabouts having met at Fort McMurray on this fourth day of August in this present year 1899, Her Majesty's Commissioner, James Andrew Joseph McKenna, Esquire and having had explained to them the terms of the Treaty unto which the Chief and Headmen of the Indians of Lesser Slave Lake and adjacent country set their hands on the twenty-first day of June in the year herein first above written do join in the cession made by the said Treaty and agree to adhere to the terms thereof in consideration of the undertakings made therein.

In Witness whereof Her Majesty's said Commissioner and the Headmen of the said Chipewyan and Cree Indians have hereunto set their hands at Fort McMurray, on this fourth day of August in the year herein first above written.

Signed by the parties thereto in the presence of the undersigned witnesses after the same had been read and explained to the Indians by the Rev. Father Lacombe and T.M. Clarke, Interpreters.

A. LACOMBE O.M.I.
ARTHUR J. WARWICK
T.M. CLARKE
J.W. MARTIN
F.J. FITZGERALD
W.G.H. VERNON

J.A.J. McKENNA Treaty Commissioner
ADAM X BOUCHER Chipewyan Headman
SEAPOTAKINUM X CREE Cree Headman

The Indians of Wapiscow and the country thereabouts having met at Wapiscow Lake on this fourteenth day of August in this present year 1899 Her Majesty's Commissioner the Honorable James Hamilton Ross and having had explained to them the terms of the Treaty unto which the Chief and Headmen of the Indians of Lesser Slave Lake and adjacent country set their hands on the twenty-first day of June in the year herein first above written do join in the cession made by the said Treaty and agree to adhere to the terms thereof in consideration of the undertakings made therein.

In Witness whereof Her Majesty's said Commissioner and the Chief and Headmen of the Indians have hereunto set their hands at Wapiscow Lake on this fourteenth day of August in the year herein first above written.

Signed by the parties thereto in the presence of the undersigned witnesses after the same had been read and explained to the Indians by Alexander Kennedy

A.E. SNYDER, Insp. N.W.M. Police
CHARLES RILEY WEAVER
J.B. HENRI GIROUX, O.M.I. P.Ph.
MURDOCH JOHNSON
C. FALHER, O.M.I.
ALEX. KENNEDY, Interpreter [Signature in Cree Character]
H.A. CONROY,
JOHN McLEOD
M.R. JOHNSTON

Recorded 13th March 1900
Lib 163 Fol 288

JOSEPH POPE
Dep. Registrar General of Canada

J.H. ROSS Treaty Commissr
JOSEPH X KAPUSEKONEW, Chief
JOSEPH X ANSEY Headman
WAPOOSE X Headman
MICHAEL X ANSEY Headman
LOUISA X BEAVER Headman

The Cree Indians of Sturgeon Lake and the country thereabouts having met at Lesser Slave Lake on this 8th day of June in this present year 1900, James Ansdell Macrae Esquire, and having had explained to them the terms of the treaty unto which the Chief and Headmen of the Indians of Lesser Slave Lake and adjacent country set their hands on the 21st day of June, in the year 1899, do join in the cession made by the said Treaty, and agree to the terms thereof in consideration of the undertakings made therein.

In witness whereof the said James Ansdell Macrae, Esquire, and the Headmen of the said Cree Indians, have hereunto set their hands at Lesser Slave Lake on this the 8th day of June in the year first above written.

Signed by the parties thereto in the presence of the undersigned witnesses after the same had been read and explained to the Indians by Peter Gunn & Albert Tate, Interpreters.

ALBERT TATE
PETER GUNN
GEO. HOLMES
MYLES O'C. MacDERMOTT
W.J. O'DONNELL
A. CHEESEBROUGH Const.
R. FIELD Const.

Recorded 14th January 1901
Lib: 163 Fol: 442

JOSEPH POPE
Dep: Registrar General of Canada.

J.A. MACRAE
MEE-SOO-KAM-IN-OO-KA-POW X
WILLIAM PEE-YU-TAY-WEE-TUM X
MUK-COO MOOSE-OS X
ALEXIS PA-PASS-CHAY X
THE CAPTAIN X

The Beaver Indians of the Upper Peace River and the country thereabouts having met at Fort St. John on this 30th day of May in this present year 1900, Her majesty's Commissioner James Ansdell Macrae, Esquire, and having had explained to them the terms of the treaty unto which the Chief and Headmen of the Indians of Lesser Slave Lake and adjacent country set their hands on the 21st day of June, in the year 1899, do join in the cession made by the said Treaty, and agree to adhere to the terms thereof in consideration of the undertakings made therein.

In witness whereof Her majesty's said Commissioner, and the following of the said Beaver Indians have hereunto set their hands at Fort St. John, on this the 30th day of May, in the year herein first above written.

Signed by the parties thereto in the presence of the undersigned witnesses after the same had been read and explained to the Indians by John Shaw, Interpreter.

JOHN SHAW Interpreter
W.J. O'DONNELL

Recorded 14th January 1901
Lib: 163 Fol. 443

JOSEPH POPE
Dep. Registrar General of Canada

J.A. MACRAE Commissioner
MUCKITHAY X
AGINAA X
DISLISICI X

TACHEA X
APPAN X
ATTACHIE X
ALLALIE X
YATSOOSE X

The Slave Indians of Hay River and the country thereabouts having met at Vermillion on this twenty-third day of June, in this present year 1900, Her Majesty's Commissioner, James Ansdell Macrae Esquire, and having had explained to them the terms of the Treaty unto which the Chief and Headmen of the Indians of Lesser Slave Lake and adjacent country, set their hands on the twenty-first day of June in the year 1899, do join in the cessions made by the said Treaty, and agree to adhere to the terns thereof in consideration of the undertakings made therein.

In witness whereof Her majesty's said Commissioner and the Chief & principal men of the said Slave Indians have hereunto set their hands at Vermillion on this 23rd day of June in the year 1900.

Signed by the parties thereto in the presence of the undersigned witnesses after the same had been read and explained to the Indians by Louis Cardinal

LOUIS X CARDINAL
Witness, G. ARTHUR BALL
ALFRED SPEECHLY WHITE
ISAIE GAGNON
GEO KNAPP
H.J. LAROCQUE
MARTIN X OUELETTE
Witness G. ARTHUR BALL
WILLIAM LETENDRE
J.A. MACRAE Commissioner
ALEXIS X TATATECHAY
FRANCOIS X TOHATEE
GIROUX X NAHDAYYAH
KOKA X
KACHWEESALA X

Recorded 14th January 1901
Lib: 163 Fol: 444

JOSEPH POPE
Dep: Registrar General of Canada

The Indians inhabiting the South shore of Great Slave Lake, between the mouth of Hay River and old Fort Reliance, near the mouth of Lockheart's River, and territory adjacent thereto on the mainland or on the islands of the said lake, having met at Fort Resolution on this 25th day of July in the present year 1900, Her Majesty's Commissioner James Ansdell Macrae, Esquire, and having had explained to them the terms of the Treaty unto which the Chief and Headmen of the Indians of Lesser Slave Lake and adjacent country set their hands on the 21st day of June 1899, do join in the cession made by the said treaty, and agree to adhere to the terms thereof in consideration of the undertakings made therein.

In witness whereof Her Majesty's said Commissioner and the Chief and Headmen of the said Indians have thereunto set their hands at Fort Resolution on the 25th day of July in the year herein first above written.

Signed by the parties thereto in the presence of the undersigned witnesses after the same had been read over and explained to the Indians by Revrd Father Dupirer, W.R. Norn, A. Mercredi.

W.R. NORN
ALEXANDRE MERCREDI
THOS. J. MARSH
F.C. GAUDET, [Indian characters]
(The mark of Michel Mandeville), [Indian characters]
(The mark of Chief Pierre Squirrel)
CHARLIE NORN
RICHARD FIELD

Witnesses
T.C. RAE
OLIVER MERCREDI
J.S. CAMSELL

Recorded 16th January 1901
Lib: 163 Fol: 445

JOSEPH POPE
Dep: Registrar General of Canada.

J.A. MACRAE, Commissioner,

For the Dog Ribs:
DRIED X GEESE, Chief
WAY-MI-AH X H.M.
CRAP-WA-TEE X H.M.,

for the Yellow Knives:
SNUFF X, Chief
TZIN-TU-X H.M.
ATE-EE-TEN X H.M.

Chipewayans:
LOUISON X AHTHAY, Chief
OLIVER X AJJERICON

Slaves of Hay River:
SUNRISE X, H.M.
LAMELISE X, H.M.

Chipewayans:
VITAL [Indian characters]
LAMOELLE
PAULETTE [Indian characters]
CHANDELLE

KNOW ALL MEN BY THESE PRESENTS, THAT WE, the undersigned Chief and Principal men of The Sarcee Band of Indians resident on our Reserve in the District of Alberta in the North West Territories and Dominion of Canada, for and acting on behalf of the whole people of our said Band in Council assembled, Do hereby release, remise, surrender, quit claim and yield up unto OUR SOVEREIGN LADY THE QUEEN, her Heirs and Successors forever, ALL AND SINGULAR, that certain parcel or tract of land and premises, situate, lying and being in the Sarcee Indian Reserve in the North West Territories and Dominion of Canada containing by admeasurement be the same more or less and being composed of a road sixty feet wide across the said Sarcee Indian Reserve and shown colored in red on attached Plan.

TO HAVE AND TO HOLD the same unto Her said Majesty THE QUEEN, her Heirs and Successors forever, in trust to be used for road purposes and upon such terms as the Government of the Dominion of Canada may deem most conducive to our welfare and that of our people.

AND WE, the said Chief and Principal men of the said The Sarcee Band of Indians do, on behalf of our people and for ourselves, hereby ratify and confirm, and promise to ratify and confirm, whatever the said Government may do, or cause to be lawfully done, in connection with the dedication of the said portion of land for road purposes.

IN WITNESS WHEREOF, we have hereunto set our hands and affixed our seals this Third day of January in the year of Our Lord one thousand nine hundred Signed, Sealed and Delivered, in the presence of

A.J. McNEIL, Indian Agent
G. HODGSON, Interpreter
BULL HEAD (Chief) [L.S.] X his mark
his BIG PLUME (Minor Chief) [L.S.] X his mark
BIG WOLF X (Minor Chief) [L.S.] X his mark

JIM BIG PLUME [L.S.] X his mark
JACK SARCEE [L.S.] X his mark
CROW COLLAR [L.S.] X his mark
TWO GUNS [L.S.] X his mark
DOG [L.S.] X his mark
TWO YOUNG MEN [L.S.] X his mark
MANY SWAN [L.S.] X his mark
AFRAID OF GRASSHOPPER [L.S.] X his mark
HIT FIRST [L.S.] X his mark
WOLF [L.S.] X his mark
JACK HEAD ABOVE WATER [L.S.] X his mark
BULL COLLAR [L.S.] X his mark
DODGING A HORSE [L.S.] X his mark
TOM HEAVEN FIRE [L.S.] X his mark
YOUNG BULL HEAD [L.S.] X his mark

DOMINION OF CANADA, North West Territories, District of Alberta

To Wit:
Personally appeared before me, Alexander James McNeil the Indian Agent of the Band of Sarcee Indians in the District of Alberta in the North West Territories, and Bull Head Chief of the Band of Indians.

AND the said Alexander James McNeil for himself says:

That the annexed Release of Surrender was assented to by a majority of the male members of the said Band of Indians of the Sarcee Reserve of the full age of twenty-one years then present.

That such assent was given at a meeting or council of the said Band summoned for that purpose and according to their Rules.

That he was present at such meeting or council and heard such assent given.

That he was duly authorized to attend such council or meeting by the Superintendent General of Indians Affairs.

That no Indian was present or voted at said council or meeting who was not a member of the Band or interested in the land mentioned in the said Release or Surrender.

And the said Chief Bull Head says:

That the annexed Release or Surrender was assented to by him and a majority of the male members of the said Band of Indians of the full age of twenty-one years then present.

That such assent was given at a meeting or council of the said Band of Indians summoned for that purpose, according to their Rules, and held in the presence of the said Chief Bull Head.

That no Indians was present or voted at such council or meeting who was not an habitual resident on the Reserve of the said Band of Indians or interested in the land mentioned in the said Release or Surrender.

That he is a Chief of the said Band of Indians and entitled to vote at the said meeting or council.

Sworn before me by the two Deponents Alexander James McNeil and Bull Head at the City of Calgary in the District of Alberta N.W.T. this 10th day of January A.D., 1900, having been first interpreted and explained to said Bull Head

D.L. SCOTT, A Judge of the Supreme Court of the North West Territories. George Hodgson sworn as Interpreter. A. J. McNEIL BULL X HEAD

Accepted by the Governor in Council on the 5th Feb. 1900

JOHN J. McGEE Clerk of the Privy Council
Recorded 23rd February 1900. Lib. 150, Fol. 644.
JOSEPH POPE Dep. Registrar General of Canada

The Treaty No. 8 Tax Judgement: The Facts and Some Thoughts

C. RODERICK WILSON

Introduction

On 7 March 2002 Justice D.R. Campbell of the Federal Court of Canada ruled that Treaty No. 8 First Nations people were exempt from paying taxes. The ruling was not that they were exempt from paying certain federal taxes, but that they were exempt from paying any tax. Predictably, most people who commented on the ruling in the days and weeks thereafter were outraged. Part of that outrage came from a simple reading of the text of the treaty: it nowhere stipulates that exemption from taxation is part of the treaty. In fact, taxes are not mentioned in the treaty.

On what basis, then, did Justice Campbell make his ruling?

The Facts

The Case

Docket T–2288–92, between Charles John Gordon Benoit, Athabasca Tribal Corporation, The Lesser Slave Lake Regional Council, and Kee Tas Kee Now Tribal Council, plaintiffs, and HER MAJESTY THE QUEEN IN RIGHT OF CANADA, defendant, and The Attorney General of the Province of Alberta, and the Canadian Taxpayer Federation, Intervener.

The material that follows consists largely of quotations. These are from the written judgement of the case by Justice D.R. Campbell, reviewing the facts of the case, his reasoning, and the judgement. Page numbers refer to Justice Campbell's decision.

Treaty Making

'In the summer of 1899, in order to open the Peace-Athabasca country for settlement and commerce, the Government of Canada made promises to the Cree and Dene people which were to endure as long as the "sun shines and the water runs." In the course of securing agreement to what is Treaty 8, certain assurances were made by the Treaty Commissioners acting for Canada' (p. 2).

'On May 29, 1899, the Commission party left Edmonton, expecting to arrive at Lesser Slave Lake by June 8, 1899. Mr. Laird and Mr. McKenna and their party traveled to Athabasca Landing and then to Lesser Slave Lake, arriving there on June 19, 1899, because of unfavorable traveling conditions. Mr. Ross and his party traveled over the Assiniboine trail to Lesser Slave Lake, arriving at Lesser Slave Lake on approximately June 5, 1899.

'On June 20, 1899 the Commissioners met the Cree of Lesser Slave Lake. On that day the terms of treaty that the Government offered were conveyed in a meeting with the Cree of Lesser Slave Lake.

'Treaty Number 8 was drafted and put in written form at Lesser Slave Lake following the meeting with the Cree on June 20, 1899' (p. 14).

Similar meetings were subsequently held up and down the major rivers of the area, ending on 25 July 1900 at Fort Resolution on the south shore of Great Slave Lake.

The Treaty Report

'The "Report of Commissioners for Treaty No. 8", directed to the Honourable Clifford Sifton, Minister of the Interior and Superintendent General of Indian Affairs, is . . . dated September 22, 1899, and contains the following quoted passage:

'"As the discussions at the different points followed on much the same lines, we shall confine ourselves to a general statement of their import. There was a marked absence of the old Indian style of oratory. Only among the Wood Crees were any formal speeches made, and these were brief. The Beaver Indians are taciturn. The Chipweyans confined themselves to asking questions and making brief arguments. They appeared to be more adept at cross-examination than at speech-making, and the chief at Fort Chipweyan displayed considerable keenness of intellect and much practical sense in pressing the claims of his band. They all wanted as liberal, if not more liberal terms, than were granted to the Indians of the plains"' (p. 16).

'"There was expressed at every point the fear that the making of the treaty would be followed by the curtailment of the hunting and fishing privileges, and many were impressed with the notion that the treaty would lead to taxation and enforced military service. They seemed desirous of securing educational advantages for their children, but stipulated that in the matter of schools there should be no interference with their religious beliefs. . . .

'"Our chief difficulty was the apprehension that the hunting and fishing privileges were to be curtailed. The provision in the treaty under which ammunition and twine is to be furnished went far in the direction of quieting the fears of the Indians, for they admitted that it would be unreasonable to furnish the means of hunting and fishing if laws were to be enacted which would make hunting and fishing so restricted as to render it impossible to make a livelihood by such pursuits. But over and above the provision, we had to solemnly assure them that only such laws as were in the interests of the Indians and were found necessary in order to protect the fish and the fur-bearing animals would be made, and that they would be as free to hunt and fish after the treaty as they would be if they had never entered into it. . . .

'"*We assured them that the treaty would not lead to any forced interference with their mode of life, that it did not open the way to any imposition of any tax, and that there was no fear of enforced military service*"' (p. 17; emphasis added).

Principles of Interpretation

'While the objective at hand is to determine whether the Commissioner's words constitute a treaty promise before embarking on the final interpretation of the Treaty itself, I find that the admonitions of the Supreme Court of Canada . . . are important to keep in mind; a sensitive and contextually practical approach should be adopted. Also, with respect to analysing the meaning of words spoken so

as to conclude whether they constitute a term of the Treaty, a highly technical grammatical approach, involving putting weight on any difference in meaning between the phrases "we promised", "we assured them," and "we had to solemnly assure them," should be avoided unless there is evidence that the difference was actually understood by the Aboriginal People concerned' (p. 73).

'In order to maintain the Honour of the Crown in interpreting the actions of the Treaty Commissioners, it must be assumed that they had no intention to mislead, and that the words used, as far as the Commissioners were concerned, were honestly meant and intended to be relied upon. I find that, by the successful negotiation of the Treaty, the Aboriginal People understood this to be the case' (pp. 74, 75).

The Court's Finding

'I find that all statements of commitment made by the Commissioners were intended to be accepted by the Aboriginal People as promises, and the Aboriginal People placed a high degree of trust in the Commissioners in accepting their word. On this basis, I find the tax assurance to be a Treaty promise, and, as such, is a Treaty term' (p. 75).

'For the reasons provided, I declare that:
(a) the Plaintiffs are entitled to claim the benefits of Treaty No. 8, including the Treaty Right not to have any tax imposed upon them at any time for any reason;
(b) the Treaty Right was not extinguished prior to April 17, 1982; and is now protected from extinguishment by the *Constitution Act, 1982* and is binding upon Canada to honour and uphold;
(c) the imposition of any tax by Canada on the Plaintiffs is an unjustified breach of the Treaty Right' (p. 178).

Some Interpretive Comments

About Treaty No. 8 Negotiations

That the Native people gathered at Slave Lake in 1899 had serious concerns and a list of specific questions to be answered before they would sign treaty is not to be wondered at. After all, they had by then been hearing about treaties and talking to other Indians who were living under treaties, for almost 30 years. Certainly they had questions to ask and points to negotiate.

Oral Testimony

All peoples around the world have ways of remembering important things. This may or may not involve writing. (It would likely do some of us good to reflect on the ancient founding peoples of the Judeo-Christian-Islamic tradition, for instance, who told and retold stories for centuries in an oral tradition before they became 'people of the book' and the stories were written down.) The Cree and Dene people of Treaty No. 8 also had 'rememberers' who gave testimony at the trial about what was said at the treaty negotiations. That testimony was important, but it has not been emphasized here for two reasons: first, because it was substantially supported by the written report of the Commissioners; and second, because most of the people reading this are more accustomed to giving credence to written statements.

Written Testimony

The written testimony of the Commissioners on the question of promises about taxation and other matters is, to put it bluntly, unambiguous. Treaty No. 8 people were assured by the Commissioners that no tax would ever be imposed on them. Curiously, most of the media critics of this decision seem to overlook the testimony of the Commissioners. That is, in criticizing the 'absurdity' of giving credence to oral testimony, they overlook the fact that in this instance the oral testimony and written testimony were congruent.

Fairness

Most critics of the decision end up saying that the decision is not fair. The first point to make in this connection is that this is a question the Court did not consider at all. The only question, really, that the Court considered had to do with determining what had been negotiated in Treaty No. 8 and in ensuring, 'for the honour of the Crown', that this was respected.

A second point to make with respect to fairness and honour has to do with the historic record of the last century. The reader may wish to reread the sections of the Commissioner's report cited above. How many of these promises, these supposedly mutual understandings, were wholly followed through?

Conclusion: What Now?

The defendant in the case, the federal government, almost immediately filed with the Federal Court of Appeal. A stay was granted, meaning that until the appeal has been heard, the tax regimes that were in place will continue as they were. In the end it is very likely that the case will ultimately be heard by the Supreme Court of Canada.

On the other hand, it may not. Even as we all wait for the case to make its way through the court system, the disputants entered into direct discussion in the fall of 2002. If it can be achieved, a negotiated settlement is probably to be preferred.

In any case, it needs to be remembered that in the case we have been considering, and in any future court cases on this issue, the Court has not been engaged in making law. Judges ask, 'What is the law?', not 'What should it be?' It is politicians who ask whether or not the law is popular. The courts have said that, regardless of whether the law pleases an average voter, the honour of the Crown demands that it be upheld.

If, after the Supreme Court has ruled in this matter, there is widespread dissatisfaction with the ruling, it is possible that the Parliament of Canada could act. *But, it could not act alone, unilaterally.* As Justice Campbell noted in his judgement, 'the promise given by Commissioner Laird that Treaty Rights last forever cannot be fulfilled by quietly passing general tax legislation. In my opinion, the promise that Aboriginal People would control any change to the terms of the Treaty, at the very least requires a focused and completely open consultation with those Aboriginal People affected to reach a consensus on change if Canada considers that a change is needed. There has been no such consultation' (p. 172). As noted above, since Justice Campbell wrote these words, consultation is at last occurring. There is reason to hope that an agreement can be achieved.

INDEX

Page numbers in **bold type** indicate figures, maps, and tables.